1 2

3

4

5

OFFICIAL RESIDENCES OF RULERS.

1—The Vatican at Rome. 2—White House, Washington. 3—The Tuileries, Paris. 4—Buckingham Palace, London. 5—King's Palace, Berlin.

THE NEW WORLD

COMPARED WITH

THE OLD:

A DESCRIPTION OF THE

AMERICAN GOVERNMENT, INSTITUTIONS, AND ENTERPRISES,

AND OF THOSE OF OUR GREAT RIVALS AT THE PRESENT TIME, PARTICULARLY

ENGLAND AND FRANCE.

BY

GEO. ALFRED TOWNSEND.

An Elegant Octavo Volume, Illustrated with Eighty Engravings.

HARTFORD, CONN.:
S. M. BETTS & COMPANY.
CHICAGO, ILL., GIBBS & NICHOLS.
PHILADELPHIA, PENN., JOHN BIGELOW & CO.
NEW YORK, J. D. DENNISON.
H. H. BANCROFT & CO., SAN FRANCISCO, CAL.
S. J. STRICKLAND, AUBURN, N. Y.
1870.

PREFACE.

THE volume which is introduced by these lines is intended to diffuse cosmopolitan political information in as picturesque fashion as the subject will permit, or the author can present it. Much is said in our day about our position amongst states, and our privileges amongst peoples. I have tried in these pages to ascertain the truth under both heads, and I consider the three years I have spent in Europe as a poorer qualification for the task, than the access I have been so cheerfully accorded to the fine Library of Congress.

The work was at times embarrassed by improvements in the institutions of Europe: by a change of front in the French Imperial Government, by the Revolution in Spain, by the unfinished condition of Germany and Italy, by the Disraeli Reform Bill, and by Gladstone's disestablishment of the Irish Church in the United Kingdom. The title of the book might more truly have been "The Old World Compared with the New," as what is described of America is mainly meant to arrest attention and fix the eye upon the successive European institutions; but the book will read either way, and it is not impossible that an Englishman might take it up and compare our civilization with his. The inquiry was so profitable to myself that I felt almost chagrin when I came abruptly to the limit of the volume, and, reading it over now, I remember much that I had intended to tell, sacrificed in the consciousness that one cannot bind the globe into a book.

Perhaps that which impressed me most in this research was the superiority of European authorities upon America to our own literature of Europe. We have believed the contrary, and have made outcry upon foreign travellers and writers amongst us; but we have never sent a De Tocqueville abroad nor apprehended our own future with the intelligence of a Cobden. Our travellers in Europe have been mainly provincial in mind, and in observation superficial; some of them write full of wonder, and some with lofty village scorn. The very best of our travellers was Fenimore Cooper, whom we berated for his frankness as heartily as we took our foreign critics to task. In Hawthorne, we sent one Consul abroad who looked about him, but wrote too little. In our diplomatic establishment there is scarcely one experience, save Jefferson's, which is marked by the fine contemporary analysis of both the politician and the traveller. Within the past ten years, however, several philosophic foreigners have become naturalized amongst us, and these have laid the foundation of an American political literature upon Europe; the tone of our foreign correspondence in the newspapers and reviews has also improved since the civil war, and we are throwing out of our schools those pernicious guides to a true estimate of continental politics,—histories of Europe based upon English opinion.

For fifty years our boys have been taught that Pitt's statesmanship was the wisest, and Wellington's sword the brightest; that the French Revolution was only infidel and circumscribed by the "Reign of Terror," and that everybody but ourselves is incapable of Republican government. Against this English Toryism a reaction as baneful has been led by certain American clergymen, sitting at the feet of Cæsar, and these have covered the land with indiscriminate praises of the Napoleons. Between the two schools, our youth escape altogether the moderate period and party of continental Europe, which is in affinity with our own temper and institutions, and has sent hither the most intelligent and friendly travellers. The great names in political economy, reciprocity, and international philanthropy have been lost to us in the rivalry of merely warlike reputations. Peel is obscured by Bismarck, and Alison is read instead of Martineau. Our Academies and Colleges would do well to begin the study of modern history with the year 1815, for all prior to that time will be read and retained by the student of his own will; whereas the attention, carried up to a giddy climax in the story of Napoleon, relaxes at his downfall, and listens languidly to the "History of the Peace," which is the truer and more elevating history of our era and of European glory.

The sole object of this comparison is to popularize political information, and wherever a quotation could be made judiciously, it has been preferred to original statement, as carrying authority, and as being, besides, a sample of foreign thought, idiosyncrasy, or oratory. Personal conviction upon disputed points has been evaded by citing opinion from both sides; but the general conviction is retained throughout that we have the happiest government, and that only popular defection or neglect can overthrow it. The publishers have wished me to print a list of authorities consulted in the preparation of the book; but this custom has been so frequently abused by writers who seek to establish authenticity merely by parading a catalogue, that I shall confine myself merely to some general indication of books still in print and procurable; other authorities will be named in the text.

Harriet Martineau's "History of the Peace" is incomparably the best and fairest book upon English affairs since 1815. It has been issued in an American edition of four volumes, specially edited by the author.

The "Statesman's Year Book," annually published by Macmillan and Co., of London, is a book of nearly eight hundred pages, containing a succinct account of every government of note, and of the colonies of each, as well.

Many hand-books of Church and State have been issued in England, and of these one of the cheapest is published by Murray, London.

The only political history of note in America is that of Jabez Hammond, "The Political History of the State of New York," in three volumes, and but few copies are now in circulation; it recites with impartial faithfulness the rise of parties between the close of the War of Independence and the death of Silas Wright.

Dr. Edward Fischel's work on the English Constitution has been translated into English, and published by Bosworth and Harrison of London; it is close, entertaining, and more censoriously just than similar English books.

Libraries are all supplied with Benton's "History of the Working of the American Government for Thirty Years," which is full on many points, and on some dogmatic. A very useful book on the "Laws and Government of the States and the United States" is that of William B. Wedgwood, published in 1866. New York. An abridgment of the United States Census and an abridged Blue Book have also been circulated by private publishing houses.

The English Black Book is a caustic, partisan, and somewhat sensational account of abuses, sinecures, and evils in the English political system; Jenckes's Report on the American Civil Service is a more careful book upon a part of the parallel subject.

The political history of the Continent of Europe is to be found in an immense variety of publications, few of which are in English. Kinglake's sketches of parties in France are severe and bigoted, but in many respects just. On the French Church I have consulted the "*Almanach du Clergé pour l'an de Grâce*, 1867;" on legislation, politics, and finance, the works of Casimir Périer and Adrien Huard.

A good book on Germany, particularly on North Germany, is much needed in America. I have read, in the French, Eugene Véron's History of Prussia down to the battle of Sadowa, with advantage.

"Russia and its People," by Count Gurowski, is a pithy and savage book; for a charming view of citizen life in Russia, one cannot do better than to read Turgenieff's novel of "Fathers and Sons," nicely translated by Consul Schuyler, and published in New York. "The Russians in Central Asia," by Valikhanof, and Veniukof, is a book pertinent to our new Asiatic relations, and issued in English, London, 1865. The cheapest compendium of travel, railway fares, distances, steamship routes, cities, etc., to be found in Europe or America, is "Bradshaw's Special Guide for the Continent," imported by August Brentano, New York, every month, at the price of about three dollars, currency. Other English guides to Europe are offensive and partisan, particularly Murray's; and American guides to Europe are worthless, being based upon them.

To conclude: many of the statistics cited here will be found to vary at different periods, and with different authors. The publishers design to keep the book in these respects up to the latest information. I hope that some reader may grow interested in the great contemporary questions here discussed, and hold a truer mirror up to government, so that we may become larger politicians in the sense expected of a republican, who is at once a citizen and a sovereign.

LIST OF ILLUSTRATIONS.

CONTENTS.

CHAPTER I.

WASHINGTON AND LONDON.

CHAPTER II.

THE QUEEN AND THE PRESIDENT.

CHAPTER III.

THE BRITISH ARISTOCRACY.

CHAPTER VI.

THE PRIME MINISTER AND THE CABINET.

CHAPTER VII.

CHURCH AND STATE.

CHAPTER X.

LOCAL GOVERNMENT IN THE STATES, COUNTIES, AND PROVINCES.

CHAPTER XI.

BRITISH PROVINCES AND PROVINCIAL CITIES.

CHAPTER XII.

BRITISH COLONIES AND AMERICAN TERRITORIES.

CHAPTER XIII.

THE BRITISH AND AMERICAN ARMY AND NAVY.

CHAPTER XIV.

BRITISH AND AMERICAN FINANCE.

CHAPTER XV.

POLITICS AND POLITICAL PARTIES ON BOTH SIDES OF THE SEA.

CHAPTER XVI.

CHAPTER XVII.

AMERICA AND ENGLAND AS INFLUENCED BY EACH OTHER.

CHAPTER XVIII.

NEW YORK AND PARIS.

CHAPTER XIX.

NAPOLEON III, AND NAPOLEONISM.

CHAPTER XX.

THE FRENCH GOVERNMENT.

CHAPTER XXI.

POLITICS AND POLITICIANS OF FRANCE AND THE CONTINENT.

CHAPTER XXII.

A GENERAL VIEW OF CONTINENTAL FINANCE AND GOVERNMENT.

CHAPTER XXIII.

THE NEW WEST AND THE NEW EAST.

CHAPTER XXIV.

EUROPEAN AMERICA.

CHAPTER I.

WASHINGTON AND LONDON.

A comparison of the capital cities of America and England.—Their conception, growth, public buildings, political and commercial influence, benefactors, revulsions, tragedies, and social and intellectual advantages.—Probable future of Washington and London.

IF the reader will stand on the dome of the Capitol at Washington, he will see beneath him the American nation in epitome. The broad, clear, shallow river between whose forks the capital city lies, was named by the Indians, whose nomenclature survives them in the streams, lakes, and mountains of the land. Across the Potomac lies Virginia, named for the invincible Virgin Queen, in whose reign Shakespeare wrote, Spain decayed, and the English planted in the New World. On the other side is Baltimore, almost within view, the metropolis of what was once the colony of the Stuart Catholics, and named for their protector. The counties of Maryland and Virginia, which enclose Washington, are further suggestive of the simple origin of the State. In Rappahannock, Shenandoah, and Alleghany, we hear the sounds of the sparse aboriginals, beyond whose era lived here no clearly defined human species. In Fairfax, Fauquier, and Loudon, we recall the proprietors and patrons of early English colonization. Charles, Prince William, and Prince George were of the royal families whose subjects immigrated here, and Clarke, Jefferson, and Washington were of the first great generation of native men who founded the independent republic. The capital city, like the nation, has been born within the memory of living people. The last of the old folks who saw vessels filled with stone for building the "Departments" come up the Potomac, the archives of the infant state landed near by the base of the Capitol, and the dignified figure of Washington enter the suburbs of the embryo and swampy city, is not yet deceased. There were people at the funeral of Lincoln who remembered the funeral of Washington. They or their immediate parents talked with the Indians who held an annual council on the banks of the little creek, Tiber, which winds round Capitol Hill. The memory of one man can swing from that time of primitive government to this, — when thirty-five millions of people, living on two oceans and in two zones, are represented in Washington, and their consuls and ambassadors are in every port and metropolis of the globe, —from the pine wilderness to the government city, from the lonely farm of Davy Burns to the solid habitations of a hundred thousand people, having little other vocation than what the state affords them.

The landscape of the city is new, crude, and imposing, like the nation. The dwellings are of mixed and indifferent construction, — quadrangles of red brick run up and covered with roofs of the once cheap cypress shingle, some pretentious, some durable, many of mere plank or plaster, and heterogeneous of form as of material; here the newly-imported French Mansard roof, there an attic coated with patent-right contrivances of tar and pebbles, or dark-blue slate from the quarry. Porticos, balustrades, verandas, bay-windows, and church-spires, eked out between the carpenter and the architect, are revealed above and amidst the mass. The suburbs are plentiful with cabins or "shanties;" many vacant lots are disclosed; the upturned soil has the dark virgin colors; and looming here and there through the tranquil tenements the monumental offices of the government are seen, — the long, granite façade of the Treasury, the white porticos of the Patent Office, the red sandstone towers of the Smithsonian Institute, the mansion of the President, and the plainer buildings of war, navy, and state. At last, beneath the spectator's feet, the Capitol itself, enthroned within sight of all the lofty amphitheatre of ridges which environ Washington, salutes them with the statue of Freedom, poised serenely upon its shield and sheathed sword, beautifully nondescript, like the hopeful but undeveloped destinies of the state. If this figure of bronze, which faces Eastward, toward Europe, could remember and speak, it might explain why every hill-top in the horizon is capped with a freshly dismantled fort, and tell of recent days when the tranquil navy yard, under its shadow, was surrounded with transports and ships-of-war, coming and going silently in the night, or saluting the city by day with cannon. Civil war, vigorous as the nature of our institutions, has already made the landscape of the capital historic, and once in our brief history a foreign enemy has burnt the public buildings to the ground. Personal tragedy has consecrated the streets of the city. Eighteen magistrates have presided here. As far as human anticipations may go, Washington is vindicated as the seat of government, and by material and inspired considerations is to remain the American capital.

The city was conceived in the opinion of the wisest founders of the state that a free legislature should sit remote from the violence and temptation of great commercial cities. It was fixed midway between interests which threatened in the beginning to take sectional outlines and organizations. The love of Washington for the neighborhood of his estate and his preference for this spot decided the precise site of the city. It was called in his honor, with the consent of the legislature, and surrounded with a small municipal district named for the discoverer of the American continent. That its grave and ardent founders did not project a capital for a century, but for all time, is seen in the spacious and effective ground-plan of the streets and squares, for which our impatient generation has not provided consistent buildings. But without manufactures, or foreign commerce, the sequestered city now stands eleventh in the land in relative populousness, and the ratio of its increase at the present time is greater than that of any Eastern American city, except Philadelphia and New York. Essentially what its founders meant it to be, a city of public offices and residences, it is idle to speculate whether Washington will ever become a busy metropolis, in the sense of trade and physical industry. It is inland, without accommodation for deep ships; but it has coal and reliable water-power near by. Baltimore has outstripped it in accumulation of capital and in enterprise, and although Washington is better placed commercially than Paris, Vienna, or Berlin, its established rivals, its need of stable public spirit, and the friendlessness of it in the national councils, will probably make the social and intellectual delights its chief attractions. Unlike Rome,

> " That sat upon her seven hills,
> And from her throne of beauty ruled the world,"

Washington is actually governed by its transient occupants, Congress having exclusive jurisdiction over it; and what little experience the city has had in self-government is of doubtful example to the state. At present there is universal manhood suffrage in Washington, whites and blacks sitting in the two councils, and the mayor is elective. But it rests within the discretion of the dominant Congress to abolish the city government at any time, and resume exclusive administration over all the District of Columbia. The suggestion has been frequently made that the municipal city should be governed by a commission of private citizens, unsalaried, like those who compose the boards of trustees of many colleges and bequests, or administer the Central Park, of New York. It matters little to the country at large how the resident people of Washington live politically, — whether they demonstrate, as at present, a crude and unqualified municipal democracy, disfranchised nationally, or become representative, like the empire at whose head they live; but all our tastes, patriotisms, and sensitivenesses are concerned in seeing the capital made worthy of the land, its avenues paved, its hospitalities improved, and the unsightly environs of its public buildings made healthy and picturesque. We need not have an embellished capital city; we should have a neat one; less is required to be added than to be finished. The work, however, moves on apace, and it may be doubted at present whether the scholar, the man of social tastes, wealth, and leisure, can find in America a more congenial residence than Washington, — New York and Boston not excepted.

This city, therefore, is the deliberative evolution of original Christian republicanism. No oracle commanded it. No augury fixed its site. It was not countenanced by flights of sacred birds, like Rome, nor were its foundations baptized in blood. Its only Virgil has thus far been the humorously servile Irish poet, Tom Moore, creating contemptuous satire upon Washington, for the aristocratic market; and in view of the influence of this capital upon mankind, we may almost accept with pride his statement: —

"And what was Goose Creek once *is* Tiber now."

From this clear sky of Washington, and almost limpid atmosphere, bringing near the eye the distant green forests and the bare gray heights, showing every roof and object in the basin of the city, and suggesting exquisite sites and opportunities for future growth, let us abruptly change the scene to the capital of the British empire.

Standing on the dome of St. Paul's Cathedral, London lies beneath us in the pall of smoke and fog, its outlines lost like its origin, — the vague suggestion of its mighty self, like the smoke of a volcano.

Here is the capital of that empire from which our own is most directly derived. The eyes of the men, who, with sheathed swords, stood round the corner-stone of Washington city, had often looked with earnest though outraged loyalty toward this ancient metropolis.

Here was the habitation of the American sovereign. Here deliberated the parliaments which made laws affecting every ship, every trunk of ship timber, every pound of tobacco, and every ounce of gold and silver in America. Hence came the yearly parcels of books which Washington read in his childhood, and Franklin noticed in his newspaper. The London pamphlets and journals were their New York and Chicago "Tribunes," their "Nation," "Independent," "Atlantic," and "New York Ledger." The "sights" they talked of were all in London,—Westminster Abbey, the Tower, Temple Bar, St. James's Palace. Here were the spiritual leaders of the leading American sects; hence came the great preachers and bishops to Newport and Philadelphia. Braddock, Wolfe, Abercrombie, and the military commanders of our forefathers received their commissions here, and their aspirations were like Nelson's, for "a peerage or a tomb in Westminster Abbey." Here Pocahontas kissed the hand of the sovereign of Virginia, John Smith read the proof-sheets of his exploration of Chesapeake Bay, Franklin came to receive insult while he pleaded for the rights of Pennsylvanians, and Washington's modest recital of his trip to the Ohio was here committed to the printer and the bookseller. As the ancient world looked to Rome with obedience or fear, those looked to London. It was the birthplace of the English Bible and prayer-book, the grave of Bunyan and Milton, the theme and theatre of Shakespeare. We have not lived, we shall not live, to see the American city which can be the London to us that this was to our forefathers, or is to the existing Englishman. Around it lie the associations of nearly twenty centuries, stretching back to the page of Tacitus. Here it stood, doubtless, when the idle procession followed Jesus, bearing his cross to the hill of crucifixion in Jerusalem. When the sovereign in London declared war against France or Spain, the drum beat along all our Atlantic and frontier settlements, our privateers put to sea, and our women dreamed of painted savages marching down from Canada and Louisiana. The scandal of the court that was talked by our ancestors — the latest favorite, the revolting execution of the latest traitor, the beauty of the lord mayor's daughter — brings vividly before us the apparition that London was to the imaginations of our great grandparents. In every American town some giddy head was full of the freshest toilet worn at Whitehall palace; some grim dissenter or embryo republican denounced the profligacy of the court; and, over all, the intense sentiment of subject toward king prevailed, that which we faintly revived in the American word "loyalty," during the recent rebellion.

Let us stand here, on St. Paul's, as we stood on the dome of the Capitol at Washington, and look upon London, as if by some miracle it had been swept of fog and smoke, and lay beneath us distinctly.

A dense mass of red-tiled houses and blackened chimney-stacks, ten miles long and six miles wide. Ten miles to go without the sight of a green field! Six miles from hedge to hedge, from bird to bird! This is at least three times the size of New York Island, and ten times the size of the actually settled city of New York. All this wonderful extent of houses, in which lodge every night three million six hundred thousand people,— the greatest city of the modern world, and perhaps the greatest of history in population,* — stretches in solid parallelogram on both sides of a river which takes the same general course as the Potomac, flowing south-eastward. Washington lies in the "fork" of the Potomac and Anacostia, about a hundred miles from the Chesapeake Bay; London may be said, in like manner, to lie in the fork of the Thames and the little River Lea, sixty miles from the English Channel. The tides rise and fall ten miles above

*It may be the wish of some reader to know the populousness of London and Rome, in their highest prosperity, relatively. I therefore subjoin the following from Dr. Lord's "Old Roman World."

"The city of Rome virtually contained between three and four millions of people. Lipsius estimates four millions as the population, including slaves, women, children, and strangers. Though this estimate is regarded as too large by Merivale and others, yet how enormous must have been the number of the people when there were nine thousand and twenty-five baths, and when those of Diocletian alone could accommodate three thousand two hundred people at a time. The wooden theatre of Scaurus contained eighty thousand seats; that of Marcellus would seat twenty thousand; the Coliseum would seat eighty-seven thousand, and give standing space for twenty-two thousand more. The Circus Maximus would hold three hundred and eighty-five thousand spectators. Lipsius estimates the circumference of the city at forty-five miles, and Vopiscus at nearly fifty. The diameter of the city, according to Strabo, must have been eleven miles.

"The Coliseum alone would seat all the male adults of the city of New York. At the Circus Maximus more people witnessed the chariot races at a time than are nightly assembled in all the places of public amusement in Paris, London, and New York combined, —more than could be seated in all the cathedrals of England and France."

According to more critical testimony, London has already passed Rome in population, if not in superficial measurement. The estimate of the population of London, in this book, is based upon its probable increase by 1870. In 1861 it contained two millions eight hundred thousand people. Modern London covers seventy-eight thousand acres of ground, or one hundred and twenty-two square miles, which, according to Mr. P. Cunningham, was half the area of Babylon.

London, three miles above Washington. The River Thames, from its rills to the sea flows two hundred and thirty miles, the Potomac four hundred miles, or longer than all England proper.

This River Thames, whose smoky course we see, passing by long arms or "reaches" under more than a dozen bridges, — a black, oozy, surly tide, charged with the refuse of three and a half millions of people, — is in great part responsible for the power of London. To our American eyes it seems a puny river, — a thousand feet from shore to shore, less than a fifth of a mile. The little steamers which run as omnibuses upon it, dropping their funnels at every bridge, are mere needles to our fine floating-palaces. Nevertheless, it has been more serviceable than any river in the world, and at this time six hundred steamers and three thousand sailing vessels belong to its waters, while forty thousand craft of steam and sail enter and depart from it every year. The Romans embanked it when they conquered England. Up its waters the Northmen pirates sailed on errands of robbery, and various little creeks, on whose sites London streets are now built, were used by these robbers to penetrate far into the country. Since England became an independent kingdom, but one instance has occurred of a foreign enemy sailing up its channel, except as a captive. In 1815, the year Napoleon fell, — when Washington lay in ashes, burnt by British perhaps from this very city, — the first steamboat was seen upon the Thames. It was named the "Margery," had been built in Scotland, and sailed nearly round England to reach London. The biggest ship which has ever been known to man was launched upon this little Thames, the "Great Eastern," and she safely put to sea, while we esteemed it a doubtful enterprise to send down the Potomac the United States frigate "Minnesota," after we had launched her from the Washington Navy Yard. It is this strong little stream which carries away from London one hundred and fifty millions of dollars' worth of exports every year. To accommodate its vast shipping enormous artificial docks have been excavated below the city, covering between four hundred and five hundred acres, and costing nearly a hundred millions of dollars. To keep the river deep dredging machines are constantly at work, which take millions of tons of ballast a year from it, and this alone sells for one hundred and fifty thousand dollars. The bridges across the Thames, one of which passes the stream by only three arches, cost from less than half a million to five millions of dollars, and one of them alone cost five-sevenths as much as the Capitol at Washington. A tunnel, which cost three millions of dollars, penetrates from shore to shore beneath the river bed, but this is neither as long nor as useful as the Chicago lake tunnel. The great marvel of this river is, that it has kept its channel clear and deep for these two thousand years, never filled by the offal of the great nation on its shores, but equal to their industry now as in the beginning, the ocean welcomed by it twice every day; and though tawny and grimy with toil, it is as youthful, as generous, and as beneficent as ever, promising as hopefully for the eras and the empires which may succeed to its dominion.

The valley of the Thames, in which London lies, is bounded by ridges of hills to whose distant bases the vast suburbs extend, — cities in themselves. From these hills one can look down into the great crater of smoke, with St. Paul's, on which we stand, showing its dome and cross three hundred and sixty-five feet above the ground, — as many feet as there are days in the year. The ground surface of the city itself is undulating, with a general elevation toward either ridge, and here and there, in the heart of the city, are abrupt eminences, chief of which is Ludgate, or the hill of St. Paul's, on which we stand. Looking through the dense mass of houses, we see few open squares or clearings of any kind, except to the west, or up the Thames, where a series of green parks begins at the elbow of the river, a mile from our feet, and stretches to the boundaries of the city. By these intersecting parks, St. James's, Green, and Hyde, one can walk from the Thames, nearly three miles westward to Kensington Palace, where Queen Victoria was born, passing on the way Buckingham Palace, where she resides, and St. James's Palace, where she holds her court. And at the point where this series of parks starts from the Thames, stands Westminster Palace, commonly called the Parliament buildings, which corresponds to the Capitol of Washington, being the palace of legislation. Beside Westminster Palace is Westminster Abbey, the burial place of the monarchs of England, which was founded in the year 1221, or two hundred and seventy-one years before Columbus found America. Now, facing about, and looking east, as the river flows, we can see, half a mile from St. Paul's, on which we stand, a cluster of large buildings in the densest quarter of the city. The strange old hall, with a heavy face, mediæval-looking, like a Flemish "Hotel de Ville," is the Guildhall, or seat of city government, corresponding to the city halls of New York and Washington. Near by it is a large, sculptured classical building, with a portico and pillars, which is the residence of the Lord Mayor of London. Between these two are the Bank of England and the Royal Exchange. The bank has a capital of seventy-five millions of dollars; the Exchange building cost seven hundred and fifty thousand dollars; and the Lord Mayor gets, besides his house, rent free, a salary of forty thousand dollars a year, or nearly double that of the President of the United States. The Guildhall was the seat of city government before Columbus was born, and London, as a corporation, is older than Spain or Holland as kingdoms.

The eye of the observer, pitched from the dome of St. Paul's, will at once take in the contrary nature of this group of banks and city halls and the group of palaces first described. St. Paul's in the middle, the cathedral of the city; Westminster a mile up the river, the seat of Parliament and the Queen; the city hall and the banks down the river half a mile, — that is the position.

Now, strictly speaking, the Westminster end is not in London at all, for of this mighty mass of habitations, enclosing three millions and a half of people, only about one-twentieth, or, in numbers, one hundred and thirty thousand people, live in the city of London. The rest is a grand series of suburbs, not subject to the city government, but ruled by the English ministry from their capitol at Westminster. London, the parent city, like a hoary patriarch, stands upon its ancient charter around Guildhall, surrounded by its offspring. Within the limits of its ancient walls, now destroyed, the power of its Mayor is confined. Grown rich, by the privileges and opportunities of its charter, it is the seat of trade, banking, and exchanges, while Westminster, or the West End, is the suburb of the court and aristocracy, and the social resort of Londoners and Englishmen. The other suburbs are parasites and excrescences of these two, the City and Court. Across the river, from Court and City, are the suburbs of the poor, Southwark and Lambeth, with nearly the population of Philadelphia. North of London is the suburb of clerks and business people, Finsbury, with the population of Brooklyn. Down the river from London is the suburb of the sailors, Tower Hamlets, named from the famous old Tower of London, with nearly the population of New York. North of Westminster is the suburb of the tradesmen of the court, and those who like to snuff the air of gentility, Marylebone, with the population of Boston and Chicago. Westminster itself has the population of Baltimore. Within the past year (1868) two new parliamentary districts have been established, Chelsea and Hackney.

When we come to examine the plan of London streets, the task seems hopeless of conveying to the mind any methodized, memorable notion of them. Our American towns were mainly laid out deliberately by the surveyor, beginning with Philadelphia, which was apparently conceived in some revulsion of the mind of William Penn against the inscrutably mixed lanes of the neighborhood of his father's house in London. There are three American cities whose original streets make something of a maze, — Quebec, Boston, and New York,— but this is mainly due to the natural configuration of the ground on which they stand. As Boston and New York expand, however, their streets straighten and cross at right angles. Washington city was carefully laid out by an engineer officer upon two plans: a city of streets, for the people to live upon, and a city of wide avenues to exhibit the public buildings to advantage. London is the growth of less deliberate times, and it is by reference to her conditions at various periods that we lay hold upon the successive evolutions of her thoroughfares.

In the first place, there is old London, in the East, the walled city, and within its small circumference we find the most involved tangle of streets, adapted in part to the ancient enclosure; for London Wall and Barbican are street names to this day, commemorating the defences on whose site they stand. Out of this mighty maze go the highways to the country, and they take the names of the gates in the wall through which they passed, such as Ludgate, Aldgate, Bishop's Gate, and Newgate. These country roads, pouring into London through the gates, converged upon the Guildhall, the seat of government. Other streets, running parallel with the walls, connected these gate streets; but in the ancient time the right of thoroughfare was not appreciated as now, and churches, abbeys, religious houses, and so forth, compelled people to go round them. Cities, in the sense of the middle ages, were gatherings of incorporated tradesmen and artisans, called guilds or companies, somewhat like the present trades-unions. Guildhall means the council-hall of the Guilds. Therefore Old London was largely composed of streets of tradesmen, slipping in between privileged reservations of churchmen, courtiers, and the like, and a host of streets still survives, indicating their former character, such as Cheapside, Cloth Fair, Threadneedle Street, and Hozier Lane. So we recall the religious houses of former times in "Great St. Thomas Apostle's Cloak," Paternoster Row, and Holy Well Street. Lombard Street, the centre of banking, takes name from Lombardy, the country of the Jewish bankers who settled in London after their expulsion from Italy and anglicized the pawnbroker's three golden balls, the ancient arms of Lombardy. Jewry was the quarter of the poor Jews. The mansions and associations of noblemen, knights, and monarchs are revived in Knight Rider Street, Garter Lane, Earl Street, and Tudor Street; and here, where we stand, the central and most lofty monument in London, St. Paul's, rests upon the foundations of successive Christian temples, reaching back to the seventh century and perhaps upon the site of heathen temples a thousand years further. This is the grandest Protestant church in the world, as St. Peter's, at Rome, is the grandest Catholic church. St. Peter's stands upon the supposed site of the martyrdom of St. Peter. And St. Paul, or his immediate disciples, are supposed to have been the apostles of Britain. St. Paul's and Westminster, the two poles of the mighty aggregation called London, were founded at the same time. Both have been rebuilt. In Westminster lie the early monarchs of England; in St. Paul's her greatest commanders, Nelson and Wellington. Westminster, the city of the Abbey church, may be called the capital of England. Guildhall, under the shadow of St. Paul's, may be called the capital of London city.

Looking down from St. Paul's upon the dense and intricate old city, one can see the landmarks of the richest and most influential municipal corporation ever known to man,— a corporation of bankers, mechanics, tradesmen, and sailors, which by purchase or contention has wrested from the throne and the aristocracy repeated privileges, and moulded, jointly with the nation at Westminster, the present form of the English government. Holding the purse, the arts, and the mob, the centre of agitation and thought, the home of a sagacious and enterprising democracy, the refuge of authors, orators, and politicians, London has preserved every privilege, substantial or ceremonial, to the present time. Within the walls of the city proper, her mayor takes precedence of the sovereign, and walks before him. A toll of two or four cents is still collected at the city gates upon the carts and carriages of all strangers. The old city has an income of two million of dollars a year. Twenty thousand "freemen" vote in her elections, or about one-seventh of her population. Nearly fifteen thousand houses are compressed within her ancient walls, whose combined rents exceed eleven millions of dollars, and land round about St. Paul's is worth five millions of dollars an acre. When night descends upon the ancient city of London, her vast warehouses and multitudinous shops are deserted. One-half her people withdraw into the outlying suburbs. Her resident population grows thinner every year, while her lusty offspring without the walls increase and multiply continually.

Dismissing the *city* of London as a separate subject, and considering hereafter herself and her suburbs as an entirety under the general name of London, we observe that her principal thoroughfares run from east to west, and make the figure of an elongated hour-glass, as expressed in the following diagram: —

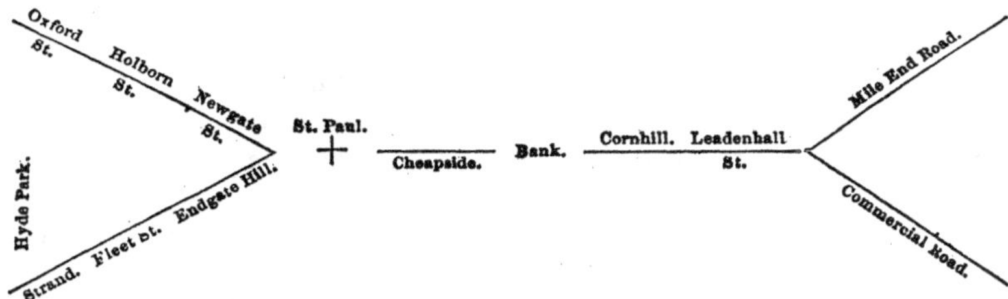

Curling within and around, and crossing this diagram, go twenty-eight hundred streets, whose added lengths make three thousand miles, traversed by five thousand cabs and omnibuses. Four hundred miles of telegraph wire and two hundred telegraph stations carry news between the three hundred thousand houses which compose the city. Four and a half millions of dollars are spent in cab fare every year by Londoners. Six million two hundred and seventy thousand letters are delivered to them yearly. Three hundred and sixty thousand gas lamps light their streets; six thousand two hundred policemen patrol them. Her five hundred and fifty charitable institutions spend ten millions of dollars a year. The smoke of five millions of tons of coal, which prepares the food of her people, is seen to trail opaquely away thirty-two miles. Fifty millions of gallons of porter, ale, and spirits are consumed in London, which is five millions of gallons in excess of the water drunk.

The water itself comes partly from the Thames, at once the sewer and the well of London, or it is brought by an artificial river thirty-eight miles, — less distance than by the Croton Aqueduct of New York. Two million one hundred thousand four-footed beasts are yearly sacrificed to the appetite of London. Ten million head of game and fish feed the same necessity. Thirteen thousand cows give milk for London. Eight hundred and fifty churches give prayers. Seven thousand lawyers give counsel. Twenty-five hundred bakers give bread. Fifteen thousand eating and coffee houses accommodate strangers, and five thousand drinking houses give beer and spirits.

To these superficial statistics many of equal marvel might be added. As a port of revenue, London has no rival in the world. One-half the entire customs of England are collected at her piers, or nearly sixty millions of dollars a year, while Liverpool, next in importance, collects only twelve millions. The entire income of the English government, derivable from all sources, is only six times the customs of London.

Within the past twenty years the spirit of public improvements has been at work in and beneath London to increase the comfort of her people, to beautify, modernize, and enlarge her highways, and to obviate some of the evils arising from her slow, cumbrous, and monstrous evolution. Twenty-one millions of dollars have been spent in improved sewerage alone, between 1860 and 1869. Fifty-six millions of dollars have been expended in underground railways, in embanking the Thames, and in many minor improvements. The public works of London, in progress or already completed, are more important than those of any nation in the world, America and France excepted. Her underground life is more wonderful every hour of the year than the proudest day of imperial triumph above the streets of ancient Rome. Through the old tunnel of the Thames the railway trains thunder at last. By pneumatic despatch the mails go almost with the promptness of thought across the city.

Subterranean railways make the traversing of the great city no more than a walk around a block. One of these roads crosses the river twice on bridges which cost millions, to carry omnibus passengers at a few cents a head. And the sewers of Paris, which M. Victor Hugo has presented to literature with much vividness, are gutters to the sewers of London, which are adapted to the rise and fall of tides, and are designed with almost the exquisiteness of the venous and arterial system in man.

The monumental aspect of London is heterogeneous yet huge, like the history and the eras it illustrates. St. Paul's cost nearly four millions of dollars, and was thirty-five years in course of construction. The Crystal Palace, a pleasure house, near by London, cost

5

upwards of seven millions of dollars, which was, according to the architect of the United States Capitol, Mr. Clark, three-fourths the cost of the latter building. The finest private residence in London, Stafford House, cost with its furniture and paintings, one million two hundred and fifty thousand dollars. There are probably nearly as fine residences, exteriorly, in New York, Philadelphia, and Boston. A single railway depot cost four millions of dollars. The House of Parliament cost ten millions of dollars. The contents of the British Museum are probably more valuable than all the paintings, statues, libraries, and curiosities which can be collected in the United States. One boast of this institution is that its library of seven hundred thousand volumes (to which seventy-five thousand are added every year) contains twice as many American books as the best library in America; the building in which all these are housed cost five millions of dollars. The oldest great monuments of London are the Tower, built by William the Conqueror; the Temple, built A. D. 1185, and Westminster Hall and Abbey. Arches, obelisks, and statues illustrate almost every hero and reign. Yet London cannot be called a splendid city in the sense of art; for her riches have always exceeded her tastes. Her monuments are more memorable by their associations than by their art.

The city, as an apparition, is known throughout the world by its swarthy and vapory complexion, covered with fog and smoke entangled in each other, and sometimes the twilight usurps the place of mid-day; highway robbery goes forth to do its work, and the lamps of gas burn consumptively. The political organization of London is further remarkable to us who live under simple municipal charters, sometimes embarrassed by State interference. It contains a "lordship," a "lieutenancy," some thirty "villages," five "watering-places," four "boroughs," two "episcopal cities," three "towns," and it extends into four counties.

The social and intellectual life of London embraces whatever leisure, taste, genius, riches, or profligacy can be contributed by the kingdom. The true "season" is at its height in spring, when the Royal Academy opens, court removes to London, the Queen holds drawing-room and levees, the opera commences, Epsom and Ascot races are held, and Parliament sits. The newspaper and periodical reading of nearly the whole kingdom is supplied by London. The literature descriptive of London city is more extensive than all the literary remains of the ancients extant, and few modern nations or races have illustrated so many plays, novels, and histories as this city alone. Unlike Rome it has rivals, but the growth of their enterprise and immigration is matched by the natural increase of London, whose huge bulk exudes every year a city of the size of Providence, Buffalo, or Cleveland. This is the leviathan city, the monster of the fogs. This is the metropolis of Protestantism. By the privileges of its charter and its sturdy spirit, it has in turn divided the nobles, defied the kings, and exercised hospitality toward oppressed mankind, but notably toward oppressed Protestants. These, flying from France, from Flanders, from the German Empire, and from Savoy, brought money and skill to make their adopted city the banker, the silk-weaver, and the merchant of the world. It is by the vast fortunes laid away in London that many of our American railways are built, and by the same assistance much of our war for the Union was maintained.

We have in America no metropolis of corresponding influence, either achieved or in promise. It is not probable that we shall ever have an American London. The day of independent municipal republics seems to have gone by, and all our American cities maintain their local self-government with difficulty. In Paris the emperor's *Prefect* marshals the police; in New York they are responsible to the legislature at Albany. London alone, of the great cities, administers herself after her ancient forms.

But at their rate of progress, with their harbors so much more spacious and convenient to the sea, and with their enlightened public enterprise, it is to be apprehended that New York and San Francisco will become the chief ports of the two oceans, receiving and discharging for that London of the New World: the rich and happy continent which lies between them, covered by a charter more excellent than London city's! Those young and vigorous ports retain less treasure than London, perhaps, in their coffers, but it lies near by in the mine. Their arts and monuments are yet crude, but their institutions are the masterpieces of Christian freedom and human charity. Their common schools, rooted in the law and the origin of the State, are fairer edifices in the sight of man's happiness and destiny than Westminster Abbey or Westminster Palace. London has no system of public schools conceived in the spirit of ours in America. Her private schools number sixteen hundred; but ignorance, aggravated by the presence of an aristocracy, develops "from Saint James's to Saint Giles's" in those shapes of caricature and subserviency, crime and folly, which illustrate the pages of Dickens and his contemporaries, and have no corresponding people in America. Except by her money and her trades, London does not influence America in any marked degree. The burden of influence is the other way. It is from Washington that the century is moved.

I have made this sketch of London city for the purpose of localizing the views I am to give of the British sovereign, parliament, and people. In subsequent chapters London will continue to afford us descriptions.

1 2

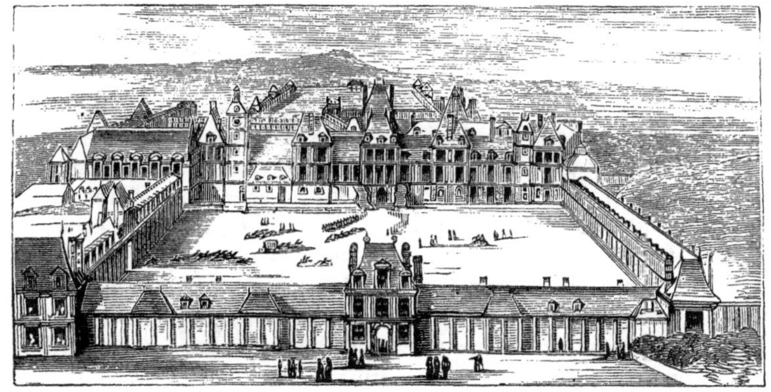

3

4 5

COUNTRY SEATS OF RULERS.

1—Ulricksdal, Sweden. 2—Windsor Castle, England. 3—Fontainebleau, France. 4—Soldiers' Home, Washington. 5—Tivoli, Rome.

CHAPTER II.

THE QUEEN AND THE PRESIDENT.

A comparative sketch of their ceremonies, dignities, public duties, places of residence, social amusements, salaries, powers, and personal influence in the state. — Description of the royal household: the birth, coronation, marriage, and family relations of the queen.

THE President of the United States is, if not so sacred, a more powerful personage than the Queen of England. His salary is twenty-five thousand dollars a year. Her private purse is three hundred thousand dollars a year. His perquisites are some bushels of coal to light his fires, a gardener or two, a couple of soldiers to guard his door, and he lives in a mansion which cost three hundred thousand dollars, and which is furnished once every four years at a cost of twenty-five thousand dollars. The Queen has many residences, the least of which cost more than the President's palace. Her minutest household expenses are met by the state, a large number of courtly attendants and officials are attached to her person, and seven thousand six hundred picked troops take turns in guarding her. One million and a half of dollars every year are paid to support her various households and to pay her tradesmen's bills, and all her children receive separate incomes, sufficient to support their rank.

Standing before Buckingham Palace and recalling the plain "White House" at Washington, we can account for Mr. Anthony Trollope's description of the home of the American Chief Magistrate. "The President's House," he says, "or the White House, as it is now called all the world over, is a handsome mansion fitted for the chief officer of a great republic, and nothing more. I think I may say that we have private houses in London considerably larger. It is neat and pretty, and with all its immediate outside belongings calls down no adverse criticism."

The Queen has four palaces in London, all situated along the margin of the great series of parks which reach from the Thames, at Westminster, to the environs of London. Kensington Palace, the Queen's birthplace, where she has resided only for short intervals these many years, is an old brick edifice, near the outskirts of London. Buckingham Palace, her city residence, St. James's Palace, her place for holding court, and the fragment of Whitehall Palace, where she occasionally gives alms or hears prayers, are all situated upon the borders of St. James's Park, a kite-shaped enclosure of ninety-one acres. Each of these buildings is far more costly and elaborate than the President's House at Washington, and excepting the fragment of Whitehall they are all larger. But it may be doubted if either of them is so chaste, so exquisite, or so complete as the White House at Washington. St. James's Palace is a confused series of low brick tenements and saloons, of the exterior appearance of a group of battlemented stables with a stack-yard in the middle. Kensington Palace resembles an old barn-like boarding-school or convent. Buckingham Palace is a huge, forbidding, blackened pile, repeatedly altered and enlarged, one front of which alone cost twice as much as the White House. Probably four millions of dollars have been expended in the construction and ornamentation of these four palaces.

The President of the United States is permitted to take quarters for some months of the summer in a cottage at the Soldier's Home, a military asylum near Washington city. The Queen of England has, probably, a hundred castles, fortresses, and mansions which belong to the crown, and stand ready to open their gates at her will.

But there are three palaces, especially, which are reserved for the Queen, and in which she spends all the time not given to London. I enumerate these palaces in the order of their importance.

WINDSOR CASTLE. — An hour's ride by railroad from London, in the midst of a noble park and forest of twenty-three hundred acres, has been for seven hundred years a favorite residence of English sovereigns. It is a mighty castle on the River Thames, whose battlements and many towers are visible for a great distance. The royal standard denoting the presence of the Queen floats over the tallest tower fully half the year. A court-yard of vast dimensions lies within the castle, and upon this open many of the apartments. The cost of this ancient and vast structure cannot be ascertained, but, in 1824, to restore a small portion of it Parliament voted one and a half million dollars. The stables alone cost one hundred thousand dollars. Within this castle is St. George's Chapel, one of the most elegant Gothic churches in the world. A single apartment of Windsor is two hundred feet long and thirty-four broad, or nearly three times as large as the celebrated East room at Washington. Here, the greater part of the life of Victoria has been passed, and for several years the Queen has been seen but a small portion of the year at her London palaces.

BALMORAL CASTLE. — The scene of many of the domestic events related in the Queen's recent books. This castle is entirely modern, and was built by Queen Victoria in Aberdeenshire, Scotland, a hundred miles north of Edinburgh, or upon the latitude of Labrador and Hudson's Bay. The Scotch Dee River runs beside it. It is a hundred and twenty by two hundred feet in dimensions, built entirely of granite in the Scotch baronial style, with a single tower at one end thirty-five feet square and one hundred feet high. The ballroom is the principal apartment, being sixty-eight feet by twenty-five in dimensions. Behind this castle rise the Grampian Hills, where Norval's father fed his flocks; some of the peaks of which are upwards of four thousand feet high. Balmoral was designed by Prince Albert, Queen Victoria's husband, who purchased it for the royal children, with thirty thousand acres of farm and mountain land near by.

OSBORNE HOUSE. — After Windsor, the favorite country house of the Queen, on the Isle of Wight, within the lovely harbor called the Solent, and overlooking Southampton water; here pass many lines of steamships, and notably the Hamburg and Bremen steamers from New York. Cowes, the town near by, is the head-quarters of the English Yacht Club, and here the American yacht "Henrietta" dropped anchor after winning the race across the Atlantic in 1867. Osborne was originally Oysterbourne; or, as we would name it, Oysterbay. The Queen bought the old place in 1840, with five thousand acres of ground, and erected a splendid mansion in the Italian style, with a tower above it ninety feet high.

The grounds slope to the salt-water side, where ride at anchor the fleet and elegant steam yacht of the Queen, which latter cost three hundred thousand dollars. In this yacht she can circumnavigate her kingdom or visit the neighboring coast of France.

The Queen of England is the ideal and ornamental head of the British Empire. The President of the United States is a hard-working man of many cares, who is held to a strict responsibility for his public behavior. Not so with the Queen. A cabinet of politicians administer her realm. Her will has long since ceased to be regarded in affairs of state, for, as it is a maxim that the sovereign can do no wrong, her ministers take care to rule the state according to their own counsel, for they are ostensibly responsible to Parliament, and might possibly be made to suffer for her obstinacy or error. Since the expulsion of James II., and notably since the American Revolution, the House of Commons has absorbed all political power in England. It is as if the House of Representatives at Washington said to the President, "We will relieve you of the cares of state, but your office and person shall retain all their ancient title and respect; you shall never be punished, but your prime minister who reigns in your name must be changed as often as we disagree with him." Thus, while the Queen is apparently the most powerful ruler on the earth, she is no more than an effigy, laden with jewels, covered with honors, surrounded by a court, and protected by a troop. The present Queen has made but one effort in the course of her long reign to have her way in any political question whatever, and that singularly was to keep her own maids of honor around her whom a new cabinet wished to displace. She was obliged to give way.

Queen Victoria is an hereditary sovereign, descended from James I., son of Mary, Queen of Scots. Her reign, which in glory and duration rivals that of Queen Elizabeth, seems to be a recompense for the sorrows of her beautiful ancestor. The great-grandson of James I. was George I., Elector of Hanover. George III., the King whom our revolutionary forefathers denounced, was Victoria's grandfather. Her father, the Duke of Kent, was one of George III.'s fifteen children, far down in the list, and it seemed improbable that he or his child would ever reach the throne. He was quite poor, badly treated, and, while abroad in Germany, whither he had gone to find cheap living, he married a widow, who was daughter to the Duke of Saxe-Coburg. The deaths of several intermediate heirs to the crown making it possible that he still might succeed to it, the Duke of Kent hastened to embark for England in 1819; but he had not money enough for the journey home. His family refused to send it to him and he had to borrow it from some humble people. Soon after he reached the dull old Palace of Kensington, Victoria, his only child, was born on the 24th of May, and they called her the Mayflower. She was christened Alexandrina Victoria. Eight great noblemen and ecclesiastics were present at her birth, amongst whom was the Duke of Wellington, who had fought the battle of Waterloo four years before. One month afterward the child was privately christened from a gold font by the Archbishop of Canterbury. In little more than six months her father died, deeply in debt. Victoria's early youth was passed in dependence. Her mother knew what it was to be "dunned" by creditors as well as the father of Abraham Lincoln, yet her income was never less than the salary of the President, even when poorest.

By passages from the life of Queen Victoria we can best illustrate what it is to be a "constitutional" Queen in our century. The public incidents of her life are mainly these: Her proclamation, her coronation, her marriage, and the birth of her heir, the Prince of Wales.

The proclamation of the Queen may be compared to the announcement of the President-elect by the two houses of Congress on counting the electoral vote. The office of President never expires; "the King never dies." On the same day that King William IV., her uncle, died, the head of the church, the head of the cabinet, and the Lord Mayor of London proceeded to old Kensington Palace, and the Prime Minister gave up to this young girl, just turned her eighteenth birthday, the seals of office. All the cabinet signed the oath of allegiance to her. She made a little speech to them, written for her by the Prime Minister. Then she returned to them the seals of office. The official stamps were ordered to be re-engraved in her name, and the prayers of the Church of England altered in like manner. That same afternoon, while the dead King was lying on his bier, hundreds of carriages came to Kensington Palace bringing visitors to offer homage and congratulation. That night the Prime Minister wrote a proclamation, which was next day sealed with the new great seal, and, being read aloud at Kensington Palace, was circulated around the world. At the reading of this proclamation, which occurred at ten o'clock in the morning, Kensington Palace was the scene of the following ceremonies, as described by McGilchrist, the biographer: —

"All the avenues to the old palace were crowded, every balcony, window, and housetop being crammed with the better class of spectators. The space in the quadrangle in front of the window where Her Majesty was to appear was crowded with ladies and gentlemen, and even the parapets above were filled with people.

"At ten o'clock the guns in the park fired a salute, and immediately afterward the Queen made her appearance at the window of the tapestried anteroom adjoining the audience chamber, and was received with deafening cheers, — cheers all the more hearty that her appearance was a surprise, for few had known that she was to be there present. She was dressed in deep mourning, with a white tippet, white cuffs, and a border of white lace under a small black bonnet,

6

which was placed far back on her head, exhibiting her light-brown hair simply parted in front. She viewed the proceedings with intense interest, standing during the whole rehearsal of the proclamation; and, although she looked pale and fatigued, she returned the repeated rounds of cheers with great grace and dignity. All were touched with the pale face, wet with tears, calm and simply grave, the gravity being enhanced by the plain black dress and bands of brown hair, giving an aspect of Quaker-like neatness. On either side stood Lords Melbourne and Lansdowne, in their state dresses and blue ribbons, and close to her was her mother, who was dressed similarly to the Queen.

"In the court-yard were Garter King-at-Arms, with Heralds and Pursuivants in their robes of office, and eight Officers-of-Arms on horseback, bearing massive silver maces; Sergeants-at-Arms, with their maces and collars; the Sergeant Trumpeter, with his mace and collar; the trumpets, Drum-Major and drums; and Knights Marshal and men. On Her Majesty showing herself at the presence-chamber window, Garter principal King-at-Arms, having taken his station in the court-yard under the window, accompanied by the Duke of Norfolk as Earl-Marshal of England, read the proclamation, containing the formal and official announcement of the demise of King William IV., and of the consequent accession of Queen Alexandrina Victoria to the rule of these realms. The proclamation was brief, and to the point: —

"'Whereas it hath pleased Almighty God to call to his mercy our late Sovereign Lord, King William IV., of blessed memory, by whose decease the imperial crown of the united kingdom of Great Britain and Ireland is solely and rightfully come to the High and Mighty Princess Alexandrina Victoria, we therefore, the lords spiritual and temporal of this realm, being here assisted with these of his late Majesty's Privy Council, with numbers of other principal gentlemen of quality, the Lord Mayor, Aldermen, and citizens of London, do now hereby with one voice and consent of tongue, proclaim that the High and Mighty Princess Alexandrina Victoria is now, by the death of our late Sovereign William IV., of happy memory, become our only lawful and rightful liege lady, Alexandrina Victoria I., Queen of Great Britain and Ireland, Defender of the Faith, — to whom we acknowledge all faith and constant obedience, with all humble and hearty affection, beseeching God, by whom kings and queens do reign, to bless the Royal Princess Alexandrina Victoria with long and happy years to reign. God save the Queen!'

"At the termination of this proclamation the band struck up the national anthem, and a signal was given for the Park and Tower guns to fire, in order to announce the fact of the proclamation being made. The air was rent with cheers by those within the area, which were taken up by the tens of thousands outside. The moment she was proclaimed Queen, she turned round, threw her arms about her mother's neck, and wept without restraint. When her uncle, the Duke of Sussex, presented himself, to take the oath of allegiance, and was about to kneel in her presence to kiss her hand, she gracefully prevented him, kissed his cheek affectionately, and said, 'Do not kneel, my uncle, for I am still Victoria, your niece.'"

Three weeks afterward the young Queen moved to Buckingham Palace, and held her first court levee. This leads us to describe a royal reception.

The Queen's receptions are divided into *levees* and drawing-rooms, which are quite different affairs, although we generally confound the terms in America.

A *levee* is an occasion for the presentation of gentlemen, only, to the Queen.

A "drawing-room" is an occasion for the presentation of ladies, chiefly, to the Queen.

Each of these opportunities is advertised in the London daily papers with directions as to the coming and going of carriages. Unlike the receptions of our chief magistrate, the utmost care and circumspection are exercised in admitting persons to these levees and drawing-rooms. Court dress must be worn. The name of the person wishing to be introduced, with the name of the nobleman, gentleman, or foreign minister wishing to introduce him, must be sent to the Lord Chamberlain several days before presentation, and the latter is supposed to send the cards to the Queen that she may personally pass upon them.

The Queen and her household, indeed, would be less ceremonious and censorious about the quality of visitors to St. James's Palace, if it were not for the ludicrous and reverend jealousy of the common people and the newspapers. In 1862, a man who had been convicted of swindling was accidentally introduced to the Queen, and the press of the entire country was filled with indignant complaints about it. All this seems queer to us, used to the hurly-burly of a night at the White House; but perhaps it might be well if we also took the honor of the President more out of the custody of politicians.

Any English person who has been introduced to the Queen can make his ambassador in any land introduce him to the sovereign thereof.

The ceremony of presenting addresses to the Queen, greatly stickled for by Englishmen, is also regulated after the severest fashion. Not more than four persons can present an address, although it may be signed by a million, and the bearers are permitted to offer no comments or speeches whatever. The latter provision, if insisted upon at Washington, would probably put an end to all petitioning.

On her first reception the Queen wore a rich lama dress, her head glittered with diamonds, and her breast was covered with the insignia of the Garter and other orders. A pair of embroidered velvet slippers covered feet, which, resting on a cushion, were observed and admired by all as "exquisitely small."

The first official ceremony of the new girl Queen was the dissolution of Parliament; for the Queen is a part of Parliament, and her attendance upon the opening, the proroguing, or the dissolving thereof, is made an occasion of considerable pomp.

It is with this imposing procession that the Queen opens, prorogues, or dissolves Parliament:—

Six grand carriages, each drawn by a set of bays, precede her immediate party. These carriages are driven by servants in powdered wigs, knee-breeches of silk or velvet, silk stockings, and buckled shoes, and footmen in like gorgeous livery stand behind them.

The first carriage contains three Gentlemen Ushers, and the Exon in Waiting. The second carriage contains a Groom in Waiting, and three Pages of Honor in Waiting. The third carriage contains the Equerry in Waiting, and the Groom of the Robes. The fourth carriage contains the Clerk, Marshal, the Silver Stick in Waiting, the Field Officer in Waiting, and the Comptroller of the Household. The fifth carriage contains the Captain of the Yeomen of the Guard, the Lord in Waiting, and the Treasurer of the Household.

The sixth carriage contains the Lady in Waiting, the Lord Steward, and the Gold Stick in Waiting. All these officials are clad in georgeous state-dress. These six carriages are followed by the Queen's marshalmen, the Queen's footmen of state, and a party of the yeomen guard. After all this follows the grand state coach, which cost nearly forty thousand dollars, was constructed in 1762, or fourteen years prior to the independence of America, by the design of Sir Wm. Chambers, a celebrated architect, and was painted by Cipriani. In this coach sits the Queen. Her crown has gone before her, carried by one of the Lord Chamberlain's chief officers upon a velvet cushion. The Lord Chamberlain and the Vice Chamberlain conduct her to this carriage. None ride with her except the Mistress of the Robes and the Master of the Horse. Eight magnificent cream-colored horses draw this gorgeous coach.

The ceremony which the Queen performed within the Houses of Parliament will come more properly in the chapter upon the "House of Lords."

About four months afterward she visited in grand state the ancient Corporation of London, or that part of London which exclusively has a city charter and was anciently surrounded by walls. This also is a celebrated royal ceremony in England, and it illustrates how jealously London city insists upon all its hereditary honors and privileges. Her dress was pink satin shot with silver. She rode from Marlborough House, her temporary residence, — now the property of her son, the Prince of Wales, — to the Guildhall, or City Hall of London. All along the way banners, evergreens, mottoes, and her portraits blew in the dark fogs of the narrow streets. At Temple Bar, one of the ancient gates of London, she found the way barred before her, but there the Lord Mayor and aldermen dismounted from horseback, and presented her with the keys of the gate. Then they were swung back and permitted her to enter, but before her coach the Lord Mayor rode all the length of the city, with the jealous sword thereof held aloft, while behind her followed the mounted aldermen. Around St. Paul's cathedral the *guilds*, or voting companies of tradesmen, were crowded upon their "hustings" or voting-places, to intimate that they had a voice by right in her government. An address of welcome and fealty was presented to her, and the boys of the charity schools sang the national anthem of "God save the Queen." At Guildhall she was regaled with a magnificent banquet, at the expense of the city of London, and she returned to Westminster over the same route, — illuminated in the night.

The first message which the Queen sent to Parliament was to ask for a moneyed income for her German mother. This was promptly granted, and one hundred and fifty thousand dollars a year was the sum fixed, equal to six years' salary of the President of the United States. After this the Queen observed the strictest formal etiquette toward her mother, to quiet any suspicions that the old foreign lady was influencing her in the state. Her mother was always placed at her left hand at dinner, which is in the palace quite a ceremony of itself. The old lady, relieved of "duns" and well-provided for, lived down to 1861, the same year the Queen's husband died.

About a year after her proclamation, the young Queen, now past nineteen years of age, was solemnly crowned at Westminster Abbey. We are all familiar with the ceremony of inaugurating the President of the United States. It costs the government nothing. It consists of a speech to the people and the taking of an oath at the hands of the highest judge in the land. Some of our presidents have ridden to the Capitol alone on horseback, "hitched" their own horses to the fence, taken the oath, untied the horse again, and ridden back to the White House. Whatever festivities we have, incidentally, are of the spontaneous movement of the people. Washington was inaugurated at the New York City Hall. Jefferson was the first President inaugurated at Washington. Madison was the first at Washington who addressed the crowd. There have been two days when the country was without a President, the fourth of March falling upon Sunday. After these simple reminiscences we may better conceive the extraordinary pageant of crowning an English sovereign, when we are told that Victoria's coronation cost three hundred and fifty thousand dollars, which was not much beyond a quarter of the expenses at the coronation of the worthless George IV.

This ceremony of coronation is the most gorgeous pageant witnessed in the British Empire, where the well-known loyalty of the people makes it a popular holiday as well as a right ancient ceremony. It happens not more than once or twice in the lifetime of a reader, although there was one Englishman, "Old Parr," who had lived in the reigns of ten sovereigns, namely: Edward IV., Edward V., Richard III., Henry VII., Henry VIII., Edward VI., Mary, Elizabeth, James I., and Charles I.; in all one hundred and fifty-two years; he was the Methusaleh of modern times.

To see Victoria's coronation in June, 1838, four hundred thousand people visited London. One million dollars in gold were paid, in the aggregate, merely for window-room to look out upon the procession. One ambassador paid eight thousand dollars for a chariot in which to ride in the pageant, and another hired one for a few hours for twelve hundred and fifty dollars. Marshal Soult and the Duke of Wellington, ancient opponents, were amongst the thousands who honored the Queen. The procession passed over a route not above two miles long, starting from Buckingham Palace and describing a semicircle through Westminster to the grand old Abbey, but not entering the city of London proper, at all. In the procession marched or rode all the executive parts of the government, the

Queen's household, her troops, and the foreign ambassadors, while the nobility and the lords and dignities of the church waited in full dress in the Abbey from daylight till nearly noon.

Contemporary accounts of the spectacle of this procession and of the scene within the Abbey when the Queen arrived there, excite the imagination to the utmost. The day was beautiful for London. At dawn the guns of the grim and bloody old Tower, several miles from the Palace, expressed themselves in salvos. London was full of ringing bells and heraldic banners, of cannon and cheering, of drink and pleasantry. The procession moved soon after breakfast-time, and very wonderful it was as a testimonial to the power of the British Empire. The most novel feature of the procession, says one writer, was the carriages of the foreign ambassadors, with their jagers in gorgeous or grotesque uniforms. These came in the order in which they had arrived on their special missions to the coronation; the carriages of the regular resident ambassadors came in their appointed order of precedence. Next followed the members of the Royal Family, the Duchess of Kent, the Queen's mother preceding the carriages of the surviving sons of George III. To the Queen's barge-master, with forty-eight watermen, succeeded twelve of the royal carriages, containing the ladies and gentlemen of the household. Next came mounted, three and three, the high functionaries of the army, amongst them the great Duke of Waterloo. And after came royal huntsmen, yeomen, prickers, marshalmen, foresters, and a host of other minor functionaries, — the whole of the mounted household troops being here and there interspersed at intervals in the cavalcade with the gigantic Horse Guards, helmeted and most conspicuous. Then came the grand state coach containing the Queen, with the Duchess of Sutherland, Mistress of the Robes. On either side of the carriage rode Lord Combermere, Gold Stick in Waiting, and the Earl of Ilchester, Captain of the Yeomen of the Guard. The Earl of Albermarle, as Master of the Horse, and the Duke of Buccleuch, as Captain-General of the Royal Scottish Archers, rode behind. A squadron of Life Guards brought up the rear.

At Westminster Abbey this splendid procession came to a halt. Above its music, plumes, and emblazoned banners, with the gorgeous royal standard, blue, yellow, and crimson, advanced above all the rest, rose the solemn twin towers of the great cathedral, two hundred and twenty-five feet, grimy and venerable, and buttresses and flying buttresses, carvings of saints and kings, pinnacles and transepts, showed hoary as sooty frostwork in the bright sunshine. The doors swung wide open, and nobles of state and bishops appeared to receive her. Music burst suddenly through the solemn vastness of the abbey-church as the sovereign entered, making the deep arches and vaulted roof tremble, and all the painted windows within shed their soft colors upon the tombs and effigies of kings, as well as upon the brilliant congregation, filling far-off galleries and swarming over the floors of stone. Down the long length of the nave and choir, four hundred and sixteen feet; up into the carved groinings, one hundred feet, held to their places by entwined trunks of stone; into the grand transepts, two hundred and twenty-five feet from rose-window to window, the coronation anthem poured. As the Queen retired to her robing-room the procession formed in the nave and slowly marched toward the altar, which was laden with magnificent gold plate, and beside which stood St. Edward's chair. Besides the elements which are common to all great English royal processions, and which it is, therefore, not requisite to recapitulate, the regalia, which only appear on such occasions, were thus distributed: St. Edward's staff, the golden spurs, the sceptre with the cross, the curtana, and two swords of investiture, were borne respectively by the Duke of Roxburgh, Lord Byron, Duke of Cleveland, Duke of Devonshire, Marquis of Westminster, and Duke of Sutherland. The coronets of the princes of the blood were borne by noblemen; their trains by knights' or peers' sons. Next came the Earl-Marshal, Duke of Norfolk, with his staff, Lord Melbourne with the sword of state, and the Duke of Wellington with his staff as Lord High Constable; the Dukes of Richmond, Hamilton, and Somerset bore the sceptre and dove, St. Edward's crown, and the orb; the Bishops of Bangor, Winchester, and London carried the patina, chalice, and Bible.

The Queen, who was supported on one side by the Bishop of Bath and Wells, on the other by the Bishop of Durham, wore a royal robe of crimson velvet, furred with ermine, and broidered with gold lace. She wore the collars of her orders, and on her head a circlet of gold. Eight peers' daughters bore her train, most of them friends of her childhood, and distinguished by their personal attractions. About fifty ladies of rank, occupying various positions in the household, succeeded, and the procession was concluded by officers of state and yeomen of the guard.

The splendid attire of some of the foreign ambassadors attracted more attention than even the sovereign to whose court they were accredited. The costume of the Austrian Prince Esterhazy, says one authority, was by far the most gorgeous; his dress, even to his boot-heels, sparkled with diamonds. The Turkish Ambassador seemed especially bewildered at the general splendor of the scene; for some moments he stopped in astonishment, and had to be admonished to move to his allotted place.

As the Queen advanced slowly to the centre of the choir, she was received with hearty plaudits, and the musicians sang the anthem, "I was Glad." At its close, the boys of Westminster School, privileged of old to occupy a special gallery, chanted "Vivat Victoria Regina."

On this the Queen moved to a chair, midway between the chair of homage and the altar, and there, after a few moments' private devotion, kneeling on a fald-stool, she sat down, and the ceremony proper began.

First came the "recognition." The Archbishop of Canterbury, accompanied by some half-dozen of the greatest civil dignitaries, advanced, and said, "Sirs, I here present unto you Queen Victoria, the undoubted Queen of this realm; wherefore, all of you who have come this day to do your homage, are you willing to do the same?" On this, all Her Majesty's subjects present shouted, "God save Queen Victoria!" the Archbishop turning in succession to the north, south, and west sides of the Abbey, and the Queen doing the same. The bishops who bore them then placed the patina, chalice, and Bible on the altar; the Queen, kneeling, made her first offering, — a pall, or altar-cloth, of gold. The Archbishop having offered a prayer, the regalia were laid on the altar; the litany and communion services were read, and a brief sermon preached, by various prelates.

The preacher was the Bishop of London, and his text was from the second book of Chronicles, chapter xxxiv., verse 31: "And the king stood in his place, and made a covenant before the Lord, to walk after the Lord, and to keep his commandments, and his testimonies, and his statutes, with all his heart, and with all his soul, to perform the words of the covenant which are written in this book." After the sermon the Queen swore, the Archbishop of Canterbury putting the oath as follows: —

"*Archbishop of Canterbury.* — Will you solemnly promise and swear to govern the people of this United Kingdom of Great Britain and Ireland, and the dominions thereto belonging, according to the statutes in Parliament agreed on, and the respective laws and customs of the same?

"*Queen.* — I solemnly promise so to do.

"*Archbishop.* — Will you, to the utmost of your power, cause law and justice, in mercy, to be executed in all your judgments?

"*Queen.* — I will.

"*Archbishop.* — Will you, to the utmost of your power, maintain the laws of God, the true profession of the gospel, and the Protestant reformed religion, established by law? And will you maintain and preserve inviolably the settlement of the United Church of England and Ireland, and the doctrine, worship, discipline, and government thereof, as by law established within England and Ireland and the territories thereto belonging? And will you preserve to the bishops and clergy of England and Ireland, and to the churches there committed to their charge, all such rights and privileges as do, or shall, appertain unto them, or any of them?

"*Queen.* — All this I promise to do."

The Queen then went to the altar and laid her hand upon the gospels, taking the following oath: "The things which I have heretofore promised I will perform and keep. So help me God."

The Queen then kissed the gospels at the altar and signed the oath. The choir meantime sang, "Veni, Creator, Dominus." The Church of Scotland is protected by a separate oath, taken at a different time.

Next in the order of coronation was the anointment. The Queen sitting in King Edward's chair, four knights of the garter holding the while over her head a canopy of cloth of gold, her head and hands were anointed by the Archbishop of Canterbury; after which he said his prayer, or blessing, over her. In quick succession followed the delivery of the spurs, sword of state, etc. The Dean of Westminster, having taken the crown from the altar, handed it to the Archbishop, who reverently placed it on the Queen's head. This was no sooner done than there arose from every part of the edifice a tremendous shout, "God save the Queen!" accompanied with cheers and the waving of hats and handkerchiefs. At the same moment the peers and peeresses put on their coronets, the bishops their caps, and the kings-of-arms their crowns, the trumpets sounded, the drums were beaten, and volleys fired from the tower and park guns.

The crown — that symbol and metaphor of all sovereignty, spiritual as well as temporal — was especially made for Queen Victoria's coronation, and is quite a different affair from the crown we generally conceive. It weighs one pound and three-quarters, or little more than a man's winter hat, and is a cap of purple velvet, enclosed by hoops of silver, and studded with many diamonds and precious stones, amongst which are a splendid ruby and a matchless sapphire. Many of these stones had entered into the composition of other crowns, worn as long ago as the discovery of America. The whole of this comfortable crown is estimated to be worth £111,900 sterling, or about $559,500, which is, after all, only about three months' income of Mr. Alexander T. Stewart, the New York merchant, or less than the frequent turn of an "operation" in Wall Street.

The royal crown proper of England, however, is a circle of gold enriched with stones and pearls, and heightened with four crosses pattée and four fleurs-de-lis alternately. From these rise four arch-diadems, adorned with pearls, which close under a mound, ensigned with a cross pattée. It weighs eight pounds. With this heavy ornament was crowned George III., the last King of the thirteen American colonies. After the benediction and Te Deum, the Queen was "enthroned," or "lifted" as the formulary has it, from the chair in which she had first sat into the chair of homage, where she delivered the sceptre, etc., to noblemen, while she received the fealty of her more distinguished subjects. The Archbishop first knelt and did homage for himself and all the spiritual peers; next came the princes of the blood, who merely touched the crown, kissed her left cheek, swore the oath of homage, and retired without kneeling; then the peers in succession came, — seventeen dukes, twenty-two marquises, ninety-four earls, twenty viscounts, and ninety-two barons. Each peer knelt bareheaded, and kissed Her Majesty's hand. Lord Rolle, who was upwards of eighty, stumbled and fell in going up the steps; the Queen at once stepped forward, and held out her hand to assist him. While the peers were doing homage, the Earl of Surrey, Treasurer of the Household, threw silver coronation medals about the choir and lower galleries; and when the homage was completed, the members of the House of Commons, who occupied a special gallery, indicated their loyalty by giving nine lusty cheers. It was almost a quarter to four when the procession came back along the nave.

The return cavalcade along the streets was even more attractive than that of the morning, for the royal and noble personages now wore their coronets, and the Queen her crown.

In the evening, the Queen entertained a hundred guests to dinner at Buckingham Palace, and at a late hour witnessed from the roof fireworks in the park.

The Duke of Wellington gave a ball, to which two thousand guests were invited. All the cabinet ministers gave state dinners; a fair was held in Hyde Park; and a grand review of troops by the Queen, and a great banquet was given at Guildhall.

About seven months after her coronation the Queen was married to Albert, her cousin, the second son of the Duke of the little state of Saxe Coburg in Germany. His father and mother had been divorced while he was a child. The match had been really made by Victoria's mother and his relatives, particularly by the old King of Belgium, Leopold, father of "Carlotta," the brief Empress of Mexico. He had met the future Queen when he was seventeen years old. His income at home in Germany was twelve thousand dollars a year, and he received his education at Bonn on the Rhine. He was younger than the Queen by a few months. Before he came to England the Queen sent him the order of the Garter, the highest insignia of English knighthood, and a present of diamonds, both the honor and the present being of value to his poor estate. There was considerable opposition to the match, and the Queen was in no hurry to marry anybody, but she committed some indiscretions while a virgin Queen, and her ministers were anxious to put her under the control of a husband. No member of the royal family in England is allowed to marry an English subject, and the choice on the Continent is limited to Protestant princes. There are few Protestant princes equal in rank or wealth to those of England, and therefore the hand of the powerful Queen was in great request.

This restrictive law, justly denounced by many English people, compels the princes of England, if they dare marry at home, to beget illegitimate children only, and the same has been the case in Victoria's time, — virtuous women and wives ranking before the law as mere mistresses. The object of the law is to prevent ambitious suitors making civil feuds in the nobility at home.

Young Albert came courting to England by the advice of old Leopold in 1839, four months before his marriage. The young Queen received him at Windsor, was charmed with his manners and appearance, and in a week decided to accept him.

A magazine article published not long ago in England gives the following undisputed account of his wooing: —

"The Prince played the part of a royal lover with all the grace peculiar to his house. He never willingly absented himself from the Queen's society and presence, and her every wish was anticipated with the alacrity of an unfeigned attachment. At length Her Majesty, having wholly made up her mind as to the issue of this visit, found herself in some measure embarrassed as to the fit and proper means of indicating her preference to the Prince. This was a perplexing task, but the Queen acquitted herself of it with equal delicacy and tact. At one of the palace balls she took occasion to present her bouquet to the Prince at the conclusion of a dance, and the hint was not lost upon the polite and gallant German. His close uniform, buttoned up to the throat, did not admit of his placing the Persian-like gift where it would be most honored; so he immediately drew his penknife, and cut a slit in his dress in the neighborhood of his heart, where he gracefully deposited the happy omen. Again, to announce to the privy council her intended union was an easy duty in comparison to that of intimating her wishes to the principal party concerned; and here, too, it is said that our Sovereign Lady displayed unusual presence of mind and female ingenuity.

"The Prince was expressing the grateful sense which he entertained of his reception in England, and the delight which he experienced during his stay from the kind attentions of royalty, when the Queen very naturally and very pointedly, put to him the question upon which their future fates depended: 'If, indeed, your Highness is so much pleased with this country, perhaps you would not object to remaining in it, and making it your home.' No one can doubt the reply."

Prince Albert's testimony tallies with the above; for we have extant a copy of a letter he wrote to his grandmother immediately after his betrothal.

Prince Albert wrote to his grandmother: —

"The subject," he says, "which has occupied us so much of late is at last settled. The Queen sent for me alone to her room a few days ago, and declared to me in a genuine outburst of love and affection that I had gained her whole heart, and would make her intensely happy if I would make her the sacrifice of sharing her life with her; for she said she looked on it as a sacrifice. Since that moment Victoria does whatever she fancies I should wish or like, and we talk together a great deal about our future life, which she promises me to make as happy as possible. Oh, the future!"

The entire courtship of the Prince and Queen lasted five weeks. The engagement was first communicated to the ministers, then to relatives, at last to Parliament. The latter prince-ridden body was asked to vote Prince Albert two hundred and fifty thousand dollars a year. After some severe debate, which made angry both the Queen and old Leopold, this sum was reduced to one hundred and fifty thousand, — enough, one would think. To avoid further debate, Prince Albert refused to be made an English peer. A vessel was sent to Calais to bring the Prince to England; his bride and her mother received him at the door of Buckingham Palace, and that night he paid formal visits to all the members of the royal family. The next day but one they were married. A description of the marriage ceremony will be interesting to the ladies, besides necessary to make plain the real life of a living sovereign.

Prince Albert set out from Buckingham Palace, we are told, dressed as a British field-marshal, and with all the insignia of the Garter, the jewels of which had been a personal present from the Queen, having on one side his father and on the other his brother, both in military uniforms. He entered his carriage amid tremendous cheers, and the enthusiastic waving of handkerchiefs by a bevy of ladies privileged to stand in the ground lobbies of the palace, and was escorted to the chapel of St. James's Palace by a squadron of the Life Guards. On the return of the carriages which carried the Prince and his company, Her Majesty was in turn apprised that all was in readiness for her departure. She, too, was enthusiastically received, "but her eye was bent principally upon the ground." In the same carriage with the Queen rode the Duchesses of Kent and Sutherland. It was noticed as she drove along that she was extremely pale, and looked very anxious, though two or three incidents in the crowd caused her to smile.

On her arrival at her old brick palace of St. James, the Queen was conducted to the presence chamber, where she remained with her maids-of-honor and train-bearers, awaiting the Lord Chamberlain's summons to the altar. Meanwhile, the colonnade within the palace, along which the bridal procession had to pass and repass, had been filled since early morn by the élite of England's rank and beauty. Each side of the way was a parterre of white robes, white relieved with blue, white and green, amber, crimson, purple, fawn, and stone color. All wore wedding favors of lace, orange-flower blossoms, or silver bullion, some of great size, and many in most exquisite taste. Most of the gentlemen were in court dress; and the scene during the patient hours of waiting was made picturesque by the passing to and fro in various garbs of burly yeomen of the guard, armed with their massive halberts, slight-built gentlemen-at-arms, with partisans of equal slightness; elderly pages of state, and pretty pages of honor; officers of the lord chamberlain, and officers of the woods and forests; heralds, all embroidery, and cuirassiers in polished steel; prelates in their rochets, and priests in their stoles, and singing-boys in their surplices of virgin white.

Within the chapel, in which the altar was magnificently decorated and laden with a profusion of gold plate, four state chairs were set, varying in splendor according to the rank of the destined occupants, respectively for Her Majesty, Prince Albert, the Queen Dowager, and the Duchess of Kent. The Archbishops of Canterbury and York, and the Bishop of London, having taken their places within the altar-rails, a flourish of trumpets announced the procession of the bridegroom. As the Prince passed along, the gentlemen greeted him with loud clapping of the hands, and the ladies waved their handkerchiefs with at least equal enthusiasm. In a few minutes the procession of the bride was announced by trumpets and drums. It was of six or seven times the numerical strength of the bridegroom's, and the beauty of the twelve bridesmaids, all daughters of peers of the three highest grades, was specially commended. The Duchess of Cambridge led by the hand her then child-daughter, the Princess Mary, "and the mother of so beautiful a child was certainly not to be seen without much interest." The Duchess of Kent appeared "disconsolate and distressed;" while the Duke of Sussex, who was to give away the bride, was "in excellent spirits." The Queen herself looked "anxious and excited, and paler even than usual." She was dressed in a rich white satin, trimmed with orange-flower blossoms. She wore a wreath of the same, over which was a veil of rich Honiton lace, worn so as not to conceal her face. She wore as jewels the collar of the order of the Garter, with a diamond necklace and ear-rings.

After the conclusion of the marriage rite, the Queen hastily crossed to the opposite side of the altar, and kissed the queen dowager and her mother, who were standing there. She then took Prince Albert's hand, and passed down the aisle. On the return to Buckingham Palace, it was observed that the Prince, still retaining the Queen's hand in his own, whether by accident or design, held it in such a way as to display the wedding-ring, which was more solid than is usual in ordinary weddings. When the Queen had been led into the palace by her husband, it was observed that her morning paleness had entirely passed off, and that she entered her own halls with an open, joyous, and slightly flushed countenance.

After the wedding breakfast the young couple departed, at a quarter before four, for Windsor, amid the cheers of the undiminished multitude. Her Majesty's travelling-dress was a white satin pelisse, trimmed with swan's-down, with a white satin bonnet and feather.

The marriage thus commemorated was one of the happiest royal attachments ever made. Doubtless the bride and groom already loved each other, or soon learned to do so. The poor Prince was obliging and modest; he made a prudent counsellor to the Queen, and seldom excited public criticism. He had the German domestic virtues,— love of method, thrift, and the open air. His wife became busy with child-bearing, and therefore made no trouble nor interference with the state. He turned the energies of his household to saving money, making good investments, and marrying off his children as well as possible; and unless his sons should turn out profligates, the private estate laid up by Victoria and Albert is enough to make them very rich and powerful, even if they should lose the English crown.

After marriage, house-keeping, and of the Queen's practice of this first of female arts we have some close and entertaining glimpses in her own books, called "Early Years of the Prince Consort," and "Journal of our Life in the Highlands." But the testimony of third persons is perhaps more valid, and from one of these, Lord Lennox, we obtain the following account of a state dinner in Buckingham Palace. Anybody who has dined in the White House at Washington can draw the comparison.

"At each end of the dining-hall, buffets, seventeen feet high and forty broad, were set. They were of rich fretted Gothic framework, covered with crimson cloth, and brilliant with massive gold plate. Immediately opposite the queen was set a pyramid of plate, its apex being the tiger's head captured at Seringapatam, and comprising the 'Iluma' of precious stones which Lord Wellesley, the Governor-General of India, presented to George IV. The table, which was laid for a hundred guests, extended the whole length of the hall. All down the centre, epergnes, vases, cups, and candelabra were ranged, the celebrated St. George's candelabrium being opposite Her Majesty. The hall was splendidly illuminated, and two bands of the guards discoursed sweet music from a balcony. The yeomen of the guard stood on duty at the entrance. The repast, which did ample justice to the merits of the Queen's renowned cuisinier, Francatelli, was entirely served in gold plate, and the attendance was so faultless that there was less bustle and confusion than usually attend a repast shared by a party of ten or a dozen. At a quarter to nine grace was said; and after the dessert and wine had been placed on the table, the Lord Steward rose and proposed, without remark, 'The Queen.' The Queen simply, when the toast had been drank, bowed her acknowledgments. After a brief pause, the health of Prince Albert was drank standing, as the Queen's had been, the band playing the 'Coburg March.' At half-past nine the Queen rose, and, accompanied by the Duchess of Kent, was followed by all the ladies to the drawing-room."

The Queen and her family, however, have never been recognized as possessing genius. The Hanoverian dulness marks their countenances, and no Prince of that line could ever have earned great credit in private life.

Guizot, the French statesman, who was the Queen's guest at dinner in 1840, remarked on the want of animation and interest in the conversation, whether at the dinner-table or in the drawing-room. Politics of any kind, home or foreign, were, apparently to his surprise, strictly avoided. When the gentlemen joined the ladies, which, throughout the Queen's reign, has been at a very short interval after the departure of the latter from the dining-room, they all sat on chairs round a circular table set before the Queen, who occupied a sofa. Two or three of her ladies engaged themselves in fancy work; Prince Albert challenged some one to a game of chess. Lady Palmerston and M. Guizot, "with some effort," carried on a flagging dialogue. The conversation being thus flat, M. Guizot took to looking at the pictures on the walls, of which there were but three, hung over the different doors of the apartment. He was very much astonished at the extraordinary contrasts in the subjects of these pictures. They certainly were most incogruous. One was Fenélon, the second the Czar Peter, and the third Anne Hyde, the discarded wife of James II. He asked one of his fellow-guests whether the combination was intentional or an accident? But he could get no satisfaction on the subject. No one had remarked the combination, and no one could tell the reason for it.

At the levee which he attended the day following, he was still more astonished and perplexed. "I regard," he says, "with excited esteem the profound respect of that vast assembly, courtiers, citizens, lawyers, churchmen, officers, military and naval, passing before the Queen, the greater portion bending the knee to kiss her hand, all perfectly solemn, sincere, and awkward. The sincerity and seriousness were both needed to prevent those antiquated habits, wigs, and gags, those costumes which no one in England now wears except on such occasions, from appearing somewhat ridiculous. But I am little sensible to the outward appearance of absurdity when the substance partakes not of that character."

Promptly on marriage-time Victoria's first child was born, now wife to the heir of the crown of Prussia. Less than a year afterward the heir to Victoria's crown, the present Prince of Wales was born, and a state bulletin thus announced the fact: —

"BUCKINGHAM PALACE, Nov. 9th.

"This morning, at twelve minutes before eleven o'clock, the Queen was happily delivered of a Prince, His Royal Highness Prince Albert, Her Royal Highness the Duchess of Kent, several Lords of Her Majesty's Most Honorable Privy Council, and the Ladies of Her Majesty's Bedchamber, being present. This great and important news was immediately made known to the town by the firing of the Tower and Park guns; and the Privy Council being assembled as soon as possible thereupon, at the Council Chamber, Whitehall, it was ordered that a Form of Thanksgiving be prepared by his Grace the Archbishop of Canterbury, to be used in all churches and chapels throughout England and Wales, and the town of Berwick-upon-Tweed, on Sunday, the fourteenth of November, or the Sunday after the respective ministers shall receive the same.

"Her Majesty and the infant Prince are, God be praised! both doing well."

The Prince of Wales was born in dark and ominous times, in the starving days of 1841; yet all due exhibitions of loyalty were made.

Upon the announcement of the happy accouchement, the nobility and gentry crowded to the palace to tend their dutiful inquiries as to the sovereign's convalescence. Amongst other, came the Lord Mayor and civic dignitaries in great state. They felt peculiarly proud that the Prince should have been born on Lord Mayor's day; in fact, just at the very moment when the time-honored municipal procession was starting from the city for Westminster. In memory of the happy coincidence, the Lord Mayor of the year, Mr. Pirie, was created Sir John Pirie, Baronet. On the 4th of December, when he was twenty-five days old, the queen created her son by letters patent, Prince of Wales and Earl of Chester: "And him, our said and most dear son, the Prince of the United Kingdom of Great Britain and Ireland, as has been accustomed, we do ennoble and invest with the said Principality and Earldom, by girding him with a sword, by putting a coronet on his head, and a gold ring on his finger, and also by delivering a gold rod into his hand, that he may preside there, and direct and defend those parts." By the fact of his birth as heir-apparent, the Prince indefeasibly inherited, without the necessity of patent or creation, these dignities, — the titles of Duke of Saxony, by right of his father; and, by right of his mother, Duke of Cornwall, Duke of Rothsay, Earl of Carrick, Baron of Renfrew, Lord of the Isles, and Great Steward of Scotland.

It is this young man who is to succeed, in all probability, his virtuous and now widowed mother.

Victoria, unlike many ladies in private life, never objected to increasing her family. She has borne nine children. She adorned the female character, and showed herself to be a healthy, spirited, yet modest lady, happy as she is good, until, in 1861, her sturdy German husband died. If the English throne is to continue, the offspring of Prince Albert will long occupy it, and to associate his death with their future careers these passages of bereavement in the palace are appended.

Shortly after midnight the great bell of St. Paul's, which is never tolled except upon the death of a member of the royal family, boomed the fatal tidings over a district extending, in the quietude of the early Sabbath morn, for miles around the metropolis.

The Queen, the Princess Alice, and the Prince of Wales, who had been hastily summoned from Cambridge, sat with the dying Prince until the last. After the closing scene the Queen supported herself nobly, and, after a short burst of uncontrollable grief, she is said to have gathered her children around her, and addressed them in the most solemn and affectionate terms. "She declared to her family that, though she felt crushed by the loss of one who had been her companion through life, she knew how much was expected of her, and she accordingly called on her children to give her their assistance, in order that she might do her duty to them and the country." The Duke of Cambridge, and many gentlemen connected with the court, with six of the royal children, were present at the Prince's death. In answer to some one of those present who tenderly offered condolence, the Queen is reported to have said: "I suppose I must not fret too much, for many poor women have to go through the same trial."

Prince Albert was buried at Windsor and this is the inscription over his costly tomb, prepared, it is said, by the Queen's own hands; the original is in Latin.

"Here lies the most illustrious and exalted Albert, Prince Consort, Duke of Saxony, Prince of Saxe Coburg and Gotha, Knight of the Most Noble Order of the Garter, the most beloved husband of the most august and potent Queen Victoria. He died on the fourteenth day of December, 1861, in the forty-third year of his age."

Hitherto I have given sketches of pageants only, such as connect the sovereign with the state. She is the nominal ruler over a "United Kingdom" of thirty millions of people, nineteen millions of whom inhabit England proper, and in her numerous colonies live about two hundred millions more, savage or civilized, four millions of whom are close beside the United States. Her parent kingdom, the island called "Great Britain," is the largest island in Europe, and the sixth in size in the world. At the time of the American Revolution the United Kingdom contained less than eight millions of people. At present the assessed wealth of that kingdom is thirty-two billions of dollars, — double the wealth of the United States; its imports and exports amount to seven hundred millions a year, and its debt is about four billions and one hundred millions. Each one of these vast items affords a volume of suggestion, which the present is not the place to consider. The aggregate of them unquestionably indicates the mightiest empire of modern times, from which we, as a detached part, rank certainly not more than two places separated. This United Kingdom owes the backbone of its power to the fusion of northern nations in it. By its insular position it was relieved from the ravages of other than civil war, and it bred hardy sailors on the long indented line of its coast. Its acceptance of the reformed or Protestant religion made it a grand asylum for the free-spirited, ingenious, and persecuted Protestants of the Continent. It is the Roman Empire of Protestantism, and the Queen now at its head is a descendant of that Elector of Saxony who protected Martin Luther. When the Spanish Armada perished off the English coast, the sea changed masters. Coal, iron, tin, lead, and flax were the adventitious possessions of a race thus predestined. With scarcely an exception its kings have been unworthy of such a kingdom. Elizabeth and Oliver Cromwell stand almost isolated in its long list of wicked, errant, or sluggish sovereigns, and the state has made progress in almost every case, proportionate to its aggressions upon the monarch. With the present expensive but otherwise harmless royal family, the United Kingdom has gained upon its past rapid and solid progress, and perhaps the poet, Tennyson, was even more excellent as a philosopher when he wrote of Victoria: —

"Her court was pure; her life serene;
God gave her peace; her land reposed;
A thousand claims to reverence closed
In her as mother, wife, and queen.

"And statesmen at her council met,
Who knew the seasons, — when to take
Occasion by the hand, and make
The bounds of freedom wider yet,

"By shaping some august decree,
Which kept her throne unshaken still,
Broad-based upon her people's will,
And compassed by the inviolate sea."

CHAPTER III.

THE BRITISH ARISTOCRACY.

Their number, origin, wealth, privileges, habits of life, estates, and influence on the nation.

If, as some have contended, titles of honor are founded in human happiness, gratitude, and love of distinction, happy should we be in America, who are all either "general," "colonel," "major," "squire," "chief," "boss," "captain," "cook," or "judge." One of our humorists has said, that in the height of the war he threw a stone at a dog, which, missing, hit six brigadier generals. "And," he naïvely concludes, "it was not a good day for brigadiers either."

Soberly speaking, there are here no legalized titles but those of officers of the army and navy. Following colonial precedents, the President of the United States is sometimes called "His Excellency," but seldom by well-bred persons. "Honorable," used as a prefix to the names of members of Congress and others, is likewise an instance of deference or compliment, having no more authority than the "Esquire" which we now append by vicious habit to every male person's name, and which, like the word "Professor," used by mountebanks, charlatans, and school-teachers indiscriminately, has fallen into disfavor amongst people worthy of it. The universal habit here of addressing people by these fictitious titles is our defence against ever being compelled to accord them. When a sovereign in Europe wishes to bring a certain order of knighthood into disrepute, he confers it upon Tom, Dick, and Harry. So, to be addressed by the bare and respectful term of plain "Mister," is still the most honorable prefix known to Americans.

But, if we look about us, we shall find abundant relics of an aristocracy, in the names of our streets, counties, and villages. New York has Kings, Queens, and Dutchess County; Virginia has Princess and Princesses. In some part of the United States the estate of every nobleman in England is probably commemorated. The counties of New York and Massachusetts abound in such revivals. Maine, New Hampshire, New Jersey, and New York will suggest a title of nobility to every Englishman. While the author is putting this chapter to writing, his newspaper relates the death of one of the last of the Fairfaxes, the patrons of Washington. Near by the capital city live the Calverts still, descendants of Lord Baltimore. The great republic has absorbed these into simple citizenship; but the kingdom from which their titles were derived, continues to our day that ancient aristocracy recognized by our forefathers. There exist those badges, which, to retain or win, made Sir John Johnson a tory, and Benedict Arnold a traitor. In no country of Europe is the aristocracy so well defined or so powerful as in modern England. Legislatively it is irresponsible, being hereditary; and while the House of Commons is the instrument of British legislation, the aristocracy, by their social and landed power, control a majority of places in it. A late English Review took the poll of the House of Commons, and showed that it contained two hundred and fifty persons, or more than one-third, either peers or related to peers, while out of the whole number of six hundred and fifty-eight members there were not two hundred who had not either "title, office, place, pension, church patronage, or immediate relatives deriving large sums from government abuses."

In the United States our "best families" have derived their position, either directly or by inheritance, from wealth, chiefly acquired by commerce, manufactures, or speculation in lands, staples, and enterprises. Not one of these people can be a "gentleman" in the English sense. With us, "gentleman" refers to the feeling and the breeding; with the English the "gentry" is a rich, leisurely, anciently derived class, yet untitled; and, strange as it may seem, there are English "gentlemen" whose descent is so anciently established that a title would impair it: such regard, with haughty contempt, the new-made baronets or peers whose honors came from brewing good ale, or building railroads, or writing histories.

Over English society the shadow of the aristocracy rests like the pillar of fire by night which guided the Hebrews. Its patronage, its lineage, its carriage, its unassailable place at the summit of society and government — and, also, we must admit, the fine undegenerate graces of its members — enable it to absorb, corrupt, or charm the entire character of the common people. One by one the commons bow down to it, — now the aged knees of Carlyle, now the pregnant hinges of the poet Kingsley, now in mid-flourish the young radical Disraeli abases himself. It is impossible for an American to conceive the vigor and influence of this aristocracy until he has visited England, and even then, if he should come within the circle of its social power, he might become its apologist. Then he can understand how mightily this aristocracy appeals to every ambitious young Englishman, lying, so to speak, across the threshold of his life, charming him with its conversation, helping him with its means and its favor at court, appealing to his imagination by its castles and woodlands, incorporating itself with his traditions, until he discovers himself its defender, and lays down his life in its worship and service. This was the highest motive of Nelson, to which I have referred already, — "A peerage, or a tomb in Westminster Abbey" amongst the bones of peers.

It is from the United States that the English aristocracy has met its great opposition in our century. When Bright, Cobden, Hughes, Cobbett, Beales, and the young republicans of this and the last generation moved upon the aristocracy, it was with the history and constitution of the United States unfolded like the gospels. When, twenty years ago, Bright and his friends, in and out of Parliament, raised the question as to whether the English government might not accept some profitable suggestions from the polity of the United States, a laugh went up from the forward partisans of the aristocracy too loud to be merry. Authors and novelists, under the patronage of this landed aristocracy, hastened to America to misrepresent it. And when, in 1861, the towering republic cracked from crest to centre, the talent and vigor of the British kingdom were developed against us in the most insidious, mocking, and persistent literature which has signalized the art of printing. If the republic is prospered in the future as in the past, men will not wonder half so much, at the end of the next century, at the cruise of the "Alabama" as at the leaders of the "Times" and the speeches of the peers. In them the British aristocracy reached high-water mark; America maintained her unity, and British panegyric has been since as fulsome as its previous misrepresentation was abortive.

In the principal American staple, cotton, the landed aristocracy of England met a no less powerful enemy. To us it was the *fleur de lis* of a temporary aristocracy; to the British aristocracy more destructive than the wars of the red and the white roses. It built up in England mighty *guilds* of manufacturers, raised Manchester against

Westminster, produced Richard Cobden and the anti-corn law league, and routed the landed interest under its own prime minister, Sir Robert Peel.

"Nothing is so sacred as aristocracy," said Charles Kingsley in 1865, "unless it be the monarch."

And the most relentless enemy of the English aristocracy has been the dissenting church, which threw the Bible into the scale against both peers and king. It made Oliver Cromwell in England, and New, or Better, England in America. Those three batteries, never at rest, have steadily played upon the aristocracy, — New England, Manchester Cotton, Presbyterianism. And, at last, intellect wavers in its fealty to the nobility and gentry, for it has its choice of patrons now. We have come down to that remarkable period when Mr. Disraeli, after serving the aristocracy for so many years, finds it more honorable to refuse than to take a peerage. Yet, says his biographer, speaking of his first retirement from the cabinet: —

"He had gained for all his future life the magical prefix of 'Right Honorable' to his name."

But the period is more remarkable in this, that John Bright is a cabinet minister, he who said: —

"You may have an ancient nobility in grand mansions, and parks, and great estates, and you may have an ecclesiastical hierarchy, covering with worldly pomp that religion whose virtue is humility. But, notwithstanding all this, the whole fabric is rotten, and doomed ultimately to fall; for the great mass of the people on whom it is supported, is poor, and suffering, and degraded."

This book, however, is not written for partisan objects, and we shall find good reason, in our descriptions of the aristocracy, to account for their influence upon the British population. Let us address ourselves to this description.

How began the British aristocracy? In the year 1066, A. D., the Duke of Normandy, of France, overthrew the Saxons at Hastings, in England. His army was rewarded with all the estates of the Saxons. This was the last and greatest property revolution that ever happened in Europe. The brutal conqueror and his soldiers seized the entire kingdom. The Indians were treated with far more ceremony and fairness by the English colonists in America. At a swoop every Saxon's right went down; it was the most exhaustive robbery in history. To William the Conqueror's officers the oldest English noblemen trace their lineage, and probably with truthfulness in some cases.

9

For instance, the Marquis of Westminster, said to be the richest peer in England, shows every in and out of his pedigree, back to one Lord of Grosvenour, in the County of Normandy, France, a hundred and fifty years before the latter followed the fortunes of Duke William to England.

With the estates of the Saxons, the Norman barons and counts found local names to append to their titles. Many of them married, in the second or third generation, Saxon women; as, for example, the present Lord Derby's family name is Stanley; for his Norman ancestor, Adam de Aldithly, married Mabella Stanley, a Saxon woman.

The Saxons were already more civilized people than the Normans. King Alfred had lived, who was said to have been the Saxon founder of Oxford University, whereas Duke William could not read, and he signed his name to all his state papers extant with a "cross."

The English peers of the present day, who do not trace their lineage to some officer of William the Conqueror, derive their titles by the favor of William's successors, the kings of England, and a multitude of causes led to this favor. Some peers are descended from the illegitimate children of the monarchs; for, although "aristocracy" is a compound Greek word signifying "the government of the best," and good birth is defined by Aristotle to be "ancient (long-inherited) wealth and virtue," yet I doubt whether the most barefaced American politician of our time would commend to office such beings as began many ducal lines in England. It was a frequent custom for the sovereign to give a husband an office, a title, or a grant of land, and take his wife for a mistress. This was the case close down to the reign in which we write. Dukes, a grade higher, were the fruit of intimacies between the king and some actress. Many families were ennobled for military service, for opportune loans of money to the king, or for mere reward of good company. In a later part of this chapter I will give some examples under each of these heads.

How originated the present grades of British peers?

The *sovereign* is the head of the British aristocracy. Then follows her family, the *princes*, or those immediately of the royal blood. Then come three *royal dukes*, partly of royal blood, twenty-six *dukes*, thirty-eight *marquesses*, two hundred and two *earls*, sixty-one *viscounts*, and two hundred and five *barons*, — in all close to five hundred and fifty peers, or nobles, including fourteen women, peeresses in their own right (1854). Besides these peers there are nearly nine hundred *baronets*, who are not noblemen, and cannot sit in the House of Lords, but are allowed the prefix of "sir," which gives them rank and precedence, without privilege. They belong to the aristocracy, however, and so do the *gentry*, or untitled folks of ancient family.

Let us go back into the origin of these titles, for curiosity's sake.

The Duke and the Count were Roman titles, military words (Latin *dux*, from the Latin verb *ducere*, to lead) invented by the later Roman emperors. The count was half-magistrate of Roman provinces; the duke was the general of the same. When the northern nations descended upon Rome they appropriated these titles. Very soon the military dukes turned about and put themselves ahead of the count-magistrates. After a time, the duke became so powerful in his distant province, that he held it in his own right; and this was the case with the Duke of Normandy when he invaded England. Himself and several other French dukes had reduced the possessions of the crown of France to a couple of cities. A marquess was the guardian of the Roman frontier marches, and this title, also, the nations of the middle ages appropriated from Italy.

There were no dukes in England, except the Conqueror, Duke of Normandy, till two hundred and sixty-nine years after the Conquest, the only titles in William's army being Baron and Count. The first British duke was the Black Prince, so created by his father, King Edward III. Afterward several sons of kings were made dukes. Queen Elizabeth found on her accession only one duke remaining, — Norfolk, — and him she executed. James I. made George Villiers Duke of Buckingham. Charles II. made fifteen dukes, six of whom were his illegitimate children. The number of peers of all classes has steadily increased in England. There are now two hundred more than there were in the American Revolution, and three hundred and eighty more than in the time of Queen Anne. The eldest ducal family now in England is that of Norfolk; among the wealthier ducal houses are Devonshire and Bedford. The Queen addresses a duke officially, as "Our right trusty and right entirely beloved cousin and counsellor," which must have required of the young Queen Victoria the devotion of a quarter's schooling to get it by heart. A duke's letters are endorsed, "His Grace," or, "The most noble, the Duke of ——." It was from the Duke of York that New York was named, and not from York city, and Maine took its name from the tradition that the Duchy of Maine, in France, was an English possession. Almost every English duke has ascended through lesser degrees of nobility to his eminence. Thus, the Duke of Wellington was Lord

Wellesly, and his place was just missed by one of the Wesleys, founders of Methodism. With his title this last of the great dukes received about fourteen millions of dollars to support it. The Duke of Bedford is also Marquis of Tavistock, Baron Russell of Cheneys, Baron Russell of Thornhaugh, and Baron Howland of Streatham. His eldest son takes, by courtesy, the second title.

Marquess, the second rank of nobility, is old as the reign of Richard II. The first marquess was Robert Vere, raised from Earl of Oxford to Marquess of Dublin. The oldest marquessate existing is that of Winchester. Probably the richest is that of the Marquess of Westminster, who owns almost the whole of that vast and luxurious district of London called Belgravia. A marquess is addressed, "My Lord Marquess."

Earl is a Scandinavian title of lost antiquity. When first unearthed it was applied to the custodian of an English county. Shrewsbury is the eldest earl; and the second in time — perhaps the first in wealth and power — is Derby, whose name and whose son's name (Lord Stanley) are well known to us in America as associated with our late civil war, and the treaties attempted to be negotiated after it.

Viscount, as an English title, goes back to about the time of the discovery of America, and the eldest viscount is he of Hereford. This was the rank of Lord Palmerston, English prime minister during our recent civil war, whose title expired at his death.

Baron is a title of vague origin. The eldest extant, Le de Spencer, dates as remotely as the year 1264.

The term "cousin," applied by the sovereign to all peers save a baron, arose from the fact that there was one English monarch, Henry IV., who was related to every earl in the kingdom.

The above five grades of nobles constitute the peers of England, and they make a body nearly twice as numerous as both houses of the United States Congress. They were created in two ways besides original military rank and investiture of lands, namely, by Writ of Summons, to come to Parliament and help the Queen with counsel, or by Letters Patent, naming the exact rank and the circumstances under which the patent is conferred. In former times with every such writ or patent an estate was given. At present it is an expensive favor to be made a peer. The stamps on a duke's patent cost one thousand seven hundred and fifty dollars in gold. A baron pays for his creation two thousand one hundred dollars in gold. The privileges of the peerage are now of little consequence, if we except right of exemption from sitting on juries, freedom from common arrest, privilege of seeing the Queen on public business, and trial by one's peers in cases of treason and felony.

The baronets, next below the peers, were created out of the pecuniary necessities of James I., who wanted money, first to settle Ulster, in Ireland, then to "plant" Nova Scotia, the present discontented neighbor of the United States. He asked five thousand five hundred dollars a head to make baronets in this way.

The sovereign creates a peer to be, in himself and his issue, defender and adviser of the crown and protector of the royal prerogatives. The nearer a peer is to the throne, in office or duty, the closer is he to the fountain of honor and power. Hence many of the nobility are merely attendants upon the Queen.

Madame d'Arblay, a lady of the court of the wife of George III., tells many stories illustrative of the absurd deference of the aristocracy at that court during the American Revolution. Her employment was to robe the Queen-Consort, and to keep her snuff-box well replenished. No person was allowed to drive past the royal family on the road; none could sit or eat in their presence, nor pass by the open door of any room in which they were, nor speak to them unless requested. If met by them anywhere, the courtier must stand still, and go backward, if retiring. When they entered any room, all the people within it had to rise, fall back against the wall, and give the princes all the middle of the room exclusively, and when they entered the house of any nobleman they brought along what persons they pleased, ecclesiastics or concubines, and had entire control of the host's mansion. Madame D'Arblay used to be ready to drop from hunger and long standing, but the Queen took no notice of it. Commenting on the above, an English historian, Mr. John Wade, writing in our own time, quaintly says: —

"As princes are of ancient institution, these rules have, doubtless, a sage and politic meaning."

The great offices around the sovereign held by peers are: —

1. The Lord Great Chamberlain, custodian of Westminster Palace, decorator of Westminster Hall and Abbey for state trials and coronations, ticket-giver for Parliament; in short, the Queen's Sergeant-at-Arms. This office is hereditary, and, owing to some split or other in the lineage, it is now held by two noblemen, relations.

2. The Earl-Marshal, a sort of Queen's proclamation maker, the preparer of programmes for royal christenings, etc. The Duke of Norfolk is hereditary Marshal.

3. Hereditary Grand Almoner. This noble functionary does nothing whatever but toss medals round Westminster Abbey at the Queen's coronation.

The other offices around the sovereign are filled by the Queen by writ, that is, the prime minister of the political party in power nominates for them, and they are part of the spoils of victory. Some of the names of these ennobled servants are Lord Steward of the Household, salary, 10,000 dollars; Treasurer, ditto, 4,500 dollars; Comptrollers, ditto, 4,500 dollars; Master, ditto, 5,600 dollars; Lord Chamberlain, 10,000 dollars; Vice-Chamberlain, 4,500 dollars; several Lords in Waiting, 3,500 dollars; several Grooms in Waiting, 1,750 dollars; a corps of Gentlemen at Arms and a corps of Yeomen of the Guard, select soldiers and "gentle" officers, paid from 5,000 dollars, captains, to 300 dollars, privates; Groom of the Stole, who watches the Queen's bed, nominally, 10,000 dollars; twelve Lords of the Bedchamber, defunct or nearly so, 5,000 dollars a head; Mistress of the Robes, 2,500 dollars; ten Ladies of the Bedchamber 2,500 dollars a head, nine Bedchamber Women 1,500 dollars; eight Maids of Honor, 2,000 dollars; Master of the Horse, 12,500 dollars; Clerk Marshal and Chief Equerry, 5,000 dollars; eight Equerries and Pages of Honor, 3,750 dollars to 1,000 dollars; Master of the Buckhounds, 8,000 dollars. Contrast all this array of sinecures with the household officers of President of the United States, namely, two Secretaries and a Marshal of the District of Columbia. If he wishes more help he must get a private soldier or two detailed. The Queen's coachmen, postilions, and footmen cost almost sixty thousand dollars a year besides. All this useless court must be maintained by the social argument of an aristocracy, who might else outblaze the sovereign, and that the Queen's poor relations may not be laughed at by the peers they receive enormous pensions. Old Hampton Court Palace, near London, is a home for decayed nobility who must not be turned into the street. This palace costs a hundred and fifty thousand dollars a year to keep it up, exclusive of numerous pensions paid its inmates.

An English statement said of the Duke of Grafton: —

"This hereditary pensioner is paid annually, out of the excise revenue, forty-two thousand dollars, and out of the post-office revenues seventeen thousand dollars. The original pensioner was one of the numerous illegitimate offspring of Charles II.; for whose royal amours the people of this age are still called upon to pay. These pensions have now (1857) been paid to the Dukes of Grafton for a period of one hundred and seventy-three years; so that the maintenance of this single peerage alone has cost the English people, in hard cash, no less a sum than ten millions two hundred and ninety thousand dollars!"

I have said that the English aristocracy are the proudest nobles in Europe. This rises mainly from their greater riches. In ancient lineage they can at best trace their origin to the countries of their neighbors on the Continent. The Queen's house, that of Guelph, claims Italy for its origin. Tennyson sang in his welcome of the bride of the Prince of Wales: —

> "Saxon and Norman and Dane are we,
> But each all Dane in our welcome of thee."

If there is any advantage in English over foreign aristocracy, it is that the former was created directly by the sovereign, and has never been obliterated by a revolution, like the *ancien noblesse* of France.

The Venetian aristocracy sprang from rich commercial houses; that of Florence, from bankers and money-lenders. In Germany and France the possession of land was almost the exclusive source of titles, and hence *von* and *de*, prefixes, in German and French (meaning "of"), denote the estate of the noble. Baron Von Humboldt means "The Baron of Humboldt," and it is an affectation, generally speaking, for an American to retain the prefix *de*. By buying a fine estate, a Frenchman generally assumed to ennoble himself, and hence, when the French Revolution broke out, there were eighty thousand French families claiming to be noble, "not three thousand of whom," says an English writer, lugubriously, "were of ancient lineage." The French aristocracy was crushed out by one decree of the French National Assembly (Republican) on the 18th of June, 1790, which said: "An hereditary nobility is an institution incompatible with a free state," and all titles, arms, and liveries were forthwith abolished. Two years afterward all the records of the nobility were burned. The present French nobles are merely descendants of Napoleon's marshals and officers. All this will be explained in the chapter on French peers. Spain claims to have the purest nobility in Christendom. The word "hidalgo" means the "son of Somebody," and the class at large goes by the name of *grandees* there.

The British aristocracy, however, keeps its position by wealth, the profits of the vast estates hereditary in it, and British law and legislation are all suborned to keep these intact. There are in England, it is said, no more than thirty thousand proprietors of the land; in Scotland and Ireland only nine thousand. The laws which perpetuate this monstrous system are called entail and primogeniture, and that the possession of land may not be burdensome to the aristocracy, it is taxed inconsiderably, while the landless masses pay the enormous expenses of the court, the army and navy, and the civil list.

The cost and character of some of these vast aristocratic estates will stagger an American reader. The largest real-estate incomes of America are probably derived from corporations like Trinity Church, New York, or the Pacific railroads; and from a few private estates in the chief cities, like those of Longworth in Cincinnati, Girard in Philadelphia, and Astor in New York. What shall we say of the Marquis of Westminster, on whose ground, in the fashionable part of London, dwell three hundred thousand people? or of Earl Derby, who owned the whole site of one manufacturing town of fifty thousand inhabitants? The Duke of Bedford is scarcely less opulent in London real estate. And these extravagant possessions were the gift of kings in barbarous times, transmitted intact under the protection of laws no less extraordinary.

In this country of the United States, we travel long lines of railway, and see that the farms and dwellings are almost uniform. The people, rich or poor, follow the impulses of emigration. It is rare to find three generations of one family living upon the same family estate. In England, however, the contrary is the rule. Few quit the ancient home, be it castle or cottage. The conditions of men do not change. The splendid modern mansion of the nobleman, supplied with water and gas by modern contrivances, stands beside the picturesque ruins of his immemorial forefathers. The ivy-covered towers and battlements overhang the Mansard roof and the polished panes of modern window-glass. Only time has done its work of disintegration; the name of the estate is the same; the family is the same; the tenantry of the living lord are children of the peasants of his barbaric ancestors. This is the difference between England and America: the land is the enemy and conqueror of the one; the other is the conqueror of the land. When mother earth decides against the poor, then are they poor indeed.

Let us take up some illustrations of the estates of English noblemen.

The Marquis of Westminster has four immense and elaborate country seats, namely, Eaton Hall, Halkin Castle, Motcombe House, and Fonthill, in the County of Wilts. Besides these he has a splendid city residence on Grosvenor Square. His pictures are valued at three quarters of a million dollars. His income has been said to be two hundred thousand dollars a week. The motto on the arms of this gentleman is, "The virtue, not the mere lineage, of race;" but his possessions are great enough to comprehend both.

The Duke of Bedford, who owns a great part of that district of London called Bloomsbury, derived his possessions from a characteristic accident. His ancestor was a plain squire, John Russell, who lived on the English coast, near Weymouth, in the time of Henry VII. At that precise time an Archduke of Austria was about sailing from his province of Flanders to Spain. A storm arose in the English Channel, and drove him, much "demoralized," into the port of Weymouth. Now, plain John Russell's relative was sheriff, or something of the sort, to that part of the country. He posted off, rapidly to the court, to tell of this mighty visitor, and left the Archduke in the company of John Russell. John proved to be a good fellow at an anecdote, a ride, or a dinner, and when the sheriff came back the Austrian was so much infatuated with plain John Russell that he insisted upon carrying him up to court. The people at court were also delighted with Russell. He was retained there as a courtier, and ennobled. In process of time he received an estate out of the grand general confiscation of Abbey lands, and then Charles II., long afterward, made his posterity Dukes of Bedford. The present Duke, inheritor of John Russell's good luck, is also the descendant of that Lord Russell who was executed for treason by the Stuarts, and brother of Lord John Russell, the late English prime minister and contemporary of William H. Seward. He is said to pay Lord John, the genius of the family, an annuity for keeping up the family talent. The latter has also three residences, or, as they are called in English parlance, a "seat," a residence, and a "town house." Lord John Russell was made a peer in 1861. His eldest son is called Viscount Amberly, while the eldest son of the Duke of Bedford gets the title of Earl Grosvenor. The motto of them all is, "What will be, will be!" The motto and arms of a peer are presented by the sovereign when the patent of creation is issued. These are prepared by an old institution called the College of Heralds, and the science of heraldry is as immovably maintained in England as the Lord's Prayer.

The book of the peerage is regularly issued in London at the first of every year, and it is a huge, gilded volume, like a New York street directory in size, of thirteen hundred pages. It tells all the deaths, marriages, and births of peers and baronets in the year expired, names the children of peers who have married commoners, recites extinct and disputed titles and those "in abeyance;" and all this is exhibited with a solemnity of diction and a minuteness of detail which would seem ludicrous to an American. The volume for 1868 was the thirtieth edition of this ponderous dictionary of dignities.

So immense was the Duke of Queensbury's estate that the mere legacy duty upon the settlement of it amounted to seven hundred thousand dollars. A property lawsuit between the Talbots and Berkleys lasted one hundred and twenty years. Frequently great families intermarry to unite their landed estates. Thus, in the Cavendish family there are two dukes. The father of the present Duchess of Hamilton, John Fauqhar, gave one million four hundred thousand dollars for his estate of Fonthill Abbey, second-hand, and the money which reared this extravagant property came from slave labor in Jamaica. The Duke of Athol planted at one time fifteen thousand acres of woodland.

The life of the British aristocracy should be, in the sense of self-love and the gratification of dominion, delightful beyond comparison. At the head of the court and politics of a boundless empire, chief possessors of an insular kingdom singularly endowed by nature, and grand and various in its landscapes, visited by such dews as make the foliage green, the grain and grasses big and juicy, and the cattle and the horses large and strong, — to be a separate and a grander class in such a kingdom must be a more national dream of empire than Alexander ever realized.

Take a single exemplification, — the Duke of Devonshire, of the family of Cavendish. One of his numerous estates is Chatsworth, or the "Palace of the Peak," in Derbyshire. This nobleman belongs to the house of Cavendish, and he is called, in the parlance of England, "a noble and generous landlord." Chatsworth is about forty miles from Manchester. The estate is twelve miles in circumference. There are eighty acres of mown lawn in the gardens alone, and forty acres in the arboretum, or nursery of specimen trees. The estate is entered by a grand gate, and over the splendid woodlands the great mansion is seen to rise, far off, a square palladian building, of vast proportions, erected in the time of William III. At the gate is a hotel for the accommodation of visitors, who are permitted to see the palace and grounds freely. Some little distance off is the village of Edensor, owned entirely by the Duke, in the midst of which is the parish church which he controls almost absolutely, filled with the monuments of the Cavendish family. Entering the park, one sees close before him the River Derwent, crossed by a stone bridge, with statues above all the piers, and the velvet lawn beyond, cropped close to the river's brink, is adorned with frequent figures in stone, marble, and bronze. The house itself, containing the masterpieces of the sculptor, Grinling Gibbons, is decorated with marbles from all foreign countries; the windows are composed of the largest panes of plate glass, and all the sashes are gilded. A grand vestibule and hall, filled with noble statuary, and effigies wearing the armor of the Cavendish ancestors, leads to a noble series of state apartments, hung with rich tapestries, embroidered in remote times, and exhibiting such scenes as the voyages of Ulysses and episodes of the Crusades. Canova, Thorwaldsden, and the best modern sculptors, have made this mansion illustrious with their works. The noblest paintings of the masters of the middle ages line the walls. Through armories, drawing-rooms, dining-rooms, great state bedchambers, amongst whose furniture are the coronation thrones of George III. and William IV., — which were the perquisites of former Dukes of Devonshire, as lords chamberlain, — by billiard rooms, through museums, filled with articles of science and virtuoso, one wanders until he tires of splendor, and then seeks relief in the gardens, the like of which, public or private, we do not possess in America. There are gates made of a single stone, moving upon a pivot; vast houses of glass, wherein float, in great tanks of water, *Victoria regias*, whose leaves will almost support a man's weight, yet are fluttered by the artificial motion of a wheel in the water. "There are forty thousand rhododendrons alone," says the description of the gardens. The conservatory is probably the most extensive in the world. It is approached by an artificial gorge of rocks, made up of great masses tossed wildly together, and through this a carriage-way leads, by such cunning curves, that one does not see the conservatory until he comes bolt upon it. There is no necessity for dismounting; the carriage-road makes the circuit of the inside of the mighty glass building, which covers one acre, is two hundred and seventy-six feet long, one hundred and twenty-six feet wide, and sixty-five feet high, is supplied with fuel by a subterranean tramway, and warmed by seven miles of pipes. These pipes alone cost seven thousand five hundred dollars, and the building contains forty miles of sash bars. From an interior gallery one can look down upon a jungle of tropical trees, fruit, and flowers. Here grow the banana, the India rubber, and the dragon tree, the talipot, palm, and the American magnolia, and lotus and papyrus float in tanks. Without there rises a tower, surmounted by the ducal flag, approached by a cyclopean aqueduct of lofty arches, which carries up water from a reservoir of six acrès near by. This water is distributed to the numerous fountains, one of which is a single *jet geant*, flung up lonesomely in the solitude of a screen of lime-trees, whose tops it tries to reach, two hundred and sixty-seven feet in the air. Another, and the greatest fountain, is a colossal flight of steps, surmounted by a temple. Touch a valve, and from every crevice of this temple water will burst, which, tumbling in cascade down the flights of steps, disappears in the ground at the bottom.

The stables of the Duke are also marvellous in the number and breed of the horses, the number of which is not stated, but in 1862 the author counted the horses in the stable of the Earl of Derby, and found them to pass one hundred and fifty. The hounds were not less remarkable in breed and number. All the grounds are filled with rabbits, hares, pheasants, and deer. Picked cattle graze in the moist meadows, of stature and stride novel to Americans. There are lodges all round the park, and game laws, besides, are made in the Duke's favor. His many farms are spread round the country, for he owns not only the park, but all the outlying landscapes; yet Chatsworth is only one of his "seats." Others are Oldcotes and Hardwick Hall, the latter the prison of Mary, Queen of Scots, which bears, in its architecture, the monogram of "Old Bess of Hardwick, the greatest member of the house of Cavendish." She was the wife of an usher to Cardinal Wolsey, who obtained his share of the monastery lands, seized from the church, for the spoil of the courtiers. She was married four times, to men of large estate, in every case, and intermarrying her children with those of her husbands, their combined lands and riches were transmitted to her posterity.

An instance of a different origin is that of Blenheim Park, presented to the Duke of Marlborough for gaining the battle of Blenheim. The mansion alone cost a million and a half of dollars, and it is carved in trophies, surrounded by triumphal arches, columns, and statues, adorned with hanging woods above a lake of two hundred and sixty acres, which is in turn crossed by a noble bridge. The old oaks and cedars are planted in battalions to reproduce the plan of the battle of Blenheim. Twenty-seven hundred acres comprise this park, and the circuit of it is twelve miles.

These are scarcely exceptional instances. Similar noble estates lie in every part of the United Kingdom. With education, means, and taste, the aristocracy has refined horticulture and agriculture beyond any previous condition they have gained. The hospitality of these large estates is unbounded, after one has passed the arctic circle of an English introduction.

N. P. Willis, while a member of the American legation in England, had extraordinarily rare chances to observe the home life of English noblemen. I take some pages from his description of a week spent at Gordon Castle, which Mr. William Howitt, an English authority, has pronounced "the most perfect and graphic description of English aristocratical life, in the country, which was ever written."

"Dismounting at Gordon Castle, in the midst of its noble park, I followed a boy through a hall lined with statues, deers' horns, and armor, and was ushered into a large chamber, looking out on a park, extending, with its lawns and woods, to the edge of the horizon. 'Who is at the castle?' I asked, as the boy busied himself in unstrapping my portmanteau. 'Oh, a great many, sir.' He stopped in his occupation, and began counting on his fingers a long list of lords and ladies. 'And how many sit down to dinner?'—'Above ninety, sir, beside the Duke and Duchess.'—'That will do;' and off tripped my slender gentleman, with his laced jacket, giving the fire a terrible stir-up on his way out, and turning back to inform me that the dinner hour was seven precisely.

"A tall, white-haired gentleman, of noble physiognomy, but singularly cordial address, entered, with a broad red ribbon across his breast, and welcomed me most heartily to the castle. The gong sounded at the next moment, and in our way down he named over his other guests, and prepared me, in a measure, for the introduction which followed. The drawing-room was crowded like a soirée. The Duchess, a tall and very handsome woman, with a smile of the most winning sweetness, received me at the door, and I was presented successively to every person present. Dinner was announced immediately, and the difficult question of precedence being sooner settled than I had ever seen it before in so large a party, we passed through files of servants to the dining-room.

"It was a large and very lofty hall, supported at the ends by marble columns, within which was stationed a band of music, playing delightfully. The walls were lined with full-length family pictures, from old knights in armor to the modern dukes in kilt of the Gordon plaid; and on the sideboards stood services of gold-plate, the most gorgeously massive and the most beautiful in workmanship I have ever seen. There were, among the vases, several large coursing-cups, won by the Duke's hounds, of exquisite shape and ornament.

"I fell into my place between a gentleman and a very beautiful woman of perhaps twenty-two, neither of whose names I remembered, though I had just been introduced. The Duke probably anticipated as much, and as I took my seat he called out to me, from the top of the table, that I had, on my right, Lady ——, the most agreeable woman in Scotland! It was unnecessary to say that she was the most lovely.

"I have been struck everywhere in England with the beauty of the higher classes, and as I looked around me upon the aristocratic company at the table, I thought I had never seen 'Heaven's image double-stamped as man and noble,' so unequivocally clear.

"The band ceased playing when the ladies left the table; the gentlemen closed up; conversation assumed a merrier cast; coffee and liquors were brought in, when the wines began to be circulated more slowly, and at eleven there was a general move to the drawing-room. Cards, tea, music, filled up the time till twelve, and then the ladies took their departure, and the gentlemen sat down to supper. I got to bed somewhere about two o'clock; and thus ended an evening which I had anticipated as stiff and embarrassing, but which is marked in my tablets as one of the most social and kindly I have had the good fortune to record on my travels. At breakfast the Duke sat laughing at the head of the table, with a newspaper in his hand, dressed in a coarse shooting-jacket and colored cravat; the Duchess was in a plain morning-dress and cap of the simplest character; and the high-born women about the table, whom I had left glittering with jewels and dressed in all the attractions of fashion, appeared in the simplest *coiffure*, and a toilet of studied plainness. The ten or twelve noblemen present were engrossed with their letters or newspapers over tea and toast, — and in them, perhaps, the transformation was still greater. The *soigné* man of fashion of the night before, faultless in costume and distinguished in his appearance, — in the full force of the term, — was enveloped now in a coat of fustian, with a coarse waistcoat of plaid, a gingham cravat, and hob-nailed shoes for shooting; and in place of the gay hilarity of the supper-table wore a face of calm indifference, and ate his breakfast and read the paper in a rarely broken silence. I wondered, as I looked about me, what would be the impression of many people in my own country, could they look in upon that plain party, aware that it was composed of the proudest nobility and the highest fashion of England.

"Breakfast in England is a confidential and unceremonious hour, and servants are generally dispensed with. Between breakfast and lunch the ladies were generally invisible, and the gentlemen rode or shot, or played billiards, or kept in their rooms. At two o'clock, a dish or two of hot game, and a profusion of cold meats, were set on the small tables in the dining-room, and everybody came in for a kind of lounging half-meal, which occupied perhaps an hour. Thence all adjourned to the drawing-room, under the windows of which were drawn up carriages of all descriptions, with grooms, outriders, footmen, and saddle-horses for gentlemen and ladies. Parties were then made up for riding or driving. The number at the dinner-table of Gordon Castle was seldom less than thirty; but the company was continually varied by departures and arrivals. No sensation was made by either one side or the other. A travelling-carriage dashed up to the door, was disburdened of its load, and drove round to the stables, and the question was seldom asked, 'Who has arrived?' You are sure to see new faces at dinner, and an addition of half a dozen to the party made no perceptible difference in anything. Leave-takings were arranged in the same quiet way. Adieus were made to the Duke and Duchess, and to no one else, except he happened to encounter the parting guest upon the staircase, or were more than a common acquaintance."

He is a poor nobleman who has not also a fine 'town house' in London, to which he repairs in the spring, and takes his place at court and in society. But the real life of the aristocrat is in the country, where he is not overshadowed by the sovereign, but all the county turns out to his fox-hunt; his "patronage" is solicited by every mountebank and cricket-club, and flattery lifts him above the degeneracy of a mere voluptuary's life. He is not simply rich, but he is a peer of the realm. Still, this o'erdeserved human state leads to inflated heights of self-esteem, and often to depths of baseness.

While Hamilton, Jefferson, and Washington were types of the American Revolution, the English statesman, Fox, their warmest admirer,—he who addressed Washington in terms of reverence, and was also Bonaparte's friend, lived the life of a roué and a gambler. His father gave him guineas for the gaming table while yet a lad, "that his spirit might not be broken," and left him seven hundred and fifty thousand dollars to pay his debts. Within a few years he was deeply embarrassed as before. Said Gibbon, the historian: —

"Fox prepared himself for the holy work of emancipating the clergy, by passing twenty-two hours in the pious exercise of hazard. His devotion cost him five hundred pounds an hour — in all eleven thousand pounds."

Again a wild friend found him, after a night's debauch at the gaming table, calmly perusing Herodotus in the original Greek. He exclaimed that Fox seemed in no whit repining: —

"What would you have me do," said Fox, "when I have lost my last shilling?"

The great Lord Chatham, under whose administration Quebec and Canada were annexed to the English colonies, turned his stomach with strong ale, till gout and temporary fits of insanity marked his career; while William Pitt, the humiliator of France and Bonaparte, died of dyspepsia, induced by close attention to the bottle, so that Malmsbury remarked, "He died of old age at forty-six as much as if he had been ninety."

There are few books more entertaining in criminal literature than "Romances of the Peerage," "Crimes of the Nobility and Gentry," and others of standard authority. In our own day the giddy careers of the Duke of Hamilton and of the Marquis of Hastings are fresh in the mind of the reader. Gossip alleges that at least one of the children of the Queen lacks "balance" for his eminence. It is, indeed, an anomalous, though an ancient, condition of society, for a few people to hold all the honors, control all the intellect, and possess nearly all the land in a kingdom. This will not stand the test of an age of mass-meetings and cheap newspapers. In the interest of the land, laws have been mainly made in England down to the repeal of the corn laws. It will hardly be credited now, that, under the plausible and selfish cry of, "Protect the British farmer!" the millions of British people had to pay a high duty on imported wheat down to 1849. This tax was the cause of starvation and hunger throughout the kingdom, yet it was imposed entirely in the interests of the landholders, the aristocracy. The Duke of Wellington coerced the passage of its repeal through the House of Lords, himself under the coercion of Sir Robert Peel, the enlightened prime minister.

A few Americans have been ennobled or knighted in England. The title of Lord Lyndhurst, which expired about 1866, was shared by his lady, formerly Susan Clarke, of Boston. He had been an American Tory. The illegitimate son of Benjamin Franklin was knighted for his toryism in the American war, and Benjamin West, our Pennsylvania colonial artist, became "Sir Benjamin."

I have omitted reference to the various orders of knighthood in England. These confer honor and are much coveted; but they do not confer nobility, and the honor is not hereditary. The orders of British knighthood are, The Garter, The Thistle, Saint Patrick, The Bath, The Star of India, and one or two more, of no consequence. The Garter, with its well-known motto of "*Honi soit qui mal y pense*," is the proudest order of knighthood in England, perhaps in Europe, with the sovereign at its head, and twenty-five knights. It was founded in 1350, meets once every year at St. George's Chapel, Windsor, and the installation fees are twenty-two hundred dollars. Amongst its present members are Louis Napoleon; the Kings of Belgium, Denmark, Portugal, and Prussia; Derby and Russell, the statesmen, and the second Duke of Wellington. The Thistle is a Scotch order of eighteen knights. The Knights of St. Patrick, Irish, number twenty-four. The Bath is a military order, with nearly a thousand officers, knights.

Such is an outline of the British aristocracy, and if we come to examine the causes of their anomalous influence over an active and practical kingdom, we shall find these resolved to two, — their social monopoly and their monopoly of the land. As a country, particularly a small country like England, grows richer and more densely peopled, the high circles of society and the land become less accessible. Riches seek recognition; cramped people want land. And going still one degree further in our inquiry, the land monopoly is the parent of the social monopoly. A beggared and landless aristocracy has no chance for perpetuation, as the history of the Venetian and French nobility in our century proves. The British nobles, seizing all the land, first from the Saxons, then from the Catholic church when they discarded it, adopted the laws of entail and primogeniture, by which their great estates were transmitted unbroken. Perhaps this is not the least of the causes which have driven millions of British subjects to America and Polynesia, — a longing to own the land monopolized by so few at home. The land is the best riches. It is most grudgingly held in England. The millions pay rent, the hundreds receive it. The better the skill and enterprise of the millions, the dearer grows the rent of the land under their feet. An aristocracy, thus endowed, is not the shadow of an ancient lineage merely. It is a powerful circle, which, despite the democratic tendencies of the age, keeps its ranks unbroken and commands homage. Yet, despite its social graces, and the appeal it makes to our love of pomp and luxury, its virtues touch our imagination alone; for by the light of this century it is as baneful and unjust as the worst relic of barbarism which has perished. The first step to take in its overthrow is to do justice: Tax the land! Remove the burdens of an extravagant government from the poor and landless, and lay them upon the ground. Thus taxed, acre by acre, the vast estates and parks will become expensive luxuries, and must, though reluctantly, be broken up. With land available, the commons will feel a new independence, and industry and patience will rear a rival court; wealth, virtue, and intellect will compose a new aristocracy.

1

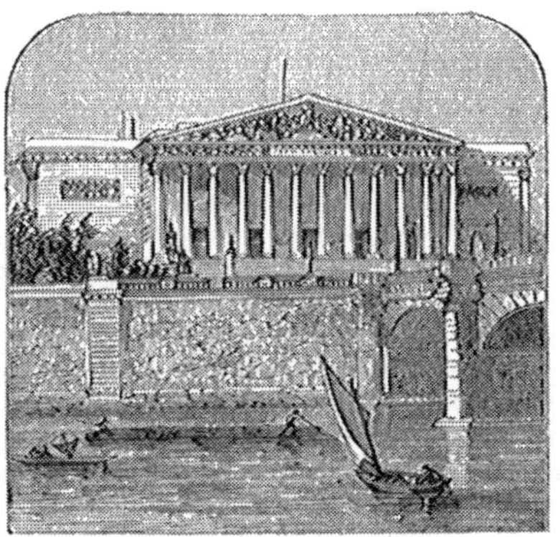

2

3

4 5

HOUSES OF THE LEGISLATURES.

1—Modern Capitol, Rome. 2—Palace of the Corps Legislatif, Paris. 3—Capitol, Washington. 4—Houses of Parliament, London. 5—Parliament Houses, Ottawa, Canada.

CHAPTER IV.

THE SENATE AND THE HOUSE OF LORDS.

United States Capitol and British Houses of Parliament compared. — Sketches of Westminster Hall, Abbey, and Palace. — The House of Lords architecturally. — The lords and the senators in their seats, relatively. — Officers of the House of Lords. — Business of that body. — Descriptions of various scenes in that house. — Opening of Parliament. — Impeachment. — Trial of a peer. — Riotous scenes. — Parliamentary law and manual.

A MILE from either arm of the Potomac River, on a commanding hill, ninety feet above tide-water, stands the United States Capitol. It is of Greek architecture, — in order, Corinthian. Two white marble wings, connected by a middle building of white freestone, over the latter of which rises a white dome of iron, — that is the Capitol at Washington. Take three dominos, and place two of them lengthwise against the ends of the middle one, stand a pullet's egg on the middle domino, and you obtain a suggestive miniature of the building. It is the most extensive and costly edifice on the American continent. It cost twelve millions of dollars, covers one hundred and fifty three thousand one hundred and twelve square feet, or about three and a half acres of ground, is seven hundred and fifty-one feet long by two hundred and thirty-nine feet wide, and the dome is more than two hundred and eighty-seven feet high, or two hundred and seventeen feet, clear, above the main building.

The Capitol, as it stands, is the work of many persons, of whom but two or three are noticeable. Dr. Thornton made the first design, said by Washington to combine "grandeur, simplicity, and convenience." The architects retained but two or three features of Thornton's design, and preferred one by Mr. S. Hallet. B. H. Latrobe, of an enterprising Maryland family, began to rebuild the Capitol on Hallet's plan, after the British burned it, and a Mr. Bulfinch completed it. It was thirty-five years after the laying of the corner-stone before a completed national Capitol existed in America.

John Quincy Adams was the first of our presidents who ever sent a message into an entire Capitol building. In like manner the extension of the Capitol has already (1869) occupied nearly twenty years. Washington laid the corner-stone of the old, Webster of the new Capitol. The Brunelleschi of the house is Thomas U. Walter; the Ghiberti of it is Thomas Crawford.

Walter is incomparably the national architect. He built the Girard College, at Philadelphia; and on that building and the wings and dome of the Capitol, his fame will rest.

This dome is the most ambitious structure in America. It is a hundred and eight feet higher than the Washington Monument, at Baltimore, sixty-eight feet higher than that of Bunker Hill, and twenty-three feet higher than Trinity Church tower, New York. It is the only considerable dome of iron in the world, and it is, in this respect, significant of the era of the republic and its industry. It is, also, the only piece of ornamental architecture undertaken by the republic which is at all worthy of our wealth and art. We must have halls for Congress, and custom-houses and post-offices; but we need not have domes. In this isolated case the country has consented to an expensive edifice for other than practical considerations. More than all, the dome is the real monument of the great war for the Union and the overthrow of American slavery. It was begun in 1856, with the rise of the Republican party; it was finished in 1865, when the Confederate flag surrendered on the last field, and the defeated party came back to plead for representation under the dome of the Union. The echo of almost every hammer driven upon it, was returned by a cannon. No day, not the darkest day of the war, saw the workmen frightened from its scaffolds. With Early thundering on the east, and Lee far in the northern rear, and Beauregard at Fairfax Court-house, and Mosby and Gilmore almost at Arlington, the flies at work upon this eyrie of liberty crawled steadily up their filament ladders; the steam-whistle blew the signal for every girder, as they sent it aloft; like a steamship at sea, with the storm of war beating across every horizon, the engine under the dome never put out its fires; its lanterns burnt every night.

The successor of Mr. Walter is Mr. Clarke, his pupil. Mr. Clarke occupies a wooden cabin, in a green park across the way from the Capitol. There he sits, much of the time, making models and drawings, ciphering up the cost of marble per foot and paint per keg, with Mr. Sears, his chief assistant, at a desk near by, and an apprentice or two draughting in India ink.

Mr. Clarke is a large, intellectual-looking man, with heavy eyebrows and little beard. He was a pupil of Mr. Walter, the real architect of the dome and the Capitol extension. Mr. Walter's photograph hangs over Mr. Clarke's head, — a stout man of, say, sixty years of age, with a luxuriant head of white and gray hair, white beard all around his jaws, and a weary look, as of a man who had to climb a great deal, and was too fat for it. He and Mr. Clarke are both Philadelphians; but Mr. Walter retired, satisfied that his work was in the best of hands; and Mr. Clarke, having built the new library and carried out all the designs of his predecessors, is engaged in the conscientious work of making the Capitol building a more harmonious edifice.

Here is the Capitol as Mr. Walter found it: A building of freestone, painted white, supporting three wooden domes, all the cost of which had been under two millions of dollars. It was three hundred and fifty-two feet long, and one hundred and twenty-two feet deep.

Here is what Mr. Walter did: He built a dome of iron on top of the old freestone Capitol, and a marble wing against each end of it. The dome cost about one million one hundred thousand dollars, and the wings cost six million five hundred thousand dollars. To make the old Capitol proportion itself well to the additions, short corridors connected it with the wings.

Here is what Mr. Clarke has done: Finished up the designs of Mr. Walter, completed the dome, worked out of the inside of the old Capitol a noble library, suggested and superintended all manner of details, as statuary, ventilation, heating, rectifying old mistakes, and teaching taste and harmony.

And this is what Mr. Clarke wants Congress to do: Move the front of the old freestone Capitol forward, and rebuild it of marble; put the present front on the rear of the Capitol; extend the park of the Capitol so as to make it eligible for drives, and reform the architecture of the interior of the dome, which is now a monotonous succession of orders, so as to make two entablatures only, and not three. To rebuild the central freestone building will cost two millions of dollars, and to buy the land for the enlarged park will cost one million two hundred thousand dollars.

This Capitol, standing in a wide, vacant, lofty area of new lots and green parks, is surpassed by but one legislative palace in the world, — the Houses of Parliament, at Westminster, London.* These make

* The Parliament House at Melbourne, Australia, is four hundred and fifty feet long, two hundred and twenty feet wide, and seventy-four feet high. The style of architecture is Roman Doric, and the building is surmounted by a tower and cupola upwards of two hundred

one grand mass of Gothic buildings, situated upon a flat plain on the brink of the River Thames, so low that the river often overflowed the Parliament entrances in former times.

This mass of buildings covers nearly eight acres, or four acres and a half more than the Capitol covers. Its length is nine hundred and forty feet, its width about half as much, and the height of its tallest tower is three hundred and forty feet, or fifty-three feet higher above the ground than the dome at Washington. It contains over one hundred staircases, eleven hundred apartments, and more than two miles of corridors. Sixteen miles of steam-pipes heat it; four hundred and fifty statues already adorn it, and there are spaces for more than two hundred more. The plan of it was selected from ninety-seven competing designs. The architect was made a baronet. He was twenty-one years at work upon it, and it cost three times his original estimate, or, ultimately, about ten millions of dollars, in gold. This sum is about equal, all things considered, to the cost of the Capitol of the United States, which is proof that public works in England are more conscientiously and more cheaply built than in America. The Parliament Houses would have cost us from twenty to thirty millions, as we should have had to use depreciated currency, dear labor, and to have made of the work a political "job." The new court-houses in New York are said to have cost nearly as much as the vast Houses of Parliament. I have made a statement of these details merely to prepare the mind of the reader for a more consecutive description of this grand palace of Westminster.

If one will descend the hill of St. Paul's Cathedral, whence we have already obtained a general view of London, and continue westward along Fleet Street, he will pass under Temple Bar, or arch, after a walk of twenty minutes, and the same Fleet Street prolonged before him will take the name of "The Strand." Twenty minutes' walk further will bring him to the end of the Strand, at an open square, full of statues, and faced with fine hotels, and here, one of the

feet high. There are two legislative chambers, seventy-two feet long by forty wide; a library forty feet square; two reading-rooms, and two restaurants, each of the four being fifty by twenty-five feet.

The Parliament House at Ottawa, Canada, is to cost half a million dollars in gold. The style is Italian Gothic. The building is to be five hundred feet long, and to support a tower one hundred and eighty feet high. The two legislative halls are eighty-two by forty-five feet. The building is rendered imposing by being placed on the bold bluff of the Ottawa River, one hundred and fifty feet above the water. [See, further, the chapter on "Canada and Australia."]

The above are the chief legislative palaces of the British colonies.

underground railways of London has established its principal depot. The spot of confluence is called Charing Cross, and it is, except only London Bridge, the spot of densest confluence in London or the world.

At Charing Cross the streets break up and radiate. Go to the right by the first street and you enter St. Giles, the abandoned quarter of the "West End," in ten minutes. Or go to the right by the second street, and in five minutes you are in the Haymarket, the street of night-walkers and the region of theatres. Or go straight on, across the square, and in ten minutes you are in Pall Mall and St. James, the quarter of gentlemen's clubs and noblemen's palaces. But turn to the left, by the broad street called Whitehall, and in ten minutes you are at Westminster.

Whitehall, like all the streets we have pursued since quitting St. Paul's, follows the windings of the Thames River, and is within rifle-shot of it.

Immediately on entering Whitehall one sees that the buildings grow large and imposing. Soldiers, sentinels, mounted couriers, and numerous policemen appear. To the right of this wide street are the offices of the navy, the army, the treasury, the foreign secretary, and those other offices that we call in Washington by the general name of "The Departments." Behind these stretches the series of green parks, with the palaces on their further borders. To the left are the police headquarters, — whose chief officer is a baronet, — and a colossal fragment of the ancient palace of Whitehall, where Wolsey and Elizabeth dwelt, and where Charles I. was beheaded; the republicans who condemned the latter to die were hanged, drawn, and quartered at Charing Cross behind us.

It is these objects which revive to us the past bloody and memorable associations of English history, and while yet in the glow of their remembrance, we have come to the end of Whitehall; the River Thames is close to the left of us, crossed by a magnificent bridge, and right before us, separated by an open piece of ground called Palace Yard, are Westminster Abbey and the Houses of Parliament. Here, for nearly a thousand years, the Kings of England have been crowned, the royal court has been pitched, Parliament and State trials been held, and the enemies or victims of kings have been pilloried and executed.

To the right stands the glorious Abbey Church, the oldest association of the spot, where, to this day, the House of Lords worships on occasions of thanksgiving. Built in front of it, so that there is but a narrow graveyard between, is the Church of St. Margaret, where the House of Commons worships on similar days of rejoicing.

To the left, across the Palace Yard, is Westminster Hall, dating back to the year 1087; it stands on the spot of burial of Edward the Confessor, one of the last Saxon kings, at whose grave William, the Norman Conqueror, was crowned King of England, and William Rufus, the Conqueror's son, built this grand old hall, which is to-day the vestibule of the Houses of Parliament.

The Abbey is a Gothic cathedral of blackened gray stone, whose two great towers and front face across the parks, to the Queen's Palace. Its rear or choir is toward Parliament, with gloomy cloisters and carved chapels attached thereto, like a garden and outhouses to a dwelling. St. Margaret's Church is newer, but it carries its spire with no more straightness than the old buttresses and pinnacles which swarm around the cathedral.

The Palace Yard, between, is a cab-stand for the carriages of members merely, but before this book shall become old, it will be beautified and enclosed most probably; so will the Capitol at Washington be cleared of its common surrounding buildings, and made to exhibit itself more grandly.

But the Palace and the Abbey can never rise out of the ground like our marble Capitol, which is placed upon a hill, like the Acropolis at Athens, or the Capitol at Rome. The Parliament Houses afford no one grand view from any side. They lie below the level of the surrounding streets. The approaches to the bridge of Westminster are lifted above their lower windows. From the Thames bank, opposite, there is an unbroken view of the river façade, but there the Abbey is almost out of sight. From the parks, the confused towers of Abbey and Palace show imposingly, but the body of both buildings is lost. From Whitehall we cannot see the Abbey plainly, for the intervening Church of St. Margaret, and we observe only one end of the Palace. The fourth side is yet more buried in blocks of common houses, inhabited in many cases by needy or base persons. In short, Westminster Palace (the proper name of the "Houses of Parliament") is built upon its present site out of respect to the ancient traditions thereof, with the characteristic respect of Englishmen; but the situation is obscure and bad on all accounts of solid foundations, picturesqueness, and health. The sewer of the Thames, beneath its windows, emits foul odors and dangerous vapors.

The graveyard of St. Margaret, close by, is said to breed disease. A bed of concrete, twelve feet thick, had to be laid, before the architect dared proceed with his work, and the coffer dam and river wall alone required nearly three years to complete them. The foundations of Washington Capitol, on the contrary, were laid by nature, durably and imposingly, and the dome of the Capitol is thirty-seven feet higher above tide water, therefore, than the tallest tower of Westminster.

These natural defects omitted, the Houses of Parliament, which are new as the newest parts of the American Capitol, constitute the largest building which has been erected in England for many centuries. Excepting Milan Cathedral, and perhaps a few other Gothic churches, it is the most elaborately ornamented building of the Christian era. It is built of magnesian limestone, brought from Yorkshire, the color of which is somewhat like that of the New York brownstone, and this is supported upon river terraces of granite. The interior is of Caen stone from France, and of fine brick, and the trusses and girders are of iron. The style of architecture is Gothic, of that variety called Tudor, favorite three hundred years ago; and fretwork, gilding, pinnacles, and statuary are profusely embroidered upon the entire palace. Upon this English Gothic are engrafted studies from the famous city halls and civil edifices of Belgium and Flanders, such as the belfries and *hotels de ville* of Antwerp and Brussels, Lille and Bruges. If from some lofty place one could look down upon the whole edifice at one view, he would see that it is a vast, irregularly oblong building, broken by pinnacles, bays, and buttresses throughout its long outline. From the centre rises a dome surmounted by an open stone Gothic lantern and spire, reaching the heighth of three hundred feet. At each end are unlike towers, besides, — one eight feet square and three hundred and fifty feet high; the other forty feet square and three hundred and twenty feet high. The long river front is further ornamented with a pair of wing-towers at each end, — the two pairs, seven hundred feet apart, — almost the whole length of the American Capitol, — and each of these wing-towers has crested roofs, open-winged pinnacles, and gilded vanes, most exquisitely wrought.

Remembering all this, we shall presently be able to go on with perspicuity. A vast Gothic parallelogram, with a dome and spire in the centre and a tower at each end, — this is the situation on the land side. A similar parallelogram, with a dome and spire in the middle and two towers at each end,—this is the view on the water side. Now, what is remarkable about those two towers on the side of the land, is this: the nearer and more slender one is the clock tower, with a huge clock in the swollen top of it. This clock shows four illuminated dials, each thirty feet in diameter; it chimes the quarters, and strikes the hours, on a bell weighing eight tons. The farther and greater tower is the largest square Gothic tower in the world. It weighs twenty-eight thousand tons; the dome of the Capitol but four thousand; the Victoria tower is ascended by four hundred and seventy-two steps. The architect, Sir Charles Barry, would not allow it to be built up at a greater speed than thirty feet a year, for fear of settling. In the front of this tower is an arch sixty-five feet high, in which the great state carriages of the Queen and her suite are driven. This tower is the principal marvel of the building, and it is called in honor of the Queen. The clock tower rises up from the side of the approaches to Westminster Bridge, and if you will stand by that tower and strive to look down the profile of the building, you will find the Victoria tower cut off from your view by a great old battlemented hall, which has placed itself lengthwise along the front of the Palace, and parallel with it, as if striving to measure lengths. This old hall is of a different color and of a pattern less florid than the Palace. It is moved, so to speak, against the Palace, like a steam-tug against the side of a full-rigged ship, and at its head rise two strong towers of stone, while the rear or stern of it reaches just to the middle of the Palace.

This is the ancient and spacious Hall of Westminster, built by King William Rufus, and celebrated for its exquisite carpentery. To retain it in his general pile of Westminster the architect has thus ingeniously swung it alongside the new Palace, and made it the principal entrance hall.

The people enter Parliament Houses by walking into Westminster Hall from the end of the Palace, near the clock tower. This takes them for nearly three hundred feet down the face of the Palace. Then turning to the left, at what was formerly the foot of the hall, they penetrate the Palace proper to the area beneath the central dome.

The Queen, on the contrary, always drives into the Palace under the Victoria tower, at the opposite end. There are no other notable public entrances.

These are the more bulky outlines of the great building, but its details are intricate and rich with turrets, niches, figures of queens, kings, and statesmen, and exquisite pinnacles and bands of sculpture between the stories, illustrative of heraldry, seals, and arms. Every detail is wrought with nicety. The noble towers appear to lengthen themselves as we observe them, rising with the eye and the wonder of their measurer; but the elaborate Palace is not the product of any of those ages when Gothic architecture was a revelation of the mind, and consonant with man's existing faith and art. It is a bran new imitation, successful and prodigious, but without memories or inspirations of its own. It shows the power of British science, but is in nothing besides the Britain of the century in which it was reared. It is a perfect rose, —in wax. The same can be said of the United States Capitol, but it will not be felt; for the Greek architecture was akin to the Greek freedom, reviving which, the various peoples of the eighteenth century revolutionized, — ourselves the first. Every republicanized nation, as it shook off its fetters, returned to classical models for laws, heroes, and architectures. In Paris they built the Pantheon; at Washington, the Capitol.

While we look up at the blossoming outlines of this wonderful Palace, the story of its site may be vividly called before us. This spot was a little island beside the Thames once, called Thorney Island. In the seventh century a small monastery was founded here. The later Saxon kings built a palace beside it. The Norman Conqueror, anxious to flatter the conquered and take advantage of all superstitions, was also crowned here, beside the good King Edward's tomb, on Christmas day. Here he gave thanks for his victory also. His successors continued to ornament the site, at the expense of the good citizens of London, who, said Henry III., sneeringly, "called themselves barons on account of their wealth." Here the fabric of Parliament was built up. In a nook of the Great Abbey Church the House of Commons sat for three hundred years. The great hall, now vestibule of the new Parliament Houses, was meantime the rendezvous of the peers. The great courts of law were set up on this site. Here the captive King of France was received most royally. Here the barons in armor extorted privileges from the sovereign. Here direful anathemas were pronounced amidst the quenching of tapers. Here single combats were fought out in the sovereign's presence. Clerk of these works of Westminster was once Geoffrey Chaucer, the earliest of our great poets. After Agincourt, the victor came here in glorious state. Then the River Thames was the royal highway, filled with barges, and traitors were sent hence to the Tower.

In the yard of this Palace perished Raleigh. In the vaults of it waited Guido Fawkes, with match and gunpowder, and he also, with his co-conspirators, was hanged here. Here Charles I. was tried, and Cromwell inaugurated. Down to our own time all great state trials have been held here, not the least notable of which was that of Warren Hastings, which occurred in the latter years of George Washington's life, and was concluded four years after the ground was bought for Washington city. The year Mrs. John Adams moved into the unfinished White House, its first tenant, the Irish Parliament was here annexed to the English. The novel of "Barnaby Rudge," by Charles Dickens, will give one an interesting idea of the dreadful religious riots which raged round Parliament in the closing years of the American Revolution. The year before our second war with England broke out (1811), Percival, the Prime Minister, was murdered in Parliament. The year the Missouri compromise was passed, the King of England (Geo. IV.) was prosecuting his wife in Westminster Hall for divorce. The year Andrew Jackson was inaugurated President for the second time, slavery in the British Colonies was abolished here. The next year following, 1834, or twenty years after the British had burnt the Capitol at Washington, the Houses of Parliament took fire and burnt to the ground. As a temporary Capitol (afterwards the Old Capitol Prison) was set up at Washington in one hundred days, so in one hundred and twenty-five days the British Parliament met in the restored ruins of their Palace. The oldest part of the present American Capitol, the centre, was completed in 1825; twenty-five years afterward the wings were commenced; in 1856 the new dome was commenced. In 1840 the corner-stone of Parliament Houses was laid. Neither Palace nor Capitol are yet entirely completed.

Let us now enter the Houses of Parliament. Passing up a few steps we enter Westminster Hall, sixty-eight feet wide and forty-two feet high. The roof is splendidly carved in oak, and ornamented with many royal devices. Formerly it was hung with guidons, standards, and battle ensigns. To repair this roof in 1820, — nearly five hundred years after its first construction, — old ships-of-war were broken up, and their stout and storied timber was employed. Statues of kings flank this great hall, and when we have walked to its further end, two hundred and thirty-nine feet, we mount a flight of steps, sixty-five feet in height, lighted by a grand Gothic window, of stained glass, forty-eight feet high by twenty-five feet wide. Turning to the left, we take a passage at right angles to the great hall behind us, ninety-five feet long, thirty feet wide, and fifty-six feet high. This splendid hall is all of one level; it is decorated with frescoes, and marble statues of Hampden, Mansfield, Clarendon, and other statesmen.

This second hall, when we have traversed it, terminates in an octagon seventy feet square, which lies directly beneath the central dome and spire, that we have noticed without. From this octagon, which is at the centre of the Parliament Houses, corridors pass by the right to the House of Peers, and by the left to the House of Commons. Taking the passage to the right, we are in the lobby before the House of Peers.

The peers' lobby is thirty-eight feet square; four lofty arches open out of it, and the archway leading to the House of Lords is closed with gates of massive brass, which are eleven feet high, and weigh a ton and a half, and are richly decorated.

The bronze doors leading to the United States House of Representatives are seventeen feet high. They weigh ten tons, and are altogether more remarkable than those of the House of Lords.

The House of Lords' chamber is ninety-one feet long, forty-five feet broad, and forty-five feet high, almost an exact double cube. The United States Senate chamber is not so high by nine feet, but it is twenty-one feet longer and thirty-seven feet broader. The Senate chamber has a separate seat and desk for each senator, or less than a hundred places in all. These commodious desks are arranged in semi-circular fashion, so that all the senators face toward the Vice-President. The senate galleries will accommodate a thousand persons. The House of Lords, however, gives benches to two hundred and thirty-five peers, who face each other in rows lengthwise. The galleries in the House of Lords give place to few spectators, and that part of the chamber which, with us, is filled by the presiding officer and his clerks, is generally unoccupied, in the peers' chamber, for there stands the Queen's seat, the empty throne. The Senate chamber is surrounded by walls of a buff color; the ceiling is of iron, handsomely embossed and gilded, and the only light afforded is through panes of enamelled glass in the roof. There are neither paintings nor statues in the Senate chamber. The House of Lords, on the contrary, is most gorgeously decorated. Six lofty windows, in painted glass, on either side, show full-length portraits of past kings and queens. Three archways, in either end, show fresco paintings of allegory, or English history. Between the windows and the arches, are canopied niches, whose pedestals are supported by angels, bearing shields, and in the niches stand the bronze effigies of those barons who forced the great charter from King John. The flat ceiling is magnificently charged with monograms, mitres, croziers, shields, and heraldic symbols, and these are crossed by massive beams, gilded like solid gold, and all inscribed with mottoes of loyalty and religion. Busts, arms of bishops and peers, and infinite feudal cognizances, spangle the sides, borders, recesses, and ceilings. There is a reporter's gallery, and behind it a "strangers'," or spectators', gallery. At the opposite end from the throne is the bar, a sort of screen and railing at which counsel plead, and to which come members of the House of Commons. Next to the throne is the clerks' table. Nearer the body of the house are the crimson-colored woolsacks, or cushions, of the officers of the House of Peers. The carpet on the floor of this beautiful chamber is of a deep-blue ground, spangled with gold-colored Norman roses. The members' seats, reaching lengthwise, leave a fair open space at each end, and four superb brass candelabras light the area between, each seventeen feet high, and weighing twelve hundred pounds.

The empty Royal Throne is always the object of the greatest attention. It consists of a chair and footstool mounted upon a low platform, and covered with a triple canopy. The legs of the chair rest upon lions. The back of it is bordered with crystal and velvet, and surmounted by the lion and unicorn. Roses, thistles, shamrocks, and other devices are carved upon various parts of this seat, which stands upon a low platform covered with scarlet carpet, fringed with gold, and powdered with white roses and lilies. The Queen's footstool has carved sides, and a crimson velvet top, embroidered with roses and lilies. There are chairs near by, for the Prince of Wales and the sovereign's Consort, both splendidly gilded and carved.

On either side of the throne, doors open into the Prince's chamber, a smaller apartment, ornamented with Tudor fireplaces, with paintings and with portraits; and behind this chamber a royal gallery, one hundred and ten feet long, and forty-five feet wide, splendidly decorated with frescoes and stained glass, reaches back to the Queen's robing-room, near the Victoria tower.

The number of peers differs somewhat every year, but it may be said to be at present in the neighborhood of four hundred and sixty, including minors.

The following was the list in 1868: —

Princes of the blood royal	4
Dukes	20
Marquesses	18
Earls	109
Viscounts	22
Barons	215
Peers of Scotland	16
Peers of Ireland	28
English and Welsh Bishops	26
Irish Bishops	4
Total	462

Besides these the greater judges are generally summoned, to assist and advise the House of Lords. It will thus be seen that there are six times as many members of the House of Lords as of the United States Senate, but the number generally sitting bears about the same proportion to the House of Commons as do our senators to our representatives. The speaker of the House of Lords is called the Lord Chancellor, who is the custodian of the Queen's Great Seal, an important judge, and an officer of vast power and patronage. His salary is fifty thousand dollars a year; he has an official residence, holds his office at the Queen's pleasure (which means as long as his party keeps in office), and he retires upon a pension of twenty-five thousand dollars a year.

On the table before this "bewigged and begowned" Lord Chancellor, who sits uncomfortably balanced upon a crimson pillow-case, called the "woolsack," are placed the mace and the seal-bag. The first is his presumed gavel, and the second contains the great seal. The mace is five feet long, silver gilt, elaborately chased and carved with a crown, orb, and cross. The seal-bag is of crimson silk, embroidered in gold, fringed with gold bullion, tied by a silken cord, and inside of this bag the precious seal is further tied up in a leather pouch and a silk purse. The seal is merely a pair of silver dies, six inches in diameter and three quarters of an inch thick, in which melted wax is poured to take an impression of the device engraved there. The seal of Victoria represents that monarch, robed and crowned, on horseback, and on the reverse side the same good lady is enthroned between Justice and Religion. When the Queen comes to die this seal will be cut into four pieces and deposited in the Tower.

They used to break up the great seal, and give fragments of it to the poor, perhaps "to cure the king's evil."

The Lord Chancellor need not be a peer; he is not addressed by those who claim the floor, but they address themselves to "My Lords;" neither has he the right to decide who has the floor, nor the right to keep order. His office is costly, showy, and nondescript.

The Queen appoints deputy speakers when the Lord Chancellor is absent or debating.

The Chairman of Committees is a peer who presides in committee of the whole, and at some other times; he is not a political officer, and is usually re-elected every session; he gets twelve thousand five hundred dollars a year, and the counsel who assist him get seventy-five hundred dollars.

The Clerk of the Parliaments gets twenty thousand dollars a year, a residence and a pension. He is appointed by the Queen, and his assistants are appointed by the Lord Chancellor.

The Sergeant-at-Arms is the sheriff of the house; he carries the mace before the Lord Chancellor, keeps order in the lobbies, and gets seventy-five hundred dollars a year.

The foregoing officers correspond to the officers of the United States Senate. The Lord Chancellor resembles our Vice-President, but gets forty-two thousand dollars more salary than the latter. The Senate has also a Secretary, an Executive Secretary, and a Sergeant-at-Arms; but the House of Lords has another officer whose duties are mainly ceremonial; he is called the Gentleman-Usher to the Black Rod. He is a Knight of the Garter. He ushers the Queen into Parliament. He carries messages to the House of Commons. Peers charged with crimes are committed to his custody. This officer is a sort of connecting link between the sober business of Parliament and the fantastic artificiality of the court.

As in the Senate chamber, the two political parties choose, of their own will, opposite sides, so in the House of Lords the long seats on the Lord Chancellor's right hand are occupied by the administration party, with its leaders on the front bench. On the Lord Chancellor's left, facing the administration party, sit the opposition. If there are neutrals, as is frequently the case, they take the cross benches in front of the Lord Chancellor.

This is the House of Lords or Peers, — a body constituted to support the rights of the crown, and having full powers in all legislation, except the voting of money. Its members can vote by proxy. All bills of amnesty and those affecting the rights of the peerage, emanate from the crown and are introduced into this house.

The House of Lords is the highest tribunal in the land; it tries appeals from the Court of Chancery and impeachments made in the House of Commons. When a grand jury indicts a peer, he is tried by his peers.

The Queen never comes to Parliament except with solemn ceremony to open, adjourn or dissolve it. A hundred and fifty years ago the sovereign was a frequent spectator.

The sixteen Scotch peers who sit in Parliament are elected every year by the eighty-four nobles who constitute the peerage of Scotland.

There are over two hundred Irish peers, only twenty-eight of whom are representatives in the House of Lords.

Those ceremonials and representative sittings of the House of Lords, of which we propose to give examples in the present chapter, will comprise:

First, the Queen's appearance in the House of Lords to open, prorogue, or dissolve Parliament.

Second, a trial by the House of Lords, acting in its capacity of jury for the trial of a peer.

Third, some characteristic points of debates in the House of Lords.

Before we enter into these descriptions it is necessary to say that the two chambers of Lords and Commons comprise but a small part of the vast bulk of the Parliament Houses. These two chambers are conveniently near each other, but, besides them, there are eleven courts open to the sky, and eighteen official residences within the Parliament Palace limits. Libraries, committee and refreshment rooms, conference and reading rooms, are parts of this great building; telegraph offices connect Parliament with the clubs — where members commonly loiter out the evenings — with the city of London, with the Continent of Europe and with the Atlantic Cable. There is, however, an extensive part of the Palace, in the rear of the House of Lords, devoted entirely to the convenience of the Queen.

In a former chapter the sovereign has been described as she proceeds with her court to open Parliament in state. That description concluded with the Queen's entrance to the Victoria tower.

The Victoria tower stands at that corner of the Parliament buildings immediately opposite the public entrance we have made use of when passing into Westminster Hall. The Queen and her suite drive under the Victoria tower, and the Queen, descending, mounts by a grand stairway lined with statues of sovereigns to what is called her robing-room. Her carriage, meantime, passes on below to a large court-yard within the Palace, where it turns and comes back to the foot of the staircase under the Victoria tower, to await her descent.

In the United States Capitol there is one small apartment, in the rear of the Senate, called the President's room, lined with vari-colored marbles, and excessively frescoed. The President is never seen in this room more than two or three times a year, when he comes at the close of a session to sign bills immediately upon their passage.

The Queen, however, is an integral part of Parliament, and a large part of the Parliament Palace is devoted to her uses. The great square tower, which is so expensive and so majestic a part of the Palace, is merely a sort of triumphal arch under which she may pass, and nearly all the space between this tower and the rear of the House of Peers is taken up by her staircase, guard-room, robing-room, and gallery. When the queen has been escorted by her suite up the royal staircase, she passes through the "Norman porch," which is embellished with statues and paintings of the Norman sovereigns, to her robing-room, — a small but exquisite chamber painted with scenes from the legend of King Arthur and the court of chivalry.

Here the queen is robed by her attendants, everything being convenient in the way of accessories, — mirrors, toilet articles, whatever could fit out the most fastidious belle for a ball, — and, besides the garments in which she is arrayed, she is fitted with her crown, and the sceptre is placed in her hand.

The two Houses of Parliament have, meantime, been three days organizing, taking oaths, etc., in anticipation of this event, and the House of Peers is now waiting for the Queen, while the House of Commons is waiting for the House of Peers. The peers are all in their robes; the Lord Chancellor is ready with the Queen's speech, which she has got pretty nearly "by heart," meantime, as her prime minister wrote it for her; the Gentleman-Usher to the Black Rod, with his rod in his hand, is itching to bow the way before the Queen to her throne. At last they are all ready; cannons fire, outside; the Queen moves on, with her richly clad household and grand officers behind her, the Black Rod scraping before; and the splendid royal gallery, with its gilded ceiling, is crowded on both sides with peeresses and people of distinction, who have come to see the ceremony. The sovereign clears the long gallery, passes the vestibule called the "Prince's chamber," and appears before Parliament.

Here let us take up the scene, as continued from our second chapter, of Victoria's first opening of Parliament. We are indebted for much of it to Mr. James Grant, a celebrated Parliamentary reporter.

So early as twelve o'clock, M., the interior of the House of Lords, on the day Victoria opened Parliament, was nearly filled by peeresses and their daughters; by one o'clock it was quite full; and so great was the anxiety to obtain a view of the young Queen, just eighteen years of age, that even the gallery of the House of Lords was filled with the female branches of aristocratic families by twelve o'clock, all, as in the body of the house, in full dress. Lady Mary Montague has given a graphic description of the siege which a troop of duchesses, countesses, and other titled ladies, laid to the door of the gallery of the House of Lords, when, in her time, some interesting debate was expected, and how, when they found, after a ten hours' assault, the gallery was not to be taken by storm, they succeeded in effecting an entrance by stratagem. The ladies, in the present case, were not under the necessity of attempting an entrance into the gallery by sheer physical force, for they had, in most cases, procured a Lord Chamberlain's order of admission; but several of them effected an entrance by the persuasive eloquence of their pretty and fascinating faces, accompanied by a few honeyed words, which the officers could not resist.

Similar persistent efforts on the part of the ladies are made to enter the Senate chamber when the President is inaugurated. On such occasions the Sergeant-at-Arms, acting under orders from the Vice-President, keeps the galleries and doors.

"Some of the British peeresses, on the occasion we are describing, carried the joke still further, and actually took forcible possession of the front seat in the gallery, which is always specially and exclusively appropriated for the gentlemen of the press. This seat is capable, on an emergency, of containing, including a back form, about thirty persons, and yet, on this day, only three reporters were fortunate enough to obtain admission; and even they, but for the accidental circumstance of having taken possession of their places the moment the door was thrown open, would also have been among the excluded. And what does the reader suppose would have been the consequence? Simply, that not a word of the important proceedings in the House of Lords on the opening of Parliament by the

Queen, beyond a copy of the speech, which is always sent from the government offices to the newspapers, could have appeared in next day's papers.

"The three reporters already referred to, when they saw the rush of the ladies to take possession of the unoccupied seats, felt, in the first instance, inexpressible surprise; but, on recovering themselves, the predominant feeling in their minds was one of gratitude to their stars that they had been fortunate enough to possess themselves of their places.

"There they sat," moans Mr. Grant, "for two long hours, amidst a large assemblage of the fairest of the fair, literally hidden from the sight of those who were lucky enough to get a peep into the house from the door, by a forest of waving plumes of feathers of the richest kind. By one o'clock the house had an appearance which, I am convinced, may be said with truth, it has seldom, if ever, presented before. The whole of the benches on the floor and the two side galleries were occupied by the female portion of the families of the peers, all attired in their costliest and most magnificent dresses. I will not attempt to describe the effect produced on the mind of the spectator by the dazzling splendor of the jewelry they wore."

The nearest approach we Americans can make to such a scene is grand opera night on the advent of some youthful new *prima donna.*

All the ladies had to sit about two hours before the arrival of the Queen, and while there were no proceedings in the house; and yet everything was quiet. Meantime opera-glasses were employed upon each other as liberally as we make use of them in our full-dress public assemblies.

A little before two o'clock, a discharge of artillery announced that Her Majesty was on her way to Parliament. This made great flutter amongst the ladies, and some wished they were outside, while everybody outside wished they were in.

A short time passed away, and the striking up of a band of music on the outside announced the near approach of Her Majesty. A few moments more elapsed, and the thrilling tones of the trumpet intimated that Queen Victoria, though as yet unseen, was proceeding along the passage to her robing-room, and would be in the midst of them presently.

Here the ladies in the House of Lords indulged in lively anticipation of the Queen's wardrobe. They were not left long in doubt, for after various noises in the rear of the throne, and a few seconds more of fluttering, Victoria entered the House. The peeresses and all present simultaneously rose. The young girl Queen, laden with jewels and precious garments, bowed in by the usher, according to his best knowledge of "deportment," and followed by the nobility of her court, climbed fair and blushing up the steps of the throne. Her Majesty, having taken her seat on the throne, desired the peers to be seated. The intimation was known to be equally meant for the ladies. The Commons were then summoned into the royal presence.

In the interval before their coming, the brilliant audience scanned the Queen's childish face and slender figure with mingled respect and criticism. She had been tutored to keep her self-possession, but maidenhood was sensitive beyond royalty, and by the rules of etiquette none dared approach to soothe her or to relieve her, and as yet she had no husband whose near presence and sympathy she could feel.

Very soon, however, the wild buffaloes of the House of Commons were heard approaching.

No sooner had the door been opened, in obedience to the mandate of the Queen, which leads into the passage through which they had to pass, on their way to the bar of the House of Lords, than you heard a patting of feet as if it had been of the hoofs of some two or three score of quadrupeds. "This, however," says one present, "was only one of the classes of sounds which broke on the ears of all in the House of Lords, and even of those who were standing in the royal passages leading to it. There were loud exclamations of 'Ah! ah!' and a stentorian utterance of other sounds, which denoted that the parties from whom they proceeded had been suddenly subjected to some painful visitation. All eyes, not even excepting the eyes of Her Majesty, were instantly turned towards the door of the passage whence the sounds proceeded. Out rushed, towards the bar of the House of Lords, a torrent of members of the lower house, just as if the place they had quitted had been on fire, and they had been escaping for their lives. The cause of the strange, if not alarming, sounds, which had been heard a moment or two before, was now sufficiently intelligible to all. They arose, from what Mr. O'Connell would call, the mighty struggle among the members, as to who should reach the House of Lords first, and by that means get nearest to the bar, and thereby obtain the best place for seeing and hearing. In this mortal competition for a good place, the honorable gentlemen exhibited as little regard for each other's persons as if they had been the principal performers in some exhibition of physical energy in Donnybrook Fair. They squeezed each other, jammed each other, and trod on each other's gouty toes.

"The most serious sufferer, so far as I have been able to learn," adds Mr. Grant, "was one of the honorable members, who had his shoulder dislocated in the violent competition to be first at the bar. Even after the M. P.'s were fairly in the presence of their sovereign, there was a great deal of jostling and jamming of each other, which extorted sundry exclamations indicative of pain, though such exclamations were less loud than those before alluded to. The Irish members played the most prominent part in this unseemly exhibition, and next to them the English ultra radicals; the tories cut but a sorry figure in the jostling match. The liberals were, as the saying is, 'too many for them.' I thought with myself, at the time, what must the foreign ambassadors and their ladies, who were present, think of English manners, should they, unhappily, form their notions on the subject from the conduct, on this occasion, of the legislators in the lower house? It was a rather awkward exhibition for a body of men arrogating to themselves the character of being 'the first assembly of gentlemen in Europe.'"

Her Majesty having taken the oath against popery, which she did, in a slow and serious, yet audible manner, proceeded to read the royal speech, which was handed to her by the Lord Chancellor, kneeling on one knee. The most perfect stillness reigned through the place while Her Majesty was reading her speech.

The speech being ended, Victoria descended from the throne, and with slow and graceful steps retired from the House to her robing-room, a few yards distant, nodding, as she did on her entrance, to most of the peeresses as she passed.

In a few moments, by the cheers outside, it was known that she was returning to her palace, and her route was marked by the same affectionate testimonials as before.

On the conclusion of the Queen's speech, both Houses adjourned, as is usual on such occasions, till five o'clock, when they again met to discuss the royal oration, and to consider the propriety of voting an address to Her Majesty, expressive of the gratitude of the Legislature for her most gracious speech.

In both Houses there was a large attendance of members, while the galleries were crowded with strangers.

In proceeding along the passage which leads to the reporter's gallery in either House, immediately previous to the commencement of the debate, it was an interesting sight to witness the reporters of the evening newspapers, with a number of boys all ready to be despatched to their several offices, with the copy in piecemeal so soon as prepared, sitting at a table, with the necessary apparatus of pen, ink, and paper before them, and each more eager than the other to give a practical proof of the accuracy and expedition.

Divest this scene of its stars, garters, insignias, and extravagant ceremony, and it will be seen to resemble very much any ordinary state pageant in the United States. Here, however, women cannot be eligible to office at the present time, whereas, in the English government, a woman stands at the pinnacle of the edifice of state.

Similar scenes happen when the sovereign prorogues, or stops, Parliament for a stated time, and when she dissolves it, or commands its official life to cease.

No Parliament can sit longer than seven years, nor more than six months after a sovereign's death. When a sovereign dies, Parliament must meet instantly, even if it be Sunday. The Queen cannot prorogue Parliament more than eighty days, although when they meet again she may again prorogue them. In 1867–68 was held the third session of the seventh Parliament of Victoria's reign. At the same time the forty-first Congress of the United States was in session.

It frequently happens that Parliament is opened with no more dignity by the sovereign than we count our electoral votes in joint Senate and House.

I have fallen upon a very humorous instance of the manner in which William IV. appeared, reading the royal speech prepared for him by the politicians. He was Victoria's uncle. The day the King opened Parliament was unusually gloomy, which, added to an imperfection in his visual organs consequent on advanced years and to the darkness of the old House of Lords, especially in the place where the throne is situated, rendered it impossible for him to read the royal speech with facility. Most patiently and good-naturedly did he struggle with the task, often hesitating, sometimes mistaking, and at others correcting himself. On one occasion he stuck altogether, when, after two or three ineffectual efforts to make out the word, he was obliged to give it up, when, turning to Lord Melbourne, the Prime Minister, who stood on his right hand, and looking him most significantly in the face, he said, in tone sufficiently loud to be audible in all parts of the House, "Eh! what is it?" "The infinite good-nature and bluntness with which the question was put," says a looker-on, "would have reconciled the most inveterate republican to monarchy in England so long as it is embodied in the person of William the Fourth." Lord Melbourne having whispered the obstructing word, the King proceeded to toil through the speech, but by the time he got to about the middle, the librarian brought him two wax tapers, on which he suddenly paused, and, raising his head, and looking at the Lords and Commons, he addressed them, on the spur of the moment, in a perfectly distinct voice, and without the least embarrassment, or the mistake of a single word, in these terms: —

"My Lords and Gentlemen, —

"I have hitherto not been able, from want of light, to read this speech in the way its importance deserves; but, as lights are now brought me, I will read it again from the commencement, and in a way which, I trust, will command your attention."

He then again, though evidently fatigued by the difficulty of reading in the first instance, began at the beginning, and read through the speech in a manner which would have done credit to any professor of elocution, — though it was clear he labored under a slight hoarseness, caused most probably by cold. The sparkling of the diamonds in the crown, owing to the reflection caused by the lighted candles, had a fine effect. Probably this was the first occasion on which a King of England ever read his speech by candle-light, at the opening of his Parliament.

This sovereign was Victoria's predecessor on the throne, and during his reign the celebrated "Reform Bill" was passed, which the House of Lords so strenuously opposed that a creation of new peers in mass was threatened. The King was largely controlled by the Lords' party in the crisis, but he was obliged to yield at last, and I shall instance the sort of debate that preceded his appearance, to demonstrate that the House of Peers is frequently coarser and more boisterous than our Senate.

"Their Lordships," says the newspaper report, "met at three o'clock. The House was crowded in every part. The Lord Chancellor having, as was understood, left the woolsack for the purpose of receiving His Majesty, Queen Victoria's uncle, whose arrival had been announced by the firing of the Park guns, and the cheers of the multitude assembled outside the House. The King had come to dissolve Parliament.

"The Earl of Mansfield rose and said: I move that the Earl of Shaftesbury do take the chair *pro tempore*.

"The Earl of Shaftesbury took his seat on the woolsack.

"Lord Wharncliffe: I believe there can be no doubt in your Lordships' mind as to the purpose for which we have this day met.

"The Duke of Richmond rose amidst the greatest confusion: I rise to order. Some noble Lords are not in their places. I move the standing order of the House, that they do take their places.

"A noble Lord: I dissent from the suggestion of the noble Duke.

"The Duke of Richmond: I maintain it is a standing order of the House that the noble Lords take their proper places on such an occasion as the present, and if that order be not complied with, I will move another standing order, 'That persons not members of the House be ordered to withdraw.'

"The scene of confusion which here ensued defies description. A number of peers, in all parts of the House, were calling out, 'Order! order!' at the full stretch of their voices, while the peeresses who were present, — of whom there were many in full dress, — were greatly alarmed. In the midst of the scene a noble Lord, supposed to be Lord Lyndhurst, made some observations which were not heard.

"The Duke of Richmond: I have to complain of the use of such language as that which has just fallen from the noble Lord; and I shall move that the standing order against offensive language be read. [Renewed uproar, which it is impossible to describe.]

"When it had somewhat subsided, the Marquis of Londonderry's voice was heard. He spoke in a very loud tone, and exhibited the utmost violence of manner. He said: I rise to order. I maintain that I am in possession of the House. I rise to accuse the noble Duke of bringing forward a very unfounded charge. I am not aware of any offensive language being used on this side of the House which could provoke the remarks of the noble Duke.

"The Marquis of Clanricarde: After what has fallen from the noble Marquis, it is most desirable that the noble Duke should persist in his motion for the observance of the standing orders of the House.

"The Marquis of Londonderry: I call on the noble Duke to mention any offensive language which has been used by the noble Baron (Lord Lyndhurst). It appears to me that the noble Duke begins to think that he is to be the hero of the *coup d'état* on this occasion, and that he fancies he can smother that feeling which is essential to the expression of the sentiments of noble Lords on this most extraordinary meeting. It appears to me that the noble Duke is endeavoring to set aside the right of peers to declare their sentiments, by having recourse to so miserable an expedient as that of moving the standing orders of the House. The cries of 'Order! order!' which now resounded through the House were deafening. They were mingled with shouts of 'Order of the day!' during which, Lord Wharncliffe rose and said: Without wishing to provoke a discussion on the subject, I am anxious that it shall be entered on the journals of the House, that I, in my place yesterday, did give notice that I would move an humble Address to His Majesty, not to exercise his undoubted prerogative of dissolving Parliament. I now beg leave to read the address to your Lordships.

"The noble Lord here read the address, which was to the effect, that it appeared to the House that under the extraordinary circumstances in which the country was placed, and the excitement then existing in the public mind, a prorogation or dissolution of Parliament was likely to be attended with the most disastrous consequences. (Loud cries of "Hear! hear!" from the tory benches.) The Lord Chancellor at this moment entered the House, and addressed their Lordships in the most emphatic manner in the following terms: 'My Lords, I have never yet heard it doubted that the King possesses the prerogative of dissolving Parliament at pleasure; still less have I ever known a doubt to exist on the subject at a moment when the lower house has thought fit to refuse the supplies.'

"Here there were tumultuous cries of 'Hear! hear!' mingled with shouts of 'The King! the King!' and tremendous uproar.

"The Lord Chancellor having retired from the House to receive His Majesty, confusion reigned. The Marquis of Londonderry called on Lord Shaftesbury to take the chair. [Cries of 'Order! order!' 'Lord Shaftesbury!' 'Shame! shame!' 'The King!' and the greatest uproar.]

"The Earl of Shaftesbury having taken his seat on the woolsack, a scene of confusion ensued, of which it were impossible for words to convey any idea. When it had partially subsided, the Marquis of Londonderry rose, with much warmth of tone and violence of gesture, and said, 'As long as I hold a seat in this House, I will never consent to—' [The uproar was here renewed with such tremendous violence as to prevent the noble Marquis from proceeding further.] It having again partially subsided, the Earl of Mansfield rose, and said, 'My Lords, such a scene as this I never before witnessed in your Lordships' house, and hope I never shall see anything like it again. I have heard from the noble and learned Lord on the woolsack, with the utmost surprise, that it is the undoubted right of the crown to dissolve Parliament when the House of Commons refuses the supplies. The noble and learned Lord had indeed, perhaps, with wilful ignorance, declared this to be the fact. I will use no intemperate language, but I will nevertheless assert, as far as God Almighty has given me the means of understanding, that the crown and the country are now about to be placed in a most awful predicament, unparalleled at any previous period.'

"The noble Earl was proceeding in somewhat the same strain, when loud cries of 'The King! the King!' announced the approach of His Majesty, who, on entering, immediately mounted the throne with a firm step, and, begging their lordships to be seated, he, after one or two forms had been gone through, delivered his speech dissolving the Parliament."

The "Times" account of this extraordinary affair concludes thus: "It is utterly impossible to describe the scene that presented itself in the House from the commencement of the proceedings up to the very moment of His Majesty's entrance. The violent tones and gestures of noble Lords; the excitement, breaking down the constitutional usages, not to say civilities, of life, astonished the spectators, and affected the ladies who were present with visible alarm. In a word, nothing like this scene was ever before witnessed within the walls of Parliament."

There are several striking examples of trials of peers by the House of Lords, but I have selected, to illustrate this function of the superior House of Parliament, the trial of Lord Kingsborough for the murder of Henry Gerald Fitzgerald. The latter was a natural son, and a man of bad passions. He seduced the former's daughter, his own cousin, and, after being exposed, again attempted to decoy her from her father's house. In this attempt he was discovered, and while engaged in a deadly struggle with her brother, Lord Kingsborough shot him dead. This case fills many interesting pages of such books as the "Romances of the Aristocracy," and "Tales of Noble Families," — a class of books very popular with British females of high and low degree. The parties were Irish, but the "stage business," as one denominates it, is precisely the same nowadays.

It is from the enterprising annalist, Burke, that I derive this sketch.

It was on the eighteenth of May, 1798, the year before Washington died, that the trial took place in the House of Lords. Much interest was excited by the affair, as, since the case of Lord Byron, in England, nothing of the kind had been known. It was a tragedy new alike to the actors and the audience, and the imaginations of either were proportionably raised beyond the level of ordinary occasions. The usual place of meeting, a small though handsome chamber, being too confined for the business on hand, the peers marched in grand procession into the House of Commons. First came the Masters in Chancery, with the robed judges of the inferior courts; next came the minor orders of nobility not entitled to vote, and the eldest sons of peers; lastly, the peers themselves advanced, two by two, all save John Fitzgibbon, the first Earl of Clare, who walked, in solitary dignity, without a companion. "We will not," says Burke, "dwell upon the bowings and the bendings employed by the various subordinates in the preliminary discharge of their duties, neither will we stop to recount all the crossings to the right and to the left, and the reverences to His Grace, the Lord High Steward, on the woolsack. If they occupied much time, and to little purpose, we will not commit the same error by repeating them. It is enough for the present purpose to have noticed that such was the case."

When these ceremonies had been gone through, the royal commission was read aloud, appointing the Earl of Clare, Lord High Steward, all the peers standing up the while with their heads uncovered. To this succeeded the reading of the writ of *certiorari*, with the return to it, the indictment before the grand jury, and the finding of a true bill by Boyle and Fellowes. Finally, the Clerk of the Crown called upon the Sergeant-at-Arms to do his duty, whereupon the latter came forward and cried: "Oyez! oyez! oyez! Constable of Dublin Castle, bring forth Robert, Earl of Kingston, your prisoner, to the bar, pursuant to the order of the House of Lords. God save the King!"

A profound silence followed this summons, every eye and ear being stretched in anxious expectation of the prisoner. After a delay that seemed more than long enough to the excited audience, though it could not have lasted many seconds, the Earl was ushered in by

Constable and Deputy Constable of Dublin Castle, the latter being on his left hand, and carrying an axe, with the edge turned from him, in token that he had not as yet incurred the last fatal penalty of the law. He then bowed lowly to the High Steward, and again to the peers on either side, after which he knelt to the bar, — "a degree of humility," says the reverent Burke, "that might have become guilt when soliciting for mercy, but hardly seems appropriate to a man facing his judges in the bold consciousness of innocence."

The degradation, however, if it really were such, was short-lived. He was directed by the High Steward to rise, whereupon he repeated the former ceremonial, which this time was acknowledged by all present, and Lord Clare thus addressed him from the woolsack: —

"Robert, Earl of Kingston, you are brought here to answer one of the most serious charges that can be made against any man, — the murder of a fellow-subject. The solemnity and awful appearance of this judicature must naturally discompose and embarrass your Lordship. It may, therefore, not be improper for me to remind your Lordship that you are to be tried by the laws of a free country, framed for the protection and punishment of guilt alone; and it must be a great consolation to you to reflect that you are to receive a trial before the supreme judicature of the nation; that you are to be tried by your peers, upon whose unbiased judgment and candor you can have the firmest reliance, more particularly as they are to pass judgment upon you under the solemn and inviolable obligation of their honor. It will also be a consolation to you to know that the benignity of our law has distinguished the crime of homicide into different classes. If it arise from accident, from inevitable necessity, or without malice, it does not fall within the crime of murder; and of these distinctions, warranted by evidence, you will be at liberty to take advantage. Before I conclude, I am commanded by the House to inform your Lordship, and all others who may have occasion to address the court during the trial, that the address must be to the Lords in general, and not to any Lord in particular."

"This last remark, in all likelihood," says the same critic, "proceeded from the general non-acquaintance with such proceedings, they having slept so long in abeyance." The Clerk of the Crown next commenced the usual interrogatories: —

"How say you, Robert, Earl of Kingston, are you guilty, or not guilty, of this murder and felony for which you stand arraigned?"

"Not guilty," replied the noble prisoner.

"How," resumed the clerk, "will your Lordship be tried?"

"By God and my peers."

"God send you a good deliverance!"

Proclamation was then made by the Sergeant-at-Arms:—

"Oyez! oyez! all manner of persons who will evidence upon oath before our sovereign Lord, the King, against Robert, Earl of Kingston, the prisoner at the bar, let them come forth and they shall be heard, for he now stands at the bar upon his deliverance."

To this appeal there was no answer, and, after a short delay, that the witnesses, if there were any, might have time to come forward, Lord Clare demanded of Curran, the counsel for the accused, whether due notices had been served of the removal of the indictment into the High Court of Parliament. This demand was met by evidence showing that such notices had been served on the widow and children of the deceased; and again proclamation was made, requiring any witnesses for the crown to come forward with their testimony. None replying to this second summons, the peers in succession pronounced their verdict of "Not guilty, upon my honor;" when Lord Clare informed the accused of his unanimous acquittal, upon which the latter made three low bows and retired. Not the least impressive part of this ceremony, if we look only to the imagination, was the symbolical form which now concluded it. The white staff being delivered to the High Steward, he held it in both hands, broke it asunder, and declared the commission was dissolved.

It is this identical form of trial which is liable to be revived to-day. An instance of appeal lately made from the highest under tribunals to Parliament was that of Mrs. Yelverton, proceeding against her dishonorable husband, though "a gentleman" in the English sense. The peer commanded more mercy than the woman, and, to the disgust of the English Commons, the wife's plea was rejected.

A notable example of condign punishment visited upon a peer was the case of Earl Ferrers, about a hundred years ago. He butchered his steward for rendering some testimony in favor of the Earl's divorced wife, and was condemned to be hanged and anatomized at Tyburn. He proceeded to the gallows in his wedding-suit, congratulating the people on the way that they were to see "a gentleman" die. Drunkenness and indecency, the usual accompaniments of an English execution, marked hangman and spectators, but the gentleman was hanged with a silken cord.

Frequently, at the trial of peers, swords have been drawn in the Hall of Westminster by retainers of the various contestants. This has not occurred for some years, and one of the last illustrations of the sort was the trial of Lord Gray, of Work, indicted for seducing Earl Berkley's daughter. The latter would not quit her paramour, and the Earl's friends put it to the arbitrament of cold steel.

The history of England is fruitful in episodes of impeachment. We have had two or three such trials in the United States, and the latest of these is yet in the memory of the youngest reader. It was the arraignment of a President before the Senate on impeachment by a vote of the House of Representatives. The trial was long, dramatic, and futile, and, in a certain sense, reactionary upon its abettors. In like manner Warren Hastings, Governor-General of India, was tried on presentment of articles of impeachment for seven years, and he, also, was acquitted.

When the House of Commons impeaches, a member rises, makes the motion, and offers his proofs. If the House concurs, this member, with several of his friends, goes up to the bar of the House of Lords, and impeaches the offender. The trial is held in Westminster Hall, the Lord High Steward presiding, and Commons attend in Committee of the Whole. The peers vote guilty or not guilty, "upon my honor!"

If guilty, the Speaker of the House of Commons demands judgment. Either the House of Commons can rescind, or the crown can pardon, after conviction.

When the House of Lords "divides" on a vote, or passes through tellers, the division is ordered by the cry of "Not content!"

No motion in the Lords need be seconded.

The House of Lords is called "an estate." Sometimes it is considered as two "estates," one being the lords spiritual, the other the lords temporal. Parliament, properly speaking, is composed of the crown, these two, and the Commons. We have fallen into a fashion of calling our House of Representatives "Congress," as the English often improperly call the House of Commons "Parliament."

A petition addressed to the peers must begin: "To the Right Honorable, the Lords Spiritual and Temporal, in Parliament assembled."

The longest Parliament ever assembled was in 1661, A. D., which existed more than sixteen years and a half, and one of the shortest was in 1830, which expired in less than six months.

The House of Lords has exclusive jurisdiction in matters affecting the peerage. The Irish peers in it are elected for life by the body of the Irish nobility, and the sixteen Scotch peers are also elective.

Three peers present constitute a quorum in the House of Lords. This house seldom holds sessions on Wednesdays or Saturdays, and it meets at five o'clock, P. M. If a peer gets in the rear of the Lord Chancellor's woolsack, he is not considered to be in the House of Lords, and cannot vote there. If a peer undergoes examination before a select committee of the lower house, he sits with his hat on. So jealous are the peers of their own superior station that, although the law prescribes joint committees for the transaction of business between the two houses, no such committee has been appointed for a hundred years. No motion made in the Lords needs to be seconded. If several peers rise to speak together, the peers, and not the speaker, say who shall be heard.

By right, the peers take specified seats, according to their relative dignity and the antiquity of their peerage; but this is seldom insisted upon. Young noblemen on attaining majority take their places without paying fees or without ceremony, while newly created peers must pass both gauntlets. Peers and Commons alike sit with their hats on, after the manner of a Quaker meeting.

Protestant and Catholic peers take different oaths. The Scotch peers show their certificates of election. Except the Princes of the blood and the Lord Chancellor the peers take the oath in bodies. Peers, with writs of summons, present their writs kneeling on one knee to the Lord Chancellor. The House of Lords is daily opened with prayers, after which strangers are admitted by ticket. When sitting as a court anybody can enter.

In the United States, the President has the power of vetoing bills, returning them, with his objections, to the house in which they originated. His assent is signified by merely taking up a quill and signing them, and toward the close of a session he occupies a room in the Capitol building for the express purpose of signing bills as rapidly as they are passed. Or they need not be signed at all; for if he neglect them for ten days they become laws.

The Queen has, also, the veto power, but she dare not exercise it in the present state of English public opinion. The last refusal to sign a bill passed by Parliament occurred in the time of Queen Anne, 1707. Victoria gives her royal assent either by special commissioners, or in person, robed, crowned, and seated on her throne in the House of Lords. The bill is read by its title, and the assent is rendered for the Queen, by the Clerk of the Parliament, in Norman French:—

"*La Reyne le veult.*" [The Queen wills it.]

To bills of supply he gives her answer:—

"*La Reyne remercie ses bons sujets, accepte leur benevolence, et ainsi le veult.*" [The Queen thanks her good subjects, accepts their kindness, and wills it."]

A bill becomes an act immediately when the royal assent is rendered.

The following chapters will take up in detail many functions of the peers performed jointly with other branches of the government.

Such is the House of Peers, imperfectly portrayed, and the reader has been reminded of its likeness to the American Senate in many particulars. The Senate, indeed, in many of its traditions and parliamentary laws is copied from the House of Lords.

The Senate, like the House of Lords, never completely expires, but laps over from Congress to Congress, from administration to administration. It is the conservative body, with less direct responsibility to the people than the lower house, and it is closely interwoven with both the executive and the legislative government. It appoints to office jointly with the President. It passes bills jointly with the House. Its President is generally the Vice-President, who goes up to the chief magistracy in certain contingencies. It is a court to try judges and presidents. As the House of Commons must come to the Chamber of Peers when the Queen opens Parliament, so does the House of Representatives come up to the Senate when the President is inaugurated. The Senate is partly of Roman, and partly original, but chiefly of English, origin, created by the written constitution of the country, and set going nearly at the beginning. The House of Lords was the original Parliament of England, wrested from the absolute tyranny of the throne, and the House of Commons, in turn, was coerced from the Sovereign and the Lords. With us the people were first; with the English the King was first.

In the growth of time the latest body has become the most powerful of all, both in America and England, and the Senate and the House of Lords are at present the most honorable, and yet the most unpopular bodies in either government. In 1867 the House of Representatives consented to the passage of a Tenure-of-Office Bill, giving the Senate a veto power over the President's removals. This act vastly strengthened the Senate, yet led to troubles which perplexed the state, and in the end raised in certain extreme minds a question identical with a mooted one in England, — whether the Senate and the House of Lords alike were not dangerous and irresponsible bodies. Bitter experience has taught the House of Lords to consent to such legislation as the Commons demands. The Senate in like manner generally gives way to popular will. If the House of Lords holds out, the only relief is to create enough new peers to outvote them. But we cannot create more senators except by admitting more States, and over this the Senate has joint legislation. The senators are elected by State legislatures, and in several cases where the latter bodies are demoralized, it is claimed that gross corruption enters into the choice. But, collectively, the United States Senate is the finest body of legislators in the world, physically, at least. In 1867 they were of the average height of five feet ten and a half inches, and above the average weight of one hundred and seventy-one pounds. The English peers are also of dignified bearing, and frequently of handsome presence. But the tendency of thought and indignation in England is no less against the aristocracy in its social and landed, than in its legislative, relation. In every land rationally governed there must needs be a body midway between impulse and tyranny, popular passion and absolute magistracy. But whether this body shall be hereditary, and invigorated by occasional accessions from the people, or indirectly elective, is the dilemma of English thinkers at the present day. Americans think that there can be but one conclusion upon this question. What has preserved the British aristocracy is mainly this: that it is the most accessible and democratic aristocracy in history. Its abuses are from the past, its virtues are from the present.

CHAPTER V.

THE HOUSE OF COMMONS AND THE HOUSE OF REPRESENTATIVES.

Comparison of their places of meeting, parliamentary laws and behavior, and rise and development in the state.— Individual exemplifications of their leaders and oratory.— England considered in her constituencies. — The reform bills of 1832 and 1867. — Statement of the relative merits of the English and the American manner of representation. — Various scenes in the House of Commons.

By this time we are well acquainted with the Houses of Parliament. We see that the chambers of the Commons and the Peers occupy the same relation to each other architecturally, as the Senate Chamber and the Hall of Representatives at Washington. But those two chambers in the Parliament Houses are deeply buried in the core of the buildings, while in the American Capitol their counterparts occupy the body of the two large wings.

Hidden in their vast Gothic palace these British chambers of legislation are no more than a couple of seeds in a melon. "The palace itself," as a reviewer says, "delights only those who see in it a stone embodiment of the British Constitution — the slow, irregular, but picturesque growth of ages." Others, like Lord Brougham, believe that it is "barbarous in the extreme to erect a Gothic structure for parliamentary purposes in the middle of the nineteenth century."

Be this as it may, we have now but to return from the House of Lords along the main corridor which passes under the great central dome, and, crossing the lobby of the Commons, we enter the House or Chamber of Commons. The Speaker of the House in his chair and the Queen, when enthroned in the Lords, face each other four hundred and fifty feet apart, and midway between them is the Octagon.

The Speaker of the House of Representatives, in like manner, faces the President of the Senate, and midway between them is the Rotunda. The Hall of Representatives is one hundred and thirty-nine feet long, ninety-three feet wide, and thirty feet high, and galleries running quite round it give seats to twelve hundred spectators. The shape of the hall is rectangular, and the Speaker sits on one of the wide sides, facing the main door of entrance. His chair is placed upon a conspicuous platform; a marble bar or table stands before him, and this is again enclosed by the marble bar of the clerks. As with the senators, each representative has a desk especially assigned to him, and a comfortable chair. In the fortieth Congress there were two hundred and thirty-two members.

The Hall of the House of Commons is seventy-five feet long, forty-five feet wide, and forty-one feet high, or only about half the size of the Hall of Representatives, with galleries on three sides. It is a rectangular chamber, but the Speaker sits on one of the short sides, or at the end, facing the main door of entrance. Over the head of the Speaker, as in the American Congress, is a reporters' gallery. Behind and above the reporters' gallery in the House of Commons, is a sort of bird cage, with wire gauze in front, and this is the only place which ladies are allowed to enter; for by rule they are forbidden in the House of Commons. There are places for only sixty "strangers" or spectators, and these can be vacated by the whim of any member crying out: "Mr. Speaker, I see strangers in the House!" The Speaker sits under a canopy, carved with the royal arms, and he wears a white wig and a black gown. Before him is the clerk's table, whereon is placed the Speaker's mace, a weapon of so little real use as to deserve the name which Cromwell gave it of the "fool's bauble." The seats run lengthwise down the house, on each side of the Speaker's chair, and there are short cross-benches by the door. No member has a desk or table; all sit as in church pews, with a pulpit in the middle, or, as I once heard a profane American say, "The arrangement of seats is like that of a pit for dog-fighting, open at the ends." There were six hundred and fifty-eight members in the House of Commons in 1868, but seats for only four hundred and twenty-eight. The average attendance is three hundred. The Chamber of Representatives at Washington is approached through the noble semi-circular hall of the older Capitol, with columns, sculpture, and light, worthy of a Roman Senate House. Out of this a short aisle, closed with massive and elaborate gates of bronze, leads to the light and airy lobby which completely encloses the new Hall of Representatives. Opening from this lobby are committee rooms, post offices and telegraph offices, and magnificent marble stairways, which lead to the lobbies and galleries above. That side of the lobby which lies behind the Speaker's chair is the private lobby of the Speaker and members, and along it are the office rooms of the Speaker, the Clerk, and the Sergeant-at-Arms. From this lobby two splendid bronze stairways descend to the committee rooms, restaurant, etc., in the basement. These lobbies have no official use, but are merely places for conversation or promenading.

In the House of Commons, the two long lobbies on either side of the Speaker have actual uses, and they are called "division lobbies," that to the Speaker's right hand being for "ayes," that to the left for "noes." When a division is called for, to precisely ascertain the vote upon any question, the two political parties muster their members, and the House is filled. Two minutes only are allowed after the moving of a question for absentees to appear, and these are marked by a sand-glass, which the Speaker turns upside down. Then the door is closed, and he puts the question.

"I think the ayes have it!" he says, when they have voted orally. "No! no!" from the other side.

"The ayes to the right, the noes to the left!" he says. Then everybody leaves his seat, and goes out of the door to the right or to the left, according to his vote, the doors being cut through the long benches. Two tellers are appointed for each door, picked from both political parties. The members re-enter in single file, are counted by the tellers, and a clerk, in wig and gown, standing at a little box, takes the numbers. The four tellers then form abreast, and retire backward, bowing, while that teller whose party has won the vote takes the right-hand side.

In the House of Representatives, when tellers are demanded, the members merely walk through a couple of tellers down the main aisle of the Hall, and return to their seats by the side aisles.

The Hall of Representatives is even more elaborately ornamented than the Senate Chamber, and gilded overhead between the painted skylights. It contains, like the Senate, separate galleries for ladies, gentlemen, and the foreign diplomatic body. The House of Commons is much plainer than the House of Peers. It has twelve side windows, painted with the arms of boroughs; the ceiling is flat, with the ends inclined, and the house is lighted by skylights, with gas jets above them. The floor is of perforated iron, covered with mats, and hot or cold air is admitted at will below. The benches are painted green, and the walls are panelled with oak.

Take a meeting-house, and put half-a-dozen rows of benches lengthwise down it on each side, sloping up in gentle tiers, so as to leave the space in the middle open. In the centre of the open space put a table; at the foot of the open space put a chair under a canopy, something like an old-fashioned bed. Cut an aisle across the long seats, paint the benches green, and grain the walls oak. Now, fill the seats with men, with their hats on, and put wigs and robes on the Speaker, and a few other officers, and a sword on the Sergeant-at-Arms. The general effect will be that of a Quaker meeting, sitting as a jury, with some Episcopalian bishops amongst them as judges. This is the House of Commons superficially.

We have often made complaints of the acoustic properties and accommodations of our Halls of Congress, but Parliament has altogether the worst of the two bargains. The "British Almanac" for 1869, says: —

"When designing the Houses of Parliament, in all that enormous space room could only be found for something less than two-thirds of the members of the House of Commons; and the building, erected at a cost of millions, as the place of meeting of the Legislature, is actually so constructed, that no arrangements can be made for more than two-thirds of the working sections of it being present at the most important discussion. Even a prominent member of the ministry stood, for hours, 'unable to get a seat.' The peers have less difficulty to be seated than to be heard." It has been seriously proposed, indeed, that both bodies shall vacate the Palace of Parliament, except on ceremonial occasions, and remove to separate buildings.

In a severer tone, a humorous reviewer in the "London Quarterly" for 1857, says: —

"This, then, is the room in which laws are made for some one hundred and forty millions of people, and in which, through ages to come, in all human probability, laws will continue to be made for Britain and her dependencies. . . . . The roof looks like the inside bottom of a huge barge. The chamber was, originally, far more handsome, but the principle of acoustics had not been studied, and opposition members were incessantly rising and attacking clauses which the government had struck out ten minutes before, while the supporters of the ministers were defying their antagonists to divide on amendments of which they had announced the withdrawal. It was felt that either the architectural beauty of the chamber must be sacrificed, or pantomime and the speaking-trumpet must be introduced into the British constitution."

The Capitol of the United States is not above criticism in these respects, but it is a far more commodious and sensible edifice than its vaster and more elaborate rival.

Dismissing the architecture of the palace henceforward, we come to the composition of the House of Commons as it existed in 1868.

Through the enactments of the Reform Acts of 1830–32, the House of Commons consisted of six hundred and fifty-eight members, who were returned, as follows: —

English County Members,	143	471
——— University,	4	
——— Cities and Boroughs,	324	
Welsh County Members,	15	29
——— Cities and Boroughs,	14	
Scotch County Members,	30	53
——— Cities and Boroughs,	23	
Irish County Members,	64	105
——— University,	2	
——— Cities and Boroughs,	39	

The effect of the Reform Act of 1867 will be considered further along in the chapter.

The Speaker of the House of Commons is chosen by each Parliament for the whole of the session, and from amongst its own members. If, during that Parliament, the political sentiment of the country changes, the Speaker still keeps his place. Mr. Shaw Lefevre was Speaker from 1839 through three Parliaments. He receives twenty-five thousand dollars a year and a furnished residence, and at the close of his official life receives a peerage and a pension of twenty-thousand dollars. He is also a member of the Queen's Privy Council. He gives only the casting vote, "names" for censure contemptuous members, and in extreme cases orders members into custody. The Queen is permitted by law to refuse to confirm the Speaker after the House elects him; but if she should really do this the country would start up in violent agitation.

This officer is, in almost every respect, the model of the office of Speaker of the American House of Representatives. He gets about four times the salary and perquisites of the American Speaker, however.

The chairman of Committees of the Whole House is also chairman of the Ways and Means Committee, and some other committees of the House. He is a censor and inspector of all private bills; his salary is seventy-five hundred dollars a year, and the office is a political one.

The Clerk of the House of Commons holds for life. He is appointed by the Queen, and appoints his own clerks, of whom there are thirty-six. He presides at the election of a Speaker, and his office is almost identical with that of the Clerk of the House of Representatives at Washington. His salary is ten thousand dollars, and his two principal assistant clerks receive seventy-five hundred, and five thousand dollars a year respectively. The Clerk's in America is a political office, and he is dismissed at every change of party, and also in some cases by the party which elected him.

The Sergeant-at-Arms of the House of Commons is a sort of constable to the Speaker.

He appoints the doorkeepers, porters, and pages, is the ceremonial officer of the House, and is paid six thousand dollars a year, with an allowance for house-rent. He wears a sword at his side.

The Sergeant-at-Arms in 1868 was a nobleman, three of the clerks were baronets, and the superintending short-hand writer was the same official in both Houses. In the United States, the sergeant's office, through "constructive" mileage, the rendering of duplicate and fraudulent accounts, and the use of funds entrusted to the Sergeant for his own influence and profit, has become discreditable. The following persons are ineligible for membership in the House of Commons: government contractors, police justices, sheriffs, mayors, bailiffs, judges of the superior court, tax, custom, and stamp officers, foreigners, clergymen, pensioners of the crown, bankrupts, English peers, Scotch peers, and Irish peers sitting in the House of Lords. Nobody but members is allowed to perambulate the House of Commons, whereas, in America, ex-members can claim the privilege of the floor. A county member must own property worth three thousand dollars a year; a borough member one-half that amount.

A member accepting any office under the executive government has to be re-elected to retain his seat in the House of Commons. He cannot resign his seat in the Commons except by accepting an office under the crown, and there are various nondescript and sinecure places of this kind filled for no other purpose.

In America the House of Representatives is composed of citizens elected from congressional *districts*. Territories, or districts not formed under State government, send a delegate merely. The number of districts in a State is regulated by population, according to a census taken every ten years, and while these districts cannot be arbitrarily increased in number, they are sometimes *gerry-mandered* or altered in their boundaries to accomplish partisan objects. Neither counties, cities, nor any of the fixed local distinctions, are recognized in Congress. The city of New York is composed, nationally, of a certain number of congressional districts merely, and it often happens that part of a city, and part of the next county, are united to make one district. Thus the republic is like a network of unequal squares thrown over the surface of the ground. The ground is the history of population, the net is the government of it. The ground is the original colony; the net is the nation. Looking through the open thread of the Federal state we see particular neighborhoods in their county or corporate circumstances. Boston as Boston has no member in Congress. Yet look through the districts of the net, and you can see who sits for Boston by accident.

The contrary is the case in the House of Commons. There every member represents an original settlement and not a part of a census. Our Congress is representative or popular. The English House of Commons is the representative of neighborhood traditions, venerable charters, and original and arbitrary divisions of the soil. By a fixed routine of population, ascertained by deliberate census, we reconstruct Congress every ten years. A new State is formed out of newly populated territory, and it gains or loses in districts as it retains population. Not so in England, where there have been but two reorganizations of Parliament in history, — one in 1832, another in 1867.

Every member of the House of Commons represents either a county, a city, a borough, or a university. Let us see if we know precisely what each of these terms means.

1. Counties were formed by the Saxons before the time of Alfred the Great, and the Normans found them intact and well defined when they landed. A county is an administrative division of the English government, like the District of an United States Marshal and Court. For example, there are two divisions of Pennsylvania, each having a court and officers. In England and Wales there are fifty-two counties, in Scotland thirty-three, and in Ireland thirty-two. Pennsylvania alone has sixty-five counties, or the same number that Scotland and Ireland possess together, and yet it has scarcely more people than the single county of Lancashire in England. Every county is presided over by a Lord Lieutenant, who is the head of the militia,

and it has also a Keeper of the Rolls, a Sheriff, a Receiver General of taxes, a Coroner, Justices and Clerks of the Peace, and Courts of Assize, County, and Hundred. These English counties, in the main, correspond to the States of the American Union, yet are not sovereign like our States, but are rather viceroyalties. The members of Parliament who come from the counties have been elected by the proprietors and occupiers of the land.

2. A city in the true English sense is a town corporate, with a bishop and a cathedral church. The word cathedral is derived from a bishop's throne or chair, deposited in it. A town corporate is a town capable of using its name like a person in business and of suing and being sued. The first free cities of modern times were in Italy, and their example was imitated in France, Flanders, and Germany. They bought or wrested their rights from the Prince, and were mainly composed of trades-unions or guilds. Such are some English cities to this day in a parliamentary sense, as I have shown in the chapter on London, — a collection of mercantile and trading associations, made up of "freemen," who vote for members of Parliament. With us a city gets its charter from a State, but this entitles it merely to local self-government, and gives it no representation in the Legislature. Politically an English city is quite a different thing from an American city.

3. Borough is a word of Saxon origin, said to have meant "walled town." The Normans found eighty-two boroughs when they arrived in England. Each borough held its own fair or market, and maintained its borough court The borough was a sort of confederated neighborhood, generally rallying about a castle or village, and showing or claiming to have once received a charter. It was often governed by a little oligarchy of landholders, or by a guild or series of guilds. After the House of Commons was established in England, each of these boroughs claimed the right to send a member or members to Parliament. In 1830 there were one hundred and seventy-one English boroughs.

4. A university is an ancient and honorable endowment, requiring representation to protect and dignify it. Oxford, Cambridge, Dublin, and the University of London are represented in Parliament. Oxford University members are voted for by Doctors and Masters of Arts, whose names are on the books, amounting to three thousand seven hundred and eighty-six electors. Cambridge has four thou-

sand nine hundred and forty-nine electors. Dublin has one thousand seven hundred electors.

I have said nothing in this chapter about the members of the Cinque (five) Ports, which are a set of old, decayed maritime towns, which were once admitted to Parliament because of their gallantry in naval warfare, and there they stick, to this generation.

To see the inequality of English representation observe the difference between Sandwich, one of these Cinque Ports, and London city in 1868. Sandwich had two members, who represented about nine hundred voters; London proper four, who represented about eleven thousand voters.

Portarlington, Ireland, gives about eighty votes, and has a member; while Birmingham, which gives ten thousand votes, and elects John Bright, has only two members.

Looking over the House of Commons, we see that all the members represent traditional neighborhoods, counties, or corporations in this way. But in the time in which we write, a Reform Bill is about to go into operation, and this will affect the electors of Parliament, though not materially the number and appearance of the House itself. Before we take up this new bill, therefore, let us ask ourselves the question, as we keep the House of Commons in view, What was the origin of this body, and why did it need reforming?

Parliament, a word of French origin, had its beginning in the Norman House of Lords. The Lords, resisting the Kings, invited the counties to give them support and to contribute delegates. About the middle of the thirteenth century the House of Commons was clearly defined. Henceforward it was the instrument of voting money, — little more. Excepting some single splendid episodes, as of the Stuart and Puritan Parliaments, the history of the House of Commons from the time of Henry VI. to 1830 was a series of brilliant personal apparitions, without aggregate virtue, or love of freedom. "Time had augmented its deformities," says an author,* "till it had degenerated into a mere mockery, obvious to the minds of all by the ludicrous contrast of old Sarum and Gatten with representatives, — Birmingham and Manchester without a voice. By nomination boroughs, close corporations, and the peculiarities of the county franchise, only one interest was substantially incorporated into the Legislature. Land was omnipotent; commerce, manufactures, ship-

* Mr. John Wade.

ping, — all that had created the material greatness and opulence of the realm were dumb. An oligarchy ruled, and the laws it made, the measures it supported, and those it proscribed, savored of the character, the interests, and the prejudices of their authors. By patriotic and enlightened men, parliamentary reform was deemed the sole corrective of the constitution." The Reform Bill, so called, extinguished fifty-six effete boroughs, which had been sending one hundred and eleven members to Parliament. It cut thirty boroughs down to one member. It gave one hundred and fifty-nine members to eighty-two county constituencies, and distributed amongst the better boroughs and the cities one hundred and forty-three members. Yet, after all this so-called reform, it was said by Earl Gray, the chief supporter of the bill, that "it was the most aristocratic measure that ever passed the House of Commons;" and we can readily imagine this to be so, if, as the appendix to the Reform Bill of 1867 shows, two hundred English and Welsh boroughs, with a population of eight million six hundred and thirty-eight thousand five hundred and sixty-nine persons, had only four hundred and eighty-nine thousand and seventy-one registered voters, including nearly fifty thousand who voted on some ancient qualifications, and were called Freemen, Potwallers, Scot and Lot voters, etc.

To this miserably little extension of the franchise is yet ascribed the progress of England in the last forty years. It called into political existence the manufacturing cities, repealed the corn-laws, carried free-trade, and gave opportunity to John Bright and Richard Cobden. Poor as the gift was, it was opposed bitterly by nearly every nobleman, and at the head of these stood the Duke of Wellington. The noisy scenes in the preceding chapter illustrate the feeling amongst the peers when this bill was pressed. It will be further considered in the chapter on Political Parties in England.

The next extension of the franchise was granted in 1867, and as, at this writing, it has not gone entirely into effect, my notice of the matter will be brief.

The royal assent to this important act, entitled "The representation of the people's act, 1867," was given on the 15th of August in that year. It will not probably pass into entire operation till the latter part of the present year (1869).

Scotland, Ireland, and the two English universities are excepted from the operations of this act. It provides that every man above twenty-one years of age, of the following classes, shall be registered as a voter, and shall vote for a member or members to serve in Parliament:—

1. Who has occupied a whole dwelling, either as tenant or owner, for one year, and paid the poor rates, or taxes.

2. Who has lodged in a part of one house for a year, where his rooms, unfurnished, cost not less than fifty dollars in gold a year.

3. Who owns real estate, chattels, or has a bank account bringing a clear income of twenty-five dollars a year, and who pays taxes thereon.

4. Who rents and occupies land worth sixty gold dollars a year, and pays poor rates.

By the same act four corrupt boroughs are disfranchised and everybody in them who took bribes is disfranchised by name. In contested elections where three members of Parliament are to be selected no person shall vote for more than two, nor shall any hired election agent, canvasser, etc., vote at all. All boroughs with less than ten thousand people return but one member. London in the aggregate gets four more members, making fourteen in all for three millions of people; while New York State, with nearly four millions, has thirty-one congressmen. Twelve new boroughs are created. The city of Manchester gets three members, and the boroughs of Liverpool, Birmingham, and Leeds three apiece. The University of London gets a member. Londoners can live twenty-five miles out of the city and still vote there.

If anybody pays another person's taxes to get his vote, he and the second person shall be punished for bribery. Several counties are divided into boroughs. Twenty-three little boroughs return but one member hereafter.

This Reform Bill answered the expectations of the English masses very imperfectly. It was tendered by a tory or anti-popular ministry to retain power, and fell far short of the intentions of the opposite party. *

* Reform Bills were passed for Scotland and Ireland in July, 1868. In Scotland the franchise for boroughs is the same as in England, but seventy dollars in gold must be the annual tenure, or rent, paid for land in the counties. Seats are given to the universities of Glasgow and Edinburgh. Glasgow gets three members in Parliament, with four hundred thousand people, while Philadelphia, with five hundred and fifty thousand people, has not quite five members in Congress. To make room for several new Scotch county members, seven English boroughs were disfranchised. In Ireland, the occupation franchise in towns was reduced to twenty dollars, and for lodgers fifty dollars yearly rent paid for unfurnished

We publish in the United States a little pamphlet directory of each session of Congress. It is compiled by clerks, and is exceedingly meagre and often imperfect. In England, however, there are many directories of Parliament, gleaned with care and minuteness, and expressed with elegance. By running through any one of these "Companions" or directories, we get some quaint insight into the character of Parliament.

First, the names of all constituencies are given, their population, the number of votes polled in each and of their registered electors. Then there is a short biography of every member, his parentage, age, profession, office, church patronage, political principles and pledges, public acts, and the name of his clubs and residences.

An English M. P. is always a club man, and club life in England is intimately associated with political life. Out of Parliament a member is generally sought at his club, where, perhaps, he takes his meals, receives his letters, attends to the desires of his constituents, and whence he is summoned by telegraph on occasion of party necessities to cast his vote with his party.

I give below some extracts from the Parliamentary Companion for 1868.

"BOSTON. — (The original of Boston, Massachusetts), Lincolnshire.

John Wingfield Malcolm, ...	546
Thomas Parry, ...	465
Meaburn Staniland, ...	453

"On petition, March, 1866, a scrutiny being made, fourteen votes were struck off Mr. Parry's number, which gave a majority of two to Meaburn Staniland.

"On Mr. Staniland accepting the Chiltern Hundreds, new writ, March, 1867, Thomas Parry was returned to Parliament.

"*Constituency.* — Corporation and freemen paying scot and lot, and the ho. of 10*l.* Population, 17,803. Registered electors, 1,093, including 148 freemen."

Explanation. — Staniland, the name in italics, was the unsuccessful candidate, but Parry's seat being contested, Staniland received it. Then Staniland accepted office under the government, or took the sinecure place called the Chiltern Hundred, a sort of fictitious hole to put weary pegs in. A new election was ordered at Boston, and Parry was elected at last by the holders of

apartments. Dublin city has two members, Dublin county two, and Dublin University two, which would make, if they were at all representative, six members for a city and county of more than four hundred thousand people,—the same number that New York city has in Congress.

property, with ten pounds a year by "scot and lot" right, an ancient privilege, and by members of the town companies, or "free men."

"YORK CITY. — (I instance this as a quaint manner of comparison between Old York and New York cities, although the American city was not named for the English one, but for the Duke of York, afterwards James II.)

James Lowther, ...	2,079
George Leeman, ...	1,854
Joshua P. B. Westhead, ...	1,792

"*Constituency.* — Freemen, freeholders, and the ho. of 10*l*. Population, 43,385. Registered electors, 4,724, including 2,571 freemen."

Explanation. — Only one person in ten is an elector in York. The electors are members of the city guilds, property owners, and those who pay fifty dollars a year rent.

"HERTFORD, BOROUGH. — (I instance this as an odd sort of comparison with the city of Hartford, Connecticut, where this book is published.)

Right Honorable William H. Cowper, .	—
Sir Minto Farquhar, ...	—

"On the death of Sir Minto Farquhar, new writ June, 1866.

Robert Dinsdale, ...	—

"*Constituency.* — Freemen and the ho. of 10*l*. Population, 6,769. Registered electors, 602, including 96 freemen. The Marquess of Salisbury has considerable influence in this borough, as has also Earl Cowper."

Explanation. — The new writ referred to above required a new election. The same thing takes place in any American constituency on the death or retirement of a congressman.

"BRISTOL, GLOUCESTERSHIRE. — (This town is instanced to show the constituency of Sir Morton Peto, the baronet, who was a prominent railroad stockholder in America, and made us a visit before his failure in 1866.)

Francis F. H. Berkeley, ...	5,296
Sir S. Morton Peto, ...	5,228
Thomas Francis Fremantle, . . .	4,269

"*Constituency.* — Freemen and freeholders, and the ho. of 10*l*. Population, 154,093. Registered electors, 14,324, including 1,707 freemen."

Turning from Bristol constituency to another part of the book, we find the name and history of its representatives: —

"PETO, Sir Samuel Morton, bart. (Bristol), son of the late William Peto, Esquire, Cookham, Berks, by the daughter of Ralph Alloway, Esquire, of

Dorking Surrey. Born at Woking, 1809. Married (1st) 1831, his cousin, Mary, eldest daughter of Thomas de la Garde Grisel, Esquire, of Stockwell Common, Surrey. (She died May, 1842.) Married (2nd) 1843, eldest daughter of Henry Kelsall, Esquire, of Rochdale, Lancashire. A member of the firm of Peto and Betts, contractors for Public Works. Constructed the Crimean Railway without profit to himself in 1855, and for his services was made a baronet. A Magistrate and Deputy-Lieutenant for Suffolk, and a Magistrate for Norfolk and Middlesex. A liberal (radical); in favor of the extension of the franchise to the working-class, vote by ballot, and "complete religious freedom to every denomination." Sat for Norwich from July, 1847, till December, 1857; for Finsbury from May, 1859, till July, 1865, when he was elected for Bristol. Residences and clubs, Kensington Palace Gardens, West, Chipstead, Seven Oaks, Kent. Reform club, Auchlyne, Killin, Perthshire."

Explanation. — The above shows what family influence Sir Morton Peto has, hints at his wealth and idiosyncrasies, and shows that he has a town residence in London, an English country house, and a Scotch estate.

No salary is paid to a member of Parliament. A senator, or a congressman of the United States, is paid five thousand dollars a year. The Speaker, as we have said, is generally re-elected at the beginning of Parliament as long as his political party retains power. In 1866, for example, the Right Honorable John Evelyn Denison was proposed for Speaker by Mr. Monsell, seconded by Earl Grosvenor, and for the third time unanimously re-elected. Mr. Sergeant Yelverton, who was elected during the reign of Queen Elizabeth, gave a good description of the qualifications required in a Speaker, whether for Parliament or Congress. "He that supplieth this place ought to be a man big and comely, stately, and well spoken, his voice great, his courage majestical, and his purse plentiful and heavy." If two candidates are nominated for Speaker, the house divides, or settles the vote by tellers.

Notwithstanding the fact that no salary is attached to the place of an M. P., the privileges, social opportunities, and honors of the place are held in so great request that bribery and chicanery are freely used to accomplish elections. In the United States, a congressman is invariably a resident in the district which he represents; but this is not of necessity the case in Parliament, and if a man is needed in the House of Commons, he can be passed round by his party from borough to borough till he is elected somewhere. The limited franchise, and the power of landholders to influence or compel the votes of their tenants, lead to many abuses, but there is also a corrupt and purchasable class of voters in England, whose degradation is an annual theme of parliamentary inquiry. Looking over some of the documents upon English election frauds, I find that in Harwich, consisting of one hundred and twenty voters, one Attwood, the tory candidate, spent thirty-one thousand dollars in one election, and his opponents enough more to make in all forty-five thousand five hundred dollars. Another investigation showed that in Nottingham eighty-five thousand dollars were spent on a constituency of four thousand five hundred people, or about twenty dollars to a man. The reader of novels, who wishes to find in pleasant narrative form the manner of conducting an English election, may do so in Thackeray's "Newcomes," or in George Elliott's "Felix Holt, the Radical." The daily newspapers are adjuncts to the most shameless parliamentary corruption, in witness of which see the following advertisement from the London "Times" of July 1st, 1847: —

"To PARLIAMENTARY CANDIDATES. — Messrs. —— and Co., of —— Street, London, have all the machinery requisite to carry out the election of an M. P., including registry, canvass clerks, etc., and writers of eminence would be placed at the disposal of candidates. Borough or county registers expeditiously arranged."

Quoting the above, a number of the "Westminster Review" enters into the discussion of election and bribery, and says of the abuses of landlord and tenant: —

"Let a map be made of the island according to the estates of the four and twenty thousand proprietors who own it, and color the estates according to the politics of their landlords. You will discover in this way the character of the votes of the tenants. They are merely the voting-machines of their farms. The rich man, who buys a ten-pound house in a small borough, just buys a ten-pound vote. The attorneys in many large boroughs make sure that scarcely any man shall get in without paying black-mail to them. The House of Commons is thus made a club of rich men, when it ought to be a workshop for the people."

The same fearless "Review" continues: —

"The maintenance of a property qualification is indefensible on any principle of justice, right, or expediency. It has been the mere bulwark of class elevation. It does not insure intelligence; for the inadequacy of parliamentary intelligence is everywhere apparent. It does not even color the every-day fallacy of the patriotism of property; for we have bankrupts, spendthrifts, and blasé gamblers and speculators in the legislature, — men only saved from the disgrace of a prison by the privileges of their position."

The House of Commons never had a manual prepared for it, regulating order and precedence, till 1857, when Thomas Erskine May undertook the work, and this should be consulted by any reader who is minutely curious about parliamentary law. In America Thomas Jefferson wrote a manual in the early years of the republic, and John M. Barclay, Journal Clerk of the House of Representatives, has very recently made a digest of the Rules of the House, which is said by Mr. Speaker Colfax to be the best book of the sort extant. The House of Representatives has had some notable Speakers, of whom Henry Clay had probably most will, N. P. Banks superior "presence" and bearing, and Schuyler Colfax much readiness.

The House of Representatives was created when the constitution was adopted essentially as it exists. The House of Commons is a history of creepings-up, — at first an intimidated body, permitted to meet by way of compliment, to vote money else wrested from it; now the great political estate of the realm, with absolute and exclusive power to vote or withhold money. The Senate can alter an appropriation bill of the House of Representatives, or suggest a field of expenditure. The peers cannot amend nor originate any appropriation bill, but must either entirely accept or entirely reject it. Not even the standing army can be maintained except by an annual vote of the Commons, and yet this powerful body in all formal matters is subservient and deferential to both the sovereign and the peers. In theory the House of Commons is intended to protect the liberties of the people, who are the tax-payers, while the House of Peers is intended to protect the rights of the Sovereign. I shall take up the House of Commons and treat of its manner of organization, so as to make a connected narrative jointly with the proceedings already described in the Chamber of Peers.

A new Parliament is summoned by the Queen, who, in her Council of State, commands the Lord Chancellor (or President of the Peers), to issue the summons. The Lord Chancellor, in obedience directs the Clerk of the Crown to issue writs, signed with the Great Seal, to all the Sheriffs of counties in the realm. Then each Sheriff, receiving his order, directs the returning officers of the municipalities, boroughs, etc., in his county to conduct the election. The election itself will be considered in the chapter on Political Parties. After the elections are over, the Sheriff sends the results back to the Clerk of the Crown, who publishes the names of the new members in the gazettes. Then the Queen, by proclamation, appoints the time of meeting, and as we have already seen, goes in person, or sends commissioners, to open Parliament.

Victoria has enacted this form seven times.

When the Commons meet together, the first business, as in Congress, is to elect a Speaker. The Clerk of the House, being a permanent officer, presides, and some member, addressing him, makes a nomination. When the Speaker has been chosen, he is escorted to his chair by the mover and seconder of his nomination, and there he returns thanks to the House. Immediately the mace, the symbol of his office, is taken from under the table before him and laid in full view upon the top of the table. Some elderly and influential member then goes gravely up to the Speaker, and shakes hands with him. The House at once adjourns.

The next day the Commons meet again and go up to the House of Lords, where they are received by the Lord Chancellor, the presiding officer of that body. On behalf of the Queen the Lord Chancellor approves of the Speaker elected, and the Speaker then, in behalf of his House, asks that all the ancient rights and privileges of the Commons may be continued. The Chancellor, in the name of the Queen, confirms these rights. Then the House returns to its chamber.

The next two or three days are spent in taking oaths of allegiance, which the Speaker administers, and the oath has been a subject of trouble for many years, being obnoxious to many sectarians and folks with scruples. It was not till 1858 that Jews were formally admitted to Parliament, and in 1833 Moravians and Quakers had to be especially qualified. In 1852 Viscount Clancarty, a Protestant, was refused permission to take the Roman Catholic oath, which he preferred. In 1851 Alderman Salomans, a Hebrew, was rejected from Parliament for refusing the regular oath, and in 1829 O'Connell refused to take the oath of supremacy.

No business can now be done till the Queen formally opens Parliament. The Commons on that day wait in their chamber till the Black Rod, the ceremonial officer of the Peers, comes to summon them. He stands without and strikes the door three times with his rod. The door being opened, he walks up the middle of the floor escorted by the Sergeant-at-Arms of the House, and bows three times with great impressiveness. Having expressed to the Speaker the

Queen's commands that the Commons attend her immediately in the Chamber of Peers, the Black Rod walks out backward, bowing still. The House proceed in some order to the Chamber of Peers, and, hearing the speech, return to their own chamber, where they generally pass some small formal bill to prove their independence, and again adjourn.

The Clerk of the Crown has meantime given the Clerk of the House a list of members returned, and any contests are introduced by petition and referred to their proper place for consideration. The House now proceeds, like the Peers, to answer the Queen's opening address, and when this has been done, paragraph by paragraph, and debated, the Commons proceed to the Queen's palace with their answer, the Speaker in a state coach. Once they kept the Queen waiting half an hour, — in 1845, — and the nation expressed great indignation. The scene of presenting the answer is an interesting one ; but if the Queen be at Windsor or elsewhere, a committee from both Houses proceeds there with the reply. In either case the Speaker and the Lord Chancellor walk together, and are ushered to the Queen's presence by the Lord Chamberlain. The Parliament is now ready for straightforward business, and you will observe the political parties in it at once, yet both parties go by the Queen's name, one being Her Majesty's Ministry, the other Her Majesty's Opposition. The front bench of the House of Commons on the right hand of the Speaker is called the Treasury bench ; for there sits the leader of the administration, or Prime Minister, whose official title is "First Lord of the Treasury." His colleagues are around him, and on the bench facing them sit the vigilant and unappeasable opposition. The members who represent London city proper claim the right to a part of the front bench. Every seat has a brass plate on the back of it, with the name of the member who claims it. Forty members present make a quorum. As in the American Congress, there are fixed days for certain kinds of work.

The House early in the session resolves itself into a Committee of Supply, to consider the estimates of money required to support the different services ; namely, Army and Navy, the Civil Services, Salaries of Custom, Inland Revenue, and Post Offices, Packet (ship) Service, and Fortifications.

Then the House resolves itself into a Committee of Ways and Means, to devise the means of raising the supplies of money already granted.

Finally, at the end of the session, they pass the annual Appropriation Act. The chapter on "Finance" will take up the above matters in detail.

The right of petition, which John Quincy Adams so magnificently vindicated in the American Congress, is a fundamental principle of the British Constitution, and has been exercised from the earliest times. In the year 1868, one thousand seven hundred and seventy-six petitions, officially signed and sealed, were presented, and seventeen thousand eight hundred and sixty-five altogether. More than two and a half millions of names were appended to these petitions. The petition of the Chartists some years ago for a republicanized government was so immense that it was rolled into the House of Commons like a huge cart-wheel. These petitions are crammed into bags, and carried out, to be considered, let us charitably suppose.

One of the great periods of a parliamentary session is the discussion upon the "Budget," which is derived from the French word *bougette*, a bag.

It is an annual speech, with a comparative statement of the expenditures and receipts of the country in the year passing and the years past, and a justification and explanation of the same.

Expunging resolutions, such as were passed blotting from the journal of the House of Representatives a censure of President Jackson, are sometimes passed in Parliament, as in 1782, in the case of John Wilkes, and in 1833, in the matter of Sir Robert Peel and William Cobbett.

Petitions from London city are presented by the Sheriffs thereof, in red gowns and occasionally by the Lord Mayor. The Lord Mayor of Dublin also appears for the same purpose at rare opportunities.

No member of the House of Commons can speak insolently of the Queen, nor urge her private opinion to affect any matter of legislation. Seldom does any member answer newspaper articles in his place, and a member of one house seldom makes any reference to the other house. These matters are less scrupulously observed in the American Congress. The President is quoted to influence or defeat a bill, and is frequently spoken of with acrimony and invective. As to newspaper articles, there are many congressmen who are known to fame in America only for explanations on this head.

There is a good deal of button-holing and claim-urging in the lobbies of Parliament; but the floor is carefully guarded from the access of corrupt or impudent attorneys. Respectable counsel are licensed to plead claims before committees, and this arrangement is found to give credit and intelligence to the prosecution of claims. On the score of personal avarice and corruption, members of the House of Commons have not a like opportunity with congressmen, and the allegation and investigation of charges against personal honor are less frequent in the British than in the American Legislature. The House of Commons can punish contempts of its authority, give its committees right to send for persons and papers, and commit offenders to prison till the close of the pending session. Congress holds, and frequently practises, the same authority. Congress generally meets at noon, and holds night sessions when business has unduly accumulated. The House of Commons meets at four o'clock, except on Wednesdays, when it meets at noon. If business accumulates unduly, it holds day sessions. All great debates in the Commons take place by gaslight.

The essential difference between Congress and Parliament is the presence of the executive government in the Legislature. There sit the Cabinet Officers and the President (Prime Minister) of the state, developing their policy, answering questions of moment, struggling to retain the confidence of a majority of the House, and voting upon measures of their own proposition. The House of Commons is thus the concentrated theatre of political agitation. A presidential election is liable to take place within it at any time and by its whim or impulse the wealth and influence of the entire administration may be transferred from one party or sentiment to another.

The debates of Parliament are printed in the newspapers, but without authority, and it is a breach of privilege theoretically for reporters to be present, or for publishers to circulate the proceedings. Like many other things in the English government, which are illegal, but inevitable, this transgression has become a formidable right. Newspaper reporting in the House of Commons began during the American Revolution, and Dr. Johnson was one of the earliest notetakers. After the close of the British wars, in 1814, when the legislative proceedings monopolized attention, the work of publishing the debates was earnestly and fully undertaken. The debates of the American Congress are reported at the cost of the government, and a daily paper, called the "Globe," contracts for the work. A large corps of phonographers are engaged, who are paid by the column. Many of these were taught their art at the public High School of Philadelphia, an institution which makes phonography a specialty.

The head of the corps, until recently, and one of the earliest shorthand writers in America, was Mr. Richard Sutton, who began his career, I think, in the reporters' gallery of the English Parliament. The publication of the debates is a subject of considerable expense in the United States, but they are rendered with remarkable exactness and promptitude. At the opening of each session at noon, daily, the "Globe" is found on every member's desk, containing a perfect transcript of the debates of the previous day. The "Globe" does not print the documents, bills, acts, memorials, and other papers which assist legislation. These are committed to the government printer, who has a great establishment near by the Capitol, and they are reproduced in folio, or in stitched pamphlet form, for ready use and reference. Collected together, they make the permanent public documents, and are bound, registered, and numbered.

Attached to the House of Commons are two similar officers, the Printer of Journals and the Printer of Votes. But the government has no such institution of its own as the great-printing office at Washington, which is alleged to be the most complete establishment in the world. The debates of Parliament are digested and reported with pains and cleverness in the London "Times," and other papers. The "Times" was formerly considered the most perfect newspaper which existed; but this encomium does not hold good in many respects at the present day. There is editorial gravity without much conclusiveness in it; but in the promptitude of its news, and the amount and variety of its matter, it is now surpassed by many journals in America, while late developments have shown that its management is quite as unscrupulous and avaricious as that of papers elsewhere. It contains, daily, seventy-two columns of matter, or seventeen thousand five hundred lines, or upwards of one million pieces of type. Its daily circulation was set down at fifty-nine thousand copies in 1867, of which thirty-three thousand are distributed in London. It employs one hundred and ten compositors of type, and twenty-five pressmen. There is no strong newspaper at the Capitol of the United States; but in former days influential organs of opinion were maintained there, chief of which in different fields were the "Intelligencer" and the "National Era," in the latter of which appeared parts of "Uncle Tom's Cabin," the anti-slavery novel.

In both Parliament buildings and Capitol there are very many committee rooms; for much of the work of large legislative bodies has to be considered by select committee, while the Legislature, in whole, is the ultimate body to accept or reject the act. Committees of Congress generally consist of from six to ten or twelve persons; of the Commons, from twenty to thirty persons. The leading Committee of Congress, Ways and Means, was composed, in 1868, of nine members; while the whole of the House of Commons is resolved into that committee in England. Committee duty is compulsory in the Commons, and Smith O'Brien, once refusing to serve, was committed to custody for contempt.

To an American, the excess of forms, and the reverence for them, is the leading distinction of the English government, and of the House of Commons, its most practical manifestation. The Speaker must be elected by the Commons, and the selection communicated to the Queen. She "graciously" gives her consent, and the poor Speaker meantime makes himself ridiculous with excuses, timidities, and compliments. Next the superstition of the Mace is most apparent. There is no more use for the Mace than for the crowbar, and if the Speaker of the House of Representatives employed a war-club he would have as much reason. This Mace is laid before the Speaker of Commons while he sits in his place, is carried before him when he rises, and is put beneath the table when he leaves the chair. The absurdity of the Mace and the Sergeant-at-Arms is illustrated in a very amusing manner by the quarterly reviewer for 1857: —

"The most amusing ceremony," he says, "in which the bauble figures, is when a Master in Chancery comes with a message from the Lords: The Sergeant-at-Arms goes reverently up to the Speaker and announces the fact, and the Speaker kindly lends him the Mace, that he may receive the Master in a more imposing manner. Armed with — almost staggering under — the gilded load, the Sergeant walks down the House to fetch the Master. The pair form in line, and come marching up to the table, the Master being more splendid in regard to costume, but the Sergeant borrowing the reflected glory of the Mace. They bow at various stages of the journey, and the Master having arrived, delivers the message of the Lords, the Sergeant standing by him with his grand weapon, and looking as if he were ready to castigate him on the spot if he should show any lack of reverence. Then they retreat, *pari passu*, bowing whenever it occurs to them, and in this retrograde movement the Sergeant has an advantage, his legs being unincumbered, whereas the legs of the other are in chancery, and his gown is traitorous. Finally, the Sergeant, having seen his companion back to the bar, comes up again, with more reverences, to return the Speaker his Mace, and then bows himself back to his own chair after these six promenades.

"Strangers," adds the sarcastic reviewer, "do not always look respectfully upon this ceremonial, but nothing is so wholesome as etiquette between neighbors."

Violent combats and interchanges of violent language in the American Congress have been a source of discredit to us at home and abroad; but it must not be inferred that there is not also much ignorance, ill-breeding, and boyish behavior in the House of Commons. In the month in which I write, May, 1869, I find this communication from a correspondent of the "London Pall Mall Gazette," who dates from the House of Commons, and signs himself "A Bloated Aristocrat": —

"I read," he says, "with great interest, yesterday, your ingenious article on 'Manners in England and America.' It pleased me so much that I shall take care to send a copy of it to a gentleman, a member of the House of Commons, who was lately seen, in the reading-room of that assembly, to take his boots off preliminary to the enjoyment of his newspaper. Lounging in one chair, with his feet reposing in their stockings upon another, he made, in the sunshine, a very striking, if not quite an agreeable, figure. To be sure, Tuesday was a very warm day, but that, I venture to think, is no excuse for this particular breach of good manners. Sir, pray print my letter as a hint to the gentleman in question; otherwise, when the dog-days come in, he may be encouraged to strip himself still further, and that would really be offensive. Besides, bad manners are contagious, even (though you might not think it) in so august an atmosphere as ours."

"Among the smaller recreations of the House," says a review, "is the raising a terrific cry when a member new to parliamentary manners accidentally walks between the Speaker and the member speaking;" but this breach of etiquette is the rule rather than the exception in the House of Representatives. The great majority of members of the House of Commons speak as educated men should do, but one frequently hears a member dropping his h's like the vulgarest cockney, saying, for example: —

"I am too 'appy to leave the haffair hin the 'ands of the 'ouse!"

The Scotch and Irish accents, in all their forms, are heard in the House of Commons, but the Scotch speak very little, and the Irish very much. Long speeches are as frequently made as in America.

Mr. Gladstone and Mr. Disraeli have, several times, spoken above five hours apiece. No instances of late date have happened of personal affrays in Parliament, but many duels have been fought on account of words spoken in debate. To send or accept a challenge is now a breach of privilege. Coarse and taunting words and bitter repartees are as common in the English as in the American Legislature. I have selected from the debates two or three of the more aggravated instances of such personal collisions.

That most truculent of all members of the House of Commons, Daniel O'Connell, often figured in brawls and skirmishes on the floor, and I recite here from the records, one particular instance: —

"Mr. O'Connell rose, and said, 'The honorable member (Mr. Shaw) has expressed his opinions in a manner which can do no good service to his cause. There was a determination about him amounting almost to a spiritual ferocity. He seems to think that the Protestant religion consists of pounds, shillings, and pence."

"Mr. Shaw [with great vehemence]: 'I deny that I said the Protestant religion consists of pounds, shillings, and pence. But the church establishment of any country must be supported by money, and that church which the state endowed with money became the established church. In such a situation stands the church which the honorable and learned member for Dublin has sworn not to subvert, and which he now attempts to subvert.'

"Loud cries of 'Order! order!' now proceeded from the ministerial side of the House. The Irish members shouted the words with one voice.

"Mr. O'Connell [with the greatest warmth and violence of gesture]: 'I call the honorable Recorder to order. He has made use of a false assertion.'

"Here Mr. O'Connell's voice was drowned amidst the deafening cries of 'Order!' which proceeded from all parts of the opposition side of the house. A number of honorable members rose at once, and accompanied the words with a corresponding violence of gesture. It is impossible to describe the confusion of the scene.

"Mr. O'Connell resumed: 'The honorable member has accused me of having sworn one thing and done another. It is quite out of order for a member to utter falsehoods.'

"Here the opposition almost in a body shouted, 'Order! order!' at the full stretch of their voices, mingled with cries of, 'Chair! chair!' It was sometime before any measure of order was restored. When the uproar had somewhat abated, Mr. Finn said, 'I pronounce the expression which has been uttered by the learned member for the Dublin University to be an atrocious calumny.' 'The latter terms were pronounced with an emphasis,' says a sensitive reporter, 'and were accompanied with a vehemence of gesture that defy description.'

"The confusion and uproar which now ensued, owing to the cries of 'Chair! chair!' and 'Order! order!' which burst from the opposition side of the House, with the rising of many of the members from their seats, exceeded anything which can be imagined. In vain did Mr. Bernal endeavor, as chairman of the committee, to restore order. His voice was lost amidst the deafening noise which prevailed. Some degree of quiet being at length restored, Mr. Shaw rose, and with great warmth, said, 'The honorable member for Dublin knows that when he used the word falsehood —' Here Mr. Shaw's voice was again drowned amidst renewed uproar and confusion, caused by the rising of seven or eight of the Irish members at once, each of them, at the same time, speaking in the loudest and most indignant tones. It would have been impossible to hear a single word either of them said, owing to so many persons speaking and shouting at the same instant; but that difficulty was greatly increased by the shouts of 'Chair! chair!' which burst from the opposition side of the house. When the uproar had again partially subsided, Mr. Bernal said, in a most vehement and impassioned manner, 'If I cannot restore and preserve order, I must dissolve the committee at once. It is impossible for me to maintain order when seven or eight honorable members all get up and speak at once.'

"The determined manner and sharp rebuke of Mr. Bernal had, to a very great extent, the desired effect.

"Then Mr. Shaw, still laboring under great excitement, and speaking with much warmth of manner, said, 'The honorable member (Mr. O'Connell) has charged me with being actuated by a spiritual ferocity; but my ferocity is not of that description which takes for its symbol a death's-head and cross-bones.' [Tremendous cheers from the opposition, with uproar from the Irish members on the ministerial side of the house.]

"Mr. O'Connell (addressing himself to Mr. Shaw personally, and not to the chairman): 'Yours is a calf's-head and jaw-bones.' [Deafening cheers from the ministerial side of the house, with cries of 'Order! order!' 'Chair! chair!' from the opposition.]

"Mr. Bernal again interposed his authority as chairman, when, having once more restored order, the business of the committee proceeded without any further material interruption."

The parliamentary annalist, Grant, gives a still more indecent scene in one of his books of sketches.

"I shall allude," he says, "to only one more scene of this kind. It occurred towards the close of a recent session. An honorable member, whose name I suppress, rose, amidst the most tremendous uproar, to address the House. He spoke, and was received, as nearly as the confusion enabled me to judge, as follows: 'I rise, sir [ironical cheers, mingled with all sorts of zoölogical sounds], I rise, sir, for the purpose of stating that I have — ["Oh! oh!" "Bah!" and sounds resembling the bleating of a sheep, mingled with loud laughter.] Hon. gentlemen may endeavor to put me down by their unmannerly interruptions, but I have a duty to perform to my con— [Ironical cheers, loud coughing, sneezing, and yawning, extended to an incredible length, followed by bursts of laughter.] I say, sir, I have constituents who on this occasion expect that I — [Cries of "Should sit down," and shouts of laughter.] They expect, sir, that on a question of such importance ["O-o-a a-w," and loud laughter, followed by cries of "Order! order! order!" from the Speaker.] I tell honorable gentlemen, who choose to conduct themselves in such a way, that I am not to be put down by — [Groans, coughs, sneezings, hems, and various animal sounds, some of which closely imitated the yelping of a dog, and the squeaking of a pig, interspersed with peals of laughter.] I appeal — ["Cock-e-leeri-o-co!" the imitation, in this case, of the crowing of a cock was so remarkably good, that not even the most staid and orderly members in the House could preserve their gravity. The laughter which followed drowned the speaker's cries of "Order! order!"] I say, sir, this is most unbecoming conduct on the part of an assembly calling itself de — ["Bow-wow-wow," and bursts of laughter.] Sir, may I ask, have honorable gentlemen who can — ["Mew-mew," and renewed laughter.] Sir, I claim the protection of the chair. [The Speaker here again rose and called out "Order! order!" in a loud and angry tone, on which the uproar in some measure subsided.] If honorable gentlemen will only allow me to make one observation, I will not trespass further on their attention, but sit down at once. [This was followed by the most tremendous cheering in earnest.] I only beg to say, sir, that I think this is a most dangerous and unconstitutional measure, and will therefore vote against it.' The honorable gentleman then resumed his seat amidst deafening applause."

In exhibitions of oratory recent times afford few great examples either in England or America. The historic or artificial standard of manhood is better maintained on the continent of Europe, and at present France and Spain can perhaps instance more fervid speakers than either Parliament or Congress. Favre, Berryer, Olivier, and Pelletan, in France, Castelar, and some others, in Spain, rank higher than contemporary English or American orators. Of one of Castelar's speeches Mr. George Smalley wrote from London in May, 1869 :—

"He spoke upon the impulse of the moment, without a note, without the least preparation. Such a mighty oration has not been delivered in the Cortes within the memory of man. Gravid with historical facts, which poured from his memory in torrents, he battered the Canon's position to pieces, and pulverized every argument based upon them. Frequently the applause from every part of the House interrupted him, and when he had brought his peroration to a close — a peroration unequalled for beauty of diction, force of language, and sublimity of imagery — the excitement was so great that the members of the chamber, irrespective of party, rushed up to him and congratulated him, Rivero leading the way, and embracing him on both cheeks. The scene was bewildering. The effect of the oration has not worn off yet. The young orator has received upwards of three hundred telegrams from all parts of the country, thanking him for this service to the cause of religious liberty and freedom of thought. There is a proposition that the Cortes shall print the speech by tens of thousands, and outside, all parties are uniting to present him with a testimonial. But these compliments, merely personal, and however deserving of record as indicating the esteem in which his marvellous powers are held, are really empty results, compared with the effect his terrible attack upon the church and the coalition has had politically."

Our American oratory is best developed upon the "stump," or by attorneys at the bar. In the legislature our public men are merely debaters. The most able exhibitions of oratory witnessed in Congress during late years were those on the trial of the Impeachment of Andrew Johnson, President, when the speeches of William S. Groesbeck and William M. Evarts were able, both as pleas and as pieces of literature. No member of the House of Commons is allowed to read his speech.

It is doubtless within the curiosity of the reader to wish to compare the best specimens of parliamentary oratory, English and American. I have been at pains, therefore, to cull two contemporary passages from eminent gentlemen of either nation, illustrative not only of the same event, but of the general purpose of this volume. These are Mr. Disraeli, late English Prime Minister, and Mr. George Bancroft, late American Cabinet Officer. The occasion was the passing of eulogiums upon the death of Abraham Lincoln.

Said Mr. Disraeli, in the House of Commons: —

"In the character of the victim, and even in the accessories of his last moments, there is something so homely and innocent, that it takes the question, as it were, out of all the pomp of history and the ceremonial of diplomacy; it touches the heart of nations, and appeals to the domestic sentiment of mankind. Whatever the various and varying opinions in this House, and in the country generally, on the policy of the late President of the United States, all must agree that in one of the severest trials which ever tested the moral qualities of man he fulfilled his duty with simplicity and strength. Nor is it possible for the people of England at such a moment to forget that he sprang from the same fatherland, and spoke the same mother tongue. When such crimes are perpetrated the public mind is apt to fall into gloom and perplexity, for it is ignorant alike of the causes and the consequences of such deeds. But it is one of our duties to reassure them under unreasoning panic and despondency. Assassination has never changed the history of the world. I will not refer to the remote past, though an accident has made the most memorable instance of antiquity at this moment fresh in the minds and memory of all around me. But even the costly sacrifice of a Cæsar did not propitiate the inexorable destiny of his country. If we look to modern times, to times at least with the feelings of which we are familiar, and the people of which were animated and influenced by the same interests as ourselves, the violent deaths of two heroic men, Henry IV. of France, and the Prince of Orange, are conspicuous illustrations of this truth. In expressing our unaffected and profound sympathy with the citizens of the United States on this untimely end of their elected chief, let us not, therefore, sanction any feeling of depression, but rather let us express a fervent hope that from out of the awful trials of the last four years, of which the least is not this violent demise, the various populations of North America may issue elevated and chastened, rich with the accumulated wisdom, and strong in the disciplined energy, which a young nation can only acquire in a protracted and perilous struggle; then they will be enabled not merely to renew their career of power and prosperity, but they will renew it to contribute to the general happiness of mankind."

It is probable that no more excellent instance of Disraeli's remarkable power and grace in eulogy can be instanced than this. He and Mr. Bancroft are alike literary men and statesmen. The latter's culture is no higher above that of the average of congressmen than is Disraeli's above the average of members of Parliament. I put Mr. Bancroft's comparison between Lincoln and Lord Palmerston, therefore, beside the above, and leave the relative merits of both to the judgment of the reader.

"Palmerston," said Mr. Bancroft, "traced his lineage to the time of the conqueror; Lincoln went back only to his grandfather. Palmerston received his education from the best scholars of Harrow, Edinburgh, and Cambridge; Lincoln's early teachers were the silent forest, the prairie, the river, and the stars. Palmerston was in public life for sixty years; Lincoln, for but a tenth of that time. Palmerston was a skilful guide of an established aristocracy; Lincoln, a leader or rather a companion of the people. Palmerston was exclusively an Englishman, and made his boast in the House of Commons that the interest of England was his shibboleth; Lincoln thought always of mankind as well as of his own country, and served human nature itself. Palmerston, from his narrowness as an Englishman, did not endear his country to any one court or to any one people, but rather caused uneasiness and dislike; Lincoln left America more beloved than ever by all the peoples of Europe. Palmerston was self-possessed and adroit in reconciling the conflicting claims of the factions of the aristocracy; Lincoln, frank and ingenuous, knew how to poise himself on the conflicting opinions of the people. Palmerston was capable of insolence towards the weak, quick to the sense of honor, not heedful of right; Lincoln rejected counsel given only as a matter of policy, and was not capable of being willingly unjust. Palmerston, essentially superficial, delighted in banter and knew how to divert grave opposition by playful levity; Lincoln was a man of infinite jest on his lips, with saddest earnestness at his heart. Palmerston was a fair representative of the aristocratic liberality of the day, choosing for his tribunal, not the conscience of humanity, but the House of Commons; Lincoln took to heart the eternal truths of liberty, obeyed them as the commands of Providence, and accepted the human race as the judge of his fidelity. Palmerston did nothing that will endure; his great achievement, the separation of Belgium, placed that little kingdom where it must gravitate to France; Lincoln finished a work which all time cannot overthrow. Palmerston is a shining example of the ablest of a cultivated aristocracy; Lincoln shows the genuine fruits of institutions where the laboring man shares and assists to form the great ideas and designs of his country. Palmerston was buried in Westminster Abbey by the order of his queen, and was followed by the British aristocracy to his grave, which, after a few years, will hardly be noticed by the side of the graves of Fox and Chatham; Lincoln was followed by the sorrow of his country across the continent to his resting-place in the heart of the Mississippi valley, to be remembered through all time by his countrymen, and by all the peoples of the world."

The speeches of John Bright form exceptions to the average mediocrity of British oratory, but they are so familiar to this country that I need not quote from them. He probably stands at the head of Anglo-Saxon parliamentary orators. Mr. Gladstone and Mr. Disraeli rank as the finest running debaters. The writer and compiler of this book has heard the leading orators of both the Lords and the Commons declaim, but his personal verdict upon their rhetoric and their degree of ability would not, perhaps, have the same value to readers of different sympathies that English criticism itself might possess. I have therefore looked over the files of the Manchester, Dublin, and Glasgow newspapers, to glean some of the descriptions of English public men, which are so spicily written by their London correspondents, "many of whom," says Dr. Shelton Mackenzie, editor of the "Philadelphia Press," himself a practised eye and hand in parliamentary literature, "are highly educated men, who generally are students in some of the Inns of Court, and will become lawyers in a few years. Lord Campbell, it is remembered, began his career in London as a reporter on the 'Morning Chronicle,' and ended it as a peer and Lord Chancellor of England; the late Sir James Dowling, Chief Justice of New South Wales, and Sir James Hannen, now a judge of the Court of Queen's Bench, also were newspaper reporters, and numerous other instances might be mentioned."

This type of young man is bound to attend every evening in the reporters' gallery of Lords or Commons, and describe, as an eye-witness, the striking points of debates, and the manner, method, and appearance of members. This he does usually with great freedom, often with great ability.

Here is a sketch of Lord Palmerston, Prime Minister of England during our civil war, and generally our enemy: —

"Though for near sixty years he was a member of the House of Commons; though of these he was forty-five in office, twenty-five in the cabinet, and seven at the head of the government, yet he seldom spoke on any great question of domestic interest, — Ireland, for example, with which his ties were unusually close, and his sympathies as earnest as it was in his nature to feel, — without reminding us that the impress of his thought was never stamped upon any great subject of home policy. He spoke, in his last year, of Irish emigration, in words exceedingly like those which he used on the same subject in 1828, and it is obvious that the question made little, if any, progress in his mind from that day to his death."

At the head of the Conservative or Tory party in the House of Lords was Lord Derby, the father of Lord Stanley, who negotiated the unpopular treaty on the Alabama claims with Mr. Reverdy Johnson in 1869. The Earl of Derby was no less our enemy than the ostensible "Liberal," Palmerston, and it may be interesting to know what stature and compass of man he was. In this we are assisted by the analytic mind of Mr. Grant, the veteran of the reporters' gallery: —

"Of Lord Derby's vehement career as a reformer, while great abuses stared him in the face; of his generous anti-slavery policy; of his rash and violent personal collisions with Mr. O'Connell and Mr. Shiel; of his superficial treatment of the Irish Church question, and his wish to relieve the grievances of Catholics without infringing the privileges of Protestants; of his deepening conservatism as the current of liberal principles began to run stronger and deeper; of his gallantry in adhering to his obsolete protectionist prejudices, even when Sir Robert Peel abandoned them; of his pro-Austrian feeling when Austria was threatened by France and Italy; of his pro-Southern feeling when the South (United States) was invaded by the North, — in all stages of his career alike Lord Derby's political motives have consisted very much of strong class-impulses and fastidious personal tastes, to which it is impossible to find any consistent intellectual clue. His political influence has chiefly arisen from sharing strongly the tastes and prejudices of a class, while possessing a literary feeling too large and refined to admit of his expressing these prejudices in any gross or revolting way. A commonplace intellect and an imperious will, combined with more sensitive perceptions and cultivated tastes than most of his order possess, have enabled him to throw these prepossessions into an effective, chivalric form, that has given them a weight they seldom deserved. And no nobleman of anything like Lord Derby's eminence has ever shown so little power of learning as he has done. His speech on assuming office in 1852, after the free-trade controversy had been discussed and decided for six years, was a model of dense economical ignorance, — almost of incapacity to think on such subjects at all."

Scarcely in more complimentary terms is Lord Derby's son, Stanley, considered: —

"Conservatism and radicalism," says Grant, "might, in a certain sense, really unite under Lord Stanley; for conservatism would be gratified by the cold shoulder which he uniformly turns to imaginative or enthusiastic liberalism; and radicalism would be gratified by the cold shoulder which he uniformly turns to sentimental or traditional conservatism. Lord Stanley is as incapable of refusing a common-sense reform from any fear of the abstract danger of change as of joining in a demand for reform from any anticipation of Utopian benefits, or any chivalric devotion to abstract justice. Hence, he is what the chemists would call a neutral or earthy base."

Lord Stanley is said to have once observed, "My father would be a very able man — if he knew anything;" and Lord Derby, when asked why he had not sent his translation of the Iliad to his son, is rumored to have replied, that he was waiting till it should be printed in prose, and published in the form of a blue-book.

The most dashing character in Parliament is Disraeli, a politician of Jewish descent, and of excellent literary attainments, about whose rank and character there is great diversity of opinion. In his face there is a dazzling, saucy look, which at once excites your interest. You see that, if not a great man, he is an intensely clever one; and though, on reflection, you see more display than reality in his performance, and are not sure that he is in earnest, or that he means what he says, or that he is sustained and prompted by any great principle, you feel that as an orator he has few rivals. When he soars, as he occasionally does, you tremble lest he should break down; but Disraeli never attempts more than he can achieve; and, when nearest to pathos, he saves himself by a happy flight; but, even in his highest efforts, he preserves the same doggedly cool and unconcerned appearance, and will stop to suck an orange, or, actually (as he did in his great budget speech), to cut his nails! It is true there are times when he displays a little more feeling.

The conservative party in England never had a more illustrious nor more useful exemplar than Sir Robert Peel, the British Jefferson, the son of a cotton trader, and the abolisher of the corn laws, who died in 1850. He was a remarkably good-looking man, rather above the usual size, and finely proportioned. He was of a clear complexion, full, round face, and red-haired. His usual dress was a blue surtout, a light waistcoat, and dark trousers. He generally displayed a watch-chain on his breast, with a bunch of gold seals, of unusually large dimensions. "He can scarcely," says a contemporary, "be called a dandy, and yet he sacrifices a good deal to the graces. I hardly know a public man who dresses in better taste." This was when Peel was in the prime of life, being forty-seven years of age. His whole appearance indicated health. His constitution was excellent, and his temperate habits seconded the kindly purposes of nature. He was capable of undergoing great physical fatigue, and, says an author, "I have known him to remain in the House for three or four successive nights till one and two o'clock, not only watching with the most intense anxiety the progress of important debates, but taking an active part in the proceedings, and yet be in his office, transacting business of the greatest moment, by ten o'clock on the following morning."

In 1868 one hundred and ninety-two new private bills were introduced into the House of Commons, of which one hundred and seventy passed, — a fact which shows much less special legislation than the American Congress indulges in. Both bodies are huge manufactories of statute law. The pleasures of sitting in Parliament are highly appreciated by Englishmen. The spacious courts, cloisters, and promenades of the great building are free to a member. He can smoke his cigar on the river terrace, seeing vessels come and go, and the mighty mass of men and horses traversing Westminster Bridge. Near by is his club, where are the newspapers and serial literatures of the world at his disposal. He is beset with invitations to entertainments, made presiding officer and orator of city and suburban meetings, and when he returns to his district after Parliament adjourns he is received with ceremony and a banquet. But a working member of the House of Commons is quite as busy as any industrious congressman. The social world of London is much vaster than Washington, and its allurements and seductions are more various. In London, Parliament is a mere episode of that gigantic life which condenses into a city the riches and population of a nation. At Washington, Congress is the city, and the city is little more than a deserted watering-place with the waiters retained after Congress has departed. The private vices of members of Commons are much the same as those of congressmen. There are profligate persons in both bodies. A prize-fighter has been seen seated in either legislature. When the national horse-race is held at Epsom Parliament adjourns.

If we come to ask ourselves which body is the better one to represent the people, we can best answer in the opinion of the people themselves. A few private voices are raised in America for qualified suffrage, limiting the ballot to intelligence, to property, to color, or to some other accident or inheritance. In England the demand for universal suffrage and equal chance to sit in Parliament is a formidable roar, with the passion of revolution in it.

"I go further than Bright," said a young Englishman at Southampton to me. "I want right!"

Wealth and democracy are the great elements of politics in this century, and it is more likely that we shall be debauched by the first than limited in the second. The agitation in England is the other way. Wealth constitutes the House of Commons, and democracy is undermining it. The House of Representatives is democratic beyond limitation, and only money can contend with numbers there. The abuse of representation in England is that a man can elect himself to Parliament. The abuse here is that a man can nominate himself for Congress. The corrupt Englishman buys the constituency. The corrupt American steals the machinery of nomination. If the English Parliament is corrupt, there are millions of English people guiltless of it, because millions are disfranchised. If the American Congress is corrupt, an American cannot be guiltless, because all are electors. This government can only degenerate by default of interest in it, and, amongst the numberless schemes of law, not the least significant is one to compel every elector in America to deposit his vote.

The effect of all the enginery of the century is to make the legislature absolutely popular. Even in the despotism of France every citizen votes for his representative in the lower house of the legislature. Grudgingly and by degrees the English Parliament is popularizing its constituencies. In 1832 the wicket was unlatched. In 1867 the gates were set ajar. In a little while the gates will be thrown wide open, and vote by ballot will be the means of sending representative citizens to Parliament. Many agreeable old traditions must perish before this can be done. The "freeman" must become a citizen, the "borough" disappear in a district, the ancient privilege expire in the census. But these English laws will be the enactment of all Englishmen. Money will be assessed, not upon the back like a stripe, but upon the ground. The extravagant fiction of the monarch and his family must then be maintained by the virtues of the Princes, and even then it must, like every illusion, expire, if by nothing else, by its own self-respect. To be enshrined like a jewel-laden idol, complimented with a form of worship, made legally immaculate, and dowered with money and attendants in profusion, this age is too practical and irreverent to continue this play when democratic Parliaments come to be.

The paying of salaries to legislators must come with popular Parliaments. The state has no right even to a rich man's time without compensating him. As to the English custom of giving the executive government place in the Legislature, that has been proposed in Congress within a few years, and it is a question of no little importance. The English have found it wise and convenient. It brings the magistrate and the reformer together. The one feels the earnestness of the other, and communicates his knowledge in return. It makes falsehood in the speechmaker superfluous, and meets inquiry with promptitude. We must guess at a minister's intention in America. In England he is asked in Parliament to reveal it.

The English Parliament, because of its want of representative character, is not up to the requirements of the nation. "What is there specially to admire in either House?" says the "Saturday Review," 1867. "In the leaders of either there is an utter want of creative force. They cannot suggest anything, or do anything, or remedy anything; they can only view things in the light of an educated mind, and that comes to so very little. They have no motive power in themselves, and they receive none from the nation. They cannot give us an army, they cannot give us popular education, they cannot conciliate Ireland, they cannot do anything for the poor. Their intentions are admirable, and so is their public spirit; but they are impotent."

CHAPTER VI.

THE PRIME MINISTER AND THE CABINET.

Explanations of the executive governments of Great Britain and America. — Relative opportunities for statesmanship. — Accounts of divers administrations and sketches of their methods of action in developing certain policies. — The prime minister and the president at home. — An English foreign minister and an American secretary of state corresponding with each other. — Architecture of the executive departments in London and at Washington. — Party politics and public duty. — Salaries and perquisites of officials at home and abroad.

THE title of this chapter might have been "The Prime Minister and the President;" for the President of England is, in fact, the Prime Minister, while the Queen's place is analogous to nothing here unless it be the fainter phantom that we call The People. We say The Sovereign People; the English say The Sovereign; and as the most practical nation must have some emblem, symbol, or personality to cherish in its emotions, we love our Flag where they love their Queen. "Our dear Queen!" cries the English child. "Our old Flag!" say American boys going to battle. The American flag, appealing to the sensuous and artistic part of our nature by the gorgeousness of its colors and the purity of its symbols, — the stars shining from the sky, — was one of the happiest suggestions of our fathers. It has had an influence in the state akin to the Cross in the Crusades, the Eagle to the Romans, or the Marsellaise Hymn to the French Republicans.

It has been often said that the President of the United States has more power than the English Sovereign. The English Sovereign has personal influence, and there is great respect for her opinion. She is made rich. and lives luxuriously, but she is without other power than this. The President of the United States is more powerful than an English Prime Minister, and this is probably what the above allegation means. The people's electors directly elect the President for a fixed term of years. If he becomes obnoxious to either the people or to Congress, there is no getting rid of him but by a vexatious trial, and during his term of office he has control of many thousand officials whom he may coerce to his will. But the British Prime Minister can be changed at the will of the House of Commons, which meets annually; and in this respect lies the excellence of that form of government which is more immediately obedient to the Legislature than our own President.

The Prime Minister is the Queen's responsible self; he who rules the realm in her name, and can be punished for her mistakes. She must put him aside when the House of Commons, by voting want of confidence in him, expresses that desire. Thus the Prime Minister is the Queen's manager sitting in Parliament. He stands at the rudder, and is the commander of the ship of State, but around him are the underwriters whom he must conciliate, and prove to them that his course is the true one. Being responsible, the Prime Minister dare not hold his place after he has been sufficiently rebuked by the votes of Commons. He therefore advises the Queen to send for the leader of the opposite political party, who becomes Prime Minister, and continues on with the administration in the name of the Queen.

Let us construct this form of government for America so as to make it palpable what would be the appearance of the United States with a Prime Minister at the head of it.

Here is King Ulysses Grant to represent the Queen. He belongs to no political party, but sits in uniform at the top of the State, its hereditary ornament and sovereign, incapable of resigning, never to be elected out, not to be punished nor banished. He descended to us from his father, and his son "Buck," is to take his place inevitably. We derived him without our consent, and can only expel him from his place by rebellion, which is high treason, and the penalty thereof death. In the early days of his family, two hundred or three hundred years ago, King Grant was his own minister and did as he pleased, spent our money with or without our consent, and put any of us whom he might dislike into the Tower, his jail. But being a lazy, luxurious tyrant, he found it convenient to rule us through some able favorite, a Cardinal, or a Duke. We could not dethrone the King, so we turned all our animosity upon his favorite minister, whom it was not high treason to hate, and in course of time this minister occupied so dangerous a place between the hate of the people and the freak of the King, that he was obliged to say to the King: —

"Your majesty! I cannot be your minister unless you keep within the law, for the people will hang me for executing your commands."

The people, also, rose up against the Grants after a time, cut off the head of one King Grant, drove two others out of the country, and at last the King agreed that he would rule entirely through his ministers, who were, in turn, to rule according to the laws, and to be changed whenever the House of Commons wished.

Now, there are two political parties in the country, and they have each sent to the House of Representatives as many members as they could elect relatively. The House of Representatives elects a Speaker. The two parties seat themselves on opposite sides of their legislative chamber, and some one sagacious and eloquent statesman becomes the leader of each party. This may be, for example, Mr. Thaddeus Stevens for the Radical party, and Mr. George Pendleton for the Conservative party. The King, Grant, at once selects Mr. Stevens for his Prime Minister, because Mr. Stevens' party has the majority of members of the House of Representatives. He requests Mr. Stevens to form a Cabinet for him, which shall conduct the business of the nation, fill the executive offices, collect the revenue, and direct the policy of the State. Mr. Stevens can either comply with this request or decline the honor, according to his opinion of his own capacity under the circumstances.

We will suppose that Mr. Stevens accepts the place of Prime Minister. He looks round the country and through both Houses of Congress to discover the ablest men of his party whom he can obtain. There are, perhaps, seventy great offices to be filled; but as seventy men would make an unwieldy Cabinet, only about sixteen of the greatest officers are indicated for the Cabinet. Mr. Stevens makes himself the First Lord of the Treasury, and, perhaps also, the Chancellor of the Exchequer. He is known by the title of Prime Minister, or Premier. He takes the seals of office from the King, Grant, as the sign of his authority to rule in the King's name, and so selects his Cabinet that they will be popular with the House of Representatives as well as useful to the State. His own salary is twenty-five thousand dollars a year. As his Cabinet depends upon the will of Parliament for its continuance, himself and several of his colleagues must also have seats in Parliament; but to accomplish this they all require to be re-elected by their constituents. The government being formed, Mr. Stevens, or that member of the Cabinet who is the leader in the House of Representatives, begins work by recommending to the House, in the King's name, that they pass supply bills to carry on the country, and estimates are suggested of the amount required for each department. Mr. Stevens also writes the speech with which the King, Grant, opens Parliament.

As in all politics to the victors belong the spoils, without which politics would have no selfish stimulus, Mr. Stevens puts his friends in all the great political offices, but he cannot, in the name of King Grant, do that which President Grant has the privilege of doing, — change all the clerks, laborers, and lackeys of the government. The opposition party, with Mr. Pendleton at its head, is jealous of Mr. Stevens and the Radicals, because they hold so many rich offices. Therefore every wily energy of the opposition is exerted to destroy the confidence of Parliament in the Cabinet. The Prime Minister must be ready to explain every troublous matter, and to convince Parliament that the country is being well governed He brings up his annual "budget," to show the good state of the country financially, satisfies apprehensions about the foreign affairs of the State, explains why the cattle disease rages, and accounts for the Houses of Parliament costing more than the original estimates. He also aims to bend Parliament to his political convictions, and, being a Radical, he wishes to extend the franchise to such Chinese, French, Africans, and Italians as may be in the country. In this the House of Representatives is not up to his standard, and he loses some of the support of his party or of certain neutral members. Finally he is beaten by a decided vote, as he pushes his views. He is then bantered by Mr. Pendleton, and the other party with his failure, and asked why he does not give up the task of governing. He meets with an adverse vote once or twice more, and sees that he has lost the confidence of Parliament. So he takes the seals of state back to the King, and resigns his place, saying: —

"Sire (or, your Majesty), I advise you to send for Mr. Pendleton to make up a new ministry which will be acceptable to Parliament."

Perhaps, however, Mr. Stevens may think that the people of the country are with him in opinion, and he may take the resolute step of advising the King to dissolve the Senate and House and order a new election of Representatives. If this election should confirm the sentiments of Parliament, Mr. Stevens will have no alternative but to resign, and let Mr. Pendleton take possession of seals, offices, and honors.

This is the English form of government, which I have thus suppositítiously transferred to America. Let us now see the actual Cabinet which the President, the elected magistrate of the people, gathers around him. And here we come to a remarkable fact, which is this: that in neither America nor England is there any such organization as a Cabinet named or provided for by law. There is no record kept of the existence of either body, and in England the names of the Cabinet officers are known, but they are never announced officially. Each member of the Cabinet, as he is also an administrative officer of the State, is recognized in the latter capacity, but not as a Cabinet officer. Neither Parliament nor Congress ever prescribe when or where a Cabinet shall meet. It is a little conspiracy of great officers to divide the magistracy of the State; and the word "cabal" is composed of the initials of the names of the members of a certain historical English Cabinet. For example, there is in England a First Lord of the Treasury, and in America a Secretary of the Treasury. These are recognized administrative officers. But when the Head of the Treasury, in either case, enters into secret council at Cabinet meeting, the law has no knowledge of such meeting. Congress or Parliament can request the Secretary of the Treasury to furnish it with information upon any branch of his department; but he is never required to tell what happened in Cabinet meeting, or to disclose how opinion was divided there upon any subject. One leading English authority, Lord Chief Justice Campbell, has insisted, however, that the Cabinet, "by our Constitution, is in practice a defined and acknowledged body for carrying on the executive government of the country."

The President of the United States is the Chief Magistrate by name and by act for a fixed term of four years, charged with the execution of the laws, sworn to the defence of the Constitution, made Commander-in-Chief of the army and navy, and entrusted with the granting of pardons. He can only be removed by death, or conviction on impeachment, and, so far as we know, a President has never been anxious to resign. He is elected by the voters of each State going to the polls on a certain day, and casting ballots for electors. These electors meet together at a point in each State, and ballot separately for President and Vice-President. They send detailed statements of the result to the President of the Senate, at Washington. Then, on a fixed day, the Senate and the House meet together, with the President of the Senate presiding, and in the presence of them all the statements are unsealed, and the ballots read. He who has the votes of the majority of the electors for President is declared President for the next four years. If there be no choice, the House of Representatives chooses by ballot a President from amongst the three names highest on the electors' lists, each State delegation casting only one vote. If there should still be no person receiving a majority, the Vice-President becomes President.

The new President, being inaugurated, selects his great officers of state within a day or two; for his duties are so numerous and various, that he must have chief clerks over some of the important branches. These chief clerks bear the name of Secretaries, and must be appointed at once, because all the smaller clerkships should be filled by them. The Secretaries are called as follows, and are considered relatively honorable in this numerical rank:—

1. The Secretary of State and of Foreign Affairs.
2. The Secretary of the Treasury.
3. The Secretary of War.
4. The Secretary of the Navy.
5. The Secretary of the Interior.
6. The Postmaster-General.
7. The Attorney-General.

The names of these are sent in to the Senate, which, sitting with closed doors, and with a Secretary sworn to keep its secrets, considers the nominations, and resolves, by a majority, either to confirm them, or to reject them. If confirmed, they remain the President's chief clerks during his will, and are paid a salary of about eight thousand dollars apiece, as clerks or Secretaries.

Now begins their relation of Cabinet officers, which, as I have said, veils its existence from the laws of the land, or, in the words of an English statesman, Sir G. Cornewall Lewis, is "merely a voluntary meeting of certain ministers; for the archives of the country contain no means of distinguishing between a *Cabinet* minister and any other." The President, having some public design upon his mind, finds that the execution of it will affect each of the seven great clerkships or "departments" of the government. It would be awkward to go visiting each Secretary, or to send for each one separately. So he calls them all together, and places his plans before them. Under some of the Presidents, executive acts are said to have been passed by the vote of the majority of the Cabinet. Under some of the more imperious Presidents, Cabinet councils were called between long intervals. General Garfield, a Representative in Congress, has said to me that Mr. Lincoln seldom called Cabinet meetings, and that his Secretary of the Treasury complained that the Cabinet was reduced to a series of chief clerks. The Constitution of the nation says only this, hinting toward a Cabinet: "He (the President) may require the opinion, in writing, of the principal officer in each of the executive departments, upon any subject relating to the duties of their respective offices." Besides being false syntax, this paragraph is in nothing explicit, as to the subject of the Cabinet, which keeps no Secretary, and therefore does no writing.

The United States Cabinet Ministers meet in the office of the President, for the Cabinet has no existence without the Chief Magistrate, and until 1868, when Congress enacted a bill, called the "Tenure-of-Office Law," the right of the President to remove a Secretary was not disputed. Out of this law, and the alleged disregard of it arose our most memorable impeachment.

While the relative harmony, intellect, and character of a Cabinet have no influence to change the duration of a President's term of office, they materially affect the popularity of his administration.

We elect Presidents in America as a reward of signal services, more frequently in the field of war than on the plane of statesmanship; but we regard the choice of his Cabinet as frequently more vital to the country than his own character. Each Cabinet officer has, by our present regulations, the absolute power of removal and appointment over the large body of lesser clerks and laborers in his department. In more important appointments the President sometimes interferes. But it is seldom that a new President has the mortification of seeing his Cabinet officers rejected by the Senate, however crude the selections may be. In 1869 the Senate even confirmed Mr. A. T. Stewart, of New York, for Secretary of the Treasury, when, by a law obsolete in the memory of men, it was discovered that his mercantile pursuits rendered him ineligible. The vast "patronage" of the President, in honors and offices, generally secures his earlier appointments respectful attention.

In the English government the selection of a Cabinet is altogether a more delicate and important matter, for upon the strength of his Cabinet associates depends the political existence of the Prime Minister. In both countries a shrewd mixture of political and social notabilities is required to make an effective Cabinet, for the administration must commend itself to the respect of the people, and also be equal to the tactics of its partisan opponents, who are not apt to be scrupulous. In America, also, it is esteemed impartial to consult geographical attachments, two Cabinet officers from one State often causing complaint. Personal favoritism also enters into the composition of Cabinets, as it is natural that the President should wish one or two trusted friends at his side. President Jackson brought Major Eaton, his neighbor, to Washington, and raised him to a ministership, much to the annoyance of his Cabinet, as I shall relate hereafter. General Grant made his townsman and chief-of-staff, General Rawlins, Secretary of War. The majority of each Cabinet being politicians, intrigues not uncommonly begin within the Cabinet circle with the intent to affect the succession to the President or Prime Minister. Instances of this sort occur in recent administrations of both America and England.

There are two or three remarkable coincidences between the office of President and that of Prime Minister. The first is in the average duration of their terms of office. In one hundred and fifty years, or from 1715 to 1866, there were thirty-eight Prime Ministers for England, — an average term of three years and eight months, which is nearly the exact period between the inauguration of one President, and the election of his successor. Again, the salary of both President and Prime Minister is the same. Neither of them is directly elected by the people, the source of power in America, nor appointed by the Sovereign, the source of power in England. In one case the electors intervene, in the other, Parliament must be satisfied. The House of Commons can terminate the career of a minister, by voting want of confidence in him, and the House of Representatives can impeach a President, and with the concurrence of two-thirds of the Senate, remove him. Both President and Prime Minister represent a political party. Both are the dispensers of the great offices of the State. If a Chief Justice dies during the administration of a certain Premier, the latter, like the President, fills the place. Both offices are the pinnacle of political ambition in their several countries. To either office the most popular or the ablest statesman is generally elevated by his party, although it frequently happens that some comparatively obscure gentleman, or some soldier merely, slips past a more formidable colleague. Instances of this sort in America were General Harrison passing over the head of Henry Clay, Mr. Polk anticipating Mr. Van Buren, and Mr. Lincoln outstripping Mr. Seward. Analogous cases in England were the administrations of the Earl of Aberdeen, in 1852, and, previously, of the Duke of Wellington, of whom Miss Martineau says: —

"All that had been previously surmised of the Duke of Wellington's unfitness for civil government seemed orally confirmed by himself, and he was formally deposed in the accustomed way, by a majority of the House of Commons voting against him. Next day brought the glad tidings of his resignation."

The English Cabinet, in the summer of 1866, consisted of these officers, fifteen in number: —

1. *First Lord of the Treasury.* — Earl of Derby; sixty-seven years old. Salary, twenty-five thousand dollars. He was also Prime Minister, or *Premier*, and appointed, as his colleagues, the members of the Cabinet succeeding.
2. *Lord High Chancellor.* — Lord Chelmsford; seventy-four years old. Salary, fifty thousand dollars. The best-paid officer in England. He corresponds in some degree to our Vice-President, being President of the House of Lords.
3. *Lord President of the Council.* — Duke of Marlborough; forty-six years old. Salary, ten thousand dollars a year. He controls the department of education, and attends the Queen at the council table. He belongs to the Privy Council, which formerly managed the country jointly with the Sovereign.
4. *Lord Privy Seal.* — Earl of Malmesbury; sixty-one years old. This officer keeps the Sovereign's private seal, and was formerly of high authority in the State, but the privy seal is of little note nowadays, and the office is little more than honorary.
5. *Chancellor of the Exchequer.* — Right Hon. Benjamin Disraeli; sixty-three years old. Salary, twenty-five thousand dollars a year, and the second officer in importance in the Cabinet. He is the English Secretary of Treasury.
6. *Secretary of State for the Home Department.* — Right Hon. Gathorne Hardy; fifty-four years old. This officer is the head of the government police and militia, and is entrusted with the maintenance of the public security. He renders up fugitive criminals from the United States.
7. *Secretary of State for Foreign Affairs.* — Lord Stanley; forty-two years old; son of Earl Derby, the Prime Minister. He is the nominator of Ambassadors and Consuls, issues passports, negotiates treaties, and keeps England in correspondence with all foreign governments. This office concerns us more than any other Cabinet position in England.
8. *Secretary of State for the Colonies.* — Duke of Buckingham; forty-five years old. This officer, like all the five Secretaries of State, receives twenty-five thousand dollars a year, and has charge of the immense colonial possessions of England. We have a Secretary of the Interior, who corresponds to him in some degree.
9. *Secretary of State for India.* — Sir Stafford Northcote; fifty years old. The English Empire in India is so vast and so important, that the custody of it is entrusted to a special Cabinet officer.

10. *Secretary of State for War.* — Right Hon. Sir John Parkington; sixty-nine years old. This officer is, in all material respects, the counterpart of our Secretary of War.
11. *First Lord of the Admiralty.* — Right Hon. Henry Thomas Lowry Corry; sixty-five years old. This officer is the English Secretary of the Navy, and he has a wider jurisdiction than the American Secretary, the British Navy being perpetual, and of monstrous size.
12. *President of the Board of Trade.* — Duke of Richmond; fifty years old. Salary, ten thousand dollars. The commerce, railways, and commercial statistics of England, being of vital consequence, are intrusted to a special Cabinet officer.
13. *Postmaster General.* — Duke of Montrose; sixty-nine years old. Salary, twelve thousand five hundred dollars a year. He has control of fifteen thousand offices, and dispenses three millions of dollars a year.
14. *Chancellor of the Duchy of Lancaster.* — Right Hon. Colonel John Wilson Patten; sixty-six years old. An honorary appointment, mainly, with a salary of ten thousand dollars, and filled by a statesman of rank. The Duchy of Lancaster is a bit of private interest of the Queen's, which yields her sixty thousand dollars a year.
15. *President of the Poor Law Board.* — Earl of Devon; sixty-one years old. Salary, ten thousand dollars. The custodian of the mighty pauper establishment of England; the most extraordinary feature of the kingdom, not excepting its shipping.

By running over the Cabinet list above, it will be seen to be exactly twice the size of the American Cabinet, excluding the Prime Minister. These fifteen officers govern England with the support of the House of Commons. Yet, though dependent for their political existence upon the Commons, nine of them are seen to be peers, and one is a baronet. This conclusive evidence of the subserviency of all powers in England to the aristocracy is made the subject of satire by the German writer on the English constitution, Dr. Fischel, who quotes from Bulwer, "Could the king choose a Cabinet out of men unknown to the aristocracy? Assuredly not! The aristocratic party in the two houses would be in arms! What a commotion there would be! Imagine the haughty indignation of my Lords Grey and Harrowby! What a 'prelection' we should receive from Lord Brougham 'deeply meditating these things.' Alas! the King's ministry would be out the next day, and the aristocracy's ministry, with all due apology, replaced."

The main features of this chapter, which is directed like the entire book toward satisfying curiosity rather than making disquisitions, will be: —

1. An account of the origin of Cabinets.

2. Some scenes in Cabinet meetings at home and abroad.
3. Sketches of certain administrations in England.

The Sovereign of England is traditionally the possessor of certain inherited and inalienable absolute powers called prerogatives. The earliest Kings of England were unrestrained tyrants, until the barons forced them to consent to certain restrictions of their arbitrary power. When James the First, who reigned during the settlement of Virginia, was on his way from Scotland to be crowned in London, he had a thief hanged up at a town of Newark, through which he passed, merely to show "that he was God's representative, and had a right to place himself above all law." His son, Charles I., in whose reign New England and many of the other States were settled, declared "that he was responsible to God alone for his acts." Down to the time of the expulsion of James II., a hundred and eighty years ago, the monarch of England surrounded himself at pleasure with a few confidential advisers, called Privy Councillors. This body, the Privy Council, exists yet in England, but its former importance is diminished, and the Cabinet, which was formed out of a faction in it, or, as we would say, by a "corner" in it, is now nearly absolute. There are at this time probably a hundred or two hundred Privy Councillors, and they are all entitled by this appointment to be called "Right Honorable." Being Privy Councillors, they have access under certain regulations to the Queen's presence; but only those sit at her Privy Council table who are specially summoned. In America the great body of honorable and influential citizens who can have access to the President may be considered his Privy Council, and this includes whoever is worthy, and who is requested by the President to give him information or suggestions. When President Grant called in the Quakers to advise him about Indian affairs, they were of his Privy Council, in the English sense. In England the majority of Privy Councillors are peers, and the members of the Cabinet are almost invariably attached to this effete body, which, however, has a few duties left to it, and certain committee work to do. We have reason to remember it, for the celebrated "Orders in Council" passed during the French and English wars in 1806, to the annoyance of our ship-owners. For thirty years there has been no meeting *en masse* of this large Privy Council, which is one of those cumbrous and useless appendages to a useless monarch, embarrassing the study of the English constitution, and accomplishing no good to man nor to the nation.

Looking back over the later days of the Privy Council we have no reason to wonder that it was overthrown by a small minority within it. Clarendon, the Lord Chancellor of Charles II. was one of the last of the great councillors, and he was impeached of high treason on the ground of common fame, without the examination of witnesses by the Commons; upon which the Lords resolved that he could not be committed in the absence of any special charge of treason. The articles of impeachment, which were seventeen in number, might have been drawn closer, and several transactions of Clarendon been more fully known, as subsequently revealed. There is good reason for believing that he was the principal adviser of a standing army to be raised and maintained by a forced contribution, and of the corrupt sale of Dunkirk to the French King. In his secret correspondence with the French court, he betrayed state matters, which it was the interest of the country should be concealed; and was not only himself a traitor, but made the King a similar delinquent, by soliciting money from the King of France to minister to the licentious profusion of his own Sovereign. Clarendon was thus guilty of the enormous iniquity of rendering a lavish Prince dependent on the wages of a foreign power, to enable him to elude the control of Parliament. Avarice was his flagrant vice; and it was observed by Evelyn, who was friendly towards the Chancellor, that he "never would nor did do anything but for money." He had, too, the weakness of ostentation; built a large house — Dunkirk House, it was called from its surmised origin — of unparalleled magnificence, storing it with choice pictures and furniture, that excited the surprise of all who remembered his recent poverty. Parliament felt so strongly hostile to him, that Charles declared his inability to protect him, and advised his withdrawal from the kingdom. This advice he adopted, and on a dark November night he escaped to France. He was old and infirm, vastly proud withal, and after bearing his misfortunes with little dignity, died in exile seven years after. In those days the Privy Council chamber was also a torture chamber.

After the Stuarts were expelled in 1688, a section of the Privy Council took charge of the State, and, with a single exception, England has been governed by a Prime Minister and Cabinet ever since. The exception was on the death of Queen Anne, the year after South Carolina was settled, when the Cabinet had resolved to restore the Stuarts to the English throne. Two Dukes of the Privy Council strode into the Cabinet meeting, and a general meeting of the Privy

Council was summoned, so that, despite the treason of the Cabinet, the Hanoverian succession and the era of Victoria was ensured.

The English Sovereign does not attend Cabinet meetings, and therefore the Prime Minister rules in her name, doing pretty much as he pleases, consonant with the support of the House of Commons. This custom began with George I., who could not speak English, and he therefore kept away from the Cabinet. In former days when a minister ruled adversely to the House he lost his head. Now he only loses his official head. Ministers are not responsible for their acts in these days, although they make great show of responsibility.

To make this subject as plain as possible I propose to compare the material features of the official life of a Prime Minister with the same features of the life of an American President. And first, the beginning of an administration.

In 1868 General Grant was elected President. On the fourth of March, more than three months afterward, he was inaugurated. The author was a witness of this state ceremony, and it was pronounced the finest pageant of its sort ever seen at the capital of the republic. Multiplied ways of travelling, increased speed, low excursion fare, and a more nomadic and inquisitive spirit, augment the visiting crowds to Washington city every four years, so that it is wise to say that each quadrennial inauguration is more extraordinary than the previous one. When Jefferson was inaugurated, as has been often told, there was no procession; the President, in a homespun suit, — the best "protection" to American industry,— rode unattended on his nag to the Capitol, and hitched his horse to the palings outside. Within, he took the oath of inauguration in calm dignity, uttering an address, which, for concise, clear statement, and frank expression of great truths only yet half popularized, far exceeded the literary merits of his Declaration of Independence. After Jefferson, the government became gradually more federalized; and Jackson, fond of personal parade, made his inaugurations triumphal receptions. Harrison and Taylor, being military heroes, got the dramatic support of the military spirit. Then the inaugurations were partisan merely, down to Lincoln, when the North showed its enthusiasm. At last we have come to Grant, and to his inauguration came representatives from thirty-five millions of people. The contiguous State of Pennsylvania alone is now almost as populous as the republic of Washington, and the neighboring city of Baltimore — only one hour from the capital — is as large as all the great American cities, in 1776. Of course the inauguration was a great gathering, by physical as well as sympathetic reasons. It was an entirely hearty inauguration, the testimonial of intellect to modesty, and not, like that of Lincoln, a turn-out of drollery to see "Old Abe;" or like that of Harrison, a pantomime of "Hard Cider." I saw here the most distinguished Americans, and if Gen. Grant had been a Protestant Bishop, he could not have been spoken of with more heartfelt respect. No grisly humor attached to him; no nickname gave him fictitious popularity. He refused to let the light of military victory shine upon him, and in his unobtrusive manner he came shyly with a friend to the Senate Chamber and read his little speech, and again withdrew to duty. It is only a high plane of citizenship that can appreciate such silent character, and every eye that quietly looked upon Grant riding on the avenue was a huzza without passion. The age of hero-worship seemed to have expired, and that of business to have begun.

Did you ever go to one of the modern Sunday night preachings in a theatre? There is a mixed audience come to the worship of novelty; the gilt and mirrors and fictitious laces round the private boxes shine and shimmer, and down through the painted scenes comes a preacher with a Bible, and says: —

"Let us pray!"

So seemed to me this inauguration, all spangled with triumph, as Grant came to his people and asked strength to do his simplest and best. No rhetoric, no gesture, no "deportment," nothing of the French melodramatic, nor of the old Pagan Republic, but a revival of Jefferson, without Jefferson's idealisms. The President-elect rode to the Capitol with Gen. Rawlins, his Galena townsman. Two good nags drew his carriage. A long procession went before and behind. He subscribed to the civil forms of the occasion, bowing to the popular salutations, and his dress was plain black, without a tittle of the soldier in it. There was much music, ringing of bells, banners, and huzzas; but the intensest study was the shy little man in the carriage, without a flush on his face, but with deep, reflective marks there, made by poverty and war. When he arrived at the Capitol, he found the top, the stairs, the projections, the balustrades, the abutments of that large marble edifice as full of people as a candy capitol might be of flies. The area before the Capitol was clear, save of a few; but in the park beyond, the trees were full of clinging human fruit, and between the huge sitting-statue of Washington and the eye a silent, orderly multitude looked up to where the long façade of the

Capitol projected its three great porticoes. The middle portico was the focus of all rays of light, of music, of attention. Two long flags drooped down the central Corinthian columns, and between them burst the peal of invisible drums beaten in the rotunda. From the bases of these columns fell a temporary flight of stairs to a platform railed, and draped in colors. This was all, except the stately building reaching to the clouds, and the peering, tiptoe multitude on trees, fences, carriages, and house-tops, while amongst the mass on frail scaffolding of timber, photography, like a carrier pigeon perched, to seize the spectacle, and fly down the generations with it. Grant alighted in presence of all these, and with Senator Cragin, of New Hampshire, a gentleman, with large, baldish, florid forehead, he walked out of the view of the people, they huzzaing. The Senate was a packed mass of ladies in the galleries, and on the floor folks of distinction, amongst them the gold-fringed, sworded, cocked-hatted members of foreign legations. The new Vice-President, Colfax, made a little speech, and the retiring Vice-President, Mr. Wade, went out of what is called active life. Grant entered the Senate, with his usual shy unconsciousness, bowed to the chair, and sat awhile, suffering examination. When the time came to go before the people, he was prompt and sedate. The procession moved deliberately through the long lobby and aisle to the rotunda, where the band of music made the iron ribs of the dome overhead tingle, and, filing to the left, the President-elect walked into the daylight, descended the flight of stairs, and stood before the roaring, surging people. There were the judges in their long, black robes, to administer the oath of office; there was his wife, happiest joy of all, her love and confidence crowned in this,— poverty appeased and obscurity vindicated; there she stood amongst her relatives, by her father, and her sister's husband, with her pride too big not to beam except for tears; — there was everybody of honorable descent, talent, or station, and the air was full of glad salutations, the people saying for the moment unselfishly: —

"Hail, our accepted one!"

The music throbbed its last; the huzzas ceased; the General took the oath of office to Chief Justice Chase, with his arm and spread hand lifted. He looked up to the large presence of the Chief Justice, burnt by the fire of battle — the Judge possessed by gentler inspirations. All grave and grand allegory was depicted in their two figures, — the burning torch of the wilderness was inverted, and the slayer without a sword took the oath of peace. Together they stood, who came to these two magistracies by different roads, — the younger man by the harder and the wearier route, — one taking all the dignities of the other; and now, that the conflict of their ambition is over, how like they are in wishes, in wisdoms! The one by the study of books, the other by the study of active life, stand now upon the same results, both progressive, both conservative, and probably mutual admirers. General Grant drew forth his speech carefully, and folded it back, wetting his finger at his lip. Then he read in a quiet way, audible near by, no further; and while he did so his daughter was passed to his side, and she put her hand upon his arm as if to support him. So he stood, strengthened by childhood, looking into the multitude and pronouncing his designs, like the captain of a ship plunging out of battle into storm.

The President then rode to the White House, his official residence, at the head of the procession of firemen, soldiers, political clubs, militia, and mounted citizens. He found this building ready for his occupation, having been evacuated the previous day by the former President. That night he completed the list of his Cabinet, and next day sent it to the Senate, which, sitting with closed doors, confirmed it. The same day, or a day or two afterwards, there was a Cabinet meeting, and a new American administration had fairly commenced.

Let us now turn to England and describe the inauguration of Sir Robert Peel, the first Prime Minister elected in the reign of Queen Victoria.

When the girl Queen came to the throne, she found the Whig party in power, with Lord Melbourne Prime Minister. The Queen's childish associates and her family had all been Whigs in feeling, and, knowing little of politics, she threw herself, with all a woman's fervor, upon the Whig side. Her household was filled, according to custom, with ladies chosen from the great Whig families, and these, being almost as wily politicians as their husbands and fathers, made the Queen an enthusiast in their cause. She disliked the name of "Tory" or "Conservative," — the latter word being a liberalized form of the former, — and was particularly opposed to the leading conservative statesmen. In the enjoyment of the society of her distinguished and obliging household, the young girl seemed to have no apprehension of any violent change in her confidantes dependent upon the whim of politicians, or the exigencies of state. This was to be part of her destiny, however; for in 1839, Lord Melbourne, the Whig Prime Minister, announced in the upper house, a fact long patent, that the Whig ministry did not possess the confidence of Parliament, and that they had resigned.

But an unexpected determination of the Queen arrested the popular judgment and restored them to power. Her Majesty refused to dismiss the ladies of her household, considering them probably not politicians of any party. This, however, Sir Robert Peel made an indispensable concession ere he would undertake to form a new ministry; and the Queen, not acquiescing, and resorting to the advice of Lord John Russell, a Whig who approved her determination, the old whig ministry was reinstated. A Cabinet Council mooted the point in dispute, and agreed that the constitutional usage of changing the servants of the royal household on a change of ministry extended only to those who were members of Parliament, not to ladies. Parliament appears to have acquiesced in the ministerial version of the prerogative, being doubtless reluctant, if dissentient, to press an adverse construction on a question so personal to a girlish sovereign. It had the effect of prolonging the existence of the ministry for two years longer, though the votes of the Commons had designated its incompetence to administer the affairs of the nation. There is little doubt that, in a constitutional point of view, the Queen was wrong, and was made the instrument of the wily Whigs. Besides this, she was blunt with Sir Robert Peel, and told him that she entirely approved of the conduct of the retiring ministers. The Queen lived to regret her folly, and Peel had the satisfaction in two years more of seeing the country sustain him. The Whigs were routed, and a change of ministers became compulsory. The Queen, meantime, had been married, and, under the discipline of a husband, had learned to leave state affairs entirely to the Cabinet, so that when Sir Robert Peel came to the palace a second time, obedient to her summons, she was resigned to lose her old acquaintances of four years, from the Mistress of the Robes, who may be called the Female Prime Minister of the household, down to the Ladies of the Bedchamber.

Scarcely a word was spoken at the dinner-table, when the Queen took her last meal with her old household, and, when she was with ladies afterwards, tears and regrets broke forth with little restraint; these were natural and amiable. It was no fault of hers — nor of theirs — that their connection was made dependent on the state of political parties; the blame rested elsewhere, though the suffering was with them. Everybody pitied the young sovereign, and saw and felt the hardship; but there were many who looked forward cheerfully to an approaching time when she would know a new satisfaction in reposing upon an administration really strong, efficient, and supported by the country, and on a household composed of persons among whom she could make friends without the fear of their removal from any other cause than her wish, or their own.

Somewhat resembling the above is the scene between Mr. Duane, Secretary of the United States Treasury, and President Andrew Jackson. The latter wanted to use the former for a partisan object, and Mr. Duane would neither be used, nor would he resign, but insisted upon being dismissed by the President. The Secretary gives the following as part of the conversation Jackson had with him: —

"*President.* — 'I suppose you mean to come out against me?'

"*Secretary.* — 'Nothing is further from my thoughts; I barely desire to do what is now my duty; and to defend myself if assailed hereafter.'

"*President.* — 'You have been, all along, mistaken in your views. Here is a paper that will show you your obligations; that the executive must protect you.'

"*Secretary.* — 'I will read it, sir, if such is your wish; but I cannot anticipate a change of opinion.'

"*President.* — 'A secretary, sir, is merely an executive agent, a subordinate, and you may say so in self-defence.'

"*Secretary.* — 'In this particular case, Congress confers a discretionary power, and requires reasons if I exercise it. Surely, this contemplates responsibility on my part.'

"*President.* — 'This paper will show you that your doubts are wholly groundless.'

"*Secretary.* — 'As to the deposits, allow me, sir, to say my decision is positive. The only question is the mode of my retirement.'

"*President.* — 'My dear Mr. Duane, we must separate as friends. Far from desiring that you should sustain any injury, you know I have intended to give you the highest appointment now in my gift. You shall have the mission to Russia. I would have settled this matter before but for the delay or difficulty' (as I understood Mr. President), 'in relation to Mr. Buchanan.'

"*Secretary.* — 'I am sincerely thankful to you, sir, for your kind disposition, but I beg you to serve me in a way that will be truly pleasing. I desire no new station, and barely wish to have my present one blameless, or free from apprehension as to the future. Favor me with a written declaration of your desire that I should leave office, as I cannot carry out your views, as to this (deposits), and I will take back this letter.'

"*President.* — 'Never have I had anything that has given me more mortification than this whole business. I had not the smallest notion that we could differ.'"

Afterwards the President sent a note to Mr. Duane, which concluded with the well-known words, "I feel myself constrained to notify you, that your further services, as Secretary of the Treasury, are no longer required."

To proceed with the installation of Sir Robert Peel as Prime Minister: Parliament opened; the two leaders of the rival parties, Russell and Peel, met each other cordially in the House of Commons, and shook hands. When the Commons went up to the Lords' chamber, it was found that the Queen's speech was read by permission, as she had declined to open Parliament herself, on account of the partisan character of the speech which had been composed for her by the old Whig ministers retiring; also, perhaps, because she felt somewhat ashamed of her self-will two years before. The first votes taken in both houses showed that the Whig ministry could not work harmoniously with either body. In a few days a Whig minister in each house declared that the ministers had resigned their offices. Then the old ministers, in plain clothes, took carriages, and drove up to the Queen's palace. A great crowd stood around the gate, cheering, groaning, laughing at the retiring administration; and the dejected ministers, being formally introduced into the presence of the Queen, delivered up their seals of office. In a short time, the victorious new ministers drove up in splendid state coaches, and were cheered with the greatest enthusiasm by the crowd. They were obliged to wait until the Queen had taken an affectionate leave from the old ministers. Finally, Sir Robert Peel, the new Prime Minister, for whom the Queen had sent by the advice of his rival, was admitted to see Victoria, and she gave him her hand to kiss. The Duke of Wellington, who was to be a colleague of Peel's, was also admitted, with three or four other members of the incoming Cabinet, and they all reverently kissed the Queen's hand. The Queen and her husband then went to another apartment, and organized a formal meeting of the Privy Council. The members of the new Cabinet came in and took the oath of Privy Councillors "to advise the Queen according to the best of their cunning and discretion; to advise for the Queen's honor and the good of the public without partiality through affection, love, meed, doubt, or dread; to keep the Queen's counsel secret, to avoid corruption, to help and strengthen the execution of what shall be resolved; to withstand all persons who would attempt the contrary; and to observe, keep, and do all that a good and true councillor ought to do to his sovereign lady the Queen."

After taking the oaths, the new Cabinet took lunch with the Queen and the rest of the Privy Council, and high-bred conversation upon state topics was indulged in, every effort being made to conciliate the shy young Queen, particularly by the new Tory young ladies of the household, her ancient aversion, whom the Ministry had also introduced to her. These she was now compelled to accept for her everyday attendants and acquaintances, not mistress of her own household, though a Queen. Everybody was very stately and deferential to her nevertheless, and at last the new Cabinet withdrew masters of the state so long as the Commons should agree to leave them there. The new ladies of the household were left behind; for now the palace was their home. Immediately the Whigs vacated some sixty great offices of government, and Peel and the Tories possessed themselves of them. Sir Robert Peel, master of the situation, now took his place in the House of Commons, on the front bench, to the right of the Speaker. A new Lord Chancellor presided over the peers, and the Duke of Wellington took the ministerial bench in that house. Crowds were in attendance on all these occasions to see the ceremony of installation of a new government; the streets were full of pictures of the new Cabinet ministers, and in Parliament the late ministry began to assail the new.

Amusement for observers was afforded on the revolution in the ministry in seeing the eminent men of the country change seats on the reassembling of Parliament. The new Tory ministers had lost no seats in the process of their re-election; and they, therefore, assembled their whole number. Some of the Whigs went over and occupied the front benches of opposition; some seemed at a loss where to place themselves after having sat in the same seats for ten years, with only a short interval. One or two members, too radical to belong to any party, would not move, but sat composedly among the Tories. The next interest for strangers was in hearing the Prime Minister's statement as to how the new government meant to proceed. The Chancellor of the Exchequer arose and said he must ask a vote of twelve million five hundred thousand dollars to carry on the new government. With this large grant requested, the new government was fairly installed and thrown upon the resources of its own ability and the support of its party.

The same is the procedure at the present time. The Queen reigns; the Prime Minister rules; the House of Commons, holding the purse-strings of the monarchy, dismisses Prime Ministers at will. If the Prime Minister holds to his dangerous eminence, despite repeated warnings from the tellers of Commons, revolution is imminent. The Prime Minister may prorogue Parliament, or he may dissolve it and demand a new election, but in the end he must yield to public opinion, and the Queen, for her own safety's sake, must bid him good-by.

I have given an instance of the Queen's disagreement with a Prime Minister. To show another curious instance of the jealousy with which the Cabinet watch the Queen's movements, we may cite the incident of Victoria visiting King Louis Phillippe, of France, in 1843, as expressed in the diary of a Mr. Raikes, a bosom-friend of the Duke of Wellington: —

"I went down," says Raikes, "to Walmer Castle, and found the Duke walking with Mr. Arbuthnot on the ramparts, or, as it is called, the platform, which overlooks the sea. . . . . . After the company had departed, at ten o'clock, I sat up with the Duke and Arbuthnot till twelve o'clock talking on various topics. . . . . . I see that the government was evidently opposed to the Queen's visit to Eu, in France. It was a wily intrigue managed by Louis Phillippe, through the intervention of his daughter, the Queen of the Belgians, during her frequent visits to Windsor with King Leopold, and was hailed by him with extreme joy, as the first admission of the King of the Barricades within the pale of legitimate sovereigns. The Duke said, 'I was never let into the secret, nor did I believe the report then in circulation, till at last they sent to consult my opinion as to forming a regency during the Queen's absence. I immediately referred to precedents as the only proper guide. I told them that George I., George II. (George III. never went abroad), and George IV. had all been obliged to appoint councils of regency; that Henry III., when he met Francis I., at Andres, was then master of Calais, as also when he met Charles V., at Gravelines; so that in these instances, Calais being a part of his dominions, he hardly did more than pass his frontier, — not much more than going from one county to the next. Upon this I decided that the Queen could not quit this county without an Act of Regency. But she consulted the crown lawyers, who decided that it was not necessary, as courtiers would do.' I myself (resumes Raikes) did not believe in her going till two days before she went. Peel persisted afterwards that he had told me of it; but I knew I never heard it, and it was not a thing to have escaped me if I had."

This will be curious reading for many Americans, who suppose that a Queen is guardian of all her private movements, and is not only absolute in her own realm, but free to visit every other. Few persons would think of questioning the movements of an American President, and an English Prime Minister is also free to visit whither he will. We have never had, however, an instance of a President going abroad during his term of office, but if the Chief Magistrate would like to go to Mexico, Cuba, or Canada, for a short trip, few would object, provided he left the public business in good hands.

Quarrels between Cabinet officers are not rare in either America or England, and it sometimes takes all the shrewdness of a President to prevent his administration from falling to pieces.

During the midst of the great civil war in the United States, the Secretary of State and the Secretary of the Treasury were reported to be at variance, and in the middle of summer Washington was thrown into a ferment by the resignation of Mr. Chase, as Secretary of the Treasury. The publication, some weeks before, of the "Pomeroy Secret Circular," in the interest of Mr. Chase as a Presidential candidate, had created much talk and considerable bad feeling in the party. The President, Lincoln, however, took no part in the discussion or criticism which followed. "On the contrary," says Carpenter, the artist, "he manifested a sincere desire to preserve pleasant relations, and harmonize existing differences in the Cabinet. In proof of this, I remember," continues the same authority, "his sending one day for Judge Lewis, the Commissioner of Internal Revenue, and entering into a minute explanation of a misapprehension which he conceived the Secretary of the Treasury to be laboring under, expressing the wish that the Commissioner would mediate on his behalf with Mr. Chase."

Many sincere friends of Secretary Chase considered his resignation at this juncture unfortunate and ill-timed. The financial situation was more threatening than at any period during the war. Mr. Chase's administration of the Treasury Department, amid unparalleled difficulties, had been such as to secure the confidence and satisfaction of the masses, and his withdrawal, at such a time, was regarded as a public calamity, giving rise to the suspicion that he apprehended national insolvency. The resignation, however, had been twice tendered before. The *third* time it was accepted. During this period, Mr. Carpenter, an artist at the White House, says, "I never saw the President under so much excitement as on the day following the event. Without consultation or advice, so far as I ever could learn, he sent to the Senate, the previous afternoon, the name of Ex-Governor Tod, of Ohio, for the successorship. The nomination was not popular, and great relief was experienced the next morning when it was announced that Governor Tod had declined the position. Mr. Lincoln passed an anxious night. He received the telegram from Governor Tod declining the nomination, in the evening. Retiring, he laid awake some hours, canvassing in his mind the merits of various public men. At length he settled upon Hon. William P. Fessenden, of Maine, and soon afterwards fell asleep. The next morning he went to his office and wrote the nomination. John Hay, the Assistant Private Secretary, had taken it from the President on his way to the Capitol, when he encountered Senator Fessenden upon the threshold of the room. As Chairman of the Finance Committee, he also passed an anxious night, and called thus early to consult with the President, and offer some suggestions. After a few moments' conversation, Mr. Lincoln turned to him, with a smile, and said, "I am obliged to you, Fessenden, but the fact is, I have just sent your own name to the Senate for Secretary of the Treasury. Hay had just received the nomination from my hand as you entered." Mr. Fessenden was taken completely by surprise, and, very much agitated, protested his inability to accept the position. "The state of his health," he said, "if no other consideration, made it impossible." Mr. Lincoln would not accept the refusal as final. He very justly felt that with Mr. Fessenden's experience and known ability at the head of the Finance Committee, his acceptance would go far towards re-establishing a feeling of security. He said to him, "Fessenden, *the* LORD *has not deserted me thus far, and he is not going to now.* You must accept!"

They separated, the senator in great anxiety of mind. Throughout the day Mr. Lincoln urged almost all who called to go and see Mr. Fessenden, and press upon him the duty of accepting. Among these was a delegation of New York bankers, who, in the name of the banking community, expressed their satisfaction at the nomination. This was especially gratifying to the President, and in the strongest manner he entreated them to see Mr. Fessenden, and assure him of their support."

In England Cabinets often fall apart, because the Prime Minister is deserted by some one strong colleague whose ability or influence is necessary to conciliate the House of Commons. The defeat of a ministry in Parliament is held to be quite as disgraceful as the repudiation of an administration at the polls in this country. The defeat and retirement of Earl Grey, the chief supporter of the beneficent Reform Bill of 1832, is as affecting as the retirement of some American Presidents.

The old statesman, now in his seventy-first year, had to take leave of power. He was worn and weakened by the toils and responsibilities of office, and he was conscious of having fallen somewhat behind the time, earnest as he was in saying that the times went too fast, and not he too slow. The close of his term of power was mortifying, if not ignoble, in its character, affording but too much excitement to the taunts and vindictiveness of adversaries, — taunts and triumphs which were not spared even on this occasion. Twice he rose and murmured a few words, stopped and sank down upon his seat. The House cheered him, and he seemed unable to rise. The Duke of Wellington occupied a few minutes in presenting petitions, in order to give Lord Grey time to recover himself. When the old man rose a third time, he spoke feebly and tremulously, but he gathered strength as he proceeded, and spoke so as to interest all feelings, of friend or foe, except where overpowering prejudices hardened some hearts and minds against all reverent emotions and clear convictions. The Duke of Wellington vehemently asserted that Lord Grey had deserted his sovereign, and his review of Lord Grey's Government was little short of malignant. "The old man retired," says the historian, "amidst universal if not unmingled sympathy and respect, to enjoy the repose which his years required, in the bosom of a family by whom he was adored. He had had the last experience of civic glory." This sad departure from the glory of power is compared by Miss Martineau, in her admirable book called the "History of the Peace," to the insult which the same Earl Grey poured out upon Mr. George

Canning, when the latter was routed as Prime Minister three years before. At that time Canning sat in the House of Commons and Grey in the House of Lords, and the latter made a speech upon the demise of the former's administration, cold, hard, cutting, and cruel, so that the thought of it rankled in the victim to the last. They never spoke to each other nor met again.

The extremest personal instance we have had in America of a dispute between Presidents was in 1869, when the incoming and the outgoing Presidents not only refused to speak to each other, but would not ride to the inauguration ceremony in the same carriage, nor, in fact, in the same procession.

As an instance of violent rupture in an American Cabinet we may cite the famous contest in the administration of President Jackson, over the character of Mrs. Eaton, whose husband was a Cabinet officer. The latter had married a tavern-keeper's daughter, and the wives of his colleagues would not visit her. President Jackson sympathized with the lady, and strove in vain to raise Mrs. Eaton to the level of her political sisters. The result is humorously told by the biographer, Parton: —

"Could the Cabinet be other than an unharmonious one? It was divided into two parties upon the all-absorbing question of Mrs. Eaton's character. For Mrs. Eaton were Mr. Van Buren, Major Eaton, Mr. Barry, and the President. Against Mrs. Eaton were Mr. Ingham, Mr. Branch, Mr. Berrien, and the Vice-President. The situation of poor Eaton was most embarrassing and painful, for the opposition to his wife, being feminine, it could neither be resisted nor avenged. He was the most miserable of men, and the more the fiery President strove to right the wrongs under which he groaned, the worse his position became. The show of civility kept up between himself and the three married men in the Cabinet was at last only maintained on occasions that were strictly official. Months passed, during which he did not exchange a word with Mr. Branch, except in the presence of the President.

"After enduring this unhappy state of things for nearly a year, the President's patience was completely exhausted, and he was determined that his Cabinet should either be harmonized or dissolved. For the next fifteen months there was the semblance of harmony among the members of this ill-assorted Cabinet. The President, however, did not often consult the three gentlemen who had families. The time-honored Cabinet Councils were seldom held, and were at length discontinued. Mr. Van Buren maintained and strengthened his position, as the President's chief counsellor and friend. The President spoke of the Secretary of State by the name of 'Van,' and called him 'Matty' to his face. It was decreed that Jackson's Cabinet should be dissolved upon this question. A dissolution of the Cabinet, except at the end of a presidential term, had never before occurred in the United States, and has occurred but once since. So unexpected was this event (the general public having received no intimation of the Eatonian scandals, and not immediately discerning the connection between the Cabinet explosion and Mr. Calhoun's pamphlet), that a slight rumor of some approaching change was ridiculed in the Jackson papers, within three days of the announcement of Mr. Van Buren's resignation. It produced a prodigious sensation. At that day all official distinctions were more valued than they now are, and a Cabinet Minister was regarded as an exceedingly great man. It seemed as if the republic itself was shaken, when the great city of Washington was agitated, as all the hive is wild when the queen bee is missing. It added to the effect of the dissolution, that the leading editors would not, and the editors-in-ordinary could not, give any sufficient explanation of the event. Some vague allusions to 'Madame Pompadour' found their way into print, but the Jackson papers hurled fierce anathemas at those who gave them currency."

The English Privy Council bears the same relation to the Cabinet that the hand does to the mind, the former body having the power to do what the latter body conceives to do. It often happens that an influential Privy Councillor is a member of the Cabinet, though he has no department to control, as if, for example, Mr. A. T. Stewart, of New York, being a friend and preferred confidant of President Grant, were to go into the Cabinet while he had no office to administer. To be struck off the sovereign's list of Privy Councillors is an extreme example of the royal displeasure, and no instance of the kind has happened since 1805. The Privy Council exists six months beyond the death of one sovereign into the reign of the successor. The present large dimensions of the Privy Council would be a reason for dispensing with it in administration, if there were no other, for it is not adapted for despatch or secrecy. In the Privy Council of Victoria, are Judges, Bishops, the Speaker of the Commons, the Ambassadors, the Commander-in-Chief of the Army, the Paymaster of the forces, and many other persons. Members of the Royal Family are not sworn in as members of this body, but are merely introduced, except the brothers of the sovereign, who must take the oath. The Queen, in Privy Council, can issue proclamations binding on the subject, and in extraordinary emergencies, or, when Parliament is not sitting, may even issue orders in contravention of law. Still, in any such extreme cases, the Privy Council must seek indemnification of Parliament. The Queen, in Council, appoints the Sheriffs for England and Wales, regulates quarantine, and lays or removes embargoes; but the Cabinet is generally at the bottom of these acts. The Privy Council has considerable control over insignificant colonies, and is supposed to be absolute over the Channel islands, which lie between England and France, and are of Norman population. Whatever the sovereign can do in person, as marrying off her daughters, is done in Privy Council. The Privy Council meets once a month, or oftener, at the Queen's Palace, six members constituting a quorum, and it generally consists of the Cabinet, the Archbishop of Canterbury (who is the highest churchman in England), and the great officers of the Queen's household. Every member of the Privy Council ranks higher than a Judge or a Baronet, and one degree lower than a Knight of the Garter. When the Queen is not present this ceremonious old body is called the Lords in Council. Acts of Privy Council effecting important matters are considered in these days extraordinary and almost arbitrary, and if promulgated without the consent of the ministers would probably lead to the resignation of the Cabinet, and to a panic throughout England. It sometimes happens in America that the President and Cabinet resolve upon some momentous act, which is more properly, perhaps, the province of the legislative body.

The most important act ever agreed upon by a President and Cabinet was the Act of Emancipation, the subject of many eulogies and paintings, and of this Mr. Lincoln has left us an account in his own homely words: —

"It had got to be midsummer, 1862," he says. "Things had gone on from bad to worse until I felt that we had reached the end of our rope on the plan of operations we had been pursuing! That we had about played our last card, and must change our tactics or lose the game! I now determined upon the adoption of the Emancipation policy, and without consultation with, or the knowledge of, the Cabinet, I prepared the original draft of the proclamation, and, after much anxious thought, called a Cabinet meeting upon the subject. This Cabinet meeting took place, I think, upon a Saturday. All were present, except Mr. Blair, the Postmaster-General, who was absent at the opening of the discussion, but came in subsequently. I said to the Cabinet that I had resolved upon this step, and had not called them together to ask their advice, but to lay the subject-matter of a proclamation before them, suggestions as to which would be in order after they had heard it read.

"Various suggestions were offered. Secretary Chase wished the language stronger in reference to the arming of the blacks. Mr. Blair, after he came in, deprecated the policy, on the ground that it would cost the administration the fall elections. Nothing, however, was offered that I had not already fully anticipated and settled in my own mind, until Secretary Seward spoke. He said, in substance: 'Mr. President, I approve of the proclamation, but I question the expediency of its issue at this juncture. The depression of the public mind, consequent upon our repeated reverses, is so great that I fear the effect of so important a step. It may be viewed as the last measure of an exhausted government; a cry for help; the government stretching forth its hands to Ethiopia, instead of Ethiopia stretching forth her hands to the government.' His idea was that it would be considered our last shriek on the retreat (this was his *precise* expression). 'Now,' continued Mr. Seward, 'while I approve the measure, I suggest, sir, that you postpone its issue until you can give it to the country supported by military success, instead of issuing it, as would be the case now, upon the greatest disasters of the war.'

"The wisdom of the view of the Secretary of State struck me with very great force. It was an aspect of the case that, in all my thought upon the subject, I had entirely overlooked. The result was, that I put the draft of the proclamation aside. From time to time I added or changed a line, touching it up here and there, anxiously watching the progress of events. Well, the next news we had was of Pope's disaster at Bull Run. Things looked darker than ever. Finally, came the week of the battle of Antietam. I determined to wait no longer. The news came, I think, on Wednesday, that the advantage was on our side. I was then staying at the Soldier's Home, three miles out of Washington. Here I finished writing the second draft of the preliminary proclamation; came up on Saturday, called the Cabinet together to hear it, and it was published the following Monday.

"At the final meeting of September 20th another incident occurred in connection with Secretary Seward. I had written the important part of the proclamation in these words: 'That on the first day of January, in the year of our Lord one thousand eight hundred and sixty-three, all persons held as slaves within any State, or designated part of a State, the people whereof shall then be in rebellion against the United States, shall be then, thenceforward, and forever, free; and the executive government of the United States, including the military and naval authority thereof, will *recognize* the freedom of such persons, and will do no act, or acts, to repress such persons, or any of them, in any efforts they may make for their actual freedom.' When I finished reading this paragraph, Mr. Seward stopped me, and said, 'I think, Mr. President, that I should insert after the word "*recognize*," in that sentence, the words "*and maintain*."' I replied that I had already fully considered the import of that expression in this connection, but I had not introduced it, because it was not my way to promise what I was not entirely *sure* I could perform, and I was not prepared to say that I thought we were exactly able to 'maintain' this.

"But Seward insisted that we ought to take this ground, and the words finally went in.

"As nearly as I remember, I sat, at the time, near the head of the Cabinet table; the Secretary of the Treasury and the Secretary of War were at my right hand, the others were grouped at the left.

"Secretary Stanton, whom I usually found quite taciturn, referred to the meeting of the Buchanan Cabinet, called upon the receipt of the news that Col. Anderson had evacuated Moultrie and gone into Fort Sumter.

"'This little incident,' said Stanton, 'was the crisis of our history, — the pivot upon which everything turned. Had he remained in Fort Moultrie, a very different combination of circumstances would have arisen. The attack on Sumter, commenced by the South, united the North, and made the success of the Confederacy impossible. I shall never forget our coming together by special summons that night. Buchanan sat in his arm-chair in the corner of the room, white as a sheet, with the stump of a cigar in his mouth. The dispatches were laid before us, and so much violence ensued that he had to turn us all out of doors.'"

The Act of Emancipation will always be regarded as of Mr. Lincoln's own contrivance, assisted therein by prominent members of Congress and of his Cabinet. It was proclaimed rather as an act of war than of justice, and is one of those few great tableaux of our history which are displayed, not upon the floor of legislation, but in the secrecy of executive council. The correspondingly great act of an English Prime Minister was the Reform Bill of 1832. This was the work of Earl Grey and his Cabinet, acting in the name of King William IV., Victoria's predecessor. At the same time, Lord Brougham was Chancellor, Lord Durham was the Lord Privy Seal, and Lord Althorpe was Chancellor of the Exchequer. This bill was the English act of emancipation to several millions of English people, who had no part in their government. It rescued Parliament from the control of the landed aristocracy, and made it more the representative of the nation. It also improved the morals of the government, and corrected much of its extravagance and corruption. For twenty years the abuses in public institutions, chartered companies, the church establishment, in charitable foundations, the management of the public revenue, and crown revenues, had been a constant subject of exposure in England. It was discovered and shown that the government had not fulfilled its legitimate purposes; that it had been carried on more for the benefit of the Cabinet administrators than the community; that public services were extravagantly, unequally, or inadequately paid; that public money was squandered in the maintenance of sinecures and undeserved pensions; and that peer and commoner, their relatives and dependents, participated in the general corruption. Even the ministry of the Duke of Wellington had not been free from opprobrium. Official patronage was abused, and Cabinet ministers were found creating offices and putting their sons into them, and then abolishing the offices and receiving in lieu compensation pensions. The progress of this Reform Act was much slower and more complicated than the American act of Emancipation. The first step was to get the conservative ministry out, which was accomplished by defeating the Duke of Wellington, Prime Minister, in the House of Commons, on a motion, made from the liberal side, to examine the accounts of his civil list. The King then requested of Lord Grey to "form a government." Lord Grey replied that he would undertake this task, provided a reform bill should be made a question for Cabinet consideration. The King, who was afterward called "The Reform King," immediately consented to this proposition, and delight was exhibited over the whole nation. Only the aristocracy and the parasite supporters of their political party felt sullen at their threatened loss of power. Lord Grey, the Prime Minister, took charge of the bill in the House of Lords, and Lord John Russell, though not a Cabinet minister, presented the bill in the House of Commons. In these days of democratic triumph in England, that Reform Bill does not seem to have been a sweeping measure; but in 1831 it was considered by the aristocracy no less than revolutionary. Indeed, as Russell read the list of boroughs to be disfranchised, the members from those boroughs thought he was jesting, and interrupted him with laughter.

For seven nights the bill was bitterly debated, and nearly eighty speeches were delivered upon it; the whole country was aroused; political unions were formed over all the kingdom; vast masses of disfranchised men, like our Wide-Awake and Union Leagues, prepared to march upon London by tens of thousands to present their mammoth petitions to Parliament.

In the fullest House of Commons ever known to have divided on a vote, the ministers, with three hundred and two members voting for their bill, had still a majority of only one vote. At the next stage of the bill the ministers were defeated by a majority of eight votes; then the Tory, or Conservative, party refused to vote supplies to the ministers; the ministers, therefore, determined to resign, and waited on the King to give up their seals of office; the King refused to accept their resignations, seeing how fearfully the country was excited, and the ministers then advised him to dissolve Parliament. To this the King was loth to consent, for Parliament had scarcely yet begun the business of the session, and the average duration of an English Parliament is more than three and a half years. While the ministers were reasoning with the King to thus precipitately break up Parliament, both bodies were in session, having been up nearly all night in a state of the highest excitement.

In the House of Lords the aristocrats were even saying that the King had not the right to dissolve Parliament. Hearing this, the old monarch cried out that he would show them what he could do, and said that, if he could not have a state coach promptly, in which to proceed to Parliament, he would take a hack. Cannon boomed, after the usual habit, as the King drove rapidly to the House of Lords, where was happening the riotous scene which I have described at length in the fourth chapter of this book.

One peer, Lord Mansfield, had to be pulled down to his seat by those around him before he would stop his speech, even in the King's presence.

That day, the 22d of April, 1831, was the political crisis of the history of England in the nineteenth century.

A general election was ordered all over the country. It was attended with the extraordinary agitation which will be described in a succeeding chapter.

The reformers were successful all over the country, and in two months a new House of Commons assembled, pledged to support the new Reform Bill. For two and a half months the hot debate raged in that chamber, and then Earl Grey's ministry and the bill were sustained by three hundred and forty-five votes against two hundred and thirty-six in the opposition. The country was covulsed with joy, and the whisper now was, "What will the House of Lords do?" A member of the Cabinet, attended by a hundred Commoners, carried the bill up to the surly Lords. Only one Bishop voted for the bill; twenty-one Bishops voted against the bill. The churchmen, less liberal than the secular aristocrats, defeated the cause of reform, and the House of Lords rejected the Reform Bill by forty-one votes. The country was in gloom, and curses loud and deep were uttered against Lords temporal and Lords spiritual. Then the King prorogued Parliament, or adjourned it for a long recess, in order that the Lords might hear the growls of the people. Riots occurred all over the kingdom in the interval; then, after reassembling, the House of Commons passed the bill the second time. Again a member of the Cabinet carried the Reform Bill up to the House of obdurate aristocrats. After a long delay the bill was again defeated in the House of Peers by thirty-five votes.

Now the last desperate measure of the Cabinet was suggested, to create enough new peers to outvote the unyielding aristocrats. The King fought hard against this extreme measure, and, at last, he sent a circular letter, dated from his palace, to each of the peers. The Duke of Wellington, always an inveterate enemy of the people, accepted the suggestion of this letter, by absenting himself from the upper house when the vote was taken, and one hundred peers followed his example. The Reform Bill was finally passed, after more than two years' struggle, by both houses, and the King appointed a commission to signify his royal assent to it.

Such was the manner, and attended by such excitement, in which a little, incomplete measure of justice was forced by a Prime Minister and his Cabinet upon a weak King, an illiberal aristocracy, and a servile House of Commons; but more was accomplished than the mere passage of this act. It showed how agitation, organization, and outcry, even from the disfranchised classes, could make themselves felt in a partial and narrow government. It was the same agitation which accompanied the proclamation of the Emancipation Act in America.

In the Cabinet there are often disagreements upon matters of vital consequence to the nation. At one time Lord John Russell denounced Lord Palmerston, and compelled his retirement, for interfering in the politics of the Continent without consulting his superiors. Prime Ministers have frequently prosecuted the editors of the country for speaking harshly of them and their official acts. In former days, and even within the past twenty years, Prime Ministers were in the habit of using money to corrupt Parliament, and it was in this way that, against the will of the English people, Lord North continued himself in power during the whole of the American Revolution, bribing Parliament to endorse him, and wheedling the King.

Parliamentary corruption, under George II., had become an undisguised element in the government, and still more dangerous to civil liberty was the retention in its service of a body of hireling public writers. For these practices Sir Robert Walpole appears to have been justly reprehensible. Both Mr. Hallam and Lord John Russell admit the corruption of this minister, but the latter doubts whether his government was more so than that of the half century which preceded and that which followed it. The direct bribery of Parliament is supposed, by Mr. Hallam, to have continued to the end of the American war.

If we examine the list of American Presidents and contrast it with British Prime Ministers, we shall probably find that the latter affords the most renowned names. Many of our American Presidents have been the accidental suggestions of party conventions. An English Prime Minister must be strong enough to "form a government;" yet the American President who, next to Washington, most commands the respect of the world, was one of those very accidents, and he was ushered from obscurity to history on the shoulders of a party wherein not one man in ten thousand had ever heard his name. An English Prime Minister may be everything but obscure. Mr. Canning, one of the greatest, was even poor. But amongst English Premiers have been found poets, historians, jurists, novelists, and men of manifold acquirements; our Presidents of late years have not been remarkable either for the extent or the variety of their learning.

The English government, as influenced by "party," should be conceived of as a pedestal of bronze, whereon, according as circumstances urge, one or other party leader is uplifted; it is of little moment whether to-day Lord Derby, or to-morrow Lord John Russell, or the next day Mr. Gladstone, takes his stand thereon, the pedestal will still remain solid and unshaken. This kind of government would not suit a democracy; for who could have formed a ministry in 1861? We should have fallen into anarchy at that time had we been obliged to depend upon the influence of mere statesmen, none of whom were of the same mind. But the constitution so clearly prescribed the time and method of electing a President, that the country, or that part of it which sustained the Union, was in no doubt about whom to rally. In England, where there is such uncertainty, the King is still at the head of the nation. The King never dies, and if he lose his sanity, as has happened with some English Kings, a Regent is appointed to govern in his name.

In the thirty-eighth Congress a bill was introduced by some admirers of the English government and particularly supported by Mr. George H. Pendleton of Ohio, providing that the President's Cabinet officers might have seats in Congress, and leave to debate there. This proposition was debated with much earnestness, but in the end it proved to have no popularity.

General Garfield, one of the warmest supporters of this bill, said in the debate: —

"The British ministry is nothing more nor less than 'a committee of the House of Commons.' I believe that no nation has a ministry so susceptible to the breath of popular opinion, so readily influenced and so completely controlled by popular power, as is the ministry of Great Britain by the House of Commons. Let one vote be given against the plans of that ministry, and it is at once dissolved. It exists by the will of the House of Commons.

"It does not, therefore, become gentlemen to appeal to our ancient prejudices, so that we may not learn anything from that great and wise system of government adopted by our neighbors across the sea."

To this it was answered that what the United States needed was not quicker susceptibility to feel the breath of popular opinion; and Mr. S. S. Cox, also of Ohio, and a member of Mr. Pendleton's party, made a very humorous and vigorous speech against the movement, in which he said: —

"If the Executive, by its Cabinet, were in contact with the Legislature, the people would lose, through the aggressions of power, and the persuasions of corruption, their share of the government, and the Legislature, representative of their interests, would become the pliant instrument of the Executive. The democratic element of our institutions would be expunged, and the power which in England reached Parliament and people to corrupt and enslave would here be used for the same purpose."

Very frequently American Cabinet ministers visit Congress, in which, by rule, they have the right of access; but no particular attention is paid to them. During the trial of the Impeachment of Andrew Johnson, nearly all the Cabinet Ministers were present in the Senate, and some gave testimony. Ministers are responsible here no more than in England, where, according to the best authorities in law, ministerial responsibility, in the modern constitutional sense, cannot exist, from the fact that the law does not recognize a "ministry," but only individual advisers of the crown, whether presiding over a department or not. Impeachment is not restricted to the ministry; every high officer of state may be brought before the supreme court of law, as was the case with Warren Hastings, the Scotch Lords in 1715, and in 1746 with the four Scotch Lords Balmerino, Cromartie, Kilmarnock, and Lovat.

Thus, on the impeachment of Sir Adam Blair and some others for high treason, the House of Lords, after full deliberation, resolved to proceed on the impeachments. The opinion of Blackstone, that a Commoner cannot be impeached before the Lords, for any capital offence, is contrary to the latest resolution of the supreme tribunal.

Frequently the statesman in England, whom the King called to "form a government" is not at the head of the political party to which he belongs. An attempt was made in America, on the election of Thomas Jefferson, to set aside the public will by a shrewd bargain between the Whigs and Aaron Burr, who was an unscrupulous adherent of Mr. Jefferson. Mr. Jefferson arranged with the governors of the neighboring States to march their militia upon Washington city if this plot should be consummated.

But one of our Presidents has been assassinated, and we have never given his widow a pension. When Percival, who had been Prime Minister and Speaker of the House of Commons, was shot dead in the lobby by a lunatic, the grant of Parliament mounted up to this, — Fifty thousand pounds for the children; two thousand pounds a year to their mother, — this two thousand pounds per annum to revert to the heir on the death of the widow, to be enjoyed by him for life; and one thousand pounds a year for life to the eldest son, on his coming of age. When this grant was made, no one dreamed of the destination which awaited a part of this monstrous provision. In the shortest possible time that decency would permit, Mr. Percival's widow married again. The wife of Mr. Lincoln repeatedly petitioned Congress for a pension of five thousand dollars a year. Apprehensions, which revived the case of the widow of Percival, militated against this moderate request.

Notwithstanding the almost powerless condition of the monarch in England, the present Queen, with all her virtues, has been three times subject to attempts upon her life. Before her marriage she was annoyed by lunatics who wanted to wed her, and who stopped her horse or stole into her palace. A boy, named Oxford, fired two pistol-shots at her as she was riding near Hyde Park with her husband in 1840. Oxford was put in a lunatic asylum for twenty-seven years, and then expelled forever from British possessions. He seems never to have been a lunatic, and he ascribed his crime to inordinate vanity, probably the inspiring principle of Booth's assassination. After the Queen had been several times fired upon subsequently, Parliament passed an act punishing her persecutors with flogging as well as perpetual imprisonment amongst lunatics. President Lincoln was fired upon one night as he rode to the Soldier's Home; but the perpetrator of the act was not discovered, and news of the incident was suppressed. A deliberate attempt was also made upon the life of President Jackson. There are few sovereigns in Europe who have not been attacked, and Prime Ministers have been repeatedly mobbed. The Duke of Wellington had to nail up his windows at Apsley House to resist volleys of stones, and Lord Castlereagh, a high Cabinet officer, was driven by public execration and his own perversity to commit suicide; the nation rejoiced over his death as if a battle had been gained over a foreign enemy.

The British Cabinet holds its meetings at the Foreign Office, which corresponds to our State Department, or at the residence of the Chancellor of the Exchequer, who has an official residence close by the Houses of Parliament and the Queen's city palace, in a little lane called Downing Street, which is, in truth, the Capitol of England.

No instance is on record in recent times of an English Cabinet minister revealing the secrets of Cabinet meetings. Lord Brougham once charged this upon Lord Durham; but it proved to be a slander. It was Parliament in England which abolished slavery in the British colonies at the suggestion of the Cabinet, nearly thirty years in advance of America. The slave-trade had been abolished in 1807, and by a later statute, following the example of the United States, declared to be piracy; but the act of 1833 abolished slavery itself in the West Indies. The eight hundred thousand slaves were not at once declared free, which would have been precipitate, and tended to disorder, but their gradual emancipation was definitely prescribed. All children under six years of age, or born after August 1, 1834, were declared free! All registered slaves above six years became apprenticed laborers, divided into two classes. The term of apprenticeship of one class, namely, those employed in agriculture, expiring in 1838, and of the other class two years later. These terms of apprenticeship were anticipated by the masters setting the negroes free before the expiration of them. The most difficult question to settle with the planters was the amount of compensation to be paid to them as the price of emancipation. At first a loan of fifteen millions of pounds was thought of; but this was deemed an inadequate equivalent, and subsequently the loan was transmuted into a gift of twenty millions of pounds. It was by the proceeds of slave labor in the West India Islands that the fine future of William E. Gladstone, the present distinguished English statesman, was acquired. His father gave him five hundred thousand dollars during his lifetime, and left him much by will. He went to Parliament at the age of twenty-three, was a member of the administration at twenty-five, and at twenty-nine denounced emancipation in a speech. He has lived to become almost a radical.

We are in the habit of considering William Pitt the greatest of English ministers, but the doubtful results of his policy upon English happiness has gone far to impair his reputation. He was the statesman of a selfish period. "He had no popular sympathies," says one critic, "though he certainly would have had if the people had ever come before his eyes, or he had had that high faculty of imagination which might have brought them before the eye of his mind. To him the people were an abstraction, and he had no turn for abstractions."

A Prime Minister has, practically, no such absolute power over the Cabinet as a President, although he is generally obeyed by his colleagues. A rupture in an American Cabinet would be a public scandal, but in England a similar breach might overthrow the Prime Minister. The study of politics in any country shows that jealousy, envy, and intrigue are associated with the dispensation of power. John Bright remarked in 1868 : — " I have seen so much intrigue and ambition and selfishness and inconsistencies in the character of many statesmen, so called, that I have always been rather anxious to disclaim the title." Mr. Disraeli, once Prime Minister, avows for himself pretty much what Mr. Bright charges. He says : " The truth is, a statesman is the creature of his age, the child of circumstances, the creature of his times. A statesman is, essentially, a practical character, and when he is called upon to take office he is not to inquire what his opinions might or might not have been upon this or that subject. He is only to ascertain the needful and the beneficial, and the most feasible manner in which affairs are to be carried on. I laugh at the objections against a man, that, at a former period of his career, he advocated a policy different to his present one. All I seek to ascertain is, whether his present policy be just, necessary, expedient. Whether at the present moment he is prepared to serve his country according to its present necessities."

Frequently a British King and his Prime Minister are on ill-terms with each other. George III. upbraided Pitt bitterly, and Queen Victoria, as we have seen, disliked Sir Robert Peel for many years. Scarcely more confidence has marked some American Cabinets. Adams, Hamilton, and Jefferson, in Washington's administration, were almost enemies. Andrew Jackson was, perhaps, the most exacting master of a Cabinet that we have ever had. He ruled by prerogative almost entirely, and we have this sketch of his manner in office, in the diary of a witness : —

" Cabinet Council, the fourth of May, 1838. Present, the Secretary of State, Livingston ; of the Treasury, McLane ; of War, Cass. The Maine boundary question was under consideration. Mr. Livingston had asked me for a rule to draw up some lines upon a map. After some minutes' search I entered the President's office with a rule in my hand. The map was on the table before the President. Mr. Livingston was at his side, looking over the map with him, and making some remarks on the measure under consideration. He had just uttered the idea that its adoption would, probably, raise a clamor, when the President interrupted him with the words, ' I care nothing about clamors, sir, mark me ! I do precisely what I think just and right.' As he uttered the last, his forefinger came down perpendicularly upon the map."

The English people have looked at our form of government, simple as it seems to be, with a good deal of curiosity. One of the latest of them, the popular writer, Mr. Anthony Trollope, says of this subject: —

"It will be alleged by Americans that the introduction into Congress of the President's ministers would alter all the existing relations of the President and of Congress, and would, at once, produce that parliamentary form of government which England possesses, and which the States have chosen to avoid. Such a change would elevate Congress and depress the President.

"No doubt this is true. Such elevation, however, and such depression seemed to me to be the two things needed."

ECCLESIASTICAL EDIFICES.

1—Winchester Cathedral, England. 2—Rheims Cathedral, France. 3—Notre Dame, Paris. 4—Trinity Church, New York. 5—Interior of St. Paul's, London. 6—St. Sophia Mosque. 7—St. Peter's, Rome.

CHAPTER VII.

CHURCH AND STATE.

An account of the established church in England, and of its influence upon America. — Sketches of the church dignitaries, cathedrals, and parish institutions of the United Kingdom.

By this time we have seen the complicated character of the British government: a Queen with immense revenues, yet ruled entirely by a partisan Prime Minister and a Privy Council. But the Queen at her coronation, as has been described, is invested with a spiritual as well as a temporal sceptre. She stands at the head of the Established or Government Church of England, — a feature of national life which is comparable with nothing in this country.

Let us begin the examination of the subject of Church and State by some geographical notices.

Forty miles from London, near the mouth of the River Thames, is the old town of Canterbury, which stands upon the flat lands of the county of Kent, a snug little old-fashioned town, out of which rises the enormous bulk of a great cathedral, so high, broad, and venerable that it has been likened to a natural mountain upheaved there.

About two hundred miles north of London, in the middle of the large county of York, stands the city of York, once potential, now merely venerable, and this old town is also ridden by the towers and walls of a mighty cathedral.

These two cathedrals give the names to the two greatest dignitaries of the Established or Government Church of England. At the head of this Church is the Queen. She is its Pope, exercising nominal sovereignty, both temporal and spiritual, as the Czar of Russia is the sovereign head of the Greek Church. Below the Queen are the Archbishops of Canterbury and York, the former being known as the "Primate of all England," the latter as the "Primate of England." These two dignitaries keep their name and rank precisely as their predecessors bore them when the Roman Catholic Church was the Church of England, and a long and bitter quarrel on the score of precedence between the two primates was settled by a Pope of that day. The Archbishop of Canterbury is altogether the most powerful of these two churchmen, and far from being content to reside in the little town of Canterbury, he inhabits a palace in London, while the Bishop of London is altogether his subordinate.

He is the first peer of the realm, and has precedence over all government functionaries, and the entire clergy. In rank he comes immediately after the Princes of the Blood. He is privileged to have eight chaplains, whereas a Duke may only have six at most. His title is "His Grace and Most Reverend Father in God." He subscribes himself "By Divine Providence, Archbishop;" whereas other bishops only write "By Divine permission." When speaking of him and the Archbishop of York, the wonted form of expression employed is, "He is enthroned;" whereas the other bishops are merely said to be "installed."

The title of a Bishop is "Right Reverend Father in God," and he ranks after a Secretary of State, if the latter be a Bishop; otherwise after Marquises younger sons.

The Bishop of London is the "Dean in Ordinary" of the Chapel-royal. He nominates a sub-dean. The royal domestic chaplain is the "Clerk of the Closet;" and has the right to say grace at the Queen's table. With him officiate forty-eight other chaplains, who celebrate divine service daily in the Chapel-royal. The Queen's palace is thus kept as resonant with prayers and chantings as the Vatican at Rome. At the Chapel-royal seats are appropriated to the nobility; the service is chanted by boys three times a day, and great jealousy is exercised with regard to the admission of strangers. The Bishop of London lives in a fine residence in the fashionable part of the town, close by the Queen's palaces; he is paid fifty thousand dollars a year.

The residence of the great Archbishop of Canterbury is a quaint old brick palace, within sight of the Houses of Parliament, and on the opposite side of the river, in the district called Lambeth. It is surrounded with large grounds, and its brick towers are conspicuous above the verdure which surrounds it. For six hundred years the Archbishops of Canterbury have lived on this spot. There are twenty-five thousand volumes in the library of this palace, and its tenant, besides the fine archiepiscopal home, had an income of seventy-five thousand dollars in gold a year. In a pleasant old parish church, adjoining Lambeth Palace, several of the Archbishops of Canterbury are buried.

No information regarding the number of persons belonging to the Episcopal Church and those adhering to other religious creeds in England, is given in the latest official census books. It appears, however, from the returns of the Registrar-General, that, in the year 1861, out of a total number of one hundred and sixty-three thousand seven hundred and six marriages, one hundred and thirty thousand six hundred and ninety-seven were solemnized according to the rites of the Established Church: these figures refer only to England proper. In 1860 there were fifty-four thousand and nine churches in the United States, with property valued at one hundred and seventy-one million dollars, and church accommodation for nineteen millions of people. This shows that we have a church to about every five hundred and eighty persons. The Protestant Episcopal Church in the United States may be considered as a legitimate branch of the Established Church of England, except in the political affiliations of the latter. There are nearly two thousand two hundred Protestant Episcopal Churches in the United States; and the membership is supposed to be about eight hundred thousand; their church property was valued, in 1860, at twenty-two millions of dollars.

At the time of the Revolutionary War, there were not more than eighty clergymen of the Church of England established north of Maryland and Virginia; in the two latter States they had legal establishments of their own, but in the Northern States were supported by missionary societies in the mother country. The largest grant of land ever made to an American church has now become the famous Trinity Church Corporation of New York city; the original grant, however, was inconsiderable. The first independent Protestant Episcopal Bishops of the United States were consecrated in the old Palace of Lambeth, which we have described, and by the Archbishop of Canterbury, according to a special act of Parliament. Two of these Bishops were Philadelphians, and one represented Trinity Church, New York.

The following is a part of the ceremony, at the installation of an English Bishop, as performed at the present day, by the Archbishop of Canterbury: —

"After the Gospel and the Nicene Creed and the Sermon are ended the elected Bishop (vested with his rochet) shall be presented by two Bishops unto the Archbishop of that province (or to some other Bishop appointed by lawful commission), the Archbishop sitting in his chair, near the holy table, and the Bishops that present him saying: —

"'Most Reverend Father in God, we present unto you this godly and well-learned man to be ordained and consecrated Bishop.'

"Then shall the Archbishop demand the Queen's mandate for the consecration and cause it to be read. And the oath touching the acknowledgment of the Queen's supremacy shall be ministered to the persons elected, as it is set down before in the Form for the Ordering of Deacons. And then shall also be administered unto them the oath of due obedience to the Archbishop, as followeth: —

"*The Oath of Obedience to the Archbishop.* — 'In the name of God, I, N., chosen Bishop of the Church and See of N., do profess and promise all due reverence and obedience to the Archbishop, and to the Metropolitical Church of N., and to their successors. So help me God, through Jesus Christ.'

"Then the Archbishop and Bishops present shall lay their hands upon the head of the elected Bishop, kneeling before them upon his knees, the Archbishop saying: —

"'Receive the Holy Ghost, for the office and work of a Bishop in the Church of God, now committed unto thee by the imposition of our hands in the name of the Father, and of the Son, and of the Holy Ghost. Amen. And remember that thou stir up the grace of God which is given thee by this imposition of our hands, for God hath not given us the spirit of fear, but of power, and love, and soberness.'

"Then shall the Bishop elect put on the rest of the Episcopal habit, and, kneeling down, *Veni Creator Spiritus* shall be sung or said over him, the Archbishop beginning, and the Bishops, with others that are present, answering, by verses, as followeth: —

"'Come, Holy Ghost, our souls inspire,
And lighten with celestial fire.
Thou the anointing Spirit art,
Who dost thy sevenfold gifts impart.

"'Thy blessed Unction from above
Is comfort, life, and fire of love.
Illumine with perpetual light
The dulness of our blinded sight.

"'Anoint and cheer our soilèd face
With the abundance of thy grace.
Keep far our foes, give peace at home
Where thou art guide, no ill can come.

"'Teach us to know the Father, Son,
And thee, of both, to be but One.
That through the ages all along,
This may be our endless song:

"'Praise to thy eternal merit,
Father, Son, and Holy Spirit.'"

From the three American Bishops, apostolically consecrated as above by the English Primate, have sprung the more than forty Bishops who administer the affairs of the American Protestant Episcopal Church at the present time. The Protestant Episcopal Church in America, relieved from its association with politics, has become one of the most flourishing and popular denominations in the republic, — a fact which significantly shows the ability of any Christian church to support itself without the assistance of the temporal government.

There is an ostensible division of the territory of the United States into parishes, according to the polity of the American Episcopal Church. But this is very different from the English parish system, and also quite different from the civil parishes of Louisiana.

An English parish may be considered as an ecclesiastical territory, like the Papal State, yet, by the changes of time, it has become a temporal as well as a spiritual community. By the common law, every land-owner or lease-holder residing in a parish is a parishioner. Every parishioner has the right to take part in the parish church government, provided he fulfil the obligations which the parish imposes upon him. A meeting of parishioners constitutes a vestry, and the rector, or parson, presides over the same. The Church in England, being recognized by civil law, has power over all parishioners, whether they be Christians or Jews. The vestry, or the minister, or both, appoint church-wardens, who keep the Church in good repair and take care of its furniture. Every parish has one Church, and some have two. The assembled vestry, or the church-wardens, levy the church-rates upon all lands and houses in the parish, and these rates are recoverable at law. But no church-rates are paid upon royal property, ecclesiastical property, or by the "patron," — he who owns the parish Church and appoints the pastor. All persons must pay these church-rates, whether they belong to the Established Church or not; Jews, Dissenters, and Catholics must thus pay for the support of a Church with which they have no sympathy, perhaps, in any respect. This is one of the crying evils of the British government, and every year motion is annually made in Parliament to abolish these despotic church-rates.

Quakers, by special statute, can make the parish pay back the church-rates which have been extorted from them. In several thousand English parishes Dissenters, Jews, and Catholics make a majority in the parish vestry, and summarily reject the church-rates; in other words, they meet as part of the Church, and vote against paying any money to the Church.

Out of the popular unwillingness in England to pay rates to the support of the Church have grown many notable lawsuits, chief of which was the great Braintree case, which passed from court to court like any civil case. This suit arose on this wise: —

The parish Church of Braintree being very much out of repair, a monition issued from the Consistorial Court of London, commanding the church-wardens to summon a vestry for a specified day and hour, and ordering the parishioners then to attend, and make a church-rate. A vestry having been convened, a rate was proposed and seconded. An amendment, in effect, "that no rate be granted," was moved and seconded, and, on a show of hands, carried. The majority of the parishioners who had negatived the granting a rate, having quitted the vestry, the church-wardens in the minority continued to remain in the vestry, and reproposed and carried the necessary rate. The legality of the rate thus made was argued in the Consistorial Court of London before Dr. Lushington, who decided that the rate was invalid. From this decision an appeal was prosecuted in the Arches Court, and the Dean of Arches, reversing the decision of Dr. Lushington, held that the rate was a legal and valid church-rate.

The decision of the Arches Court was brought under the consideration of the Court of Queen's Bench upon motion for a writ of prohibition restraining the judge of the Arches Court, the church-wardens of Braintree, and all other persons, from proceeding in the matter of the rate.

The Queen's Bench decided that the rate was well made, and refused the writ of prohibition. A writ of error was brought on the judgment in prohibition, and the Court of Exchequer Chamber affirmed the decision of the Queen's Bench. Upon further appeal to the House of Lords that judgment was reversed, and it is now finally settled that the minority of the vestry have no power to bind the majority, and that a church-rate at common law can be legally imposed only by a majority of the parishioners duly convoked and assembled in vestry for that purpose.

In many respects the Church of England has been liberalized by act of Parliament. In 1854, the arrogant regulations of the two established universities were rescinded, and in 1869, Mr. Gladstone, the Prime Minister, struck a vital blow at the Irish Church, a branch of the English Church establishment. So bitterly did the Bishops and some of the peers oppose this measure in the House of Lords, that a new creation of peers was threatened. And, curiously enough, the champion of the Irish establishment, in all its uncharitableness, was a statesman of Jewish extraction, whose race had been denied civil toleration in England down to the time of Cromwell, and had been kept out of Parliament even in Mr. Disraeli's lifetime. The career of the Jews in England, where they have risen to great power, and within a few years past have been admitted to many dignities, is not the least significant thread in the liberalization of England.

A rich Jew of Amsterdam, Manasseh-ben-Israel, had previously petitioned in vain the "Long" and the "Barebones" Parliaments. Cromwell was more tolerant. He succeeded, notwithstanding the violent opposition he had to contend with, in establishing that, by his special commission, Jews might settle in England. Manasseh-ben-Israel received a pension from the Protector.

Jews, who have lived seven years in any English colony, are naturalized, *ipso jure.*

The pertinacious opposition against the admission of Jews to Parliament had partly a secret reason; it was feared that if the formulæ of religious oaths were removed opulent Mohammedans and Hindoos might succeed in buying their way to Parliament; hence, only by special resolution of either house are the words "On the true faith of a Christian" omitted in favor of Jews; the entrance to Parliament remaining still barred to Mohammedans and Hindoos.

This latter question is to the Englishman what the question of Chinese and Japanese naturalization is to us. If England could be republicanized, as many Americans suppose, the heathens in her single colony of India would outvote the entire British race.

Cromwell, whom I have referred to above, was a dissenter, and there is no ecclesiastical, nor even civil recognition of his administration kept in England.

Notwithstanding his stern and victorious Protectorate, both the man and the era of the Commonwealth are omitted from all legal documents, and many so-called historical documents of England. The reign of Charles II. is reckoned from the death of his father, the decapitated king. Thus, almost the only years, eleven, in which the English people have been classed as citizens and not as subjects, and represented at the head of the State by a hero of their own class, are swept away from their records by a fulsome and futile act of stultification. At the present day the criminal King, Charles I., is called "the martyr" in magazine articles and novels, while the body of Cromwell lies in a ditch amongst the remains of many other men as far in advance of English literary sentiment at the current time as their era is remote. And amongst a certain kind of celebrations patent still in England is that of "The Restoration," which may be described as the transition from glory to the shambles. There is not a statue of any English republican set up in London, except, perhaps, Milton. On the contrary, the meanest of the Stuarts and Hanoverians are well commemorated. It is certain that if "reform" means anything in England, it will some day make sentiment, and at Charing Cross the effigies of the regicides may be expected to stand, within our own century perhaps, on the site of their brutal executions.

The history of the dissenting denominations in Great Britain is far more vivid and interesting than that of the Established Church.

The English Reformation was unaccompanied by the stirring episodes which marked the German reformation. The English clergy in the main part quietly consented to be transferred from allegiance to the Pope to the control of the King, and the immense ecclesiastical estates with which William the Norman had invested his bishops were distributed amongst the nobles, to appease their scruples. The king himself took the lion's share. The great Abbey lands, which were almost at a stroke transferred from the Church to the State, have been mainly absorbed in the large manors of the aristocracy; some of them have found their way to colleges, schools, and charities, and others belong to the crown lands down to the present time. But the remains of the beautiful Gothic edifices, which belonged to the Catholic age of England, are objects of beauty and interest over all the kingdom, covered with green ivy, which clambers up the long shafts and traceries of their portals, and blows in and out of the rich oriel windows suspended above. The American visitor beholds them almost with superstition; for our ruins are confined to certain Indian mounds and the old stone windmill at Newport.

The English Reformation, indeed, was not at first a rebellion in doctrine, but a civil contention with the Pope. One of the best continental critics has said of it, that "the haughty sentiment of the Englishman, fancying for himself a national God of his own, a Deity providing for the affairs of other nations by the way merely, was loth to endure that a foreign prince beyond the realm should exercise any jurisdiction upon his spiritual concerns." No sooner had the King asserted his own independence than he began to persecute the dissenters from his own church most unmercifully. The history of these persecutions is intimately woven with the settlement of the United States.

By the Act of Uniformity, it was enacted that no person should thenceforth be capable of holding any ecclesiastical promotion or dignity; or of consecrating or administering the sacrament, until he should be ordained priest according to Episcopal ordination; and, with respect to all ministers who then enjoyed any ecclesiastical benefice, it directed that they should, within a certain period, openly read morning and evening service according to the Book of Common Prayer, and declare before the congregation their unfeigned assent and consent to the use of all things therein contained, upon pain of being *ipso facto* deprived of their spiritual promotion. This act is really the test-act of the English hierarchy. By its enforcement in 1662, two thousand four hundred of its most efficient and devoted ministers were deprived of all promotion.

In the year 1789, the Dissenters made an application to Parliament for the repeal of the Test and Corporation Acts, and the old spirit was at once revived. A torrent of insult and abuse was let loose upon the petitioners; a cry was raised that the Church was in danger, and a meeting was held in Manchester, "to consider of and consult about the impropriety of the application to Parliament of the Protestant Dissenters to obtain a repeal of those salutary laws, the Corporation and Test Acts, the great bulwarks and barriers for a century and upwards of our glorious Constitution in Church and State." The High Church party carried the day, and the Dissenters were defeated. Among the resolutions passed at this meeting was the following: "That the religion of the State be the religion of the magistrate, without which no society can be wisely confident of the integrity and good faith of the persons appointed to places of trust and power." This meeting was followed by the formation of a "Church and King Club," the members of which wore uniforms with a representation of the Collegiate Church engraved upon their buttons; and the standing toast at their numerous convivial meetings was, "Church and King, and down with the Rump." As a counterpoise to the operations of this club, some of the more moderate Churchmen and Dissenters, zealous reformers, resolved to form an association of their own, and hence was begun the "Manchester Constitutional Society," which soon comprised a considerable number of members.

The exclusiveness of the established clergy is sufficiently demonstrated by the fact that they do not allow the bodies of Dissenters to be interred in their church-yards. It would seem that there is no objection to the burial in such church-yards of Dissenters who have been baptized in infancy; the only service, however, allowed at the burial is that of the Church of England. A bill tending to modify this was thrown out. Statutes against blasphemy have been in force even in our century. In 1824, eleven clerks at Carlisle were sentenced to fines and imprisonment for having sold Tom Paine's works. The Lord Chancellor Eldon, in 1822, refused protection to the copyright claimed in Byron's "Cain," because the book was of a blasphemous nature. The same Lord Chancellor, in the following year, rejected the prayer of Dr. Lawrence, the celebrated physician, for protection against the infringement of copyright of his lectures, because he denied therein the immortality of the soul. Under the same system Shelley was even deprived of the guardianship of his own children, as being a blasphemer.

In the British navy there is no recognition of any other worship than that of the Established Church, and no permission even to Roman Catholic sailors to absent themselves from its habitual celebration on board ship.

In the British army the practice is somewhat more diversified. Under the general orders of the service, Roman Catholic soldiers have for some time been everywhere exempted from attending the service of the Church. In Ireland their officers resort to their chapels in company with them, in order to prevent their being tampered with by political harangues; but the precaution hardly meets the supposed necessity, as the sermons are often in Irish. There was, until recently, no similar exemption for Protestant Dissenters, probably because no rule of their religious communities in general forbids their attendance at the worship of the Establishment, but in July, 1839, an order was issued forbidding the exaction of compulsory attendance from any soldier of a persuasion other than that of the Church.

At each military home station divine service is performed by local clergymen of the Church Establishment, in England; and in Scotland, either by those of the Establishment, or of the Episcopal communion, as the regiment may be Scotch or English. Episcopalians and Roman Catholics were entitled, in Scotland, before the recent order, to repair to their respective churches. The troops stationed in the forts in Scotland are allowed the services of a Presbyterian clergyman at the public expense. Thus it would appear that the principle of the army is, a full toleration of all Dissenters, a recognition of the Established Church of Scotland, in Scotland, and of the Church of England generally.

While Ireland has been saddled with an expensive Church establishment, and the English Dissenter must pay his church-rates annually, the Scotch people, more fortunate, are permitted to have a different doctrine and organization. While King Henry VIII. and his Archbishop, Cranmer, were establishing a gorgeous Episcopacy in England, John Knox, a Scotch clergyman, who had been travelling on the Continent, returned to Edinburgh, and founded the Calvinistic Church. As Scotland was not definitely annexed to England until a comparatively recent period, it was permitted to have a separate Church establishment.

The Scotch Church is a perfect democracy, all the members being equal, none of them having power or pre-eminence of any kind over another. There is in each parish a parochial tribunal, called a Kirk session, consisting of the minister, who is always resident, and of a greater or smaller number of individuals, of whom, however, there must always be two selected as elders. The principal duty of the latter is to superintend the affairs of the poor, and to assist in visiting the sick The session interferes in certain cases of scandal, calls parties before it, and inflicts ecclesiastical penalties. But parties who consider themselves aggrieved may appeal from the decisions of Kirk session to the presbytery in which it is situated, the next highest tribunal in the Church The General Assembly, which consists partly of clerical and partly of lay members, chosen by the different presbyteries, boroughs, and universities, comprises three hundred and eighty-six members, and meets annually in May, and sits for ten days; but it has been the custom to appoint a commission, to take up and determine any matters it may have left undecided. The Assembly is honored during its sittings with the presence of the representative to the Queen, who bears the title of Lord High Commissioner. He cannot interfere in any way with its proceedings. All matters brought before the Assembly are decided, after debate, by a vote. The dissenters from the Church are very numerous, and are variously estimated as comprising from one-half to two-thirds of the entire population. The largest body is the Free Church, formed from a secession in 1843. Next is the United Presbyterian Church, recently formed from an amalgamation of several bodies of seceders, some dating as far back as 1741. The Established, the Free, and the United Presbyterian Churches may be said to divide the Scottish nation among them. In doctrine they are identical, and only differ as to the propriety of their relation to the State.

There is an Episcopal Church in Scotland which includes a large portion of the nobility and gentry, and is said to be growing. Its members were estimated, in 1863, at twenty-two thousand.

The Scottish establishment has commonly been jealous, in the extreme, of admitting either the term or the idea of regal headship. In the "Second Book of Discipline" it is stated that "it is a title falsely usurped by Antichrist, to call himself the head of the Church." Some of the English sovereigns have been enthusiastic advocates of their Church establishment, chief of whom was James I., a Scotchman.

In a controversy between some of his northern sages, when the question was "whether the practice of smoking tobacco was a sin," the respondent maintained that it was lawful to get drunk with brandy, but not to smoke; because the Holy Scripture saith, "that which proceedeth out of the mouth defileth a man, while that which entereth into it doth not defile him." King James was the oracle,— the type of his time,—its pedantry, ignorance, and superstition. This "wise fool," as Sully termed him, dedicated one of his literary performances to Jesus Christ. When James left his Scotch throne to become King of England, the Presbyterians expected that he would protect their theology in that country; the King's reply was, "No Bishops, no King."

To the English Church we owe the noble translation of the Bible, which all English-speaking denominations use; and also the beautiful prayers of the Episcopal liturgy. The English Church is entitled to high respect for its venerable character.

It is the eldest of free churches that revolted from the Catholicism of Rome, commencing in the denial of the papal supremacy by Henry VIII.; but it was not till the next reign that the theology of Protestantism really began to be introduced. Under King Henry innovations had been limited to the sovereignty of the Church and its temporalities, but under Edward VI. a new doctrinal worship was sought to be raised on the basis of the ancient religion. This was the vital commencement of the existing liturgy and ecclesiastical establishment, of which the chief founder was Archbishop Cranmer, assisted by the zealous reformers, Bishops Hooper, Ridley, and Coverdale.

The Established Church had its period of persecution in the reign of Queen Mary, and against its independence was directed that grand armada which perished in the English seas, and marked the last tableaux of the greatness of Spain. Several of the English sovereigns have not been believers in the theology of the church of which they were the head. James II. was a Catholic; William III. was a Calvinist; and Queen Victoria is said, with good reason probably, to be a believer in Spiritualism.

From the American Episcopal prayer-book have been expunged those prayers and ceremonials which refer to the connection between the Church and the State. From an English Liturgy in the Congressional library, I quote some prayers in use to this day in the English Church.

PRAYER ON THE ANNIVERSARY OF THE DEATH OF CHARLES I.

"Infatuate and defeat all the secret counsels of deceitful and wicked men against us: abate their pride, assuage their malice, and confound their devices. Strengthen the hands of our gracious Sovereign Queen Victoria, and all that are put in authority under her, with judgment and justice to cut off all such workers of iniquity as turn Religion into Rebellion, and Faith into Faction; that they may never again prevail against us, nor triumph in the ruin of the Monarchy and thy Church among us. Protect and defend our Sovereign Lady the Queen, with the whole Royal Family, from all treasons and conspiracies. Be unto her an helmet of salvation, and a strong tower of defence against the face of all her enemies; clothe them with shame and confusion, but upon Herself and her Posterity let the Crown forever flourish."

PRAYER ON THE ANNIVERSARY OF DRIVING OUT THE SON OF THE ABOVE KING CHARLES I., NAMELY, JAMES II.

"We bless thee for giving his late Majesty, King William, a safe arrival here, and for making all opposition fall before him, till he became our King and Governour. We beseech thee to protect and defend our Sovereign Queen Victoria, and all the Royal Family, from all treasons and conspiracies. Preserve her in thy faith, fear, and love; prosper her Reign with long happiness here on earth, and crown her with everlasting glory hereafter."

PRAYER ON THE ANNIVERSARY OF THE DISCOVERY OF THE GUNPOWDER PLOT.

"O God, whose name is excellent in all the earth, and thy glory above the heavens; who on this day didst miraculously preserve our Church and State from the secret contrivances and hellish malice of Popish conspirators; and on this day also didst begin to give us a mighty deliverance from the open tyranny and oppression of the same cruel and bloodthirsty enemies. We bless and adore thy glorious Majesty, as for the former, so for this late marvellous loving-kindness to our Church and Nation in the preservation of our Religion and Liberties. And we humbly pray, that the devout sense of this thy repeated mercy may renew and increase in us a spirit of love and thankfulness to thee its only Author; a spirit of peaceable submission and obedience to our gracious Sovereign Lady Queen Victoria; and a spirit of fervent zeal for our holy Religion which thou hast so wonderfully rescued, and established a blessing to us and our posterity. And this we beg for Jesus Christ his sake. Amen."

PRAYER FOR THE LORD LIEUTENANT OF IRELAND.

"Almighty God, from whom all power is derived, we humbly beseech thee to bless thy *Servant* the *Lord Lieutenant* of Ireland, and grant that *he* may use the Sword which our Sovereign *Lady* the *Queen* hath committed into his hand, with justice and mercy, according to thy blessed Will, for the protection of this People, and the true Religion established amongst us. Enlighten *him* with thy Grace, preserve *him* by thy Providence, and encompass *him* with thy Favor. Bless, we beseech thee, the whole Council; direct their consultations to the advancement of thy Glory, the good of thy Church, the honor of *her* sacred Majesty, and the safety and welfare of this kingdom: Grant this, O merciful Father, for Jesus Christ his sake, our only Saviour and Redeemer. Amen."

It is a singular fact that the English statesman, who is chiefly responsible for the breaking up of the Established Church in Ireland, has always been a rigid defender of the Established Church in England. Mr. Gladstone wrote a book upon the Church and the State, about thirty years ago, which is useful, as showing the views of an enlightened Englishman upon a subsidized religion. Of the divorce between Church and State, as practised in our country, he said: —

"We must not imagine that the present condition of the United States can afford a conclusive test of the effects which are to be generally anticipated from the absence of public religion. In the great society of nations, the customary rule will very much modify the temper even of those who depart from it. Perhaps the greatest portion of the real change will be suspended until such departure has become, or tend to become, the rule. If the day shall ever come when North America, still adhering to her present maxims and policy, shall lead the world; when in religion, in art, in science, in morals, in manners, she shall give the tone to Europe instead of receiving it from Europe; when the old civilization shall have fallen into decrepitude, and shall at a distance and feebly tread in the guiding footprints of the young one, — that day, and none earlier, will make full proof of the results of the divorce of religion from the State."

That day has quite come. The combined churches of America outnumber those of England. The religious sentiment of this country is as influential, and its missionary and charitable establishments as enterprising and complete, as the combined "establishments" of the United Kingdom.

The same distinguished statesman thus affirms the natural reliance of religion upon government, which may interest the American reader unused to seeing statesmen express themselves upon such questions: —

"It is clear that God has relations and reckonings with men in their national capacity. How are those relations to be conducted by a government which has not a religion? The law is not the act nor the voice of an individual, nor of a number of individuals as such; but it is a public instrument, proceeding from a public power, and that power the greatest upon earth; and yet, under the proposed system, that power will be without religion.

"The union is to the Church of secondary though great importance. Her foundations are on the holy hills. Her charter is legibly divine. She, if she should be excluded from the precinct of government, may still fulfil all her functions, and carry them out to perfection. Her condition would be anything rather than pitiable, should she once more occupy the position which she held before the reign of Constantine. But the State, in rejecting her, would actively violate its most solemn duty, and would, if the theory of the connection be sound, entail upon itself a curse."

The practical piety of the English Church people has never been questioned by any observer, but the subsidization of religion by the State has led to the gravest political and moral evils in England.

The dignitaries of the Church are themselves members of a great political corporation, and, as such, bound up with the parliamentary government. The hereditary aristocracy looks on the Church as its domain; it grants out, by the agency of the Cabinet, all the places in the gift of the Crown, and both in the Chapters and in the Bishops' *sees* has its members and partisans combined into one serried phalanx. The Church has consequently become a thoroughly mundane and political institution, and cannot any longer assert for itself an existence apart from the State. This is the testimony of a distinguished English critic. In the bosom of the English Church itself, there is the strife of party, its members being divided into the "high church," the "broad church," and the "low church." These parties have also been styled the "attitudinarians," the "latitudinarians," and the "platitudinarians." The distinctions between them are not, however, readily appreciable; of so subtle and dialectic cast are they, that only the initiated can rightly enter into them.

Political ballads and speeches upon the subject of the Church are as familiar in England as they are with us, upon the Lobby, the Caucus, and the Nominating Convention. Here are some instances of songs sung by the Orthodox undergraduates of Oxford University: —

"Old mother Church disdains
The vile dissenting strains
That round her ring;
She keeps her dignity,
And, scorning faction's cry,
Sings with sincerity
'God save the king.'

"Sedition is their creed;
Feigned *sheep*, but *wolves* indeed,
How can we trust?
Gunpowder Priestly would
Deluge the throne with blood,
And lay the great and good
Low in the dust.

"History, thy page unfold;
Did not their sires of old
Murder their King?
And they would overthrow
King, lords, and bishops too,
And, while they gave the blow,
Loyally sing."

The above song, it need scarcely be said, is sung to the music of "God save the King," which is the national anthem of England. The following partisan-ecclesiastic hymn is also curious, and not very respectful: —

"Peers, knights, and squires in league combined,
Protect your Good Old Mother;
For should the beldame slip her wind,
You'll ne'er see such another.

"Two hundred years and more the Dame
Has tightly held together;
Her glorious motto, 'Still the same,'
In spite of wind and weather.

"Her babes of grace, with tender care,
She feeds on dainty dishes;
And none but they have had a share
Among the loaves and fishes!"

Not only is the Church degraded by this familiar mention, but the churchmen themselves, driven into partisanship, have become the most reactionary and intolerant class of English subjects. Of the great English reforms, such as the Reform bills of 1832 and 1867, few churchmen have been supporters; they have always been the latest to hear the cry of the poor, as in the last days of the corn laws; and of the degradation of ecclesiastics into politicians, we require no better examples than were afforded us during the struggle over the Irish Church in 1869 in all the English newspapers.

At what we should call a Church Conference, a Bishop — not a dissenter — publicly wished that "Bill" Gladstone, as he elegantly called the Prime Minister, might go to what Mr. Mantilini, with regard for the feelings of his wife, called the demnition bow-wows; but the Bishop of Cork named the place more directly. The same Bishop said in the same Church conference, "The bill had yet to go through the House of Commons, where it would be licked into shape. When it went into the House of Lords he trusted it would be licked in another sense. He hoped they would lick it like a bear, and leave nothing but the bare skin, and make Mr. Gladstone a present of it to stuff and put in his museum, and, as Milton said, 'grin on it.'" The assembled clergy applauded his grace, whereupon a Mr. Puxley added, "Let them hope that their dear Queen, God bless her! would not perjure herself. Let her own good sense tell her whether it is right for her to perjure herself. It was a cowardly thing of Gladstone to take this opportunity, when a poor woman was on the throne, to confuse her, and endeavor to make her commit perjury. If Prince Albert were living he would not dare do it. The poor Queen relied on her ministers to advise her, and Gladstone, the traitor, the renegade, was one of them."

Very many of the English clergymen pay no further attention to their churches than to draw the stipend thereof, but employ curates to read the prayers and the sermons.

The "Pall Mall Gazette" said, in 1869, that in England, from London to the Land's-End, there is hardly a Bishop fit for work. The Bishop of Winchester, eighty years of age, is disabled by paralysis. The Bishop of Salisbury has broken down, both in body and mind. The Bishop of Bath and Wells is also disabled. As for the Bishop of Exeter, he is now in his ninetieth year, and for at least ten or twelve years has quite withdrawn from visitations and confirmations. Yet these prelates cannot be induced to resign.

American readers are not unaware that the rectorships of English churches are considered both political and ecclesiastical offices. In every administration there is a Lord Chancellor, who has at his disposal about seven hundred "livings" belonging to the crown, and when the clergyman of a parish dies during his term of office, the Lord Chancellor fills the place with one of his partisans or friends.

Besides the rights of presentation pertaining to the Queen, the Lord Chancellor, the Prince of Wales, the higher clergy, and the chapters, there are three thousand eight hundred and fifty peers, peeresses, baronets, parsons, gentlemen and gentlewomen, in the enjoyment of such patronage. How very intimately the Established Church is bound up with the governing class may, from this simple fact alone, be readily apprehended.

Archbishops and Bishops are nominally elected by the Deans and Chapters, but are really appointed by the Prime Minister, in the Queen's name. It is a quaint subject for an American to think of a politician distributing bishoprics. A civil commission of lay politicians, called the "Ecclesiastical Commissioners," keeps the Church straight, and watch out for its estates, sales, etc.

The British curates are a poor class of people, who are about as well paid as country preachers in America.

"Convocation" is a kind of effete ecclesiastical Parliament. A few years ago this body met, and in its two bodies, the Upper House (composed of an Archbishop and his Bishops), and the Lower House (composed of Deans, Archdeacons, Proctors, and Clergy), a book called "Essays and Reviews," indicted by free-thinking clergymen, was condemned; the proposition was entertained of reforming the Book of Common Prayer; the marriage of a man with his deceased wife's sister was laboriously discussed, and some little harmless flunkeyism was addressed to the Queen.

English rectors and ecclesiastical officers are good fox-hunters, and they amuse themselves in ways which an American clergyman would hardly pass favorably upon. But they are eminently "conservative" in all matters of opinion, and this, in England, covers multitudes of sins. Some persons may be curious to ascertain the difference between the forms and doctrines of the Roman Catholic, and the English Established Church. The liturgy of the former is in Latin; of the latter, in English. The English Church forbids the veneration of images of saints, and of the Virgin, and denies the doctrine of transubstantiation, or that the body of Christ is not actually present in the Lord's Supper. But the confessional has not been abolished in the English Church. It has simply fallen out of use, and a relic of cellbacy remains in the fellowships of the colleges. In no nation in Europe is the State so closely identified with the Church as in England, and in none apparently is the time more distant when State and Church will be divorced. The English Church Establishment extends to all its vast colonies, to India and to Canada. We have but to cross the line of the St. Lawrence to find how closely it is identified with the army, the Governor-General, and the office-holding classes.

The architecture of English churches is of amazing splendor to an American. The largest and finest of our church edifices are exceeded by the smallest English cathedrals, many of the latter having required a century to construct them.

How many have heard of Ripon Cathedral? Yet its nave is a hundred and seventy-one feet long, and ninety-seven feet wide, and its towers are one hundred and sixty-one feet high.

The Cathedral of Litchfield is three hundred and seventy-five feet long; its roof is sixty feet high; it has three spires, one of which is one hundred and eighty-three feet high.

The towers of Worcester Cathedral rise to the height of a hundred and sixty-two feet.

Gloucester Cathedral is four hundred and twenty feet long; eighty-four feet high; and its towers rise to the height of two hundred and twenty-five feet.

Westminster Cathedral, as has been recited, is four hundred and sixteen feet long; two hundred and three feet wide, and one hundred and one feet high; and St. Paul's cathedral cost nearly four millions of dollars in the time of Queen Anne.

The latter is the only great church which has been built in England in Protestant times, all the others having been Catholic property before the time of Henry VIII.

An American in England can employ his time delightfully in passing from town to town, looking at the quaint or grand churches and church-yards. There are no such fine public cemeteries in England as we possess; for we commit our dead, in all the great towns, to beautiful parks. In all England there is scarcely one noble civil cemetery like ours at Boston, Rochester, Louisville, or Cincinnati.

Canterbury, the ecclesiastical city, of which the great Archbishop is the representative, was once a rival in influence of London and Winchester. It was eclipsed, however, on the extinction of the Kingdom of Kent, by the royal cities of London and Winchester, and in spite of the great reputation of Archbishops Lanfranc and Anselm, Canterbury itself was comparatively little heard of until the murder of Becket in the cathedral (1170) lifted it at once to an equality with the most sacred shrines of Europe. St. Augustine, the former patron saint, gave place to the new martyr, and pilgrimages were made to his shrine from all parts of England, one of which was made the thread of the "Canterbury Tales," one of the earliest epic poems in the English language. At present, Canterbury contains no more than eighteen thousand people. Pleasant glimpses of life in the old town may be found in Dickens's novel of "David Copperfield." On the site of its fine cathedral stood the earliest Christian church in England. The present cathedral is one of the finest and oldest in England.

The Archbishop of Canterbury has charge of twenty other Bishops, while the Archbishop of York controls only seven. The former has for his Dean, the Bishop of London; for his Chancellor, the Bishop of Winchester; for his Vice-Chancellor, the Bishop of Lincoln; for his Precentor, the Bishop of Salisbury, and for his Chaplain, the Bishop of Winchester. He crowns the sovereign of England, while the Archbishop of York crowns the sovereign's consort.

York Cathedral, called the Minster, from the word *Monasterum*, is a magnificent old pile of magnesian limestone, finished about twenty years before the discovery of America. Its roof is a hundred feet above the floor, clear space; its nave and aisles are one hundred and four feet broad; the length of the cathedral is four hundred and eighty-six feet; its transepts are two hundred and twenty-three feet long, and ninety-four feet broad; its towers are two hundred and one feet high. There is a peal of twelve bells in its tower, one of which weighs twenty-two thousand pounds. Not many years ago a religious lunatic burnt the massive timber roof of this old cathedral, and it cost, to replace the same, three hundred and twenty-five thousand dollars. It is a singular commentary upon English society that Sir Edward Vavasour gave the stone to restore this cathedral about twenty years ago from the same quarry from which his ancestors had built it in the fourteenth century. The jurisdiction of an Archbishop is called his "Province," of a Bishop, his "See;" the latter holds his own courts. The three greatest Bishops are those of London, Durham, and Winchester. Durham is worth forty thousand dollars a year, Winchester, thirty-five thousand dollars, and Ely, twenty-seven thousand five hun ed.

The salaries of some of the London churches are appended as matters of curiosity: St. Olave, 9,455 dollars; St. Botolph, Bishop's Gate, 8,250 dollars; St. Marylebone, 6,250 dollars; St. George's, Hanover Square, 3,500 dollars.

One of the most delightful cathedrals in England is that of Winchester, which is within an hour's ride of Southampton, where many Americans disembark. It is the longest cathedral in England, namely, five hundred and sixty feet, of which three hundred and ninety feet can be seen at once, from the entrance; the nave is seventy-eight feet high, and with its aisles eighty-six feet wide; the breadth of the transepts is two hundred and eight feet, and its unfinished tower is one hundred and thirty-five feet high.

Besides their salaries, the English Bishops have charge of a great many churches, and "present" to them, often it is supposed for a consideration. The colonial Bishop of Quebec get 9,950 dollars a year; of Toronto, 6,250 dollars; Montreal, 4,000 dollars; Nova Scotia, 2,750 dollars; Newfoundland, 6,000 dollars; Jamaica, 15,000 dollars; Barbadoes, 12,500 dollars. American Episcopal Bishops seldom receive above 5,000 dollars. A Bishop has a council of his own called "the Dean and Chapter," the latter composed of Canons. A Dean gets about 5,000 dollars a year, and a Canon 2,500 dollars. Westminster Cathedral has a Dean with 10,000 dollars a year. An Archdeacon and a Rural Dean are the Bishop's judicial officers and inspectors. A church parson is called a Rector. To see something of the life of a British rector, read Mrs. Gaskell's Life of Charlotte Brontë.

The following was the Irish Church Establishment a few years ago, and it was probably not materially changed down to the time fixed for the disestablishment of the same: —

Archbishop of *Armagh with Clogher, Primate,* . . .	Salary, £12,087
Bishop of Meath, with Clonmacuoise, ...	" 4,068
" Derry and Raphoe, ...	" 8,000
" Down, Connor, and Dromore, ...	" 4,204
" Kilmore, Ardagh, and Elphin, ...	" 6,253
" Tuam, Killala, and Anchonry, ...	" 4,600
Archbishop of Dublin, with Glandelagh, and Kildare, .	" 7,786
" Ossory, Leighlin, and Ferns, ...	" 4,200
" Cashel, Emly, Waterford, and Lismore, .	" 5,000
" Cork, Cloyne, and Ross, ...	" 2,498
" Killaloe, Kilfenora, Clonfert, and Kilmacduagh,	" 3,870
" Limerick, Ardfert, and Aghadoe, ...	" 4,973

The above makes about three hundred and thirty thousand dollars a year paid to twelve bishops, or nearly enough to discharge the salaries of all principal executive officers of the government of the United States, who reside in Washington.

The total revenues of the Irish Established Church, in 1861, were nearly three millions of dollars, and there were alleged to be nearly seven hundred thousand communicants, or about fifteen members to every one hundred Roman Catholics. There were nearly as many Presbyterians in Ireland as Churchmen, and there were only three hundred and ninety-three pews in all Ireland. The latter fact shows that there must have been very little encouragement to do business in that island.

The Irish Established Church has been a scandal and an oppression almost from its beginning, and hundreds of murders and crimes have been committed in the attempts to collect tithes from the unwilling people. Although the government has done everything in its power to discourage Catholicism and promote its own Church, the latter is always in straits, and it is now about to be given up. Such is the result of mingling temporal and spiritual government.

The Roman Catholic Irish Church is under four Archbishops, of Armagh, Cashel, Dublin, and Tuam, and twenty-three Bishops. Among the whimsicalities of the English government is the support of a Catholic college, called Maynooth.

The support of the College of Maynooth was originally undertaken by the Protestant Parliament of Ireland, in the anticipation, which has since proved miserably fallacious, that a more loyal class of priests would be produced by an education at home than by a foreign one, and that a gradual mitigation in the features of Irish Romanism would be produced, when its ministers were no longer familiarized with its condition in continental countries, where it still remained the religion of the State, or was brought into contact with the revolutionary principles then so prevalent in France. "Instead of which it has been found," says Gladstone, "that the facility of education at home has opened the priesthood to a lower and less cultivated class, and one more liable to the influence of secondary motives."

In amount this grant is niggardly and unworthy. In principle it is wholly vicious; and it can hardly fail to be a thorn in the side of the State of these countries, so long as it may continue.

There are but eight Roman Catholic Bishops in the United States. I give their names and addresses below:—

Most Reverend Jos. S. Alemany, San Francisco, Cal.
" " Francis N. Blanchet, Portland, Oregon.
" " Peter R. Kenrick, St. Louis, Mo.
" " John McCloskey, New York city.
" " J. M. Odin, New Orleans, La.
" " Jno. B. Purcell, Cincinnati, Ohio,
" " Martin John Spaulding, Baltimore, Md.
" " James Duggan, Chicago Ill.

Within the past few years a strong Roman Catholic movement has taken place within the English Church, and led by Dr. Pusey and other "High Churchmen," a Ritualistic party has sprung up, with imitators in America. An infidel movement, led by Bishop Colenso, has also been one of the results of putting politicians into the pulpits. A very interesting article in the "New York Tribune" in June, 1869, gave the complete *status* of the Roman Catholic Church throughout the world.

While the breach between the Roman Catholic Church and the Protestant Churches is at present either fully as wide as it was three hundred years ago, or even wider, there are some notable exceptions. There are men and parties in several of the churches that have generally been accounted among Protestants that regard a union with Rome as practicable and desirable. Others, while not going so far, consider the difference between the Roman Catholic and the Orthodox Protestant Churches as insignificant in comparison with those which separate the Orthodox Protestants from the Rationalistic tendencies of modern times, and they, consequently, advocate a coalition of all

Christians who believe in the divinity of Jesus Christ and the inspiration of the Scriptures, against those who deny these docrines. Guizot, once Prime Minister of France, is one of the best-known representatives of this class of men, and he, at a recent meeting, expressed the opinion that Pius IX., in convoking the Council of 1869, exhibited an admirable wisdom, and that "from this assembly, perhaps, will issue the salvation of the world; for our societies are very sick; but for great evils there are great remedies." Guizot is a Protestant. In Germany, a Protestant writer, Reinhold Baumstark, has issued a pamphlet on the Council, which breathes a similar spirit, and has had a very wide circulation. But nowhere, outside the Roman Catholic Church, was there so friendly a disposition towards the Council and towards the object of its convocation, as among a part of the Ritualists of the Church of England. There is an organized party, counting such men as Dr. Pusey among its members, which is even now ready to recognize an honorary Presidency of the Pope over the entire Christian Church, and which believes that the thirty-nine articles of the Church of England can be harmonized with the decrees of the Council of Trent. This party hopes and prays for the success of the Council, and some of its members advocate the sending of representatives to Rome to stipulate the conditions of their submission. All of which is interesting reading, to say the least.

The most vigorous and prosperous denomination in America is the Episcopal Methodist, with its own Bishops. And it is a curious fact that, while John Wesley and the British Methodists have never had Bishops, the republican Methodist Church has a hierarchy. This church was a secession, or rather a revolution, from the English Established Church.

The great sepulchre of the Dissenters in England is Bunhill Fields burying-ground, where are buried Bunyan and all the great lights of the independent churches.

Church and State has several times crept into American politics, as in the contentions over the Bible in the public schools, the Anti-Catholic party of 1844, etc. Our people have been wise enough heretofore to respect the clergy in all religious questions, and to entertain a wholesome jealousy of them in politics. The latest politico-theological movement is to insert the name of the Deity in the Constitution.

CHAPTER VIII.

THE OFFICE-HOLDERS AND THE OFFICES IN AMERICA AND IN ENGLAND.

An account of the executive departments and their occupants. — A sketch of the civil service in both countries, and an account of the judiciary.

A STRANGER visiting Washington city requires no guide to show him the public offices. They stand revealed above the outlines of the straggling city, and are chiefly enormous temples in Greek and Roman architecture, perverted into the abodes of business clerks. Conspicuous amongst these buidings is the Treasury, an expensive edifice of granite, surrounded with huge monolithic columns, which stands immediately under the windows of the President's House; the Patent Office and the Post Office, which occupy an eminence in the middle of the city; the War and Navy Departments, and the head-quarters of the Commander-in-Chief, — plain brick edifices adjoining the President's House; the State Department, in the environs of the city; and the Agricultural Building, near the Potomac River.

The principal government buildings in England, corresponding to our "Departments," lie in central London, and particularly in the neighborhood of the Houses of Parliament, upon a broad street called Whitehall. Some of the very largest offices, however, connected with the government, lie in remote parts of London, and others in the suburbs. The head-quarters of the Army and Navy, the Treasury, and the Palaces make one general group, as with us. The Treasury is a vast building, but is not as imposing as our own Treasury, and in it are housed the Board of Trade, the Home Secretary, and the Privy Council. In the council-room of the Lords of the Treasury, and at the head of their table, stands to this day the empty throne of the Queen. Any account that I might give of many of these departments would be obsolete in a short time, for magnificent new edifices are now being constructed, and several of the old buildings will speedily be demolished.

These new *Public Offices* of Great Britain, now nearly completed, will make one vast edifice in Italian architecture, to contain Foreign,

Colonial, East India, and many other bureaux and departments. The site of the building cost two hundred thousand dollars, and on the structure one million dollars have already been expended. About the old offices many curious recollections cluster, some of which are associated with important episodes in American history; but it may safely be said that the earlier generations of American legislators provided for their public buildings in a more generous manner than any other people.

In the old Colonial Office, which stands in Downing Street, just off Whitehall, Nelson, England's greatest sailor, and Wellington, her greatest soldier, met the only time in their lives. They were in an anteroom waiting to get an audience with the Secretary of the Colonies; just as, during our civil war, many of our ablest generals became acquainted with each other while awaiting an audience at the War Department.

The public business of the United States, since the civil war, has outgrown even the noble dimensions of our public buildings, and new structures are loudly demanded by the heads of Executive Departments. Many persons think that the soberest of our Executive Departments, architecturally, are quite as consistent and effective as our more ambitious structures; that the Navy Department is in better taste than the Treasury, and the War Department, in its plain brick dress, is better than the great classical Patent Office.

The English government, like our own, is much cramped for room to accommodate its officials, and the India Board is driven into a hotel, just as our State Department inhabits an Orphan Asylum. We pay, at Washington, about two hundred thousand dollars a year in rents, which would suffice to construct one fine new department annually.

Many public buildings in America are constructed under contracts, and the cry is often raised that peculation occurs between the officials and the contractors; but the history of public edifices in England is marked by the same excess of appropriation over estimates. It is only in severe despotisms, such as the French and Russian Empires, where the cost of public works is unchallenged. The number of civil officials employed in Great Britain considerably exceeds the census of the same class in the United States.

The total number of officers in the United States Customs, during the administration of Washington (then called "the External Revenue"), was seven hundred and thirteen less than the present force of the New York Custom-house, and their annual compensation amounted to 439,567 dollars; the number of officers in the Internal Revenue was four hundred and ninety-three, and their compensation was 113,000 dollars; the number of officers connected with the Land Office eight, and their annual compensation 4,765 dollars; the number of Postmasters nine hundred and ninety-four, with an annual compensation of 69,900 dollars; while in all other departments of the civil establishment, including the officers at the seat of government, and in diplomatic service, there were four hundred and fourteen receiving annually a total of 445,000 dollars. These were the small beginnings of a service which now numbers more than fifty-three thousand persons, and whose annual compensation amounts to about 30,000,000 dollars.

The English census, of 1851, gave sixty-four thousand two hundred and twenty-four salaried civil functionaries, — a goodly crowd of officials, assuredly, considering the vast number of town and municipal offices, purely honorary, and the total absence of government railway functionaries, etc., with which the continent swarms. The average salary of mere clerks, in England, being paid in gold, is higher than the remuneration of the same class in the United States. In the higher offices, the salaries in England are from three hundred to five hundred per cent. greater than in our own country. Let us take the case of the judiciary in both countries.

The judicial system of England is much involved, the number and variety of courts being very great. There is an Attorney-General, as with us, but he is not a member of the Cabinet; the English have also a Solicitor-General, and a Queen's Advocate. The Attorney and Solicitor-General have seats in Parliament, and are subject to the mutations of politics. All prosecutions in England are made in the name of the Queen. An English indictment is headed, "The Queen *versus* ——— ———" In an American indictment, in a Federal Court, "The United States *versus* ——— ———" Our judicial institutions are derived almost directly from the English. We have a National series of Courts, and a series of State Courts; Courts of Equity or Chancery, and Courts of Common Law. The Supreme Court of the United States is composed of a Chief Justice, with a salary of 6,500 dollars a year, and seven Associate Justices, with 6,000 dollars a year; there is also a local Supreme Court for the District of Columbia, with extensive jurisdiction, whose Chief Justice is paid 4,500 dollars a year, and his three Associates, 4,000 dollars each;

there is a separate Orphan's Court, a separate Levy Court, and there are about sixty United States District Courts distributed over the country, each having a Judge, with not more than 4,000 dollars a year, an Attorney and a Marshal, whose fees often far exceed the salary of the Judge. The United States is divided into eight circuits, to which the Supreme Court Judges pay annual visits. The United States has been exceedingly fortunate in the character and longevity of its Chief Justices, Marshall, Taney, and Chase having been men of irreproachable lives, and wide experience in almost all the fields of human duty; each of these Chief Justices had been an active politician, and reached his place in the line of political promotion. The United States Judges hold office during life, or good behavior; they are appointed by the President. The Judges of the State and County Courts, in America, are almost all elected by the people, and frequently improper persons mount to those sacred offices on the shoulders of a partisan rabble; the basest instance of this sort on record has occurred in our own generation, when a speculator, without other acquirements than ill-gotten money, has deliberate partnership with a Judge on the bench, and dictates his own decrees of spoliation.

The United States cannot be sued by a citizen, but Congress has established a Court of Claims, consisting of five Judges, which investigates claims for money due by the Federal Government. Its decisions, however, are not always final, as they can be reversed by Congress.

It is treason to kill a superior judge, in England, where treason is not strictly limited to levying war against the State, as with us; no person has ever been convicted of treason in America, although there have been several trials on indictments for the offence.

The highest Judge of Common Law, in England, the Lord Chief Justice of the Queen's Bench, is paid 40,000 dollars a year; the Chief Justice of the Common Pleas is paid 35,000 dollars a year; the Chief Baron of the Exchequer is also a Judge, with the salary of 35,000 dollars a year; there are twelve Associate Judges, with 25,000 dollars a year, each; these fifteen Judges constitute what may be called the Supreme Court of England, and, like our Supreme Justices, they travel through the kingdom, which is divided into eight great circuits; every Judge taking his Marshal with him, and before the day of railroads the entrance of a Judge into a County seat to hold assize was made the occasion of pompous celebration; the

Lord Lieutenant and the Sheriff, with an armed band, escorting the Judge into the town.

The dignified manner of conducting law proceedings in England, tends to create a deep impression. The Judges do not sit in resplendent chambers; the localities which serve as law courts at Westminster have not an imposing aspect; but the rich official costume of the Judges, and the wigs and gowns of the Barristers are calculated to establish a salutary restraint between the Judge, the parties interested, and the public. This outward dignity is ordinarily combined with great calm and gentleness on the part of the Judge, and with an utter absence of all prejudice as against the accused, in the conduct of the proceedings. Of brow-beating on the part of the presiding Judge, and high-sounding invectives launched by the public prosecutor against the accused, there is in England no trace.

This has not always been the case, however, especially in times of political excitement and persecution. In the indictment against Sir Walter Raleigh, Sir Edward Coke began his speech for the prosecution with these words: "Thou art the lowest and most abominable traitor that has ever lived; I am at a loss for words to mark out thy viper-like treason; I will prove that never a more detestable viper lived in the world than thou. Thou art a monster; thou hast an English face, but a Spanish heart; thou viper, I thou thee, thou traitor." Coke behaved in the same way towards Essex. The name of Jeffreys, an English Judge, has become infamous through all the nations.

In the United States, the Supreme Court thereof, at Washington, is at the head of the entire Federal Judiciary system, and takes cognizance of cases arising, both in law and in equity. The English have two great and distinct systems of jurisprudence.

At the head of the Equity Courts is the Lord Chancellor, or President of the House of Lords; he is a partisan officer, and loses his place when his party goes out of power. The other Equity Judges hold their places for life; they are named as follows: the Master of the Rolls, the Lords Justices of the Court of Appeal in Chancery, two in number; the Vice-Chancellors, three in number; the Chancellor always receives a peerage. The Lord Chancellor is the best-salaried officer in England; of the fifty thousand dollars a year which he receives, twenty thousand is paid him for presiding over the House of Lords. The Master of the Rolls gets 30,000 dollars a year; the two Justices of Appeal get 30,000 dollars a year each;

and the three Vice-Chancellors 25,000 dollars a year each, or as much as the President of the United States. After fifteen years' service, or when disabled, the Judges both of Equity and Common Law receive handsome annuities. The Master of the Rolls retires upon 18,750 dollars a year; the Chief Justice of the Queen's Bench upon 19,000 dollars a year; the Lord Chancellor upon 25,000 dollars a year; the Judges of Appeal, upon 18,750 dollars a year; and the Associate Judges of the higher courts upon 17,500 dollars a year. It is these enormous annuities which make the English government so costly; but, we take the other extreme in America, and pay no pensions in any but the military services, and give our greatest officials such paltry salaries, that we may well wonder that corruption is not more general amongst them. Attached to these courts in England are numerous officers; for example, there is an Accountant-General attached to the Equity Court, who takes charge of the vast property under its control; this officer has had as much as two billions and a quarter of dollars' worth of property lodged in his charge; he is paid 15,000 dollars a year salary and keeps twenty-six clerks, several of whom receive 4,000 dollars a year. Another officer attached to the Equity Court is the Clerk of the Petty Bag, who makes out certain great writs, and is paid 3,000 dollars a year. There are also two officers called Masters in Lunacy, who look into the estates of lunatics. There are also eleven Commissioners in Lunacy, three of whom must be physicians, and three barristers, who are paid 7,500 dollars a year each, and who investigate the conduct of lunatic asylums.

In America almost every State has its own lunatic asylum, and many of the larger cities have corresponding municipal institutions. In some of the States there are salaried officers who have charge of their inspection. The government of the United States maintains one excellent insane asylum near Washington, where are placed the insane of the army and navy, and of the District of Columbia.

There is also, substantially, a Court of Bankruptcy, in England, whose Commissioners receive ten thousand dollars a year, and have plenty to do.

Imprisonment for debt is still the rule in England, although it has been abolished in almost all civilized countries. The principal London jail for debtors, in Whitecross Street, has been examined at great leisure by Mr. George Francis Train, and some other American gentlemen involuntarily residing in England. Almost every vestige of imprisonment for debt has disappeared from all the States of the

Union. After the civil war in the United States, Congress passed a bankruptcy law, fair and equitable to both debtor and creditor. The English have also a court for the relief of insolvent debtors.

We shall now consider some of the governmental departments and bureaux in both countries. Several bills have been introduced into the American Congress to establish a department of Home Affairs; but none of these propositions have been entertained.

The British Home Secretary is the great police officer of the kingdom, and has charge of the militia, prisoners, and almost all minor matters of internal government. He has police authority over the entire United Kingdom, except Ireland, which is ruled by a Lord Lieutenant. The following are the bureaux under the control of the Home Secretary: —

1. *The Police Courts establishment.* A newspaper called the "Police Gazette," is published in London twice a week, and is distributed gratuitously; it contains lists of stolen property, suspected offenders and deserters from the army and navy. Bow Street has been, for a century, the great head-quarters of the English police system; it is said to have the shrewdest police detectives in the world. The English police frequently come to America to apprehend felons, and the case of the murderer of Müller, who was seized on his arrival in New York in 1865, is still fresh in the memory of the reader. London and vicinity, like New York and vicinity, constitutes a grand police department, which is controlled by two commissioners appointed by the Home Secretary; each of the Commissioners receives six thousand dollars a year and house-rent.

The London police establishment costs about two million dollars a year, and employs about six thousand men. The Home Secretary appoints four Inspectors of Prisons, who make the tour of all the jails in England and Wales every year; they receive four thousand dollars a year and travelling expenses. There are also Directors of Prisons appointed by the Home Secretary.

2. *Inspectorships of Factories, Mines, etc.* — Labor in mills is minutely regulated by law in England; small children are forbidden to work, and the government exercises a humane fatherhood over the daughters of operatives; so in mines, children under ten years of age cannot be apprenticed to work in them, and Inspectors make the rounds of all the mines in the kingdom, and report annually upon the condition of their laborers in the collieries. There are also Inspectors of Anatomy, who see that the medical students dissect no body

which has not been obtained by fair means; it was formerly a custom in England to kill people for the sake of selling their carcasses to the medical schools.

3. *Registration Office.*—Births, marriages, and deaths are minutely and promptly registered in England, as in almost every civilized government except America. The Registrar-General takes charge of the census in England.

4. *Tithe, Copyhold, and Enclosure Commissioners.*—Tithe Commissioners arrange for the commutation of church-rates; the Enclosure Commissioners see that land and commons are kept well fenced, and they attend to drainage; they receive seventy-five thousand dollars a year, but the office will probably be abolished.

The majority of the duties entrusted to the English Home Department reside in the separate States in America, and there has always been a strong party in the republic to protest against the transfer of any of these functions to the Federal government. After the extinction of slavery, a counter-movement was developed in favor of stripping the States of many of their old privileges, and centralizing them in the Federal government. This is, perhaps, one of the leading issues in the politics of the present day; whether the States shall retain many of their former powers, or sink into mere counties, subject to the powerful sovereignty of the Federal State.

The Poor-Law Board, in England, exercises an important influence on the condition of the poor throughout the United Kingdom; the head of the Board is styled its President, and his office is considered a partisan one; he receives a salary of ten thousand dollars a year. Ireland has now a special commission of this sort. There is also a National Board of Health,—whose President receives ten thousand dollars a year,—and a Special Commissioner of Sewers.

A Metropolitan Building Commission sees that only safe houses are put up in London. This subject is entirely a matter of municipal control in America; in the larger cities, the construction of wooden buildings is now generally forbidden.

A great number of Commissions of Inquiry are appointed in England by the executive government; in America the duties which they perform are intrusted to Committees of Congress.

The American Patent Office is both a great national edifice, and a great national instrumentality. It is almost the only bureau in the executive government, which is self-supporting. The building is four hundred and six feet long, and two hundred and seventy-five feet deep. Models of all patents issued in the United States are here exhibited, in four great galleries, which are unitedly more than thirteen hundred feet long. About fifty thousand patents have been issued by this office, since 1836, while in England, not much more than half this number are recorded. In 1860, only about three thousand patents for inventions were issued in England. In the same year, four thousand eight hundred and nineteen were issued in America. The American Patent Office has an income of about two hundred and fifty thousand dollars a year. Around the building swarm a host of patent agents. It has a fine library for the use of inventors, and is one of the most unique and characteristic places of resort in the United States.

The English Patent Office is under the control of the Courts, and is not, as with us, subject to the Home or Interior Secretary. There is a museum of patents in London, which would be insignificant, except that it contains some historical models, such as Arkwright's original spinning and carding machine, Trevithick's original locomotive, Watt's beam engine, and Millar's first steam engine for ships. The South Kensington Museum may be called the English Patent Office, and grand museum of English science and art besides.

The Public Record Office, in England, is an immense establishment, — a vast fire-proof edifice in Chancery Lane, where are stored the most ancient, uninterrupted, and complete series of archives in the world; a fine reading-room is connected with the Record Office. America is sadly in need of a building of this sort, and we have no adequate organization nor place, for preserving, indexing, and making available, our colonial and historical documents. The British burned some of the best American Records in 1814. Public attention has been awakened to the necessity of collecting and preserving American documents, and all the great States in the Union now have historical societies, with libraries and officers. Mr. William H. Seward, our most distinguished Secretary of State, has taken the lead in encouraging a national taste for the collection and preservation of American antiquities.

The English government has expended more than two million dollars in Commissions of Inquiry affecting the public records.

In the chapter upon Finance, the reader will find a sketch of the Custom House and Internal Revenue offices; in the chapter on Colonies and Territories, offices in Ireland, and Consuls and Ambassadors will be described. Other subjects, affecting the relation of office-holders to offices, are distributed through the book, and can be readily found by the help of the index.

Agriculture, in England, has not been so intimate a subject of government investigation and control in the last twenty years as it formerly was. The main interests of England, at present, are her mines, her manufactures, and her commerce. While she is using every energy to preserve these, the peculiar condition of her landed classes makes agriculture a matter of individual encouragement. But in the United States, our great staples for export come from the ground, not from the mills; we have established agricultural colleges in all the larger States, subject to their control, and these are endowed munificently with national lands. A special department has been created at Washington, to exercise vigilance over our agricultural interests; to direct immigrants in the choice of lands; to import seeds, and scatter them over the country gratuitously, and to encourage the introduction of new fruits, grains, and plants.

The Commissioner of Agriculture receives about four thousand dollars a year, and has a large number of employés, entomologists, statisticians, chemists, etc.

The Agricultural Building stands over the Tiber Canal, on a high, breezy knoll, a few minutes' walk from Pennsylvania Avenue, and close by the Smithsonian Institute. It is a brick building, trimmed with brown stone, three stories high, exclusive of the attic, under a Mansard roof. It is a hundred and sixty odd feet wide, and surrounded by a farm of nearly forty acres. The building cost one hundred and forty thousand dollars, for its construction, furniture, and complete outfit, being almost the only public building that has not cost more than the sum voted for it. The terraces in front of this building are in excellent taste, and the farm is to be laid off in *arboreta*, to represent every tree capable of being adapted to our climate. Fish are also to be artificially spawned here. The building, within, is practically a museum of American cereals, fruits, birds, insects, etc.; a laboratory for the analyzation of soils, and a library. It is very interesting, and seems to be shrewdly managed.

The timber interests of the United States have not been guarded for government uses, as in England, where there are large forests, nominally belonging to the crown, which are nurseries of ship timber. The naval exigencies of the future are already agitating the minds of men of foresight, and the eastern part of the United States is almost as bare of good timber as are the British islands at present.

The Chief Clerk in the English Admiralty Office gets 5,000 dollars a year; his first class clerks receive from 3,000 dollars to 4,300 dollars a year; his third class clerks receive 1,050 dollars.

The Chief Clerk of the American Navy Department gets 2,200 dollars a year; other clerks receive from 1,800 dollars to 1,200 dollars a year. The chiefs of naval bureaux get 3,500 dollars a year.

In the British Museum, which corresponds to our Congressional Library somewhat, the salaries of attendants are from 1,500 dollars to 400 dollars. In the House of Commons, the clerks receive from 5,000 dollars to 1,250 dollars. In every large American city, the government has built an edifice for the Post Office and the Customs.

In the English Custom's Department, clerks receive from 1,500 dollars to 800 dollars. Gaugers receive from 2,500 dollars to 725 dollars. American Custom's clerks are paid from 1,800 dollars to 1,300 dollars a year. Gaugers are paid about the same sums.

In the English Exchequer, a chief clerk receives 4,500 dollars; a common clerk, from 700 dollars to 1,750 dollars. The chief clerks of the Treasury Department of the United States receive 2,200 dollars a year, and subordinate clerks from 2,000 dollars to 1,000 dollars a year.

In the English Inland Revenue, which corresponds to our Internal Revenue, clerks receive from 4,000 dollars to 650 dollars. The Commissioner of Internal Revenue, in America, gets 4,000 dollars a year, which sum is supposed to keep him pure, amidst all of the assaults of the "Whiskey Ring," and other immaculate organizations.

In the English War Department, salaries range from 4,000 dollars for first clerks, to 450 dollars for messengers. In America, salaries run from 2,500 dollars to 725 dollars. Female clerks are employed in many American Departments. They are paid from 1,200 dollars to 600 dollars a year. Copyists are paid ten cents per hundred words.

Clerks in the English Treasury and War Office have seven weeks' holidays during the year; in the Post Office a month; in the Home Office about eight weeks; in the Customs near five weeks.

In the United States civil service, twenty-eight days is the average holiday; we give Jack too much work, and little play, and have, therefore, a good many dull boys.

American clerks take their stations at nine o'clock, and quit them either at three or four o'clock. No English clerk, in the civil service, begins work before ten o'clock, and the majority do not begin work until twelve o'clock; they quit work either at five or seven o'clock.

Little pains are taken, in America, to provide the public with information upon the statistics, and other concerns of government. Every two years a great "Blue Book" is published, with the name and the salary of each official, and we take a decennial census at considerable expense; the last of which filled nearly three thousand pages, and comprised five bulky volumes. The government publishes no "Moniteur," like France, nor "Gazette," like England, but advertises its wants in the daily newspapers at Washington and other cities.

The English keep a State Paper Office; this has been for three centuries a depository of the official correspondence of the country; all the great state papers are classified and examined by clerks in this department. The State Paper Office has been combined with the Public Records Office in London.

The United States government has all the facilities for advertising its own sales, and proposals for purchase, either in the "Globe," which prints the debates of Congress, or from the government printing office; but these advertisements are generally used as party patronage, and distributed amongst the stipendiary press.

The "London Gazette" is the authorized medium for making known to the public state intelligence, orders in council, etc. A full series of the "Gazette," from its commencement, may be found in the Library of Congress, at Washington.

In this "Gazette" are inserted all Royal Proclamations, Acts of Council, Diplomatic Dispatches, Laws signed by the Queen, Appointments under the State, and Court Decrees. Copies of this important paper are transmitted to all friendly governments.

Every year the "Gazette" office publishes a book of state intelligence, well indexed, costing one dollar and a quarter. The English monarchy is popularly supposed to spend a great deal of money in corrupting the journals of its own and of rival countries.

The Stationery Office of England is almost as old as the United States government. It purchases wholesale all stationery, and this single duty involves a national outlay of nearly one million and a half of dollars. There are two leading officers of this department: *Storekeeper*, with the salary of two thousand dollars a year, and twenty-four clerks, three examiners of paper, and about twenty warehousemen; *Comptroller*, four thousand five hundred dollars a year's salary, and a residence.

The Treasury Department controls the Stationery Office. Stationery in America is given out by separate officers in each of the Executive Departments, and much fraud and scandal attend the purchase and distribution of it. We should have a Stationery Office. In England the government keeps its own mill to make bank-note paper. We are about to adopt the same system.

The English Board of Trade and Plantations, which formerly was of great consequence, and which regulated many of our American Colonies, is now entrusted with a part of the inspection of railways, with the collection of statistics upon trade, and with many other matters which apparently belong to different departments; for instance, it has charge of the

Corn Returns' Office. — This bureau takes charge of the statistics of the price of corn, — corn, in England, being a word used to signify grain.

Registry of Designs' Office. — Designs, or patterns as we would call them, being of great consequence in connection with English manufactures, this office registers original designs, charges a fee, and gives a copyright upon the design of from nine months to three years.

Joint Stock Companies' Registration Office. — The English have found, as we shall find, that stock companies must be watched, and, therefore, they compel the registration of every corporate company, its designs, and its members, and also compel the payment of a fee for registration. These registry papers are open to inspection on the payment of a fee.

Department of Science and Arts. — This subject will be considered more particularly in the next chapter.

Coal Whippers' Office. — An immense amount of coal is discharged from vessels at the wharves of London. The laborers who unload the coals were required to be registered; for this purpose the Board of Trade appointed three commissioners, the city of London one, and the Coal Factory's Society one. Only registered persons were employed, and a fee was charged to pay the expense of this coal whippers' commission.

Merchant-Seamen's Registration. — English seamen must register, procure a ticket, and generally pay a fee.

The Trinity House. — There are three institutions bearing this name in England, one at Hull, one at Newcastle, and one in London. The principal one is in London, and its revenues amount to one million and a half of dollars a year.

Trinity House has charge of the commercial navy of the country, the keeping of light-houses, pilots, navigation laws, and the regulations about ballastage. This institution shows how thoroughly republican is the seamanship of England. The seamen have made England the great nation that she is, — the greatest nation in the modern world. In America we have of late paid little national attention to our mariners.

The London Trinity House is a corporation composed of thirty-one elder brethren and a limited number of younger brethren, selected by ballot from the masters of British vessels. This corporation is thoroughly republican, and its constitution shows that the vital concerns of seamanship require the actual administration of the working seamen. This corporation also gives relief to worn-out seamen, and its establishment in Hull relieves upward of a thousand persons a year. Trinity House is subject to the Board of Trade in most matters.

We have permitted all the affairs of our merchant marine to run down. All the strong specific legislation is for the manufacturers.

The English Treasury is the chief department of the English government; and, since the civil war in America, the Treasury is the chief department of the American government. In the chapter on Finance we shall consider this department in both governments.

The English Post Office, which now forms one of the great public departments, was not established till the seventeenth century. In 1649 a weekly delivery of letters to all parts of the kingdom was instituted, and in 1657 the office was placed upon nearly the present plan. In 1784 mail-coaches were first run, and the sluggish pace of the post was greatly accelerated. Gradual improvements and changes continued to be made till 1840, when the new system of a uniform rate of postage and the principle of prepayment was brought into operation. The history of the English Post Office is very interesting, and is fully related by Harriet Martineau. Here are some of the main items in it: —

Coleridge, the poet, when a young man, was walking through the Lake District, in the North of England, when he one day saw the postman deliver a letter to a woman at a cottage door. The woman turned it over and examined it, and then returned it, saying that she could not pay the postage, which was a shilling. Hearing that the letter was from her brother, Coleridge paid the postage, in spite of the manifest unwillingness of the woman. As soon as the postman was out of sight, she showed Coleridge how his money had been wasted, as far as she was concerned. The sheet was blank. There was an agreement between her brother and herself that, as long as all went well with him, he should send a blank sheet in this way once a quarter; and she thus had tidings of him without expense of postage. Most people would have remembered this incident as a curious story to tell; but there was one mind which wakened up at once to a sense of the significance of the fact.

It struck Mr. Rowland Hill that there must be something wrong in a system which drove a brother and sister to cheating, in order to gratify their desire to hear of one another's welfare. He immediately proposed a reform in the whole postal system. Mr. Hill proposed to reduce the cost of all letters not exceeding half an ounce in weight to a penny. The shock to the Post Office of such an audacious proposal was extreme.

"He kept the idea in circulation, however, and at last it was adopted. No one has done so much as Mr. Rowland Hill in our time in drawing closer the domestic ties of the nation, and extending the influences of home over the wide-spreading, stirring, and most diverse interests of social life in our own country. And from our own country the blessing is reaching many more, and cheap postage is becoming established in one nation after another."

Benjamin Franklin is generally alleged to have been the founder of the American Post Office, but since the adoption of railways we have made our main strides in republicanizing the Post Office, which, however, does not pay its expenses to this day, but leaves a large deficit to be made by Congress. We have adopted many good ideas from the English, such as maintaining a money-order system, postal cars, and a free delivery by carriers. No Post Office is better administered than ours, except with regard to extravagance The English have a pneumatic despatch for mails in great cities.

Letters are inviolate in England, and cannot be opened except by the Secretaries of State and the Lord Lieutenant of Ireland. Between 1843 and 1853 only six letters were opened. We are even more particular in America, although we have seized telegraphic despatches in two or three instances. There is a movement now in all the nations to make the telegraph adjunct to the Post Office. Mr. E. B. Washburne is at the head of this movement in America.

The English Post Office is subordinate to the Treasury; the leading officers of the Postal Department receive ten thousand dollars, six thousand dollars, and four thousand dollars a year. The Postmaster-

General receives twelve thousand five hundred dollars a year. Nearly twenty thousand persons are connected with the English postal service, and their combined salaries exceed three millions of dollars.

The mails leave London twice a day for all parts of the kingdom and for the continent, except for the small islands which lie near by the English coast. Through the postal-order system of England fifty millions of dollars are transmitted every year. The Franking privilege covers petitions to Parliament, and letters between the various departments. One feature of the English postal system is that of stamped newspapers, which go through the Post Office several times for the price of the original stamp. The *poste restante* of Europe is equivalent to our general delivery window.

The postage collections in the United States on the correspondence exchanged with Great Britain and countries on the continent of Europe, amounted to $1,090,244.03 in 1868, and the postages collected in Europe amounted to $616,223.73. The excess of collections in the United States was $474,020.30.

The estimated amount of United States postage upon the letter mails exchanged with Great Britain and the continent of Europe was $793,700.64; in the same year with Canada and the British North American Provinces, $176,179.55; and with the West Indies, Brazil, Mexico, Japan, and China, and Central and South America, $128,098.87; making in all $1,097,979.06.

The number of letters exchanged with foreign countries (exclusive of the British North American Provinces) was 11,128,532; of which 5,900,307 were from, and 5,228,225 received in the United States.

The postal franking system is the great cause of the annual deficit in the American Post Office. The Postmaster-General in 1868 said: —

"I have had occasion frequently during the past year to call attention of members of Congress to the use of their names in sending mailable matter free under a fac-simile frank. Three dollars will buy the fac-simile frank of any member of Congress, and the use of it by claim agents and business men in cities in sending books, periodicals, letters, and business circulars, defrauds the department out of immense sums of money. It is estimated that the loss of the department, by this species of abuse of the franking privilege, has amounted to from one million to one million and a half of dollars during the past year."

The crowning shame of America is her debauched and partisan

civil service, which has been almost entirely reformed in England, where it had to make a long struggle before it could be purified and organized upon a business and non-partisan basis.

The mismanagement of the Crimean war gave rise to this now well-known agitation for administrative reform, which resulted in the partial opening up of the appointments in some, and the complete opening in others of the public departments. Mr. Layard was the first to raise this important matter. Mr. Gladstone, "heartily wished him God-speed," and said that he saw with unfeigned satisfaction that the state of public feeling was likely to take the direction given to it by Mr. Layard. He believed, in contradistinction to the popular opinion, that the system of patronage was the weakness, not the strength, of the executive. What he wanted was a change in the basis of the whole system of the civil service; perfectly free competitions for admission by the test of examination, and subsequent promotion by merit and efficiency alone. The public, he held, had a right to be served by the best men it could get for the price it offered. And he contended, not only that the existing system did not give the best men, but that it created a vast mass of collateral evils connected with the dispensation of patronage, which kept a large class of men in a state of expectancy wasting their lives in solicitation. How truly can we say this of our American civil service at present!

The term "civil service" is a phrase popularly used for general convenience, and represents the large body of men by whose labors the executive business of the country is carried on. It has been officially stated that the civil service of England includes more than fifty thousand officers, which would make a class more than twice as numerous as the clergy. Deducting, however, four thousand as office-keepers, messengers, etc., seventeen thousand as inferior revenue officers, postmen, etc., and fifteen thousand artificers and laborers employed in the various government dock-yards, we may calculate that there are, in round numbers, seventeen thousand civil servants of the higher class who are engaged in the various public offices of the United Kingdom. The civil service was in a condition quite as bad as ours at present when the reformers took hold of it.

For many years the unsatisfactory condition of the permanent civil service had attracted considerable attention, as well out of Parliament as in, until, in 1853, a commissioner was appointed with a view to the improvement and reorganization of that body. In the same year Sir Stafford Northcote and Sir Charles Trevelyan addressed a report to the Lords of the Treasury, stating their opinion that "the right of competing for appointment in the civil service should be open to all persons of a given age, subject only to the necessity of giving satisfactory references to persons able to speak to their moral character." The Queen's speech, at the opening of Parliament in 1854, contained the following passage: "The establishment required for the conduct of the civil service, and the arrangements bearing upon its condition, have recently been under review, and I shall direct a plan to be laid before you which will have for its object to improve the system of admission, and thereby to increase the efficiency of the service." No such plan was laid before Parliament, but on the 21st May, 1855, her Majesty issued an order in council, appointing commissioners for conducting the examination of young men proposed to be appointed to any of the junior situations in the civil establishments, and authorizing them to give certificates of qualification before such young men entered on their duties. After due consultation with the heads of the several departments of the civil service, a scheme of examinations was prepared, and the first examination took place on the 30th June, 1855, since which time examinations have been held nearly every week. The principle of examination has not only been twice affirmed by resolutions of the House of Commons, but has been formally sanctioned by two acts of Parliament.

Government situations in England are ordinarily obtained in this way. A member of Parliament, whose political opinions coincide with those held by the party in power, is asked by an influential constituent to get a place in government office for a relation or a friend. The member of Parliament applies to the parliamentary Secretary of the Treasury, who has the distribution of patronage, or to the political head of some department. The Secretary of the Treasury, or the head of the department, willing to gratify a parliamentary constituent, accedes to the request, and presents the member's protegé with a nomination to one of the junior clerkships in his gift. The person nominated does not, however, as a matter of course, enter the public service, for no interest, however powerful, can confirm an appointment unless the nominee is able to obtain a certificate of fitness from the Commissioners of the Civil Service appointed by the crown.

Before granting their certificate the Commissioners ascertain: —

First. That the nominee is within the limits of the age prescribed for the department to which he desires to be admitted.

Secondly. That he is free from any physical defect or disease which would be likely to interfere with the proper discharge of his duties.

Thirdly. That his character is such as to qualify him for public employment.

Fourthly. That he possesses the necessary knowledge and ability for the proper discharge of his official duties.

Great pains are taken in England to see that a clerk has been honest in his previous career, and this form of letter is always addressed to his previous employers: —

"CIVIL SERVICE COMMISSION, S. W.

"SIR: — Mr. ——, a candidate for the junior situation of ——, having stated that he was employed by ——, I am directed by the Civil Service Commissioners, to request that you oblige them by filling up and returning to me, in the enclosed envelope, the 'statement' hereto annexed. The postage need not be paid. I am to add that your answer will, if you desire it, be regarded as confidential, and that the word 'confidential' should in that case be written on the envelope. The favor of an early answer is requested.

"I am, sir, your obedient servant,

"——

"QUESTIONS.

"1st. Are you related to the candidate? If so, what is the relationship?

"2d. Are you well acquainted with the candidate?

"3d. Will you have the goodness to mention the dates of his entering and quitting your employment, and his reasons for leaving?

"4th. How long have you known him?

"5th. Is he strictly honest and sober, intelligent and diligent?

"6th. Do you believe him to be free from pecuniary embarrassment?

"7th. What do you know of his education and acquirements?

"8th. Has he ever been in the service of the government? and if so, in what situation?

"9th. What has been the state of his health since you have known him?

"10th. Are you aware of any circumstance tending to disqualify him for the situation which he now seeks?"

This reformed civil service has been one of the greatest blessings that was ever conferred upon England.

In 1865, it appeared that the total number of nominations since the commencement of the civil service in May, 1855, amounted to twenty-nine thousand seven hundred and sixty-three. The number of competitors for the superior situations, in 1864, was seven hundred and ninety for two hundred and fifty-one places, out of which five hundred and seventeen received nominations. Of the remaining two hundred and seventy-three, two hundred and forty-one fell below the standard of competence, nineteen failed in respect of age, five in respect of health, and eight in respect of character. For the inferior offices, — letter carriers, etc., — out of two thousand three hundred and eighty-four, one thousand nine hundred and thirty-one certificates were granted.

The practice of renominating unsuccessful candidates within a short time after their failure having led to abuses, the Lords of the Treasury have fixed three months as the shortest period after which they will grant a second nomination, and in the Admiralty and War Office an interval of six months is required. A third chance is rarely offered to the unsuccessful candidate.

We have no such examinations in the United States, but appointments depend upon favor.

The most important competitive examination that has taken place in England, since the establishment of the commission, was that for eight vacancies in the office of the Secretary of State for India. It was thrown open to all comers; and, out of seven hundred and eighty-nine applicants, no less than three hundred and thirty-nine actually presented themselves for examination at Willis' rooms, London, on the 18th of January, 1859. The examination lasted three days, six hours each day, interrupted only by a break for refreshment, and on the 11th of February the names of the successful competitors were declared. Seven of the successful candidates offered themselves for a voluntary examination in extra subjects, and obtained honorary additions to their certificates for proficiency in Greek, Latin, German, French, Political Economy, Euclid, Algebra, etc. The total of marks was one thousand five hundred and fifty, but the highest only reached one thousand one hundred and thirty, while the lowest was eighty-four. Of the successful competitors one was a sub-editor of a newspaper, one a school-assistant, two were school-masters, and three clerks.

In contradistinction to the above examination take the testimony of Mr. S. M. Clarke, who filled a high government place in America. He says: —

"I was referred for examination in August, 1856, to a Board of Examiners appointed by the Secretary of the Treasury, consisting of Mr. Rodman, then Chief Clerk, and Major Barker and Mr. McKean, two prominent fourth-class clerks. The 'full particulars of such examination' were as follows: I was instructed by the then Secretary to appear before this board at a given time and place to be examined. I put in my appearance at the time and place stated in my instructions. Major Barker commenced the 'examination' by saying, 'You are from New York, I believe, Mr. Clarke?' I replied that I was. He then commenced a detailed narrative of his first visit to New York, and gave me an interesting and graphic account of the disturbance created in his mind by the 'noise and confusion' of the great city. The delivery of this narrative occupied, as nearly as I remember, about half an hour. I listened to it attentively, endeavoring to discover some point in his discourse which had reference to my 'examination.' I failed to discover any relevancy, and therefore made no reply. At the close of his narrative, without any further question, he said to his associate examiners, 'Well, gentlemen, I presume there is no doubt but that Mr. Clarke is qualified.' Whereupon they all signed the certificate, and my 'examination' closed."

All American statesmen have borne testimony against the custom of appointing partisan clerks.

Mr. Nathan Sargent, Commissioner of Customs, tells this little incident of his own career: —

"General Taylor, through Mr. Clayton, Secretary of State, first tendered me the office of Secretary of the Mexican Commissioners; which I declined on the ground that I did not understand the Spanish language. General Taylor was pleased to say that I was the first man he ever knew who declined an office because he did not consider himself fit for it; and then offered me the office of Recorder of the Land Office, which I should have declined if I could without giving offence."

To General and President Andrew Jackson and his vindictive nature we owe the demoralized condition of the civil service. He was the first President to turn everybody out of office who would not become his personal follower and *clacquer*. His best friends protested against it in vain, amongst them Major Lewis Jackson, his relative, who said: —

"I embrace this occasion to enter my solemn protest against it, — not on account of my office, but because I hold it to be fraught with the greatest mischief to the country. If ever it should be carried out in extenso, the days of the republic will, in my opinion, have been numbered; for, whenever the impression shall become general that the government is only valuable on account of its offices, the great and paramount interest of the country will be lost sight of, and the government itself ultimately destroyed. This, at least, is the honest conviction of my mind with regard to these novel doctrines of rotation in office."

After Jackson began his partisan and personal proscription, the city of Washington was seized with panic, and all enterprise there declined. The system of proscription is still in vogue, and Washington energy continues to be depressed.

"Thirty-three houses," said a newspaper, just after Jackson's proscription began, "which were to have been built this year, we learn, have been stopped in consequence of the unsettled and uncertain state of things now existing here; and the merchant cannot sell his goods or collect his debts from the same cause. We have never known the city to be in a state like this before, though we have known it for many years. The individual distress, too, produced in many cases by the removal of the destitute officers, is harrowing and painful. Many of the oldest and most respectable citizens of Washington, those who have adhered to its fortunes through all their vicissitudes, who have 'grown with its growth and strengthened with its strength,' have been cast off to make room for strangers, who feel no interest in the prosperity of our infant metropolis, and who care not whether it advances or retrogrades."

In spirited words the virtuous Josiah Quincy condemned this quadrennial revolution in the public departments. Speaking of a dead office-holder, he said: —

"The poor man shall hardly be dead, he shall not be cold long, before the corpse is in the coffin, the mail shall be crowded to repletion with letters, and certificates, and recommendations, and representations, and every species of standing sycophantic solicitations, by which obtrusive mendicity seeks charity, or invites compassion. Why, sir, we hear the clamors of the craving animals at the treasury trough, here in this Capitol. Such running, such jostling, such wriggling, such clambering over one another's backs, such squealing because the tub is so narrow, and the company is so crowded."

Henry Clay bore similar testimony to the system of rotation in office: —

"It is a detestable system, drawn from the worst periods of the Roman republic, and if it were to be perpetuated — if the offices, honors and dignities of the people were to be put up to a scramble, and to be decided by the results of every presidential election, — our government and institutions becoming intolerable, would finally end in a despotism as inexorable as that of Constantinople."

A movement is now on foot, at the head of which is Mr. Jenckes, of Rhode Island, to reform the civil service, in America; but this has been attacked, by Mr. Woodward, Democrat, of Pennsylvania, and by General Logan, Republican, of Illinois, on the ground that a permanent civil service is a European and monarchical institution.

Appealing to a prejudice, these gentlemen are doubtless fearful that, by reforming the civil service, their hold upon the small offices, as a means of partisanship, may be imperilled.

Another crying evil, in America, is the miserable salaries paid by government. My impulse has once been, that the clerks of the government are paid enough. By an actual inquiry into the subject, I am satisfied that the salaries of the majority of clerks in Washington are insufficient, and the argument that plenty of people are waiting to take less seems to me to be conceived without regard to the respectability and honor of the public service. I know from experience that three thousand dollars is a little sum to keep even a very little house, and a very little family, in Washington, while the American boarding-house is a "hash house" of character, particularly in Washington. The system of "shaving" salaries in vogue in Washington is an evidence of the incompetence of hire. Four-fifths of all the salaries are hypothecated before the month is half over, and the clerk pays ten per cent. a month for the advance. The result is beggary at the end of the year, misery, and a collection among the other impoverished ones to send the bankrupt home. I know that this is poor saving on the part of the government. If those extravagant fees were cut down, such as are received by the Sergeant-at-Arms of the House, and officials with perquisites, and if the useless office-holders were discharged, the salaries of really useful clerks could be advanced to suit the times, without loss to the government. Meanness is not economy. The excess of single men in government service has led to a social debauchery. The back alleys of the town swarm with the abandoned, and these are supported upon the wages of men too poor to marry, but human enough to sin.

This is the testimony of the Secretary of the Interior, who said: —

"The income of office will not equal the outlay, if the incumbent lives in a style at all compatible with the proprieties of his position, and the relations which a decent regard to to the just claims of society compel him to maintain. The high offices of the country should be open to the poor as well as to the rich; but the practical effect of the present rate of compensation will soon be to exclude from executive councils all who have not ample resources independently of their official salaries.

"It is a singular and disreputable anomaly, that the chiefs of bureaux of the War Department each received in pay and emoluments, during the last fiscal year, a larger compensation than the Chief Justice of the United States. Recent legislation recognized the just claims of the Judges of the District Courts, and of the Supreme Court of this District; but Congress, in the absence of political pressure, omitted to make a becoming provision for the Justices of the Supreme Court of the United States."

The same Secretary made this suggestion:—

"The proposition to erect and furnish houses for the Vice-President and Cabinet ministers may not meet with more favor now than when it was originally made. I earnestly recommend, therefore, that fifty per centum be added to their present salary, and to the Justices of the Supreme Court. It will even then be much less than is allowed to officers of a similar grade, by any other first-class government. The cabinet ministers will not receive more than is now paid, in coin, to several of our foreign representatives, who discharge much less laborious duties, in capitals not more expensive than Washington. Since the salaries in question were fixed at the present rate, Congressmen have, by successive statutes, nearly quadrupled their own, and I do not doubt that the members of that honorable body will render, in some degree, to others, the justice already secured to themselves."

To show how small salaries debauch public officers, let me cite the following statement of an old office-holder, at Washington, to whom I applied for information as to the difference between the nominal salaries of government officials and their actual incomes:—

"State Department: the salary of the Secretary is eight thousand dollars a year, but he actually costs the government nearer eighty thousand dollars a year.

"Many of the clerks about the establishment never think of moving without retainers, and poor devils, why should they? for the average nominal salary of State Department clerks is about fifteen hundred dollars. Think of it, thirty dollars a week! thirty dollars a week in a city where the whole of this sum is demanded for the merest accommodation; and yet a clerk in the State Department is liable to make the acquaintance of Ministers Plenipotentiary, and of Secretaries of Legation. In fact, the affairs of our State Department can be known to almost any prying foreigner, who has only to apprize himself of the necessities of a State Department clerk, to find the key to the bottom of our archives. There is a gentleman of the State Department, whom I know, with a salary of, say forty dollars a week. He has, according to the best of my information, about ten children; this gentleman I believe to be a faithful and devoted servant of his Department,yet his salary, reduced to gold, is about six pounds a week, and, reduced to English marketing, it is about three pounds a week. Now, to bring disgust to the face of a confidential clerk of the English Foreign Office, tell him that his correspondent in America receives three pounds a week to do plenty of work, and keep his counsel.

"We have had some good foreign secretaries in our country, but as things stand at present it is a rich man's office. Seward, probably our best secretary, got even with his mean salary, by going freely into the pleasures of office; his printing at the congressional office cost the government considerably more than Lord Stanley's salary, and the pleasant old gentleman would hardly cross the river to Arlington, without getting the loan of Welles' most luxurious steamer. Looking upon his salary as zero, he gave bountiful encouragement to the Atlantic Telegraph, and to the Foreign Steamship companies, and an American hardly ever went abroad but he met some jolly bearer of despatches for the State Department, watching the CAN-CAN at the Ball Mabille, and assisting our formidable Secretary of State to help somebody to get something for his keeping the United States out of a foreign war.

"As to Mr. Gideon Welles, about whom I have just spoken, people say that he was not a very efficient officer. History will not join in this verdict, but he was so poor, after serving the government eight years, that he had to fire up a fine vessel-of-war to take his household furniture from Washington to New London.

"In the hottest time of the war, when to know which way Mr. Stanton's nose turned up was worth a thousand dollars an hour to contract-hunters, the salary of clerks stood at a starvation figure, and yet fifty per cent. of these clerks were under temptation to reveal the secrets of their bureaux.

"I can tell you two or three cases, but you will not care to print them, because you can hear of thousands of the same kind in a day's excursion around Washington.

"There was Th——, a first-class penman and book-keeper who had been turned out of the Interior Department for political suppositions, and he became so poor, in 1862, that he went to the wharves on the Potomac and got a job as a stevedore on an army supply vessel. When he had worked there like a Mick for several months, the quartermaster, an old brute, came out one day and asked, with an oath, if there was any man in the gang who could write. Th—— spoke out; accoutred as he was, he plunged in, made a magnificent assistant, and for all his labor and responsibility received what?

"Six hundred and fifty dollars a year!

"Amongst the contract-hunters who came to that wharf was a shipping merchant from a northern city. He became acquainted with Th——'s condition and ability; the government clerk and the merchant struck a partnership. In eighteen months Th—— was worth eighty thousand dollars, and this was not probably a third part of the gains of his moneyed partner.

"Here somebody made two hundred thousand dollars; here something lost it. I think it was the mean nation, which paid a man thirteen dollars a week, when he had thirteen chances a day to hook thirteen thousand.

"Need I remind you of the case of young ——, a navy clerk, who obtained more than a hundred thousand dollars by forgery, which required him to imitate about thirty names on each set of a series of warrants, which ran through two months. He was in love with a beautiful girl; his salary was a thousand dollars a year; he was liable to be chucked out of place to-morrow, though he did his best. He hooked the money; he married the girl; they took him almost from her side at the altar to the penitentiary.

"Of course he was a regular bad 'un, but how did he get into the government service? and what an accident that they got him out!

"On which hobservation, ask Mr. Jenckes of Rhode Island.

"And now, my dear sir, to come to the Treasury, I feel as if I were measuring up the ocean in a gill measure to try to tell you the stories of its civil list with one steel pen.

"Go there, and on a marble plate in a prominent room, printed at his own suggestion in golden letters, you will see a name amongst several, which is an index to the kind of precocious villainy which storms the party-caucus and manages the civil services. Mention it to any observer in Washington, and he will say, 'Dog! he enriched himself upon plundered cotton; he used his office merely to catalogue the claims against the Treasury, and resigned it to prosecute them.' In this case original sin was doubtless sufficient to account for the man, but had he been hauled into court, and made to face the penitentiary, his plea of excuse would have been:—

"'Good people, how could I maintain my honors with my appearance and thirty-five hundred dollars a year?'"

Here I leave my ancient office-holder and correspondent. He writes not elegantly perhaps, but with a cheerful indignation which may bring this subject home to the reader. In the civil service of our government are many accomplished and faithful men, to whom a civil service bill would be a relief, a social promotion, and better compensation. It is well known that the executive departments are overcrowded by the unscrupulous greed of merely political Congressmen to pension their retainers, and worse, upon the Federal service. The people must cry out for this reform; it might be called the vital reform of all the reforms needed. With the drones out of government service we could afford to pay the true clerks well, and the Executive Departments would cease to be mere soup-houses, where the unworthy crowd out the poor.

The English government has passed through this question, and the reformed civil service has proved to be a decency and a blessing on which the whole kingdom applauds itself; scrupulous, intelligent, orderly, patriotic, working clerks have replaced the old party hacks, and the vast clerical operations of the British kingdom are responsibly conducted by gentlemen almost as well paid as the clerks of private employers.

In the account of London offices, above given, little is said about their architecture; but as a rule they are not finer buildings than our own.

The building of the General Post Office in London stands in the densest part of the old city, near St. Paul's Cathedral; it is a fine building, but not more remarkable than the General Post Office in Washington. Generally considered, the public offices of London do not present as imposing appearances as the departments at Washington; all great London buildings, whether constructed of marble or granite, tarnish and blacken in that sooty atmosphere, while the public buildings of Washington compare in size and style with the largest of the world, yet keep almost as white as if freshly erected.

One of the largest public offices in London is called the Somerset House. It stands upon the Strand, or on the bank of the Thames, and contains several of the greatest offices of the government. The Inland or Internal Revenue Office occupies nearly one-half of the building; the Audit Office and part of the Admiralty and several other bureaux are established here. About nine hundred government officials have desks in Somerset House, and their combined salaries are nearly one million and a half of dollars a year. The leading Commissioner of Internal Revenue gets the highest salary in the building, or twelve thousand five hundred dollars a year; the same officer in the United States receives six thousand dollars a year. In the basement of Somerset House are presses and fonts of type to make stamps, stamped labels, etc. So large is Somerset House that it contains thirty-six hundred windows.

Another great government office in London is Burlington House, formerly the residence of a nobleman, situated on the street called Piccadilly; it covers one hundred and forty-three thousand square feet of ground, and cost seven hundred thousand dollars in gold.

It is not one of the good signs of the times in America that everybody wants office, and the unscrupulous methods by which offices are obtained strikes every stranger at Washington. "A universal thirst after salaried public employment," says Montalembert, "is the worst of all social maladies; it infects the whole body politic with a venal and servile humor, which in no way excludes, even among those who may be the best paid, the spirit of faction and anarchy. It creates a crowd of hungry suitors, capable of every excess to satisfy their longings, and fit instruments for every base purpose as soon as they are in place. A population of place-hunters is the most despicable of all people. There is no ignominy of which it is not capable."

MONUMENTAL STRUCTURES.

1—Alexander Column, St. Petersburg. 2—Column Vendome. 3—Arc De Triomphe, **Paris.**
4—Bunker Hill Monument. 5—Washington Monument. 6—Statue of **Columbus.**

CHAPTER IX.

NATIONAL ART AND EDUCATION.

The schools, universities, and institutions of art and literature in England and America. — A particular account of Oxford and Cambridge.

WE have now reached a subject in which the extremes of poverty and munificence are manifested by our country. Compared with Great Britain, or, indeed, with any modern nation, we are splendidly endowed with elementary schools, and enjoy in cheap and convenient variety all the advantages of public libraries and popular literature. The American people give voluntary and general support to the printing-press, which may be called the main engine of republicanism. But to the very highest developments of education, and to monumental art, the State does not think it wise to extend its organized assistance. We are, therefore, in the infancy of a great state, if measured by our architectural monuments and by our largest universities. The demands of the period with us are not for culture, but for usefulness. The most imposing of our institutions is, perhaps, the Patent Office, — that mighty depository of the mechanical triumphs of our nation, displayed in the course of our grand campaign toward reducing the wilderness and utilizing the products of the ground. But the most thorough and beneficent of our general i stitutions is, undoubtedly, our vast system of commo schools; for which we tax the people, in *lieu* of the grie ous churc -rates levied upon unwilling millions of Englishmen.

In 1865 there were twe ve thousand nine hundred and fifty schools, or departmen s of scho s, for the laboring classes in all Great Britain, taught by bout tw lve thousand teachers, and attended by one million two hu dred nd forty-six thousand children.

In the Stat o N York, alone, in 1862, there were one million hree hundred an t enty-three thousand scholars of the public schools.

The British gov nment made the first grant for general education in the year 1834; e sum was one hundred thousand dollars. In

MONUMENTAL STRUCTURES.

1—Alexander Column, St. Petersburg. 2—Column Vendome. 3—Arc De Triomphe, Paris. 4—Bunker Hill Monument. 5—Washington Monument. 6—Statue of Columbus.

CHAPTER IX.

NATIONAL ART AND EDUCATION.

The schools, universities, and institutions of art and literature in England and America. — A particular account of Oxford and Cambridge.

We have now reached a subject in which the extremes of poverty and munificence are manifested by our country. Compared with Great Britain, or, indeed, with any modern nation, we are splendidly endowed with elementary schools, and enjoy in cheap and convenient variety all the advantages of public libraries and popular literature. The American people give voluntary and general support to the printing-press, which may be called the main engine of republicanism. But to the very highest developments of education, and to monumental art, the State does not think it wise to extend its organized assistance. We are, therefore, in the infancy of a great state, if measured by our architectural monuments and by our largest universities. The demands of the period with us are not for culture, but for usefulness. The most imposing of our institutions is, perhaps, the Patent Office, — that mighty depository of the mechanical triumphs of our nation, displayed in the course of our grand campaign toward reducing the wilderness and utilizing the products of the ground. But the most thorough and beneficent of our general institutions is, undoubtedly, our vast system of common schools; for which we tax the people, in *lieu* of the grievous church-rates levied upon unwilling millions of Englishmen.

In 1865 there were twelve thousand nine hundred and fifty schools, or departments of schools, for the laboring classes in all Great Britain, taught by about twelve thousand teachers, and attended by one million two hundred and forty-six thousand children.

In the State of New York, alone, in 1862, there were one million hree hundred and twenty-three thousand scholars of the public schools.

The British government made the first grant for general education in the year 1834; the sum was one hundred thousand dollars. In

1853 the vote of money was one million three hundred thousand dollars, and at present it amounts to three million dollars and more a year. In twenty-three years the government has spent thirty-four million dollars for educational purposes, of which two-thirds went to the Church of England's schools, and the rest was distributed amongst the dissenting denominations and Catholics. Public schools in England are called National Schools; and educational administration in England is confided to the Education Department, — a branch of the Privy Council, — but the actual work is done by its Secretary, and a large number of Inspectors. The latter are paid two thousand two hundred and fifty dollars a year each, with travelling expenses, while the Secretary of the Committee receives six thousand dollars a year. America has a stronger exhibit to make.

There were more than one hundred and thirteen thousand schools in America in 1860, employing one hundred and forty-nine thousand teachers, and attended by nearly five and a half millions of scholars, and nearly five millions of these scholars attended the public schools. There were in America, besides, twenty-seven thousand seven hundred and thirty libraries, containing about thirteen and a half millions of volumes, and four thousand and fifty-one newspapers, circulating nine hundred and twenty-eight millions of copies a year. There were, also, four hundred and forty-five colleges in America, in 1860, attended by fifty-five thousand students.

Nearly the whole of this noble system of schools is the work, not of the nation, but of the separate States and cities; for the general government leaves to the people, in their corporate capacities, the regulation of all those affairs not strictly delegated to the Federal State. In Great Britain the State is made the encourager and conservator of education and art, as well as of industry, and the public schools feel the contact of this patronage. The National Schools of England are little more than pauper institutions, and take hold of the popular affections as do the work-houses and the agencies of out-of-door relief. But the common schools of the United States, maintained by the will of the people, partake of our republican spirit, and are comparable to the best private schools in the world. The sons of the rich are sent to them as well as the sons of the poor, and in this way the successive generations of the republic begin, equalized in charity, nationalized in manners, and taught to remember the rights of all and to be self-reliant, rather than to depend upon adventitious conditions. Into this great hopper of the public schools every immigrant or native mother pours her children. They emerge with all their original individualities, but bereft of most of their superstitions and arrogances, ready to take their places in the line of citizenship.

Education in England, as I have said, is not managed by the cities or the States as with us; it is a national affair, and is managed by a Committee of the effete Privy Council. Upon this Committee sit the Lord President of the Council, the Secretary of State, the Chancellor of the Exchequer, and four other eminent members of the government.

About three millions and a half of dollars are now voted for national schools, to which the children of citizens in middle life seldom go; and, with the usual regard paid in England to authority, the school-teachers frequently have residences built for them.

The Secretary of the British Education Board receives a salary of six thousand dollars a year, and there are a great number of School Inspectors, who receive, besides travelling expenses, two thousand two hundred and fifty dollars a year apiece.

At the Philadelphia High School, which was one of the best institutions of its kind in America, the Principal is paid only two thousand two hundred dollars a year, and has no official residence. In fact, no officials in America are given official residences, except the President and some of the State Governors.

When Washington city was planned, spaces were left to accommodate the different States with sites for residences for their Senators and Representatives. None of the States, and none of the Congressional Districts have been generous enough to avail themselves of these opportunities, and, as a consequence, many members of Congress, and even some of the cabinet officers, are unable to bring their wives to Washington city. Licentiousness is, therefore, said to abound under the shadow of the Capitol, and we have it on the authority of a Senator, that one of the Representatives from one of the greatest whiskey-distilling districts in the United States recently turned his house into a gambling-saloon, and there plundered his friends whom he had invited under his roof.

In the year 1860, before slavery was abolished, one person in six of the entire American population attended school. Since that time a noble series of elementary schools have been established in the South by the Freedmen's Bureau, and by the magnificent bequest of Mr. George Peabody, an American banker, of London, who had previously endowed the latter city with cheap lodging-houses. The need in England is for life, for shelter; the cry in America is for light, for schools. In the year 1860 there were one million two hundred and eighteen thousand persons in the United States who could not read and write. Of these not quite one-half, or about one person in forty of the native population, were native Americans.

The condition of the people is far different in Great Britain. A recent report of the British Registrar-General shows that thirty-two and seven-tenths per cent. of the male minors who married in 1841 were obliged to sign the register with marks. This proportion diminished year by year till 1866, when it was twenty-three per cent. The progress of education among women has been still greater. In 1841 forty-eight and eight-tenths per cent. of minors were unable to write their names; but in 1867 there were only twenty-three per cent. In the whole quarter of a century, from 1842 till 1866, the proportion of men who write has risen from being only two-thirds to be three-fourths, and of women, from being a half to be two-thirds. But the spread of education over the kingdom has been very unequal. It appears from a Parliamentary return, issued in the session of 1867, that more than a third of the Welchmen who married in the year 1865 had to "make their mark;" very nearly a third of the men of Hertfordshire, Cambridgeshire, and Norfolk were put to the same predicament; more than a third of the men of Suffolk, thirty-five per cent. of the men of Bedfordshire, thirty-eight per-cent. of the men of Staffordshire, and forty per cent. of the men of Monmouthshire. In all Lancashire one man in every four who married had to "make his mark." Foremost among the ignorant districts, so far as concerns women, stands South Wales, with more than half its women unable to write their names; and in North Wales, Monmouthshire, Staffordshire, and Lancashire the number exceeds forty-six in one hundred. In Bedfordshire, two women in every five who married in 1865 had to make their mark. In the eastern counties, and in many counties in the southern half of England, more women signed the marriage register in 1865 than men.

With regard to the British army the proportion of ignorant men is not less formidable. Of every thousand recruits examined in the year 1864 in English districts, two hundred and thirty-nine were unable to read or write, thirty-seven able to read only, and seven hundred and twenty-four able to read and write. In Scotch districts the numbers were respectively, one hundred and sixty-three, one hundred and fifty-seven, and six hundred and eighty. In Irish districts the result appears as three hundred and eighteen, one hundred and four, and five hundred and seventy-eight. Compared with the results for 1861, there is a decrease in the proportion of uneducated in England, but scarcely any difference in Scotland and Ireland.

There is no more remarkable indication of the need of public or common education in England than the numerous dialects which pervade the rural counties. Many of these are not merely the mal-pronunciation of habit, or the terms of locality, but coarse and harsh vocabularies, unintelligible to English-speaking people. Even in London, the large population called "Cockneys" speak a dialect not above the elegance of an American negro slave's in former days. Wherever one goes, throughout the British Islands, he finds dense ignorance, rude or servile mannerisms, and gross appetites. A small portion of the people are educated far above the needs of magnanimity, and they despise their common countrymen, while the poor are thrown together in parish or National Schools, unleavened in most cases by the companionship of the children of the better classes. By these strong walls, built between the various grades of childhood, the "conservatism" of England is thought to be secured; but it is the pride of a wealthy American father, in all but exceptional cases, to commit his son to the public teacher, and let him enter into competition with the average human nature on trial there. The result has proved, according to the best testimony, that there is less selfishness, haughtiness, and vice in the American common schools than at Eton or Harrow, the nurseries of the British aristocracy.

There were in America, in 1860, in addition to the scholars of the public schools, nearly half a million lads and girls attending private academies, of which latter there were nearly seven thousand established. There were, besides, upwards of four hundred and fifty incorporated colleges attended by fifty-six thousand students. These academies and colleges, collectively, had an annual income of more than twelve millions of dollars. These institutions are not associated with the public school systems of the different States; many of them are richly endowed by religious bodies, by the legislatures of the States, or by private benefactors. Almost every State has one or more universities, and those of some of the newest of the States compare favorably with the best in the land. Amongst the most flourishing and individual of these schools are the University of Michigan, at Ann Arbor, the Cornell University, at Ithaca, New York, and Oberlin College, in the State of Ohio. Taken together, the private or pay schools of the United States are, alone, probably more numerous and better attended than the private schools of England. Counting our vast system of public education at nothing, the pay schools of America match those of Great Britain, omitting the British National Schools. The American colleges of some single States, if collected into groups or universities, would outnumber the colleges of Oxford and Cambridge together. Ohio, for example, has forty-five colleges, with more than seven thousand students. All New England is in one point of view a grand academy, to which go scholars from all parts of the republic. In England there are particular schools of great antiquity and of rich revenues, which engage in the preparation of boys for college; a few of these may be enumerated.

Christ's Hospital in London, otherwise known as the Blue Coat School, is purely a charitable establishment; the pupils have retained their distinctive dress, a blue gown, yellow leggins, and no hat, ever since its foundation, and are obliged to wear this dress continuously, even in vacation. At the universities these charity scholars are known by their long hair. Charles Lamb went to this school, as well as Coleridge and Leigh Hunt. Its revenues are more than three hundred thousand dollars annually. At the opposite end of London, beside Westminster Abbey, is a school of a very different sort; it is called Westminster, and was once the Court School; for a long time it rivalled Eton, but was lately reported to be in a terrible state of decay. "The position of the school in the heart of a great city," says a critic, "had doubtless something to do with corrupting the boys' morals, but would not entirely account for their low and ungentlemanly habits; nor could their general ignorance of everything but vice be attributed to any other cause than gross neglect on the part of those who had control over them." At this school were trained Ben Jonson, Cowper, Gibbon, Lord John Russell, and many boys destined to greatness; the institution is three hundred years old.

Charter House School, in London, was the nursery of John Wesley, Thackeray, Blackstone, and Havelock; it was founded in the year 1611. I visited it in 1863, and found the names of Martin and John Van Buren on its registry book. At St. Paul's School, under the shadow of the great cathedral, were educated Milton and Marlborough. The two most renowned country schools in England are those of Harrow and of Eton, the latter situated close by the Queen's palace of Windsor. Harrow has the reputation of being a great place for the quasi-aristocracy, — the sons of rich commoners, — as Eton is for the sons of noblemen. Eton was founded fifty years before the discovery of America; at present it has nearly eight hundred scholars, and is richly endowed. Here were scholars many future prime ministers, and great churchmen and soldiers: Wellington, Hallem, Chatham, Fox, Canning, and Admiral Lord Howe.

The best idea an American reader can get of these British schools and of the two great universities will be afforded by Charles Astor Bristed's "Five years at an English University," and for pleasant, pure reading there are no books more popular than those of Mr. Thomas Hughes, "Tom Brown at Rugby School," and "Tom Brown at Oxford." The first of these books is a conscientious account of an American boy's experience at Cambridge, and I have availed myself of it freely in describing life at that great university.

American criticism is generally adverse to the social life of English schools, as indeed is much of the ingenuous portrayal of the same by the late English novelists.

The Etonian boys of nineteen are as old in appearance as the New Yorkers or Bostonians of twenty-one. They all wear white cravats and men's black beavers; caps are forbidden; to be an "Eton man" is a badge of high-breeding though not always of good-breeding. The school, perched on the Thames by the base of Windsor, is a sort of juvenile court. A feature of all these schools is the interest endowed for them in the great universities. Out of its seven hundred odd pupils only about one-tenth are collegers. These collegers are the nucleus of the whole Etonian system, and the only original part of it, the paying pupils (called *oppedans*, or town boys) being, according to general belief, an after-growth. The collegers are educated gratuitously, and such of them as have nearly but not quite reached the age of nineteen are elected, when a vacancy occurs, to go to King's College at Cambridge, and they are there provided for during life, or until marriage.

Amongst the many colleges of America there are two which have heretofore taken precedence over all others, by reason of their age and fine endowments, and by the eminence of their *alumni*. A long day's ride from Washington city, but little further from New York than is Oxford from the city of London, stands Yale College, in the pleasant town of New Haven, the city of the Elms, — a series of venerable or modern buildings in the green public squares, with churches and houses of justice or legislation intermixed.

Yale College, like Harvard, is named for a private benefactor,

Elihu Yale, who was born at New Haven in 1648, and lies buried at Wrexham, in North Wales. He quitted America when a child, and never returned to Connecticut; he rose to be governor of the East India Company, and became rich; his united bequest to Yale College amounted, however, to only about five hundred pounds. The conception and infancy of the college date back about one hundred and eighty years; but the earliest of the present buildings at New Haven were finished about the year 1780. Nearly eight thousand persons had graduated at New Haven up to the year 1862; there were about forty-five instructors in the college at that time and six hundred students. As at Harvard, there is an academic department at Yale, besides colleges of law, science, medicine, and theology. There are forty thousand books in the college library, besides several subsidiary libraries belonging to societies. The alumni of the college have made it several handsome bequests,—more than two hundred thousand dollars having been given in two separate subscriptions. Yale, however, is not so richly endowed as Harvard. It is, if not more conservative in politics than Harvard, more conservative in its religion, still adhering to the forms and doctrines of the Congregational Church. In both these great American universities there is a radical and a staid faction, contending for their control; at present the more radical university seems to be about as far ahead as Oxford outstrips Cambridge in material things; but both these universities are firmly established, and their interior policy and regimen attract almost as much attention in America, as do Oxford and Cambridge in England.

It would be very pleasant in this chapter to sketch the pleasant College of Dartmouth, in the lowlands of New Hampshire; the University of Pennsylvania, in the heart of the great city of Philadelphia; Brown University, on the heights above Narragansett Bay, and Ithaca University, on the green slope of Cayuga Lake. I have only room, however, for an outline of the American Cambridge.

Three miles from Boston city, on the banks of the broad, brackish River Charles, in the midst of the pleasant suburb of Cambridge, stands Harvard University. The town of Cambridge was named after Cambridge in England, by the founders of the college which stands here, many of whom had graduated at the English University of that name. Cambridge town, in England, at the present time, is probably not as populous as Cambridge in Massachusetts. Several years ago the two Cambridges had but about two thousand difference in population. John Harvard was born in Middlesex County, England, the county in which London stands, in 1638. He died at Charlestown, Massachusetts, and left about eight hundred pounds to found a college, and also a small library; but Cambridge University was really the work of the settlers of Boston and the town round about; it properly began six years after the settlement of the Boston region. This college received a limited State support down to the year 1814; but the bulk of its wealth was the gift of private individuals. It has received bequests amounting to more than one million of dollars; in its library are about one hundred and twenty-five thousand volumes. There are more than a dozen large buildings upon the fourteen acres which constitute its premises, and one of its colleges is in Boston city. It has about seven hundred and fifty students, generally speaking. In theology it is generally considered a Unitarian institution; but the sentiment of its undergraduates, alumni, and patrons has grown more and more progressive, until at present its President is a young man, and its overseers and corporation belong to what is called the advanced or youthful party, in politics, philosophy, and religion.

From Yale and Harvard let us turn to the two ancient universities of England.

Cambridge is fifty-seven miles from London. Oxford is fifty-two miles from London. Cambridge dates back to about the year 1230, A.D. Oxford is said to have been a seat of learning as early as the year 802, A.D.

The Associations of both Oxford and Cambridge are scholastic, and historical in a high degree. Cromwell three times represented Cambridge in the House of Commons, and Bacon, Newton, Coke, Dryden, and Byron were among the graduates of this venerable university. At Oxford were burned Ridley, Latimer, and Cranmer, the earliest Bishops of the English Church. The library at Cambridge contains more than two hundred thousand volumes; the Bodleian Library, at Oxford, contains nearly three hundred thousand volumes. The revenue of Oxford is two million three hundred thousand dollars in gold, a year. It has thirty-five professors, numerous tutors, six hundred "Fellows," and thirteen hundred students. The revenue of the university-proper, however, is only about thirty-eight thousand dollars a year; the rest going to separate colleges, to prizes, and to fellowships. At Cambridge there are seventeen colleges. Government gives the professors about six thousand dollars a year, collectively, and the revenues of the university proper are thirty thousand dollars a year. Both colleges have had magnificent bequests. One museum, at Cambridge, is endowed with five hundred thousand dollars in gold, and one college has a separate library of fifty thousand volumes. Oxford has a magificent printing establishment and a theatre connected with it. At both colleges there are professorships of Arabic, Sanscrit, and other oriental branches. Both these universities originated in monastic schools, which, after a time, had secular imitators; these latter hired inns, and other buildings, where they lived in association, with superintendents, stewards, and other officers appointed by themselves. From those poverty-stricken inns have grown up the vast series of colleges which constitute these two noble universities, both of which, by right of usefulness, of intelligence, and of property, are represented in the Parliament of Great Britain. For many years, Mr. Gladstone, the present enlightened Prime Minister, was elected by Oxford University.

The great University of Oxford possesses nineteen colleges, and five halls, presided over by their respective "Heads." The university has always been governed by statutes of its own making, which in 1626 were digested into a code.

The style of the corporation is, "The Chancellor, Masters, and Scholars of the University of Oxford." The Chancellor holds his office for life, is usually a nobleman of distinction, who has been a member of the university, is elected by the members of Convocation, and attends only on extraordinary occasions. The Vice-Chancellor, the highest resident officer, is annually nominated by the Chancellor from the Heads of Colleges, but of late has generally held office by reappointment for four years. He convenes all courts and meetings, enforces the laws, punishes delinquents, licenses taverns in the city, and is a magistrate for Oxford, Oxfordshire, and Berkshire. He appoints four deputies, or pro-vice-chancellors, from the Heads of Colleges, who exercise his power when he is unwell, or necessarily absent from the university.

The following are the names of the colleges composing the Universities of Oxford, with the students, as reported a few years ago: —

University,	72
Balliol,	101
Merton,	45
Exeter,	171

Oriel,	87
Queen's,	63
New,	34
Lincoln,	40
All Souls,	4
Magdalene,	55
Brasenose,	99
Corpus,	47
Christ Church,	211
Trinity,	81
St. John's,	49
Jesus,	44
Wadham,	72
Pembroke,	66
Worcester,	68

Halls:—

St. Mary's,	18
Magdalene,	73
New Inn,	6
St. Alban,	9
St. Edmund,	22
Litton's,	5

Balliol, judged by the standard of the class lists, and University prizes, is a far better college than Christ Church, or Brasenose, or, indeed, any other in Oxford.

Take one college at Oxford, to example the rest,—Christ Church: It was commenced by Cardinal Wolsey, in 1526, but when the King disgraced him, the former seized the funds appropriated to building the college, and changed its name from Cardinal's to King's. One side of this college is four hundred feet long, broken in the centre by a bold gateway, over which rises a tower and dome, containing a bell which weighs seventeen thousand pounds, and whose clapper weighs three hundred and forty-two pounds; every night, at ten minutes after nine, this bell, by one hundred and one strokes, gives notice to all the colleges to close their gates.

The gateway under the great bell leads into a vast court, more than two hundred and forty feet square, and surrounded with superb architecture; in the centre of the court plays a fountain, and from one corner of it, where stands a statue of Cardinal Wolsey, a beautiful staircase leads to the College Hall, which is one hundred and fifteen feet long, forty feet wide, and fifty feet high, and finished by Wolsey himself. In this hall the English sovereigns are received when they visit Oxford, and many plays have been enacted here before the kings. A Cathedral is attached to this college, and fine stone cloisters. A magnificent Portrait Gallery, of historical personages associated with this college, is one of its attractions. A meadow of fifty acres extends from the college to the pleasant river's brink, and promenades under elm-trees lead to the junction of the Cherwell and Isis, where lie moored the barges from which the collegians cheer the racing-boats, while the green meadows are on racing days crowded with spectators. From this college Locke was expelled; here Cranmer was confined before his execution; here William Penn attacked the Christ Church students, and tore their white surplices from their backs.

These are but a few of the larger features of this magnificent college, which is replete with exquisite patches of stained glass, and quaint or florid sculpturing. An American scholar can spend a month in Oxford, inspecting Christ's Church and other colleges, and here, in 1869, appeared many of our Yale and Harvard boys, to watch the university boat race between Harvard and Oxford. In and around all these colleges will be seen the students in their academical costumes, which are not worn in America except on show occasions, and then in a very modest and reduced form.

The English academical costume consists of a gown, varying in color and ornament according to the wearer's college and rank, but generally black, not unlike an ordinary clerical gown, and a square-topped cap, which fits close to the head like a truncated helmet, while the covered board which forms the crown measures about a foot diagonally across. To steal caps and gowns is no more an offence against the eighth commandment, in Cambridge, than to steal umbrellas.

A remarkable class of men at the English universities are the "Fellows," who reside in the university, and devote themselves to teaching or to learning. The Fellows, who form the general body from which the other college officers are chosen, consist of those four or five Bachelor scholars in each year who pass the best examination in classics, mathematics, and metaphysics. This examination being a severe one, and only the last of many trials which they have gone through, the inference is allowable that they are the most learned of the college graduates. They have a handsome income, whether resident or not; but if resident, enjoy the additional advantages of a well-spread table for nothing, and good rooms at a very low price. The only conditions of retaining their fellowships are that they take orders after a certain time, and remain unmarried. Of those who do not fill college offices, some occupy themselves with private pupils; others, who have property of their own, prefer to live a life of literary leisure, like some of their predecessors, the monks of old. The eight oldest Fellows at any time in residence, together with the Master, have the government of the college vested in them. We have no such leisurely class in America; all who live in the college are undergraduates. Yet it might be well for our literature if some such fellowships were attached to our universities, that some excellent students might have leisure for authorship. There are, nevertheless, many drones and hangers-on about the English universities.

Oxford has numerous professors, who are utterly unoccupied. They are engaged in spasmodic efforts at getting hearers, and are forced, against their will, into lazy apathy. "As a whole," says one critic, "the public teaching of the university is unwillingly contemptible.

"One must either pity the men who have no one to teach, or one must despise the men who continue the same functional gabble to successive aspirants for a certificate.

"Some of the ablest Oxford professors lecture to women and strangers. I have gone in to a lecture on a subject of the profoundest interest, and I have seen there three or four Fellows, and so forth, of the lecturer's college, one or two citizens, and an ambitious undergraduate, who took notes for ten minutes, and slept for fifty. It is in vain that founders of professorships annex penalties to a slovenly performance of public offices."

The sums of money invested in these fellowships is very great. Rich men, dying, endow so many fellowships in this college.

There is no less than a sum of four hundred thousand dollars per annum bestowed on those who desire, or receive, as the case may be, eleemosynary aid in Oxford as undergraduates.

The annual value of the fellowships and college headships, buildings included, is at least seven hundred thousand dollars.

The annual value of ecclesiastical benefices connected with the colleges is at least one million dollars, and the income of the university, including its trust estates, according to one estimate, will bring the gross total to not much less than two million five hundred thousand dollars per annum.

It was the case a few years ago, and probably will continue in the

English universities, for the university to control much of the city in which it stands. The town officers are sworn in by, and subject to, the university authorities, and the Proctors have a right to enter almost any house or premises, put down all disorderly houses, and expel from the place all the notorious prostitutes, of whom there are many hundreds, as well known as if they were under a Parisian registration.

It may be that these sensual attractions partially account for the unproductiveness of many Oxford fellowships, for a recent graduate of Oxford says: —

"I find my own university, the richest in the world, — far richer in its income than all the universities of continental Europe from St. Petersburg to Cadiz, — far behind, in its literary labors, some of the smallest of most modern establishments in the pettiest German principality or dukedom."

The cost of education at Oxford, payable in gold, is fully twice as much as the combined fees at Yale or Harvard. It can rarely happen that the annual expenditure of an undergraduate's residence is less than one thousand dollars at Oxford, and, according to the best testimony, the opportunities to spend money there are very considerable, though, out of this annual expenditure, college bills amount only to between four hundred and five hundred dollars. These bills include tuition provided by the college, rent of rooms (unfurnished, the furniture being purchased and transferred on entering and leaving rooms); kitchen and buttery, — the former of these two providing dinner, the latter commons and beer. The college does not supply the undergraduate with tea, coffee, or sugar; but most of the colleges arrange for the undergraduates' washing and coals, and these items are included in the bill.

This is an outline sketch of the great University of Oxford, which is typical of the peculiar nation of which it is one of the ornaments. Its separate colleges have local and particular connections.

For instance, Exeter College has a large west country connection, and a very considerable clerical one.

Balliol and University are strongly occupied by a Scotch and north of England connection. Jesus is almost entirely Welch. Trinity is powerfully Wykehamist.

Queen's is eminently limited to Cumberland, Northumberland, and Westmoreland. Brasenose is a good deal beholden to Manchester, and so in their degree with the rest.

Down to 1832 there were in England but two ancient universities. In that year a university for the study of theology was founded in Durham. The Bishop of the diocese is the "visitor," and the Dean the "Warden." It is now attended chiefly by the sons of wealthy farmers. The London University was founded by royal charter on the 28th of November, 1836. It is empowered to confer the degrees of master of arts, and of doctor of laws, of medicine, and of science. There are two colleges in direct relation with it, namely, University and King's College. The Fellows and the Chancellor are nominated by the Queen; the Vice-Chancellor by the Senate.

The first view of Cambridge, town and university, is quite as quaint, if not as fine, architecturally, as Oxford. Like almost all old English towns there are narrow and winding streets of crazy old buildings, filled with ancient sign-boards. Among these narrow, ugly, and dirty streets are tumbled in, as it were at random, some of the most beautiful academical buildings in the world. However their style of architecture may vary, according to the period at which they were built or rebuilt, they agree in one essential feature: All the colleges are constructed in quadrangles, or courts; and, as in course of years the population of every college, except one, has outgrown the original quadrangle, new courts have been added, so that the larger foundations have three, and one has four, courts. Sometimes the "old court," or primitive part of the building, presents a handsome front to the largest street near it; but frequently, as if to show its independence of, and contempt for, the town, it retires from the street altogether, showing the passer-by only its ugliest wall and smallest, shabbiest gate.

When Mr. Bristed appeared before this old university and selected the college he meant to attend, he wrote a very pithy description of the place: —

"You enter by a portal neither particularly large nor very striking in its appearance, but rather the reverse, into a spacious and elegant square. There are neat grass-plots and walks, a fountain in the centre; on one side stands a well-proportioned chapel; in one corner you catch a glimpse, through a tantalizing grating, of a beautiful garden, appropriated to the delectation of the authorities. In a second court you find sounding and venerable cloisters, perhaps a veritable structure of monkish times, if not, a satisfactory imitation of that period. And you look on the walls, here rich with sculptured ornament, there covered with trailing and festooning ivy."

At Cambridge, as at Oxford, there are many colleges, and all these colleges have equal privileges and rights, with one exception; and, though some of them are called halls, the difference is merely one of name. But the halls at Oxford, of which there are five, are not incorporated bodies, and have no vote in university matters; indeed, are but a sort of boarding-house, at which students may remain until it is time for them to take a degree. "I dined at one of those establishments," says Mr. Bristed. "It was very like an officers' mess. The men had their own wine, and did not wear their gowns."

Mr. Bristed spent five years at Cambridge, and it is his opinion that an English university course is far more thorough and effective than one at Yale or Harvard.

"Were I to be questioned by an educated foreigner — an Englishman, or Frenchman, German, Hollander, or Dane — upon the standard of scholarship in our New England colleges and universities, I should be obliged to answer," he says, "not having the fear of the American public before my eyes, that it was exceedingly low, and that not merely according to *his* idea, but according to the idea of a boy fitted at a good school in New York. When I went up to Yale College in 1835, the very first thing that struck me was the classical deficiency of the greater part of the students and some of the instructors. A great many of the freshmen had literally never heard of such a thing as prosody; they did not know that there were any rules for quantity. It may be imagined what work they made with reading poetry. Nor could their teachers, in many instances, do much to help them. One of our *classical* tutors did not know the quantity of the middle syllable in *profugus*, — almost the first word in the Æneid. The etymological part of Greek grammar (to say nothing of the syntax) was very imperfectly understood by the majority, and of those who made pretensions to scholarship there were not ten in a class who could recite three consecutive sentences of decent Latin prose.

"Yale is the largest college in our country, and one of the two most distinguished. The result of my inquiries has not led me to believe that Harvard is any better off. That the other colleges throughout the country, many of which derive their instructors from these two great New England colleges, are, if anything, in a worse state, may be easily inferred."

Mr. Bristed's testimony as to the relative morality of the English and the American universities is severely rendered against the former, and what he says will be confirmed by any traveller who is informed upon the social life of the young men of the higher classes in the British Islands.

The American graduate, who has been accustomed to find even among irreligious men a tolerable standard of morality, and an ingenuous shame in relation to certain subjects, is utterly confounded at the amount of open profligacy going on all around him at an English university; a profligacy not confined to the "rowing" set, but including many of the reading men, and not altogether sparing those in authority. There is a careless and undisguised way of talking about gross vice, which shows that public sentiment does not strongly condemn it; it is habitually talked of and considered as a thing from which a man may abstain through extraordinary frigidity of temperament or high religious scruple, or merely as a bit of training with reference to the physical consequences alone; but which is on the whole natural, excusable, and perhaps to most men necessary. Some instances of representative wickedness at Cambridge are of a sort to make an American turn up his eyes. Let me give them as cited from the authorities: —

"You want to know what this row was between Lord Gaston and Brackett, — well, it happened this way: Brackett had brought his *chère amie* down from London. Gaston made her acquaintance. Brackett goes there one night and finds the door locked; so he kicked the door open, and gave Gaston a black eye. Then Gaston wanted to challenge him, and said he didn't care whether he was turned out of the university or not (this is the penalty for being concerned in a duel); but his friends agreed that, *as Brackett was going into the church*, they had better make it up," etc.

"A young woman of previous good character went to a fellow of King's College to procure an order of admission to the chapel on Sunday evening. He made her drunk and seduced her. The reader will probably agree with me, that if the corporation of King's had expelled him from their body it would not have been a punishment beyond his deserts. What did they do? They suspended him from his fellowship for two years, which was equivalent to a fine of four thousand pounds or thereabout."

Not less repulsive is it to an American to find English university students taking reactionary positions in politics. The same authority says: —

"I first had full personal experience of the uncharitableness shown by these youthful Tories towards their liberal countrymen. Many of them, who seemed to have taken up the Romish idea that a blind devotion to their church establishment could atone for any irregularity in their lives, looked upon a Liberal as no better than a Dissenter, and a Dissenter as only one step above an Atheist. A professed Radical was regarded as a strange monster always to be suspected."

It would be a grievous offence in the eyes of American students if I omitted mention of the great rowing matches at the English universities. At Oxford these take place upon the Isis; at Cambridge, upon the Cam. The Cam being a very narrow stream, scarcely wider than a canal, it is impossible for the boats to race side by side. The following expedient has therefore been adopted: they are drawn up in a line, two lengths between each, and the contest consists in each boat endeavoring to touch with its bow the stern of the one before it, which operation is called bumping; and at the next race the bumper takes the place of the bumped. The distance rowed is about one mile and three quarters.

Yale and Harvard race each other upon the beautiful lake called Quinsigamond, near Worcester, Massachusetts,—a lake which is about half a mile wide. During the race on the Cam there is wonderful activity and excitement, and the river brink is alive with people and nags. One account says of the scene in racing week that,—

"Men and horses ran promiscuously along the banks, occasionally interfering with each other. A dozen persons might have been trampled under foot, or sent into the Cam, and no one would have stopped to render them assistance. The cockswain of one of the boats looked the very personification of excitement; he bent over at every pull till his nose almost touched the stroke's arm, cheering his men meantime at the top of his voice. The shouts rose louder and louder. 'Pull, Trinity!' 'Pull, Keys!' 'Go it, Trinity!' 'Keep on, Keys!' 'Pull, stroke!' 'Now, No. 3!' 'Lay out, Greenwell!' For the friends of the different rowers began to appeal to them individually. 'That's it, Trinity!' 'Where are you, Keys?' 'Hurrah, Trinity! inity!! inity!!!' and the outcries of the Trinitarians waxed more and more boisterous and triumphant, as the men, with their long, slashing strokes, urged their boat closer and closer upon the enemy.

"Cambridge was turned into a show place for that day only. Gold-embroidered gowns of noblemen mingled with the red gowns of Doctors of Divinity and Physic. Crowds of well-dressed strangers thronged the beautiful college grounds, looking as unamused as the great Anglo-Saxon race usually does when it gets together in a crowd.

The Senate House was thronged. All manner of big-wigs graced the scene, and augmented the dignity of the Duke of Northumberland. Some one of the Royal Family was there, — I forget who, but recollect two officers pushing the people out of his way. Prince Albert came up to be made something or other, and put on some extraordinary dress. Illustrious foreigners were not wanting. Edward Everett and Baron Bunsen were created D. C. L.'s, and had red gowns put over their diplomatic uniforms." The scandalous conduct of some members of Oxford University to our distinguished countryman, when the same degree was conferred on him there some time later, is notorious.

In 1865 and '66 I wrote for the "New York World" accounts of the races at Lake Quinsigamond, and my companion was an Englishman, whom I may call Tom Brown. There were many cabs and stages between Worcester and the Lake, but quantities of strange vehicles also, which could be enumerated under no possible head, — buggies served up at the country blacksmith's, dearborns which might be laden with hay, but which creaked abominably under the human freight of the father of the family, peak-visaged, and calculating costs upon the rump of his horse, as upon a slate; the old lady meditating apple-butter and the cost of education.

With these went ponies and saddles, which ought to have been "fit into the revolutionary war," and furniture carts in which half-tipsy sons of sires were singing in their sleep. The road was undulating, and parallel with a railroad, and a part of the way went across some swampy bottoms, and at last struck a hill-top, whence the sweep of hills to the north and south was as beautiful as the roll of the West Riding moors. Below lay the lake, dark and shining like ebony, and to the right meandering among many islets, and everywhere shadowing woods of chestnut and oak, but to the left, a single reach of unbroken water, rising straight to the further distance, where in the end of the perspective the buoy lay, like a white feather. A causeway divided this clear arm of the lake from the west, in which was an arch, through which a small steamboat was now passing.

Tom Brown saw all this at a glance, and that nature which beats down all reticence and prejudice brought from his lips an honest admission: —

"I say! this thing can't be beat, out of Westmoreland. Who the deuce wouldn't row his arms off here?"

The carriages and nags were all collected along the causeway, and in the woods on either side; a railway turn-off to the right was dropping passengers by hundreds, who filed across the meadows and the road, and went down a slope into the woods. The scene was orderly, yet animated, and nobody was visible who seemed to be poor or outcast.

"Where are all your beggars?" said Tom Brown; "don't they come to see your races?"

"There are no beggars here."

We two left the crowd to the left, and went down to see the boats. They lay in a couple of unostentatious plank-houses, on the brink of the lake, and were rakish shells, each resembling a very long, and pointed cigar, scooped out in the middle, and guided by a rudder not bigger than a sheet of foolscap.

Tom Brown said they were neither quite so long, nor quite so narrow, as the highest university barges. Their crews were dressing as he approached, in handkerchiefs, silk shirts, and cotton drawers. They looked like work, and he bet his money on Yale.

The scene along the lake borders was neither so eccentric, nor so densely peopled, as upon the Cherwell, or the Cam, during the British university races, but the knobs and capes of the lake were plentifully inhabited, and all the woodsides bordering it revealed groups of spectators, while the surface of the water was spotted with swift-darting craft, from the skeleton boat, manned by the single, conceited oarsman, in red shirt, to the punt giving lodgment to a family. The brass band, on the boldest cape, played fitful airs, chiefly military, but spending most of their time in picking out the tubes of their cornets with pen-knives, and little attention was paid to the Worcester regatta, for nobody in the country has much interest in what Worcester is doing; but by and by the college boats came on the ground.

Then the excitement rose to fever heat, though Tom Brown remarked that the disorder was not so coarse as in England, where ladies and grandfathers wagered, and "demmes" were as frequent as compliments.

They gave the stakes to the keeping of one of the many Generals floating about, and scarcely had the agreement been made, when the signal gun reverberated, and the two college crews came dashing up the lake.

Tom Brown watched the scene with his old interest. The scream of the partisans, the waving of ladies' cambrics, the flutter, and thunder, and alarm were lost on his ears. He only saw the two long, lean, rakish shells dart forward, the oarsmen bending, till from waist to scalp their bodies lay horizontally; and then the quick, vehement erection, which made the tough oars quiver, and gave the craft an impetus, like the ricochet of a shell, while every oar-lock vibrated.

Head and head they come, the swifter, but more fitful sweep of Harvard giving them for a time the advantage; but the dip of Yale is like the method of the piston, — certain, equal, and irresistible, and as they pass, so bending to their task, that they only feel the proximity of the world, and divine the direction, and hearing, as folks in a vacuum, the peal of the cheers on shore, the twelve rowers put their souls in the shaft, and feel their hearts beat at the top of the paddles, and only know that the air is cloven, as by two lean and famished birds, and count, from time to time, the call of "steady," from the tremulous coxswain.

Still, the cries of the cape, left far behind, reach up to them, but they have only intuitions, no sense, nor perception, nor cognition. Away and away, each can hear the breathing of the other; the buoy boat approaches; the woods draw nearer; the winds are so still, that the hard-drawn breath of every toiler is plainly noted while they ride. Fiercely pulls Harvard, with the reputation of its old pulls dependent upon it.

Regularly and strongly labors Yale, too well indoctrinated, to do other than feather every oar, and make every stroke a reputation of its predecessor.

And so, passing the stake boat, Tom Brown saw every impetus give Yale her golden hope, till, with wild gratulation, she returned past the cape, and shot across the starting-rope, like a flashing pendulum.

Directly, the victors returned, the flags they fought for borne before them, and beaten Harvard went soberly home, hopeful of a better year.

That night the boys made the town of Worcester ring. They burst the door-panels, and shied their pillows into the street.

Leaving the universities we come to the public libraries, of which the largest in America is the Congressional Library in the Capitol at Washington. It now contains, in round numbers, about one hundred and eighty thousand volumes, which is more than that of Harvard

College, which outnumbers all others in the Union, except this. But let us compare it with some European libraries: —

	VOLUMES.
The Imperial Library, in Paris,	1,084,000
" Royal Library, in Munich,	818,600
" Library of the British Museum, in London,	615,000
" Bodleian, in Oxford,	282,000
" University Library, in Cambridge,	200,163
" Arsenal Library, in Paris,	208,000
" Royal Library, in Berlin,	510,000
" Imperial Library, in Vienna,	370,000
" Royal Library, in Dresden	302,800
" University Library, in Gottingen,	305,000
" Grand Ducal Library, in Darmstadt,	304,000
" Royal and University Library, in Breslau,	352,000
" Town Library, in Brussels,	210,000
" Vatican, in Rome,	324,000
" Imperial Library, in St. Petersburg,	475,000
" Royal Library, in Copenhagen,	428,000

Some notice of the British Museum has already been made, in the chapter on London; we could have no such library and museum in America, even if we collected in one spot all the pictures, libraries, and scientific collections in the republic. The National Gallery, and the Kensington Museum contain the great art collections of London; they are spacious edifices, and our collected art treasures would probably make a sorry show in them. A small, but promising Art Gallery has recently been endowed, in Washington City, by W. W. Corcoran, a banker. An Academy of Design was erected in New York, a few years ago; but its annual exhibitions attract no such attention as those of the Royal Academy, in London. American artists have attracted attention abroad chiefly for their landscapes, and some of our sculptors, as Story, Powers, and Miss Hosmer, are well known in England, but we have neither the institutions nor the patrons to encourage art in America; some of our best artists, as Boughton and Vedder, live abroad, and rely upon foreign support.

American medical education was confined to Philadelphia for many years, where there are two renowned colleges, the Jefferson and the medical department of the University; but medical students generally resort to the greatest cities, where they have a versatile practice in the hospitals, and New York seems to have had the favor of medical students since the civil war.

St. Bartholomew's Hospital in London contains five hundred and eighty beds, and it relieves seventy thousand patients a year, and has an annual income of one hundred and fifty thousand dollars. Guy's Hospital is endowed with more than one million dollars. Medical students pay two hundred dollars a year for lectures, practice, and all privileges. St. Thomas Hospital has an income of one hundred and fifty thousand dollars a year; it receives fifty thousand patients annually, and its splendid new hospital, which stands immediately opposite the Parliament Houses, was built out of a part of about one million and a half of dollars which it received from a railroad company for its former building at London Bridge.

We have several law schools in America, and young men generally read law in the offices of attorneys with us, while in England they live together in great buildings.

The Inns of Court. There are four great Inns of Court in London: Inner Temple, Middle Temple, Lincoln's Inn, and Gray's Inn; these Inns are voluntary households of law students and lawyers. The annual yearly rental of the offices in the Inns of London is more than five hundred thousand dollars.

Monumental art in America is ambitious, but not of a remarkably national character. In London there is a statue of George Peabody, by an American — Story; but this is almost the only case of American sculpture getting government patronage abroad.

I sometime ago spent part of a day in the shaft and workshops of the Washington Monument, — a mournful instance of the short-livedness of public impulse, and the defects in the machinery of miscellaneous private enterprise. This monument is already raised to the height of one hundred and seventy-five feet. It has cost nearly two hundred and fifty thousand dollars, and is raised to more than one-third its total height. The foundations are perfectly secure, and capable of supporting all the height yet to be added. There are stones from all parts of the world, ready to be inserted in the shaft, or subsidiary temple; but work has been suspended upon it for about twelve years.

The monument was discouraged, because the people believed that the contributions being dropped into post-office boxes, all over the country, were stolen and never applied to the edifice, and also because the artists and art critics kept up a steady fire of deprecation upon the plan of the monument. This plan was an obelisk, surrounded with a Greek temple. There is no notion at present of adding the temple, but the monument association hope to raise money enough to finish the obelisk. It is easy to do this, and it ought to be done, for the unfinished shaft in the capital city is a record of popular impotence worse than if a monument to Washington had never been begun. This age and people are no exception to the human passion for monumentalization. If ten thousand churches and schools would give twenty-five dollars apiece, this monument could be finished. The interior of the shaft is of twenty-five feet diameter, between the inner sides of the walls, and so thick are the walls that the exterior diameter is fifty-five feet. The material is marble, from Maryland. Within, there is a yawning chasm of shaft, very impressive to look up into, and see at the farthest height a scaffold hung, from which a rope droops dizzily, and on the floor the dampness splashes, and the darkness lies all round the year, save when some melancholy visitor puts his head within, and feels dejected over the suspended gratitude of the land of Washington. I hope no more great monuments will be commenced, but hope a feeling will be revived to see this one finished. The memorial stones to decorate some portions of the shaft represent all companies, lands, and ages, — lava from Vesuvius, aerolites shaken out of crazy satellites or planets, rocks of copper and of porphyry stones from Jerusalem and Mecca,— everything but the Pope's stone, which not the builders, but the mob rejected.

The finest monument in America is probably the Washington monument at Richmond, Virginia, unfinished. In the great city of New York we have but one fine public statue, while the United Kingdom is a great museum of colossal ornamental works. The Albert Memorial, the finest monument erected in our generation, stands in Hyde Park, London, and it cost six hundred thousand dollars. It is a splendid Gothic canopy and spire, and it is one hundred and sixty feet high, and covers, with its flights of steps, a square of one hundred and thirty feet each way; colossal groups of statuary surround it; the Prince Consort is enshrined above. Close by this magnificent monument stands the marble arch, which cost four hundred and fifty thousand dollars.

CHAPTER X.

LOCAL GOVERNMENT IN THE STATES, COUNTIES, AND PROVINCES.

Sketches of some American states and some English counties, with their comparative populations, rights, and resources.

THE names of American States perpetuate the Indian names of their great rivers and lakes, or bear the names of their colonial proprietors. The English Counties retain their old Saxon names, some of them as Kent, Sussex, and Surrey having been Saxon kingdoms. In America a State has jurisdiction over all the incorporated cities within its boundaries, but in England many of the large towns rank as "Counties Corporate," and the officials of the surrounding County cannot control them. We have in this country different laws in the different States, and even different codes of law. In Louisiana, justice was administered by the *code Napoleon* instead of the English common law. So in England there are old distinctions of privilege and administration between the great Counties, but these are of little consequence to our inquiry, and need not be recited. The English County, like the American State, is mainly a judicial district, but it has less independence. A State with us exercises large powers of sovereignty, charters railway and traffic companies, and between its pretensions and the progress of the Federal government has arisen our most deadly collision. As in America, the administrative districts of England are these Counties, corresponding to our States; the County Governor is called the Lord Lieutenant; the Sheriff and his deputies constitute the main constabulary force; the other officers of County governments are Justices of the Peace, Coroners, and Knights of the Shire. The police system, however, throughout all England is controlled by the Home Secretary, a member of the Cabinet. There is no voting by ballot, in any of these Counties; those only count as electors who can vote for Parliament members; few of the County offices are elective, but are held at the disposal of the King's ministers. With us a State is a turbulent and organized territory, having all its own machinery driven by its own will. An English County is an ancient territory which sends a part of the members to Parliament. The Lord Lieutenants hold their offices for life; and, unlike our State Governors, neither receive salaries nor are strictly accountable for their party politics. When a vacancy occurs in a Lord Lieutenancy, by death or resignation, it is filled by the Cabinet, which is a political body; but only four cases are on record of the removal of these officers for opposing a dominant national administration. When a Lord Lieutenant is appointed, he appears before the Queen's Council and takes the oath; a Lord Lieutenant, however, has military authority mainly, while the Sheriff of each County is the principal judicial officer; both Lord Lieutenants and Sheriffs are considered to belong to the Lord Chancellor's department, the latter officer being the great conservator of the peace. An English Sheriff is in almost all respects like the Sheriff of an American County; he executes all processes of the King's Courts, serves writs, arrests, takes bail, has charge of jails, and is responsible for the execution of criminals; like the Lord Lieutenants, Sheriffs are appointed by the Queen's administration on nomination by the County Judges; several persons are generally nominated, and the Queen designates who shall serve by pricking the parchment list with a punch opposite his name. The Sheriff gets no salary; he serves one year, and is, during that time, the most eminent subject in the County; except for this social consideration. few persons would care to serve as Sheriffs. Several ladies have filled this office in past times.

In the County in which London is situated the citizens have the chartered right to appoint their Sheriffs, and, in the County of Cornwall, the Prince of Wales names the Sheriff, for he is the Duke of Cornwall. Lancaster, in England, used to be the property of a nobleman, who became King, and it is governed, in part, by a separate Cabinet officer, as the private appendage of the sovereign.

The English County, like the American State, is a district of historic, and not of legislative construction; the Counties, therefore, are very unequal in size. From time immemorial, England has had forty Counties, and Wales, twelve. The largest of all the English Counties is Yorkshire, which has about the area of Connecticut and Rhode Island together, and is for convenience divided into four districts, three of which are called Ridings, — a corruption of the word "Tithings," which latter means a district composed of three Hundreds. In the State of Delaware, in the United States, Counties are also divided into Hundreds. None of these small divisions, in England, have the right to create railway monopolies like some of our States, or to embarrass traffic passing across them. The general Parliament is their Parliament in all matters affecting great interests. Each English County is bound to maintain a Jail and House of Correction; both Counties and towns can be compelled to erect Lunatic Asylums; these institutions are visited periodically, by the Justices of the Peace; they are maintained by rates levied on the County or town, and over the whole series of them, Parliament, or the Cabinet exercises the rights of inspection and interference. Within the past ten years the condition of English prisons has greatly improved; all the greater penitentiaries and the convict stations are out of control of the Counties, and belong to the government.

In no part of England is flogging now permitted, and steps have been taken to abolish it in the Army and the Navy; but on the convict stations flogging is in full vogue, though the sentiment of the nation is expressed against it even there. We retain the whipping-post in but one State, Delaware. In each of the three court-house villages of Delaware the whipping-post is an old and familiar ornament. It was removed from Wilmington, the principal city, many years ago, but you can see it in Georgetown and Newcastle, and in Dover, the State capital. The legislators, if in session, at the time of court, can hear the screams of the whipped in the green jail-yard, behind the State House, and if they like, look out of the Representatives' Hall, upon the flogging. This whipping-post looks like an old pump without a handle or a spout, the fissure in which the handle, if supplied, would work, being devoted to the pillory board, which is passed through and pegged fast. In this board the offender's head and wrists are locked tight, and he stands in the hot sun, or rain, as it may be, exposed to the taunts of tavern loafers, — his friends, probably, yesterday or to-morrow. To the sides of the whipping-post, three feet above the ground, a pair of iron clamps are fastened; these pass over the wrists of the condemned, and are locked to staples below, so that he stands with his back bowed, hugging the post. Behind him stands the Sheriff, or his deputy, applying the raw-hide. The boys, the negroes, sometimes the girls, come round to be amused, for in a dull town like Dover, a whipping is a fall of manna in the wilderness. The consequences of the punishment do not stop with the bloody bare back of the criminal; they extend to the young spectators, and make them coarse and insensible; they give the State a name, which its neighbors abhor, and involve our common nationality in the shame of their stripes. They brutalize the State of Delaware; its women and its men together sharing the effects of the infliction, which is morally worse than to be whipped. White men are said to be seldom beaten here.

At the town of New Castle, some cunning imitator of the virtues of the guillotine has invented a cat-o'-nine-tails, with wire extremities, every blow of which cuts into the tendons like a knife-blade, and often into the loins. More than twelve (one hundred and eight) blows of this instrument are said to be perilous to life.

The pillory is no less brutalizing, being a blow at one's pride, which is the last article of man that a good State can appeal to, and to the spectators it makes a ribaldry of punishment, so that they laugh at the pilloried one, and do not pity him.

The people of Delaware, from the Governor down, argue for the continuance of these two Asiatic institutions, saying, chiefly, that the whipping-post is a better preventative than the jail, and that only negroes "catch it."

The most populous County in England is Lancaster, which in 1861 had two and a half millions of people, or was about equal to the population of Ohio in 1860. The second County, in populousness, was Middlesex, in which the bulk of London lies, with two and one-fifth millions, or a million and a half less people than New York State, in which the American London lies. The third County, in rank, is York, with a little above two millions, somewhat greater than Illinois. The fourth County is Surrey, also embracing a part of London, which contains one hundred and fifty thousand less people than Alabama. Stafford and Kent follow next, being about as populous as Wisconsin and South Carolina. Wales, altogether, contains about one million one hundred thousand people, or about as many as Tennessee. The smallest English County is Rutland, which has one-sixth the population of Delaware. Warwick has a third as many people as Rhode Island. England and Wales are more densely populated than any other country in Europe, except Belgium, containing about three million seven hundred and forty thousand houses, and upwards of twenty millions of people, or nearly three hundred and fifty to the square mile. In many English Counties the population is decreasing. England has doubled in population in the course of half a century; the women outnumber the men, in England, five per cent.

Passing from State to State, in America, the traveller sees few striking differences in the garbs, the habitations, or the farms of the people; but in England there are customs and traditions inherent in each County, which the laboring people preserve from year to year. These are of infinite amusement to the American, and in the small space of England proper there is more variety of life and condition than in all America. Almost every parish has its common, where pasture the cows, asses, and goats of the poor. Every parish has one church, and of these, alone, there are twelve thousand in England; they are frequently of great antiquity, dating back to the earliest days of Christianity in Britain, and their picturesque towers, and roofs of thatch, or tile, or slate, are studies for wayfarer and architect alike. In every parish there is a work-house, and many of the poor are also paid weekly stipends, who do not inhabit this asylum. "To come upon the parish," is the English phrase for relying upon charity. Not only are there commons in the villages, but along the roadsides in many parts of England there are barren tracts, which yet give root to bushes of furze, whose beautiful yellow flowers make their lonesomeness bloom. Gypsies and cricketers betake themselves to these commons and wastes, for England has been a favorite kingdom for the former named these many centuries. Throughout the whole of these Parish and County jurisdictions, the power of the landholder shows itself, interwoven with all the conditions of life, and responsible for the most of them.

The large manufacturing cities of England lie, in many cases, upon the manors of these aristocrats, and when the manor of Manchester was subsequently purchased by the Corporation, in 1845, the purchase money amounted to no less than one million of dollars. The power of the English magistrate is dependent upon his wealth and rank more thoroughly than upon his office, and, in fact, like the Swiss landlords, who are also magistrates, and pass upon the justice of their own accounts, the English magistrates are mainly taken up with the conservation of their own laws, lands, and privileges. They control the church "living," in many cases, and it is to their interest to enforce the church-rates, which pay the salary of their parson, — perhaps a relative. They keep game, and much of their administration is the punishing of "poachers" upon it. By the theory of English law, the sovereign is the only person who has the right to pursue game, and whoever wishes to acquire such right must obtain a license from the crown. This right has been transmitted to the landed gentry, and Blackstone says that "the only difference between the old

Norman forest laws, and the new game laws, is that formerly there was only one great hunter through the land, whereas, at present, a petty Nimrod reigns in every manor-house. To be able to shoot a partridge upon land which he leased, required, down to 1830, fifty times as much income as to be a parliamentary elector. At present a man may shoot game on his own land, by buying a license, or he may lease a field for shooting to a licensed gunner. In this way the great landed proprietors frequently receive large sums of money every year, by selling out a week's or a month's shooting on their grounds. Dealing in game is allowed by license and trade certificate, but poaching by night and killing game out of season are punished severely. The game laws have made almost as many criminals in England as the use of alcohol. The prevalence of game in America has made our laws lax in respect to it, and in the eastern part of the United States there is probably less game at present than in Great Britain, where it is preserved. We have no such oppressive land monopolies as the English, and need fear the inauguration of no such game laws as have been maintained with them; but a land without birds is almost as poor as a land without trees. We are taking steps in many of the States to guard the fish and the game, and not to rob posterity altogether.

In America we find that very small States retard the interests of their greater neighbors. Delaware maintains the whipping-post, because she has not the population to support large penitentiaries and State institutions. But in England there is among the governing classes a strong preference for little jurisdictions and small constituencies.

One of the most noteworthy points of a late address of Mr. Gladstone was that portion of it in which he spoke most strongly in behalf of small nomination boroughs. He said he regarded them as supplying the race of men who were trained to carry on the government of the country, the masters of civil wisdom, like Mr. Burke, Sir James Mackintosh, Mr. Pelham, Lord Chatham, Mr. Fox, Mr. Pitt, Mr. Canning, and Sir Robert Peel, all of whom sat first for small boroughs. If there was to be no ingress to the House but one, and that one the suffrages of a large mass of voters, there would be a dead level of mediocrity. The extension, the durability, of our liberty were to be attributed, under Providence, to distinguished statesmen introduced into the House at an early age. But large constituencies would not return boys, and therefore he hoped the small boroughs would be retained.

Two of the most alarming evils of our American system of government are, the corruption of the State Legislatures, and the application of universal suffrage to the selection of Judges and the disposition of municipal finances. In the great cities, particularly in the greatest of our cities, the taxes are imposed by partisans chosen from the destitute and debauched classes, and it seems impossible, according to present indications, that New York city will ever get, by the present system, a purer form of government.

Justices of the Peace, in England, are selected from the richest and most respectable people. Rich merchants, clergymen, great landed proprietors, and leading lawyers are invested with this office; they are generally appointed for the whole County, by the Lord Chancellor, on formal application from the candidate himself. There are about eighteen thousand Justices in England, only thirteen hundred of whom are paid, and yet nearly one-half are arduously engaged in dealing out justice So honorable is the possession of even a petty office esteemed in England! These Justices of the Peace are the minor magistrates of the kingdom, and commit all paupers, keep the highways free, demand bail, and have jurisdiction over the small offences of everybody but peers. These Justices need not give open hearings; they have no control over cases affecting bequeathed property, but can compel the payment of tithes and wages, and they arbitrate between master and workman. Like all other subjects these Justices of the Peace are answerable to the law; but their motives are considered in extenuation of their acts. The combined Justices of the Peace in one County appoint the Constables thereof, but great variety in the manner of appointing and controlling the police exists amongst the different Counties.

London, excepting the city proper, is divided into twenty-three district courts, whose magistrates are paid salaries, and unlike our American police justices they must be barristers-at-law of seven years' standing.

Within the Counties, Coroners, Knights of the Shire, Poor-law "Unions," and Boards of Health are elected by the freeholders of the County. In the large towns the "gentry" are no longer the Justices of the Peace, magistrates being appointed for that purpose. About the office of Justice of the Peace, Lord Coke says, "that if it is administered in a fitting manner the whole of Christendom has not its equal." It is a pity that this sentiment does not control the appointment of petty magistrates in the United States. A property qualification is required for this office throughout England, except in the case of peers.

Eighteen or twenty towns constituted municipal Counties, chief of which are London, York, Chester, Bristol, Nottingham, Exeter, and Newcastle. These Counties have their own sheriffs, coroners, and militia. But now upwards of two hundred towns in England are not subject to the government of the Counties in which they are situated. The tax-payers elect a Mayor, who serves for one year, and can be a magistrate for a year succeeding. The town government consists of a Board of Aldermen and a Council. The Mayor presides over the Council. Aldermen serve for six years. Common Council meets once a quarter. Except in some minor details, where some musty old privilege or nuisance is tolerated or compromised, English municipalities at the present day are nearly counterparts of our American city governments; but, in our American cities, we attach too little importance to the municipal legislatures, and in the English cities they attach too much. We consign the vast property interests of beautiful cities, like New York, Philadelphia, and Cincinnati, to bodies of councilmen who often have no interests in the town, and no acquaintance with decent society.

The least consequential cities of England are guarded in all their municipal interests with that jealous respect for property rights which is characteristic of the entire English government.

A representative American State may be cited to show how our separate sovereignties are governed.

As an example, take the State of New York. It has had six distinct forms of government, — Dutch, English, Revolutionary, — besides three Constitutions, and another Constitution proposed (1867). In a few paragraphs I will consider these various forms of government, in order to show the democratic growth of State government.

The Dutch established civil government in 1621, — nearly two hundred and fifty years ago, — on the basis of the Dutch Roman Law, with a Director-General and Council, and embarrassed right of appeal to the home government of Holland. New York (Amsterdam) city was incorporated in 1653.

The English captured the colony in 1664, and governed as arbitrarily as the Dutch for twenty-seven years. The Captain-General, who was much the same officer as the Captain-General of Cuba in 1869, held his office during the pleasure of the English government, and received twelve thousand dollars a year, exclusive of fees. His council consisted of about a dozen members, and every councillor was called "The Honorable."

During the Revolution, the British set at rest most experiments upon the temporary form of government by capturing the city and establishing martial law in it. What New York State has grown to be in our day is a more interesting consideration.

The New York Civil Service List is a book of six hundred pages, very carefully edited, and a model for the United States Blue Book, which is much less satisfactory.

It is at once a history of the State, and a personal record of all its officials, from the year 1621 to the present time. As I look over this book I am reminded of how far enterprise, State pride, and talent go to diminish the political and social sins of New York State.

A stranger, unacquainted with the inside affairs of the worst-governed city in the New World, looks in vain for the outward evidences of *decadence*. He sees the lamps duly lighted every night far into the naked country, until the whole island blazes. A policeman is never out of sight. Gangs of workmen go steadily up the streets, laying huge cubical blocks of paving-stone. One never feels able to believe his body endangered here, provided he shall not go into dens of danger. The magnificent Court House rises slowly to completion. The Central Park grows more elaborate; the town strides past it; the city gets a surer, grander hold upon the island every year, encroaching on the purlieus, fixing the sockets of its East River bridge to cross an arm of the salt sea, and casting its determined eye upon Hell Gate, resolving that some day the "Great Eastern" ship shall tread up Long Island Sound, as up the long nave of some cathedral, to anchor fast at the piers of the city. Like Paris, New York is a better protector of the stranger than of her own citizens. To the one she turns her monuments; to the other, her tax-gatherers.

In like manner with the State. At Albany they are laying the piers of the great State Capitol, to rival the *Hotel de ville* of Paris in its mediæval elaborateness.

The Civil Service List which I take up shows that the State of New York probably exercises more powers of sovereignty than any State in America, Massachusetts scarcely excepted. The Governor appoints foreign commissioners, wreck-masters, and other dignitaries.

The Governor's staff have actual duties and material to consider, and are not, as in many States, altogether ornamental appendages. They are Brigadier-Generals, and are salaried, as well as their aides. The State has a Bureau of Military Statistics, with a museum of trophies and mementoes. The Secretary of State is a powerful officer, with diversified duties. The canals of the State are its property, and the chief sources of its revenue and corruption.

Bank and Insurance Companies are put under rigid censorship. There are three immense State prisons, in the three corners of the triangle, the newest of which is at Clinton, near Lake Champlain, among the Adirondacks. The Superintendent of Schools has more multifarious duties, if he performs them well, than the similar officer of many kingdoms.

The Regents of the University are general custodians of the higher academies and State colleges, who receive no salaries. There is also a Board of Railroad Commissioners. The State holds and restricts the city of New York, very much as an army holds a hostile town in time of war, being as jealous of the city as is the English government of London.

The salary of the Governor of New York is 4,000 dollars; and on the last popular vote for this office eight hundred and fifty thousand ballots were cast. He has a private Secretary and private Door-keeper. The Lieutenant Governor gets six dollars a day; four of the Governor's staff get 2,400 dollars each a year, and their aides get 1,800 dollars; the Secretary of State gets 2,500 dollars; the Comptroller and Treasurer, 2,500 dollars each; the State Engineer, 2,500 dollars; the Auditor of the Canal 2,500 dollars; the Attorney-General, 2,000 dollars; Canal Commissioners, 2,000 dollars each; several Canal Appraisers, 2,000 dollars and expenses; the Superintendent of Insurance companies, 5,000 dollars; and of banks, 5,000 dollars; three Prison Inspectors, 1,600 dollars; Superintendent of Schools, 2,500 dollars; Inspector of Gas-metres, 1,500 dollars; Judges generally 3,500 dollars; Members of the Legislature three dollars per day, and the Speaker four dollars.

These salaries are inadequate, in the main, to keep honest poor men in office, and it is notorious that, in the general demoralization of a commercial age, New York has one of the most corrupt Legislatures in America.

There are in New York nineteen incorporated cities, of which Ogdensburgh is probably the smallest. The terms city, town, and village have more definite and traditional meanings in this State than we generally allow in our loose commonwealths. Above all other political powers in the State are these two, — The State Capitol and Tammany Hall.

In 1860 New York State contained three million eight hundred and eighty thousand seven hundred and thirty-five inhabitants, and next year will probably show four million five hundred thousand, allowing the same increase as in the previous decade. This is one-fourth more people than Scotland, and, as New York is about one-fourth greater than Scotland, their relative density is nearly the same. It is about a million less than the diminishing population of Ireland, and, the changes being the same, in another ten years New York will be more populous than Ireland. It is nearly one-third the population of Spain. It is half a million past that of Portugal. It is almost exactly that of Belgium, and a third greater than Holland, the parent country of New York. It is a million past that of Sweden. It is a fourth the population of Prussia. It is double that of Switzerland, and, if we estimate the present population of London at three millions, it is London and a half, and it is one-half more people than composed the United States in the war of the Revolution, and four and a half times all the people on the Pacific coast of the United States at the present day.

The property of the State Government of New York is about eighty millions of dollars. It owns about three thousand miles of railroad, or nearly as much as Prussia.

With powers of such magnitude, far exceeding those of the most powerful County in England, it is refreshing to mark the ignorance of some British commentators upon our States, one of whom, Mr. Anthony Trollope, says: —

"Nothing has struck me so much in America as the fact that the State Legislatures are puny powers. The absence of any tidings whatever of their doings across the water is a proof of this. Who has heard of the Legislature of New York or of Massachusetts? It is boasted here that their insignificance is a sign of the well-being of the people; that the smallness of the power necessary for carrying on the machine shows how beautifully the machine is organized, and how well it works. 'It is better to have little government than great Governors.' That glory, if ever it were a glory, has come to an end. It seems to me that all these troubles have come upon the States, because they have not placed high men in high places. The less of laws and the less of control the better, providing the people can go right with few laws and little control. One may say that no laws and no control would be best of all, — provided that none were needed. But this is not exactly the position of the American people."

The same writer is more to the point when he says that "the two professions of law-making and of governing have become unfashionable, low in estimation, and of no repute in the States. The municipal powers of the cities have not fallen into the hands of the leading men. The word politician has come to bear the meaning of political adventurer, and almost of political blackleg. If A calls B a politician, A intends to vilify B by so calling him. Whether or no the best citizens of a State will ever be induced to serve in the State Legislature by a nobler consideration than that of pay, or by a higher tone of political morals than that now existing, I cannot say. It seems to me that some great decrease in the numbers of the State legislators should be a first step toward such a consummation. There are not many men in each State who can afford to give two or three months of the year to the State service for nothing; but it may be presumed that in each State there are a few. Those who are induced to devote their time by the payment of sixty pounds can hardly be the men most fitted for the purpose of legislation.

"It certainly has seemed to me that the members of the State Legislatures and of the State governments are not held in that respect, and treated with that confidence, to which, in the eyes of an Englishman, such functionaries should be held as entitled."

The Channel Islands, which lie in the British seas, are regulated internally by their old Norman laws. The writs of the great courts of Westminster are not served here, but the Queen's commission must be produced. Parliament must mention the islands by name, if they are to be governed by any of its acts. For a good account of Guernsey, one of these islands, read Victor Hugo's story of "The Toilers of the Sea."

The Isle of Man, in the Irish Sea, is governed by its own Legislature, composed of two bodies, the "Council," and the "House of Keys," and by a Queen's governor. An inhabitant of Man is called a Manx-man.

Scotland retains many individual customs. The government grants about one-third of the benefices of its established church. Common law and equity are not under two heads as in England, and every act of Parliament applies to Scotland, unless the terms of the law make the exception. There is no grand jury in Scotland, nor must the petit jury unanimously agree. The Supreme Court in civil cases is the Court of Session, consisting of thirteen judges, with "inner" and "outer" houses, and the Court of Justiciary is the supreme tribunal in criminal cases, composed of five select judges of the Court of Sessions. The head President of the Court of Sessions gets 27,000 dollars a year; he is the head of the select bench. The Lord Justice Clerk gets 22,500 dollars, and is at the head of the minor bench. The other judges get 15,000 dollars a year. The law officers are the Lord Advocate, with salary and fees of 15,000 dollars a year, and the Solicitor General, with 5,000 dollars a year. The revenue of the English Established Church in Ireland, up to the time of its legislated decease in 1869, was nearly three millions of dollars in gold a year.

The Scotch people gave a dynasty — and the worst one — to the English throne, and being a shrewd and business-like people, they have greatly prospered by the union between the two ancient kingdoms. They retain their national church, and have no foreign Lord Lieutenant to preside over them; on the contrary, the English royal family has a residence in Scotland.

Very different in intention and reception is the government of Ireland. Practically, the government of Ireland and every step of importance connected with it, are under the immediate control of the English Cabinet. On matters of revenue, the Lord Lieutenant of Ireland is instructed to correspond with the Treasury; but on all other subjects with the Home Secretary of State, who is deemed personally responsible for the government of Ireland, and is in close correspondence with the Lord Lieutenant, advising him, and keeping him informed of the views and opinions of the Cabinet upon all the more important questions connected with his government. For the issue of instruments under the Great Seal of Ireland, he receives Her Majesty's authority by warrants under her sign manual. No person professing the Roman Catholic religion can hold the office. The Lord Lieutenant's duration of office depends upon that of the ministry of which he is a member. His salary has generally been one hundred thousand dollars per annum, with a residence in Dublin Castle, and another in Phœnix Park.

All acts of Parliament extend to Ireland, unless they be expressly excepted. There is a special Privy Council for Ireland, consisting of fifty-eight members, each member of which is entitled "Right

Honorable." There is a Secretary of State, removable like the Lord Lieutenant, on a change of administration, with a salary of fifteen thousand dollars a year, and a permanent under-Secretary with ten thousand dollars a year.

The Lord Lieutenant of Ireland is thus one of the most important officers of the British government. He has the highest salary, — even above the Lord Chancellor and the Prime Minister; he can pardon criminals in Ireland; he has charge of the police, and is the superior of the army general in command of Ireland. He is, in short, a military governor, and keeps Ireland in subjection, prevents insurrection, and exercises the pretence of civil powers, but the reality of arbitrary ones.

I feel the same disinclination to compare the behavior of Ireland and Scotland as parts of the British Kingdom that I should to compare Esau and Jacob, Ishmael and Isaac. Two warm temperaments, one burning to genius, the other to business, the Scotchman has become prosperous by submission, the Irishman wretched by resistance. Neither had a like religion with the nation that absorbed them. The Scotch Presbyterian is no less a foe to the English hierarchy than is the Irish Catholic; but the Scotch were never the creatures of demagogues, the dust of faction, nor the forward partisans of their ecclesiastics. Democratic in church government, every Scotchman thought for himself in civil government; every Scotchman saw that the geographical modern law forbade England and Scotland to be two governments, and he worked for his place in the compound government.

Two destructive things have underlain Ireland: a priesthood controlled from abroad, and an unstable national character. The Irishman has genius, wit, music, valor, — but not convictions. He follows leaders everywhere, and is betrayed by them or betrays them. It is impossible to believe that, under any circumstances, Ireland or England could have been happy or peaceful, divided. The Irishman would have been, abroad, the Northman pirate preying upon his neighbor; at home the Orange and the Ribbon bands exterminating each other. To this irreconcilable enemy the arrogant Englishman must be either a master or a victim. Yet Irish individualism has been one of the glories of the English nation. Grattan, Wellington, Goldsmith, proclaim it. The Irish nation, like the Jewish race, seems fated to illustrate all lands, and control, as a unity, in none. They are to England what the American Indian is to us: the theme of allegory and drama, the type cf generosity and valor, but also the race of short truces and frequent forays. In peace they fall into tribes and plunder each other. In war they violate international law and the terms of hospitality, moving upon England by way of Black Rock in Canada. Dispersed among the other races, they are an element of vigor and industry; but collected, as in the great American cities, they make us write such verdicts against them as we do, with pity. No American can speak in praise of English rule in Ireland. No American can speak in praise of Irish behavior under England. Two men have lived in Ireland who rank as benefactors: Father Mathew, the apostle of temperance, and Daniel O'Connell, who procured the enfranchisement of Irish Catholic subjects. O'Connell showed all the genius of his race, amongst whom he was a gentleman, and also all its turbulence. The latter years of his life were passed in nervous retirement, and after his discharge from jail in Ireland for agitating for the repeal of the act of union between Ireland and England, these are the particulars of his life, well told by an historian: —

"Released from jail one evening, he went home to his own house. The next morning early, he went back to his prison, to be carried home in triumph. The whole city of Dublin was abroad to see; and it was two hours from the time when the procession began to leave the jail gates before the car could be brought up. The car — invented for the occasion, and never seen again but at his funeral — lifted him a dozen feet over the heads of the crowd. He stood at his full height, and was crowned with the repeal-cap. He was portly, and apparently in good health; but his countenance wore that anxious expression which was now becoming habitual to it.

"He was invited to England, and feted there, and made use of for the anti-corn law cause. But he was never really formidable again, and he knew it. He had no policy, no principle, nothing to repose upon; and only his ingenuity and audacity for a resource. Then he was seen in London streets, walking slowly and stooping, while supported by two of his sons; and members of the House complained that they could not hear his now short speeches, because of the feebleness of his voice. He retired to Hastings, on the coast. He desired that the newspapers might be kept away from him, and all tidings of Ireland. No one was to be admitted who would speak of Ireland. He so watched the countenance of his physician when looking at his tongue, and was so alarmed by any gravity of countenance at the moment, that his physician had to remember to look cheerful and pleased.

"Next he went abroad, hoping to reach Rome, and die under the blessing of the Pope. But he sank too rapidly for this. He was carried to Paris, Marseilles, Genoa; and then he could go no further.

"The final symptoms, consequent on a long decay of the digestive functions, came on in May, 1847; and on the fifteenth of that month he died."

This is, perhaps, a severe treatment of the character of O'Connell, who is now a feature of statuary in Dublin, but Harriet Martineau says thus further of him: —

"Ireland has been abundantly cursed with barbarous despots, but it may be doubted whether any one of them, in the long course of centuries, has perpetrated such effectual cruelties as the despot whom his victims called their Liberator, and hoped to see their King." He was, in the opinion of this writer, the pervertor of the seriousness which covered the Irish nation after Father Mathew's discourses, into mischievous political intemperances. The latter days of O'Connell were clouded by the calumnies of the hot-headed "Young Ireland" party, of whom Miss Martineau says: "The latest phase of the lives, and opinions, and influences of the Young Ireland party, tells the moral very well: John Mitchell, a fanatical champion of the slave-power in America; Meagher, in military command in the service of the north; O'Brien, issuing his manifesto from Ireland, in behalf of the Confederates and their despotism, and the Irish in New York, slaying negroes in the streets, and rising up against law and order, — these are apt illustrations of the spurious kind of Irish patriotism, which would destroy Ireland by aggravating its weakness, and rejecting the means of recovery and strength!"

I have referred thus particularly to O'Connell and Ireland, because he was the Irish Calhoun, advocating the withdrawal of Ireland from the English Parliament, while Smith O'Brien and John Mitchell were like the later State-Rights party in America, making their appeals to the sword. For a thorough idea of Irish politics, though a partisan one, read the story of the "Knight of Gwynne," by Charles Lever, which recites the condition of Ireland in 1800, when her Parliament was merged with that of England, through the efforts of an Irish statesman, Castlereagh.

We live, at present, at a period of American history, when the central government is all-powerful, but it must ever be remembered, — and this we shall see further when we come to France, — that liberty in a republic is best guarded, when by means of cities and states, power is distributed throughout the territory, instead of residing in a single spot. This is the comment of the wise and discreet De Tocqueville, the best foreign observer upon America: —

"The Union is a great republic, in extent, but the paucity of objects for which its government provides, assimilates it to a small State. Its acts are important, but they are rare. As the sovereignty of the Union is limited, and incomplete, its exercise is not incompatible with liberty; for it does not excite those insatiable desires of fame and power which have proved so fatal to great republics. As there is no common centre to the country, vast capital cities, colossal wealth, abject poverty, and sudden revolutions, are alike unknown; and political passion, instead of spreading over the land like a torrent of desolation, spends its strength against the interests and the individual passion of every State.

"Nevertheless, all commodities and ideas circulate throughout the Union as freely as in a country inhabited by one people. Nothing checks the spirit of enterprise. The government avails itself of the assistance of all who have talents or knowledge to serve it. Within the frontiers of the Union the profoundest peace prevails, as within the heart of some great empire; abroad, it ranks with the most powerful nations of the earth; thousands of miles of its coast are open to the commerce of the world; and, as it possesses the keys of the globe, its flag is respected in the most remote seas. The Union is as happy and as free as a small people, and as glorious and as strong as a great nation."

CHAPTER XI.

BRITISH PROVINCES AND PROVINCIAL CITIES.

Sketches of the leading towns and cities of Great Britain and Ireland, and their points of similarity with places in America. — A chapter to supply the place of a map. — Glimpses of daily life in town and country.

In the United States the loudest roar is in the conflict of parties; next is the clash of great interests; then the challenge between city and city. In cities modern freedom began, where in Italy and Flanders the tradesmen bought their liberties of their Lords, and maintained them by courage or advantageous alliances. In England, as we have seen, there are now many municipalities like our own, — small republics in the heart of the British Empire, — and also a few old-time cities, like London, governed by their guilds or trades-companies. Of cities of the latter sort we have no examples, nor are any of our cities independent of the State in which they are situated, but derive their charters from the States, and acknowledge the same as liable to be altered by the State Legislatures. English cities have this important advantage, — that they are, in nothing material, subject to the County which encloses them. The greatest of the English cities is called the Metropolis, and the secondary cities go by the name of the Provincial cities. Middlesex, the County of London, is called the Metropolitan County, and the other rural districts are called Provinces. London is the British metropolis in all respects of population, commerce, legislation, money, capital, and social influence. We have no undisputed metropolis in America, and it is affectation or bluster for any one city to allege it. New York is at present the commercial metropolis, and Washington is the political metropolis. But San Francisco has commercial opportunities which almost outpromise New York, and if, in the destiny of events, Havana should become ours, it may yet lay claim to this title. Neither the political nor commercial pivot of the United States is yet fixed with certainty, but this is a common point in Great Britain, long ago ascertained.

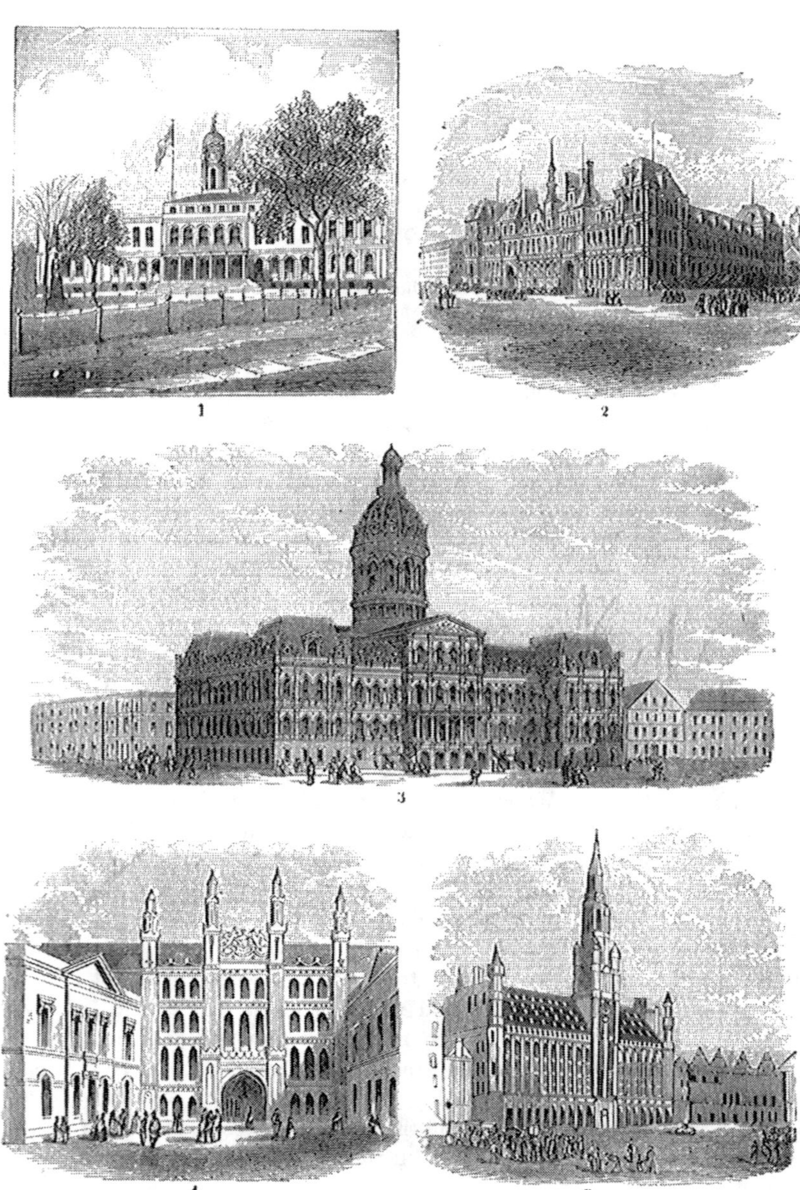

SEATS OF MUNICIPAL GOVERNMENT.

1—The City Hall, New York. 2—The City Hall, Paris. 3—New City Hall, Baltimore.
4—The City Hall, London. 5—The City Hall, Brussels.

An American visiting England will disembark at Southampton, on the south coast, or at Liverpool on the north-west. He may also find steamers to Cork, and to Londonderry, in Ireland, or to Glasgow, in Scotland, or even to London. But practically, all great passenger trade between the United States and Great Britain goes to Liverpool, which is the seaport of Manchester, Bradford, Leeds, Sheffield, and Birmingham, and which grew into importance almost entirely by the American trade. When steamship commerce began across the Atlantic, the city of Bristol made earnest show of rivalry with Liverpool. Bristol equipped a steamship, and sent it to New York, but before it could get off, the Liverpoolers despatched an old tub of a tug, which barely lived to New York, but beat the Bristol ship some days, and exhausted the glory of the feat. Bristol had, in 1861, but one hundred and fifty-five thousand people, while Liverpool had four hundred and forty-four thousand. Bristol has no such series of great towns in the rear of it as Liverpool, nor a railway system exhaustive as her rival's; but Bristol is still the third city in England, commercially, and inhabited by a more generous and benignant people than Liverpool; it never produced, in our periods of trouble, such enemies as the Lairds and the Spences. Liverpool is one of the most depraved and selfish cities in the world, having neither the independence of Manchester, nor the beauty of Bristol. Southampton and Hull follow Bristol, in importance, as commercial towns in England, the former having about fifty thousand people, and the latter, one hundred thousand.

The city of Baltimore in America has recently made earnest strides toward commercial importance, and sanguine expectations have been formed of the growth of Norfolk, Charleston, and Portland. There are many remarkable harbors in America which have declined in importance by reason of the decline of our commerce; witness Newport, New Bedford, and New London. As a rule, the ports of Europe are poor compared with those of America in depth of water and extent of anchorage ground.

In populousness, the principal American cities stand to British cities, thus: —

MANUFACTURING CITIES.				COMMERCIAL CITIES.			
America.		*Great Britain.*		*Great Britain.*		*America.*	
Philadelphia,	600,000	Manchester,	475,000	Liverpool,	445,000	Baltimore,	300,000
Cincinnati,	275,000	Birmingham,	300,000	Glasgow,	390,000	Boston,	200,000
Pittsburg, Alleghany, etc.,	200,000	Dublin,	265,000	Bristol,	155,000	New Orleans,	150,000
		Leeds,	210,000	Belfast,	155,000	Buffalo,	85,000
		Sheffield,	190,000	Newcastle,	115,000	Charleston,	45,000
Louisville,	80,000	Wolv'rhampt'n,	150,000	Plymouth and Devonport,	115,000	Richmond,	45,000
Newark, N.J.,	110,000	Bradford,	110,000			Portland,	30,000
Albany and Troy,	90,000	Stoke,	101,000			Cleveland,	70,000
		Preston,	94,000	Hull,	100,000	Detroit,	50,000
Providence,	55,000	Bolton,	85,000	Portsmouth,	100,000	Chicago,	300,000
Lowell,	40,000	Blackburne,	70,000	Sunderland,	85,000	St. Louis,	200,000
Manchester, N. H.,	25,000	Merthyr-Tydril, Wales,	85,000	Edinburgh,	170,000	Milwaukie,	60,000
		Paisley,	55,000	Cork,	75,000	San Francisco,	120,000
				Dundee,	95,000		
				Aberdeen,	75,000		
				Southampton,	50,000		
				Greenock,	45,000		

In the above list I have given the presumed population of both British and American cities, in 1866. The census has not yet been taken in America, for 1870, and between the jealousy of American cities it is probable that some persons may take exception to my figures. I think that the above estimates are nearly correct, however, for many cities in both countries have fallen off in the past ten years rather than increased. Some towns, like Edinburgh and Dublin, are neither commercial nor manufacturing towns, or are both.

Over the broad belt of the United States reside probably thirty-five millions of people. In the small British islands dwell thirty millions. There are two main islands of the United Kingdom, *Great Britain* (which comprises England, Wales, and Scotland) and *Ireland.* For the channel and sea which divide these two islands substitute the plains and deserts west of the Mississippi, and we may construct an Ireland on the Pacific coast of the United States. Then Galway would occupy the place of San Francisco, and Galway has but twenty-three thousand inhabitants. Portland, in Oregon, might be compared to Londonderry, or Derry, which has twenty thousand inhabitants. Dublin, the end of the chief ferry between England and Ireland, resembles in place Virginia City, the first town reached on the Pacific Railroad, after passing the desert. Cork might be put in place of Guaymas, our probable port on the South Pacific, and the terminus of a projected railway.

Following out the same fancy, and returning to the more populous island of Great Britain, we shall see that Wales is attached to England like a pair of promontories. Call the northern promontory of Anglesey, Kansas, and the southern promontory of Pembroke, Texas; then Leavenworth will compare with Holyhead, the ferry slip to Dublin, and Austin or Houston will stand in stead of Pembroke, a great naval station of England. Salt Lake city is merely an island in the desert, like the Isle of Man in the Irish Sea.

The Mississippi River, dividing the United States north and south, is our coast line. For the Ohio River substitute Bristol Channel; then Cincinnati becomes the city of Bristol. For the Illinois River substitute the Mersey; then St. Louis becomes Liverpool, and Chicago is Manchester. St. Paul in Minnesota is Glasgow in Scotland.

Behind Chicago, manufacturing articles for it to despatch westward across the plains is a cluster of rising cities, Detroit, Toledo, Fort Wayne, Cleveland. Behind Manchester, manufacturing goods to swell its mighty contribution westward, are Blackburn, Bolton, Preston, Rochdale.

Following the south coasts of Great Britain and the United States eastward, Galveston will become Plymouth, and New Orleans Southampton; Portsmouth in England stands for Mobile, and Brighton for Pensacola. Turning Florida and proceeding up the coast of the Atlantic, the Gulf Stream is the Strait of Dover as the Gulf of Mexico was the English Channel; London becomes Savannah; the Humber is the Chesapeake, and upon its various streams are Hull, its Norfolk; Nottingham, its Richmond; Sheffield, its Washington; Leeds, its Baltimore, and York, which is as much like York, Pennsylvania, or Lancaster, or Harrisburg, as anything I can think of; Newcastle-upon-Tyne is Philadelphia, both great coal ports. Edinburgh is New York, Providence is Dundee, Boston is Aberdeen, and Portland is Inverness. Birmingham is tributary to Bristol Channel, and compares in position with Pittsburg.

The above may enable the reader, without consulting the map, to keep the geography of England in mind, and there are some curious facts with regard to the colonization and civilization of the United Kingdom which readily adjust themselves to the above comparisons. England, like the United States, was settled and christianized from the East; the south-eastern parts of both empires were first settled; in the north of England as in the north of the United States, Calvinism took permanent root, while the Established or Episcopal Church fixed itself in the Southern States as in the south of England. These and many other reflections will occur to the student of a suggestive turn of mind. In this little United Kingdom dwell more than thirty millions of people. Leaving out New York and Massachusetts, there are as many people in the British Isles as in the United States; there are two hundred and thirty-nine people to the square mile in the British Kingdom, and in England and Wales three hundred and forty-seven to the square mile. Yet the greatest length of Great Britain is only six hundred and eight miles, about as far as from New York city to Toledo, Ohio; while the greatest width is two hundred and eighty miles, or the distance from New York city to Elmira. In one place the island of Great Britain is only thirty-three miles wide, or the distance from Washington to Baltimore, and the tides of the North Sea and the Atlantic rise within eighteen miles of each other.

In the New England States of America, there are about fifty people to the square mile; in the Middle States and Ohio, seventy; in the North-western States, twenty-two; and in California, two.

Before the civil war the population of our Southern States was only half as dense as that of Russia in Europe.

In England proper, and Wales, live twenty millions of people, or as many as inhabit our Middle, Southern, and seven North-western States.

Turkey is more densely peopled than our six Middle States. England and Wales comprise fifty-eight thousand three hundred and twenty square miles, or five thousand less than the New England States. Scotland contains about three millions of people on half the area of New England, which latter has about the same number of people. Ireland contains more than five and a half millions of people, or about the population of our seven North-western States. There were in 1861 three millions seven hundred and thirty-nine thousand five hundred and five inhabited houses in England and Wales. Wales alone contains about one million one hundred thousand people, or less than Massachusetts.

We divide America superficially into the New England, the Middle, the Southern, and the Western States. England proper is divided into the Northern Counties, the Midland Counties, the Eastern Counties, the Southern Counties, and the Western Counties. Our boundary lines between these sections are the Hudson, the Potomac, the Ohio and the Alleghany Rivers; the corresponding rivers of England are the Humber and Mersey, the Thames, and the Severn. The eastern part of the United States is separated from the valleys of the Mississippi and the St. Lawrence by the Appalachian Mountains, generally called the Alleghanies; so the most important range of British mountains guards the coast of the western channel, and forms the interlinking Pennine, Cambrian, and Devonian ranges. Of these latter the highest peaks are in Wales, where Mount Snowdon is three thousand five hundred and seventy-one feet high. The highest peaks of the Alleghanies are in western North Carolina, where, under the general name of the Black Mountains, they rise to the altitude of six thousand seven hundred and fifty-five feet. In Vermont the Alleghanies rise in Mount Mansfield to four thousand two hundred and seventy-nine feet, in Maine to Mount Katahdin, five thousand three hundred and eighty-five feet, and in New Hampshire to Mount Washington, six thousand four hundred and ninety-six feet. The highest mountains in Scotland rise to less than four thousand four hundred feet, and the highest in Ireland to three thousand four hundred and four feet. Scotland is the White Mountain region of America; Wales is the Adirondack country. The Blue Mountains of the United States, which are called the Highlands in New York, are also matched by a secondary range in England, which crosses that kingdom north-eastward. The larger English rivers are of nearly equal lengths with our Eastern streams; the Severn is longer than the Hudson, and the Thames larger than the Merrimac. A most thorough and complex system of canals connects all the rivers of England, and the interior of that island is a minute web of mutually contributing streams. But the British canals are not upon the grand scale of the Erie, the Pennsylvania, or the Potomac canals in America. They scarcely compare with the Chesapeake and Delaware, the Rondout, or the Raritan canals. Few masted vessels are to be seen crossing from river to river by these British canals, but chiefly small barges laden with coal or crude metallic freight. Much of the canal is creek; for what are called rivers in England are often no bigger than the Conestoga or the Brandywine creeks. The Avon, whereon

Shakespeare lived, is in many places a winding brook merely, and the same we have seen to be true of the Cam at Cambridge. English scenery, however, arranged upon this miniature scale, is more various and compendious within a small circuit than we find it in America. The arms of the salt sea, the mountainous hills, the ancient village, the barren moors, the bald tableland, the sequestered valley, the forest, are frequently found within the compass of a morning's ride. Not all the industry of a dense population has assimilated these various features to a uniform appearance; but in America nature is planned upon a broad scale, and the equal institutions and ages of the people have made all the dwellings, all the farms, all the villages within a wide circuit, look like counterparts of each other.

If we wished to select that one American city close about which lie the most diversified sceneries, it would probably be Boston. The sea and the mountains are its neighbors; lakes and broad, salty marshes are also amongst its intimate associations; the largest manufactories and some of the most cultivated farms are in its neighborhood; whaling and fishing ports are within easy reach; large islands like Nantucket lie not far over its horizon; university life can be studied in its environs; cattle, horses, and sheep of the best breed known to Europe have been imported by its gentlemen-farmers. The States of Rhode Island and New Hampshire are within thirty miles; Maine, Connecticut, and Vermont are not beyond the average of twice that distance; the Merrimac, the Connecticut, the Narragansett are within picnicking distance by steam.

But measure these by the country charms of London. Not five, but ten, dissimilar counties lie within twenty miles, and eight of them radiate from London like the spokes from a wheel-hub. Boston has been called the "Hub of the Universe," but probably by some one who had ambitiously likened it to London. In these English counties all varieties of dialect, avocation, and landscape lie; the people differ in any two of these counties more than in any two American States, and their products are more unlike than those of Connecticut and Delaware. Suppose we undertake to make the circuit of some of these counties hastily.

Berkshire, a county to the west of London, is celebrated for its pigs, many of which have been imported into America; they have thick jowls, short snouts, and upright ears; the best breed is black, with white spots. A Berkshire man says, "I telled him so smack to his head;" meaning, "I said it to his face." Windsor and Reading are the leading towns here; the latter is about half the size of Reading, Pennsylvania; the American Reading deals chiefly in beer, the English in biscuits; both of them are in counties called Berks.

Buckinghamshire, within half an hour north-west of London, is a great pasture county, and on its one hundred and fifty thousand acres of meadows feed twenty thousand milch cows, and it sends, also, to London, a hundred thousand dollars' worth of ducks every year. Straw-plait and thread-lace are its manufactures; its county-seat is the most uninteresting town in England. This county is commonly called Bucks.

Oxfordshire, between Berks and Bucks, one hour from London, is riveted to both those counties by the Chiltern Hills, nine hundred feet high. It is a poor county. Oxford city is described in the chapter on the Universities.

Kent, which comes quite up to London, is one of the richest counties in the world, as well as one of the most historic. It forms the south bank of the River Thames, from London to the sea, and like a cape thrusts itself to within sight of France. The river Medway, flowing through it, reaches the sea just at the mouth of the Thames; and at the mouth of the Medway is Sheerness, the great dock-yard; and up the Medway, ten miles, is Chatham, a naval station. The mouth of the Thames goes by the name of "The Naze." In the interior of Kent are the sizable towns of Rochester, Maidstone, and Canterbury. Dover, on the coast, maintains steam ferries, with Calais, in France, opposite, and many watering-places lie along the Kentish water line. This is the greenest and foggiest county in England, and a good deal of it is agueish. It used to be a kingdom by itself, and is full of Roman camps, ruins of abbeys, and old battle-fields. Cherries and hops are the great products here; there are sixty thousand acres planted in hops, which is half the hop crop of all England. Hop-picking in Kent is a more sprightly scene than grape-picking in France. We raise the main quantity of American hops in the interior of New York State. Paper is the chief manufacturing product of Kent.

The County of Sussex swings round south of Kent, and faces France by the English Channel. Hastings, where William the Conqueror landed, is in this county; also Chichester, where there is a great cathedral, and Lewes, the prettiest town in South England, where the breed of Southdown sheep was first developed, by Ellman. Here, also, is Brighton, the Long Branch of London, and the greatest watering-place in the kingdom, with a population of seventy thousand, and with forty thousand visitors a year. It is very expensive, costing a third more than hotel prices in London. It is more than a hundred years old, as a fashionable place, is very ugly, has a beach of "shingle," poor to American notions, and a long pier reaching out to deep water. The South-downs, in Sussex, is a range of chalk heights, fifty-three miles long, within sight of the sea. Sussex is a county of relapsed industry, but very peculiar.

Hampshire continues the circle round London to the south-west. It is commonly called Hants, and in the centre of it is the old Saxon capital of Winchester, one of the most interesting cities of England, while on its coast line are Southampton, and Portsmouth, large commercial and naval cities. In Winchester, Alfred the Great was born, and Canute was buried; it was founded before the Christian era; William the Conqueror thought it second only to London in importance; here Philip and Mary, the tyrannical royal pair, were married; Izaak Walton, prince of fishermen, is buried in the cathedral; the income of the latter edifice is one hundred and ten thousand dollars a year. There is an ancient school here, feeder to Oxford. Winchester has only fourteen thousand inhabitants, at present; the name of the town means "camp on the downs," and Chester everywhere means camp, as Manchester, "camp of tents." Portsmouth, like the name of all towns ending with "mouth," signifies the place at the mouth of the port or river; but we have misapplied the term in America. Portsmouth stands on an island three miles long, and two and a half miles wide; it contains seventy-two thousand people; its harbor is two miles wide, and on the other shore is Gosport. The Isle of Wight makes a breakwater for Portsmouth, and the channel between Wight and the shore makes the celebrated roads called Spithead, the Hampton Roads of England. Portsmouth is strongly fortified, and invested with shipping. New York is not as well defended. Its dockyard contains one hundred and twenty acres, and is the longest in England. Here lies Nelson's ship, the *Victory*, in which he died, and here, according to English history, Jack Aitken was hanged for burning down the ropery, in 1776, at the suggestion of Silas Deane, the American agent at Paris. For more about Portsmouth, see the chapter on the Army and Navy. Southampton stands at the head of a beautiful sound called Southampton Water, sixteen miles from Cowes, on the Isle of Wight. It was the original nurse of British commerce. It has nearly eight times the population it contained in 1840. Its environs are very beautiful, and its docks are spacious. The Isle of Wight is to the English coast very much what Staten Island is to New York, excepting that the latter is much smaller. Its scenery is renowned throughout the world; it is the site of one of the Queen's palaces, the seat of many beautiful villas, amongst which is that of the poet Tennyson, and at Cowes, its chief town, the famous Royal Yacht Club has its head-quarters.

Hertfordshire, north of London a few miles, is commonly called Herts. It contains many beautiful gardens, and orchards, which supply London with fruit; the English apples are far inferior to those of America, being watery, and lacking flavor. Enormous quantities of hay and straw are sent from Herts to London, but the remarkable product of the county is malt, and the town of Ware, which lies in this county, is the chief seat of the malting trade in Great Britain. The beautiful Abbey of St. Albans, a favorite resort of American and British artists, is in Herts, about thirty miles north of London.

Bedfordshire, also north of London, is almost exclusively an agricultural county; a good deal of freestone and lime goes thence to London, and there are fine old Roman ruins in the county.

Essex, to the east of London, holds the mouth of the Thames, on the north, as Kent does on the south; the two counties are of much the same size. Broad marshes from the North Sea extend into Essex, and many inlets and streams penetrate it. It was the land of the Great Briton King Caractacus. Large numbers of calves go from Essex to London. It is a wheat county, and it produces, besides, the British oyster, that small and coppery mollusk, which is the delight of London cockneys, and which, they insist, has no equal in the world for flavor. An American, used to the great oysters of New York waters, and the delicious bivalves of the Chesapeake, can scarcely be persuaded to touch the British "Native" oyster. Our American oysters have been transplanted to the coasts of France and Belgium, and to the Baltic; but the British epicure, with national obstinacy, clings to his domestic oyster, which will neither make a soup, a roast, a broil, or a fry.

The counties which have been above enumerated, immediately enclose London, and minister to its appetites; they send tons of rabbit, hare, pheasant, and partridge, to the great metropolis, and although almost within sound of its bells, they retain to this day, their ancient dialects and peculiarities. Tens of thousands of their inhabitants have never visited London; others have entered the city but once, as on the occasion of the coronation of the Queen.

There are two provincial cities of England which may be said to be of even rival political consequence with London: these are Manchester and Birmingham. Since the development of steam, and its application to machinery, these two great cities have, in a manner, resumed the activity, individuality, and influence which the great cities of the middle ages exercised. Neither Ghent, Bruges, nor Florence, were more aggressive in their best days, when their guilds maintained the honor of the corporation, than Manchester and Birmingham, with their powerful trades-unions, their debating societies, their political associations, and the community of sentiment which exists between employers and employed. These two cities may almost be said to have solely accomplished the success of the three great English movements of our century, namely, Parliamentary Reform (first, in 1832, second in 1867), the repeal of the Corn Laws, and Free Trade. And, it is probable that, but for the influence of Manchester and Birmingham, which were sturdily in favor of American union and prosperity, and were represented in Parliament by clear heads and eloquent tongues, the separation of our republic would have been recognized by the British Prime Minister, and the woes of the North and the South prolonged in consequence.

The attitude of Manchester, in particular, partook of the sublime; by the loss of American cotton many of her mills closed, and tens of thousands of operatives were thrown upon public charity. Nevertheless, the sacrificing spinners and weavers never ceased to bid America God-speed, and to decry any recognition of her ruin. Birmingham suffered less, but her spirit was the same, and the behavior of these hives of operatives was in striking contrast with the base and envious expression of Liverpool, a city which had fattened by her relations with the United States, and which had equipped the slavers which assisted to plant the curse of slavery in America. As early as 1708 slave-ships from the Mersey sailed to Africa, took aboard human cargoes, and delivered them up in Virginia and the Carolinas, whence the vessels returned laden with tobacco, sugar, and the native products of the infant world. In 1752 there were one hundred and one slave-dealing houses in Liverpool.

But two other cities exercise an approximate influence in English politics with Manchester and Birmingham, and that is of an entirely different character, namely, Edinburgh and Dublin, the latter by means of its turbulent populace and its discontented newspaper press having largely assisted to shorten the days of the Established Church in Ireland. The political influence of Edinburgh is of an intellectual sort, its solid and massive thinkers making themselves felt through their periodical reviews and books of political philosophy. Compared with the political status of American cities, Edinburgh holds the rank of Boston, the seat of original thought; Dublin the place of a former Charleston, South Carolina, the abode of destructive agitation; while Manchester and Birmingham resemble Chicago and the great cities of the north-west, powerful by their numbers and decided in their convictions; London is New York, tradesman-like, rich, conservative, and merged in its vast accumulations.

Pittsburg has been called the American Birmingham, but, while their branches of industry are the same, their appearances are widely different. Birmingham stands upon a great plain nearly at the centre of England and Wales, its multitude of chimney-stacks vomiting bituminous smoke, its mighty suburb of Wolverhampton seeming to be one of its volcanic children.

The manufacturing industry of the town is chiefly the growth of the present century. Its manufactures comprise almost every description of iron and steel goods, brass and iron founding, saddlery, fire-arms, cutlery, gold, silver, plated, bronze, ormolu, and japanned wares; papier-maché goods, toys, jewelry, electro-plated goods, buttons, steel pens, glass, tools, steam-engines, and machinery of all kinds. The steam-engines employed in its factories are supposed to have a force of between six thousand and seven thousand horse-power, and the annual values of its manufactures have been estimated at five million dollars. The immense coal and iron beds of the district by which Birmingham is surrounded may be viewed as the main source of its prosperity, which has also been greatly aided by canals communicating with the Thames, Mersey, Severn, Trent, and Humber, and more recently by railroads, which bring the metropolis and all the great towns of the north of England within a few hours' journey. This town is supposed to have been a place where arms were manufactured by the ancient Britons.

Wolverhampton, close by, is no less busy; the smelting of iron ore, and its conversion into pig, railroad, sheet, hoop, rod, and nail iron, boiler-plates, castings, etc., constitute its staple manufacture and trade; and almost every article produced from brass, steel, and tin is made in Wolverhampton to a greater or less extent. The facilities enjoyed in carrying on these important trades are very ample, and the advantages of canal communication have long been possessed by these twin cities.

Like Birmingham, Pittsburg stands in the heart of the great bituminous coal regions; it also has its energetic suburbs, one of which takes the name of its English rival. Much of its prosperity is due, like Birmingham's, to the completeness of its canal and water navigation, and, like Birmingham, it manufactures enormous quantities of ploughs, stoves, nails, bolts, cannon, railroad iron, engines, boilers, and whatever iron can be wrought into. But the natural site of Pittsburg is far more magnificent than that of Birmingham.

Pittsburg in winter is the grandest *coup d'œil* of American industry. You sail up the brown current of the Ohio, round the capes of mighty hills, past islands in fertile sleep under the snows, till before you, like a portent of some vast volcano, a wall of darkness rises against the sky. You cleave this wall, guided by the lurid lighthouses of riverside furnaces, and the snow on either side is pitted and flecked with showering bitumen. Down the sluices of the river the frequent steamers swing, pitchily breathing; huge vats and flats of coal go round the headlands in tow of some Hunnish tug; the vineyards far up the hills should bring forth in this atmosphere such scorched wine as they have in Eblis; gulfs and pits gap out of the hill faces; human insects move along the cindery cliffs; a railway train darts up the brink, like a dingy flash of lightning; suddenly, through the deepening twilight of a terrified mid-day, the outlines of something in dim relief stand across the horizon, carved against the mountain background. Two pale, diverging perspectives enclose it, — they are rivers; a blackened tower, and ribbed buttresses crown it, — a cathedral; a fringe of lace blows round this funeral city, — the white and carved line of steamboats; from either side a riven amphitheatre of mountains, their blasted summits bare, their slopes the jaws of mines, their bases dense with population, enclose this city, and leaping from its plain to them, the bridges stand like the ribs of burnt rainbows, or, standing at anchor, hear the railway trains rush through them like the roar of fire. Drawing yet nearer the clumped furnaces fall apart, and by their blaze you see the high hotels, the spires, the broad-paved levée. You hear the hammers, the cheer of stevedores, the whistle of uninterrupted engines; you smell the burning coke kilns, the gases of the ores and coals; by memory you know that at every ticking of the clock a pound of nails drops out of the din, a pocket-knife and plough every minute, a mile of railroad iron an hour, a steam-boiler a day, a steam-engine twice a week.

Entering the city, still dark, — except on Sundays or holidays, when a shaft of clear sunlight sometimes stabs through the smoke, — you see chiefly rectangular streets; at one end of the town is the confluence of railroads; at the other the confluence of rivers. The Pan Handle, the Wheeling, the Connellsville, the Pennsylvania Trunk, the Alleghany Valley, the Chicago and Fort Wayne, the Erie, the Youngstown and Cleveland, the Tuscawaras and Cleveland, join in the main into one union depot, sentinelled by a great grain elevator. Beyond this depot, six miles in the country, the huge stock-yards lie. Down the Alleghany, oil and lumber pour by day and darkness; down the Monongahela, coal and iron in uninterrupted continuity; to the eastward, for two hundred and fifty miles, there is no considerable city. Nine daily papers control this great territory, representing all party shades.

As a curious instance of opposite nomenclature we may note that the large hotels of Pittsburg take the sounding names of the "Monongahela," and the "St. Charles," while the principal hotel of Birmingham is called the "Hen and Chickens."

Manchester has also its American rivals in the series of cotton manufacturing towns which surround Boston, one of which, in New Hampshire, ambitiously calls itself Manchester. With the English city, however, the history not only of the cotton manufacture, but of the application of steam to spinning and weaving, will always be identified.

In 1763, the first spinning-jenny was constructed by Thomas Highs, a reed-maker, at Leigh, in the environs of Manchester. This was improved upon by James Hargreaves, of Blackburn, close by the same city, in 1767. Richard Arkwright, in 1769, took out a patent for spinning by means of rollers, which, in 1799, received considerable improvements from Samuel Crompton. Arkwright's patents were set aside, in 1781 and 1785, by the influence of Sir Robert Peel, in which latter year the Rev. Edward Cartwright invented the power-loom, and the trade being thus set free and furnished with the needful machines, other inventions and improvements followed, and a rapid increase in the cotton trade was the consequence. In 1789, the first steam-engine for spinning cotton was erected in Manchester, and from that year, the manufacturing prosperity of the town may date its rise. At present two hundred and fifty large mills are engaged in the making of textile fabrics in Manchester, which employ about fifty thousand persons; one hundred and fifty mills and thirty-five thousand persons are employed in cotton spinning and weaving; five mills and three hundred persons in woollen and worsted spinning and weaving; fifty-five mills and eight thousand persons in silk-throwing and small wares; five mills and one thousand five hundred persons in flax-spinning, and forty works and three thousand five hundred persons in printing calicoes, etc. Besides these distinguished branches of industry, Manchester has extensive machine shops, chemical works, breweries, and numerous other industrial establishments.

Lowell, which has been called the American Manchester, contains less than one-tenth the population of the English city; thirteen millions of dollars are invested in its cotton mills; it has thirteen thousand looms, the same number of operatives; four hundred thousand spindles, and it makes two and a half million yards of cotton goods a week; more than half a million of dollars are invested in its machine shops. All English visitors to the United States have remarked the superiority of Lowell over Manchester in the cleanliness of mills and operatives, and in the intellect and decorum of the latter. Mr. Anthony Trollope says: "Women's wages, including all that they receive at the Lowell factories, average about fourteen shillings a week, which is, I take it, fully a third more than women can earn in Manchester. But if wages at Manchester were raised to the Lowell standard, the Manchester women would not be clothed, fed, cared for, and educated like the Lowell women. The fact is, that the workmen and the workwomen at Lowell are not exposed to the chances of an open-labor market. They are taken in, as it were, to a philanthropical manufacturing college, and then looked after and regulated more as girls and lads at a great seminary, than as hands by whose industry profit is to be made out of capital. Lowell is the realization of a commercial Utopia.

"The States in these matters," continues the same superficial observer, "have had a great advantage over England. They have been able to begin at the beginning. Manufactories have grown up among us as our cities grow,— from the necessities and chances of the times. When labor was wanted, it was obtained in the ordinary way; and so when houses were built, they were built in the ordinary way. We had not the experience and the results either for good or bad, of other nations to guide us. The Americans, in seeing and resolving to adopt our commercial successes, have resolved also, if possible, to avoid the evils which have attended those successes. It would be very desirable that all our factory girls should read and write, wear clean clothes, have decent beds, and eat hot meat every day. But that is now impossible. Gradually, with very up-hill work, but still, I trust, with sure work, much will be done to improve their position and render their life respectable; but in England we can have no Lowells."

Manchester in England is very old, historically, but it obtained corporate powers and privileges so recently as 1840; it is said to have traded with the Greeks of Marseilles in woven goods very early in the Christian era; like almost all the weaving interests of England, however, it received its most valuable accessions of workmen from France and Flanders; and thus, the Huguenots, whom Louis XIV. expelled, raised against France so rich an empire that it could subsidize all the armies of Europe. The greatest names of Manchester are, perhaps, the greatest of Great Britain also, in practical usefulness and wise statesmanship, — Sir Robert Peel and Richard Cobden; to support the measures of these arose the greatest English orator of the century, — John Bright.

As Manchester was the birthplace of many appliances in the cotton manufacture, America produced the cotton gin, without which looms, mules, and spools would have been valueless. America is also author of the sewing-machine, which makes every home a miniature Manchester. In 1830, the first railroad in England was opened from Manchester to Liverpool. The cotton manufactures have permanently added two millions to the British population.

Liverpool is merely the port of entry and departure for the staples and manufactures of Manchester and its progeny. At the time of the American Revolution, Liverpool had a population of seventy-five thousand, and Manchester zealously contributed troops to put down the American rebels.

The exports of Liverpool exceed those of all other British ports combined; its docks and basins cover several hundred acres, and the Albert dock and warehouses alone cost two and a half million of dollars. Both Liverpool and Manchester are monotonous cities, but the former has some pleasant environs, and it possesses in St. George's Hall the finest edifice in the United Kingdom; it is the richest corporation in the kingdom, London excepted; and the income of the municipality is nearly one and a half million of dollars a year; there are fourteen miles of quays in Liverpool, all of which are controlled by the Dock Committee and the Corporation, jointly.

Birkenhead, the Jersey City of Liverpool, since the formation of its docks, has progressed so rapidly, that in a few years it must prove both a commercial rival and an auxiliary to Liverpool. Upwards of one hundred and twenty-five million dollars have been expended upon the improvements of the Mersey and the formation of twenty-four docks, whereby a stormy estuary and an unsafe anchorage have been converted into the most perfect harbor ever constructed. The Mersey is a short arm of the Irish sea, and the city stands almost in sight of the river's mouth. The ships from Liverpool were always competitors of those of New York; the American clipper ships outsail the English, but in the celebrated contest between the great Collins' steamship line of New York, and the Cunard line of Liverpool, the superior vigilance, economy, and caution of the English prevailed over our rash management; by accident we lost two of our finest steamers; our government subsidy was withdrawn, and the Collins' line disappeared from the sea. Scarcely inferior to its American trade is Liverpool's commerce with Australia.

Bristol has ceased to be a formidable rival to Liverpool, and it occupies the same relation in commerce to that city, which Philadelphia now yields to New York. The Bristol docks were first opened in 1809, and the old channel of the Avon was converted into one floating harbor about three miles in length. The existing manufactures of the city are glass, brassware, pens, sheet lead, zinc, spelter, chain cables, anchors, machinery, drugs, paints, dyes, floor-cloth, earthenware, refined sugar, starch, soap, spirits, tin, copper, and iron wares, bricks, beer, porter, pipes, tobacco, and hats. Hull is the principal English port on the North Sea, and stands in a similar relation to the other English seaports that Buffalo holds to America; which latter yields competition on the ocean, and aims to secure the traffic of the lakes, as Hull of the North Sea. The ships of Hull ply to Holland, Denmark, Sweden, and the Baltic; it was the city of Robinson Crusoe.

What Manchester is to the cotton trade, Bradford and Leeds are to the woollen trade. These towns lie in the great County of York, beside which nestles little Lancaster, indented and busy as New England, while York well compares with New York State. In this county is the beautiful Vale of York, the finest stretch of land in England. Wolds and moors are features of this county. This is the county of *Ivanhoe* and *Robin Hood*, as is New York of *Leatherstocking* and *Rip Van Winkle*. York City used to be the rival of London in social and aristocratic attractions. Yorkshire is the Pennsylvania as well as the New York of England, being full of coal and iron, lead, jet, alum, and marble, and its agriculture and manufactures are equally celebrated. In this county are the great towns of Sheffield, noted for its steel, Bradford, for its worsteds, and Leeds, famed for its cloth. York is the greatest of woollen countries. There are in the coal field of Yorkshire and its two adjoining counties, Nottingham and Derby, five hundred and forty-one mines, producing twelve and a half million tons of coal a year. The Flemish introduced the woollen trade here. The Yorkshire sea-coast is bold and noble, and wrapped in bracing atmospheres; in the inland west of the county are mountains high as the Alleghanies. Everybody knows the character of Yorkshire hams and rams.

According to the census made in 1861, Yorkshire contained nearly two millions of acres more than either Lincolnshire or Devonshire, the next largest English counties. It is half as large as Holland, and about the size of the Peloponnesus of Greece; it contains five thousand nine hundred and sixty-one square miles, and two million and fifteen thousand five hundred and forty-one people.

We have no places for woollen work which compete with Leeds and Bradford; New England manufactures more woollen goods than either Philadelphia or New York, which two take the next rank. Philadelphia has probably more money invested in the woollen trade than any other American city.

Bradford contains nearly one hundred and twenty thousand people, and received its first steam-engine in the year 1800; from this town come to America iron plates, bars, railway tires, and cannons; every rill for miles around is dammed up to supply the water, and every drop is economized.

The staple manufactures of Bradford are worsted stuffs and mixed worsted, alpaca and mohair, and also cotton and silk fabrics. There are not less than one hundred and twenty mills in the parish for spinning and weaving worsted, etc. Broad and narrow cloths (employing six extensive mills), wool-cards, and ivory and horn combs are made in great quantities, and in the town and vicinity are extensive dye-works. The cotton manufactures are of recent introduction, but are making rapid progress. The neighborhood abounds in coal, and about three miles south-east are the Lowmoor iron works, and a mile east the Bowling iron works, both of which are on a very extensive scale.

The position of Leeds in a coal district, and having ample means of communication with both seas and with numerous great seats of commerce, have been the sources of its eminence as a seat of manufactures. Its principal woollen fabrics consist of the finest broadcloth, kerseys, swandowns, and beavers; it makes also carpets, blankets, camlets, and shalloons, and large quantities of unfinished stuffs are brought from Bradford and Halifax to Leeds to be finished. Linen, yarn, canvas, sacking, and linen cloth are the chief flaxen goods produced. Besides the above enumerated branches, Leeds has also extensive factories for locomotives, machinery, and tools, chemical works, glass houses, potteries, tobacco mills, and soap works. It is connected with the North Sea by the Aire and Calder navigation, and with the Irish Sea by the Leeds and Liverpool Canal.

There are many other secondary cities of note in England, but it would be tedious to consider them all. Sheffield is suggested to us, however, whenever we take up our knife at dinner. The cutlery of all kinds made at Sheffield has long been famous as among the best in the world. Other important manufactures are heavy iron and steel goods, plated wares, fine metallic instruments, printing types, forks, files, and steel. Coal is abundant, and some is mined in the vicinity. The Don is navigable, and the canal basin is available for vessels of fifty tons. The mass of American cutlery is made in Connecticut, and at Rochester, Pennsylvania, penknives are made that rank with Sheffield.

Our manufactures, indeed, are slowly, but undoubtedly catching up to England's, protected by partial legislation; but our shipping, that was endeared to us by American hardihood and triumph, has well-nigh given up the ocean. We may be said to have a navy which is without a commerce to protect.

In 1860, all the United States manufactured one hundred and fifteen millions of dollars' worth of cotton goods; while England exported more than three times this value in 1866, besides the enormous quantity of cotton goods consumed by her thirty millions at home.

The United States manufactured less than seventy millions of dollars' worth of woollen goods in 1860; while England exported alone nearly one hundred and nine millions of dollars' worth in 1866.

England exported in 1866, seventy-four millions of dollars' worth of iron and steel; in 1860 the United States manufactured nearly double this amount. In all the above figures it must be remembered that the whole manufacture of America is given, and only the export manufacture for the United Kingdom.

In 1866, England produced one hundred and two millions of tons of coal; in 1860, the United States produced more than nineteen millions of tons. England exports nearly ten millions of tons of coal every year, or more than half the quantity we mine.

Apprehensions exist that the coal of England will not last till the end of the next century; the American coal-field is well-nigh inexhaustible. The magnificent deposit of anthracite coal in the American Middle States, which saves the clear skies of our Atlantic cities, is almost unknown in England. Coal in America at the pit's mouth costs nearly the same as in England, but our freights and distances are far greater. Cheap transit is one of the most involved and pressing problems for our nation.

Scotland may be said to have two distinct metropolises: Edinburgh, which is the literary, social, and art metropolis, with a population of about one hundred and seventy thousand, and Glasgow, the commercial metropolis, with a population of four hundred thousand. These two cities lie nearly opposite each other. Edinburgh, near the Firth of Forth, — an arm of the North Sea, — and Glasgow, on the River Clyde, which receives the tides of the Atlantic. The distance between the cities is about fifty miles. Edinburgh is a most beautiful city, and, like Boston in the United States, it is called the modern Athens, as much from the resemblance of its *site* to that of the capital of Attica, as from any supposed conceit that its people resemble the Athenians in intellect and civilization. Glasgow lies flat and monotonous, though in its environs are some pleasant ranges of hills. Edinburgh is a city of antiquities; like Quebec it has its old town and its new town; its principal street, called High Street, passes from the castle, which stands four hundred feet in the air upon a rock, to Holyrood Palace, where Mary, Queen of Scots, was reproved by John Knox, and where her favorite, Rizzio, was stabbed in her presence. In both Edinburgh and Glasgow are beautiful monuments of Sir Walter Scott, that in Edinburgh being a Gothic edifice, two hundred feet high, with fifty-six statues in its various niches, besides the statue of the author and his dog, in the canopy below.

In Edinburgh is the former Parliament House of Scotland, now occupied by the Courts of Justice. The hall of the extinct Parliament is a splendid apartment, one hundred and twenty-two feet long, and forty-nine broad, with an oval roof of sculptured oak. Both these Scotch cities have universities, that of Edinburgh having been patronized by Oliver Cromwell; it has thirty-two professors, and eight hundred students, and a library of one hundred thousand volumes. Glasgow University was a dark and gloomy building, in Elizabethian architecture. Benjamin Franklin, himself, fixed the lightning rod over its cupola. A splendid new university building will shortly (1869) be opened in Glasgow, to cost one million and a half of dollars. Glasgow has a Cathedral, which is the finest Gothic edifice in Scotland; it is a hundred and fifty-five feet long, or forty-two feet shorter than Trinity Church, New York. The River Clyde passes through the city of Glasgow, flowing westward, and is crossed by fine bridges; it has twenty feet of water at high tide, but is entirely artificial, at Glasgow, having been dredged and excavated. Several miles below Glasgow are the great steamship-yards, chief of which is that of the Napiers. Glasgow ranks fourth among the export ports of the United Kingdom, and Greenock, its main harbor, twenty miles down the Clyde, is of more commercial importance than Bristol. What Greenock and Port Glasgow are to Glasgow, is Leith to Edinburgh; it has been the port of the latter old city since the time of Robert Bruce; it contains thirty-four thousand people, has spacious docks, and two of its piers are one thousand yards long, each. A good sketch of the celebrated fishwomen of Leith may be found in Charles Reade's novel of "Christie Johnstone." In Glasgow is buried John Knox, the Calvin of Scotland; in Edinburgh are kept the crown jewels of Scotland, the crown itself being old as the days of Bruce. Below Glasgow, on the Clyde, is the highest chimney in the world, towering above the great chemical works of the Tennants; it is four hundred and thirty-five feet high. The chief streets of Glasgow are Argyle and Buchanan. The streets of both these Scotch cities present, after dark, the wretched spectacle of thousands of females, drunken, wanton, or destitute, and it is curious that in this kingdom, where the code of religion and morality is written with the harshness of Draco, the other extreme of licentiousness can also be witnessed to greater excess than even in London or Dublin. Scotland, indeed, is by nature the poorest part of the British Kingdom, and far more sterile than Ireland; the appetites of its people are grosser also than those of the Irish; but the practical intellect, the ingenuity, and the industry of the Scotch have made them eminent, and influential in English Councils, while the refractory, combative, and generous Irish have been well-nigh expatriated.

Glasgow means the "Dark Glen." Here James Watt made his first model of a steam-engine. When Cromwell visited this town, upwards of two hundred years ago, he went to service in the cathedral, when the preacher, Zacharie Boyd, denounced him in the most abusive terms, so that the Protector's Secretary proposed to have him shot. Cromwell replied. "He's a fool, and you're another. I'll pay him out in his own fashion." This he did by asking Boyd to dinner, and concluding it with a prayer which lasted three hours.

Edinburgh derived its name from Prince Edwin, of Northumbria, who lived in the seventh century, and founded it; the city was completely destroyed in 1544, but after the Reformation, the bigotry of the Catholics, the intolerance of Knox and the Reformers, the civil feuds amongst the nobles to obtain the Regency, made the town unsafe, and it has declined, to be at present of far less mercantile importance than Glasgow, its rival.

Greenock, the chief port of Glasgow, maintains steamship communication with New York; it contains forty-two thousand inhabitants; here James Watt was born, perhaps the greatest benefactor England ever had. It is remarkable that the Scottish Parliament refused to the last to allow a harbor to be constructed at Greenock, and that the English Parliament granted this privilege immediately after the union; hence, arose Glasgow, and that splendid Scottish marine, which supplies the great empires of the world. The steamships which run from New York to France are all built upon the Clyde.

Paisley, well known to the ladies who wear its shawls, has risen into importance within the past half century, chiefly by imitating the fabrics of India, Cashmere, and China; this town may almost be said to be a suburb of Glasgow. North of Edinburgh, on the North Sea, are the cities of Dundee, Aberdeen, and Inverness, all old cities. Aberdeen furnishes the best granite in Great Britain,— a reddish stone, out of which were built the docks of Sebastopol, and many of the finest edifices in London. Here, as in almost every city of England and Scotland, there is a bran-new statue of Prince Albert, — the most prudent and virtuous prince, probably, ever connected with the English monarchy. The harbor and pier of Aberdeen cost nearly a million and a half of dollars.

Dundee contains thirty thousand people,— more than Aberdeen. It is the third city in Scotland; it is the principal manufacturing market of linen, using one hundred and thirty thousand tons of hemp, jute, and flax, a year, and running two hundred and three thousand spindles; it also makes one thousand tons of marmalade every year, out of sugar, oranges, etc., and one million and a half of jars are brought every year from Newcastle, to enclose this luxury. Inverness is comparatively a small town; but it is singularly remarkable for the beauty of its women, and for the purity in which its people speak the English language. Its manufactures are mainly Scotch plaids, brooches, stockings, kilts, and fowling-pieces. A large part of the business of this town is letting out moors and fishing streams for the aristocratic proprietors. Inverness is the city of Macbeth, who seems to have been much libelled by Shakespeare, as he was a pious and wise chief.

Perth, situated on the North Sea side of Scotland, inland from Dundee, contains the principal penitentiary of Scotland. Ayr, on the western coast, about thirty miles below Glasgow, was the home of Burns and Wallace. The home of Burns is now a tavern, but there are many memorials to his memory close by, amongst which are the celebrated figures of "Tam O'Shanter," and "Souter Johnnie," by James Thom, who carved "Old Mortality" and his pony, for Laurel Hill Cemetery, Philadelphia, who did some fair work for Trinity Church, New York, and cut the hideous figure of Washington, which disgraces the City Hall Park, New York.

Perhaps the principal public work of Scotland is the Caledonian Canal, which connects the Atlantic and German Oceans, and was opened in 1822; its total cost was nearly six and a half millions of dollars; it is twenty feet deep, fifty feet broad at the bottom, and twenty-three miles long, exclusive of the streams into which it flows, at either end; it takes only forty-eight hours to pass through Scotland by this canal. Another great public work is the Crinau Canal, nine miles long, which crosses one of the numerous, annoying peninsulas of Scotland. Both of these canals are under government control.

John O'Groat's House was the most northerly habitation in Scotland, and, like Land's End, the most southerly promontory of Great Britain; it has enjoyed considerable notoriety.

Scotland is noted for its beautiful scenery, and the Highland Railway affords splendid opportunities to examine the country. The finest river steamboat in Europe is the "Iona," which traverses the "firths" and sounds of the Scottish coast; but she bears no comparison with second-rate, or even third-rate, passenger steamboats in America. There is not probably a single line of steamers in Europe which would please an American, save, possibly the French steamers from Marseilles to Italy, and the Orient. One of the pleasures of travel in Scotland, and indeed in all Europe, is the excellence and thoroughness of the guide-books, — a department of literature which has scarcely had its beginning in America. The smallest and most insignificant county in England has been more perfectly delineated than the cities of New York and of Washington. An American travelling over thousands of miles of country is unable to learn anything whatever of the towns which he passes. Scottish live stock is tolerably well known to Americans, particularly the Clydesdale horses, and the cattle of Fife and Aberdeen. There are six millions of sheep in Scotland. Every American child is familiar with the Shetland pony.

Scottish manufactures rival those of York and Lancashire. There are thirty-one ship-building yards on the Clyde, from which came in 1863, a hundred and seventy steamers, representing one hundred and twenty-four thousand tons. Enormous quantities of fish are caught on the Scottish coast, the value of which in 1867 alone amounted to nearly two and a quarter millions of dollars. The manufacture of snuff-boxes is quite a feature of Scottish industry, and furnishes a curious clue to British habits. There are one hundred and ninety flax factories in Scotland, and a hundred and seventy cotton factories, running altogether nearly two millions of spindles.

The country is richly endowed with coal and iron. The Scotch in modern times have been the most remarkable people of Europe. Not a nation, but only a provincial kingdom, and with an almost sterile territory, they have yet a literature comparable with any land's, an independent character, and a national faith, and they are recognized throughout the world by their philanthropic discoveries and applications. They build the cheapest and best steamships; they make splendid sailors, and steadfast soldiers; their business talents are of the shrewdest sort, and if, as Doctor Johnson said, "a Scotchman's best prospect was the highway to England," England may be glad that the Scotchman took that road. No nobler intellectual statures ever walked any path than Robert Burns, James Watt, John Napier, Walter Scott, and William Hamilton.

Yet the condition of the lower orders of Scotch is in many places terrible. Drink and poverty are the sources of their grief, and the most startling crime in British history is attributable to Scotland,—that of Burke and Hare, who killed human beings by wholesale to sell their carcasses to the surgeons. Scarcely less terrible than crime in Great Britain is justice. In no country are punishments so merciless and speedy, and until 1869 all executions took place in sight of the people on the open pavements.

At the execution of Burke, at Edinburgh, in January, 1829, the spectacle of popular rage and vindictive exultation was fearful. Shouts arose from a multitude, vast beyond precedent,—shouts to the executioner of "Burke him! give him no rope! Burke him!" and at every convulsive throe, a huzza was set up, as if every one present was near of kin to his victims. When the body was cut down, there was a cry for "one cheer more!" and a general and tremendous huzza closed the diabolical celebration.

The early history of Scotland was as tumultuous and unpromising as that of Ireland, and the country was only pacified when the Scotch Parliament was transferred to London, and the weak race of Scottish Kings passed to England, to annoy the people there for more than a century. Scotland has never contested British domination like Ireland, but neither Irish nor Scotch are considered by Englishmen to rank with themselves; England is the kingdom to which both defer. It is the richer, the more populous, the more eminent in literature and achievements. More than all, it is the kingdom of the language.

The railway system of Great Britain, which connects the provincial cities, deserves some mention here. It is not comparable to ours for length of rail, but it is a cheaper and more beneficent system, in that it does the work of England more thoroughly than our railways; that its companies are not corrupting monopolies like ours, and that they are more under the control of the central legislature.

There were two railway gauges in England for a long time; but the narrow gauge finally triumphed as in this country; the Great Western Railway in England is the principal broad-gauge road, like the Erie, and Atlantic and Great Western, in America. As long ago as 1845, Richard Cobden moved in Parliament to adopt the broad to the narrow gauge throughout England, but without success. At the present time both England and America, therefore, are troubled with the conflicting arrangements of two entirely different series of railways, whose cars cannot be transferred either in commercial or military necessities. The long saloon car is unknown in England, the cars being "carriages" there, with doors in the sides, and half the people ride backward. The cars are classified, and one pays according to his pride or comfort.

In 1833–4 there was but one railway in England, running from Liverpool to Manchester, and a short one of seven miles in Scotland. Ten years later, railways were extended into almost every part of the kingdom, and speculation ran high. Americans familiar with the gigantic lobbying schemes of railway projectors during the construction of the Pacific Railroad can appreciate this account of the same excitement in England. The journals of 1844 tell us that three hundred and thirty-two new railway schemes were proposed before the month of October in that year, involving a capital of 1,354,750,000 dollars, and for which upwards of 115,000,000 dollars would have to be deposited before an act of incorporation could be applied for. A multitude of other schemes were in an incipient state; and there were sixty-six foreign railway projects in the English market. It was believed that altogether the number of printed plans and charts which would be brought to the door of the Board of Trade, by the expiration of the closing-day, would be eight hundred and fifteen. The number which succeeded in obtaining admission was above six hundred. The closing-day was the 30th of November. "As the summer closed and the autumn wore on, the most desperate efforts were made," says Miss Martineau, "to get ready these plans. One lithographic printer brought over four hundred lithographers from Belgium, and yet could not get his engagements fulfilled. The draughtsmen and printers in the lithographic establishments lived there, snatching two or three hours' sleep on the floor or on benches, and then going dizzily to work again. Much work was executed imperfectly, and much was thrown over altogether. Horses were hired at great cost, and kept under lock and key, to bring to town at the last moment plans prepared in the country Express trains were engaged for the same purpose; and there were cases in which railway directors refused such accommodation to rival projectors."

Meanwhile the British country gentlemen had no good opinion of the noisy innovation, and there are people in England to this day who look upon the railway system as a calamity. They love to remember the old Tory days of ignorance, contentment, and repose, when only "gentlemen" talked politics, and Manchester was a market town.

In those early days of the railway, land-owners were groaning over the spoliation of their estates, for which no pecuniary award could be any compensation. Their park walls were cut through, their "dingles and bosky dells" were cut through, and their choicest turf, and their secluded flower-gardens. A serious conflict took place on one occasion, in Lord Harborough's park in Leicestershire, between his lordship's tenantry and the railway surveyors, with the force they assembled. Railways were to run, not only along the southern margin of the island, and round the bases of the misty Scottish mountains, but through the vale on which Furness Abbey had hitherto stood shrouded, and among old cathedrals, of which the traveller might soon see half a dozen in a day. It was on Easter-Monday, 1844, that excursion-trips with return-tickets were first heard of. Here began the benefits of cheap pleasure-journeys to the hard workers of the nation. The fares were much lowered; yet the extra receipts on the Dover line for three days were three thousand five hundred dollars, and on the Brighton line nine thousand seven hundred and fifteen dollars. "The process had begun from which incalculable blessings were to accrue to the mind, morals, and manners of the nation. From this time, the exclusive class was to meet the humbler classes face to face."

The excursion system has not been carried to a like perfection in America, and our ordinary railway fare, with no better accommodation than the English second-class, is thirty per cent. dearer.

The fastest trains in England carry the Holyhead and Dublin mails, and go a mile a minute, including stoppages. They are subsidized with large sums of money by government. Our best railway speed is thirty miles an hour, and our rolling stock is more cumbrous and expensive than abroad.

To cross from Wales to Dublin, Ireland, takes four hours; for every minute behind time, the postal authorities fine the steamboat company seven dollars, except in cases of fog. This line of steamers is the finest in the waters of Great Britain, but they do not bear comparison with our Hudson River and Sound steamers. It is three hundred and thirty miles from London to Dublin, and it takes ten hours to accomplish the journey.

The Irish coast is most beautiful to look upon after quitting the smoky and hazy shores of England, and no one who has seen the glorious groups of mountains which environ Dublin wonders that the Irish love their beautiful island. Kingstown is the port of Dublin, as Queenstown is of Cork. Kingstown harbor embraces two hundred and fifty-one acres, and Parliament advanced two and a half millions of dollars toward improving it. Dublin is six miles distant, and two and a half millions of passengers pass over the connecting railway every year. The city of Dublin contains about two hundred and fifty thousand inhabitants, considerably less than Baltimore. It lies in the midst of most noble scenery, the mountains forming vistas for many of its streets, and the little River Liffey passes through it, and is crossed by many bridges. It is melancholy to enter the ancient Parliament House of Ireland, now a grand bank, and many an Irishman has had such musings in its deserted House of Lords, as Gibbon while sitting on the Capitoline Hill at Rome. Most of the public buildings of Dublin suggest the Englishman's domination. The bank of Ireland cost half a million of dollars; the Four Courts cost one million of dollars. Overhanging the town is the castle, where the Lord Lieutenant lives. It is to Ireland what the Moro Castle is to Cuba, and thence issue all the orders to the military and police. The Lord Lieutenant is almost a sovereign, and here he holds court in grand style. No seat of learning in the world can boast a longer roll of great alumni than Trinity College of Dublin, which covers thirty acres of ground, and was founded by Queen Elizabeth. Its library contains most noted manuscripts, and in its museum is the genuine harp of Brian Boroimhe, which is nearly a thousand years old; there is a Catholic University in Dublin also. Dublin contains monuments to Nelson and Wellington, who are perpetuated in almost every city of Great Britain and her colonies. Nelson's Pillar is a hundred and thirty-four feet high; the Duke of Wellington's Obelisk is two hundred and thirty-five feet high.

Every citizen of Dublin boasts as much about the Phœnix Park, as a New Yorker about the Central. The Phœnix Park is more than twice as large as the Central Park, a fact which seems to be forgotten by New Yorkers, when they claim to have the largest park extant. The Central Park contains eight hundred and forty-three acres; the Phœnix Park seventeen hundred and fifty-nine acres. The Lord Lieutenant of Ireland has a residence in the Phœnix Park, but the New York Park, in its architectural adornments, is altogether superior to its Irish rival.

Amongst the monuments of Dublin is one to O'Connell, erected in 1869. There are two Protestant cathedrals in Dublin, Christ Church and St. Patrick, the latter having been almost entirely restored by the brewer Guinness. Dublin contains many institutions of learning, and beneficence. The word Dublin means, the Blackwater. The scenery in the neighborhood of this beautiful city is comparable to any in the world, and the names of many of the neighboring localities are more beautiful than those of our American Indians. But everywhere some memento is visible of the conquest and resistance of the Celt to the Saxon: military roads scaling the mountain heights, barracks of soldiery, multitudes of spies. In every Irishman's heart, the capital of his empire is not London, but Washington. Americans know Dublin for its porter, as much as for almost any other product. London is thought to produce the best brown stout, Dublin the best porter, and Burton, Nottingham, and Edinburgh, the best ale.

Belfast is a sprightlier city than Dublin, with about half the population. The name of the town means, the mouth of the ford. It lies at the base of a tall, steep ridge of hills, the highest of which reaches the altitude of one thousand one hundred and fifty-eight feet. Its harbor is called Belfast Slough, and is an exceedingly fine one, with twenty-three feet of water at high tide; about seven thousand vessels enter and clear from this important harbor every year; the value of its exports is forty-five millions of dollars, and its customs duties amount to nearly two millions of dollars. In Belfast, and throughout the north of Ireland, the working of patterns on muslin, with the needle, employs as many as three hundred thousand persons; but the great trade of this important city is in linens. The largest flax-mill in the world is that of the Messrs. Mulholland; it gives employment to about twenty-five thousand persons, which is probably the greatest number employed by any private firm in Christendom. Sixty-five millions of yards of linen are exported from Belfast, annually, and three millions of pounds of yarns and threads. Flax yields from thirty to thirty-five "stones" per acre, and there were nearly one hundred and fifty thousand acres of it under cultivation in 1861. In all Ireland there are less than a hundred spinning-mills, and about seven hundred thousand spindles. Flax is to Ireland, indeed, what cotton and corn are to America, and it is probable that before long two-thirds of that great island will be given up to its cultivation. Not only is Belfast noted for its commerce and its flax manufactures, but many important branches of manufacture and chemistry are developed here, — in particular, the making of starch. From this neighborhood come some of the hardiest elements of population in America. In Belfast and Derry originated such families as those of Alexander

T. Stewart, of New York, George H. Stuart, of Philadelphia, and John W. Garrett, of Baltimore; the first, our prince of commerce, the second of philanthropy, and the third of railway enterprise. As an instance of Belfast enterprise, I may mention that, in 1867, I found in Cincinnati, one of the largest pork-packing establishments, under the management of a Belfast firm of merchants; they came out annually, packed their pork, and shipped it home to Ireland, and although during that year they lost eighty thousand dollars, they were back again the ensuing winter, as cheerful as ever. What are called in America the Scotch Irishmen were originally Protestant Irish, who emigrated from the north of Ireland to Scotland, which lies across the North Channel, no more than forty miles from Belfast, and returned again after the religious feuds had subsided. Except as regards "society" and politics, Belfast takes precedence of Dublin. Here, however, the most bigoted intolerance prevails amongst both Catholics and Protestants. It is noted for the number of its Orangemen, so called for William, Prince of Orange, who drove the last Catholic King of England from his throne. Orangemen in the United States take the name of the American Protestant Association.

Cork, in the south of Ireland, is the city which will be forever associated with the expatriation and griefs of hundreds of thousands of Irish Americans. Whatever interest may attach to Plymouth Rock, to Jamestown, to St. Mary's, Cork will ever be the fond and lingering thought of the more recent millions of American citizens, whose parents, or who themselves, took passage from this port, for the New World, many of them never to see their native land again; many never to see land at all, but to die at sea, bequeathing their children to the new continent they struggled so hard to reach. Cork is in some respects a handsome city, in others, very dirty; it has about eighty thousand inhabitants, the population of Buffalo, and its surrounding scenery is very beautiful; there are but seven feet of water at Cork, at low tide, and the Cunard steamers, and others, which trade to America, stop at Queenstown, ten miles distant, a noble harbor, whose splendid sceneries are disgraced by the great convict prison on which they look, and where eight hundred political prisoners, and criminals, toil together, adjudged by a Christian nation to a common penalty. The chief exports of Cork are emigrants and butter.

About midway between Cork and Dublin are Waterford and Wexford, two important towns, at the latter of which is an exceedingly bad bridge, built by Lemuel Cox, an American bridge-builder. Waterford has one of the finest harbors in the United Kingdom.

There are many towns in the interior of Ireland whose mention would be familiar to the reader, but their importance exists rather in the fond memory of the immigrant, than in any respect pertinent to our theme. For example, there is Limerick, on the Shannon, which has about the population of Syracuse. Limerick has nineteen feet of water at high tide, and ought to have been a great American port but Galway and Cork have superseded it; fish-hooks and lace are the characteristic manufactures here.

Galway is a town that at one time bade fair to be the great port of the British Islands in American trade. Over one of the gates of the town stood, until recently, the following inscription, which might be appropriately set over the gates of New York: —

> "From the ferocious O'Flahertys,
> Good Lord, deliver us."

Galway is said to be the ancestral place of the great Lynch family, many thousands of whom are in America; in the thirteenth century they came to Ireland, from Linz, in Austria, where, by their bravery, they won the privilege of taking a lynx for the crest of their coat-of-arms.

Vessels drawing fourteen feet of water enter Galway, and the Adriatic, the fastest ship in the world, built in New York, but now owned in England, once crossed the Atlantic, from Galway to St. John's, Newfoundland, in little more than four days.

The last Irish city which we will notice is Londonderry, where the steamships from Montreal and Portland touch on their way to Liverpool. The bulk of the town stands more than a hundred feet above the River Foyle, which is very wide. Here, also, Mr. Lemuel Cox put up a bridge of piles, novel in Europe, at an expense of eighty thousand dollars; it proved to be a nuisance, like the Long Bridge at Washington, and was taken up some years ago. This town has been the theatre of the most miserable and desperate religious wars, and its fortifications bear characteristic names, such as "Hangman's Bastion," "Coward's Bastion," etc.

Ireland has beautiful scenery, and hospitable and impulsive people, merry if miserable. It has pleasant old ruins of abbeys and castles, and these attest that almost all its history has been war, religion, and song. It is the only musical part of the British Empire; for nature seems to have labored so perseveringly upon the Englishman's stomach, that she forgot to give him an ear; his throat, however, is powerfully, if not delicately, constructed. The lyrists of the British Empire have been Moore, — Irish, — and Campbell and Burns, — Scotch. The Englishman is the solid and epic personage, and in every variety of life is self-contained and individual, — in Milton and Shakespeare, as in the commonest cockney, clinging to his own appetites, opinions, and selfishnesses, a kingdom in himself. "My mind to me a kingdom is," says the British poet; and there he struck the great kev of observation. Solid, beefy, of strong brew is the Englishman. Behold all things created for his use! Not of the Roman race, he is in many things more Roman than his Celtic neighbors. In haughty power of intellect and force he surveys the world, and compels or advises it to his own model.

It is fortunate for America that the controlling element of her national character is derived from this strong-stomached stock, and it makes the nucleus of all other races here, though all are valuable in compounding with it. Wherever any other race than the Anglo-Saxon constitutes a local majority in America, there is some defect, either of stupidity, socialism, or corruption.

"Ten years ago," says Dilke, "the third and fourth cities of the world, New York and Philadelphia, were as English as our London; the one is Irish now; the other all but German. Not that the Quaker City will remain Teutonic. The Germans, too, are going out upon the land; the Irish alone pour in unceasingly. All great American towns will soon be Celtic, while the country continues English; a fierce and easily-roused people will throng the cities, while the law-abiding Saxons who till the land will cease to rule it. Our relations with America are matters of small moment by the side of the one great question: Who are the Americans to be?"

This quotation indicates the shrewdness, and the mistake by its very shrewdness, of the British intellect in observation. The history of the American (so to speak) race is, that the first or second generation holds to the towns, and the second or third rambles toward the frontiers. Every race alike becomes restless here. The native American is the tarantula; whom he bites must dance. We are a race of town-makers. The most contented father has the most restless child; a mighty impulse animates us all, — to go somewhere, to begin something! What we have begun our European accessions finish, but all that we do is on the basis of democracy. The republic is not a name with us, as with the French; it is a great permeating fact. The Englishman's mind is a kingdom, indeed; the American's is a republic.

Another distinction of the English character which we have retained is the love for municipal or local self-government. The perversion of municipal institutions to political ends has occasioned the sacrifice of local interests to party purposes, which have been frequently pursued through the corruption and demoralization of the electoral bodies This was the language of the Commission on English Municipal Reform: "In conclusion," they say, "we report that there prevails among the inhabitants of a great majority of the incorporated towns of Great Britain a general, and, in our opinion, a just, dissatisfaction with their municipal institutions, a distrust of the self-elected municipal councils, whose powers are subjected to no popular control, and whose acts and proceedings, being secret, are unchecked by the influence of public opinion; a distrust of the municipal magistracy, tainting with suspicion the local administration of justice, and often accompanied with contempt of the persons by whom the law is administered; a discontent under the burdens of local taxation; while revenues that ought to be applied for the public advantage are diverted from their legitimate use, and are sometimes wastefully bestowed for the benefit of individuals, sometimes squandered for purposes injurious to the character and morals of the people. We, therefore, feel it to be our duty to represent to your Majesty, that the existing municipal corporations of England and Wales neither possess nor deserve the confidence and respect of your Majesty's subjects; and that a thorough reform must be effected before they can become what we submit they ought to be, useful and efficient instruments of local government."

Upon this proposition the old Saxon idea of local self-government was adjusted so as to purify the cities, and the remarks of the British historian are indices of the strange form of government which prevailed almost down to our time.

"It was a great thing," says Miss Martineau, "to see our country planted over with little republics, where the citizens would henceforth be trained to political thought and public virtue; but it seemed a pity that the city feasts must go, the processions be seen no more, the gorgeous dresses be laid by, the banners be folded up, the dragon be shelved, and St. George never allowed to wear his armor again; and the gay runners, in their pink and blue jerkins, their peaked shoes and rosettes, and their fearful wooden swords, turned into mere weavers, tinmen, and shoemakers. Already some of us may find ourselves discoursing eagerly to children, as Englishmen used to do to wondering Americans, of the sights we once saw on great corporation days."

Since the American civil war the tide has set strongly toward governing every part of the United States by one absolute Legislature, and a central Executive. This is not Anglo-Saxon freedom, which in an essential degree consists of local government, with a central directory. The continental nations, and notably France, tried the contrary, and made a dismal end. "The republic, one and indivisible," was only another form of saying, "a strong central government," and municipal and local institutions perished under the iron hand of the one absolute Legislature. The hardest thing to capture is an archipelago, because tyranny must divide to do it; so a republic should have many centres, with one Providence watching over all.

There is no space in this chapter to describe the internal life of English communities; that will be touched upon in the chapter upon the "Influence of Government on the People." The essential feature of English cities is repose; of American cities, action.

"It is not impossible," says a French critic, "to conceive the surpassing liberty which the Americans enjoy; some idea may likewise be formed of the extreme equality which subsists amongst them; but the political activity which pervades the United States must be seen in order to be understood. No sooner do you set foot upon the American soil than you are stunned by a kind of tumult; a confused clamor is heard on every side; and a thousand simultaneous voices demand the immediate satisfaction of their social wants. Everything is in motion around you; here, the people of one quarter of a town are met to decide upon the building of a church; there, the election of a representative is going on; a little further, the delegates of a district are posting to the town, in order to consult upon some local improvements; or in another place the laborers of a village quit their ploughs to deliberate upon the project of a road or a public school. Meetings are called for the sole purpose of declaring their disapprobation of the line of conduct pursued by the government; whilst in other assemblies the citizens salute the authorities of the day as the fathers of their country. Societies are formed which regard drunkenness as the principal cause of the evils under which the state labors, and which solemnly bind themselves to give a constant example of temperance."

It might be well if there was more concern upon the question of temperance in England; for the vice of all the British Islands is the abuse of the stomach and the brain, over-eating and over-drinking. We might be said to be a nation of "gulpers," in that we eat too fast; but the British are a nation of guzzlers and gluttons, in that they eat too much.

1 2

3

4 5

NATIONAL WORKS.

1—Suspension Bridge at Niagara. 2—The Victoria Tubular Bridge. Montreal. 3—Pont Neuf, Paris. 4—Chicago River Tunnel. 5—Menai Bridge, Wales.

CHAPTER XII.

BRITISH COLONIES AND AMERICAN TERRITORIES.

An examination of the British possessions and their relative value as compared with the unorganized and territorial parts of the United States. — Treatment of the natives of India and of the American Indians. — Mr. Seward's purchases of Alaska and St. Thomas. — The conquests of England and America from the Spanish.

In this chapter there will be little reference to Australia or to Canada, which will be specially treated in the latter part of the book. Their interests enter into immediate rivalry with ours, and are so vigorous and large that they cannot well be considered within the limits of the present examination.

The British possessions may be divided into three classes: European, Asiatic and African, American and Australian. By her European possessions, England is put into close relation with continental politics. By her Oriental possessions she measures her civilization with that of antiquity. By her acquisitions in the new worlds of America and Australasia, she becomes mutual or rival pioneer with the United States.

If we could express the surface of the globe by a flat plain, with the United Kingdom at its centre, the latter would seem to be a tiny fruticose cluster of islands, clipped from the jagged vine of Europe. Three great colonial appendages would be at once manifest: India, to her south-east; British America, due west; and Australia, upon the extended line of India, and twice the distance of the other two. For the rest of her possessions, scattered about the globe, they would separately seem as tiny as her parent self.

The table hereto appended exhibits in concentrated form the Colonial Empire of this mighty kingdom, by which it will be seen that the destiny of England is to colonize the world, as our separate American destiny has been to give liberal institutions to the western hemisphere.

POSSESSIONS.	Date and Mode of Acquisition.	Area.	Population.	Exports from the British Kingdom.	Imports into Do.
		Sq. miles.	Number.	£	£
India....................		956,436	144,948,356	23,748,180	46,873,208
NORTH AMERICAN:					
Canada...............	Capitulation....1759 and Cession........1763	331,280	2,881,862	£4,332,473	£3,067,918
New Brunswick......	Settlement.....1497	27,027	252,047	476,600	540,552
Nova Scotia..........		18,671	330,857	1,263,198	152,948
Prince Edw'd Island.		2,173	84,386	160,131	64,876
Newfoundland........		40,200	122,638	429,415	343,678
British Columbia and				—	10,487
Vancouver Island....	Settlement..... —	213,000	29,671	202,474	26,804
Total North American Colonies............	....	632,361	3,701,461	6,917,291	4,207,263
Bermuda...............	Settlement.....1609	24	11,451	29,696	6,462
Honduras.............	Cession........1670	13,500	25,635	130,426	220,[illegible]7
WEST INDIES:					
Bahamas	Settlement 1629	3,021	35,487	417,326	1,385,646
Turks Islands..........	" 1629	—	4,372	12,961	2,547
Jamaica................	Capitulation....1655	6,400	441,264	642,785	723,153
Virgin Islands.........		57	6,051	—	—
St. Christopher........		103	24,440	77,890	166,960
Nevis....................	Settlement.....1628	50	9,822	11,714	20,536
Antigua................	" 1632	183	37,125	64,999	176,739
Montserrat.............	" 1632	47	7,645	834	14,927
Dominica...............	Cession........1763	291	25,666	21,107	48,910
St. Lucia...............	Capitulation....1803	250	29,444	26,623	98,597
St. Vincent.............	Cession........1763	131	31,755	35,817	140,701
Barbadoes..............	Settlement.....1605	166	152,757	366,053	702,318
Grenada................	" 1605	133	36,955	56,920	97,477
Tobago.................	Cession........1763	97	15,410	17,990	43,059
Trinidad...............	Capitulation....1797	1,754	84,438	436,815	637,816
British Guiana.........	" 1803	76,000	155,026	741,493	1,729,151
Total, West Indies....	....	88,683	1,097,627	2,925,327	5,988,537
Falkland Islands......	Cession........1837	7,600	648	15,040	17,325
AUSTRALASIA:					
New South Wales......	Settlement.....1787	323,437	411,388	4,349,371	3,319,628
Victoria................	" 1836	86,831	626,639	7,147,216	7,680,332
South Australia........	" 1836	383,328	156,605	1,741 691	964,895
Western Australia.....	" 1829	978,000	20,260	100 075	104,673
Tasmania..............	" 1803	26,215	95,201	283 056	403,559
New Zealand..........	" 1839	106,259	201,712	2,606 994	1,180,085
Queensland............	" 1859	678,000	87,775	713 545	240,550
Total of Australasia...	....	2,582,070	1,599,580	16,941,948	13,899,729
Hong Kong............	Treaty.........1843	29	125,504	—	—
Labuan.................	Cession........1846	45	3,345	—	1,153
Ceylon.................	Capitulation....1796	24,700	2,049,881	904,255	2,420,056
Mauritius..............	" 1810	708	322,517	595,462	1,311,787
Natal	Settlement.....1838	14,397	158,580	369,990	160,271
Cape of Good Hope....	Capitulation....1806	104,931	267,096	1,700,574	1,968,217
St. Helena.............	Settlement.....1651	47	6,860	59,332	14,281
Gold Coast............	" 1661	6,000	151,346	No returns	received.

POSSESSIONS.	Date and Mode of Acquisition.	Area.	Population.	Exports from the British Kingdom.	Imports into Do.
		Sq. miles.	Number.	£	£
Sierra Leone...........	Settlement.....1787	468	41,806	144,081	39,433
Gambia................	" 1631	20	6,939	67,915	29,823
Gibraltar	Capture........1704	1⅞	16,643	No returns	received.
Malta..................	" 1800	115	143,970	36.292	835,946
Entire British dependencies.............	....	4,425,327	154,527,956	56,575,807	77,993,568

The total area of the United States and territories, inclusive of Alaska, is upwards of three million five hundred thousand square miles, or nearly three-fourths of that of the British colonies.

The European possessions of Great Britain are more important in a naval and military point of view, than by any considerations of revenue or dimensions. A few islands in her immediate seas were acquired at a very early period of her history. Heligoland, a little island two miles and a half in circumference, lies in the North Sea, off the mouths of the important German rivers Elbe and Weser; it was captured from Denmark subsequent to the American Revolution, during the French wars, and at the peace, in 1814, was ceded to the British government. It is a watering-place, with three thousand inhabitants, chiefly fishermen and pilots. Gibraltar was wrested from Spain, in 1704; it contains fifteen thousand inhabitants, has withstood frequent sieges, and has been of the utmost military consequence since the beginning of modern times; its possession has always been a source of bitterness between England and Spain, and many English statesmen are of the opinion that it should be restored. The Ionian Islands, which were conquered in the Napoleonic wars, were ceded to Greece, a few years ago, with their two hundred and thirty thousand people. Malta is even a more important station than Gibraltar; it occupies a central point in the Mediterranean Sea, on the great overland highway to India, and has been successively occupied by all the great nations of antiquity. In the year 1800 the English took possession of it, suppressed the Knights of St. John, and fortified it in the strongest manner; it contains about one hundred and thirty thousand persons, and is about as large as Staten Island, in New York harbor. All these home possessions are administered by royal Governors.

All the foreign colonies of England are called "Provincial Establishments," with the exception of Sierra Leone, in Africa, which is an English Liberia, peopled with emancipated negroes, and particularly with the descendants of those American slaves who joined the British army and navy during the American Revolution; of these, four hundred were transported, and ten years later, more than one thousand negroes, of the same origin, who had settled in Nova Scotia, with the white Tories, were sent to Sierra Leone, at their own request. This colony, like Liberia, cannot be said to have proved successful; it is a charter government, specially incorporated like a city, or a trading company. The other British colonies, in Africa, are the Gold Coast, the Cape of Good Hope, and Natal, besides two islands in the South Atlantic, off the African coast, Ascension, and St. Helena. The Cape of Good Hope was treacherously seized by the English, in 1806, when its legitimate Dutch colonists were entirely republicanized, and about to adopt a declaration of independence from Holland, after the example of the United States. England has two hundred and eighty miles of gold coast in Western Africa, populated by three hundred thousand people, and captured from the Dutch one hundred years before the American Revolution. The English rule here has been of a barbarous character, and on one occasion they put a native King to death with more agonizing tortures than Cortez inflicted upon the Montezuma; part of the family of the King of Ashantee has been educated in England. In 1868 the King of Abyssinia, who was said to be successor of the Queen of Sheba proposed marriage to Queen Victoria, and no notice being taken of his proposition, he imitated the example of Napoleon, and seized, as hostages, all the English in his dominion. With the usual decision of the English ministry, an army was despatched to Abyssinia, which penetrated to the capital of the incensed suitor, killed him, routed his army, and brought his son to London to be educated. No positive determination has yet been made, as to colonizing Abyssinia by the English, for English sentiment in our day is averse to conquering more colonies.

The above colonies are all administered by royal Governors, appointed by the English Cabinet, who convoke legislative assemblies, which can enact ordinances not repugnant to the laws of England, corresponding in this respect with the power granted by Congress to the Territorial Legislatures of the United States. In 1782, after the successful revolution of the Americans, an act was passed, entitled "Statute George III., c. xii.," which was of the utmost consequence to all the colonies of England, and which goes by the name of the "Colonial Magna Charta." It provides "that the King and Parliament of Great Britain will not impose any duty, tax, or assessment whatever, payable in any of His Majesty's colonies, provinces, or plantations." Thus the American revolt was not merely an incidental blessing to civilization, but it directly enfranchised the vast possessions of England, present and future, and made Anglo-Saxon liberty a characteristic of all the English colonies. From all the courts of the British colonies appeals lie to the Queen in Council, or to the Court of Queen's Bench, in London, and as a last resort to the House of Lords. None of the acts of the British Parliament are binding upon the colonies, unless the latter be specially mentioned. The Governor of every colony has the right of pardon, and the privilege of nominating to the civil posts. He has his own Cabinet Council, which is sometimes a Court of Appeal, but the Bishops and the important Judges are appointed in London. Canada and Jamaica have the oldest Colonial Parliaments amongst the British colonies; the constitution of Jamaica is two hundred years old; the Governor, or Captain-General, is also Commander-in-chief, and Vice-Admiral; he appoints his Privy Council arbitrarily; the upper legislative house consists of certain office-holders, and of members whom the Governor appoints for life; the lower house is elective.

The Governors of all the British colonies are appointed for six years; the salary of that of Jamaica is 30,000 dollars a year; of Gibraltar, 25,000 dollars; of the Cape of Good Hope, 25,000 dollars; and the Governor of the Little Bermuda Islands, off the American coast, receives three-fifths as much salary as the President of the United States; the Governor of Canada received 35,000 dollars before the Dominion was organized, and the combined salaries of the British Colonial Governors, in North America, were considerably above 100,000 dollars a year.

But the most extraordinary salary paid to any British official is that given to the Governor-General of India, namely, 125,000 dollars a year, with a grand palace and establishment at Calcutta, and a country residence at Barrack-Pur.

The British Empire, in India, is an episode in history, which for gorgeous romance is not equalled by the story of Cortez, or of Alexander. Beginning with a little trading company, in the time of Queen Elizabeth, it obtained permission to take shelter along the shores of the Indian Ocean, and from those paltry settlements has grown the conquest of India, the subjection of its dense population, and the mingling of cold English characteristics, with the luxurious barbarian splendor of Asiatic despotism. All modern nations, prior to the settlement of America, derived their riches from India and the East, and the opening up of ocean communication with it, by turning the Cape of Good Hope, was esteemed not less remarkable than the discovery of America, which immediately preceded. The name of Vasco de Gama took rank with that of Columbus, and the great Portuguese epic poem was written by Camoens, to celebrate his voyage. For a long time the French, the Portuguese, and the English contended for precedence in India, and after the death of the last Great Mogul, who died at Delhi, in 1707, his mighty empire of the Orient fell into anarchy and sloth, and became the prey of European adventurers. It was during the French and Indian War, in which Washington rendered his earliest services to his country, that the British General Clive finally wrested Hindostan from French and native alike, enriching and ennobling himself to so great a degree that he became the victim of jealousy and slander, and committed suicide. During the American Revolution, the able and cruel Warren Hastings became the first Governor-General of India, and he, also, was made the subject of reproach, and brought to England for trial, closing his almost imperial life in mortification and neglect. After the American Revolution, Cornwallis, who had surrendered at Yorktown, became Governor of India, and he proved one of the most amiable and beneficent officials who has ever been sent there. Some Americans may be curious to know the subsequent career of our old and unfortunate antagonist, and it is nowhere better expressed than in Miss Martineau's excellent history: —

"Cornwallis," she says, "had never approved the American war, and had avowed his disapprobation at the peril of his interests; but he did not suffer the less keenly, when his surrender at Yorktown proved the death-blow of the English power in America, and caused a change of ministry and of measures at home. His virtue, however, his disinterestedness and prudence, appear to have been so unquestionable, that he did not suffer politically, or in personal character, for this misfortune; and soon after, he was Governor-General and Commander-in-chief of Bengal. The war with Tippoo distinguished his administration; and we see him the host of Tippoo's two sons, the hostages put into the hands of this kind-hearted and generous nobleman. When the Irish rebellion of 1798 broke out, we find him appealed to, to go and see what could be done; and the testimony is universal as to his benevolent endeavors to put down violence, soften rancor, and rectify injustice on every hand. This was an extraordinary life of service and dignity to have been lived by a man whose qualifications were his virtues, rather than his talents. Disinterested, moderate, prudent, brave, and benign, he commanded confidence on every hand."

Lord Cornwallis had many successors, prominent among whom were the Duke of Wellington, before his European renown began, and Viscount Canning, who was the Governor-General when the celebrated revolt of 1857 broke out. A correspondent of the London "Times" visited Governor Canning during this revolt, and his recollections of the vice-regal palace may be appropriately inserted here: —

"A residence not altogether unbecoming the Viceroy of India, but at the same time by no means overwhelming, splendid, or in faultless taste. The general effect is nearly spoiled by a huge dome, perfectly 'bald,' rising out of the centre of the roof, like a struggling balloon.

"Placed in the midst of a large open space, with green lawns, not very extensive, but covered with fine, clean-shaven sward, and aqueducts around it; and almost within an arrow-shot of the Hooghly, the Government House should be as cool as any house can be in Calcutta; and the great number of windows on the side elevations give it an appearance of airiness which the 'sunny side' by no means deserves. If that dome could be removed, or put straight, or something be got to sit on it, taking it all and all, as seen from the exterior of the fine gateways which lead to the entrance, the Government House reflects credit on the engineer's officer who designed and built it, at the cost of seven hundred and fifty thousand dollars.

"At the gateways, with nothing more formidable than canes in their hands, were real sepoys, — each in 'shape and hue' so like a British soldier when his back is turned, that at a sudden view he would beguile; tall, broad-backed, stiff-set, but with lighter legs than the Briton, and a greater curvature in the thigh. There he is, doing his regulation stride, saluting every white man who enters, civilian or soldier, dressed after the heart of army tailors, pipe-clayed, and cross-belted, and stocked, and winged and facingled, every button shining, every strap blazing, and each bit of leather white as snow, — the sepoy of whom his officers and those around him, contenting themselves with that fair outer show, know as little, if we believe what we hear, as they do of the Fejee Islanders. They cleaned the outside of the platter, and cared little for what was within. Having whitened their sepulchre, they were satisfied. But it was not the outer portals of the Government House only that were trusted to sepoys. At the doorway, at the reception rooms, in the corridors, paced up and down the old troopers of the body-guard, dressed somewhat like our lancers; tall, white-mustachioed veterans, on whose hearts glittered many medals, clasps, and crosses, won in action against Sikh and Affghan. I am not sure whether my own feeling of mild surprise, that at the Viceroy's palace not a single English domestic was visible, would not be shared in by most of my countrymen. White-turbaned natives, with scarlet and gold ropes fastened round the waist, glided about in the halls, and some of the more important added to the dignity of their appearance by wearing large daggers in their cummerbands. At half-past six o'clock I waited upon Lord Canning, whom I found immersed in books and papers, and literally surrounded by boxes, labelled 'military,' 'political,' 'revenue,' etc., etc."

The Indian revolt, which shook the British empire in India from circumference to centre, is supposed to have been a Mohammedan conspiracy, assisted by certain singular superstitions of the Hindoos that the Raj, or reign of the East India Company, was to conclude at the end of a hundred years, and it is remarkable that although the revolt was suppressed, the hated Raj did cease within the period mentioned, for in 1858 the Home Government mustered the East India Company out of existence, and succeeded to its vast but costly possessions. The real cause of the outbreak, however, was the introduction of greased Enfield cartridges into the sepoy service; for, precluded by their religion from biting off these cartridges, the sepoys became mutinous, and at Meerut, near the great city of Delhi in north-western India, the British officers attempted to punish the disobedient heathen; they revolted on the field of parade, massacred the Europeans, and within a few days captured the city of Delhi, committing terrible atrocities almost immediately throughout the whole of Bengal, and in other provinces a mighty ferment took place; the whites were butchered everywhere; a general and his army surrendered and were put to death, while the British race in India and at home was in consternation. General Havelock and Sir Colin Campbell raised the siege of Lucknow and relieved Delhi, capturing the aged King of the latter city, the heir of the Great Mogul, who was sentenced to perpetual banishment, and died in exile in 1862. At the time of the outbreak there were two hundred and thirty-two thousand native troops in Bengal, and forty-five thousand Europeans; five years afterward the European troops were doubled, and the natives cut down to one-half; the great army of Bengal was practically disbanded.

At that woful period in the history of British colonization hundreds of thousands of Englishmen began to doubt that the domination of their empire in the Orient was either a glory or a blessing; yet, so costly have been British investments in Hindostan, and so thoroughly are the politics and commerce of England interwoven with it, that to break the tie would be almost as dangerous as we believed the extinction of slavery by the North. The English debt amassed for India alone amounts to 600,000,000 dollars, while 250,000,000 dollars are invested in India railways, and 100,000,000 dollars in India banks and stocks. The English have built six thousand miles of railroad in Hindostan, and eleven thousand miles of telegraph, achievements which compare with our Pacific Railway, and overland wires. At the present time (1869) there are twenty-four millions of acres of cotton under cultivation in India, and the products of that extraordinary land are almost representative of every zone; domesticated in that vast territory the elephant is docile as the mule; the mountains rise higher than elsewhere on the globe, eighteen peaks reaching elevations of more than twenty thousand feet, and the highest attaining a point of more than twenty-eight thousand, nearly five times the height of Mount Washington; almost every description of cereal, fruit, and tree, grows on the plains or mountain slopes of Hindostan, and the dense population of that subjugated empire is gifted, patient, meditative, and laborious, almost beyond example; their literature is older than the Scriptures; in a far-past age their forefathers were active and ambitious, as their legends show, but when they had settled upon the fertile plains of the Ganges and Hindus they sat themselves down to a long trance of reminiscence, philosophy, and piety; out of which they have not wakened for these two thousand years. If the scholarship of Europe be right, the plains of India gave birth to the great western races which now dominate the earth; there we learned many of our most practical principles, — the rotation of crops, the finer arts of weaving and embroidering, the propagation of many plants and trees which now give shade to the nations of the earth. The rivers of Hindostan compare with the Mississippi, the

Missouri, and the Colorado; the sacred Ganges is nearly two thousand miles long, and the Hindus one thousand seven hundred; the former drains five hundred thousand square miles of fruitful land, the Hindus four hundred thousand. From the earliest ages the muslins of Dacca, the shawls of Cashmere, and silks and tapestries of Delhi have been known to Europe; with them were draped the palaces of the Roman Emperors, and down to our day they adorn alike the shoulders of the Queen and of the President's wife. An American may note how singularly the Hindoo system of *Caste* resembles the distribution of labor in our modern manufacturing establishments. In India every village is like an American township, — a neighborhood rather than a town, each with its head inhabitant, its register of real estate, its brahmin or priest, its school-master, astrologer, and barber; and these trades descend from father to son, in uninterrupted continuity, till it may be said that for two thousand years each family in India has been slowly plodding over the same task, until the thought and spirit have departed; ingenuity there is none; only dexterity of hand, and melancholy perseverance; without factories, and with the rudest tools, these mild-eyed natives still produce carpets, scarfs, saddles, and weapons of such exquisite perfection that they have astonished the eyes of Europeans. In the same manner De Tocqueville pointed out the tendency of modern government and manufactures to relieve the citizen of all responsibility, and set him to work upon some separate part of machinery, so that by long and patient industry his mind ceases to labor, his hands grow automatic, and his children follow along in his trade and condition, — and this is *Caste* in Hindostan.

"In proportion," says this incisive critic, "as the principle of the division of labor is more extensively applied, the workman becomes more weak, more narrow-minded, and more dependent. The art advances, the artisan recedes. On the other hand, in proportion as it becomes more manifest that the productions of manufactures are by so much the cheaper and better as the manufacture is larger and the amount of capital employed more considerable, wealthy and educated men come forward to embark in manufactures which were heretofore abandoned to poor or ignorant handicraftsmen. The magnitude of the efforts required and the importance of the results to be obtained attract them. Thus at the very time at which the science of manufactures lowers the class of workmen, it raises the class of masters.

"The master and the workman have, then, no similarity, and their differences increase every day. They are only connected as the two rings at the extremities of a long chain. Each of them fills the station which is made for him, and out of which he does not get; the one is continually, closely, and necessarily dependent upon the other, and seems as much born to obey as that other is to command.

"What is this but aristocracy?

"I am of opinion," he concludes, "upon the whole, that the manufacturing aristocracy which is growing up under our eyes is one of the harshest which ever existed in the world; but at the same time it is one of the most confined and least dangerous. Nevertheless the friends of democracy should keep their eyes anxiously fixed in this direction; for if ever a permanent inequality of conditions and aristocracy again penetrate into the world, it may be predicted that this is the channel by which they will enter."

It is over this ancient race of Hindoos, who remind us, in their personal graces, gentleness, and beauty, of the race of the Incas, that the young and unrelenting Anglo-Saxon has fastened his chain. His establishment begins in London under the ostensible sceptre of the Queen, where the Secretary of State for India, a politician, who has perhaps never visited the Orient at all, receives his salary of 25,000 dollars a year, and his under Secretary is paid 10,000 dollars; both of them rotate out of office, when there is a change of party. But there are, also, two permanent Secretaries besides, who do the real work of administration, and the Home Secretary has a council of fifteen members, each receiving 6000 dollars a year. From this small office in London the mind must next pass a fourth way round the globe, to where, at Calcutta, the Governor-General holds the highest office, filled by an uncrowned head, in the world, excepting only the American President. He has a Privy Council of five members, nominated from London, and when he adds several persons of his own selection to these, he makes a Legislative Council, in which are both Europeans and Hindoos, the former predominating. Receiving orders from this great Governor and Council, are minor Governors for the great departments of Madras, Bombay, and Bengal; but the ostensible administration throughout India is in the hands of the hereditary and despotic Indian princes, who are thus upheld in nominal importance, as Cortez and Pizarro upheld the Incas they had enslaved, and ruled the enslaved people through them. Around these Indian despots are their nobles, and all the gorgeous pageantry of an Eastern Court; but politicians in England are directing the entire government. The civil service of India is divided into two parts, of which the covenanted civil service is entirely European, and the members have passed examination in London; there are eight hundred of them, with salaries ranging from 1,500 dollars to 40,000 dollars annually. The *uncovenanted* civil service is composed of Europeans, Eurasians, or half-breeds, and natives, more than six thousand in number, some of whom are paid as low as 600 dollars a year. There is, besides, a relentless army of spies and police employed in exacting taxes from the native population, and here we may remark, that whereas land in England has been almost exempt from taxation, in subject India the principal revenue is derived from it. The article of second importance from which revenue is derived is opium, which is manufactured by the government, and forced upon China and India. If the United States would make a monopoly of whiskey, and force the Indians to consume it, we should have a government on the plains very much like that of the British in Asia.

Contrast the worst treatment of the savage Indians of our frontiers with the ordinary behavior of the English to the Hindoos, and we shall have reason to be glad that we have not utterly disgraced our race and age, whereas, according to a report of Judge Malcolm Lewin, of Madras, torture was there, until 1856, an ordinary means of government. "Corruption and bribery remained paramount throughout the whole establishment; violence, torture, and cruelty are the chief instruments for detecting crime, implicating innocence, and extorting money; exposure to the sun; putting pepper and chillies in the eyes; searing the breasts with hot irons; nipping the flesh with pincers; fastening the aggravating poolay insect upon the navel, — these were alleged to be a part of the system of government, known and acknowledged as an engine for realizing the public revenue."

"When Neill," says Russell, the "Times" correspondent, "marched from Allahabad, his executions were so numerous and indiscriminate, that one of the officers attached to his column had to remonstrate with him, on the ground that if he depopulated the country he could get no supplies for the men."

Captain Bruce, a British authority, has said more comprehensively of British rule in India, that if "our empire in that country were overthrown, the only monuments which would remain of us would be broken bottles and corks. Along the whole coast our government is popular, because the people share in the advantages of a flourishing trade. But in the interior we are hated. There is a grinding system of exaction; we take nine-tenths; and the natives feel the privation of honors and places of authority more than the weight of imposts. One of them compared our system to a screw, slow in its motion, never violent or sudden, but always screwing them down to the very earth."

Another reprehensible feature of British rule in India is the promiscuous purchased, or enforced concubinage between the British officers and native women, — a feature of Indian life so palpable and unchallenged that officers and their mistresses are equally received at the receptions of the Governor-General. This condition of morals under the eye of the Established Church, which has its hierarchy in India, is more depraved than the worst periods in the history of American slavery. This subject has been thoroughly treated by Mrs. Roberts, an English writer, to whom we owe this picture of the Governor-General's Court: —

"The suites of apartments devoted to large evening parties occupy the third story. The ball-room, or throne-room, as it is called, is approached through a splendid antechamber; both are floored with dark polished wood, and supported by Ionic pillars, leaving a wide space in the centre, with an aisle on either side; handsome sofas of blue satin damask are placed between the pillars, and floods of light are shed through the whole range from a profusion of cut-glass chandeliers and lustres; formerly the ceilings were painted, but the little reverence shown by the white ants to works of art obliged them to be removed, and gilt mouldings are now the only ornaments. The throne, never particularly superb, is now getting shabby; a canopy of crimson damask surmounted by a crown, and supported upon gilt pillars, is raised over a seat of crimson and gold; in front there is a row of gilded chairs, and it is the etiquette for the Viceroy and the Vice-Queen, upon occasions of state, to stand before the throne to receive the presentation. There is, however, nothing like a drawing-room held in this court; no lord chamberlain, or nobleman, in waiting, or any functionaries corresponding with these personages, except the aides-de-camp, who are seldom very efficient, being more intent upon amusing themselves than anxious to do honors to the company. In these degenerate days so little state is kept up, that,

42

after the first half-hour, the representatives of sovereignty quit their dignified post and mingle with the assembled crowd.

"There is no court-dress, or scarcely anything to distinguish the public rights at Government House from a private party, excepting that until lately no gentleman was permitted to appear in a white jacket. An attempt was made by Lady Hastings to establish a more rigid system of etiquette; she had her chamberlain, and her train was held up by pages. An intimation was given to the ladies that it was expected that they would appear in court plumes, and many were prevented from attending in consequence of the dearth of ostrich feathers, the whole of the supply being speedily bought up; and as it was not considered allowable to substitute native products, there was no alternative but to remain at home. The extreme horror which European ladies entertained of appearing to imitate the natives, banished gold and silver from their robes; not contented with the difference in the fashion of their garments, they refused to wear any articles of Indian manufacture, careless of the mean effect produced by this fastidiousness."

Quite different from the British government in India is the American control of the almost utterly savage tribes of American Indians. At present, all Indian affairs are managed by a Commissioner at Washington, who is subject to the control of the Secretary of the Interior, — a Cabinet officer. The present Commissioner of Indian Affairs (1869) is himself an Indian, and an accomplished officer of the United States Army, — Colonel Parker, a chief of Iroquois, the most renowned confederation of savages ever known on the Western Continent. With him, as consulting or active missionaries, are associated members of the philanthropic sect of Quakers, fast friends of the Indians, and every energy of the government is devoted to conciliating and caring for those unstable wild-men, who have, it is feared, been too often made the victims of designing traders.

In 1869, while preparing this chapter, I waited upon Mr. Taylor, the retiring Commissioner of Indian Affairs, and obtained from him his experience in the Indian office. At that time violent counsellors had proposed to transfer the management of the Indians to the War Department, and the Commissioner's remarks were mainly directed to combating this proposition.

In the Indian office proper there are about four hundred and fifty employés, only about fifty of whom are employed in the general office, the rest being distributed over the country at the various Indian agencies, some as instructors in practical mechanics, menders of tools for Indians, interpreters, millers, missionaries, school-masters, etc.

The salaries of these vary from 3,000 dollars to 360 dollars, the former sum being paid to the Commissioner, the latter to some of the half-breed interpreters.

In a few moments I was introduced to Mr. W. G. Taylor, the Commissioner. He is a middle-aged gentleman, of a singularly benevolent face, formerly a Methodist clergyman, and afterward a member of Congress from East Tennessee. Owing to the war, he was driven to the mountains by the rebels, and upwards of a year ago he took charge of this important bureau, in which he has a conscientious missionary interest. It is a popular belief, however, that among the older attachés of the bureau, those who belong to what is called the "Indian Ring," a system of plunder has long been practised. The Commissioner, being a subsidiary officer to the Secretary of the Interior, has but little more than nominal jurisdiction, but his probity and humanity are potent among all who know him, and as fairly as any man beneath Hercules can labor in this Augean stable, Mr. Taylor has given it his diligence and sagacity. Few men have more thoroughly mastered the diplomacy of the plains, and the grand council which he recently held was one of the largest collections of Indians ever assembled on the face of the globe, — possibly the very largest.

It was on the occasion of their cession of lands to the Pacific Railway, — that fiery track which flashes the signal that the domination of the red man exists no more. And possibly it was the unconscious assemblage of the Indian at his own funeral. There, he bade farewell to the buffalo, and put upon the prairie a swifter stallion than his own wild pony, welcoming to the plains with his homely formulæ of pipes and presents, the courser that is to put a belt around the world.

I had an opportunity to talk with Mr. Taylor at some length, while he gave the fresh expression of his opinions, as the latest observer, upon the status of the Indian on this Continent.

A part of the conversation I think worthy of reproduction, as the most popular form in which I can transfer some intelligent estimate of the relation of the Indian to the present generation and its succeeding one.

"Mr. Taylor, have you been much personally among the Indians?"

"Yes, sir. I have spent considerably more than half the time since I entered upon the duties of this office among the Indian tribes on their reservations."

"You find much hardship and complaint, — do you not?"

"Much, sir. The buffalo as a reliable article of subsistence no longer exists. In five years I believe that a herd of buffalo will not anywhere be seen. The Indians are reduced for supplies to the antelope, the deer, and occasionally to elk. Looking at this hard destiny, they naturally lay it at the white's man's door, to whom, chiefly, their poverty is due."

"How so, sir?"

"Well; the wild animals fly before civilization. The steam-engine and the wild buffalo cannot exist in the same perspective. If they could, our people would turn out to kill the game for mere sport's sake, while to the Indian, these great buffalo preserves are his precious herds, from which to draw subsistence."

"The Pacific Railway is really an offensive encroachment to the Indian?"

"Yes; it is something that offends their vanity by impeaching their right of possession. As we would like no man to make a road across our lot, they hold their reservations to be absolute property, as indeed they are, given them in exchange for government. We projected the Pacific Railroad into their country without their permission, and the grand council that we held two or three years ago was to arrange for their removal, and compose them to it."

"Do the Indians object to taking new reservation?"

"Certainly, when they must do it at our convenience. No people are more fondly attached to the graves of their forefathers. We fix them upon reservations, and as our resistless population catches up to their frontiers, — our vanguard, often made up of ruffians and insolent people, — collisions ensue, and then the government dispossesses the Indian, and pushes him further toward the Pacific. The Indian mind is not so obtuse that it cannot see that the world must end somewhere. Where will they push the Indian, when he gets to the end?"

"You think that many of the Indian wars begin by our disregard of the Indian's rights?"

"I do. The majority, if not all, of the Indian wars, either begin in this way, or by a failure on the part of the United States to perform its stipulations. Take the war at present (1869) going on, at a large expense. We wanted the lands of the Cheyennes and Arrapahoes, for the purposes of the Pacific Railroad; we said to these tribes, in grand council, 'We will give you other lands, and teach you upon them how to till the ground, for which we will give you ploughs and seed, and also sheep and cattle, by which you may be fed, till your land becomes productive.' Therefore the Indian consented to be removed, and he remained upon his distant reservation peaceably, so long as we fed him according to contract. Suddenly, our appropriation ran out, and we said to the Indian, 'We shall now be unable to feed you; our money is gone.' Unable to live without nourishment, the Indians, in melancholy bands, roamed back to their former lands, and what did they behold? Our people, pushing out along the spine of the railway, following up the beds of the streams, and the fertile belts, had already overflowed the country. Surprised and jealous, the Indians regarded it all with wonder and mortification.

"Well, they are hungry, and into some isolated house they go, and say, 'We are hungry! We want food!' Here is cause for affront. Perhaps the food is refused; then they take it. Or perhaps too much is exacted. Perhaps there is a lone woman in the house, and some of the young savages offer violence. In any event bad feeling begins, and war ensues, involving millions of dollars. Now, had the Indians been sustained by the government as we promised, all collision would have been prevented."

"Whose fault was it that the appropriation ran out?"

"The fault of the false position of this bureau. The government has never had an uniform policy toward the Indians; a succession of expedients has been adopted from time to time, to satisfy the Indians, but the Commissioner of the bureau is without influence, either with Congress or the President. He is an officer of the Secretary of the Interior, who meantime is busied with the vast and complicated affairs of his other bureaux, and courtesy and custom demand of the Commissioner that he should have no independent dealings, but make all his applications to the Secretary only. In fact, Mr. Townsend, the Indian Bureau, ought to be an independent department."

"Are its functions so relatively important?"

"Yes, sir; we have as many treaties with the Indian nations as we have with foreign nations. An Indian cannot understand why a political dead lock at the Capitol should make the government break its word. He demands the fulfilment of a promise as between man and man.

"If the Indian Bureau were even as independent as the Agricultural Bureau, I could go to Congress and tell them the necessities of my department. Now I must often delay, to satisfy courtesy at the expense of misunderstanding, massacre, and expensive warfare."

"Have you any notion of what should be a definite policy toward the Indians?"

"It is the province of statesmanship to meet this question. I am satisfied that the transfer of this bureau to the War Department would be unjust, provoke the helpless massacre of the Indians, and be altogether the most unstatesmanlike way to deal with them. Heretofore, we have kept the Indians in the surf of civilization, driving them ahead of us, so that their habits have not ceased to be nomadic. A Christian policy toward them would teach civilization to go beyond them, and leave them enclosed by it. The Cherokees, Chickasaws, Creeks, and Choctaws, are examples of what the stable, stationary Indian can do."

"Does any great percentage of the Indian's money get to him?"

"There is reason to believe that traders get the bulk of it. Our laws about entering the Indian reservations are honored chiefly in the breach. Any man can trade on a reservation by getting a judge and two citizens to certify that he is an honest man. With two barrels of whiskey in a wheelbarrow, and some beads, the trader comes into the reservation, takes a squaw to protect himself, and begins the systematic work of swindling.

"The cost of the Indian military expeditions is enormous. For example, the military expenditures on account of the Indians, in the territory of New Mexico alone, have exceeded four millions of dollars every year, since its acquisition from Mexico. Gen. Sumner proposed to buy out all the white citizens, and give the territory in its entirety to the Indians.

"There are, in all the United States, about three hundred thousand Indians, or not three times the population of Delaware. Ninety odd thousand of these are in the Indian Territory, where are all the civilized tribes. The Sioux are the largest of all the tribes, probably numbering twenty-five thousand, I suppose."

"You feel, therefore, Mr. Taylor, that this Indian problem is not too vague for statesmanship to take up?"

"No, sir; but it is too grave a subject to be treated as a fragment of a duty, hidden away in a recess of the Interior Department. Whatever defects have existed here are allowed to moulder, and grow in the dark. Congress cannot dismiss this subject in an hour's debate. Only by a familiar knowledge of the Indian character can we treat with the Indian, as an enlightened responsibility demands that we should, so that the ground may not descend to us, with his curse upon it."

"You have never employed Indians in the bureau clerically?"

"No, sir."

"Those who come to Washington, — do they accomplish any good result?

"Yes; they go home with formidable stories of the white man's powers, which dispose the tribes to peace. The Indian is very ignorant, except of that which is demonstrated to his senses. Hearing of the big lodges, the great canoes, and the mighty encampments does them good in a pacific way."

Since the United States became a nation, it has, in general, made acquisitions of territory, by peaceful purchase, the exception having been the war with Mexico, but even in this case a formidable portion of our people denounced the war, and in the end we paid liberally for the territory subtracted, or, in terms, one hundred dollars to every white man resident in the whole conquest.

The United States acquired Florida in perhaps a more irregular manner than any of its territory. Napoleon Bonaparte, anxious to raise money, prevailed upon the Spaniards to give him Florida, and immediately sold it to us; but this irregularity led to such uncertainty in the titles of property, that to this day the State is very sparsely settled, and in our haste to occupy it we offended the Indians, so that it is computed that the Seminole War alone cost us thirty million dollars, besides the loss of many valuable lives.

The entire purchase-money for Louisiana was fifteen million dollars; but at that time Louisiana was not the name of a State, as now; it represented the vast tract of country lying on the lower Mississippi and the Gulf.

Fifteen millions of dollars were paid to Mexico for California, so that thirty-seven millions, including seven millions for Alaska, is the sum total of our national acquisitions in real estate.

Negotiations were entered into by Mr. W. H. Seward, our Secretary of State, in 1868, to buy the Island of St. Thomas, in the West Indies; but Congress, holding that the Secretary had no right to spend money without authority, refused to ratify the purchase, and this led to considerable ill-feeling on the part of the Danish government. The people of St. Thomas testified their wish to become citizens of the United States, by voting almost unanimously for annexation. Mr. James Parton, an industrious author, has taken position that good faith requires us to ratify the treaty, and he urges the following considerations: —

"That we cannot repudiate Mr. Seward's bargain without inflicting a very great and irreparable injury upon a respectable nation, our good friend and ally.

"That if, after paying for Alaska, we refuse to pay for these islands, we stand dishonored before mankind, as having one rule for the strong and another for the weak.

"That, however erroneous may be the system which permits the Executive to commit the country to purchases of land, we have no right to hold Denmark responsible for that system, nor to reform it at her expense.

"That, when a foreign government has so much as delayed the ratification and execution of a properly concluded treaty with the United States, we have felt ourselves to be grossly wronged, and were willing to seek redress by violence.

"That these islands, in the opinion of professional men, have a great and peculiar value, which renders their acquisition highly desirable."

The advice of Washington, in the Farewell Address, is conservatively just upon this, as upon almost every international question: —

"It is our true policy," he says, "to steer clear of permanent alliances with any portion of the foreign world, so far, I mean, as we are now at liberty to do it, for, let me not be understood as capable of patronizing infidelity to existing engagements. I hold the maxim no less applicable to public than to private affairs, that honesty is always the best policy. I repeat it, therefore, let those engagements be observed, in their genuine sense; but in my opinion it is unnecessary, and would be unwise to extend them."

Far different from the conquest of India was the peaceful discovery and settlement of Australia by England, and relative results have proved it no less beneficent.

Victoria is the wealthiest of the Australian nations, and, India alone excepted, has the largest trade of any of the dependencies of Great Britain.

A party landed in 1835 upon the Yarra banks, mooring their boat to the forest-trees, and they formed a settlement upon a grassy hill, behind a marsh, and began to pasture sheep where Melbourne, the capital, now stands. In twenty years Melbourne became the largest city, but one in the southern hemisphere, having one hundred and fifty thousand people within her limits. Victoria has grander public buildings in her capital, larger and more costly railroads, a greater income, and a heavier debt than any other colony, and she pays to her Governor fifty thousand dollars a year, or one-fourth more than even New South Wales. When looked into, all this success means gold. There is industry, there is energy, there is talent, there is generosity and public spirit; but they are the abilities and virtues that gold will bring, in bringing a rush from all the world of dashing fellows in the prime of life. The progress of Melbourne is that of San Francisco. "Some of the New South Welsh," says Mr. Dilke, an author, "shutting their eyes to the facts connected with the gold rush, assert so loudly that the Victorians are the refuse of California, or 'Yankee scum,' that when I first landed in Melbourne, I expected to find street-cars, revolvers, big hotels, and fire-clubs, euchre, caucuses, and mixed drinks. I could discover nothing American about Melbourne except the grandeur of the public buildings and the width of the streets, and its people are far more thoroughly British than are the citizens of the rival capital. In many senses Melbourne is the London, Sydney the Paris, of Australia."

Liberia is the only American colony that has ever been planted on a foreign continent. This government is almost an exact reproduction in miniature of the United States. It was established for the purpose of building up an independent nation of English-speaking Africans; but the emancipation of the whole race, during the civil war, rendered foreign exile unnecessary and unpopular. The whole revenue of Liberia is not above sixty thousand dollars a year. Its most distinguished president has returned to America, and is a resident of Washington. Great Britain has probably met no more formidable opposition, in any of her Oceanic colonies, than in New Zealand, or Tasmania, where war with the native Maoris still continues. The lesser British colonies in Asia, Polynesia, and the southern hemisphere, do not require description, as their government has been already described. In a future chapter upon South America, the British islands in the West Indies will be noticed. One of the most celebrated insular colonies of England is Mauritius, or Isle de France, off the coast of Madagascar; it is described in the pretty French story of "Paul and Virginia." This island and its accessories were captured from the French, in 1810, by a grand expedition. It contains less than two hundred thousand persons, yet pays its Governor thirty-five thousand dollars a year. All the more important British colonies are assessed the salaries of their governors. Under a democratic form of government, where the people have liberty to go at large, and to agitate as they please, it is not wonderful that the inherent lust to conquer should frequently develop itself in unauthorized expeditions to the weaker coasts and islands in our neighborhood. Cuba, Central America, parts of Mexico, and Canada have, at different times, been partly possessed by bands of fillibusters; the Sandwich Islands are held in request by many of our manifest-destinarians, and American adventurers have stormed the walls of Pekin. Our government has, in every case but one, disavowed these enterprises; for the belief in the American mind that we shall peaceably succeed to the dominion of all North America is too settled to exhibit itself in these merely boyish amusements. On this continent we are the colonizing race, as the British in the East. Dutch, French, Portuguese, and Spanish have borne away prizes in past generations, but the only colonies which promise permanently to endure have been planted by the Anglo-Saxon race. Sixty years ago, France possessed two-thirds of North America. Her colonists could assimilate with the savages, but not without losing their own civilization; and the agile French half-breeds of Hudson's Bay have become the pliant instruments of the organizing English mind.

"There was once a time," says De Tocqueville, sadly, "at which we also might have created a great French nation in the American wilds, to counterbalance the influence of the English upon the destinies of the New World. France formerly possessed a territory in North America, scarcely less extensive than the whole of Europe. The three greatest rivers of that continent then flowed within her dominions. The Indian tribes which dwelt between the mouth of the St. Lawrence and the delta of the Mississippi were unaccustomed to any other tongue but ours; and all the European settlements scattered over that immense region recalled the traditions of our country. Louisbourg, Montmorency, Duquesne, Saint Louis, Vincennes, New

Orleans (for such were the names they bore) are words dear to France and familiar to our ears.

"But a concourse of circumstances, which it would be tedious to enumerate, have deprived us of this magnificent inheritance. Wherever the French settlers were numerically weak, and partially established they have disappeared; those who remain are collected on a small extent of country, and are now subject to other laws. The four hundred thousand French inhabitants of Lower Canada constitute, at the present time, the remnant of an old nation lost in the midst of a new people.

"The impulse of the British race in the New World cannot be arrested. The dismemberment of the Union, and the hostilities which might ensue, the abolition of republican institutions, and the tyrannical government which might succeed it, may retard this impulse, but they cannot prevent it from ultimately fulfilling the destinies to which that race is reserved. No power upon earth can close upon the emigrants that fertile wilderness which offers resources to all industry, and a refuge from want. Future events, of whatever nature they may be, will not deprive the Americans of their climate, or of their inland seas, of their great rivers, or of their exuberant soil. Nor will bad laws, revolutions, and anarchy be able to obliterate that love of prosperity and that spirit of enterprise which seem to be the distinctive characteristics of their race, or to extinguish that knowledge which guides them on their way."

What is to be the fate of the British colonies? In India and China, where the British constitute a mere garrison, and handful of hangers-on, it is impossible that they can keep root save by constant and wearisome struggles. Australia is almost ripe already to drop from the parent bough, and plant her own offspring in the island seas. Canada must also quit the bough, and she can but obey the law of gravitation, which will bind her to our destinies. For the lesser colonies of England, they may be retained so long as British commerce maintains its sway, but these scattered over the surface of the earth will not, of themselves, make an empire.

The United States, compact, individual, youthful, enterprising, expects to construct an empire by no such piecemeal process. She has but to open her gates, and the human sluices from both worlds pour in and people her. Her system of admitting new States into her counsels is wisely representative. The Territories of the United States are governed by a Magistrate appointed by the President, and under him an embryo Legislature meets; in Congress they are represented by a delegate, who can speak upon all matters affecting his Territory, but cannot vote. When the Territory shows signs of strength and empire, it is admitted into the Union, if its constitution is a proper one and its population adequate. Thus the work of local self-government extends itself westward. First, we formed the nation out of thirteen colonies; then we formed our wild regions into Territories, and they organized themselves and came to the capital to solicit admission; then we acquired more domain, and it developed into Territory and State successively. This process of absorption and organization will continue till we shall have formed this continent into infinite self-governments, with a common intelligence directing the vital life of all, while all shall be free to lead the separate existence of neighborhoods. England, on the contrary, conquers to bend and drain. We invite new lands into our family, and we help and influence them.

At present (1869) there are waiting for admission to the republic nine Territories, each pressing every energy to meet the requirements of the law and be recognized as integral parts of the United States. Our hardest territorial problem is the Indian, and that is a problem which the Englishman has in every colony. Providence reserved for our nation chiefly the naked and fertile land; had he packed it with people of ancient civilizations we should have the work before us that is making the Englishman despair. And what is to be our population?

An editorial writer in the "Chicago Tribune," has made a conservative answer to this question, when he says, that "it is highly improbable that the population of the United States, by the impending census of 1870, will fall short of forty millions, and it is quite likely to reach forty-one millions." Let us compare these figures with those presented by other civilized powers, in order to obtain at a glance their relative ranks in the scale of nations: —

	Population.	*Sq. Miles.*
Russia in Europe	70,000,000	2,066,000
Russia in Asia	8,500,000	5,748,000
Russia total	78,500,000	7,814,000
United States	41,000,000	3,000,000
Alaska purchase	75,000	500,000
United States total	41,075,000	3,500,000

	Population.	*Sq. Miles.*
France	39,500,000	207,000
Austria	36,000,000	230,000
Great Britain	30,000,000	123,000
German Confederation	29,500,000	190,000
Italy	26,000,000	118,000
Spain	18,000,000	183,000
Brazil	9,000,000	2,973,400
Mexico	8,000,000	830,000

In the table we have not added to Great Britain her foreign colonies and possessions. If all the subjects, Christian and Pagan, of the Queen of Great Britain, scattered over the world, were included, the number would exceed one hundred and sixty millions, and the area under her sway eight million square miles. But her Christian subjects are less than thirty-five millions of souls, which places the number still below that of the United States.

All the above enumerated population, except Russia, have their laws framed by legislative bodies elected by the people. It will therefore be perceived that in point of population the United States stands at the head of the self-governing powers. This is not remarkable to Americans, as we have, many years ago, accepted our destiny to be at the head of powers and civilizations; still the curious facts of future decades are interesting. On the basis of the average increase of the last eighty years, the United States will have in 1880 the surprising number of fifty-six million four hundred and fifty thousand; in 1890, it will have seventy-seven million two hundred and sixty-six thousand; and in July, 1900, no less than one hundred million three hundred and fifty-five thousand nine hundred and eighty-five people.

And what attached these people to us?

In part, undoubtedly, our zone, and the natural endowments of this portion of the globe. In part, and of late years, our vindicated national character and the safety of our institutions. But the magnet in America is that we are a republic! A republican people! Cursed with artificial government, however glittering, the people of Europe, like the sick, pine for nature with protection, for open vistas and blue sky, for independence without ceremony, for adventure in their own interest, — and here they find it!

We can therefore be thrilled with the idea of an empire which cannot soon dissolve. But a more melancholy vision rises upon the eye of the Englishman, and is gracefully expressed in a passage from one of his representative journals: —

"The sceptre may pass away from us; unforeseen accidents may derange our most profound schemes of policy; victory may be inconstant to our arms; but there are triumphs which are followed by no reverses. There is an empire exempt from all natural causes of decay. These triumphs are the pacific triumphs of reason over barbarism; that empire is the imperishable empire of our arts and our morals, our literature and our laws!"

Looking back to the severance of our colonies from England, we can feel how memorable was that step to the progress of mankind, by observing in the literature and politics of all lands the reverence paid to our resolution. The better Englishmen find consolation for it in the improvement of our race and the growth of liberty; the meaner, like Browne Roberts, in the apparent calamities of our allies.

"Upon this American war," he says, "the resources of our country had been poured forth with a lavish hand, and its termination left her in a state of great exhaustion, with her most bitter enemies exulting on all hands at her temporary humiliation. This exultation, however, was amply compensated for a few years after, in the calamities both of France and Spain; the former of these countries having learned, from contact with America, those revolutionary principles which soon deluged her own soil with blood, and the latter experiencing an equally prejudical effect in the loss of her South American colonies, which were not long in following the example of independence given them by their brethren of the North."

We can at this interval, and in the light of our beneficent influence in accomplishing just those things which are above decried, recall with curiosity, but without emotion, the speech which old King George III. made to the first American Minister he was obliged to receive: —

"In thus admitting their separation from the Crown of these kingdoms, I have sacrificed every consideration of my own to the wishes and opinions of my people. I make it my humble and earnest prayer to Almighty God, that Great Britain may not feel the evils which might result from so great a dismemberment of the empire; and that America may be free from the calamities which have formerly proved in the mother country how essential monarchy is to the enjoyment of constitutional liberty. Religion, language, interest, affections, may, and I hope will, yet prove a bond of permanent union between the two countries. To this end neither attention nor disposition on my part shall be wanting."

This speech and this farewell have yet to be repeated by many British sovereigns.

CHAPTER XIII.

THE BRITISH AND AMERICAN ARMY AND NAVY.

Notices of the technical institutions of war of either country, and the composition of the army and navy. — Representative episodes and personages of the services of the two nations.

"The Army and the Navy" is always the favorite toast at an English banquet. The Englishman believes that his army is as invincible as his navy, and holds the name of Wellington to be as eminent in the history of warfare as that of Napoleon. The experiences of the Crimea somewhat unsettled this patriotic superstition, but the success of the Abyssinian and Indian wars have pretty well restored the equanimity of the Briton's belief in the invincibility of his "foot-soldiery."

The Anglo-Saxon has always been a combative, not to say a military, race. The same impulse which led to Anglo-Saxon love of liberty, early declared itself in opposition to standing armies at home; and this is the distinguishing peculiarity of both our nationalities, that we have a fixed dislike to a permanent soldiery upon land, and a reverence for the prowess of our navies.

The British Navy is a permanent institution, and is not, like the Army, allowed on sufferance, and renewed from year to year. Seamen have civil privileges beyond those of the soldiery, and in the Navy "seniority" determines promotion and not purchase.

We have the same inherited notions in America with regard to our Army and Navy; our Legislatures dislike standing armies, and seldom make objection to the permanence of the Navy. As the law of England recognizes no other permanent armed force on land than the National Militia, the American Republic places its chief dependence upon its volunteers.

The Army, as it stood before the war, was the smallest organization consistent with public safety in time of peace. We had, in 1860, eleven thousand eight hundred and forty-eight enlisted men, and one thousand eighty-three commissioned officers. In July, 1866, Congress

1

2

3

MILITARY INSTITUTIONS.

1—Woolwich Academy, England. 2—School of St. Cyr, France.
3—West Point, New York.

discussed very fully what should be its future Army, and, after a long debate in both Houses, passed the law of July 28, 1866, fixing the military peace establishment. That law authorized five regiments of artillery, ten of cavalry, and forty-five of infantry. The minimum strength and the maximum strength of a regiment of each arm of the service was fixed, so that the Army might contain eighty thousand three hundred and seventy enlisted men as the maximum, while the minimum strength was forty-seven thousand two hundred and seventy enlisted men. Whether it should be in fact the larger or the smaller number, or any intermediate number, was left to the discretion of the President of the United States.

In March, 1869, as the records of the War Department showed, we had a chain of fortified posts along our coast, extending from Eastport, in Maine, on the Atlantic, to Sitka, in Alaska, on the Pacific, mounting three thousand two hundred and fifty coast guns; and we had enough enlisted men in the artillery to enable us to put two men to each gun.

The present Army of the United States consisted of nearly fifty thousand men, until the spring of 1869, when, on complaint in Congress of its expensiveness, it was reduced to about thirty-five thousand.

The British Army, in 1868, consisted of one hundred and forty thousand men; there were sixty-five thousand soldiers in India alone. It is upon the militia force of the United States that we place our chief dependence, and this was estimated in 1868 to consist of three million three hundred thousand men.

During the civil war in the South which lasted from 1861 to 1865, the Northern and Border States contributed nearly two million seven hundred thousand men to the service of the National Government; Massachusetts furnishing twenty thousand more soldiers than composed the standing army of England; four of the States gave to the army one-fifth their entire population; during the same period the Southern States had four hundred thousand men almost constantly in the field.

Great Britain draws but one in two thousand from production, and keeps but one hundred and eighty-eight thousand regular troops in time of peace, at a yearly cost of seventy-one million dollars. In 1867–8, even these figures were reduced fifteen per cent.

Great Britain's Army, including the forces in India, is estimated at one hundred and eighty-eight thousand regulars, one hundred and thirty thousand regular reserve, and one hundred and eighty-four thousand last reserve. Of the first reserve, all except two thousand regulars are pensioners and militia; while the last reserve is made up of fourteen thousand yeomanry, and one hundred and seventy thousand volunteers. The British Army recruits fourteen thousand annually, out of a population of twenty-nine million. These recruits, of course, go into the regular Army, where they serve twelve years; the reserves being, with the exception of the pensioners, little more than voluntary organizations under the patronage of the government.

The English Militia establishment is a small affair, comprising in 1867 forty-two regiments, with about ninety thousand officers and men; seven of these regiments are in Lancashire and eight in London.

At a great review of militia, held the same year, fifty-two thousand men were in line in Scotland and Ireland.

Great Britain pays in pensions more than ten and one-half millions of dollars a year.

The English Militia was allowed to fall into decay after the expulsion of the Stuarts, on account of the supposition that it was controlled by the old Tory landed gentry, who were not favorable to the revolution; still militia officers receive salaries, which is not the case in America, except when the militia are called out by the Governor. All the English militia officers, down to Captain, must have a property qualification, and a Colonel receives three thousand dollars a year. Nearly all the officers are Justices of the Peace; they are appointed by the Lords Lieutenant, or County Governors, who are the commanding officers in each county, and all the militia are under control of the Home Secretary, who is a member of the Cabinet in London. The English yeomanry is a separate body, now of little practicable account, which originated when Napoleon Bonaparte threatened to invade England.

In Ireland there are nearly thirteen thousand policemen acting as soldiers. In India there are upwards of one hundred thousand native troops, most of whom are heathens.

Out of every thousand recruits of the British Army, three hundred and twenty are Irishmen, and a hundred and twelve Scotchmen.

England has also a volunteer force of a hundred and sixty thousand men, but these are mainly holiday soldiers, like the militia soldiers of our larger American cities.

Parliament votes large sums to support and encourage the English

Militia and volunteers; in 1867 one million eight hundred thousand dollars was the parliamentary grant to the volunteers alone.

In the same year the total cost of the British Army was seventy millions of dollars. Prior to the civil war in the South, the United States Army consisted of only fourteen thousand men. Prior to the American civil war, we had no military rank higher than that of Lieutenant-General by brevet, but the remarkable services of Lieutenant-General Grant, and the increase of our regular Army, led to the revival of the rank of General, and in the same period we created Admirals in the naval service. The latter innovation was made chiefly on account of the embarrassments of our naval officers abroad in mingling familiarly with those of European nations, but the new distinction in the Army was meant to be an extraordinary form of expressing the national gratitude to General Grant.

While no movement has been made against the dignity of our Admirals, considerable feeling has been manifested against continuing the grade of General. After General Grant was elevated to the presidency, Mr. Butler, an ex-General of volunteers, made a formal attack upon the pay and perquisites of officers of the regular Army, and he gave this exhibit of the financial situation of our line officers as he proposed it. It is probable that his figures are as nearly accurate as those of any authority we can summon.

A Brigadier-General, chief of the department, has $7,606.50 if he is stationed at Washington; a Colonel has 4,392 dollars; a Lieutenant-Colonel, 3,826 dollars; a Major, 3,537 dollars; a mounted Captain, 2,725 dollars; a Captain, not mounted, 2,605 dollars; a First Lieutenant mounted, 2,177 dollars; a First Lieutenant, not mounted, 2,137 dollars; a Second Lieutenant mounted, 2,177 dollars; a Second Lieutenant, not mounted, 2,077 dollars. So that a Second Lieutenant, just out of school, gets 2,000 dollars a year, and this is outside of his commutation for his forage, and outside of his allowance for travel.

Abuses having crept into the Army, Mr. Butler, himself an officer of experience, proposed that the permanent Army establishment be fixed as follows. I use his own terms: —

"I have fixed the pay of each grade of officers in this form, subject, of course, to the better judgment of the House: Lieutenant-General to have 12,000 dollars a year, — 4,000 dollars more than the Speaker of this House, and 4,000 dollars more than the Vice-President; Major-General, 7,500 dollars; Brigadier-General, 5,000 dollars; Colonel, 3,500 dollars; Lieutenant-Colonel, 2,750 dollars;

Major, 2,500 dollars; Captain, mounted, 2,000 dollars; Captain, not mounted, 1,800 dollars; Adjutant, 1,800 dollars; Regimental Quartermaster, 1,800 dollars; First Lieutenant, mounted, 1,600 dollars; First Lieutenant, not mounted, 1,500 dollars; Second Lieutenant, mounted, 1,500 dollars; Second Lieutenant, not mounted, 1,400 dollars; Chaplain, 1,200 dollars; Aide-de-camp to Major-General, 200 dollars in addition to pay of his rank; Aide-de-camp to Brigadier-General, 150 dollars in addition to pay of his rank; Acting Assistant Commissary, 100 dollars in addition to pay of his rank; and that these sums shall be in full of everything.

"Then I provide that commutation for fuel, quarters, forage, rations, longevity-rations, servants' clothing, pay and rations, and everything of that sort in the way of allowances, shall be done, ended, cease, be got rid of, cut off, and put a stop to. [Laughter.] I provide that that great abuse shall be finally brought to an end, if it is possible to be done by legislative act. I have provided, however, when officers travel they shall have ten cents per mile."

It is probable that the future regular Army of the United States will be organized upon Mr. Butler's plan, although the grade of General has been transiently retained, at the request of President Grant, in favor of General Sherman, his successor.

The Commander-in-chief of the British Army is generally a member of the royal family, and at present he is the Duke of Cambridge, the Queen's cousin, a gentleman who, being disqualified as a member of the royal family from marrying an English woman, has children by a virtuous lady, who are yet illegitimate before the law. Down to the year 1846 the Commander-in-chief was a member of the Cabinet, but he is now controlled by it; at the same time he has the high privilege of personally communicating with the Queen, in whose name he issues all his orders. His military Secretary is an important personage, with a salary of ten thousand dollars, who holds levees at which officers and others having business to transact, find access to him. His campaigns are generally planned by the Secretary of War; but in the field he is supreme, and the enormous patronage of his office makes him powerful in peace as in war, as he recommends for all military appointments and promotions, and makes all the fees and percentages out of his own great office. He has no control whatever over the general finance of the Army, and cannot move his troops without the consent of the Secretary of War.

The position of Commander-in-chief of the British Army has been frequently abused, and in 1809 Col. Wardell, a militia officer, made a direct impeachment in Parliament of the Duke of York, the King's son and Commander-in-chief. He indicated a house in Gloucester Place, splendid with carriages, servants, and fine furniture, as the nest of the corruption he spoke of. In this house, he said, the Duke of York had placed his mistress, — a woman named Mary Anne Clarke, — who was in the habit, as could be proved, of selling offices in the Army by means of her favor with the Commander-in-chief. Mrs. Clarke had, in one instance, taken a bribe of five hundred pounds, which she paid over to a silversmith as part-payment for a service of plate, — the Duke of York discharging the remainder. Other cases were detailed, which convinced the hearers, in the midst of their consternation, that there must be some ground for the charges. The positions laid down by Colonel Wardell were, that Mrs. Clarke possessed the power of military promotion; that she took money for the use of that power; and that the Commander-in-chief shared the money. There were further allegations of Mrs. Clarke having been bribed by clergymen and gentlemen to procure appointments in the Church and the State; but the military abuses were those that the House had first to deal with.

This denunciation of the regular Army by the militia much resembles the raid on the regular Army officers by the volunteers in 1868–9.

The Generals on the English home service, comprising the "home staff," are appointed as commanding officers over the several districts, England and Wales being divided into five districts, Scotland and the Channel Islands into three, and Ireland forming a chief district, with five subdivisions. The greater colonies have in like manner their foreign staffs.

An English Field-Marshal, acting as Commmander-in-chief, receives about eighty-two dollars a day in gold, but if he be below the rank of Field-Marshal he receives forty-seven dollars a day; a General receives twenty-eight dollars a day; a Lieutenant-General nineteen dollars; a Major-General nine dollars; a Brigadier-General seven dollars; a Colonel six and a half dollars a day. To all the above seven hundred and fifty dollars a year are paid, as an additional allowance; the above are all staff officers. Cavalry Colonels in the field receive forty-five hundred dollars a year; Lieutenant-Colonels about seven dollars a day; Infantry Colonels receive twenty-five hundred dollars a year; Lieutenant-Colonels four dollars and a quarter a day; Privates in the field receive from twenty-five to thirty-seven cents a day. Officers attached to the Queen's household troops are paid much better, Colonels receiving as high as nine thousand dollars a year.

After serving eighteen years, or if disabled or dismissed by reduction of the Army, officers are permitted to retire on half-pay, a Colonel's half-pay being nearly four dollars a day, a Captain's about a dollar and seventy-five cents a day; besides, Parliament grants about seventy-five thousand dollars a year for extra pensions, which is distributed in sums of five hundred dollars to retired officers of high rank.

The most extraordinary feature of the English military service to an American observer is the purchase and sale of officers' commissions. Except a few distinguished cadets from Sandhurst College, and occasional appointments of non-commissioned officers for remarkable services, all the military commissions in the British Army are paid for, and the rate is fixed by law. A man can buy the rank of Lieutenant-Colonel in the Life Guards for about thirty-seven thousand dollars, and in the Foot Guards for forty-five thousand dollars; in the Dragoons thirty thousand dollars. A Captain's commission brings nine thousand dollars in the Dragoons, twenty-four thousand dollars in the Foot Guards, and seventeen thousand five hundred dollars in the Life Guards and Horse Guards. This is considered to be a good investment for one's money, as it pays him a good interest, gives him rank and employment, and opportunities for distinction. There are generally a great number of candidates ready to buy commissions; they must apply to the Commander-in-chief, who, when opportunities arise, selects those whom he thinks fit for commissions.

When an American officer resigns his commission he has no interest in its transfer, and he thus loses not only his yearly salary, but the capital it represents. An Army Colonel, who was about to resign in 1869, said to me that he was not only losing some five thousand dollars a year, but the eighty thousand dollars in capital which it represented.

While an Army commission in America is thus more or less dependent upon temporary political feeling, its possession may be said to confer even more honor than under a monarchical government; for in a republic, where there are no titles of honor, the Army and the Navy confer almost the sole consideration.

A recent Army critic, Wraxall, speaks in the following satirical yet truthful way, of the semi-aristocratic organization of the English Army: —

"An English officer's education is expressed by so many pounds sterling. Lord Tuppingham has been a very tiresome fellow, from the day when, to the horror of the Earl's servants, he could walk alone. He revelled in mischief of all kinds before he could write his name. You know the wondrous splutter upon paper which stands for his venerable name even now, in his thirty-second year. It was impossible to cram any serviceable knowledge into his head. But then, of what use was knowledge to the head that bore aloft, along the broad pavement of Piccadilly, such a hat? Knowledge is the necessity of the head that wears no hat. Lord Tuppingham went to Eton and learned boating. He went to Cambridge and learned smoking, and drinking, and the elements of gambling. He reached London, prepared to hold a command in the Army, to patrol the Haymarket, and mortgage his estates in St. James Street. On more than one occasion, while the play ran high, he would composedly eat plover's eggs that had just cost him one hundred pounds each. Now, with the vices, and not the studies, of Eton and Cambridge, he was 'fit for nothing but the Army.' Brave, he certainly was. He thrashed a drayman at college, and will be a prominent figure if his regiment go to the war. But then, suppose he has his men the wrong way; suppose that his cards and wine have been cultivated at the expense of his military duties; suppose that he is put on the staff before he is able to understand one of the vitally important duties of a staff officer? Lives are lost. The blood of lion-hearted men, and his own, flows in vain. Of one hundred and sixteen staff officers sent originally with the British Army to the Crimea, one hundred and nine were Lord Tuppinghams!"

Another extraordinary feature of the English Army is the military hierarchy or priesthood, composed of various ecclesiastics of the Established Church, who have actual rank as Field-Marshals, Generals, Colonels, Captains, Cornets, and Ensigns, and truly may be said to belong to the church militant.

Both England and America, and indeed all civilized nations, have military institutions for the education of young officers, and it may truthfully be said, that those of America have obtained reputation equal to those of any Continental power, and superior to that of England. The Academy at West Point is better known in Europe than any military school in England, and the periodical arrival of our Naval School fleet in European waters is made a subject of curious and reverential scrutiny. These institutions fully bear out the democratic character of our government. Some of the worthiest officers in our service have been of the poorest origin; amongst these, dismissing all recent prejudices, may be mentioned the names of Ulysses S. Grant, and T. Jonathan [" Stonewall"] Jackson.

These fountains of honor in America are the Military Academy of West Point, and the Naval School at Annapolis.

The United States Military Academy at West Point, on the Hudson River, fifty miles above New York, is the place where the officers of our regular Army are educated; they are nominated to West Point by members of Congress, each Representative having the right to select one lad to be a cadet every two years. The candidate so nominated undergoes an examination, physical and mental, and if accepted, passes through the long and exacting course of studies; if he graduates successfully, he is made an officer in the Army, and his subsequent career depends upon the exigencies of the service and his own ability. There are also numerous private and State military institutions in various parts of the Union, prominent among which are the Military Academies at Lexington, Virginia, and Frankfort, Kentucky.

In 1868, the Military Committee of Congress proposed to encourage the formation of private military schools throughout the country, and introduced a bill to provide colleges with military professors from the regular Army. The bill was disapproved, and in the debate considerable dislike of military establishments was exhibited.

In England there are several military schools, which cost altogther nearly nine hundred thousand dollars a year. Besides the Council of Military Education, there is the Royal Military Academy at Woolwich, the Royal Military College at Sandhurst, the Royal Hibernian Military School at Dublin, the Military Medical School, and the Department for the Instruction of Artillery Officers, and there are also schools and libraries in all the British garrisons, besides a military branch of the Chelsea Asylum, at London, which educates five hundred boys a year.

To show the efficiency of West Point, I need only cite General Garfield's remarks upon its record during the civil war: —

"Among the field officers, I find that of the whole number, three hundred and forty-nine thousand one hundred and thirty-five are from West Point, — thirty-nine per cent. Of the general officers, twenty-five in all, twenty-one are from West Point, and four only from civil life. Of the Army staff, numbering six hundred and eighty-one persons, two hundred and seven are from West Point, and four hundred and seventy-four from civil life, those from West Point being thirty and a half per cent. of the whole number. Of the staff department proper, however, embracing the Adjutant-General's office, the Engineer Corps, etc., two hundred and forty-nine officers in all, two hundred and twenty-nine are from West Point, and only twenty from civil life."

The picturesque and historical associations of West Point are far more remarkable than those of the English military schools, which are generally situated upon barren heaths like Sandhurst.

The Royal Military College at Sandhurst is about as old an institution as West Point, having been founded in 1799; it is controlled by a board of military officers of high rank, appointed by the Queen; at the head of it is a Governor; it has also a Lieutenant-Governor, a Major, two Captains, and Civil Professors who teach mathematics, drawing, military surveying, the modern languages, the classics, and the art of fortification.

The cadets are divided into seniors and juniors. There are but fifteen seniors, who are already commissioned officers in the Army, having served four years and exhibited high abilities. Unlike West Point, Sandhurst is self-supporting, its expenses of eighty-five thousand dollars a year being defrayed by the junior gentlemen cadets, one hundred and eighty in number. These junior cadets are either the sons of noblemen or the sons of officers, a few of whom pay nothing, being the children of distinguished military men who have died in distress. The cadets are admitted between the ages of thirteen and fifteen years by nomination from the Governor of the college to the Commander-in-chief. An aristocratic atmosphere surrounds Sandhurst, as it is the intention of the English government to keep the Army pretty well under the control of the upper classes, and fill it with the younger sons of noblemen.

The Corps of Royal Engineers is one of the most admirable organizations in the English Army; it was for many years engaged in the survey of the entire United Kingdom; to it is attached the Corps of Sappers and Miners; most of the great fortifications in England and in the Colonies, such as the powerful fort at Point Levi, opposite Quebec, are executed by the Engineer Corps.

In 1860 the English government spent ten millions of dollars in new fortifications; in 1861 eleven millions of dollars for the same object, and subsequently, down to 1866, ten millions of dollars more. At Portsmouth, which is one of the nearest seaports to London, eight millions of this money were expended, and at Plymouth, which is also on the southern coast of England, near Lands-End, one million and a half were also spent in fortifications; at Gravesend, which lies on the Thames River, more than thirty miles below London, one million of dollars were expended; at Pembroke, which lies at the southern tip of Wales, one million and a half were spent in sea walls; at Dover, the nearest town to France, one million and a quarter were spent; at Cork, where much of the American shipping enters, nearly three hundred thousand dollars were expended; at Portland, which lies nearly opposite Cherbourg, the great French naval station, one million and a half were expended; one million and a quarter of dollars were laid out on the forts of Sheerness, near the mouth of the Thames.

During the same period we Americans have nearly lost our faith in mere walls of stone, believing iron-clad ships to be the only invulnerable fortifications; we continue work, however, on the powerful fort at Sandy Hook, at the entrance of New York harbor, and unto this day the great Stevens' Battery at Jersey City is undergoing construction, superintended by General George B. McClellan, one of our ablest military engineers. The Stevens' Battery was the conception and the undertaking of a private American citizen, — a fact which shows in a marked manner the power of our government to enlist the voluntary support of its citizens, and is also an evidence of the enterprising character of the rich capitalists of New York.

If the expectations of the contrivers of the Stevens' Battery be not too sanguine, it will be an invulnerable and perfect defence of the vast interests of New York, — a floating Cherbourg or Cronstadt steaming at will through the deep waters of New York Bay, and defying the fleets of Europe to capture, for a second time, the city which was the seat of British occupation during nearly the whole of the Revolution.

Chatham, to which reference has been made in the chapter on English Provinces, is the leading naval station at the mouth of the Thames, as is Fortress Monroe at the mouth of Chesapeake Bay.

The great event in the history of Chatham and its dockyard was the burning by the Dutch fleet of many English ships-of-war lying here in ordinary. On the 7th of June, 1667, De Ruyter, with a fleet of sixty ships of the line, anchored at the mouth of the Thames. The English vessels in that river had retired, and the Dutch Admiral accordingly commenced operations in the Medway, first attacking the little fort at Sheerness, which was abandoned after a defence of an hour and a half. Although the preparations and object of the enemy had been long known, scarcely any defence had been organized. "The alarm," says Evelyn, "was so great that it put country and city into a panic, fear, and consternation, such as I hope I shall never see more; everybody was flying, none knew why or whither." After the fall of the fort the Zealand and Frieseland ships joined De Ruyter, whose fleet, now seventy-two ships of the line, blockaded the mouths of the two rivers. The attack on the ships at Chatham was made on the 12th of June. The English fleet lay between Gillingham and Chatham, — within the chain that at Gillingham Fort stretched across the river. Two large ships, the "Matthias" and "Charles V.," were placed as near this defence as posssible, so as to bring their broadsides to bear on the enemy. The chain, however, was speedily broken and the two guard-vessels set in flames by fire-ships. The next day, three eighty-gun ships, "the largest and most powerful of England," which lay off Upnor Castle, were also destroyed by the Dutch fire-ships. This disgrace was comparable to our feeling at the burning of Washington in 1814.

The English consider their greatest naval station to be Portsmouth, on the coast, south of London. Portsmouth harbor more amply combines spaciousness with security than any other in the kingdom. Though less than a quarter of a mile wide at the narrowest part of its entrance, it gradually expands to an extreme breadth of about four miles, and has an extreme length of about four and a half miles. Its outline is varied by headlands and creeks, and it is so thoroughly landlocked that even during violent storms vessels ride here in perfect security. Horsea, Pewit, and Whale Islands cover three small bays within the harbor; but everywhere the waters are so free from impediment, that even a ship of the largest size may make sail in any state of the tide. The current of ebb, being much stronger than that of flood, prevents any serious accumulation of sand, and keeps the entrance free and open. Yet the depth of the channel at the mouth, in low-water spring tides, is only twelve and a half feet; and the width at the same place, between the buoys, is only about ninety yards; so that first-rate ships, or the large steam-packets of the

Royal Steam Company, which draw seventeen feet of water, only occasionally can enter.

English, and indeed European ports at large, bear little comparison with those of the United States. There are probably no roads in the world superior to Hampton at Fort Monroe, and no ports outside of the American continent like those of New York and San Francisco.

In Portsmouth lies the hulk of the ship "Victory," in which Nelson died.

Nelson is the greatest name in the British Navy, or, indeed, in the naval history of the world. In gallantry and the capacity to inspire courage, he reminds us somewhat of Decatur; but his field was wider than Decatur's, although he was the American's inferior in coolness, discretion, dignity of character, and muscular power. Nelson remarked of Decatur that his exploit in cutting the frigate Philadelphia out of Tripoli harbor was equal to any episode in naval history. Nelson, like Decatur, fought altogether in the era of sailing vessels. His father was a clergyman, and the young Nelson commanded a frigate during the American Revolution; but it was during the Napoleonic wars that he won immortal renown, by the victories of the Nile, Copenhagen, and Trafalgar; at the former he almost annihilated the French fleet; at Copenhagen, where he fought the Danes without a previous declaration of war, he refused to retire from action when his superior officer made the signal, but, putting his hand to his only remaining eye, he looked at the discouraging flag with the blind socket of the other, and made illustrious the expression, "I don't see it!"

Fort hese two victories he was generously rewarded, and raised to the peerage; but his wounds, his restless temperament, and his licentiousness would have made his latter days wretched, but for his death in the hour of victory over the combined fleets of France and Spain at Trafalgar.

Hearing that these fleets lay in the harbor of Toulon, he offered his service to the Admiralty, and for fourteen months never left his ship but three times, and never longer than one hour; in a storm the enemy evaded him, when he cruised up and down the Mediterranean in search of them, went to the West Indies, to Ireland, along the Atlantic coast of Europe, but failed to discover them. Sick and spent, he returned to his home at Merton, near London, when suddenly he was told that his adversaries had been seen in Cadiz harbor outside of Gibraltar. He immediately started for Portsmouth, where he ordered his coffin to be embarked with him; it had been constructed out of the main-mast of a captured French ship-of-war, and he set sail amidst the greatest enthusiasm. Villeneuve, the French Admiral, was told in Cadiz, by an American, that Nelson was waiting for him outside with his fleet just beyond the horizon; this disturbing news was denied. On the 19th of October, 1805, the French fleet was seen coming out of Cadiz. They faced each other two days afterward, Villeneuve mustering forty sail-of-the-line and frigates; Nelson thirty-one. Collingwood was Nelson's second in command, a noble and virtuous character, and they fired the first shot at noon. One hour and a quarter later a musket-ball struck Nelson's epaulette, and broke his spine. At half-past four o'clock, just after the last shots were fired, Nelson expired, and by that time the combined French and Spanish fleets were sunk, dispersed, or captured, the Spanish Admiral was mortally wounded, and Villeneuve a prisoner. The French Navy appeared no more upon the sea during the reign of Napoleon.

Villeneuve was murdered in Paris, as he returned from captivity, while Nelson's memory was lavishly honored; and when he was interred under St. Paul's Cathedral, the sailors who bore his coffin rent in pieces the flag which enclosed him and kept them for mementoes. His brother was made an Earl, and given thirty thousand dollars a year; his sisters were presented with fifty thousand dollars each, and one hundred thousand was given them to buy an estate. But the earnest request which Nelson had made in his will, that his concubine, Lady Hamilton, should be maintained by the nation, could not be respected; she died miserably.

Far otherwise was Wellington honored when he returned to London after the battle of Waterloo. He had been absent from England five years. In his characteristic manner, he landed at Dover at the earliest possible moment, went straight to London, and walked into the House of Lords. He had left the country Sir Arthur Wellesley; he returned a Duke. As soon as the sloop-of-war conveying him was seen off Dover, at five in the morning of the 28th of June, the sea and shore resounded with the salutes fired from the ships and from the cliffs. Multitudes came thronging to the landing-place; and they carried the hero on their shoulders to his inn, amidst a roar of acclamation. That same evening, he was told by the Lord Chancellor, in the presence of a crowded House of Lords, that his was the only instance, in the history of the British Peerage, of an individual being, at his first entrance into that House, a Baron, a Viscount, an

Earl, a Marquess, and a Duke, — each rank being won by distinct services to the country.

Royal personages had had all the dignities heaped upon them by a single gift; but no similar instance existed of rising by patriotic service through all the ranks, before taking a seat among the peers. Then followed city and royal banquets, given in his honor, at which the royal family were solicitous to pay their tribute of homage to one who stood high above the patronage of potentates. It was in May, while in Paris, that his highest title was conferred upon him; and Parliament voted him two and a half millions of dollars, for the purchase of an estate and the support of his rank. An unprecedented offer of homage was made, in a resolution that a deputation from the House of Commons should wait on him, on his return, to congratulate and compliment him. Wellington, on being requested to appoint a time, begged leave rather to go himself, and pay his respects in person; and he appeared in the middle of the House, in the afternoon of the 1st of July. His address was simple and earnest; and it ended, like most of his public speeches, in a declaration that he was always ready for the service of his sovereign and his country.

The French force on the field of Waterloo was about seventy-two thousand men; the army under Wellington, sixty-eight thousand; the Prussians bringing thirty-six thousand more in the evening. Napoleon had two hundred and forty pieces of cannon; Wellington, one hundred and eighty. The loss, in killed and wounded, of the Allies was nearly eleven thousand, besides six thousand Prussians. That of the French was forty thousand.

The total armament of Julius Cæsar, when he invaded Britain in cavalry and infantry, amounted to thirty-two thousand men, conveyed across the channel in eight hundred first-class vessels. The number of vessels employed by William the Conqueror amounted to three thousand, but of which only between six hundred and seven hundred were of a superior construction. Supposing the Normans trebled in number that of the Romans, it must have fallen below one hundred thousand, or barely one-twentieth of the population of England.

Until within a recent period of a few months, flogging has been a feature of the entire British service.

"I have more than once heard it argued," says a British officer, "whether a strong man could bear more than nine hundred lashes, without being taken from the halberds. The punishment, too, did not necessarily cease when the delinquent's suffering overcame his physical endurance, and nature could bear no longer; but if the entire sentence was not carried into execution the first time he was tied up, a second, and possibly a third, time, after allowing a sufficient interval for the cure of his back in the hospital, was he brought out to receive the residue. Thus as the first two hundred and fifty or three hundred lashes gave the greatest pain (after which the flesh becomes numbed to further blows), the strong man took the whole of his punishment at once, without, comparatively speaking, feeling the last half of it; while the weaker man, though guilty of the same crime only as the strong one, was twice or thrice made to endure the acute torture attending the first strokes of a fresh flogging. In many regiments, too, it was the custom to flog by the tap of a drum, — that was, for a drummer to stand by and give the time to him who wielded the cat, by tapping on the drum-head with a single drumstick, at measured intervals of about two seconds. Sometimes these intervals were longer; and I have heard of half-minute time being practised, though I never saw it, which must have prolonged the torture to a most unnecessarily cruel extent. Yet excess of punishment had by no means the desired effect of repressing crime; the reverse was the fact. Flogging was too often witnessed to be greatly dreaded, and too indiscriminately inflicted to be considered at all degrading. The worst regiments in the service were those whose Colonels were too liberal of the lash; and, on the contrary, the best were those where there was but little flogging."

From this cruel infliction, Americans can understand why so many British sailors and soldiers have deserted to our milder service, and these desertions led to the assertion of the right of search which led to so many difficulties between America and England.

Far different is the treatment of the common soldier by the United States. During the civil war our Sanitary and Christian Commissions were allowed free access to the soldiery, and beautiful and compassionate women, a republic of Florence Nightingales, brightened the battle-fields and the hospitals.

The most remarkable scientific and philanthropic monument of any war is the Army and Navy Medical Museum at Washington, which occupies the sacred fane, formerly the theatre, where President Lincoln was assassinated.

The contents of the building are now of the aggregate reminder of the bruises, wounds, and agonies of the entire struggle for the Union.

In the Army Medical Museum are deposited the names and casualties of every stricken soldier, and it is a perpetual miniature of that vast field of war, whose campaigns of beneficence followed in the footsteps of its heroes, and death and mercy went hand in hand.

Here are sixteen thousand volumes of hospital registers, forty-seven thousand burial records, two hundred and fifty thousand names of white, and twenty thousand names of colored, soldiers, who died in hospitals. Here are the names and cases of two hundred and ten thousand and twenty-seven men, besides, discharged from the army disabled. Here are names and statements of one hundred and thirty-three thousand nine hundred and fifty-seven wounded men brought to hospital, and the particulars of twenty-eight thousand four hundred and thirty-eight operations performed with the knife. Read over these figures again to get a conception of the infamy of war, and the heroism of man. In them the butchered hecatombs of bullocks and heifers slain for our appetites seem to find approximation. In one year, — so methodized and perfect are the rules and registers collected in this fire-proof building, — forty-nine thousand two hundred and twelve cases of men, widows, and orphans demanding pensions have been settled in this edifice. If you look through the lower floors, you will see a hundred clerks searching out these histories, cataloguing them, classifying them, bringing the history of the private soldier down to the reach of the most peremptory curiosity, and assisting to "heal the broken-hearted, and set at liberty them that are bruised."

It is this museum which is at once the saddest memorial of the common soldier, and the noblest monument to the army surgeon. It contains a complete history of the surgery of the war, illustrated by casts, models, photographs, and preparations. There are here nine hundred medical pathological preparations, and two thousand eight hundred microscopical preparations. There is no similar Army Medical Museum in the world, and from Baron Larrey, down to Nelaton and Joubert, the published reports of this collection have delighted and surprised the savans of the world. Scarcely a leading surgeon in Europe but has written praises and sent them here.

Among the curious facts shown here are these: the average life of an American is forty years, which is better than in Prussia, and corresponds with the average in England, Wales, and France. The rate of mortality in America, in the working period of life (between fifteen and forty-five), is higher here than elsewhere in the world. Not so in childhood and advanced years, where the insurance offices seem to get the weather side of us. The mean age of a generation in America is between thirty-two and thirty-three years. The average age of all the soldiers of the late war was from twenty-three to twenty-six years; so that the average soldier is scarcely eligible to the House of Representatives. This is a higher average than the Prussian soldiery, twenty-three and a half, or the British, twenty-three. The average heighth of American men is sixty-eight inches; of recruits to the regular Army, sixty-nine inches; of recruits to the volunteer Army, sixty-seven and a half inches. Forty-seven nationalities fought on the Union side in this war, and the average of nearly three hundred and fifty thousand of them in height was sixty-six and three-quarter inches. So we are an inch and a half higher than British soldiers, and two and four-fifths higher than French. Average chest of American soldiers is thirty-five inches, of senators thirty-eight and a half; so that a life-time of politics only blows one up three and a half inches. Minnesota had the tallest men in the army, and New Hampshire the shortest, — a singular fact against our traditions. Kentuckians had the best chests, and Massachusetts men the smallest. Senators weigh on the average one hundred seventy-one and a half pounds, and soldiers one hundred forty-seven and a half.

A million drafted men, examined and reported upon, show that we are the best fighting nationality in the world, and have no right to be excused in any considerable percentage. Only three in a thousand of us have not good patriotic chests, and four and a half per thousand of us are deaf. About two and one third in a thousand are near-sighted; so that it is somewhat remarkable that so many eye-glasses are worn; and the varicoceous people are even in smaller fraction. A club-foot is one in a thousand; but imbecility, as all are aware, is more common, and goes two better. In Delaware and Missouri nobody much goes insane, but New Hampshire and Rhode Island stand well along, nearly three to the thousand. In Massachusetts, so itching is the temper of the people, nearly four in a thousand have skin diseases. Iowa and Kansas are exempted from vicious diseases, while the highest rate, thereof, was, of course, in the District of Columbia. Eighteen men to the thousand could not bite cartridges, though they were probably equal to beef-soup.

To return to the Army and Navy.

The total number of screw steamships afloat in the Navy of the United Kingdom is three hundred and forty-one; building, twenty-one.

The total number of paddle steamships afloat is seventy-three; building, one. The grand total of effective sailing-ships afloat is thirty-eight, and the grand total of steam and sailing is four hundred and seventy-four.

In 1861 the whole United States Navy consisted of forty-one men-of-war, chiefly sailing vessels. At the end of the war the Navy consisted of seventy-five monitors, four hundred and one screw or paddle steamers, and one hundred and twelve sailing-vessels, carrying in all four thousand four hundred and forty-three guns. In 1867, there were two thousand forty-eight officers, of all ranks, including one Admiral [Farragut], one Vice-Admiral, and twenty-seven Rear-Admirals. There were thirteen thousand six hundred men, and the naval expenditure, for the year ending June, 1867, was about forty-three and one half millions of dollars. We had eight dock-yards. In 1867 the English Navy cost about fifty-five millions of dollars, and was composed of sixty thousand sailors and mariners.

The number of first-class cadets admitted into the English Navy, in the year 1866, was one hundred and sixty. The Military Academy at West Point will be described in the probable chapter on the French Army. It is as beautifully situated as any castle on the Rhine.

Scarcely less picturesque is the site of the United States Naval Academy, at Annapolis, on the beautiful sheet of water called Chesapeake Bay, some forty miles from Washington.

It takes two hours to make the trip, of which one hour is spent between Washington and the place called Annapolis Junction, and another between the Junction and Annapolis. The Junction is a tavern, a station, and some woodsheds pitched in a piece of woods, near by which, on a plain, are uneasy indications of the impending birth of a town. The Annapolis road is not the property of the Baltimore and Ohio Company, and it is a profitable corporation. It traverses the ridge of the long and narrow neck between the Patuxent and the Severn Rivers, a neck of glades, swamps, scrub-pine and sassafras timber, and silent remindings of a past agricultural vigor, sapped by tobacco and smitten by war. A half-dozen of stations, incomplete unless there be a tavern-bar somewhere around, stand at the crossings of desert roads, and all the way one sniffs the air of the salt bay and its back waters. The sky and the horizon grow cool and vague, and we see, or imagine, watery mirages in the air. An appetite for shell-fish is discovered coming to one, a suggestion of yellow perch, and insane cravings to wade along some shallow beach with an umbrella and a fishing-rod. By the time you have got the appetite very bad you are at Annapolis. A brief sketch of the town may serve to freshen up the duller routine of our statistics.

From the venerable State House steeple I took this sketch of the old revolutionary city, in the summer of 1869 : —

Not above half a mile from boundary to boundary, by any diameter, the snuggest of little cities sat, to the water's edge on three sides, upon a mound-like peninsula. At the top of the mound, in the middle of the town, was the State Capitol. Two wide salt coves, coming in from the Severn, approached each other, and by the narrow neck between them came in the railway and the common road. These broad coves widened and narrowed like a chain of miniature lakes, and lying, as they did, in the greenest of foliage, I likened them to the Lakes of Killarney. The peninsula of the city itself, and the bay of the Chesapeake and Severn into which it protruded, reminded me of Monaco, the little principality city, on the Mediterranean. The shape of the peninsula is a broad lance-head, pointing, not out toward the bay, but toward the opposite side of the Severn, which is here about a mile and a half wide. On the blunt point of the peninsula is the Naval Academy. At the outlet of the cove, to the right, is the Priests' College, occupying the mansion and homestead of Charles Carroll, of Carrollton. At the outlet of the cove, to the left, is St. John's College, the oldest continuous institution of Maryland. Behind the State Capitol is the parish church of St. Ann's. Facing the Chesapeake is the market and inlet. Two miles outside is the bay. These are the main features of the little city of Annapolis, whose natural position is one of the shrewdest pickings from nature.

A series of green capes, golden-edged with beaches, introduce the bay. Behind the white light-house, on the further cape, and the light-ship moored upon the outer bar, one sees the blue-wooded line of Kent Island, the Plymouth Rock of Maryland, and the long, fruity peninsula of the Eastern Shore, that pleasant bar which keeps the Atlantic back from the noblest of our eastern estuaries. Far up and down this silent mirror of water the eye can ramble from spit to spit, from islet to island, guessing the mouths of many rivers, watching the tacking of pungies, and the steamers putting in at pleasant landings; and at the piers of the Naval Academy, with their gay buntings spread and flowing, lie at their cables the school fleet, a little navy of itself. There, at the wharf, is the frigate Constitution, in which Hull, Bainbridge, and Stewart won redeeming honors in our second war. Beyond is the Macedonian, which Decatur took from the British off the Azores in the fall of 1812. There, also, are the Dale, the Savannah, and the Santee, such models of wooden ships as made the hearts of our fathers rise. Further in the channel is the yacht America, which outsailed the English Navy in a race, and then, as a blockade-runner, outsailed our steamers. All these constitute the school fleet, which is (May) within a couple of weeks to spread sail and take the midshipmen to some distant seas.

President Polk established the Naval School at Annapolis in 1845; it includes about a hundred acres of ground, and its buildings are spacious and comfortable; they surround a large square of green, open on the water side, and near by is a beautiful park for the entertainment of the cadets. Here, as at West Point, splendid balls are frequently given; for, with all our republican jealousy of a standing Army, and a permanent Navy, the young officers of both services hold the highest rank in social life.

Every year a number of eminent gentlemen are invited by the President of the United States (who has the appointment of a few cadets at large) to visit West Point and Annapolis, and report upon their condition; the people are thus kept informed of affairs in these nurseries of our united services, and the public jealousy is allayed.

The Board of Visitors, for Annapolis, in 1869, expressed themselves as delighted with the efficiency of the school: —

"We doubt," they say, "if any institution in the world affords equal facilities for the theoretical and practical study of steam, and the steam-engine. There is, on shore, an edifice called the "steam building," in which a marine engine, complete in all its parts, even to the screw propellor, is kept ready for use, and open to the midshipmen. The department is well supplied with models, and drawings, and contains boilers in several stages of construction. The text-book in use, in 1869, was 'Main Brown upon the Steam-Engine,' an English work, deficient in some respects, and erroneous in others. It contained no analysis of American coals, nor any table showing their relative efficiency. The dozen lines devoted to anthracite coal contain several inaccuracies. It had no list of our ships, and its long list of British ships contains the names of many that are not in the service, and its table of engines in ships makes no mention of the boilers attached, which are the real exponents of the power of the machine. Some capable officer could be selected to prepare a text-book on the subject, which would be very valuable, not only to the Academy, but to many other American schools.

"The police of the grounds and buildings is admirable. Tobacco in every form and intoxicating liquors of every description are positively forbidden. Regular instruction is given in dancing, boxing, and small and broad sword exercise, and all are required to submit to gymnastic training. Ball-playing and rowing are encouraged. The result of all this care is a remarkably fine physical development, with instances of superior gymnastic skill and strength, and a very satisfactory general condition of health. During the year 1869, out of nearly four hundred students and officers, there was only about two per cent. excused from duty by reason of ill-health."

The amount of money expended, since the civil war, upon all buildings at Annapolis, including the wholly new, and the alterations, is about two hundred and twenty-five thousand dollars.

At West Point and Annapolis the government has property worth not less than three millions of dollars.

The school at Annapolis is unique and remarkable, amongst all the nations; but West Point resembles, in many respects, the great military schools of Europe.

The United States Navy is recruited by voluntary enlistments, while in France a naval conscription takes place in all the seaport towns, and in England the terrible press-gang formerly kidnapped watermen wherever they could find them.

An English authority says, of the straits to which the British Navy has been reduced by abandoning impressment, that in 1869, "in the absence of a compulsory conscription like that of France and Russia, our greatest difficulty had been in promptly increasing the regular Army by voluntary enlistment. It drove the government to the establishing of recruiting depots on the continent, and in the colonies, and to the hire of the Turkish and Sardinian contingents. But these first obstructions had been surmounted, and in the spring of 1856, England was ready with an array of vastly augmented armaments, naval and military. She had begun the war with a nucleus of only ten thousand gallant men. It had been augmented to one hundred thousand, of which seventy thousand were in the Crimea, in renovated health, strength, and discipline, ready to open the campaign. Our ships-of-war, when hostilities commenced, only numbered two hundred and twelve; when the war ended they numbered five hundred and ninety. 'The trident of Neptune is the sceptre of the world,' and Queen Victoria certainly wielded it, when at the grand marine display, at Spithead, after the peace (April 23d), she reviewed a fleet extending twelve miles, mustering three thousand eight hundred guns, forty thousand men, moved by a steam power of thirty-three thousand seven hundred and twenty horses. It was science, riches, and the heart of the people in the cause that had extemporized this magnificent novel review."

It was the scarcity of seamen to fight her battles during the Napoleonic wars, which caused England to advance the arrogant doctrine of the right of search, which was one of the causes of the second American war. Almost within cannon sound of the Capitol, the frigate Chesapeake was boarded, members of her crew ironed, and carried away, and some of them were afterward hanged. This, and other outrages, led to the eloquent reproaches of Richard Rush:—

"Men are the property of the nation. In every American face a part of our country's sovereignty is written. It is the living emblem — a thousand times more sacred than the nation's flag itself — of its character, its independence, and its rights.

"'But,' say the British, 'we want not *your* men; we want only *our own*. Prove that they are *yours*, and we will surrender them.' Baser outrage! more insolent indignity! that a free-born American must be made to *prove* his nativity to those who have previously violated his liberty, else he is to be held forever as a slave! That before a British tribunal — a British boarding-officer — a free-born American must be made to seal up the vouchers of his lineage, to exhibit the records of his baptism and his birth, to establish the identity that binds him to his parents, to his blood, to his native land, by setting forth in odious detail his size, his age, the shape of his frame, whether his hair is long or cropped, his marks, like an ox or a horse of the manger, — that all this must be done, as the condition of his escape from the galling thraldom of a British ship!"

The United States possesses seventeen million dollars of cannon, shell, and ball, which are not in use. We rifle fewer cannon, in proportion, than either England or France.

There are two steam rams in the British Navy, — the Scorpion and the Wivern, — both of which were built for the revolted government of the Southern States, during the American civil war.

The swiftest vessel-of-war in the world is the American Steam Sloop *Wampanoag*. No approach to this vessel, either in speed, or economy of fuel, or length of time of steaming at a high rate of speed has ever been made. The engineering journals of England have questioned the veracity of the captain, by inventing the statement that the speed was obtained by the assistance of sails, not knowing how else to account for it, and they declare the speed impossible under any other circumstances. It is well known in America, that no canvas was carried, — in fact, could not be carried at the speed; for when it was attempted to ascertain the vessel's speed, under steam and sail combined, the vessel's speed was so great, under steam alone, that the velocity of the wind was insufficient to add more power.

The Wampanoag is three hundred and thirty-five feet long, forty-two feet in breadth, and she draws eighteen and and one-half feet of water. The fastest steamers in English waters are the British mail vessels, which ply between Holyhead and Dublin across the shortest breadth of the English Channel; they were constructed under a guaranty to run twenty miles an hour; they are three hundred and twenty-seven feet long, thirty-five feet in breadth, and displace nineteen hundred tons. The fastest of these mail steamers runs fourteen and one-half geographical miles an hour, or crosses the Channel in three hours and fifty-five minutes. The Wampanoag runs sixteen and three-fourths geographical miles an hour, and yet displaces four thousand two hundred and fifteen tons. The Wampanoag runs at double the speed of the English mail steamer in proportion of size of boiler to vessel; it will thus be seen that the United States Government in the national navy-yards can construct swifter vessels than the best private ship-builders in England, whether on the Clyde, the Mersey, or the Thames, the Wampanoag being still a new vessel. Indeed, the hulls of United States ships and steamers have always been more beautiful and adapted to a higher rate of speed than those of any nation; our clipper ships led the mercantile navy of the world in speed; and the yacht America, which is now a part of the school fleet of the naval academy at Annapolis, carried off the honors over all England in English waters. The fastest merchant ocean steamer ever built was the *Adriatic* of the "Collins' Line." She was built for speed without regard to economy, and so completed the ruin of her owners. She is now the property of an English corporation. Her highest speed was less than sixteen miles, while the Wampanoag's was seventeen and three-quarter miles an hour. These results show that American naval constructors retain their superiority, notwithstanding the fact that we nave no steamers carrying the national flag on the Atlantic except those of the American Navy. The destruction caused by Southern privateers with the ungenerous aid of English ship-builders and English ports, drove all our better ships off the sea between the years 1861–5, or compelled their owners to sell them to foreign governments.

Since the close of the war, the high tax upon all articles entering into the composition of a ship has made it unprofitable to build vessels in this country. Our exports as well as our imports are now chiefly in foreign bottoms. The carrying trade between the United States and Europe is almost literally in the hands of Europeans. Were it not for the few ships still employed in the China trade, and the stand we are making by the establishment of a line of steamers on the Pacific, the coastwise trade, which is retained by the exclusion of foreign competition, would seem to be about all that can, under existing legislation, be relied upon for the employment of American shipping. This lamentable condition of things is justly a source of mortification to every American who remembers the past enterprise and beauty of our mercantile marine. The legislation of the country has recently been entirely in the interests of the manufacturing classes. Europeans do no longer say "Who reads an American book?" but, "Who sees an American ship?" This prostration of our marine is at this time to be especially deplored, in view of the magnificent opportunities opening to us on the Pacific Ocean, where we possess in a higher degree than any nation the confidence of the Oriental nations. Our ship-yards are going to decay, and we have not the privilege of importing the materials to construct ships, nor to buy foreign ships free of duty. At the same time we are importing immense quantities of trivial articles, which add nothing to our power and dignity of true enjoyment. The Secretary of the Treasury reported in 1869, that, two-thirds of the importations of the United States consist of articles which, in economical times, would be pronounced luxuries. The war and a redundant currency have brought about unexampled extravagance, which can only be satisfied by the most costly products of foreign countries. No exception could be taken to such importations if they were paid for in our own productions. This, unfortunately is not the fact. They are annually swelling our foreign debt, without increasing our ability to pay it. There is no department of the government which is conducted with proper economy. The habits formed during the war are still strong, and will only yield to the requirements of inexorable law. History affords no parallel case of a nation so fond of the sea as the Americans, and with such a genius for building ships, which has yet discouraged its sailor boys so entirely, and so fully succeeded in legislating its flag off the ocean. We send our mail-bags to Glasgow, to Liverpool, to Southampton, to Bremen, to Hamburg, to Antwerp, and to Brest in foreign ships; in foreign ships they return to us; the coastwise trade is all that we keep, and even this reservation was thrown up to the commercial interests by a member of Congress from Pennsylvania, in 1868, while he asked for increased tariff for his manufactures.

The most grievous feature of the decline of American commerce is, that it has discouraged our boys from going to sea, so that we can scarcely be said at present to have any native seafaring element; our navy is mainly manned by foreigners and negroes, and the maritime amusements which were formerly characteristic of the youth of all our cities are now almost entirely confined to New York city. The English, on the other hand, take every opportunity to encourage cruising, boating, and yachting, in order that the ancient naval spirit of their islands may never be broken nor weakened. There are some fifteen yacht clubs in England giving employment to over one thousand persons. The Royal Yacht Club numbers over two hundred and fifty members, the greater portion of whom are representative men in the Kingdom of Great Britain. Hon. Earl Vane is the Commodore. Fifty-nine vessels, all told, including yawls, cutters, schooners, and steamers constitute this yacht club.

The British Navy has a nomenclature mainly derived from mythology, from the names of the royal family, or from certain waspish and formidable qualities, natures, and elements.

The American Navy was in great part baptized in honor of the beautiful Indian nomenclature of our streams and mountains, but in 1869 a Mr. Borie, temporarily Secretary of the Navy, adopted in bulk the copyright titles of a large number of British ships, at which the country's good taste and individuality was justly incensed. I append the names of the very largest vessels of the two navies.

AMERICAN.	BRITISH.
COLORADO, Screw-frigate, 3,425 tons, 52 guns, some of them firing shot of 2,206 pounds, or about the weight of 7 cook stoves.	MINOTAUR, 6,221 tons, screw, 1,350 horse-power, 36 guns, 400 feet long, 59 beam, iron-clad.

AMERICAN.	BRITISH.
ROANOKE, 3-turreted monitor, 3,435 tons, 615-in. pivot guns, 350 horse-power.	BLACK PRINCE, 6,109 tons, 41 guns, 1,250 horse-power.
NEW IRONSIDES, Iron-clad frigate, 3,486 tons, 16 guns, 600 horse-power.	NORTHUMBERLAND, 6,621 tons, 1,350 horse-power, 26 guns.

Other names of British ships are Royal Alfred, Agincourt, Ætna, Royal Oak, and Viper. The iron-clad ram Dunderburg, formerly in our Navy, is now the largest iron-clad in the Navy of France, which purchased her for two millions of dollars; she carries 16 guns, and has a burthen of 5,090 tons.

In 1869 there were thirty armories and arsenals belonging to the United States, employing nearly sixteen hundred persons, of whom more than one-third were machinists and armorers. The combined monthly pay of all these persons was about ninety-four thousand dollars. In the same year the Surgeon-General's department cost sixty-five thousand dollars.

The great English musket and rifle factory at Enfield is modelled after our armory at Springfield. The American Army is at present armed with the Springfield breech-loading rifle, which is pronounced a better weapon than either the Needle or Chassepot gun.

A fine opportunity was afforded us of studying the relative merits of the French and British services during the Crimean War. While the British Navy acquitted itself with distinction, the organization and the handling of its Army were far inferior to the French, and the entire war upon the English side may be said to have been a tissue of disasters, while the French came out of it with glory at the crowning period of the siege of Sebastopol; the French captured the Malakoff, the most powerful redoubt, while the English assault upon the Redan was attended with mortification and repulse.

Russell, the "Times" correspondent was obliged to bear this testimony to the merits of the French: —

"At five minutes before twelve o'clock, the French, like a swarm of bees, issued forth from their trenches close to the Malakoff, scrambled up its face, and were through the embrasures in the twinkling of an eye. They crossed the seven metres of ground which separated them from the enemy at a few bounds; they drifted as lightly and quickly as autumn leaves before the wind, battalion after battalion, into the embrasures, and in a minute or two after the head of their column issued from the ditch, the tri-color was floating over the Korniloff Bastion. The musketry was very feeble at first,— indeed, our allies took the Russians by surprise, and very few of the latter were in the Malakoff; but they soon recovered themselves, and from twelve o'clock till past seven in the evening the French had to meet and repulse the repeated attempts of the enemy to regain the work, when, weary of the fearful slaughter of his men, who lay in thousands over the exterior of the works, and despairing of success, the Muscovite General withdrew."

The same author speaks thus of the failure at the Redan after the English were driven out: —

"The scene in the ditch was appalling, although some of the officers have assured me that they and the men were laughing at the precipitation with which many brave and gallant fellows did not hesitate to plunge headlong upon the mass of bayonets, muskets, and sprawling soldiers, — the ladders were all knocked down or broken, so that it was difficult for the men to scale the other side, — and the dead, the dying, the wounded, and the uninjured were all lying in piles together. The Russians came out of the embrasures and plied them with stones, grape-shot, and the bayonet, till step by step, pelting each other with huge stones, they retired, slipping and tumbling into the ditch, where many poor fellows were buried alive from the scarps giving way. Then came the fearful run for life or death, with men rolling over like rabbits, then tumbling into the English trench, where the men lay four feet deep on each other."

Captain George B. McClellan, an American officer, says that the failure of the English assault may be attributed partly to the fact that their advanced trenches were too small to accommodate the requisite force without confusion, in part to their not being pushed sufficiently near the Redan, but chiefly to that total absence of conduct and skill in the arrangements for the assault, which left the storming party entirely without support. Had it been followed at once by strong reinforcements, it is almost certain that the English would have retained possession of the work.

British criticism upon this war is of a very dolorous character. One authority mentions that "the natives preferred the French uniform to ours. In their sight there can be no more effeminate object than a warrior in a shell jacket, with closely shaven chin and lip, and cropped whiskers. He looks, in fact, like one of their dancing troops, and cuts a sorry figure beside a great Gaul in his blazing red pantaloons and padded frock, epaulettes, beard d'Afrique, and well-twisted moustache. The pashas think much of our men, but they are not struck with our officers. The French made an impression quite the reverse. The Turks could see nothing in the men, except that they thought the zouaves and chasseurs of the French dashing-looking fellows; and they considered their officers superior to ours."

For a fine piece of description, I instance a part of Russell's most famous letter upon the sailing of the British fleet up the Black Sea, at the commencement of the Crimean War: —

"It was a vast armada. No pen could describe its effect upon the eye. Ere an hour had elapsed it had extended itself over half the circumference of the horizon. Possibly no expedition so complete and so terrible in its means of destruction, with such enormous power in engines of war, and such capabilities of locomotion, was ever yet sent forth by any worldly power; for the conjunction of such a corps d'élite — the whole disposable British army — with a fleet of such strength, and an artillery of unequalled range, had assuredly no parallel in history. Its speed was restricted to four miles and a half per hour, but with a favoring wind it was difficult to restrain the vessels to that rate, and the transports set no sail.

"The French fleet was visible, across the whole diameter of the circle, — that is, they had a front of some eighteen miles broad, and gradually the irregular and broken lines tapered away till they were lost in little mounds and dots of smoke, denoting the position of the steamers far down below the horizon. The fleet, in five irregular and straggling lines, flanked by men-of-war, and war steamers, advanced slowly, filling the atmosphere with innumerable columns of smoke, which gradually flattened out into streaks, and joined the clouds, adding to the sombre appearance of this well-named 'Black' Sea. The land was lost to view very speedily beneath the coal clouds and the steam clouds of the fleet, and, as we advanced, not an object was visible in the half of the great circle which lay before us, save the dark waves and the cold sky.

"Not a bird flew, not a fish leaped, not a sail dotted the horizon. Behind us all was life and power, — vitality, force, and motion, — a strange scene in this so-called Russian Lake!"

The question is frequently asked, which nation would have the victory if England and America were at war. In such an event it is probable that there would be no victory, but only mutual disaster.

The American volunteer soldier of the present generation has no superior in any land, either in military experience, in ability to endure fatigue, in intelligence, in versatility, or in bravery, and notwithstanding our commercial misfortunes, the American Navy may be said, at present, to be better than at any time in its history. When we invented the monitor, we demolished with her one turret the navies of the globe; their wooden fleets fell to pieces, and they hastened, at vast expense, to rebuild them on American suggestions. We have no need to go to war with England, and we need have no fear of a foreign nation invading us. De Tocqueville forty years ago spoke in this manner of our impregnable position: —

"Placed in the centre of an immense continent, which offers a boundless field for human industry, the Union is almost as much insulated from the world as if its frontiers were girt by the ocean. Canada contains only a million of inhabitants, and its population is divided into two inimical nations. The rigor of the climate limits the extension of its territory, and shuts up its ports during the six months of winter. From Canada to the Gulf of Mexico a few savage tribes are to be met with, which retire, perishing in their retreat, before six thousand soldiers. To the South, the Union a point of contact with the Empire of Mexico; and it is thence that serious hostilities may one day be expected to arise. But for a long while to come the uncivilized state of the Mexican community, the depravity of its morals, and its extreme poverty, will prevent that country from ranking high amongst nations. As for the powers of Europe, they are too distant to be formidable.

"The great advantage of the United States does not, then, consist in a Federal Constitution which allows them to carry on great wars, but in a geographical position which renders such enterprises extremely improbable."

CHAPTER XIV.

BRITISH AND AMERICAN FINANCE.

The national debts, revenues, and expenditures of the two countries; their prospects for solvency, and their different systems of money management.

WITH a nation, as with a man, there can be no true independence, unless its credit be good, and its dealings just. It may be valorous as Paraguay, but who will lend it money unless it has thrift, resources, and business honor? It may have the genius of Ireland, but the world will not respect it, if it is perpetually impoverished. All society, all government, turn upon money as the pivotal principle; for it is the unit of prosperity, and with a modern state, even more than with an individual, is the vital element of greatness. With money laid up by the father of Frederick the Great, modern Prussia was enabled to take rank among the great powers. With money, England subsidized all Europe to make war upon France, and by her purse rather than by her sword, overthrew the greatest military genius of history. In England, the management of the national finances has always been intrusted to the most powerful statesman of his party; but in America, we have always considered the management of foreign affairs to be the most honorable post in the Cabinet, until, when the civil war of 1861 broke out, we learned for the first time that the exchequer was even more important than the map of the campaign. Within five years our public debt bounded from less than sixty-five millions to about two billions and eight hundred millions of dollars. From being the least involved of all great states, we found ourselves deeper in debt than any, except Great Britain. The national debt of the United States, on the 1st of July, 1869, was two billion four hundred and eighty-nine million two thousand four hundred and eighty-one dollars, having been reduced in four years, more than the English debt in fifty. The whole of this debt was incurred in the struggle to maintain our nationality intact. Little, or none of this mighty indebtedness was incurred in harassing our neighbors of other nations, in paying subsidies to the mercenaries and refugees of other Christian lands, or in

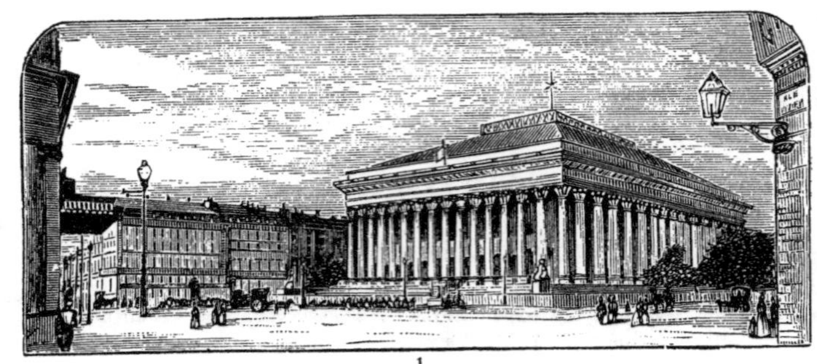

1

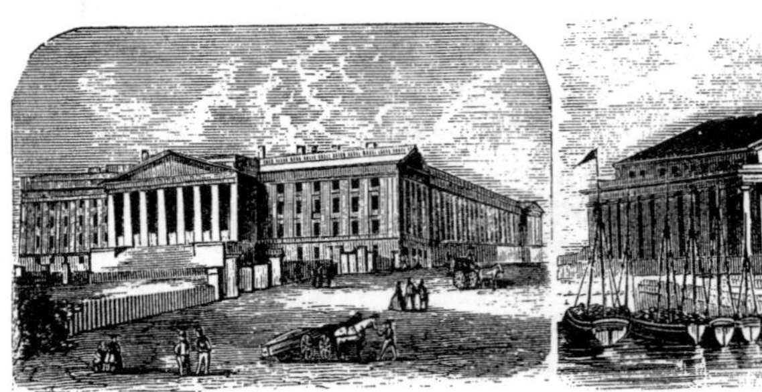

2 3

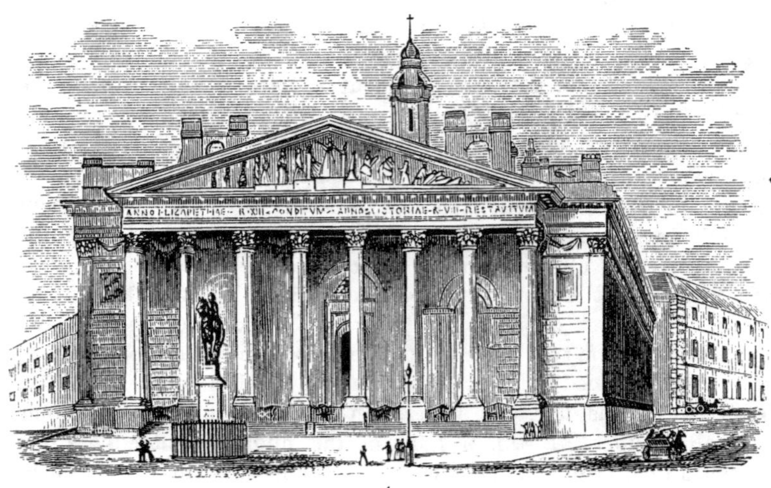

4

MONETARY INSTITUTIONS.

1—The Bourse, Paris. 2—United States Treasury, Washington. 3—The Bourse, St. Petersburg. 4—The Royal Exchange, London.

jealous interferences with the regimen of our continent. A part of it was loaned for internal improvements; the rest to save the republic for posterity. After the Revolution, in 1789–91, the debt of the United States was about seventy-five and one-half millions; by 1812 it had declined to forty-five and one-fourth millions; the second war with England brought it up to one hundred and twenty-seven and one-third millions by 1816; in 1836, this debt had been reduced to two hundred and ninety-one thousand dollars, or within the compass of a private citizen to pay it all without embarrassing himself; by 1846 the debt had risen, through the purchase of territory, Indian Wars, etc., to sixteen and three-fourths millions, and at the end of the Mexican War, in 1849, it was sixty-four millions of dollars, or little more than half the annual interest upon our present public debt. Among the many considerations arising out of our embarrassed situation, the patriotic mind can take refuge in this, that the interest of the cost incurred in war with a portion of our own nation was twice the whole principal of the cost incurred in war with the strongest power, next to ourselves, on the North American continent. With the North and South united, the cost of warfare on this continent will always be petty compared with the expense of conquering ourselves. Now let us see how the morality and extent of this account compares with that of our mother and rival. How did the British acquire their vast debt?

In the year 1689 the whole British debt was three million three hundred thousand dollars. The nation had expelled its last tyrant, and bade fair to have a prosperous future, but the new King had a passion for war, and in a few years he had run up this debt seventy-five millions of dollars, — for what? To maintain the balance of power on the Continent of Europe, where England had no possessions, but where this Dutch King had.

Queen Anne must needs win great victories under Marlborough, and she added one hundred and ninety millions to the debt.

When the American Revolution began, the whole debt of England was six hundred and forty-two millions of dollars; to conquer America, England doubled this debt in nine years. In the next nine years of peace, the debt was increased only twelve millions of dollars.

Then commenced that fatal series of wars, in which England, instigated by aristocracy and envy, strove to suppress the French Republic and France.

At the end of those tremendous and illiberal efforts, the English debt had reached the monstrous figure of four billions and two hundred millions of dollars [4,200,000,000].

In fifty years this English debt has been decreased only three hundred and thirteen millions of dollars. The Crimean War alone ran up this debt about one hundred and fifty millions.

From 1793 down to 1814, England paid in subsidies alone two hundred and thirty-one million four hundred and forty-seven thousand two hundred and ninety-five dollars, most of it to worthless Bourbon princes, and semi-civilized adventurers and courtiers of Eastern Europe.

The manner in which money was raised to meet the expenses of the American civil war attests at once the power and the weakness of our form of government. While the nation was rocking on the brink of ruin, and friends and enemies abroad alike gave up our cause, the people voluntarily came forward and took the bonds, — that was the power of the republic! But as it was contrary to our cherished notions of a popular government to wrest such vast amounts of money from the people, we were compelled to offer larger rates of interest than any other great state, — that was the weakness of the republic in time of unexpected war. As a consequence, while our capital debt is only five-sevenths that of England, we pay from ten to fifteen millions more interest annually. American rates of percentage were esteemed so high that in almost every town in Christendom there was some one who gladly became interested in our securities. Prior to the war we solicited loans from Europe to carry on the great corporate enterprises endorsed by the several States of the Union, but at present there are thousands of Germans, Englishmen, and French, who hold, so to speak, mortgages upon our national life; these had faith in the government to lend it of their savings, and it is just this part of our indebtedness which troubles us the most; for to pay the interest on those foreign bonds we must ship large quantities of coin to Europe, which is lost to circulation here. America is no longer political and social authority only in the Old World, but its finances are consulted thrice every day in every stock market in Europe; the most interesting news which is transmitted by the cable is not the number of people at the Boston Music Jubilee, nor even the opening of the Pacific Railroad, but the regular monthly statement of the public debt. We have passed out of the boyish time of national life, when we are esteemed by our genius, our cheerfulness, or courage; we have come to man's estate, with the burden of our past struggles to carry, our business responsibilities to meet, and our solvency to be vindicated for the honor of ourselves, and the capital of our children. The past history of our Union has been touching and resplendent with single episodes; we have given promise of much; we have attracted many poor and prudent Europeans to share our citizenship; but it is part of our destiny, our lot amongst the nations, the necessity of the state, as of mankind, to hold up our faith by our sacrifices, or otherwise be rejected from the front rank of creditable nations, all of whom tread the same embarrassed path. It must be confessed that in financial matters we are not considered abroad to be beyond criticism for the wisdom of our administration thereof. As in private life the last test of confidence is to loan one money, so in national life the last evidence of wisdom is to know how far to put the state in debt, and how well to recover it to independence.

Two men will always be mentioned with prominence in connection with American finance: Salmon P. Chase and Jay Cooke;—the first, as the contriver of our present monetary system, and the latter as the practical banker who popularized it. Mr. Chase's first loan was for eight million dollars, at twenty years, at six per cent.; the capitalists came forward with twenty-seven million dollars. When upwards of twenty-one million dollars had been borrowed from the banks, Congress authorized a loan, and at last passed a National Banking Act, providing for a system of National Banks, based upon government securities; this system has well-nigh superseded the State and local banks of America, so that we may be said to have partially returned to the banking system which President Jackson broke up in 1833.

The Chase banking system may be said to be as follows: Capitalists buy United States bonds and deposit them with the Treasurer of the United States, for which they receive not exceeding ninety per cent. in national bank-notes, whereby they are authorized and enabled to commence the business of banking. They receive six per cent. interest in gold on the amount of bonds purchased and deposited. As to the permanent efficiency and economy of the Chase banking system, great difference of opinion exists, and in a merely descriptive book of this kind it is impolitic to take issue thereon. The subject of finance is more imperfectly understood with us than almost any other. Multitudes of speeches have been made *pro* and *con*, and the majority of our people seem to think that we can meet the burdens of a great debt by some such patent-right contrivances as have made us eminent in mechanics. A French critic has expressed it by saying that we have no financiers, but only a great many financial inventors. Mr. Hugh McCulloch, Secretary of the Treasury in 1869, thus expressed himself on the banking question: —

"In no other country was so large a capital ever invested in banking under a single system, as is now invested in the national banks; never before were the interests of a people so interwoven with a system of banking, as are the interests of the people of the United States with their national banking system. It is not strange, therefore, that the condition and management of the national banks should be, to them and to their representatives, a matter of the deepest concern. That the national banking system is a perfect one, is not asserted by its friends; that it is a very decided improvement, as far as circulation is regarded, upon the systems which it has superseded, must be admitted by its opponents."

In the admirable preface with which Harriet Martineau introduced the American edition of her history, she probably came as near the representative expression of English financiers, as any authority that I might quote. "There is the vital subject of the currency," she says, "which it concerns every republican citizen, at all times, to attend to, when there is a danger (and there always is a danger) of a too free resort to paper money for relief from any embarrassment.

"It seems to me that no thoughtful citizen of any nation can read the story of the years before and after Peel's Bill of 1819, extending over the crash of 1825–6, without the strongest desire that such risks and calamities may be avoided in his own country, at any sacrifice. There are several countries under the doom of retribution for the license of an inconvertible paper currency; and of these the United States is unhappily one. This passage of English history may possibly help to check the levity with which the inevitable 'crash' is spoken of by some who little dream what the horrors and griefs of such a convulsion are. It may do more, if it should convince any considerable number of observers that the affairs of the economic world are as truly and certainly under the control of natural laws as the world of matter without, and that of the mind within."

The centre of gravity of the English state government, like ours, lies in its financial system; the administration of the revenues pertaining to the state alone, without any co-operation on the part of local governing bodies. "Municipal" taxation is wholly distinct;

the state deriving nothing therefor; the coffers of the state, however, often afford aid for municipal purposes. The Prime Minister is generally the first Lord of the Treasury, and under him comes the Chancellor of the Exchequer, who is real Secretary of the Treasury. Exchequer is a word derived from the checkered table-cloth over which the Norman kings and their clerks managed the revenue. As the Chancellor has to propose to Parliament the estimated expenses, or "Budget," of the State, he must be a commoner, for the House of Commons has exclusive legislation over raising revenue. Three junior Lords, one for each kingdom, constitute the commission of the Treasury.

The great branches of income flowing into the Treasury are paid into the public account at the Bank of England, with the authority of the Comptroller-General of the Exchequer, by the departments at which they are collected; and all payments on the public account are made pursuant to the warrant or order of the Board of Treasury; those relating to the larger items of expenditure, specially voted or sanctioned by Parliament, are made by the Comptroller-General; and all the civil salaries, allowances, and incidental charges, which were formerly paid at the Exchequer, are now paid by the Paymaster-General, upon special authorities from the Treasury, by drafts on the Bank of England. No moneys voted by Parliament can be drawn from the Exchequer without the warrant of the Treasury Board, nor can any payment be made from the Civil List without the same authority.

The "Budget" is the expenditure, as annually estimated by the Chancellor of the Exchequer; being only granted for one year, it necessitates the annual assembling of Parliament. From the time of Charles II., it has become the usage to grant supplies to the crown only for specified purposes. Clarendon styled this "a republican innovation." In war times an extraordinary credit is usually granted to the crown, enabling it to prosecute the war even during the recess. Ministers who, like Pitt, can reckon upon a majority in the lower house, have even emancipated themselves from all granting by Parliament. In 1797, without the cognizance of the Commons, he granted to the Emperor of Germany, by way of subsidy, six millions of dollars, and to the Prince of Conde, one million dollars. A large majority in the Commons subsequently sanctioned this unconstitutional mode of procedure as having been compelled by urgent necessity. In like manner, the Parliament, in 1859, sanctioned many millions' excess of expenditure on the Budget of 1857.

The Parliamentary Committee of Ways and Means is charged with examining the measures which the Chancellor of the Exchequer deems necessary to cover the state expenditure.

The Committee of Supplies is charged with settling the amount of the government requirements in the respective departments; its resolutions are introduced at the end of the session by the "Consolidated Fund Appropriation Bill," whereby the government is authorized to expend, for the purposes specified in the bill, the several amounts granted in Committee of Ways and Means.

The Bank of England was first incorporated in 1694, with a capital of six millions of dollars, the whole of which was lent to the government. Its charter has been renewed from time to time. The profits of the corporation arise principally from its transactions as bankers, its discounts and money dealings, from the large balances of the public moneys in its hands, from the interest of three per cent. on the fifty-five million and seventy-five thousand dollars invested as a permanent loan to the government, redeemable on the termination of the charter, and from the remuneration made by the government for the trouble and expense of managing the payment of dividends and the transfer of stock; for this latter duty the corporation is paid by a percentage, upon which a reduction was made in 1834, and a further reduction in 1844, in consideration of a release from stamp-duties (which amounted to about three hundred and fifty thousand dollars per annum), and the amount now actually paid by the public is about five hundred thousand dollars yearly. On an average of ten years the losses from forgery cost the bank two hundred thousand dollars of this sum.

This bank corporation has recently established branch banks of deposit and issue at the following large provincial towns. These banks open accounts with individuals on the approval of the corporation, and, by offering a place of secure deposit and increased facilities of discount, promote the interests of the merchants and traders in their locality. They also receive dividends and effect purchases or sales in the funds: —

Manchester,	Birmingham,	Leeds,
Liverpool,	Swansea,	Leicester,
Bristol,	Newcastle-on-Tyne,	Norwich,
Portsmouth,	Plymouth.	

The Bank of England is an institution almost precisely like the old

United States Bank, which Andrew Jackson suppressed; it was founded by a Scotchman more than two hundred years ago, and, according to his will, no Scotchman can be a Director in it. It is managed by a Governor, Deputy-Governor, and twenty-four Directors, eight of whom go out every year, and all of them must be Stockholders.

It pays seven per cent. dividend annually, and employs nine hundred persons, whose combined salaries are about one million and fifty thousand dollars a year.

Its bank-note circulation is upwards of ninety millions of dollars; there are about two hundred and eighty-four thousand stockholders; and eighty-six millions of dollars in bullion lie in the vaults.

The building covers four acres, and is situated in the heart of Old London; it is a copy of a Roman temple.

The Directors meet in a spacious parlor. The machinery for weighing sovereigns throws pieces of full weight into one box, and rejects those of light weight into another; ten of these machines have almost human intelligence, and weigh seventy thousand sovereigns a day.

When we consider the mighty power of this Bank of England, our thoughts revert to that other institution, which so warmly enlisted the support of Henry Clay and the American Whig Party, now standing in solemn majesty, in the heart of "Old Philadelphia," degraded to a mere Custom House, and thus described by Mr. Dickens: —

"Looking out of my chamber window before going to bed, I saw, on the opposite side of the way, a handsome building of white marble, which had a mournful, ghost-like aspect, dreary to behold. I attributed this to the sombre influence of the night, and on rising in the morning looked out again, expecting to see its steps and portico thronged with groups of people passing in and out. The door was still tight shut however; the same cold, cheerless air prevailed; and the building looked as if the marble statue of Don Guzman could alone have any business to transact within its gloomy walls. I hastened to inquire its name and purpose, and then my surprise vanished. It was the tomb of many fortunes, the great catacomb of investment, — the United States Bank."

It is not improbable that the Bank of England is also destined to be deserted sooner or later. Mr. Robert Lowe, an able member of the English Cabinet, gave notice of some such intention in the summer of 1869.

"The Bank of England system," says Mr. John D. Watson," largely permeates the financial, industrial, and even the social relations of that country, and has a potency compared with which the enormous power of the old Bank of the United States was as nothing. But there is a deep and increasing feeling of opposition to the bank in English financial circles. It is objected, and with good reason, that its management is illiberal and narrow; that it fails to keep pace with the progress of commercial enterprise, and that its whole policy seems to consist in embarrassing trade by making money artificially dear at the very time when it should be cheap, and cheap at the time when it should be dear. It deals with gold at one time as a mere commodity, and at other times as money, and seems to be only influenced by the one idea of retaining a certain quantity of it in England, irrespective of the true interests of the business community. In fine, it is now claimed that the time has arrived for establishing free trade in money and in banking, the same as in other departments of business."

The Bank of England is the principal bank of deposit and issue, and the most extensive in Europe, both in its capital and its money transactions. It enjoys exclusive privileges of banking, which, so far as they may be considered monopolies, may be justified by the advantages and safeguards which the corporation affords to the public. The promissory notes issued by the Bank are declared a legal tender, but by an act passed in 1819 the bank and its branch establishments are compelled to change its notes for gold on demand. The corporation is restricted from engaging in any commercial undertaking other than dealing in bills of exchange and in gold and silver, and in advancing money at interest upon valuable securities.

As connected with the state, the corporation transacts the whole of the banking business of the government; it has the management of the public debt, receiving and paying the chief part of the annuities due to the public creditors; it gives circulation to the Exchequer bills, and makes advances upon them for the public service, and also upon the prospective produce of certain branches of the revenue. It is the banker of the Treasury, the public balances being in its hands. For individuals, the corporation also acts as an ordinary bank of deposit, and makes advances to its depositors, but chiefly in times of difficulty, when extraordinary discounts are required to sustain mercantile credit.

In place of the old United States Bank, the American edifice under which the great transactions of our government are guarded, is the Treasury building at Washington. The entire structure of the American Treasury covers an area of five hundred and twenty by two hundred and seventy-eight feet, including two large courts. The Grecian Ionic order of architecture has been adopted, but it has been treated in many respects as a Roman order, being mounted on a podium or basement, crowned with an elegant balustrade. On the eastern side of the building is a colonnade composed of thirty pillars, extending a distance of three hundred and thirty-six feet north and south. On each of the other sides is a portico surrounded by a pediment. Each shaft of the columns of the porticoes is a single block of stone thirty-two feet in height and four feet six inches in diameter. The buttress caps, which partially include the steps of the porticoes, are single slabs of granite, each twenty feet square by two feet in thickness. The granite used in the construction of this building was quarried on Dix's Island, off the coast of Maine, and brought hither at great expense. Most of the larger slabs were cut after their arrival in Washington, as the risk of transporting them in a rough state was much less than if the stone had been dressed. Fronting the north entrance is a large fountain, the central base of which is twelve feet in diameter, and five feet high, and was cut from a single block of granite.. The wing is sixty-five by one hundred and ninety-five feet, with a slight projection at the front and rear.

The vault resembles a huge safe without shelves or drawers . It is composed of five thicknesses of metal, two of which are of the very best case-hardened, spring steel. The size of the vault is thirteen feet wide, thirteen high, and eighteen long, and it is secured by two massive doors, furnished with combination locks of the latest approved patterns.

Independent of the national banking system, the treasury is the head-quarters of all the great monetary operations of the government. Here is paid interest upon the public debt; here are received the immense collections from duties on imports, and receipts from the internal revenue; here have been printed, recorded, and issued, the bonds, legal-tender notes, and fractional currency of the United States; here have been deposited hundreds of thousands of dollars arising out of the sale of cotton captured during the civil war; here may be seen valuables found by the armies in their destructive marches through the South, as well as the remnant of the gold and silver coin taken from Jefferson Davis; here, also, the United States issues and guarantees the bonds of the Pacific and other railways subsidized by Congress.

While the Treasury is the centre of national business, the various mints at Philadelphia, San Francisco, New York, and Denver are engaged in coinage to the amount of millions of dollars every year. The Philadelphia Mint is surpassed by none in the world for the excellence of its machinery, and the beauty of its work. The U. S. Assay Office is in the Sub-Treasury, in New York, a grand building, which cost nearly one and a quarter millions of dollars.

The total amount of gold that was found *and coined* in the United States, east of the Mississippi River, from the earliest times up to the 30th of June, 1868, was nineteen million seven hundred and twenty-one thousand four hundred and twenty-five dollars. The total amount of gold found in all America, between its discovery and 1868, was nine billion one hundred and seven million seven hundred and twenty-five thousand eight hundred and eighty-nine dollars, while all Europe, Russia in Asia, and the Australasian Islands, including Australia, produced but two billion seven hundred and seventy-six million one hundred thousand dollars in the same time. Counting the American national debt as coin, it would take one-fourth of all the gold mined on the hemisphere to pay it off; but General Grant said in his inaugural, that it was to this "strong box" of nature that he looked for relief. When America was discovered, there were but sixty millions of gold in Europe, and one hundred and forty millions in silver. California and the territories round her have produced one thousand millions of dollars in gold in twenty years. Humboldt and Chevalier estimate the yield of Mexico, in silver and gold, to have been, since the Conquest, three billion two hundred and thirty million dollars. In the same time Peru and Bolivia together have produced two billion seven hundred and forty-five million two hundred and twenty-one thousand six hundred and forty-five dollars. Sixty-one million dollars was the largest annual annual gold yield ever made in Australia. California has several times produced ninety millions of gold a year.

The English Mint is situated close by the Tower of London, four or five miles from the Treasury Building. The Chief of the Mint is called the "Master;" his salary is seven thousand five hundred dollars a year. Sir Isaac Newton, and Sir John Herschel have filled this office, which is not a partisan one. The machinery is very intricate; the dies are hardened by a secret chemical process.

The great private mart of America for loans and banking is Wall Street, New York, which is in communication with Washington by a multitude of wires, and every operation of the government is watched by determined assiduity and cunning.

The London Royal Exchange, described, in part, in the first chapter of this book, is managed by a committee of nine members, the chairman of which is generally a member of Parliament; there are about nineteen hundred members and subscribers, and the expenses are fifty thousand dollars a year. Upstairs are Lloyd's Subscription Rooms. The great business is done here on Tuesday and Friday, late in the afternoon, in a large open court, or quadrangle, ornamented with statues. Here, standing against the several pillars, one can see the Rothschilds, the Browns, the Barings, and all the great representatives of money.

The London Stock Exchange, the greatest ready-money mart of the world, stands opposite the Bank of England. It has about eight hundred and fifty members, all of whom must be re-elected every year in committee of thirty. Fifty dollars is the yearly due. Strangers are not admitted, and, if discovered, are rigidly expelled. Bankrupts can never be readmitted until they have paid about thirty cents on the dollar. Foreigners must have resided in London five years to be eligible for membership, and forty-five hundred dollars' security must be entered for every new member. The broker's commission on home securities is one-eighth per cent.

The greatest case of "bulling and bearing" ever known in the London Stock Market was in 1814, when a person, in a nondescript uniform, appeared at Dover, opposite the French coast, and another at Northfleet, both having French money and anxious looks, and both declared that they were going with all speed to London to announce the death of Napoleon Bonaparte. The allies of these false witnesses in the Stock Exchange made all the splutter and excitement they could over this news, but Parliament and the Courts of Law took prompt cognizance of the crime, and found that at the head of it was Lord Cochrane, an ex-Admiral in the British Navy, a member of the House of Commons, and an active nobleman. He was condemned to a year's imprisonment, a fine of five thousand dollars, and to stand in the pillory. His professional career was stopped for a quarter of a century, and he was expelled from Parliament. This officer had captured Mobile in our late war; he made heroic efforts to raise his character to honor again, commanded the fleets of Chilian and of Greek independence, and was at last ennobled under another title, Lord Dundonald.

There is scarcely a foreign government debt, scarcely a European railway, mine, navigation, or trading company, that is not daily dealt in in London. But not only is London the financial centre of all European joint stock enterprises, but it is so likewise of those of almost every country on the American Continent.

A membership of the New York Stock Exchange is property, now worth seven thousand dollars, — that is, by purchase from a retiring member. The initiation fee, without purchase, is limited to ten thousand dollars. The number of members will probably be limited, so that in future the value of the seat may be considerably increased. The most extraordinary attempt ever made in America to affect the stock and gold market was in the midst of the civil war, when a startling proclamation appeared in the New York papers, signed "Abraham Lincoln," decrying the war as a failure, and ordering out a large levy of men. It was presently discovered to be a forgery, and was traced to a young man named Howard, a journalist, who had been made the instrument of Wall Street gamesters, and whose occupation gave him knowledge of the great news combination called the Associated Press. He was promptly arrested, and sent to a military fort in the harbor of New York, where he remained many months. His poverty, and the escape of his instigators, excited sympathy after a time, and by the exertions of Rev. Henry Ward Beecher and others he was released on parole.

It is not disputed that scandalous advantage was taken of the American government by its own officials, in the Treasury, as well as by outside operators during its time of trial, and subsequent to the war. Punishments in this country for offences against the state have always been lightly inflicted, and in the change of parties the public enemy is generally pardoned, but under the stern and relentless government of England, there is no offence like that against the state! Smuggling is not a mere misdemeanor, punishable with forfeiture as here, but a high crime! Every headland of the United Kingdom is patrolled by coast guards, day and night. The inevitable sailor, with the telescope under his arm, keeps a look-out on every sail. Illicit stills are pursued into Irish and Scotch fastnesses, and vengeance without remorse is dealt out to the most trifling offender.

The Lighthouse, and Coast Survey Bureaux, as well as the Revenue Cutter Service, are, in America, in charge of the Treasury Department.

The United States Revenue Cutter Service comprises twenty-five steamers, and seventeen sailing vessels. Of the six steamers on the lakes, all but one are at present (1869) out of commission, or not in use.

The United States attempted to organize a survey of its coasts in 1807, but did not really begin to accomplish anything before 1832. Our coasts and bays are surveyed in the same manner as the public lands. A Swiss mathematician, F. R. Hassler, managed the coast survey for eleven years, and he was succeeded by A. D. Bache, a descendant of Benjamin Franklin. The first base line for survey was measured by Hassler, on Fire Island beach, outside of New York harbor. France and England preceded us in establishing Hydrographic Bureaux. Before the coast survey was organized a private surveyor, Edmund M. Blunt, undertook to prepare charts of important harbors and waters at his own expense, and the "American Coast Pilot," prepared by the Blunt family, had become a book of nine hundred and twenty-six pages in 1867.

The American Light-house Board was organized in 1852 after England and France had set the example. Our light-houses were miserable until we adopted the French system of lighting. We actually subjected our vessels to the dangers of running aground on imperfectly lighted coasts, rather than import the Fresnel light from France; this might be called Protection to Shipwreck. Commodore M. C. Perry ordered the first Fresnel lights for trial, and they were placed on the Highlands of Neversink, New York harbor. Many anecdotes might be told of the difficulties which philanthropic men have had to impress upon Congress the necessity of these great public labors. Some years since there was an endeavor made to get a light-house placed on the Execution Rocks, a reef, one short mile north of Sands Point, in Long Island Sound, but it did not succeed, although asked for by a large commercial interest, until the steamboat on which there was a member of Congress, on his way to Washington, struck on these rocks, immediately after which an appropriation was made for the building of a light-house at this place.

In 1852, the bill for creating the Light-house Board was pending in Congress, but, being opposed by parties interested in keeping up our bad system, its passage was doubtful. The Baltic steamer was then at Washington, and sailed for New York. Off Sandy Hook she was detained by a fog, and could not run for want of proper buoys. A meeting of the passengers, among whom were several members of

Congress, was called on board, and their attention particularly directed to this defect, and, on their returning to Washington, they caused the above-named bill to be passed. Punch says, to make railroad travelling safe, put a director on the locomotive. To get a bill through Congress, let the members see the necessity practically.

We had, in 1866, four hundred and thirty-one light-houses, all of which have lenses. We have a few reflector lights, but they are range lights, not included in the four hundred and thirty-one.

If the four hundred and thirty-one houses were fitted with reflectors, to correspond in power with the lenses, they would consume about one hundred and sixty thousand gallons of oil annually. The consumption of the lenses is sixty-five thousand, with greatly increased light.

The number of light-stations extinguished in the civil war was one hundred and thirty-five; eighty of which have been restored. The work of restoration is going on.

The Drummond light was invented by Lieutenant Drummond, of the British Army, more than thirty years ago; he was engaged in making a survey of Ireland, and wishing to get as long a base as possible for his triangle, he endeavored to establish signals between two distant mountains, and in this endeavor he invented the Drummond light.

Every energy of the English government is bent toward increasing its commerce; for manufactures readily follow if there be buyers in foreign parts, and cheap and plentiful ships to transport the goods; to this end harbor and pilot duties are kept down to the lowest figure; while our government has done little of late toward encouraging our merchant marine.

The New Orleans charges for bringing in and towing out a ship of a thousand tons amount to over 2,500 dollars; those of New York, to about 676 dollars; and those of Boston, to about 569 dollars. The lowest of these figures would be extravagant in England.

In inland improvements, the United States compares well with England, both in the extent and cheapness of its canal and railway system, which, however, is not subordinate to the general government as in Europe.

The cost of the 14,247 miles of railroad existing in 1867 in England was nearly 2,500,000,000 dollars, while the 39,276 miles of the same year in the United States cost only 1,700,000 dollars. The English roads earned less than eight per cent. on the cost, while in the United States the earnings were nearly twenty-five per cent.; but the net earnings of the English roads are fully one-half of the gross receipts, while on our roads they are less than one-third, being not more than thirty per cent. Much of this difference arises from the high price of materials under the tariff. The various items of cost per train mileage of running trains upon the railroads of the State of New York, amount in the aggregate to one hundred and sixty-six dollars, while in Great Britain they are but sixty-one dollars and thirty-seven cents.

There were in operation in all the States, on the 1st day of January, 1869, 42,255 miles of railway, the cost of which, at 44,000 dollars per mile, equalled 1,800,000,000 dollars.

The total amount of net tonnage transported over them for the year equalled 75,000,000 tons, having a value of 10,472,250,000 dollars, a sum equalling six times their cost, and more than four times greater than the whole amount of the national debt!

Historically, the Baltimore and Ohio Railroad took precedence of all others. The opening of its first section (twenty-three miles) took place in 1830.

Massachusetts has one mile of railroad to 5.47 square miles of territory. In the same ratio the whole Union would have 600,000 miles of railway.

The Pacific Railroad is probably the greatest monument of a nation's beneficence which the history of man has to show. By the following figures, which are taken from the report of a special commission appointed by the President, of which General G. K. Warren was President, it will be seen that the United States has endorsed the bonds of the two corporations which make one grand trunk line to the Pacific, to the amount of 53,000,000 dollars.

The aid in the shape of subsidy bonds and first mortgage bonds received by each company was as follows: the Union Pacific, 525 miles from Omaha to the base of the Rocky Mountains, at 16,000 dollars per mile, 8,400,000 dollars; 150 miles across the Rocky Mountains, at 40,000 dollars per mile, 7,200,000 dollars; 360 miles, extending to Ogden, at 32,000 dollars per mile, 11,520,000 dollars. Total, 27,120,000 dollars. This is equal to 26,200 dollars per mile, and the first mortgage bonds are issued in a like amount, — 26,200 dollars per mile. Total, 52,400 dollars per mile. Subsidy bonds received by the Central Pacific road, six miles from Sacramento to the base of the Sierra Nevada, 16,000 dollars per mile, 96,000 dollars; 150 miles across the Sierra Nevada, at 48,000 dollars per mile, 7,200,000 dollars; 585 miles thence to Ogden, at 32,000 dollars per mile, 18,720,000 dollars. Total, 26,016,000 dollars, or 35,109 dollars averaged upon each and every mile of the road. First mortgage bonds in a like amount, 35,109 dollars per mile. Total subsidy and first mortgage bonds on each and every mile of the road, 70,218 dollars.

The same commission reported that nearly fourteen millions of dollars would be required to bring the Pacific railroads up to the best standards of construction and equipment.

To institute any comparison between American and English public works would be vain, the one being a broad continent, and the other a narrow island.

The canals of New York are over 900 miles long. They have cost, with their several enlargements, not less than 35,000,000 dollars, and with the river navigation and railway system of interior New York, would probably make the sum more than 200,000,000 dollars.

Some minor items of expenditure in America and England may be interesting. In 1860, 12,206 American vessels entered United States ports, exceeding the number of foreign vessels by nearly 2,000; in six years thereafter American tonnage decreased more than forty per cent., while foreign tonnage increased nearly eighty.

The coinage of England and America is quite different. America, like France, has adopted the decimal system in money, except that we divide the hundred into four parts, and coin dollars, half dollars, and quarter dollars, while the French properly divide it into fifths, and coin Napoleons, demi-Napoleons, and five-franc pieces. The English, however, have the old embarrassing system of pounds, shillings, and pence; there is no such thing as a pound in coin, but a sovereign, which is equal to about a sixpence less than a five-dollar gold piece. The English shilling is nearly equal to our quarter dollar, and is quite a different thing from the York shilling, which is equivalent to the old Mexican twelve-and-a-half-cent piece. It is probable that before long we shall all adopt the French system in money, in measure, and in weight, in which case it might be well to call the great standard coin "The Peace;" then it could be said that the empire was indeed the Peace, for it is more a piece of money, than a piece of principle.

In 1868 the British government expended six millions of dollars in public buildings and works, which was much greater than our expenditures counting out the railways.

The interest and the management of England's permanent debt in 1868, was 115,000,000 dollars; 1,500,000 dollars was spent in giving pensions; 4,000,000 dollars went to what is called the "packet service." It cost twelve and a half million dollars to collect the customs and internal revenue. The expenditures exceeded the revenue in that year six and a half million dollars.

One million paupers were fed in that year, and upwards of twenty thousand persons convicted of crime.

There are held of our bonds, 600,000,000 dollars in Europe, and 250,000 dollars of other American securities, thereby increasing our debt to Europe 70,000,000 dollars a year. The British revenue is almost entirely derived from Custom House duties and excise, or home taxation; the latter brings nearly 100,000,000 dollars a year; the Post Office clears 25,000,000 dollars, while ours gets in debt; the English receive nearly 50,000,000 dollars from the sale of stamps.

All the property in the United States is said to be worth twenty billions of dollars [20,000,000,000].

The English revenue from customs is nearly altogether derived from the duties upon a few articles, none of which compete with home products. The figures of customs revenue for two years are thus given: —

	1867.	1868.
Sugar and molasses	£5,647,787	£5,582,473
Tea	2,658,716	2,827,317
Coffee	397,190	390,161
Corn meal and flour	797,639	869,323
Spirits	4,173,027	4,298,403
Wine	1,391,192	1,468,993
Tobacco and snuff	6,455,011	6,542,250
Other imports	577,666	581,481
Sundries	200,838	104,580
Total customs	£22,299,066	£22,664,981

The expenses of collecting this revenue are small, compared to those of collecting duties on several thousand different articles, as we do in America. Our tax list makes a book nearly as large as Webster's Dictionary, and is annually changed to suit the interests of legislators and their constituents. The whole financial system of England runs smoother and more equally than ours. Ninety-six per cent. of the revenue from English excises is collected from spirits, malt, and licenses. The income tax is a fraction over two per cent.; yet the revenue from that source is equal to that collected in the United States, where the rate has been generally five per cent. England has tried both systems, — a tariff upon all articles of import, and a tariff upon a dozen leading articles, — and has found the latter to be the cheapest, and to produce fully as much revenue. One of the ablest men connected with the United States Revenue Bureau is David A. Wells. At his suggestion we reduced the tax on whiskey from two dollars to fifty cents a gallon, and we increased the revenue vastly by the change.

The annual interest on the British debt is about one hundred and thirty millions of dollars [130,000,000]. The British people pay about four and a half dollars a head in gold every year, man, woman, and child, to meet the interest on this national debt.

The joint stock companies that failed in Great Britain between August, 1862, and 1869, amounted to four hundred and eighty in number.

The American receipts from all national taxes in 1860 were 77,000,000 dollars; in 1868, from internal revenue alone, they were 191,000,000 dollars; and in 1866, from the same bureau, 309,000,000 dollars; from all sources in 1868 they were 300,000,000 dollars.

The vital defect in the American government is its civil service, which is in great part a body of merely partisan stipendiaries. Had Great Britain appointed such a class of men as we have, to collect her revenue, she would have been bankrupt thirty years ago. It is useless to qualify this strong expression; all Americans know that our revenue service, whether under Mr. Johnson or General Grant, is rotten throughout; that the question is, "What is the office worth?" and that this does not mean, "What is the salary of it to me?" or, "What is it worth to the government?" but "How much can I steal by it?" Our revenue service is venal as that of Russia. No man as President, no Congress, can take higher rank in the future, than by completely abolishing the system of making partisan appointments to assess and collect the public taxes.

The observing De Tocqueville, whom I have so frequently quoted, seemed to foresee from the character of our civil service in Jackson's administration what would be its efficiency in coming times: —

"I conclude," he says, "without having recourse to inaccurate computations, and without hazarding a comparison which might prove incorrect, that the democratic government of the Americans is not a cheap government, as is sometimes asserted; and I have no hesitation in predicting, that if the people of the United States is ever involved in serious difficulties, its taxation will speedily be increased to the rate of that which prevails in the greater part of the aristocracies and the monarchies of Europe."

The most sanguine expectations of the Americans as to paying off the national debt are based upon the value of the public lands, and the increase of immigration. During the era of slavery, our reliance to meet the cost of our imports from Europe was by the export of cotton. During our civil war, the utmost energies of England were put forth to make her colonies cotton plantations, and thereby rid herself of dependence upon the United States. The success which attended those efforts is probably one of the vital causes of the decline of American commerce and industry.

In 1864, we were told that thirty-nine sources, exclusive of the United States, contributed to the supply of cotton at Manchester; that Australia, Jamaica, French West Indies, Greece, Turkey, Brazil, Portugal, Morocco, Egypt, Italy, Austria (on the Adriatic), Hayti, Malta, Japan, China, and Venezuela were among the producers; that the average fibre of foreign cotton, in fourteen instances, was equal, for average purposes of manufacture, to the American fibre; and that in several, and in fact most, of the countries named cotton can be cultivated and exported to England at cheaper rates than American planters can afford.

It would be neglect to quit this great and involved subject without reference to the two contending principles which are now dividing parties, communities, and even families in the United States, — those of Free Trade, and High Tariff, or "Protection." The English people long ago determined this issue, and there is practical Free Trade throughout the British dominions, a Tariff being imposed upon a few articles, — chiefly those of luxury, — and directed to obtaining revenue rather than to nursing the home manufactures and products of Great Britain. The American Tariff is more partial, and is not only directed toward the collection of revenue on our frontiers, but toward placing an embargo upon many articles of foreign manufacture, so that our people shall be compelled to purchase at home, and thereby encourage, enrich, or "protect" the native miner and manufacturer. In the early history of the country, our statesmen were divided upon the subject of the Tariff, the agricultural representatives holding that, as good government was based upon the principle of the greatest good to the greatest number, no specific interest should be protected by the Tariff, but that the people should be free to buy in the cheapest market, and sell in the dearest.

The other sentiment took the position that, as our nation was in its infancy, and as its manufactures were vital to its happiness and independence, these should be protected against foreign competition, until they were able to stand alone. Amongst the advocates of the latter sentiment, none were more eminent and eloquent than Henry Clay; for he coupled with his High Tariff ideas the generous principles of Internal Improvements; but it is well known that he failed to reach the goal of his aspirations, — the Chief Magistracy, — notwithstanding the powerful special interests he favored. It was after the rise of the Republican, or Anti-slavery party in the North, that the High Tariff interest attained its principal political triumphs; for the North, needing all its energies to meet the rebellion, was little disposed to divide upon the minor Tariff issue. When the rebellion had been quelled, it was found that the High Tariff men were uppermost, constituting a majority in the Senate and the House, and up to the present writing (1869) they have succeeded in holding the Tariff up to the very highest notch. They are powerfully seconded by such vigorous journals as the New York "Tribune," edited by Horace Greeley, one of the ablest journalists that any nation ever had, while on the other hand, the "Evening Post" of New York, edited by William Cullen Bryant, the poet, and the North-western press at large, are radical advocates of Free Trade.

Symptoms of dissatisfaction with the various tariffs are manifesting themselves on every hand; in New England, Edward Atkinson, himself a manufacturer, has declared for Free Trade, on the ground that our manufactures will better thrive by the ingenuity and perseverance of their mechanics and capitalists, than by waiting like Lazarus, at the gate of the government, and asking to be subsidized. Still more remarkable is it that William Lloyd Garrison, Henry Ward Beecher, and the leading pioneers in the anti-slavery cause are also earnest advocates for the complete emancipation of trade and commerce on this continent. This is but natural, for in England Emancipation and Free Trade went hand in hand; the same banners marshalled the armies of both reforms, and men found it impossible to be advocates for freedom in the moral and political world, and yet decry its blessings in the world of commerce. At the present writing (1869) the extreme Tariff men hold the whip-hand in America; the manufacturers themselves seek admission to Congress, that they may influence their interests there, and when upon a recent occasion Mr. David A. Wells, the special Commissioner of the Revenue, advocated the reduction of certain import duties, a bill was passed by the House forthwith to strike out the salary for his office.

In England, at the time Free Trade was popularized, it was not the manufacturers, but the agriculturalists, who opposed it. They argued that the right little, tight little Island of Great Britain, having few acres to spare, could not grow wheat in competition with the barbarous Russian and the sleepless American, unless a High Tariff were put upon it, to "protect the British farmer."

Since the repeal of the "Corn Laws" in England, agriculture, so far from being crushed out, has attained perfection and importance beyond all its previous career.

"As the development of manufactures," says a recent historian, "was the grand economical feature of the last century, that of agriculture appears likely to become the distinctive feature of the present. The pernicious spell of protection is dissolved; something like a scientific education is now to be obtained by the next generation of farmers; and our sanitary researches are about to provide an ample supply of the first requisite of increased production. We may hope soon to see the agricultural population once more gaining on the manufacturing, and the rural laboring-class ceasing to be the opprobrium of our polity."

It is to be lamented that, by the collision of private and partisan interests, this merely economical question has become a subject of bitterness rather than of fair and philanthropic inquiry. In the period we have reached, it is manifest that these industrial questions are to be examined, and place-hunters and partisans, on both sides, will doubtless attempt to turn them to their own mercenary uses. The great question is, will the people be happier with a High Tariff or a Revenue Tariff? What are the natural relations of the American continent and the American mind to manufactures? Is the manufacturing or the agricultural interest most prejudicial to our individual manhood and our institutions? Must our manufacturers cling to the skirts of partisanship? Are the ingenuity and the perseverance requisite for mechanical excellence best protected by playing the sycophant to legislation, or by being cast aloof upon their own resources, like the typical American character? And is it Democratic or Republican to bolster up one interest and neglect the rest?

He would be a rash man who should undertake to settle this question in the limits of a chapter. The English have settled it in favor of Free Trade, and amongst the latest English tourists in our country, has been one, Mr. Charles W. Dilke, who has in his book, entitled "Greater Britain," given liberal interpretation to the arguments of American protectionists.

"Those who speak," he says, "of the selfishness of the Protectionists as a whole, can never have taken the trouble to examine into the arguments by which Protection is supported in Australia and America. In these countries Protection is no mere national delusion; it is a system deliberately adopted with open eyes as one conducive to the country's welfare, in spite of objections known to all; in spite of pocket losses that come home to all. If it be, as we in England believe, a folly, it is, at all events, a sublime one, full of self-sacrifice, illustrative of a certain nobility in the national heart. The Australian diggers and Western farmers in America are setting a grand example to the world of self-sacrifice for a national object; hundreds of thousands of rough men are content to live — they and their families — upon less than they might otherwise enjoy, in order that the condition of the mass of their countrymen may continue raised above that of their brother toilers in Old England. Their manufactures are beginning now to stand alone; but hitherto, without Protection, the Americans would have had no cities but seaports. By picturing to ourselves England dependent upon the city of London, upon Liverpool, and Hull, and Bristol, we shall see the necessity the Western men are now under of setting off Pittsburg against New York and Philadelphia.

"It would seem," he continues, "as though we Free Traders had become nearly as bigoted in favor of Free Trade as our former opponents were in favor of Protection. Just as they used to say, 'We are right, why argue the question?' so now, in face of the support of Protection by all the greatest minds in America, all the first statesmen of the Australias, we tell the New England and the Australian politicians that we will not discuss Protection with them, because there can be no two minds about it among men of intelligence and education.

"As far as we in our island are concerned, it is so manifestly to the pocket interest of almost all of us, and at the same time, on account of the minuteness of our territory, so little dangerous politically, that for Britain there can be no danger of a deliberate relapse into Protection; although we have but little right to talk about Free Trade so long as we continue our enormous subsidies to the Cunard liners.

"The American argument in favor of Prohibition is in the main, it will be seen, political, the economical objections being admitted, but outweighed. Our action in the matter of our postal contracts, as in the case of the factory acts, at all events shows that we are not ourselves invariably averse to distinguish between the political and the economical aspect of certain questions."

Mr. Dilke makes one curious argument, and upon a curious premise: that the western farmers are all Tariff men.

"The tendency, according to the Western farmers of Free Trade," he says, "in the early stages of a country's existence, is to promote universal centralization, to destroy local centres and the commerce they create, to so tax the farmer with the cost of transport to the distant centres, consequent upon the absence of local markets, that he can but grow wheat and corn continuously, and cannot but exhaust his soil. With markets so distant, the richest forest lands are not worth clearing, and a wave of settlement sweeps over the country, occupying the poorer lands, and then abandoning them once more."

I cannot better conclude this chapter than by quoting from the scholarly and philosophical author of "England's Greatness." "Whether reciprocated, or not, Free Trade, like many other virtues, has inherent advantages; may be administered in any quantity, and be proportionately remunerative. In its practical application it is irrespective of time or place, of old or young communities; to small or large States, it is correspondingly beneficial. Nations which trade the most will profit by it the most; but those of less traffic will benefit in proportion to the extent of their commerce.

"England, being the most mercantile community, is the most interested in its adoption; and being also the most prosperous, a forward example by her is likely most to fix attention, and be followed. Ireland was cramped and irritated, and driven to the verge of rebellion by the oppressive and pernicious nature of the protective system. The opening of her trade was the first step in her conciliation, and in drawing into more friendly sympathies with England the middle classes of her population. The same maladies continued for a longer period to alienate and retard the progress of British North America, and our West Indian Colonies, and which was alleviated by similar remedies. Their trade was fettered; they were limited in their markets, both for the sale and purchase of goods; they were constrained to trade only with the mother country, to buy dear and sell cheap, and the injury to both was aggravated by distance and freightage."

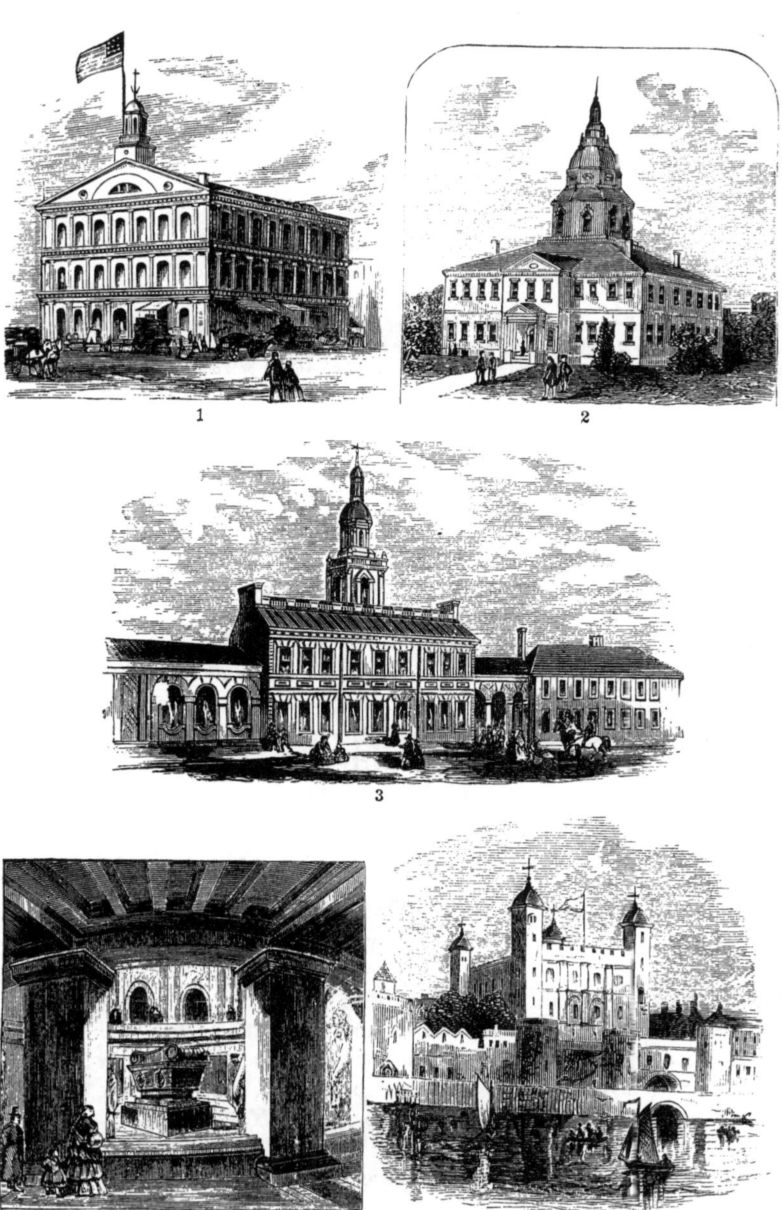

NATIONAL SHRINES.

1—Faneuil Hall, Boston. 2—State House, Annapolis. 3—State House, Philadelphia. 4—Napoleon's Tomb. 5—Tower of London.

CHAPTER XV.

POLITICS AND POLITICAL PARTIES ON BOTH SIDES OF THE SEA.

A revelation of the rise and principles of the whig, tory, conservative, liberal, republican, federal, radical, chartist, and whatsoever other parties have existed in America or England. — An electioneering campaign in England from the proclamation of an election to the close of the poll. — The philosophy of party organizations in a free state.

THE history of English politics may be said to have commenced with the expulsion of James II., the last of the male Stuarts, for prior to that time there had been revolution, and the conflict of sects and families, but not organized party politics as we comprehend it. When James Stuart was driven out of England into exile, the House of Commons obtained the assent of his dethroner, William, Prince of Orange, to a Bill of Rights, whereby Parliament and people were given leave to assemble, to petition, and to speak and print as became them, being subjects. Then began the ferment of parties and leaders, and there had already existed the nicknames of Whig and Tory, and many of the conditions of party organization.

"Whig" was a word derived from a *whey*, or *whig*, of sour milk drunk by the hunted Scotch Covenanters; and "Tory" was either the name of a robber or of a robber band, or of a robber's challenge to stand and deliver. On general principles it may be said that a "Tory" was an advocate of the monarchy in all its despotic prerogatives, and a "Whig" an advocate of monarchy limited by Parliament, by a lenient aristocracy, and by law.

But after the Stuarts had been expelled a large portion of the Tories sympathized with them, and endeavored to intrigue for their restoration; these were called *Jacobites*. At the same time a few Tories preferred that the Stuarts should not return, but that the house of Hanover should reign; these were called *Hanoverian Tories*.

The conflicts of these three parties were long, and extended to bloodshed and warfare. The Jacobites rallied around the "Pretender," as one of the Stuarts was called, when he landed in Scotland, and were defeated, hanged, and banished by hundreds. They settled in Maryland, Virginia, and the Carolinas, and in many other American States, furnishing us with some splendid family stock.

Our American ancestors were partisans of one or the other of these two English parties, Whig and Tory, and we gave these names in the Revolution to patriots and loyalists, respectively. After the Revolution we dropped for a while the old distinctions and became *Federals*, and *Republicans*, followers of Hamilton or Jefferson relatively; but after some time the word Whig was revived to indicate the successor of the first Federal party, while the term Republican became radicalized into *Democratic*. Thus, even at the present day there are mournful old men in the United States who say with some sorry fondness: "I was an old-line Whig!" thereby expressing a Scotch term of almost lost antiquity.

In England these two terms continued uninterruptedly down to the passage of the Reform Bill, when they were exchanged for *Liberal* and *Conservative;* but, meantime, the structure and policy of both parties changed repeatedly, the two organizations striving less for principles in the end than for power and the continuance of it.

It is easy to imagine the causes of origin of the two early parties in the United States; one was not all cured of reverence for English government; the other wanted a new pattern of nation, in part Roman, in part Saxon, in part original and philosophic.

"The deeper we penetrate into the working of these parties, the more do we perceive," says De Tocqueville, "that the object of the one is to limit, and that of the other to extend the popular authority. I do not assert," he adds, "that the ostensible end, or even that the secret aim, of American parties is to promote the rule of aristocracy or democracy in the country; but I affirm that aristocratic or democratic passions may easily be detected at the bottom of all parties, and that, although they escape a superficial observation, they are the main point and the very soul of every faction in the United States."

We cannot more agreeably obtain the *status* of those two early organizations led respectively by the greatest of Americans, than in the words of the same sprightly authority: —

"The party which desired to limit the power of the people endeavored to apply its doctrines more especially to the Constitution of the Union, whence it derived its name of *Federal*. The other party, which affected to be more exclusively attached to the cause of liberty, took that of *Republican*. America is the land of democracy, and the Federalists were always in a minority; but they reckoned on their side almost all the great men who had been called forth by the War of Independence, and their moral influence was very considerable. Their cause was, moreover, favored by circumstances. The ruin of the Confederation had impressed the people with a dread of anarchy, and the Federalists did not fail to profit by this transient disposition of the multitude. For ten or twelve years they were at the head of affairs, and they were able to apply some, though not all, of their principles; for the hostile current was becoming from day to day too violent to be checked or stemmed. In 1801 the Republicans got possession of the government; Thomas Jefferson was named President; and he increased the influence of their party by the weight of his celebrity, the greatness of his talents, and the immense extent of his popularity.

"The means by which the Federalists had maintained their position were artificial, and their resources were temporary; it was by the virtues or the talents of their leaders that they had risen to power."

This statement is incisive; for it may be said that the Constitution of the United States and the Farewell Address of Washington bear the Federal imprint and the tone of Hamilton, while the Declaration of Independence and the American policy were the legacy of Jefferson. Hamilton, mastering or sharing the convictions of Washington, impressed himself upon the Federal compact and the early state, while Jefferson, with whom had been, doubtless, the practical sympathies of Franklin, gave the country original republicanism, and made the American character more pronouncedly democratic than the teachings of our Constitution. To Hamilton we owe the state as a fabric, to Jefferson the people as a conviction.

The great event which influenced the formation and consolidation of political parties in England and America — and throughout the world, indeed — was the French Revolution, in part the child of our own, but made a monster of good and evil by the philosophers and magi who had predicted it, and who became its tutors, and also by the resentment of France against an obdurate aristocracy. When the Revolution began, a powerful party hailed it in America, and a less powerful party in England. Fox and Jefferson gave it countenance, and at first human millennium seemed to have come; but the embittered Tories of the monarchy and aristocracy in England, fearful that their turn was next to be, laid the basis of an opposition which never ceased till France was prostrate. They first incited the French aristocratic exiles to annoy France, and they subsidized the German powers against her, till the public exasperation of the Republicans ran to bloody excesses, — then with denunciations of these by Burke and others, they fired the English heart. The old national animosity succeeded to popular sympathy with a redeemed people, and England plunged into that costly generation of slaughter which made the meteor reputation of Bonaparte, and turned the human sluices of Europe into the channels of American emigration. During all that time the Tory party held the English government in their iron grip, while they poured money abroad like water; but in the reign of George IV., when France was ruined, Englishmen, with their usual envy, turned against their continental allies, and to break up the Holy Alliance or league of continental monarchs, the Tory party under Canning almost dissolved, and under Peel and Wellington even favored Catholic emancipation in the British realms. The sentiment of Europe is, that England went mad during these French wars, and the very excesses of the Revolution are now more readily excused than the bitter hate of its reactionary rival. A local historian of Manchester gives this illustration of the Tory party's proscriptive fashion of subduing sympathy for France.

"Many of the older inhabitants of Manchester will recollect seeing, in the public houses of their younger days, boards bearing the inscription 'No Jacobins admitted here.' These boards date their origin from the year 1792; and so late as 1825, there was one of them in a public house in Bridge Street. They were put up to prevent the discussion of reform principles in bar-parlors. We are told that shortly after the government proclamation mentioned above, and to prevent a meeting announced to be held to raise a subscription for the sufferers by war in France, a tax-gatherer, accompanied by several other persons, went round the town to all the inn-keepers and publicans, advising them, if they had any regard for the renewal of their licenses, to suffer no societies similar to the constitutional to meet in their houses; and obtained the signatures of one hundred and eighty-six inn-keepers and publicans to a document, the import of which was as follows: 'We, whose names are hereunto subscribed, being licensed inn-keepers and alehouse-keepers, within the towns of Manchester and

Salford, justly alarmed, at the treasonable and seditious conduct of a well-known set of daring miscreants, who have called a public meeting to be held on Tuesday next at the Bull's Head Inn, in Manchester, for the avowed purpose of assisting the French savages, as well as with a sincere desire of introducing similar calamities to the inhabitants of this happy and prosperous country, as those that now exist in France, take this very necessary opportunity of publishing to the towns of Manchester and Salford in particular, and to the whole kingdom of Great Britain in general, our detestation of such wicked and abominable practices. And we do hereby solemnly declare, that we will not suffer any meeting to be held in our houses, of any clubs or societies, however specious or plausible their titles may be, that have a tendency to put in force what those infernals so ardently and devoutly wish for, namely, the destruction of this county; and we will be ready on all occasions to co-operate with our fellow-townsmen in bringing to justice all those who shall offend in any instance against our much admired and most excellent constitution." This document is dated, "Manchester, September 13th, 1792."

The United States also sympathized with France, until the behavior of her Minister in America and the insolent demand of a loan which her representatives made of ours, provoked the country into a wounded neutrality, if not to resentment. But by our general sympathy with the French people, whether under the republic, the consulate, or the empire, we have kept our record clear with France, and were enabled to possess ourselves of Louisiana, her colony.

Every subsequent revolution of France, as in 1830 and 1848, created ferments in England, and led to semi-republican or ultra republican parties, chief of which was that of the "Chartists," who demanded five radical points of reform, namely: manhood suffrage, annual Parliaments, vote by ballot, remuneration of members of Parliament, and the abolition of the property qualification. The Chartists being mainly laboring men, were unfortunate in their leaders, and lacking a solid and persevering organization were intimidated by the Londoners and by the soldiery. They had prepared a petition, which was to be rolled into Parliament like a huge cartwheel, and which was said to contain five millions of names. The petition was subjected by Parliament to a thorough examination. "It weighed," says an authority, "not five tons, but under five hundred weight. The signatures were not five millions, but about a million and a half; and these were not all genuine. The Duke of Wellington's name occurred seventeen times; the Prince Consort's and even the Queen's pretended signature was there, and those of the ministers. There were nicknames, jests, and even indecent terms; and whole sheets were in the same handwriting. The five points were not likely to be obtained in such a way as this; and this is, in fact, the closing scene of the Chartist agitation in England.

"The proceedings of that day were watched from all parts of Europe; and the result produced as strong an effect on observers as perhaps any one of the revolutions of the time. The peace had been kept without the appearance of a single soldier, and by the citizens themselves re-enforcing the civic police. From that day it was a settled matter that England was safe from revolution. There were no causes for it, no elements of it; and there was a steady and cheerful determination, on the part of the people, that there should be none. No sovereign and no polity were ever safer at any time than the Queen and the constitution of England in the revolutionary years of 1848–9."

But not always by the same management are political demonstrations suppressed in England, as witness the celebrated massacre in 1819, where the people in Manchester, meeting to consider the Reform Bill, were sabred by the militia, so that the field was called "Peterloo." Of this disgraceful act Bamford, the Manchester historian, says: "On the breaking of the crowd, the yeomanry wheeled; and dashing wherever there was an opening they followed, pressing and wounding. Many females appeared as the crowd opened; and striplings and mere youths were also found. Their cries were piteous and heart-rending, and would, one might have supposed, have disarmed any human resentment; but their appeals were in vain. Women, white-vested maids, and tender youths were indiscriminately sabred or trampled on, and we have reason for believing that few were the instances in which that forbearance was vouchsafed which they so earnestly implored. In ten minutes from the commencement of the havoc, the field was an open and almost deserted space. The sun looked down through a sultry and motionless air; the curtains and blinds of the windows, within view, were all closed. A gentleman or two might occasionally be seen looking out from some houses of recent erection, near the door of which a group of persons (special constables) were collected, and apparently in conversation; others were assisting the wounded or carrying off the dead. The hustings remained with a few broken and severed flag-staves erect, and a torn or gashed banner or two drooping; while over the whole field were strewed caps, bonnets, hats, shawls, and shoes, and other parts of male and female dress, trampled, torn, and bloody. The yeomanry had dismounted; some were easing their horses' girths, others adjusing their accoutrements, and some were wiping their sabres. Several mounds of human beings still remained where they had fallen, crushed down, and smothered; some of these were still groaning; others with staring eyes were gasping for breath; and others would never breathe more. All were silent, save those low sounds, and the occasional snorting and pawing of steeds. Persons might sometimes be noticed peeping from attics, and over the tall ridgings of houses; but they quickly withdrew, as if fearful of being observed, or unable to sustain the full gaze of a scene so hideous and abhorrent."

This is the language of a native Englishman, and it shows that the great American "mob," which is always a startling feature of an English book, is sometimes a more innocent organization than an English constabulary.

"Young England" was another party, springing out of the Tories, which proposed, from a different motive, to grant principles somewhat akin to Chartism; in short, it proposed to resume a mild feudal or landed control, a benignant despotism over the poor, and let them help the Tory party to destroy the Whigs.

The true "Radical" party of England is the joint product of very liberal middle-class people in the cities, and of the more intelligent and public-spirited manufacturers; with these affiliate a few literary and scientific men, and it is powerfully recruited from the young tradesmen and clerks and from the better working-classes. The Radical party was so named by Pitt in 1798, when he denounced it, and at that time it included even a Duke of Norfolk. The Radical party of England at the present day is not, like "Chartism," "Independentism," etc., begotten of semi-French philosophy, nor of the miseries of the working-classes, but of the experience of America and of the practical philanthropy of the manufacturing mind in England. It is almost identical with the "Manchester School," and its expounders came from both the other parties; for it has sometimes acted with one, sometimes with another: coalescing with the Whigs, it carried the Reform Bill; with the Tories it wrought out Catholic emancipation and the Repeal of the Corn Laws. It is a cautious, businesslike, vigorous party, and at present seems in a fair way to swallow the Liberal party with which it is allied uneasily. When one sees "Punch" and the "Times," after twenty years of scurrility, to praise John Bright, he may know that to be a Radical is almost fashionable now. Even the "Saturday Review," a representatively vicious English periodical straining to be a more snarling sort of "Times," says that within a few years the whole scheme of Conservative belief is shaken to the foundation. "Things which a short time ago were accounted very dreadful are now spoken of as the most natural and innocent things in the world. Men like Mr. Bright, who were deemed a pest to decent society, are now flattered and courted, and hold themselves out successfully as the kind patrons of the government. There is scarcely any political opinion held so steadfastly in England that we cannot now easily conceive it fading away, and there is no man of anything like real intellectual force whose career we can anticipate. Changes in the relations of the governed to their governors, in the relations of the poor and the rich, in the relations of the Church to the State, and to modern thought, — changes that a short time ago seemed quite chimerical, — now float before every one as entering the range, not only of possibility, but of a not very remote probability."

An American sometimes speaks of his political traditions, meaning that his father was of the same party with himself; but there is no place where opinion differs so widely as at an American breakfast-table. We hear of "old line" Whigs — but where are the young Whigs?—and of "straight-out" Democrats; but the present anti-Democratic party in America derives its best strength from the sons of the enthusiasts for Jackson. An opinion here invites no spleen; an American father is apt to think his son individual and pluckful if he differs from his "traditions." From the son-in-law of Thomas Benton, the sturdiest Democrat in America, came the first Republican candidate for the Presidency; and it frequently happened in the civil war, that from the same hearthstone went a son into the army of the North, and one into the army of the South. The politician in America begins almost in the cradle; but the party man in England began in his great-grandfather. None are politicians there, in any influential sense, unless they are rich or "gentle;" and until within a few years past politics in England were guided entirely by "family" considerations. The House of Bedford is always Whig, — why so? Family! The King once cut off the head of John Russell, and that made the Russells Whigs for indefinite futurity.

The House of Derby is always conservative, — why? The Stanleys rallied round their sovereign, and that circle can never untwist. When we find a person of this type in America, we generally exhibit him as a spectacle, and treat him mildly and kindly, saying, "Lo! the poor Indian!"

There is a reason for all this English doggedness, curious as it may appear, as there is reason, also, for our family centrifugalism. We have no very strong family instinct after the second generation; we quit the family hearthstone in New York, or New England, or Maryland, and occupy some frontier neighborhood, so that our "traditions" are soon lost, and we then take party positions, not according to our memory, but according to our newspaper, our pastor, our prejudice, our immediate interest, and often according to our impulse of principle. We often vote many ways in our lives, going about from party to party as we like; sometimes because we love the candidate, sometimes because we feel the sweep of public revolution, sometimes because we have "read up" some question and changed convictions upon it.

But in cramped England there is no moving to far frontiers; there is little change of occupation or interest; the close boundaries of the island keep us to our neighborhood, and the roof-tree, like a warning tombstone, points out the party affiliations we must assume. It says, "Here my ancestors were Whigs! here are all their portraits! out of their party they chose their boon-companions, and of the same are my friends yet. It is abandoning the graveyard, it is apostasy to acquaintanceship, it is infidelity to superstition, to vault because of an author or an idea from the venerable of the old to the apparent of the new!"

Nevertheless, in England as here, there are politicians, who, by dint of the lust of power, of the hate of the rival family's promotion, and by wider experience in the world of easy pivots, often conclude to reverse an ancient principle to avoid the loss of place. These struggle hard to carry their party over, and generally succeed, after a tremendous culinary tempest, by appealing to the same old clique-spirit. "If the family of De Bodford, Whigs, cater to the new public sentiment, and elect their man, then I, De Squodford, Tory, must come down from court and privilege, and submit to be patronized, or to be sulky. Never! I will accept the hateful innovation first."

It has thus happened that the Liberal party has often been conservative, and the Conservative party truly magnanimous. At different times both have been for land, both for Free Trade. "Can any one be so blind," says Lord Brougham, "as to believe that if Burke and Fox had been ministers of George III., they would rather have resigned than make an attempt to subdue America?" — "No!" says Junius, the covert satirist, "Mr. Pitt and Lord Camden were to be the patrons of America, because they were in the opposition."

Party spirit in England is equally unscrupulous with politician spirit here.

The Whigs attempted to get into office in the time of George IV., by means of the public sympathy over the trial of Queen Caroline, his wife, just as the Republicans in America attempted to secure the Presidency by the Impeachment of Andrew Johnson. The Tories, to get Lord Melbourne's Cabinet out, got a Mrs. Norton to accuse him of criminal conversation with her, just as the American Jeffersonians accused Hamilton of a female intrigue, to drive him from office.

French Democracy, in England, was most successfully argued by Jeremy Bentham, and a Jew, Ricardo. Major Cartwright was the earliest and most persistent American Republican in England. Joseph Hume was one of the earliest Radicals. There have been many small parties in England, organized upon special issues, and in the humbler walks of English life almost every grade of opinion may be found; but in England, as here, the two great parties of Liberal and Conservative keep their ranks closed, though they sometimes change the mottoes on the banners, and the tune upon the drums.

The apparent failure of the efforts made in New England, and some of the Middle and Western States, ten years ago, to annihilate the trade in spirituous, and even in malt liquors, has recently (1869) been revived, — in Massachusetts particularly. At one time the State of Delaware maintained the anomaly of a prohibitory liquor law, and, at the same time, whipping-posts and pillories; a man could be egged in the market-place, but nowhere egg-nogged. The temperance question is a test question with a large minority of voters, in such States as Maine and Michigan, where they have refused to vote their party ticket without a temperance declaration appended to its platform. In England, attempts were made, as recently as 1869, to pass a "permissive bill" through Parliament, making it possible to embarrass or prevent the sale of liquors in any parish where two-thirds of the poor-rate payers said nay. The bill was lost by a decisive vote, though in England, as in America, the women, *en masse*, petitioned for the prohibition. Beer (strong ale) and gin are the national drinks in England, as lager beer and whiskey are with us.

Mr. John Bright has several times proposed, in England, to raise a party cry of "A Free Breakfast Table," with the object of taking the taxes off tea, coffee, and sugar. While there are stronger reasons for prohibitory liquor laws in England than with us, — as there the percentage of drunkards is greater, and is, even with women, large, — their enactment is probably very far off; for excepting a certain portion of the Dissenters, there is no great moral reform element in England, at all corresponding with the Puritan and the Methodist elements here.

The Native American, or "Know Nothing" party, of 1844, revived in 1855, was a formidable expression of the prejudice of the native-born and Protestant elements against the rapid inroads of foreigners upon citizenship, and the suffrage, and against the supposed aggressions of the Catholic Church. In 1844 the party culminated in formidable riots, and in 1856 it reared itself again upon a secret order, like that of the Jesuits it denounced. The prudence of the people believed that, with some drawbacks, immigration was still the great current of our nation's wealth and life, and not to be discouraged; and also that Protestantism could get no advantage in politics. The great party melted away as speedily as it arose, and few of its leaders now care to shoulder their propositions propounded at that time.

Another American party was raised against Free Masonry, which developed William H. Seward and Thaddeus Stevens.

In England there have been popular outcries against the Jews and Catholics, and "No Popery" is still a bitter whisper amongst the Dissenters. In 1850, the Pope proclaimed a Catholic Hierarchy for Great Britain, which caused the Queen to go beside herself, and she hastened to Lord John Russell to ask if she were supreme within her own realms. A terrible tempest of prejudice followed, and an Ecclesiastical Hierarchy bill was passed through Parliament, which became a dead letter like many American laws; everybodg yrew cool and remorseful, and the Pope's cardinals, etc., were unmolested.

The question of the ballot for women is advocated in England by John Stuart Mill, a political economist, as here by a number of able men and women; but in either country its triumph seems a long way off. Its adoption would certainly be the most formidable change ever witnessed in society and morals, probably to the advantage of men, and to the injury of women. We should cease to get drunk, and they would cease to be gentle.

Free Trade, is, as we have said, no longer the policy of any party in England; but in America it has developed into a formidable party question, although it was formidable here nearly forty years ago: —

"On the 1st October, 1831, the Free Trade Assembly, which," says De Tocqueville, "according to the American custom, had taken the name of a convention, met at Philadelphia; it consisted of more than two hundred members. Its debates were public, and they at once assumed a legislative character. The extent of the powers of Congress, the theories of Free Trade, and the different clauses of the Tariff were discussed in turn. At the end of ten days' deliberation, the convention broke up, after having published an address to the American people, in which it declared: —

"I. That Congress had not the right of making a Tariff, and that the existing Tariff was unconstitutional.

"II. That the prohibition of Free Trade was prejudicial to the interests of all nations, and to that of the American people in particular."

With its usual tact, the Democratic party, which has now been out of power several years, is setting sail toward Free Trade, with the hope of luring to its organization the million or more of Republican Free Trade voters. This was a Democratic principle long ago, and in the "late" war, we carried at our mast-heads: "Free Trade and Sailor's Rights;" but the Democratic party in 1868 declared for "Protection" in its platform, while the Republicans were afraid to speak of the subject at all. The politicians on both sides wanted both, or neither, or either; but both of them wanted the people. A movement has been made amongst the Irish voters in America, in favor of "Protection," it being argued to them that a High Tariff will cripple England; and thus it is possible that we may yet see old eastern Whigs and Irishmen coalesce against southern Democrats and western Republicans. The Free Traders are as yet of both great parties here, led mainly by James W. Grimes, James Brooks, Horace White, Murat Halstead, William C. Bryant, Henry Ward Beecher, and William Lloyd Garrison.

I have already alluded to the opinion, generally prevalent, that Sir Robert Peel was the first of English statesman. Let us see what were his public acts: —

He improved the administration of law, and renovated the police; he brought England from an inconvertible to a sound currency; he obtained Catholic Emancipation; he carried Free Trade for England; he refused a peerage, and enjoined his children to remain commoners.

When Peel died, a small but respectable party was organized upon his memory and policy, and its adherents were called "Peelites;" they were utilitarians, and believed in reduced armies and navies, non-intervention, and a simple government, but in part administered by bureaucracy.

While these are the leading English parties, there is also amongst the disfranchised in England, a formidable organization, which seeks to give the working-man a separate power in the administration of labor. It is this vast organization which is underlying England, like internal fire, sometimes forgotten, but always present, and only smouldering. When the Chartist excitement in England was highest, the operatives threatened to quit work over the whole kingdom unless their demands were acceded to.

The Trades-Union system, of America, exists in even stricter organization than in England, and enters as a power into politics, but generally, it must be confessed, in the interests of labor and poverty.

At present the Trades-Unions of the United Kingdom are by some thought to be its greatest apparent danger. They are an *imperium in imperio*, in which insufferable tyranny is exercised by workingmen over their fellows, from which there seems to be no escape but by the gradual process of education.

The laws provide protection and remedy; but recourse to that protection is prevented by the same oppression. "It is remarkable," says Harriet Martineau, "that the one intolerable despotism which at this day exists in England is found, not in the government, not in the land-owners, not in the old-fashioned rural districts, but in the modern democratic towns,—the despotism of working-men over fellow-workers in their own class, and their own trade. This is a peril which may occur in a republic, and especially if the employers possess the sort of monopoly created by a Protective system." In the United States the Federal government has already come into direct conflict with the Trades-Unions, which latter assumed to regulate prices, and prescribe the color of trades-employés in the government workshops. It is not probable that the dignity of a State will consent to compromise upon this question with merely masonic bodies, confederated not only in their own private interests, but against the wider interests of labor at large.

The following was the great popular hymn, sung at the mass meetings to agitate for the Reform Bill, and it is as historic in England as is John Brown's song with us: —

"Lo! we answer! see, we come,
Quick at Freedom's holy call:
We come! we come! we come! we come!
To do the glorious work of all;
And hark! we raise from sea to sea
The sacred watchword, Liberty!

"God is our guide! from field, from wave,
From plough, from anvil, and from loom,
We come, our country's right to save,
And speak a tyrant faction's doom.
And hark! we raise from sea to sea
The sacred watchword, Liberty!

"God is our guide, no swords we draw,
We kindle not war's battle-fires;
By union, justice, reason, law,
We claim the birthright of our sires.
We raise the watchword, Liberty!
We will, we will, we will be free."

Except at the period of the civil war, the lyric has played a small part in American politics. Our national anthem is itself an adaptation. We have had, outside of the slavery discussion, no such energetic poet as the English Corn Law rhymer, Elliott. Perhaps the only American who sent his muse upon partisan errands was Charles G. Halpine, a naturalized Irishman, who gained an important local office in New York, the Registership, valued at forty thousand dollars a year, and almost sheerly by the popularity of his rhymes on partisan topics.

The foreign element in England does not play a like important part with ours, and there are, therefore, no such pieces of literature there as this of General Halpine. The allusions to the wigwam, etc., are merely local to New York: —

"Say, here! How is it, misther —
Are you for the Boy, or no?
For he's bound to be Re-gisther,
Let the wind blow high or low.

All the Germans an' the Irish here
For him have dhrawn the skean,
For Von Halpine trinks zwei lager bier,
And Miles he 'wears the green.'

"'He's too young'? Your granny's sisther!
I tell you 'tisn't so;
An' he's bound to be Re-gisther,
Let the wind blow high or low.
All the Celtic and the Teuton vote
Are friends of his, I ween,
For Von Halpine schpeist mit pretzel brodt,
And Miles on mild poteen.

"Oh, the Wigwam wants a glysther
For to purge away her ills;
So we'll make him our Re-gisther,
An' he'll bate even Radway's pills.
All the girls are for him; this is how
That wondher came to pass, —
Von Halpine liebt ein blond-e frau,
And Miles an Irish lass.

"May my tongue be all a blisther
If I tell a lie to you,
For he's bound to be Re-gisther,
And we all must put him through.
Oh, he suits the men of every race,
This gossoon undefiled, —
Von Halpine schpeist mit Schweitzer Kaase,
An' the Boy on p'raties biled.

"So here's to Hans von Halpine,
And to Miles who wears the green;
Fill your can and dhrink it all, man,
Or in Rhine wein or poteen;
For Miles he fit mit Sigel,
And mit Asboth trinks poteen;
And you can't find Halpine's equal
For 'a-wearing of the green.'"

The Irish Catholic vote, in Parliament, is frequently a balance of power which an English politician must consult. The press of London, even more perhaps than that of New York, is written up by Irishmen, and Irish rioting in London has been witnessed in nearly equal magnitude with that of the draft riots in New York, in 1863. We have this race of combative people distributed amongst us; but had we an Ireland in America, returning upwards of one hundred Irish members to the House of Representatives, we should find the Irish problem difficult indeed to solve. Foreigners are naturalized in England with great nicety of discrimination, and by Act of Parliament for each individual case. The Home Secretary may also give a certificate, affording limited privileges to the alien, and the crown may, by patent, create "Denizens." But of wholesale naturalization, such as we extend, there is no instance in English history. It is easy for a foreign prince to reach the English throne, but hard for a foreigner to become an English subject. The greatest immigration to England was from the Low Countries, the Rhine and France, during the religious wars. The right of exile is always respected there.

By English law, extraordinary and unwonted means of influencing political elections are forbidden, such as torchlight processions, parades, bands of music, the wearing of emblems, free-lunches and free-whiskey; and although the latter of these clauses is often avoided, it must be confessed that an English campaign is generally left more to the taste, and less to the excitement, of the elector than with us. Huge torchlight processions and sensuous political exhibitions have been carried to excess here; to their abuse we owe the frequent riotous behavior of excitable classes of our people. The English candidates address the people, and frequently the opponents speak together; in general, with personal courtesy the one toward the other, a chairman being appointed. Each candidate has his election agents, who get out his bills, visit the people, and canvass the district, and these must be paid their salaries through an auditor, who is appointed by the government returning officer.

The place of nominating candidates is called the "Hustings," and is generally a mere platform, or booth, where the Sheriff reads his proclamation ordering an election, the people standing by. If only the number of nominations are made that will fill the seats, they are both (or all) declared elected. If there be more candidates than seats, the Sheriff asks for a show of hands and declares who is elected; but if his count is disputed he orders a poll. The election is then adjourned till the polling day, and meantime, all the arts of wheedling, "seeing," etc., are employed. At the election the borough, or county, is divided into districts, and there is a poll in each, where all vote, but not by ballot, and this enables every bystander to hear the choice of every voter. The poor protest against this, because their employers or landlords can punish them afterward by way of revenge for an adverse vote. The English, allege, however, that a stealthy vote takes away a man's independence; but this seems no worse than taking away both his independence and his farm.

A candidate for office in America is generally earnest to obtain the vote of some party nominating convention, or, on rare occasions, private citizens in concert nominate him, and procure him the support of a newspaper and a purse; he then takes the "stump," or makes speeches to those he solicits for his constituents. The party convention plays a lesser part in England; the candidate himself presents his name to the electors, and organizes his committee to help him canvass the district. Here is an illustration: —

"TO THE ELECTORS OF THE EASTERN DIVISION OF STAFFORDSHIRE.

"GENTLEMEN: I take this early opportunity of announcing myself as a CANDIDATE to REPRESENT your important District in the ensuing PARLIAMENT.

"For upwards of twenty years I have been connected with the county, and have furthered its canals, railways, waterworks, and public enterprises generally. My interest in the progress of the county is close, personal, and permanent.

"My political opinions are Liberal, and I have always given an active and consistent support to the principles advocated by the great Liberal party.

"I am a warm supporter of Mr. Gladstone, and should vote for the disestablishment of the Irish Church. This measure of justice conceded, the constitutional rights so long suspended will again be enjoyed by the people of Ireland in common with the other subjects of the Queen.

"I am prepared to support in Parliament an extensive scheme of National Education, believing as I do that knowledge is not merely power, but wealth, and that to educate the people is to increase their own means of enjoyment, while substantially adding to the productive riches of the country.

"Should you do me the honor to return me to Parliament as your Representative, the task of watching over the important local affairs of a county, in the prosperity of which I am so deeply interested, would be at all times a natural and agreeable duty.

"I am, gentlemen,
"Your obedient servant,
"JOHN ROBINSON M'CLEAN,
"Bridgeman Place, Walsall.

"10th July, 1868."

The want of the ballot in England is, next to the want of electors and a true electoral spirit, the pressing need. With us the pressing need is some way of escape from the thraldom of caucuses and nominating conventions, wherein our candidates are really selected, and we have no hope but that one of these may be a good one. There is no such thing in England as a vast nominating convention to adopt a platform and candidates. From his residence in London the head of the party summons his supporters to a private banquet, and there the policy stealthily agreed upon becomes the platform of the party. Says Brougham, "The game which falls a sacrifice to party are the noblest principles; the nation is deluded, and its aristocratic masters ascribe to it their own opinions. The nation itself is nothing but a toy and tool of the aristocracy."

In America the game which falls sacrifice to party is the public revenue and the public franchises; but through the strife of parties we generally get the man of our choice, and a promise, at least, of the policy we wish. The English have the defective system, and we have the defective character under the system. The people can reform our politics if they will, but only revolution, or the submission of the aristocracy, can reform the English system.

We all remember how the anti-slavery movement began in this Northern country; an author or two, a preacher or two, a newspaper or two, a novel or two, and the Quakers, — these began it. The opposition to the anti-slavery party was tremendous, and it came oftentimes from the most pious citizens; all the religious denominations were conservative; all the staid populations were deprecatory of this agitation; violence, rail-ridings, tar and feathers, were employed to stop the hubbub; it went on; it conquered the quiet elements one by one; the politicians felt the slow shifting of the wind and tacked over; we suddenly found we were all "there," when each one thought only himself "there."

Not without parallel is the case of the Reform Bill in England, which I reproduce from various authorities to show how a political reform must be carried in England: the under masses make a noise and threaten slaughter, and the upper classes relent in time, the politicians of each party taking position according to the best contingencies. With the latter part of the year 1816 arose a popular demand for a reform in the English parliamentary representation. "At this time," says Bumford, in his "Life of a Radical," "the writings of William Cobbett suddenly became of great authority; they were read on nearly every hearth in the manufacturing districts of South Lancashire, in those of Leicester, Derby, and Nottingham; also in many of the Scottish manufacturing towns. Their influence was speedily visible. He directed his readers to the true cause of their sufferings, — misgovernment, — and to its proper correction, — parliamentary reform. Riots soon became scarce, and from that time they have never obtained their ancient vogue, with the laborers of England." "Let us not descend to be unjust," says one, "let us not withhold the homage which, with all the faults of William Cobbett, is still due to his great name. Instead of riots and destruction of property, Hampden Clubs were now established in many of our large towns, and the villages and districts around them! Cobbett's books were printed in a cheap form; the laborers read them, and thenceforward became deliberate and systematic in their proceedings. Nor were there wanting men of their own class to encourage and direct the new converts; the Sunday schools of the preceding thirty years had produced many working-men of sufficient talent to become readers, writers, and speakers in the village meetings for parliamentary reform; some also were found to possess a rude poetic talent, which rendered their effusions popular, and bestowed an additional charm on their assemblages; and by such various means anxious listeners at first, and then zealous proselytes, were drawn from the cottages of quiet nooks and dingles to the weekly readings and discourses of the Hampden Clubs. One of these clubs was established in 1816, at the small town of Middleton, near Manchester; and I, having been instrumental in its formation, a tolerable reader also, and a rather expert writer, was chosen Secretary. The club prospered; the number of members increased; the funds, raised by subscription of a penny a week, became more than sufficient for all outgoings; and taking a bold step we soon rented a chapel, which had been given up by a society of Kilhamite Methodists. This place we threw open for the religious worship of all sects and parties, and there we held our meetings, on the evenings of Monday and Saturday in each week. The proceedings of our society, its place of meeting, — singular as being the first place of meeting occupied by Reformers (for so in those days we were termed), together with the services of religion connected with us, drew a considerable share of public attention to our transactions, and obtained for the leaders some notoriety. Several meetings of delegates from the surrounding districts were held at our chapel, on which occasions the leading reformers of Lancashire were generally seen together."

From these little assemblies, as with our anti-slavery lyceums, the work of reform began, and by dint of vigorous meetings, with opposition of all sorts, even to armed force, the workingmen's movement rolled on till it reached Parliament, with cries of distress and with petitions, slowly turning the hearts of the middle class, and, at last, after fourteen years it passed the House of Commons and went up to the Lords. There it was turned back, amidst the execrations of the people, who heard of its failure with despair.

The confusion in the nation that resulted in this failure is thus ably told by Cooke, who, though a partisan, is yet sufficiently accurate: —

"The House of Commons immediately passed a vote of confidence in those ministers who had carried the Reform Bill. The King interposed a short prorogation, expressly for the purpose that the bill might be again introduced. The speech was couched in terms which plainly indicated that the sovereign continued faithful. Every method was adopted which could palliate the news of the rejection of the bill, and avert the thunder-storm which threatened. The Whigs were in a great measure successful; the lightning did not strike the lofty towers of our monarchy, nor strip off the Gothic fretwork of our House of Peers; but strange sights were seen throughout the nation; and a voice had gone forth which told that the end was not yet. In London, tens of thousands of men, marching in close array and crowding all the avenues to the palace; the houses of the Tory peers in a constant state of siege, the peers themselves venturing abroad at the danger of their lives; in the metropolis of a generous people, the Duke of Wellington, whose reputation is his country's glory, unable to appear without insult and danger; in a metropolis of a people remarkable for their respect to the laws, Lord Londonderry struck senseless from his horse by a flight of stones; in the country, Nottingham Castle, the ancient possession of the Duke of New Castle given to the flames; Derby in the power of the mob, the gaol destroyed, the houses of the known Tories demolished; the city of Bristol on fire, and Sir Charles Wetherell fleeing in disguise by the light of the conflagration. Men of all grades banded together in unions, pledged at any cost to obtain Parliamentary reform; a hundred and fifty thousand assembled at Birmingham and threatening to march upon London, — these were the signs of the times, varied by public meetings all over the country, comprehending nearly the whole mass of the middle classes, and a large portion of the aristocracy, who joined in the expression of indignant surprise, that a 'whisper of a faction' should be allowed to render abortive the express desire of a nation."

The same writer continues: "Well was the national sentiment expressed and sustained by the press. Morning and evening did these batteries of reform pour their incessant fire, and the noise reverberated through the kingdom. A very large majority of the journals were in the interest of the Whigs and the people, but the combined powers of all the rest of these shrink into insignificance, when compared with that of the leader of them, a paper which, in the pride of conscious power, had styled itself the leading journal of Europe. Never was there so tremendous a party engine as the period of which we are now treating presents. The receptacle of talent sufficient to form three brilliant reputations, backed by the admiration, the applause, the obedience of a nation, it is impossible to look back upon its career without strong excitement; to see it guiding, counselling, exhorting, exciting, moving onwards, exulting in its own might; crushing at a blow the incipient reputation of any Tory in whom it discerned talent that might render him formidable, yet stooping to cherish and to draw forth into blossom the smallest bud that might be discovered amongst its own party.

"Its advocacy of the party it espoused was not confined to forcible leading articles, and to able argument; in all those numberless acts by which a party may be strengthened or injured this journal was perfect. The principal conductor of that paper appeared, placed, like the listener in the ear of Dionysius, in a focus of sound, whither the most secret whisper and the loudest clamor were alike wafted. Yet great as was the influence of the 'Times,' it only blew the flame, — it did not ignite it. The 'Times' was supporting the Duke of Wellington's administration, and repeating his declaration against reform without disapproval, when it caught the murmur of the coming storm, and with infinite tact prepared to ride it."

Other symptoms of this great political period in England liken it to the news in the North at the capture of Fort Sumter.

The mail roads were sprinkled over for miles with people who were on the watch for news from London; and the passengers on the tops of the coaches shouted the tidings, or threw down handbills to tell that the Ministry had resigned. Then was there such mourning throughout England as had not been known for many years. Men forsook their business to meet and consult what they should do. In some places the bells tolled; in others they were muffled.

The ministers resigned on Wednesday. On the morning of Thursday the news reached Manchester. It was circulated with inconceivable rapidity, and created a sensation beyond description. Its effect upon the markets was startling. Orders were at once countermanded. The shopkeepers left their places of business, and ran about asking, "What is to be done now?" The working-people in every part of the town gathered into little knots, and expressed their hatred of those whose intrigues had prevailed over the voice of twenty-four millions of people. A public meeting was held in the Town Hall, and a petition to the House of Commons unanimously agreed to. The petition prayed the House of Commons that they would assert their own collective dignity, and the indefeasible right of their fellow-subjects by determined adherence to the bill, and by refusing to vote any supplies until a measure essential to the happiness of the people and the safety of the throne should be carried into a law.

By such determined proceedings must every reform be carried in Great Britain, and yet the triumph of the Reform Bill is hailed with joy by almost every Englishman now. In 1866, when John Bright was hailed by his constituents of Birmingham with the gladness of a mighty multitude, a scene transpired to show how well the English masses recollected that vital campaign. It was an open-air meeting; two hundred thousand people were present; all was enthusiasm. The incident was thus described by an eye-witness: —

"It was at Newhall Hill that the most interesting event of the day occurred. This spot was, thirty-four years ago, the scene of the celebrated meeting of the union. The purpose of the assembly of the 7th of May, 1832, was to petition the House of Lords to pass Earl Grey's Reform Bill. The hill at that day was unbuilt upon, and covered twelve acres in extent. In dismissing the meeting its chairman, Mr. Atwood, used these words: 'My good friends, before we depart I will call upon you again to exhibit a spectacle of loyalty and devotion. Our good King is entitled to the deepest gratitude of his people. I therefore desire that you will, all of you, take off your hats, and that you will lift up your eyes to heaven where the just God rules over heaven and earth; and that you will, all of you, cry out with one heart and voice, "God bless the King!"' The united prayer went up with a sound as of thunder. It was upon this spot where the meeting to which we have thus alluded was held, that an event occurred to-day to which allusion must be made. Here four cross-roads meet, and as far as the eye could reach there was but one dense mass of people, — every avenue being choked with human beings. The carriage containing Mr. Bright was here stopped, and the honorable gentleman mounted the seat of the vehicle, and, amid the greatest excitement and cheering, pointed with his hand up Newhall Hill. The allusion was understood by the thousands who witnessed the act, and it was the signal for some of the most deafening cheers we have ever heard."

During the American war I attended several of the great meetings of sympathy with the United States, at Exeter Hall and at St. James' Hall. There were no bands, no banners, — only representative orators like Bright, Thompson, Stanfield, and Beals, and an immense outpouring of the working-classes, all earnest, decorous, and honest. I felt that others might claim to be our friends, but that these were so. Amongst them were various young "snobs" and students, saying surly things against America and making diversions. One of these said: —

"That Lincoln's only a rail-splitter and a boatman."

"Well!" said a workingman, "I think the Americans were quite right in doing honor to a poor man, one of themselves."

"Who's here for America?" said the other, — "Nobodies like Newman Hall."

"Newman Hall a nobody," said the workingman, quickly, "then perhaps you are nobody! And what is Baptist Noel?"

"Oh! Baptist Noel is a *gentleman*, I confess!"

Baptist Noel, though a friend of America, was the relative of a nobleman, and not the former fact, but the latter, made him a gentleman.

To sketch an English election is a legitimate topic of this chapter; but I know of no place where there is a consecutive account of an actual parliamentary borough contest to be found, and therefore rely upon that of Thackeray in his story of "The Newcomes," which is circumstantial, life-like, and curiously descriptive of English manners and habits. The occasion was a family quarrel between Colonel Tom Newcome and his nephew Sir Barnes Newcome, which led to the former going into the latter's district with an eccentric electioneering friend, Fred Bayham, to beat Sir Barnes for Parliament: —

"There were four candidates in the field for the representation of that borough. That old and tried member of Parliament, Mr. Bunce, was considered to be secure; and the baronet's seat was thought to be pretty safe, on account of his influence in the place. Nevertheless,

Thomas Newcome's supporters were confident for their champion, and that, when the parties came to the poll, the extreme Liberals of the borough would divide their votes between him and the fourth candidate, the uncompromising Radical, Mr. Barker.

"In due time the Colonel and his staff arrived at Newcome, and resumed the active canvass which they had commenced some months previously. The lawyer, the editor of the 'Independent,' and F. B., the adventurer, were the Colonel's chief men. His head-quarters (which F. B. liked very well) were at the hotel where we last saw them, and whence issuing with his aide-de-camp at his heels, the Colonel went round, to canvass personally, according to his promise, every free and independent elector of the borough. Barnes, his relative and opponent too, was canvassing eagerly on his side, and was most affable and active; the two parties would often meet nose to nose in the same street, and their retainers exchange looks of defiance. With Mr. Polts, of the 'Independent,' a big man, on his left; with Mr. Fredereck, a still bigger man, on his right; his own trusty bamboo cane in his hand, before which poor Barnes had shrunk abashed ere now, Colonel Newcome had commonly the best of these street encounters, and frowned his nephew, Barnes, and Barnes's staff off the pavement. With the non-electors, the Colonel was a decided favorite; the boys invariably hurrahed him; whereas they jeered and uttered ironical cries after poor Barnes, asking, 'Who beat his wife? Who drove his children to the work-house?' and other unkind personal questions. The working-man upon whom the libertine Barnes had inflicted so cruel an injury in his early days was now the baronet's bitterest enemy. He assailed him with curses and threats when they met, and leagued his brother workmen against him. The wretched Sir Barnes owned with contrition that the sins of his youth pursued him; his enemy scoffed at the idea of Barnes's repentance; he was not moved at the grief, the punishment in his own family; the humiliation and remorse which the repentant prodigal piteously pleaded. No man was louder in his cries of *mea culpa* than Barnes; no man professed a more edifying repentance. He was hat in hand to every black coat (preachers), established or dissenting. Repentance was to his interest, to be sure; but yet let us hope it was sincere. There is some hypocrisy, of which one does not like even to entertain the thought; especially that awful falsehood which trades with divine truth, and takes the name of Heaven in vain.

"The Roebuck Inn, at Newcome, stands in the market-place, directly facing the King's Arms, where, as we know, Colonel Newcome and uncompromising toleration held their head-quarters. Immense banners of blue and yellow floated from every window of the King's Arms, and decorated the balcony from which the Colonel and his assistants were in the habit of addressing the multitude. Fiddlers and trumpeters arrayed in his colors paraded the town, and enlivened it with their melodious strains. Other trumpeters and fiddlers, bearing the true-blue cockades and colors of Sir Barnes Newcome, Bart., would encounter the Colonel's musicians, on which occasions of meeting it is to be feared small harmony was produced. They banged each other with their brazen instruments. The warlike drummers thumped each other's heads in lieu of the professional sheepskin. The town-boys and street blackguards rejoiced in these combats, and exhibited their valor on one side or the other. The Colonel had to pay a long bill for broken brass when he settled the little accounts of the election.

"In after times, F. Bayham was pleased to describe the circumstances of a contest in which he bore a most distinguished part. It was F. B.'s opinion that his private eloquence brought over many waverers to the Colonel's side, and converted numbers of the benighted followers of Sir Barnes Newcome. Bayham's voice was indeed magnificent, and could be heard from the King's Arms balcony above the shout and roar of the multitude, the gongs and bugles of the opposition bands. He was untiring in his oratory, undaunted in the presence of the crowds below. He was immensely popular, F. B. Whether he laid his hand upon his broad chest, took off his hat and waved it, or pressed his blue-and-yellow ribbons to his bosom, the crowd shouted, 'Hurra! silence! bravo! Bayham forever!' 'They would have carried me in triumph,' said F. B. 'If I had but the necessary qualification I might be member for Newcome this day, or any other I chose.'

"I am afraid in this conduct of the Colonel's election Mr. Bayham resorted to acts of which his principal certainly would disapprove, and engaged auxiliaries whose alliance was scarcely creditable. Whose was the hand that flung the potato which struck Sir Barnes Newcome, Bart., on the nose as he was haranguing the people from the Roebuck? How came it that whenever Sir Barnes and his friends essayed to speak, such an awful yelling and groaning took place in the crowd below, that the words of those feeble orators were inaudible? Who smashed all the front windows of the Roebuck? Colonel

Newcome had not words to express his indignation at proceedings so unfair. When Sir Barnes and his staff were hustled in the market-place and most outrageously shoved, jeered, and jolted, the Colonel from the King's Arms organized a rapid sally, which he himself headed with his bamboo cane; cut out Sir Barnes and his followers from the hands of the mob, and addressed those ruffians in a noble speech, of which the 'bamboo cane,' 'Englishman,' 'shame,' 'fair-play,' were the most emphatic expressions. The mob cheered old Tom, as they called him; they made way for Sir Barnes, who shrunk pale and shuddering back into his hotel again,— who always persisted in saying that that old villain of a dragoon had planned both the assault and the rescue.

"'When the dregs of the people, — the scum of the rabble, sir, banded together by the myrmidons of Sir Barnes Newcome, attacked us at the King's Arms, and smashed ninety-six pounds' worth of glass at one volley, besides knocking off the gold unicorn's head and the tail of the British lion; it was fine, sir,' F. B. said, 'to see how the Colonel came forward, and the coolness of the old boy in the midst of the action. He stood there in front, sir, with his old hat off, never so much as once bobbing his old head, and I think he spoke rather better under fire than he did when there was no danger. Between ourselves, he aint much of a speaker, the old Colonel; he hems and haws, and repeats himself a good deal. He hasn't the gift of natural eloquence which some men have. You should have heard my speech, sir, on the Thursday in the Town Hall, — that was something like a speech. Potts was jealous of it, and always reported me most shamefully.'

"In spite of his respectable behavior to the gentlemen in black coats, his soup tickets and his flannel tickets, his own pathetic lectures and his sedulous attendance at other folks' sermons, poor Barnes could not keep up his credit with the serious interest at Newcome, and the meeting-houses and their respective pastors and frequenters turned their backs upon him. The case against him was too flagrant; his enemy, the factory-man, worked it with an extraordinary skill, malice, and pertinacity. Not a single man, woman, or child in Newcome but was made acquainted with Sir Barnes's early peccadillo. Ribald ballads were howled through the streets describing his sin and his deserved punishment. For very shame, the reverend dissenting gentlemen were obliged to refrain from voting for him; such as ventured, believing in the sincerity of his repentance, to give him their voices, were yelled away from the polling-places. A very great number who would have been his friends, were compelled to bow to decency and public opinion, and supported the Colonel.

"Hooted away from the hustings, and the public places whence the rival candidates addressed the free and independent electors, this wretched and persecuted Sir Barnes invited his friends and supporters to meet him at the Athenæum Room,— scene of his previous eloquent performances. But, though this apartment was defended by tickets, the people burst into it; and Nemesis, in the shape of the persevering factory-man, appeared before the scared Sir Barnes and his puzzled committee. The man stood up and bearded the pale baronet. He had a good cause, and was in truth a far better master of debate than our banking friend, being a great speaker among his brother operatives, by whom political questions are discussed, and the conduct of political men examined, with a ceaseless interest, and with an order and eloquence which are often unknown in what is called superior society. This man and his friends round about him fiercely silenced the clamor of 'Turn him out,' with which his first appearance was assailed by Sir Barnes's hangers-on. He said, in the name of justice he would speak up; if they were fathers of families and loved their wives and daughters he dared them to refuse him a hearing. Did they love their wives and their children? It was a shame that they should take such a man as that yonder for their representative in Parliament. But the greatest sensation he made was when in the middle of his speech, after inveighing against Barnes's cruelty and parental ingratitude, he asked, 'Where were Barnes's children?' and actually thrust forward two, to the amazement of the committee and the ghastly astonishment of the guilty baronet himself.

"'Look at them,' says the man; 'they are almost in rags; they have to put up with scanty and hard food; contrast them with his other children, whom you see lording in gilt carriages, robed in purple and fine linen, and scattering mud from their wheels over us humble people as we walk the streets; ignorance and starvation is good enough for these, for those others nothing can be too fine or too dear. What can a factory girl expect from such a fine, high-bred, white-handed, aristocratic gentleman as Sir Barnes Newcome, Baronet, but to be cajoled, and seduced, and deserted, and left to starve? When she has served my lord's pleasure, her natural fate is to be turned into the streets; let her go and rot there, and her children beg in the gutter.'

54

"'This is the most shameful imposture,' gasps out Sir Barnes; 'these children are not — are not —'

"The man interrupted him with a bitter laugh.

"'No,' says he, 'they are not his; that's true enough, friends. It's Tom Martin's girl and boy,— a precious pair of lazy little scamps. But at first he *thought* they were his children. See how much he knows about them! He hasn't seen his children for years; he would have left them and their mother to starve and die, but for shame and fear. The old man, his father, pensioned them, and he hasn't the heart to stop their wages now. Men of Newcome, will you have this man to represent you in Parliament?' and the crowd roared out, 'No;' and Barnes and his shame-faced committee slunk out of the place, and no wonder the dissenting clerical gentlemen were shy of voting for him.

"A brilliant and picturesque diversion in Colonel Newcome's favor was due to the inventive genius of his faithful aide-de-camp, F. B. On the polling-day, as the carriages full of voters came up to the market-place, there appeared nigh to the booths an open barouche, covered all over with ribbon, and containing Frederick Bayham, Esq., profusely decorated with the Colonel's colors, and a very old woman and her female attendant, who were similarly ornamented. It was good old Mrs. Mason, who was pleased with the drive and the sunshine, though she scarcely understood the meaning of the turmoil, with her maid by her side, delighted to wear such ribbons, and sit in such a post of honor. Rising up in the carriage, F. B. took off his hat, bade his men of brass be silent, who were accustomed to bray 'See the Conquering Hero comes,' whenever the Colonel or Mr. Bayham, his brilliant aide-de-camp, made their appearance,— bidding, we say, the musicians and the universe to be silent, F. B. rose, and made the citizens of Newcome a splendid speech. Good, old, unconscious Mrs. Mason was the theme of it, and the Colonel's virtues and faithful gratitude in tending her. She was his father's old friend. She was Sir Barnes Newcome's grandfather's old friend. She had lived for more than forty years at Sir Barnes Newcome's door, and how often had he been to see her? Did he go every week? No. Every month? No. Every year? No. Never in the whole course of his life had he set his foot into her doors! (Loud yells, and cries of 'shame.') Never had he done her one single act of kindness. Whereas for years and years past, when he was away in India, heroically fighting the battles of his country, when he was distinguishing himself at Assaye, and — and — Mulligatawny, and Seringapatam, in the hottest of the fight, and the fiercest of the danger, in the most terrible moment of the conflict, and the crowning glory of the victory, the good, the brave, the kind old Colonel, — why should he say Colonel? why should he not say Old Tom at once? (Immense roars of applause) — always remembered his dear old nurse and friend. 'Look at that shawl, boys, which she has got on! My belief is that Colonel Newcome took that shawl in single combat, and on horseback, from the prime-minister of Tippoo Saib. (Immense cheers and cries of "Bravo, Bayham!") Look at that brooch the dear old thing wears! (He kissed her hand while so apostrophizing her.) Tom Newcome never brags about his military achievements, he is the most modest as well as the bravest man in the world; what if I were to tell you that he cut that brooch from the throat of an Indian rajah? He's man enough to do it. ("He is; he is;" from all parts of the crowd.) What, you want to take the horses out, do you? (To the crowd, who were removing those quadrupeds.) I aint a-going to prevent you; I expected as much of you. Men of Newcome, I expected as much of you, for I know you! Sit still, old lady; don't be frightened, ma'am, they are only going to pull you to the King's Arms, and show you to the Colonel.'

"This, indeed, was the direction in which the mob (whether influenced by spontaneous enthusiasm, or excited by cunning agents placed among the populace by F. B., I cannot say) now took the barouche and its three occupants. With a myriad roar and shout the carriage was dragged up in front of the King's Arms, from the balconies of which a most satisfactory account of the polling was already placarded. The extra noise and shouting brought out the Colonel, who looked at first with curiosity at the advancing procession, and then, as he caught sight of Sarah Mason, with a blush and a bow of his kind old head.

"'Look at him, boys!' cried the enraptured F. B., pointing up to the old man. 'Look at him; the dear old boy! Isn't he an old trump? Which will you have for your member, Barnes Newcome or Old Tom?'

"And as might be supposed, an immense shout of 'Old Tom!' arose from the multitude; in the midst of which, blushing and bowing still, the Colonel went back to his committee-room; and the bands played 'See the Conquering Hero' louder than ever; and poor Barnes, in the course of his duty having to come out upon his balcony at the Roebuck opposite, was saluted with a yell as vociferous as the cheer for the Colonel had been; and old Mrs. Mason asked what the noise was about; and after making several vain efforts, in dumb show, to the crowd, Barnes slunk back into his hole again as pale as the turnip which was flung at his head; and the horses were brought, and Mrs. Mason driven home, and the day of election came to an end.

"Not exactly knowing what his politics were when he commenced the canvass, I can't say to what opinions the poor Colonel did not find himself committed by the time when the election was over. The worthy gentleman felt himself not a little humiliated by what he had to say and to unsay, by having to answer questions, to submit to familiarities, to shake hands, which, to say the truth, he did not care for grasping at all. His habits were aristocratic; his education had been military; the kindest and simplest soul alive, he yet disliked all familiarity, and expected from common people the sort of deference which he had received from his men in the regiment."

CHAPTER XVI.

THE PEOPLE AS AFFECTED BY THE TWO GOVERNMENTS.

An estimate of the effect of the British monarchy upon the masses of the people, and of the effect of the United States constitution upon the wealthy and intelligent. — The contrary considered. — How far are the representative English and American characters the work of their governments.

We have now nearly reached the end of comparison between England and America as nations. The term England has been used throughout, as it was the parent kingdom and cast most of the institutions of its consorts, and the name is better known in America than the proper title of "The United Kingdom." There are many conditions of life in both countries for which the state is not responsible. There are many abuses in both countries neither anticipated in the institutions of either, nor growing out of them. There is certainly nothing evil in England for which America is responsible, unless it be a part of her national debt contracted in one attempt to enslave us, and in another to intimidate us, and the balance has been struck by the present prosperous condition of British commerce, which nearly absorbed the whole of our own during our latest struggle for existence. To America, on the contrary, England as a state is responsible for much that might have hindered our progress, not the least remarkable of which endowments was slavery itself. Many reminiscences of her own social life have retarded the true growth of this country as a republic. We have had to weed out nearly all the distinctive English features of polity which remained after our war of independence, — the love of broad estates, and the haughty wish for many tenants and servants, for deference and distance between men, and distance between governors and governed, for large state powers reserved and held to influence public action, — the thousand little things which make the English notion of essentials, but are to a new and democratic state the conceits and trappings of a boy. We shook off the state church, the privy council, primogeniture, the mystery of the "presence," and kept chiefly the English common law for the administration of justice. And we have scarcely made a single step backward toward England since that period, while England has never made one great progressive step but in our direction, unless it be Free Trade. The contest between the two sets of institutions has been like the first trial between the paddle-wheel steamship and the screw steamship. They were hitched together stern to stern, and bets ran high as to how many screws the paddle-wheels could tow; the little screw, however, carried off the elder style of ship before they could adjust the bets. There can be no coming changes in the English government which will not be in our direction. Already life-peerages are mooted, and a life peer is only a longer sort of senator. The ballot must come, also, for it is more necessary for England than for us. Few men are in fear of losing farm or employment here for voting against landlord or employer; besides, the ballot in England would counteract servility, which permeates English society up to the top grade of tradesmen, and often higher. A servile fellow would carry a weapon with the ballot, with which he might give vent to his feelings sometimes; for a thoroughly fawning nation is no improvement upon a treacherous one.

The principle of English government is, no matter how the lower classes exist, so the ruling class is wise; but what wise man would not wish to be rid of the responsibility of ruling a million of poor and vulgar people? Our principle is, secure the greatest good to the many, though the few governors fare ill; for if it be so sweet in England merely to rule and assume all the responsibility for the disfranchised, then our ill-paid American office-holders must be partly paid in the pleasure of place. The sensitiveness of English opinion upon the question of arming the poor with the unit of government, the ballot, is ludicrous. An encyclopædia issued by the Scotch publishers, Chambers, of London and Edinburgh, and reissued here (1869), where it will do no harm, says, "If the suffrage were universal, the laboring class interest would be the predominant one, and serious would be the danger of class legislation as a result!" This is written in England, where, of course, there has never been class legislation! But class legislation is indeed serious, though it is questionable whether the laboring men be a class; for in America every man labors. The distress in England is that there has been class government altogether, and the government of the smallest, least laborious, and therefore least humanized class. If there be a vulgar class there, not fit to hold the unit of government, they are vulgar because the government of the few wise has never given them schools, nor access to social and administrative opportunity. The few have not been wise enough to make the many worthy. The wise few have hidden their talents of charity in the napkins of the court-table; they have been selfish, haughty, and unjust toward their fellow-countrymen, and the exodus from the British kingdom to America is like that of the oppressed Israelites from Egypt; in the western promised land they find no wise class to rule them, but undertake to be that class themselves.

Let this be accounted for. If English institutions are superior to ours, why have they failed to attract the millions of British subjects who have come to America? With more land in North America than we have, with nearly all India and Oceanica, and parts of all zones for colonies, why have the Queen's subjects failed to see the advantage of dominions ruled by her own royally-appointed Governors, — themselves of the wise few, — and come instead to a land where, if all English literature be true, there is corruption, violence, instability, miasma, — a land, in short, such as Mr. Charles Dickens sketched in "Martin Chuzzlewit"?

It was the magic name of Freedom that attracted them; not only freedom in life, wages, and locomotion, but freedom in the higher sense of equal chance before the law and before the fact, — the mention of a nation which was not diked and ditched with deference, and tradition, and made impregnable to the lowly in its central citadels; a nation where Silas Wright, or Carl Schurz, or David Broderick, could be a senator or the peer of one. And by all recent accounts of English critics, who have taken a marvellous liking to us of late, we, thus composite, are the most enlightened nation on the globe; for so we were named by Lord Houghton at a banquet in 1869.

What was the origin of this wise class in England, — too wise to be of account with only the unit of government, one ballot, for a weapon? Fischel, the German critic, says, upon authority, that "after the battle of Tewkesbury, a Norman baron was almost as rare in England as a wolf is now. When Henry VII. called his first Parliament, there were only twenty-nine temporal peers to be found; of those twenty-nine not five remain, and they, as the Howards, for instance, are not Norman nobility. A peer with an old genealogical tree is accordingly something unheard of; the real old families of the country are to be found among the peasantry. The gentry, too, may lay some claim to old blood. We owe the present peerage to three sources: the spoliation of the Church under Henry VIII., the open and flagrant sale of its honors by the elder Stuarts, and the borough-mongering of our own times.

"Nothing is more amusing," he continues, "than to read the apocryphal genealogies paraded in the peerage. The family of Lord Holland (Fox), according to Collins' 'Handbook of the Nobility,' were a distinguished tribe in England previous to the Conquest; but the Fox family itself, more modest, alleges that it derives its origin from a certain Palafox, who, in 1588, was driven ashore from the Spanish Armada. The real origin of the family is involved in obscurity; according to some, the founder was a chorister of Salisbury Cathedral, in the reign of Charles II.; others contending that he was a body-servant of this King."

Now, it has taken from two to five hundred years under the English government to make such laborers members of the ruling class, and we often find them wise enough in twenty. There is an English blacksmith, named Robert Collyer, in Chicago, whom we esteem good enough to fill the pulpit of Theodore Parker. How many years would it have taken him to have been wise enough to preach in the Chapel Royal?

English institutions are of a character to repress the aspirations of the lowly, and make them feel that the higher uses of man are too high for them to strive for. The French authority we have so often quoted admits that on passing from a country in which free institutions are established to one where they do not exist, the traveller is struck by the change; in the former all is bustle and activity; in the latter everything is calm and motionless. In the one, amelioration and progress are the general topics of inquiry; in the other, it seems as if the community only aspired to repose in the enjoyment of the advantages which it has acquired. Nevertheless, the country which exerts itself so strenuously to promote its welfare is generally more wealthy and more prosperous than that which appears to be so contented with its lot; and when we compare them together, we can scarcely conceive how so many new wants are daily felt in the former, whilst so few seem to occur in the latter. It cannot be our climate, which few Europeans like, nor our race, which our parent race has so frequently reprobated, that has made us reconstructors of the lost commonalty of England, — "those Irishmen who only brawl, those English helots who love only bitter beer," — it is the vigorous nature of our institutions which are not reformatory but inspiring; which are no royal charities, but which compel emulation by universal emulation.

"In no country on earth is an old nationality so soon absorbed as in America," observes an Englishman. "I am inclined to think the regard professed for England by American literary men is sentimental, and is produced by education and study, rather than by any feeling transmitted in families or by society."

The men who founded our government were as thoroughly reviled at the time by English critics as those who govern it now continue to be by Englishmen; descendants of the kindred of "Praise God Barebones," and the reviled class of that time, they proved worthy of De Tocqueville's splendid eulogium:—

"On the continent of Europe, at the beginning of the seventeenth century, absolute monarchy had everywhere triumphed over the ruins of the oligarchical and feudal liberties of the Middle Ages. Never were the notions of right more completely confounded than in the midst of the splendor and literature of Europe; never was there less political activity among the people; never were the principles of true freedom less widely circulated; and at that very time, those principles, which were scorned or unknown by the nations of Europe, were proclaimed in the deserts of the New World, and were accepted as the future creed of a great people. The boldest theories of the human reason were put into practice by a community so humble, that not a statesman condescended to attend to it; and a legislation without a precedent was produced off-hand by the imagination of the citizens."

Another feature of English government is, that, existing with reserved privileges for the few, who become the objects of all admiration, the hearts of the whole middle class in England are turned upward toward the aristocracy and away from the poor million at their feet. The dream of rank enters the brain of the tradesman, and he takes a taste of its realities in advance by kicking the next class below him. There is not on the globe so cruel a race as the English; they hang their criminals on the open street to make the sight of death popular; they give such sentences for petty offences as are elsewhere given for the highest crimes; we can fight rebellion five years and hang no man; but for a freak of a few poor Fenians they are hung dangling over the battlements of Manchester jail. Hawthorne, who had a literary weakness for the English nation, said that "a true Englishman is a kind man at heart, but has an unconquerable dislike to poverty and beggary. Beggars have heretofore been so strange to an American that he is apt to become their prey, being recognized through his national peculiarities, and beset by them in the streets. The English smile at him, and say that there are ample public arrangements for every pauper's possible need; that street charity promotes idleness and vice, and that yonder personification of misery on the pavement will lay up a good day's profit, besides supping more luxuriously than the dupe who gives him a shilling. By and by the stranger adopts their theory and begins to practise upon it, much to his own temporary freedom from annoyance, but not entirely without moral detriment, or sometimes a too late contrition. Years afterwards, it may be, his memory is still haunted by some vindictive wretch whose cheeks were pale and hunger-pinched."

This sense of reduction to hereditary brutality is the reason, perhaps, of the fondness of the lower English classes for prize-fighting, dog-fighting, cock-fighting, and jockeying at horse races; for many of these poor beings, permeated, like the whole of society, with reverence for the aristocracy, feel honored to climb to the social place of a ducal game-chicken or a royal bull-dog. Prize fighting in America has, it is believed, never had an American votary; all our bruisers have been imported, and have fought under "patronage." Parliament adjourns to attend a horse-race; "Guy Livingstone" was a popular book in England, brutal as it was, because it was a truthful representation of English detestation for the poor and the plebeian. One often hears, in that country, of some "gentleman" founding a hospital or a school; but what rich tradesman has done it, except George Peabody, of Massachusetts, who went at once to the relief of the London poor and the unlettered freed negroes of America? Another defect of the aristocratic government is, that it puts the mind of society upon trifles, to the prejudice of such manly questions as should make citizens. Witness this royal farce: —

The King of Hanover at the Prince of Wales' baptism, if I mistake not, was very anxious to sign the paper before Prince Albert, and when the Queen approached the table he placed himself by her side, watching his opportunity. She knew very well what he was about, and just as the Archbishop was giving her the pen, she suddenly dodged around the table, placed herself next to the Prince, then quickly took the pen from the Archbishop, signed, and gave it to Prince Albert, who also signed next, before it could be prevented. "The Queen," said Wellington, "was also very anxious to give the precedence at court to King Leopold, before the King of Hanover, and she consulted me about it, and how it should be arranged. I told Her Majesty that I supposed it should be settled, as we did at the Congress of Vienna. 'How was that,' said she, —' by first arrival?' — 'No, ma'am,' said I; 'alphabetically, and then, you know, B comes before H.' This pleased her very much, and it was done."

The above were grown-up people.

Throughout English society this reverence for triviality goes, fostered by the form of government; for the huge and beefy Englishman would be almost devoid of a love of antiquity and sentiment, were it not kept alive by the worship of a rich aristocracy descended from antiquity. Hawthorne shows how this recognition of haberdashery is maintained at the banquets of the Lord Mayor, of London: —

"There stood a man in armor, with a helmet on his head, behind his Lordship's chair. When the after-dinner wine was placed on the table, still another official personage appeared behind the chair, and proceeded to make a solemn and sonorous proclamation, ending in some such style as this: 'And other gentlemen and ladies, here present, the Lord Mayor drinks to you all in a loving cup,' — giving a sort of sentimental twang to the two words, — 'and sends it round among you!' And forthwith, the loving cup — several of them, indeed, on each side of the tables — came slowly down with all the antique ceremony.

"The fashion of it is thus: The Lord Mayor, standing up and taking the covered cup in both hands, presents it to the guest at his elbow, who likewise rises, and removes the cover for his lordship to drink, which being successfully accomplished, the guest replaces the cover and receives the cup into his own hands. He then presents it to his next neighbor, that the cover may be again removed for himself to take a draught; after which the third person goes through a similar manœuvre with a fourth, and he with a fifth, until the whole company find themselves inextricably intertwisted and entangled in one complicated chain of love. When the cup came to my hands, I examined it critically, both inside and out, and perceived it to be an antique and richly ornamented silver goblet, capable of holding about a quart of wine. Considering how much trouble we all expended in getting the cup to our lips, the guests appeared to content themselves with wonderfully moderate potations. In truth, nearly or quite the original quart of wine being still in the goblet, it seemed doubtful whether any of the company had more than barely touched the silver rim before passing it to their neighbors, — a degree of abstinence that might be accounted for by a fastidious repugnance to so many ingredients in one cup, or possibly by a disapprobation of the liquor. Being curious to know all about these important matters, with a view of recommending to my countrymen whatever they might usefully adopt, I drank an honest sip from the loving cup, and had no occasion for another, — ascertaining it to be claret of a poor original quality, largely mingled with water, and spiced and sweetened."

Further than this, the court and aristocracy being the theme of all panegyric, and their manners and habits matters of imitation, the notorious vices of both in many cases tend to debauch an entire generation. We have no court in America, and no aristocracy that is recognized except by itself. There have been chief magistrates who had their troubles, domestic and otherwise, but they hid them from the public eye, and suffered in silence, unwilling to be evil examples to their generation. There has probably never been in American society so flagrant cases of profligacy and meanness as have disgraced the English throne: William of Orange entering the kingdom with his one wife and two mistresses; all the male Brunswickers unchaste, and the fourth George the hero of a divorce court. This latter episode is worthy of reproduction, and is mildly told by a historian: —

"George III. died January 24, 1820, after a reign of sixty years. He was succeeded by the Prince Regent, whose coronation was one of the most magnificent that England had witnessed for many years. Circumstances, however, occurred, that excited the populace, and revived unpleasant remembrances of the early career of the King. When only Prince of Wales, George IV., in opposition to the Royal Marriage Act, had married Mrs. Fitzherbert, a Catholic. His father refused to acknowledge the marriage; but many persons of the highest rank, members of the royal family even, showed their disapprobation of the statute by visiting that lady, and treating her as the prince's lawful wife. George, however, was faithless; and Mrs. Fitzherbert left him forever. Embarrassed with debts to the amount of more than six hundred and thirty thousand pounds, the Prince, in 1795, consented to marry Caroline, the second daughter of the Duke of Brunswick, Wolfenbuttel. The Prince had concluded, from his father's expressions, that his debts would be paid, and his income increased. He was disappointed; the income was indeed raised from seventy-five thousand to a hundred and thirty-eight thousand pounds; but this increase was applied to the liquidation of his debts. The

Prince became embittered against his young wife; bickerings arose, and a separation followed. After dwelling many years upon the continent, Caroline heard of the death of George III., and hastened to England to claim a share of the throne of her husband. She was threatened with a prosecution if she presumed to set foot in the country; but she heeded not. Her arrival was welcomed with enthusiastic joy by the opposition and the bulk of the people.

"A bill of pains and penalties against her was introduced in the House of Lords on July the 5th, 1820. Brougham and Denman were her counsel; and by their address and eloquence they laid the foundation of their future advancement. Week after week the examination of evidence continued; but if the Queen's conduct had been unbecoming, that of her husband was notoriously worse The public, therefore, paid little attention to the charges against her; but denounced the injustice of the divorce, and the cruelty that ever since that event had surrounded her with spies, and by a variety of means had blackened her reputation in the face of Europe. The ministers became alarmed at the general clamor, and still more at the increasing diminution of their supporters in the Lords. At the second reading the bill was passed, by a majority of twenty-eight; but at the third reading, out of two hundred and eighteen peers, the ministers had a majority of only nine. They therefore deemed it prudent to abandon their project. A general illumination announced the joy of the people. Woe to the windows that were dark that night!

"In the following year the coronation took place, and Caroline presented herself at the Abbey gates, but was repulsed by the guard. The shock was too much for her; in a few days she closed her unhappy career. The populace paid to her remains the last rough tribute of their sympathy. Her body was to be interred in her native land; but orders were given that it should not pass through the city. The crowd determined that it should, and, after much tumult and some conflicts with the military, they gained their point."

The United States government calls private citizens of exalted vigilance and wide experience to political place, whatever be their grade in social life; the citizen is therefore always alert for the business of his commonwealth, and ascends to public position without embarrassment. Seldom is this true of England; few school-masters, like Amos Kendall, or shop-clerks, like Abraham Lincoln, or merchants, like Stewart, are called to the ear of the Queen. In Belfast A. T. Stewart might have grown richer than at present, but the Queen would never have become his guest.

I walked down Broadway not long ago, and coming to the corner of where Stewart's white quadrangle of iron rises, I saw the merchant himself standing in the middle of the street, directing some stone-pavers. Here was the man whose income is said to have exceeded that of the Marquis of Westminster or the Duke of Bedford. Every day he accumulated the yearly salary of the Secretaryship of the Treasury he was obliged to decline. This retail store alone is said to involve him in a daily expenditure of ten thousand dollars. Since the beginning of commerce there was probably never so great a merchant, neither in Tyre nor Alexandria, Venice nor London. And there he stood, a facile-faced, bargaining-eyed man, of light complexion, up to, or above, the good average height of slender men, consumed with the laying of a block of stone, and speaking about it to laborers and passers-by. While he stood there in plain business clothes, with a silk hat on his head, a pleasant spectacle to be one's uncle, both on account of good face and good purse, I saw a clothing-store man of lower Broadway pass by, who returned an income of above three hundred thousand dollars. Only three hundred thousand dollars! The poor fellow looked at Stewart with such shrinking yet worshipping envy that I felt for him out of the depths of my soul. The possessor of certain nickels, I ran my hand in my pocket, and held them securely for fear this desperately poor man with only three hundred thousand a year would rush upon me and rob me. From this depth of sympathy I was again recalled to the study of Mr. Stewart and his three millions of dollars, — as much money laid by as the whole United States could save out of its vast revenue every month. A splendid instance of self-denial he seemed to me, to have the purchase-money of so much pleasure or glory, and still to be a plodding business man; to be childless, and yet so devoted to the accumulation of fortune. I stepped into his store, and all its vast lower surface moved and glistened with color and invitation. Feeling like one who was entering some grand court of sovereigns, I passed by altars of gift-offering to the open area at the middle of the store, where, looking up through six floors of costly goods, through ships, villas, villages of upholstery, through armies of shirt-muslin and miles of silk stockings, and every floor moving, rustling, chattering, bargaining, I began to realize, like General Grant, that the mind which could direct all this, like the instinct which propelled the million-legged spider, might be able to get to the heart of the government finances, and distribute us back to specie payment. Down the store directly the owner walked, as plain as the plainest customer who wanted a yard of musquito netting; and almost incredulously I saw him stop to speak with an Irish woman who was underrating the cost of a yard of ribbon.

Owing to the more natural and practical basis of parties in America, party spirit seldom becomes unsocial; while in England parties growing out of social and family life often become completely estranged, and on trivial questions exhibit the malevolence of personal enemies. Old age and riches, seldom separated, are the requirements of distinction amidst these institutions of primogeniture. Youth is intimidated, and fresh and earnest individuality looked upon with suspicion. Sidney Smith, bearing testimony upon this point, alleges that it is always considered as a piece of impertinence in England, if a man of less than two or three thousand a year has any opinions at all upon important subjects; and in addition he is sure to be assailed with all the Billingsgate of the French Revolution. Jacobin, Leveller, Atheist, Deist, Socinian, Incendiary, Regicide, were lately the gentlest appellations used; and the man who breathed a syllable against the senseless bigotry of the Georges, or hinted at the abominable tyranny and persecution exercised upon Catholic Ireland, was shunned as unfit for the relations of social life.

The prevalence of crime in England is in great part the result of the aristocratic government, and so is much of the prevalent atheism there the fruit of an Established Church, with a proud hierarchy, and an inquisitive eye upon the price of rectorships. Throughout the cities of England there are clubs of socialists and infidels, some of which have sent itinerant missionaries to the United States to debauch the moral sentiment here. One of these blasphemous fellows was a certain Joseph Barker, who began public life in one of the workingmen's sceptical associations, turned dissenting preacher, again turned atheist, and made the tour of the United States, discussing the validity of the Scriptures with whatever clergymen cared to enter his arena. He returned to England just prior to the civil war, and attempted to obtain ordination in the Established Church, but this was refused until he made several defences of slavery, and attacks on the American character, when it was understood that the authorities relented, and ordained him. These associations of sceptics are multifold, in London, and the poor are mainly their supporters. The indignation of the English Republicans against their political aristocracy is always apt, in fervent minds, to extend to their ecclesiastical aristocracy; for the British Bishops are greater enemies of free institutions than the British Nobles, if possible. Hence Thomas Paine, an Englishman, and an ardent friend of freedom, was driven by the despotism of peers temporal and peers spiritual to embrace both their systems in his vigorous denunciations. His bones, which had lain in America, were exhumed by William Cobbett, another English radical, and carried home triumphantly to excite the popular favor. Cobbett arrived at Liverpool, from America. As he purposed making a public entry into Manchester, with Paine's bones, great political disturbance was anticipated, and the borough-reeves of Manchester and Salford wrote to him, so that he altered his intended route.

The policy of the English aristocracy, in foreign affairs, during the past ninety years, is condemned by all recent writers, at home as well as abroad. To save their class privileges they embarked in the wars against France, which prodigiously increased their colonies and commerce; but the former class of acquisitions has already proved burdensome. The efforts of England were impotent to suppress France; and having sealed Napoleon in the rock of St. Helena, she was most forward to recognize his nephew, and second him in another foolish war, whereby the march of Christianity to the Bosphorus was postponed. Had England been a popular government when the French Revolution began, she would have been the friend of France, and assisted the latter to liberalize the world. Out of the struggles of Pitt and the aristocrats to subdue Democracy, came the English debt which vastly increases the burdens of the poor; and her long struggle demoralized the people, so that Miss Martineau ascribes the inauguration of the crimes of the century to her disbanded troops. Compare the orderly conduct of the volunteer soldiers of the South and North, after our civil war, with the behavior of the enforced levies of England when Napoleon had been subdued: —

"Such scenes of violence went forward, in different parts of the country, that many began to be of Romilly's opinion, that the English character had undergone some unaccountable and portentous change.

"Portentous these horrors were, but not unaccountable. Many soldiers had become weary of the war, which to them had been thus far all hardships and no glory. They deserted; they could not show themselves at home, the penalty for desertion being death.

"They gathered together in gangs, took possession of some forsaken house among the hills, or of caves on the sea-shore, and went forth at night, in masks and grotesque clothing, and helped themselves with money and clothes wherever they could find them, sacrificing life where it was necessary to their objects."

This demoralization, like aristocracy itself, seems to have become hereditary in a land of caste; and British crime, partaking of the spirit of material improvements, has become formidable by science. The account of "London Labor and the London Poor," by the Mayhew brothers, shows that thieves are born into an aristocracy of their own, reared from the cradle by their fathers, and, in the process of British colonization, distributed round the globe to make property everywhere their prey. Paris knows the *Chevalier d'Industrie Anglais*, as thoroughly as we know the British burglar. In 1869 a bank was robbed in New York, by English thieves, and the newspapers were replete with descriptions of their exquisite implements, and the coolness of their preparations. Their tools were fine as the best products of Sheffield; they were of all kinds, heavy, light, coarse, fine, — about four hundred pieces in all, — designed and fitted for every professional exigency, with the nice discrimination of a dentist's set of instruments. Most of the articles were specially made for the business, it would seem, by skilled manufacturers, in this country or abroad. The "jimmies" for prying open doors were of the finest steel, beautifully finished, each of two pieces, which screwed together. There were fine steel bars, one and one-half inches thick, and four feet eight inches long, chiselled-edged at each end, and unscrewing in the middle. All the implements, including the powerful jack-screw, were constructed to be taken apart, in small pieces, or packed into a close space, or carried about in pockets.

Nothing could have been more nicely contrived than the can with a flexible tube, for filling safe locks with fine powder. The sledges of soft composition metal, which gave out no ringing sound, the two hundred brad awls, for fastening muslin against the windows, the gum over-shoes, in which the robbers could move about noiselessly, the thoughtful provision of strong cords, and of handcuffs, to gag and fetter anybody who should intrude on them unawares, were artful and scientific. The master stroke of the whole was the opening of the crack combination lock on the outer door. There were several theories proposed, to account for this; but they are all based on the supposition that by collusion, or in some other way, the burglars obtained the numbers of the combination to which the door was locked on Saturday night. "But what if they had hit upon some device to ascertain the combination, by manipulating the lock itself, making it tell its own secret, and then opened the door as easily as the man who had locked it? This is a flight of art, which the combination lock-makers had believed to be beyond the reach of mortals."

Other than these evils are directly or partly due to the nature of a government which makes the condition of life the accident of birth, hedges round the few with laws and ceremonies, and treats the bulk of its fellow-men as unworthy of its franchises. Better than this great oligarchy is a throne where there is but one family ascendant in a whole realm, and not a social and landed viceroy in every parish; and it is remarkable that at this time the monarch of England is popular with English radicals, while the aristocracy is the object of their attacks. A woman, and a good one, the Queen is removed from the conflicts of politicians, and is the magistrate, though secretly under their management. To her reach the sympathies of the people, though they are as jealously kept from access to her as the Japanese from their heavenly Emperor. A chain of aristocrats guard her person, arrogating to themselves the priestship of the temple, and often in the doors thereof playing lewdness and robbery, like the sons of Eli. Perhaps when the aristocracy is gone, the High Priest also may reel in his chair; for many believe that the present English sovereign is the next to the last.

Still, the English people are loyal to their sovereign; whatever she may be, they believe that she is all to them.

"Though we call ourselves loyal to our country and institutions," says Hawthorne, "and prove it by our readiness to shed blood, and sacrifice life in their behalf, still the principle is as cold and hard in an American bosom, as the steel spring that puts in motion a powerful machinery. In the Englishman's system a force similar to that of our steel spring is generated by the warm throbbings of human hearts. He clothes our bare abstraction in flesh and blood, — at present in the flesh and blood of a woman, — and manages to combine love, awe, and intellectual reverence, all in one emotion, and to embody his mother, his wife, his children, the whole idea of kindred, in a single person, and make her the representative of his country and its laws."

Whether this be superstition or tradition, it is pleasing and curious to us, but incompatible and undesirable in a land where the people, and not the ruler, is the source of power. The Hindoo is as loyal to his idol, but there is nothing in it, except that which he himself implants.

But while loyalty abounds, charity fails; for with all the wealth of England, — the richest country, in capital, on the globe, — there are more poor, indolent, or wicked people in the United Kingdom than in any Christian nation. Can that be a well-governed country which is at once the richest and contains the most paupers? The kingdom is cramped, but not so densely that this condition of things can be accounted for: —

There must now be 75,000 beggars in London alone, collecting, in the aggregate, several millions sterling a year. The paupers, on an area of 78,000 acres, number 145,000, and cost £1,300,000 a year. But many who get out-door parish relief also beg from societies and individuals. The real cost of the London poor, the money expended unearned, in various ways, may count up to £10,000,000. For the past five years there has been a steady increase. Vagabondism and ruffianism have also made steady progress, not only in London, but in the provinces. The Recorder of Manchester charged the Grand Jury, in 1869, that "in sobriety and general obedience to the law, Lancashire was going backward." A London paper, of May, in the same year, said, "If any one wants to see ruffianism in its most revolting state, let him take a journey to St. James Palace, at eleven o'clock, when the band plays. Here he will find an army of low-looking thieves and vagabonds, — hale, strong-looking men and hearty youths, — who follow up the band, shouting and cursing, and bonneting one another. In no other capital of Europe would such things be permitted. The band over, these fellows lie about St. James Park, on the grass, and on the benches, and round about the ornamental water."

This is a picture: St. James Palace, music, and court, and in the gardens thereof this army of paupers!

A member of Parliament, at about the same time, produced statistics to show how pauperism had increased during the last twenty-five years. In 1844, the number of confirmed paupers was 800,000, and they cost £4,976,000; in 1854, the number was 864,000, and the expenditure was £5,232,000; in 1864, the paupers had risen to 1,014,000, and the expenditure to £6,423,000; and in 1867, there were 1,040,000 paupers, and their cost was £6,939,000.

That nation may be strong, but not that people, where such things are intermingled: the shining horses, the liveries, and the benignant peers, gliding through aisles of abandoned poor; the richest men in Europe, cheered or hated by the worst, and all fellow-countrymen! It is these latter who do the fighting of England, the bleeding, and the suffering, while those — a handful — direct the empire, and hold it in their power to crush states and risings for freedom.

Let us take two examples of the "wise few," who are reared to statesmanship, and both of them eminent, and compare them with a pair of men who should have belonged to the opposite class. The first is Francis Bacon, whom Dr. Samuel Tyler, an American jurist, has thus depicted: —

"At this juncture in the progress of thought (1620), the most majestic and prophetic mind known to the history of philosophy rose up to lead men in the new career of investigation which had been begun. Trained in the practice of a jurisprudence the most technical, and in its routine the most servile, and the most obedient to authority and traditional usage of any which has been established amongst men, we see the remarkable spectacle of a Lord Chancellor of England laying aside for the moment the King's seals, to become the keeper of the seals of nature. And, in a majesty of diction unparalleled in the history of philosophy, this great thinker proclaimed to the world a new method of philosophy to guide the mighty spirit of inquiry which was abroad over the field of observation. Philosophy, no longer confined to the schools, is led forth by a politician and lawyer, out from the confines of authority, into the amplitudes. From this moment the freedom of the human mind was established. This man of business, this accomplished courtier, this cunning lawyer, this consummate orator, this leader in the affairs of the world, appears on the stage of philosophical thought, with a more comprehensive grasp of thinking, and a greater forecast than any one of even the many trained, especially to philosophy, who had preceded him."

Yet this courtier and noble, whose powers of mind have never been eclipsed, proved to be one of the most venal and corrupt politicians in history. He was convicted of base ingratitude, of tortures and thefts, and he belongs to that great array of men, educated for statesmanship, who were not fit to rule, because they considered only themselves and their class.

One other sketch of the "wise few" is afforded by Mr. Kinglake, in his summary of Gladstone, — a partisan sketch, but suggestive, as showing how the mere study of politics makes the strongest and purest mind qualmish and diplomatic, and cautious almost to superstition : —

"He was famous for the splendor of his eloquence, for his unaffected piety, and for his blameless life; he was celebrated, far and wide, for a more than common liveliness of conscience. He had once imagined it to be his duty to quit a government, and to burst through strong ties of friendship and gratitude, by reason of a thin shade of difference on the subject of white or brown sugar. It was believed that if he were to commit even a little sin, or to imagine an evil thought, he would instantly arraign himself before the dread tribunal which awaited him in his own bosom; and that, his intellect being subtle and microscopic, and delighting in casuistry and exaggeration, he would be likely to give his soul a very harsh trial, and treat himself as a great criminal, for faults too minute to be visible to the naked eyes of laymen. His friends lived in dread of his virtues, as tending to make him whimsical and unstable, and the practical politicians, conceiving that he was not to be depended upon for party purposes, and was bent upon none but lofty objects, used to look upon him as dangerous."

To these two natures, the one powerful and corrupt, the other learned and conscientious, and both qualified at great expense expressly to guide a state, oppose two other Englishmen who were sprung from lowly walks, — the one a farmer's son, the other the child of a cotton-spinner, and both of them learned how to rule a state by contact with labor, rather than by the mastery of diplomacy : —

"Mr. Cobden and Mr. Bright," says Kinglake, "were members of the House of Commons. Both had the gift of a manly, strenuous, eloquence, and their diction being founded upon English lore, rather than upon shreds of weak Latin, went straight to the mind of their hearers. Of these men, the one could persuade, the other could attack; and, indeed, Mr. Bright's oratory was singularly well qualified for preventing an erroneous acquiescence in the policy of the day; for, besides that he was honest, and fearless, — besides that, with a ringing voice, he had all the clearness and force which resulted from his great natural gifts, as well as from his one-sided method of thinking, — he had the advantage of being generally able to speak in a state of sincere anger. In former years, whilst their minds were disciplined by the almost mathematical exactness of the reasonings on which they relied, and when they were acting in concert with the shrewd traders of the North, who had a very plain object in view, these two orators had shown with what a strength, with what a masterly skill, with what patience, with what a high courage, they could carry a great scientific truth through the storms of politics; they had shown that they could arouse and govern the assenting thousands who listened to them with delight; that they could bend the House of Commons; that they could press their creed upon a prime minister, and put upon his mind so hard a stress, that, after a while, he felt it to be a torture, and a violence to his reason, to have to make a stand against them.

"Nay, more! each of these two gifted men had proved that he could go bravely into the midst of angry opponents, could show them their fallacies, one by one, destroy their favorite theories before their very faces, and triumphantly argue them down. These two men were honestly devoted to the cause of peace. There was no stain upon their names."

It was Richard Cobden, self-made, to whom Sir Robert Peel gave credit for the act which has made Peel's name eminent; and whatever Gladstone has accomplished has been in the path indicated and smoothed by Bright and Cobden thirty years ago.

We have had two men in America who were reared in the school of the wise few: John Quincy Adams and William H. Seward. Both were students in statesmanship, travellers in foreign lands, men of ample fortunes, and of the best social rank that we have. Mr. Adams was particularly of spotless character, and learned in all branches, economical or elegant. His education did not change his popular sympathies; for he was illustrious in the dignity of his life and his earnestness for freedom; but it did not enable him to conduct a more brilliant administration than Presidents of less acquirement, who better knew the needs and temper of the people.

Mr. Seward is the most admired in England of all our public men. He was an European politician, of all the boldness and *finesse* of Palmerston, and his opportunities were abundant as his promotion was long here. He rendered valuable services, and obtained the gratitude of his countrymen; but in those features of his policy wherein he followed English precedents he lost confidence, and the nation did not endorse him. He engaged in subtle treaties without the knowledge of Congress, and attempted to make grand strategy of politics, whereby, after the English fashion, a party leader might change sentiment when he pleased, and compose principles according to the condition of his liver.

It cannot be affirmed that we are ruled by the "wise few," in America; for the public sensitiveness is delicate and arbitrary here, and we are frequently too uncharitable toward our public servants. Indeed, we find that the wisest few who do rule us are often below the average morals and intellect of the mighty mass. De Tocqueville remarked this: —

"On my arrival in the United States, I was surprised to find so much distinguished talent among the subjects, and so little among the heads of the government. It is a well-authenticated fact, that at the present day the most able men in the United States are very rarely placed at the head of affairs; and it must be acknowledged that such has been the result in proportion as democracy has outstepped all its former limits. The race of American statesmen has evidently dwindled most remarkably in the course of the last fifty years."

At the same time, the race of American citizens has undoubtedly advanced; rulers and ruled were long approaching each other, and the level has been nearly reached.

"The mass of the citizens," says the same authority, "are sincerely disposed to promote the welfare of their country; nay, more, it may even be allowed that the lower classes are less apt to be swayed by considerations of personal interest than the higher orders; but it is always more or less impossible for them to discern the best means of attaining the end which they desire with sincerity."

The cure for this must be in the more thorough education of the people in subjects of government, in our schools, and in the civil service; and the latter can only be accomplished by a grand awakening of public sentiment to meet and overthrow the managers of politics. Hitherto it has been true that "the people have neither the time not the means which are essential to the prosecution of an investigation of this kind; their conclusions are hastily formed from a superficial inspection of the more prominent features of a question. Hence they often assent to the clamor of a mountebank who knows the secret of stimulating their tastes, whilst their truest friends frequently fail in their exertions."

This is still true in a marked degree. The politicians have coaxed from the people reservation after reservation of wisdom, until our benches of court are the stake of political parties, and hints have even been made toward throwing the Supreme Court into the scramble.

Chancellor Kent says, in speaking with great eulogium of that part of the Constitution which empowers the executive to nominate the judges: "It is indeed probable that the men who are best fitted to discharge the duties of this high office would have too much reserve in their manners, and too much austerity in their principles, for them to be returned by the majority, at an election where universal suffrage is adopted." This is not foreign but domestic authority, and it is true that we have reduced to the general ballot too many cloistered offices which should have been forever kept without the political arena. During the trial of the impeachment of Andrew Johnson, and afterward, certain unruly representatives, of the type of which De Tocqueville speaks below, amongst which was one Ingersoll of Illinois, from the whiskey-distilling district of Peoria, even insulted the Senate.

"On entering the House of Representatives, of Washington, one is struck by the vulgar demeanor of that great assembly. The eye frequently does not discover a man of celebrity within its walls. Its members are almost all obscure individuals, whose names present no associations to the mind; they are mostly village lawyers, men in trade, or even persons belonging to the lower classes of society. In a country in which education is very general, it is said that the representatives of the people do not always know how to write correctly.

"At a few yards' distance from this spot is the door of the Senate, which contains within a small space a large proportion of the celebrated men of America. Scarcely an individual is to be perceived in it who does not recall reminiscences of an active and illustrious career. The Senate is composed of eloquent advocates, distinguished generals, wise magistrates, and statesmen of note, whose language would at all times do honor to the most remarkable parliamentary debates in Europe.

"What, then, is the cause of this strange contrast, and why are the most able citizens to be found in one assembly, rather than in the other? Why is the former body remarkable for its vulgarity and its poverty of talent, whilst the latter seems to enjoy a monopoly of intelligence and of sound judgment? Both of these assemblies emanate from the people; both of them are chosen by universal suffrage; and no voice has hitherto been heard to assert, in America, that the Senate is hostile to the interests of the people. From what cause, then, does so startling a difference arise? The only reason which appears to me adequately to account for it is, that the House of Representatives is elected by the populace directly, and that the Senate is elected by elected bodies."

Since De Tocqueville's time the politicians have assumed to manipulate even the Senate, and some of them have cried for its extirpation. Only a grand rising of the people from their homes can rout these traders in office, few of whom command the respect of the homes of the land, but are elected by default of honest votes.

"In the United States the persons who engage in the perplexities of political life are individuals of very moderate pretensions. The pursuit of wealth generally diverts men of great talents and of great passions from the pursuit of power; *and it very frequently happens that a man does not undertake to direct the fortune of the state until he has discovered his incompetence to conduct his own affairs!!*"

If this were true forty years ago, when written, how much truer to-day! Recent travellers have noticed the same fact, that, with a government that is of the best nature, the citizens fail to perform their duties at the polls, and bequeath to the basest dregs of society the sacred offering of the ballot. The government, in its nature, is not responsible for this neglect; for it was considered, at its foundation, that the slight and infrequent duty of supporting it with his choice would be gladly undertaken by every man who had an interest or a pride in his nationality. We have been prospering in our private business, and the state has hitherto been of little importance to any of us pecuniarily; but the state is now growing greater than the nation, and the cry to every holder of the ballot must go up:—

"Help us, or we perish!"

Mr. Trollope, in 1862, noticed the carelessness of our people in this respect, and ascribed it mistakenly to a dislike for our form of government. "In all governmental matters," he says, "the people of the nation have been strangely undemonstrative. They have assented to a system which has been used for transferring the political power of the nation to a body of trading politicians, who have become known and felt as a mass, and not known and felt as individuals. I find it difficult to describe the present political position of the States in this respect.

"The millions of the people are eager for the Constitution, are proud of their power as a nation, and are ambitious of national greatness. But they are not, as I think, especially desirous of retaining political influence in their own hands. At many of the elections it is difficult to induce them to vote. They have among them a half-knowledge that politics is a trade in the hands of the lawyers, and that they are the capital by which those political tradesmen carry on their business. These politicians are all lawyers. Politics and law go together as naturally as the possession of land and the exercise of magisterial powers do with us."

Seven years afterward, Mr. Sprague, Senator from Rhode Island, discovered the same fact of the lawyers.

Many of our social errors in America are not ascribable in any respect to our government, while they afford pretext for attacks upon it. We have been so engrossed in business that we have become unsocial in all public places. Russell, of the "Times," remarked in Montreal that the Americans usually came into the salon singly; each man, with a bundle of newspapers under his arm, took a seat at a vacant table, ordered a prodigious repast, which he gobbled in haste, as though he was afraid of losing a train, and then rushed off to the bar or smoked in the passages, never sitting for a moment after his breakfast. The Englishmen came in little knots or groups, exhibited no great anxiety about newspapers, ordered simple and substantial feasts, enjoyed them at their ease, chattered much, and were in no particular hurry to leave the table. "The taciturnity of the American was not well-bred, nor was the good humor of the Briton vulgar."

Our national manners will compare favorably with those of most nations, and are far more courtly than those of the average Englishman. Woman is respected here; there is frank equality accorded and demanded between men; but it is natural that in a new, rough country, rough people should sometimes get into the marts and capitols. As a general rule our present politicians are among our worst-bred men, their associations being the worst. More men eat with their knives in Washington than in any city in America. That I may not be accused of speaking severely of the English lower classes only, I will give this instance of the worst-mannered man I ever saw in any country: —

I was writing and making notes in the library of Congress, while compiling this book, and while most busily engaged a shadow from behind fell upon my table. Thinking it some friend who was privileged to take the liberty, I did not look up for some seconds or minutes. The hand from behind picked up a piece of my manuscript, read it over, took up a second, and so forth, until finally I turned round, irritated.

There stood a total stranger, — a large, politician-like, coarse-grained, impudent-eyed man, — coolly reading my manuscript. It was so outrageous a violation of decency and so rascally a liberty, that I felt the blood go up my face like the hoisting of the British standard.

"Is that your conception of manners, sir?" I said to the man.

He looked at me like a stone with a smile on it, for a few minutes, and then said, with a contemptuous voice: —

"My God! I reckon everything here is public property, aint it? I reckon 'taint no use to put on airs here, be it? I guess not!"

Not deigning me another word, this republican genius went round all the circuit of the tables, peering in the notes and pages of every reader, lady or man, and at the end, giving me a half-defiant yet impassive look, went out at a floundering stride.

Two days afterward I saw this man, walking between two Representatives, go into the White House. He was pointed out to me as a man who had captured a valuable revenue office.

Now, consider this type of man a representative unit of the two or three thousand visitors at the White House daily. If he sees a door marked: —

"**Public not admitted here,**"

that is the particular door which he means to go through. If he cannot go through it he will peep through it. He means to "make a row" about it. His impudent stare and the coarse "feel" of his hand is upon every face or object he sees. The only sort of grace he possesses is an adjunct to cunning, when, on occasion, he can wheedle, or flatter, and put his soul through degrading gymnastics, creep on his belly, kneel and crawl like a snake, — anything but hear a "No" said without insolence or malignity.

Such is England as affected by her government, such America. We shall have grave questions to meet, which will try the virtue of our institutions; we are opening wide the gates of suffrage, heretofore ajar, and inviting hoary heathenism to become units with us in self-government. But we cannot have issues in the future more dismaying than England in the present, — all sympathy for her! — thus summed up by one of her best missionaries of peace: —

"For the United States there is no Catholic question, no Irish Church or Scotch Church question; no difficulties between Church and State, or Church and Dissenters, or about national education, on account of religious differences and claims. For the United States there is no such question of Representative Reform as convulsed Great Britain thirty-five years ago, because the republic has not yet outgrown any of its principles of representation, as England had. For the United States there is no peril of exhaustion and decay by an inappropriate and corrupted poor-law, such as that which was truly called the gangrene in the social life of England, which it was equally dangerous to remove and to let alone. The success with which the reform was at length accomplished may interest American readers; but it is to be hoped that there will never be reason for any closer sympathy. In the same way the United States have no colonial troubles to manage, no conquered countries — territories conquered centuries before the present generation saw the light — to elevate, to attach, and to make free and happy; and the best friends of the republic will ever pray that no generation of the citizens will in any age bequeath such an inheritance of difficulty and pain to its posterity. The United States have no such mass of heterogeneous and unsystematized law as England still has to digest, consolidate, and arrange; nor such anomalies of jurisdiction and administration to reconcile or abolish. The United States have no such relics of feudal times as the game laws; no such associations in our irritable, unhappy, and perverse portion of the country as Orange Societies, and Ribbon Societies, and Whiteboys in Ireland."

CHAPTER XVII.

AMERICA AND ENGLAND AS INFLUENCED BY EACH OTHER.

The critics of each country upon the other. — Causes of our mutual estrangement and consequences of it. — American ideas in England and British emigrants in America. — The peacemakers.

WITH the preceding hasty survey of England, as a subject of curiosity to us, we may conclude by a few inquiries as to which nation owes most to the other. And here is the present quality of exchange: our money is exported to England as to the richer country in accumulations, and British people are exported to us as to the richer country in prospective riches, and the better in present opportunity. England affects us as a powerful state, where the people are organized most efficiently for war and melted into its thunderbolts. The figure that struck Webster was of British drums following the course of the sun around the earth; the picture that Byron saw of America was: —

> "One great clime,
> Whose vigorous offspring by dividing ocean
> Are kept apart, and nursed in the devotion
> Of freedom."

These are the distinctions: when we are menaced by war, civil or foreign, by debt, by any of those things which test the fabric of the state, we recall the prescriptions of England, — her energies drilled, her people bred to the sea and to harness, like so many blooded animals, her powers for despotism or for peace alike kept under the watchful lash or goad of the monarchy; when England is at peace, — and peace is the wish of all the better nations now, — she looks at her festering masses, ignorant, striving in vain for release from vice, and from hard labor underpaid, for a better life and a better chance, and she has but to follow their trail to muse upon the nation that is the consuming problem of her existence.

It has been often said that we, of all nations, should have been allies, — parcels of each other, with a common antiquity, and a like religion, literature, and common law. But there is no great nation that can be the friend of England, as there has never been any such which could abide her arrogant and jealous temper. She has impulses of good, and sympathies for the weak, but no conception of the friendship of equals, no magnanimity to see the standard-bearer of her language widen its destinies and accommodate itself to its mission.

Before we took up arms, she seemed to apprehend the future that might open to us, and exerted all the violence of her prerogatives to depress us. When we revolted, she used her energies almost to exhaustion to conquer us, and when from time to time she was repulsed, she only lessened in her offers of peace the number of patriots she intended to hang.

For that period, and the period succeeding, the present generation of Englishmen is not accountable; only a few live who remember her bullying and her outrages upon the high seas, her orders in Council, the burning of our Capitol, the wasting of our coasts.

Failing in both attempts, she opened upon us by such unity and concert the more offensive batteries of the most servile press in Europe, that we have a national indictment against England which is for the present, at least, committed to every American memory. It is not an indictment which can come to trial; but it cannot come to be explained away. There is no error in the assurance of it, however it may be drawn. And that it was not the mere verbiage of irresponsible people came to proof in the latest and last crisis of our nation, when England put her fleets and stores of arms to sea with less intention to assist our malcontents than to crush the principle that both of us represented. We are not to be persuaded in a day nor a year that it is possible for us to be the natural allies of a state guilty of this long vindictiveness. The London "Times" assumed it, when in answer to the speech of Hon. Charles Sumner on England's responsibility for the ravages of the Alabama, that paper said, "We cannot be made to pay for our sentiments." The long abuse of us and the last assault upon us are directly charged by the American people to the living generation of England, and to our grievance is added suspicion of the hasty and servile congratulations which are now tendered us.

There is no foreign subject on which the representative intelligence of America is more informed than this. We know every man who said good words for us at the right time; we know the friendship of the English workingmen, — the only nobility that we recognize as of any consequence to us; and we know, as even meaner than the *pseudo* nobility, the miserable class of British tradesmen who are unworthy of any class, as they are of none, parasites of aristocracy, whether they write leaders in Furnival's Inn, or write law in Gray's Inn Lane, or write books by Blackheath, or write invoices from Blackwall. Mr. Dickens, on his second and financial errand to America, thought that a comet had better fire the earth than America and England go to war; but of the fourteen millions of people added to America since his first visit, not one could have taken encouragement to come amongst us for anything that Mr. Dickens had written.

It was as if England had planted buoys along all our coasts and placarded them with: "Keep off!" "Man-eaters dwell here!" "Beware of the Mob!" "Violence ashore!" And suddenly by an illumination of victory over a purified republic and a rescued state, we had read from the same missionary beacons: "Happy Land!" "Everlasting Alliance!" "Same Shakespeare!" "Give us your hand!"

A state debauched in honesty like this must either have a heartless national character or a treacherous government, — and it can take its choice!

The true index to British dislike of us was doubtless inspired by the suspicious malevolence of an aristocracy for a republic. The literary war upon us began with old Doctor Johnson, pensioned by Lord Bute, who attacked us during our Revolution, and George III. gave the true index to the fear of the aristocracy, when, on receiving our first ministers, he muttered "in deep emotion" his conviction that the monarchical was the only proper form of government.

Since that time we have been, not the victims, but the objects, of constant scurrility and concerted evil prophesying. Our own behavior in return has been hospitable, conciliatory, at times mildly reproachful.

All attempts made to endow scholarships of American history and literature at Oxford and Cambridge Universities have been rejected, and upon what other ground it would be hard to say, than that of repugnance to permit America to be understood, at her best, by young Englishmen. Yet this British nation, so meanly illiberal in its sentiment, is forever lecturing us upon the beauty of reciprocity; it seems that trade ought to be free current, but not history and morals. On the other hand there are many thousand Americans who look upon English political history, since the close of the French and Indian war, as well-nigh a useless study in our colleges, and one that had better be displaced by the study of European continental politics. The economic history of England began at the suppression of Bonaparte, and is of vast interest, while all its triumphs have been the rebuke of the previous century of English glory. The name of Pitt is pigmy beside that of Peel; Wellington's hollow squares disappear in Watt's hollow cylinders; the live men of England are civilized from America, and every great advance movement in England, for eighty years, has been in despite of the literature which has wasted so much advice on America. The tune of the creature has changed of late, but not his appetite, and it is unlikely that America will pay as much heed to English adulation in the future as she gave to English jealousy in the past. The "Times," which is of late our sweetheart, said of us no longer ago than 1863, in its praise of Russell's diary: —

"The United States have been a vast burlesque on the functions of national existence, and it was Mr. Russell's fate to behold their transformation scene, and to see the first tumbles of their clowns and pantaloons. It was time for him to come away, though the shame of his retirement was theirs. He did his duty while he was with them, and he has left them a legacy in this 'Diary.'"

Gather together all the literature of bigotry since the Reformation, and there will not be any parcel so filthy as fifty years of British comment on America, which served, like garbage in general, only to fertilize the land on which it was shed. As the blood of the martyrs was the seed of the church, the ink of British critics was the seed of America. And this being discovered, the British sweetheart asks us now to be thankful for it. At which characteristic impertinence we shall be probably magnanimous enough to smile. A thorough brief upon this subject is the work of Henry T. Tuckerman, entitled "America and her Commentators," which, it is to be regretted, closes before the period of that climatic vituperation during the war, when almost every chip-monk and bull-frog between John O'Groat's and Land's End swelled the riot of denunciation. It was a chorus like that the devils raised in Longfellow's "Golden Legend" around the cross they are striving to hurl from the cathedral: —

John Bull. "Hasten! hasten!
Oh ye spirits!
From its station drag the ponderous
Cross of iron that to mock us
Is uplifted high in air!

Aristocratic voices. "Oh, we cannot!
For around it
All the Saints and Guardian Angels
Throng in legions to protect it;
They defeat us everywhere!"

So rallied the desperate minions of aristocracy around the American flag, and, failing to rend it, Mr. Russell, their ablest and most unprincipled emissary, lugubriously added: —

"I never could meet any one in the States able to account for the insignia on that flag, though it has been suggested that they are an amplification of the heraldic bearing of George Washington. Strange, indeed, if the family blazon of an English squire should have become the flaunting flag of the Great Republic, which, with all its faults, has done so much for the world, and may yet, purged of its vanity, arrogance, and aggressive tendency, do so much more for mankind! Not excepting our own, it is the most widely spread flag on the seas; for whilst it floats by the side of the British ensign in every haunt of our commerce, it has almost undisputed possession of vast tracts of sea in the Pacific and South Atlantic."

No clearer indication can be had of the self-conviction of England as to her treatment of America than her universal speed at the close of our war to borrow our military inventions and extend her navy; the great inquiry of the English press became: —

"How many troops can the Yankees put in the field? How many ships on the sea?"

Then came the almost enforced confederation of the Canadas and neighboring colonies; and to this day the fear of suffering some physical return for her brutal treatment of America is apparent throughout the wide range of English periodicals. In ludicrous avarice, even greater than this fear, the Southern bondholders in England meet to ask the Federal Government to pay the notes of hand cashed by them for the price of our assassination. Impudent servility on the one hand, alarmed spite on the other, — these are the leading traits of the English nation as instanced in intercourse with us. None but a rare Christian man could forgive such a character, if he met him in social life; and yet perhaps America can rise to this rank and forget this uncivil nation.

The question is put: "Does it become us as a great state to be sensitive to abuse?" Perhaps not; yet complaint is made of us that we lack identity, and therefore cannot be a strong and sensitive state. English comment is worth just this to us: it teaches us not what we are, but who are the English people. What generous natures, open sentiments, philosophic cheerfulnesses, and cosmopolitan educations must they have who can devote fifty years of journalism to our aggravation, and yet have never produced one philosophic treatise upon America out of the Bibliotheque they have made upon us! For two centuries previously the English berated France in the same way, and at the spectacle of her heroic Revolution they beggared themselves willingly to pluck the eagle's feathers from her wing. It is this state, where every strata of society is skewered through with the cold pulse of aristocracy, which claims to be our only blood relative and progenitor; but except in a certain practicality of head and a similar language we are no longer Englishmen here, but have been humanized with all the tempers of the world. Our race resembles more the Saxon-English of the time of Alfred than the fictitious Englishman of to-day.

"The superior candor of the French writers on America is obvious to the most superficial reader," says Mr. Tuckerman. "The urbanity and the philosophical tendency of the national mind account for this more genial and intelligent treatment; but the striking difference of temper and of scope between the French and English travels in America is accounted for mainly by the comparative freedom from political and social prejudice on the part of the former, and the frequent correspondence of their sentiments with those of the inhabitants of the New World."

The difference between a French and an English aristocrat is, that one accepts the situation, and the other compels it. A thorough English democrat, like Cobden, makes use of America for suggestion rather than for demonstration, and is hence not more disinterested, perhaps, but more liberal and sensible.

Beyond the dislike of the dominant aristocracy, the English people have accustomed themselves, through years of cavilling and meddling with mankind, to become the worst observers in the world, and the most disagreeable travellers. This is their reputation in every country of Europe; waiters and commissionaires run for them, but everybody else runs the other way. Their innumerable guide-books of other lands are illustrations of bad digestion, bad manners, and no philosophy; and the majority of their commonplace books of travel are directed entirely toward the aristocratic market.

The memorable papers which first established the reputation of

Dickens curiously indicate the prevalence of this deprecatory and venal spirit in English writers on America, at a late period. The elder Weller, in suggesting to Samivel his notable plan for the escape of Pickwick from the Fleet Prison, by concealing himself in a "pianner forty," significantly adds: "Have a passage ready taken for 'Merriker. Let the gov'ner stop there till Mrs. Bardell's dead, and then take and let him come back and write a book about the 'Merrikens as 'll pay all his expenses, and more, if he blows 'em up enough."

The man who could write this passage six years before he himself wrote just that sort of book could scarcely have been careful about what the world said of his literary integrity. We have had all sorts of tramps and eavesdroppers amongst us from the land of our natural ally, and they appear to have been of little account at home, by English report. Ashe, one of the most noted of them, is openly described as a swindler; Faux as "low;" Parkinson was "a common gardener;" Fearon "a stocking-weaver." Cobbett, who is the last person to be suspected of aristocratic prejudices, and was the most practical and perverse of democrats, observed, in reading the fastidious comments of one of these impudent travellers upon an American meal, that it was "such a breakfast as the fellow had never before tasted;" and the remark explains the presumption and ignorance of many of this class of writers, who, never before having enjoyed the least social consideration or private luxury, became, like a beggar on horseback, intoxicated therewith.

Our ladies were particularly taken to task by Mrs. Trollope, a sort of peripatetic lady whose fortune was made by our sensitiveness; and we have since had an expiatory sort of book from her son Anthony, whom I have frequently quoted in this compilation. Mr. Tuckerman sums up the second Trollope thus interestingly: —

"Mr. Trollope seems extremely afraid of giving offence, continually deprecates the idea, and wishes it understood that it is very painful to him to find fault with anybody or anything in the United States; but he must censure as well as blame, and he means no unkindness. All this, however amiable, is really preposterous. It presupposes a degree of importance as belonging to his opinions, or rather a necessity for their expression, which seems to us quite irrational in a man of such common sense, and who has seen so much of the world. It is amusing, and, as a friend remarked, 'comes from his blood, not his brain.' It is the old leaven of self-love, self-importance, self-assertion, of the Englishman as such. If he had passed years instead of months in America, and grown familiar with other circles beside the circle of *littérateurs* who so won his admiration in Boston, he would have found all he has written of the spoiled children, the hard women, the despotic landlords, disgusting railway cars, western swindlers, bad architecture, official peculations, mud, dust, and desolation of Washington, misery of Cairo, and base, gold-seeking politicians of America, overheated rooms, incongruous *cuisine*, and undisciplined juveniles, thoroughly appreciated, perfectly understood, and habitually the subject of native protest and foreign report."

Enough of these wailing travellers; and it is scarcely necessary to consider the late English panegyrics upon us, which are as worthless, excepting, perhaps, the manly book of Charles W. Dilke, who recognizes the fact that America and England are not of the same blood: "America is becoming not English merely, but world-embracing in the variety of its typè; and, as the English element has given language and history to that land, America offers the English race the moral directorship of the globe, by ruling mankind through Saxon institutions and the English tongue. Through America, England is speaking to the world."

De Tocqueville ascribes our alleged sensitiveness to criticism, to the nature of our government.

"Democratic institutions generally give men a lofty notion of their country and of themselves. An American leaves his country with a heart swollen with pride; on arriving in Europe he at once finds out that we are not so engrossed by the United States and the great people which inhabits them as he had supposed, and this begins to annoy him."

There are, undoubtedly, Americans, who are fascinated by the higher social life of England, its juicy chops and steaks, its large estates, luxurious life, and high-born manners; but a still larger number are fascinated by Paris and the Continent; we go where we can get the most for our money, if pleasure be the object. Hawthorne, while Consul at Liverpool, saw even more decided preference for England amongst certain eccentric people.

"After all these bloody wars and vindictive animosities, we have still an unspeakable yearning toward England. When our forefathers left the old home, they pulled up many of their roots, but trailed along with them others, which were never snapped asunder by the tug of such a lengthening distance, nor have been torn out of the original soil by the violence of subsequent struggles, nor severed by the edge of the sword.

"A mere coincidence of names," he says, "a supposititious pedigree, a silver mug on which an anciently engraved coat-of-arms has been half scrubbed out, a seal with an uncertain crest, an old yellow letter or document in faded ink, the more scantily legible the better, — rubbish of this kind, found in a neglected drawer, has been potent enough to turn the brain of many an honest Republican, especially if assisted by an advertisement for lost heirs, cut out of a British newspaper.

"It has required nothing less than the boorishness, the stolidity, the self-sufficiency, the contemptuous jealousy, the half-sagacity, invariably blind of one eye and often distorted of the other, that characterize this strange people, to compel us to be a great nation in our own right, instead of continuing virtually, if not in name, a province of their small island. What pains did they take to shake us off, and have ever since taken to keep us wide apart from them! It might seem their folly, but was really their fate, or, rather, the providence of God, who has doubtless a work for us to do, in which the massive materiality of the English character would have been too ponderous a dead weight upon our progress."

One of the most ingenious passages in De Tocqueville is that wherein he accounts for the assumptions of many hair-brained Americans in Europe, where, it is possible, that some of his type may still go, carrying all their provincialism with them.

"An American," says this pointed writer, "is forever talking of the admirable equality which prevails in the United States; aloud he makes it the boast of his country, but in secret he deplores it for himself; and he aspires to show that, for his part, he is an exception to the general state of things which he vaunts. There is hardly an American to be met with who does not claim some remote kindred with the first founders of the colonies; and as for the scions of the noble families of England, America seemed to me to be covered with them. When an opulent American arrives in Europe, his first care is to surround himself with all the luxuries of wealth; he is so afraid of being taken for the plain citizen of a democracy, that he adopts a hundred distorted ways of bringing some new instance of his wealth before you every day. His house will be in the most fashionable part of the town; he will always be surrounded by a host of servants. I have heard an American complain, that in the best houses of Paris the society was rather mixed; the taste which prevails there was not pure enough for him; and he ventured to hint that, in his opinion, there was a want of elegance of manner; he could not accustom himself to see wit concealed under such unpretending forms.

"These contrasts ought not to surprise us. If the vestiges of former aristocratic distinctions were not so completely effaced in the United States, the Americans would be less simple and less tolerant in their own country; they would require less, and be less fond of borrowed manners in ours."

Since De Tocqueville's time we have grown more self-possessed, more attached to our institutions, and more cosmopolitan within ourselves. We have our own celebrities, and do not go in multitudes to look at foreigners, who mortify us for it. Our attention is turned from Europe to the near Orient, whence are to come the problems of multitude and mode which will speedily overflow the Rocky Mountains, and meet Europe half way on the plains of the Missouri. Destinies of colossal magnitude tower in that Asiatic mist, and with youth, but confidence, we accept them. This hemisphere was laid away for no one race; the pilgrims and they of the caravans of the earth have seen our star, and at last the English Magi also.

And ours is the government of which Emile de Girardin in "La Liberté" says (1868): "The population of America, not thinned by any conscription, multiplies with prodigious rapidity, and the day may before seen, when they will number sixty or eighty millions of souls. This *parvenue* is aware of his importance and destiny. Hear him proudly exclaim, 'America for Americans!' See him promising his alliance to Russia; and we see that power which well knows what force is, grasp the hand of this giant of yesterday.

"In view of his unparalleled progress and combination, what are the little toys with which we vex ourselves in Europe? What is this needle gun, we are anxious to get from Prussia, that we may beat her next year with it? Had we not better take from America the principle of liberty she embodies, out of which have come her citizen pride, her gigantic industry, and her formidable loyalty to the destinies of her Republican land?"

Since America was discovered she has been a subject of revolutionary thought in Europe. The mystery of her coming forth from vacancy, the marvel of her wealth in gold and silver, the spectacle of her captives led through European capitols, filled the minds of men with unrest; and unrest is the first stage of revolution. Out of her discovery grew the European reformation in religion; out of our Revolutionary War grew the revolutionary period of Europe. And out of our rapid development among great states and happy peoples, has come an emigration more wonderful than that which invaded Europe from Asia in the latter centuries of the Roman Empire. When we raised our flag on the Atlantic, Europe sent her contributions; it appeared on the Pacific, and all orientalism felt the signal. They are coming in two endless fleets, eastward and westward, and the highway is swung between the oceans for them to tread upon. We have lightened Ireland of half her weight, and Germany is coming by the village-load every day. England herself is sending the best of her working-men now (1869), and in such numbers as to dismay her Jack Bunsbys. What is to be the limit of this mighty immigration? There is extant a calculation made by the late Elkanah Watson. In the year 1815, writing on the progress of the population of the United States, he said: —

"In 1810 it was seven million two hundred and thirty-nine thousand nine hundred and three. The increase from 1790, the first census under the Constitution, has been about one-third at each census. Admitting that it will continue to increase in the same ratio, the result will be as follows: —

"In 1820	Watson	predicted	. . 9,625,734,	and it was in fact 9,638,151
In 1830	"	"	. . 12,833,645,	and it was in fact 12,866,020
In 1840	"	"	. . 17,116,526,	and it was in fact 17,062,566
In 1850	"	"	. . 23,185,368,	and it was in fact 23,191,876
In 1860	"	"	. . 31,753,824,	and it was in fact 31,445,089
In 1870	"	"	. . 42,328,432	
In 1880	"	"	. . 56,450,241	
In 1890	"	"	. . 77,266,989	
In 1900	"	"	. . 100,355,985"	

The accuracy of these calculations is truly wonderful, and gives authority to the four latter predictions. Mr. Watson added: —

"It would be almost presumptuous to stretch our minds through the ensuing century; and yet, taking as a basis one hundred million at the close of this century, and, in consideration of dense population, intestine and foreign wars, a possible subdivision, in consequence, with several republics, we will suppose the increase will be one-third in each twenty years for forty years, one-third the next thirty, and one-fifth for the next fifty years. It will stand thus: —

"For 1930, in round numbers	133,000,000
For 1940	177,000,000
For 1970	236,000,000
For 2000	283,000,000

— equal to the population of China."

But by the year 1900, what will be the drained population of China? In the first five months of 1869, nearly one hundred and fifteen thousand emigrants landed in New York.

Astounded at this increase, the timid are reflecting that it will do the country more evil than good. They are producing Old Malthus again, that sensitive British statistician, who wanted the human race to stop, for fear it would over-populate the world. By that time, perhaps, the world will stop; but we are not the people to stop it. Even the hopeful Mr. Dilke found one "old fellow who said to me, 'I don't want the Americans in 1900 to be two hundred millions; but I want them to be happy.'"

Now, Mr. Dilke, pray let us grow, — or is this the beginning of a new series of British predictions?

The influence of England upon America is now almost entirely of a passive character. We read some of her books, and sorry are we that we do not always pay for them; but the British author never could have expected so many readers under this form of government; at least he said as much. We buy a great deal of iron, and so forth, in England, and we like Spurgeon's Sermons, because we think he is in earnest. We are obliged to English capitalists who made their money out of us, for returning some of it at ten per cent. to give us railroads. We watch the reform question in England, and like Mr. Goldwin Smith and other highly-educated gentleman to come to teach us to be more profoundly and thoughtfully educated. We admire the learning of England, — for she has more learned men though not more learning men than we, — but we do not always take the advice of Mr. Carlyle. We print paper for the New York "Tribune" in the Falls of Niagara, and then allow the Falls to "shoot" themselves. Finally, we wish no war with England; for that would be too much in the line of her policy, and it would be foolish. We prefer to read instead what Mr. Russell said about that visionary war in 1864.

"If the American civil war were over in 1865," said Mr. Russell, "there would probably be six hundred thousand men under arms, and there would be at least two hundred thousand more men in the

States, who had served, and would take up arms against England with alacrity. A considerable portion of that army would indeed seek their discharge and go quietly back to their avocations; but the Irish, Germans, etc., to whom the license of war was agreeable, would not be unwilling to invade Canada, and a percentage of Americans would doubtless eagerly seek for an opportunity of gaining against a foreign enemy the laurels they had not found whilst contending with their fellow-countrymen. Commerce, indeed, would suffer; the Americans would find for the first time what it was to enter upon a quarrel, single-handed, with the British nation. They have hitherto met only the side blows and stray shots of the old mother country; and they believe they have encountered the full weight of her arm, and the utmost extent of her energies. The wicked men who are striving to engage the two States in a quarrel which would cover the seas of the world with blood and wreck, cannot be deterred from their horrible work by any appeals to fear or conscience; but the influence of the past and of the Christian and civilized people of the ex-United States will, it is to be hoped, defeat their efforts, seconded though they may be by the prejudice, religious animosity, and national dislike of a portion of the people."

This wicked class has cleaned its pipes and commenced a new tune. It followed Mr. Russell out of the country, as the children followed the Pied Piper. We hear its tootings on the other shore, to which our backs are turned for the present, and, remembering its half century of warnings and invocations, we are reminded of the best known poem in the language: —

"'Beware the pine-tree's withered branch!
Beware the awful avalanche!'
This was the peasant's last good-night, —
A voice replied far up the height:
'EXCELSIOR!'"

PART II.

FRANCE AND THE CONTINENT OF EUROPE.

NATIONAL INSTITUTIONS.

1—Hotel des Invalides, Paris. 2—Hotel Dieu, Paris. 3—Hospital at Cincinnati. 4—Greenwich Hospital, London.

CHAPTER XVIII.

NEW YORK AND PARIS.

The chief cities of the American and the European continents.

"NEW YORK and Washington Through Line" indicates the indifference of the majority of American travellers to whatever lies between. Two hundred and twenty-six miles apart, the fast trains traverse this distance in nine hours, which is perhaps equal to the highest speed attained on American railways; the passenger lies down in the sleeping-car at Washington at his usual bedtime, and while he dreams, his boots are blackened, and when he wakens it is at New York. His fare is eight dollars.

"Through Night Service, London and Paris in nine and a half hours," indicates no stopping-place between, for the majority of English travellers. The distance is about twenty-five miles greater than from Washington to New York, and there is the rough Strait of Dover between, the most travelled and the most tempestuous ocean ferry in the world, the average time to traverse which is one hour and a half. The first-class fare is about fourteen dollars. The European speed is noticeably greater, taking the changes of baggage and passengers into consideration. As we must pay extra fare for a sleeping-car, the European must pay an extra fee to the steward on the boat, and both extras are vicious in system. The second-class carriages, which cost from two to three dollars less, to Paris, are more comfortable than our regular first-class cars. The Straits of Dover are as annoying on this line as were the former ferries at Philadelphia and Havre de Grace.

There are four routes from London to Paris, and the shortest I have indicated; there is but one route, practically, from Washington to New York. The ride between both pairs of cities is marked by strong and variable scenery, and the American can trace resemblances between the steep white bluffs and rolling seas of the strait and the strong scenery at the head of the Chesapeake; between the flat and fertile fields of New Jersey and the wide and cultivated plains of France. There are a dozen important towns between, but either the city of Philadelphia or Baltimore outnumbers the combined cities between London and Paris, while London and Paris, massed together with their interlinking cities, make five and a half millions of city folks, and Washington and New York, including Brooklyn massed in the same way, make two and a third millions.

In some small degree London may be likened to New York, and Paris to Washington. To the former two there is the same gathering of masts, the same smell of the sea, the same commercial dictatorship; a like assemblage of daring capitalists and capital; similar opinions upon subjects of trade; a thunderous newspaper press; and that hold upon much of the country that the lender has upon the borrower, and the buyer upon the producer. The similarity in the landscapes of Washington and Paris has been remarked, — the same broken and lofty amphitheatre of wooded hills, the same running river, almost equal distance from the salt water, large public buildings, bureaucracy in the administration, soldiers in the streets and forts on the heights; and Paris, like Washington, is the spot toward which the continent faces. Its "decrees" can move gold up or down; its attitude in finance or toward war makes emotion from the North to the Black Sea. For the rest, Washington is only the skeleton of Paris, — and yet as a skeleton not without resemblance: its broad avenues converging upon areas strategic either for picturesqueness or for military operations, — but Paris is clothed with centuries of power and adornments; her population is greater than that of the whole assembled States of Virginia, Maryland, Delaware, and the District of Columbia. In 1820, after the desolating wars of Bonaparte, her population was but seven hundred and fourteen thousand; in 1866 her population was two million one hundred and fifty thousand. The population of New York, Brooklyn, and their suburbs is now about one million and a half.

To compare the natural site of New York with that of Paris would be unjust to the latter. If neither city existed, and some fisherman on the island of New York were transported to Paris, he would see a flat plain, bordered by hillocks, divided by a clear, running stream, and the whole, at some considerable distance, walled round with pleasant rolling heights of grass and wood. If he were to embark in his boat for the sea, he would pass by crooked courses through a valley and plain, soft, fertile, and hill-bound, like that behind him, and receiving frequent accessions from pastoral rills and little rivers, till, after two or three days' sailing, he would emerge into a wide and gentle bay with white bluffs of shore, and headlands for its gates almost in sight of each other. The headland to the right would be the site of Havre, and that to the left, of Cherbourg. Between Paris and the sea he would have passed a space left between picturesque heights, and this would be the site of Rome. His comment upon all this would have been: "It is a pastoral, and a grape and grain-growing region, but tame for a fisherman!"

If New York were also merely its foundation, and the pastoral peasant of the valley of the Seine were suddenly to be placed above it, he would feel the strong, salt neighborhood of the sea, and see a long, canoe-shaped island, just loosened astern from the solid land, moored in twice its width of water, and pointing its prow into a wide bay. This island is thirteen and a half miles long, and of an average breadth of more than a mile and a half; its entire surface of twenty-two miles is bold and granitic, and in profile resembling the cartilagineous back of a sturgeon. Its highest altitude above the tide is two hundred and thirty-eight feet. A wide, salt river flows down either side; to the right the majestic Hudson, a mile wide, unbroken by an island; to the left, the deep East River, a third of a mile wide, with a chain of slender islands abreast.

The opposite slopes of the Hudson River are high and imposing, and like driven "Palisades" of rock they stretch far rearward to the north till lost to view; the opposite slopes of the East River are green knolls that rise gracefully from the water. But where the two rivers unite at the prow of the island to enter the bay, a sentinel height stands on either side, and between these the island of the city points to the sea. Astern of this island, tidal channels make up from either river to its neighbor, and discharge in sluices at opposing tides; ahead of this island opens the beautiful bay, fifteen miles in circumference, and showing occasional small islands above its surface; at the foot of this bay, one island, almost mountainous, stands in the way, so that the waters are cramped into a strait less than two miles wide, with one small islet in the middle and bold steeps on either side; passing this strait, the waters again expand into a broader bay with less precipitous shores, where they receive accessions from other rivers, and move on by sandy spits and beaches to the ocean. But even at the ocean side one towering height holds guard, and shows itself to sails far off upon the sea. The ocean itself is only eighteen miles distant from the island of the city.

All this would the fisherman of the Seine behold, and feel the briny air, like the breath of this strong seaboard landscape, — a nature cast in hardy countenance, yet with a largeness and breadth that touch the intellect of the beholder, and make him feel that he who could live in the sight of this scenery should have high thoughts and enterprises. But as this water-bound island has two rivers, so it has two aisles to the sea; for where the tidal channels in the rear make sluices by their opposing tides, another bay opens out from the river of the East, — a little archipelago indeed, — and this again narrows to a slender channel, through which, when one has passed, a most beautiful Sound or inland sea extends eastward to the Atlantic, like the long inundated nave of a cathedral. This Sound is one hundred and ten miles long, and from two miles to twenty miles wide. The land between the two outlets to the ocean is Long Island, which is one hundred and forty miles long, and twelve miles wide.*

* The author may be pardoned for citing some verses which he published a short time ago, if they help to make plain the topography of New York. The subject of the poem is "Pan Building the City": —

"Then, for the gateways of the city, reach
A hundred leagues of golden-grainéd beach, —
Long Island, stretching to Montawk away,
And Jersey, shining to the Cape of May;
'Twixt either, jutting o'er the ocean's brink,
Stands nature's grandest lighthouse, Naversink.
Within, five rivers break into the land, —
Five mighty fingers, whose blue-veined hand
Makes a broad bay, by virgin zephyrs kissed,
Slender, but granite corded at the wrist:
The Narrows, fastest gate of Freedom. Thence,
Craggéd for picturesqueness and defence,
Dividing walls go sweeping, — to the left
By the great palisaded fresh sea cleft;
And on the right, where stark bare islets swell,
Like drifting souls caught in the gates of hell,
Burst by contending tides, which smoothly bound
In soft horizons, a most slumb'rous Sound,
Heir of the long green valleys; set between,
One island, like an arrow-head shot down,
Studded with lights and tints like diamond-sheen,
Lengthwise a sceptre, profiled like a crown,
Groom to the sea and of the land the Queen:
'Behold! Great Pan!' the Tritons cried, 'your town!'

It is this canoe-shaped island which is covered by the city of New York, — the third city of the civilized world in rank of population, the second in commerce, and the first in opportunities. There is no harbor in Europe at all comparable with it, and Rio de Janeiro, Havana, and San Francisco are the only comparable ones in the world. The Sound, which constitutes one of its ocean approaches, is a miniature Mediterranean, bordered with large towns and cities, receiving tributary rivers from old and populous valleys, and carrying an inland and coastwise commerce, which is, of itself, no despicable navy. The River Hudson is the American Rhine, and to masculine tastes its sceneries are, if not so various, more grand and striking than those of the German river. The mainland between river and Sound, from which New York island is detached, is composed of lofty and rugged hills, holding large lakes in their hollows. The sea-coasts hereabout are renowned for their beaches and the infinite varieties of game and shell-fish which harbor in them. The flat-lands at the end of the heights on the opposite bank of the River Hudson constitute the State of New Jersey, — one of the most extensive gardens of fruit and vegetables in the world. And the whole of the island of the city is accessible to its piers by the largest shipping afloat. No docks are requisite here, as in Europe, to give rest to vessels; they swim to the brink of the city, and shelter there like the ducklets beneath their mother. There is but one dock, in the English sense, at New York, — and that is at Brooklyn.

For the present let us suspend a description of the human covering of this island, and, leaving it in a state of nature as our supposititious peasant beheld it, recall the circumstances of its discovery and settlement.

The year the translation of the English Bible began (1607), Henry Hudson set sail to make a name and place in America. On his second voyage, in 1609, he entered the bay of New York, in a vessel called the *Half Moon*, and the savages from the shores swarmed out in their canoes, to see what could be done in the way of trade and stealing. This adventurous man, with a name which seems quite sonorous now

Profound the ocean, bowing at its doors;
Eternal as the eternal world its floors;
Dyed in the plumages of birds its skies;
Calm sheltered, like the strength in tender eyes;
In infinite sublimest sceneries pent;
Potential to inspire or make content;
It diadems the virgin continent!"

ascended the river which commemorates it as far as Albany; thus discovering — and apparently by collusion — both the metropolis and the State capital. On his report, which was probably as sanguine as that of any man who has been to New York, the Dutch East India Company sent two vessels out to make a settlement, for the purpose of prosecuting the fur-trade, — a business which afterward made John Jacob Astor the richest New Yorker, though he got his furs elsewhere. New York was thus settled from New Amsterdam, in Holland, in the year 1614, and it grew steadily and stolidly, under Dutch government, for fifty years. It was named New Amsterdam; and old Amsterdam, its colonizer, then had twenty thousand ships and one hundred thousand sailors of her own. The population of old Amsterdam, the parent of New York, was 261,455, in the year 1865, or less than that of Brooklyn.

The English captured this town in 1664, and, ten years later, changed its name to New York. Almost all the Dutch, including their Governor, held over, and it is to their blood that New York owes much of her commercial spirit. The most characteristic act James II. ever did for her was to forbid her a printing-press. The first grammar school was established in 1702, the first newspaper in 1725, and Columbia College, of New York, dates back to 1754. The city was prompt to revolt against British oppression, and suffered more than any other in the colonies; for more than seven years the British held it, and made it a prison and a garrison, while the most stirring deeds of the conflict were enacted in the neighborhood. Hence departed the enemy's fleets on almost all their expeditions, and, with Newport, then the rival of New York, the island city felt the hardest burdens of the conquered. On the 25th of November, 1783, the red-cross flag sailed from New York Bay, and immediately afterward the army of Washington marched over that part of the island that we have called the stern, and entered the battered old barrack village. At that time, by the closest computation, it was fifty per cent. worse off than if it had never been settled at all. The true age of New York city, therefore, is no more than ninety years; for in ten years after the evacuation it had doubled its population. It had enough bricks together to make it the seat of government for a little while; and here Washington, in his becoming velvet breeches and his hair in a bag, walked out near the spot where the "Bulls" and "Bears" contend at the present day, and said most reverently, as if he were taking a sacrament, the oath of Chief Magistrate. Here

Hamilton wrote the "Federalist," and Talleyrand saw him, with his books under his arm, going to court. Here sprang up, at the beginning of the country, the created politician, — the splendid head and carriage of De Witt Clinton; the agreeable face, and, behind it, the long, organizing head of Hamilton; the lithe, suave, cold-blooded person of Burr; the big joints and battle-inviting face of George Clinton; the gentleman, Livingston; the Man, Jay.

To this day these peculiarities remain: New York is the home of organizing politicians and organizing commercial merchants. With a nucleus of Dutch and conservative English elements, its proximity to New England has made tributary to it all that thrifty race of individual people who live on the Sound and its inflowing rivers. Brooklyn is more nearly the metropolis of New England than Boston; for Boston is chiefly itself.

This is a city, therefore, of exclusively commercial origin. An idea pervaded almost every other colony. In New England they wanted to form a Calvinistic nation; in Maryland, a school of Catholic toleration; in Delaware, a Swedish sub-nationality; in Virginia, a landed aristocracy; but here, to New York, they came solely to trade, to barter, to grow rich; and they have achieved it, they and their heterogeneous posterity. To this day there are no names more honored than those of the old Dutch settlers, Stuyvesants, Roosevelts, Livingstons, Courtlandts. Their names exist in streets and squares and "slips" and ferries. They loved their holidays and social glasses, and New York has more holidays, commercial as she is, than any American city; she is also one of the most convivial of our cities, albeit keen at a trade and particularly keen at a speculation. She is a popular city amongst Americans, and probably the most popular; for there is little jealousy, amongst her genuine natives, of any other municipality in the east, however it may be arrogated by naturalized people from other States, who bring their love of jealousy with them when they settle here. Politically, New York is conservative in its professions, but radically American in its impulses. It is the most thoroughly municipal of all our cities, and also the most cosmopolitan of them all; no New Yorker asks one's origin, though, if he finds it to be Manhattan Island, he is glad. The town is corruptly governed, because it is governed exclusively by politicians and the lower orders; but on any great national awakening there is a marked discrepancy between the votes and the attitude of New York. Her militia is organized in the dullest periods of peace; her people know what is abroad, and feel the first breath of national indignation; when her Mayor consented to see the Union broken up, her soldiers were on the march to restore it. Monumentally, she is the foremost of all cities on the western continent, and, considering the character of the age, New York is probably more representative of it, for her time of life, than any city in the world. Had she existed in the age of Gothic cathedral building, she would have piled up an edifice greater than Cologne, Milan, or Winchester.

New York, in a word, is essentially self-possessed, human, undegenerate, in the prime of youthful manhood, based upon no idiosyncrasy, warmed by no fever, the outgrowth of her splendid situation, educated without a teacher, magnanimous by her circumstances, the best exemplification of a mercantile republic, with a rabble beneath but a sound head above. No law can make her other or better, but such law as is the expression of her nature. She is wild in some things, and has her portion of the extravagances and vices; but compare these with their cotemporary fellows of London and Paris! When it is remembered that she is the third city of the world, and that human nature is not all good, let the mind rest for hope upon her splendid charities, her ready hand and liberal purse, her general co-operation, in great things, with the country of which she is a part. And what American would blot her out, — her sails, her waters, her ferment, her clear American head? Who would strike out her "Tribune," or even her "Herald," so like herself, at least in enterprise?

There is much to grieve missionaries in New York; but she is much larger than the missionary's own family, and even there all may not be perfect. When the missionary wants a text for a sermon on depravity he goes to New York; when he wants a collection for his poor church he goes to New York; in any event he goes to New York, and that is what it is to have almost a metropolis.

The city of New York, as I have said, embraces the whole of this lance-shaped island, but the densely settled city covers only the lower half; yet the entire island is lighted with lamps, supplied with water, and given paved streets far into the open country. The small channel which divides the island from the main land to the north is called by the two Dutch names of Harlem and Spuyten Duyvil rivers; across this channel lie extensive suburbs; several bridges cross it; amongst them that which does no other work than bring the water for the city from lakes thirty-two miles distant, and which of itself cost nine hundred thousand dollars, while the whole aqueduct of which it is a part cost thirteen million dollars, and will cost twenty million dollars with its extensions. The eight arches of this bridge, of hewn masonry, are each one hundred feet high. Where the Harlem River debouches into the East River, the confluence of tides from the Sound and the Bay produces a whirlpool called Hell Gate, which has been a source of vast expense, by reason of the protracted efforts to blast certain rocks in its eddies. Below and above Hell Gate, on the islands which lie in the East and Harlem Rivers are placed the county charities, the hospitals, insane asylums, prisons, houses of correction, etc., and they constitute the most magnificent series of charities on the globe, whether considered architecturally or by their efficiency. The foreign traveller, proceeding up the Sound in the mighty steamers which quit the North River, turn the point of the city, and pass the whirlpool, might suppose these great battlemented buildings to be the palaces, fortresses, and barracks of some secure potentate. Along both sides of the East River as we descend it, warehouses, mills, villas, and blocks of dwellings come to the water's edge, and at piers of piles or stone, thousands of steamers and vessels are loading and discharging cargo; there are of these piers, *par excellence*, about one hundred and twenty on both rivers, and in the large tidal docks between, thousands of smaller tugs and vessels lie, fifteen hundred boats alone being engaged in the fish and oyster trade. Opposite the island of New York, on the shore of Long Island, is a series of large towns, making one consecutive city for many miles; but the largest of the series is Brooklyn, which comprises a large city, formerly separate, called Williamsburgh, the latter lying on the slopes of East River, while Brooklyn proper clambers up the heights at the river's mouth, and extends along the bay, looking down upon New York as the Rhenish castle of Rolandseck looks down upon the island of Nonnenwerth. Between Brooklyn and Williamsburgh lies the United States Navy Yard, in a deep inlet where, in ships and shops, government has property worth twenty-five millions of dollars.

Brooklyn (Dutch word *Breucklen*, broken land) was a mere village in 1816, and it is now larger than Naples, Madrid, or Lyons, a complete city in itself, with its own Aqueduct, City Hall, and Academy of Music; between it and New York innumerable steam ferry-boats, looking like great ivory terrapins, ply swiftly, and fly their gay flags till it seems that a monstrous breed of butterflies is flaunting between a couple of rose-bushes. Below Brooklyn, the bold shores are full of villas, and on an eminence amongst them, in view of the ocean, is the Cemetery of Greenwood, three hundred and thirty acres, perhaps the most beautiful that exists. It is Brooklyn that is an offshoot of New York, and the abode of her merchants, clerks, and working people; it has been called a city of lodging-houses, and also a city of churches, and it is the Passy of Paris, — the city of homes on the hill. It lies in the same State with New York, and has the same police regulations and the same police force, fifteen hundred men in all.

Brooklyn has ambitious hopes of excelling New York in population. New York, according to the Hon. Demas Barnes, has room for a final population of only 1,872,000, counting twelve lots to the acre, and twelve persons to the lot. Her population in 1800 was 60,000; in 1820, 123,000; in 1840, 312,000; and in 1860, 814,000; and the same rate of increase would give her, in 1870, 1,300,000; and in 1880, 2,083,000; which would be more than she could accommodate. She would be completely full in ten years (from 1869), unless her increase was diverted.

All the ferries across the River Hudson, in 1868, carried 26,524,000 passengers; those to Brooklyn across the East River carried 51,550,000, almost twice as many. If to these we could add the arrivals by rail and by steamboat, the total number of persons entering New York might be obtained.

Since the consolidation with Williamsburgh, in 1855, the following was the rate of Brooklyn's increase: —

In 1855, 174,800; in 1860, 267,000; and in 1865, 350,000; and at three per cent. less than the above increase it would be: in 1870, 450,000; in 1880, 1,000,000; in 1890, 2,200,000; and in 1900, 4,800,000. This suburb of New York, therefore, compares with any of the outer districts of London.

Brooklyn paid taxes as follows: in 1855, upon 123,311,000 dollars, and in 1868, upon 149,293,000 dollars. This should have been over 200,000,000 dollars for 1868, which, at two per cent. taxation, would yield a revenue of 4,000,000 dollars. But take it at the above average, and Brooklyn will have, in 1880, 330,000,000 dollars; in 1890, 720,000,000 dollars; and in 1900, 1,580,000,000 dollars, — or an amount equal to the wealth of the nation in 1810. Brooklyn already has about the same wealth and banking capital which New York had in 1830.

At the tip of the island of New York is a green park and an old fort, turned into an immigrant depot, the whole going by the name of The Battery. From this point the eye can wander at will over the city of Brooklyn, and its Bay Ridge, till it stops at the Narrows, where the mountainous Staten Island almost closes the bay, and here are the defences of New York on that side, while the Sound also has its fortresses, in all twelve forts, and nearly two thousand guns. New York is one of the most exposed cities in the world, being but two hours' steaming distance from sea; but the character of the channel is in favor of the city's defence, and this sweeps under the guns of a powerful fort, raised almost at the edge of the ocean on Sandy Hook or Spit. Staten Island has been compared to the Isle of Orleans, and to the heights of Genoa and Palermo, for the splendor of its villas and the beauty of its shores; behind it, a stealthy passage called the Kills (Dutch) gives still a third outlet to the sea, and at either end of the Kills, through the State of New Jersey, two rivers come down from the West: the Raritan and the Passaic, — on the former of which stands the city of Newark, nine miles from New York, with one hundred and twenty thousand people; and the latter falls in a cataract of seventy-two feet, twice that distance from the same city. The State of New Jersey faces New York on the opposite side of the wide North River, and a craggy height called Bergen, on that side, corresponds to the heights of Brooklyn, the two making a pair of great jaws, between which the island of New York lies like a human tongue. At the foot of Bergen heights, on the brink of the river, lie Jersey City and Hoboken, with perhaps fifty thousand people, and here, as on the east side, the ferry-boats ply incessantly throughout the twenty-four hours of the day and night. The North River is the great highway to the West and the lakes; it is lined with populous towns, and for one hundred and fifty miles is navigable for steamers which can carry eight hundred passengers, and give them each a bed. Down this river tugs and tow-boats bring fleets of barges from Buffalo, and even from Chicago, which have come by way of the Erie Canal, — a work completed in 1825, amidst well-merited rejoicings. Twelve steam railroads enter New York, Brooklyn, and the Jersey cities. This city started the first packet line to Europe, and here were made the first experiments in steam navigation, resulting in the first successful steam vessel in the world ascending the North River. The commercial energy of the city, though greatly discouraged during the civil war, and by the subsequent apathy of the national government, is still remarkable. At one private shop here there is a dry dock four hundred by one hundred and twenty feet in dimensions, which cost two million one hundred and fifty thousand dollars. The Sailors' Snug Harbor, on Staten Island, is a richly endowed charity for the mercantile marine, with vaster property in New York real estate than all the possessions of the English Trinity House. The pilot boats, clipper ships, and yachts of New York are the fastest in the world, and, anterior to the civil war, the steamships of the city were superior to any afloat. One of the richest maritime corporations in existence is the Pacific Mail Company, with steamers which ply to the Isthmus of Darien, to San Francisco, and to China, some of them costing upwards of half a million of dollars.

When we come to examine the internal structure of New York, we shall find that it has two distinct arrangements of streets. Those of the upper and superior part of the island are rectangular, and consist of amply wide streets, named by numbers, running across the narrow island, the maximum number of which is in the neighborhood of Two Hundredth Street; these are crossed by twelve avenues, eight hundred feet apart, which will eventually reach to the northern end of the island, and these again will be diagonally crossed by a grand boulevard drive, the longest of its kind in Christendom.

The lower and pointed end of New York is the old city, and its streets have accommodated themselves to the converging shores of the city, so that many are cramped and crooked. From the Battery, where we have stood, at the cape of the island, a single broad, straight street, the axis of the island, runs along the summit of the central spine for two miles and a half; this is called Broadway, and it is the zodiac of New York, — the belt of all clustering and brilliancy, — so that a foreigner, who had explored the city, said almost with truth: —

"New York is, among cities, what one of the lower order of molluscous animals, with a single intestinal canal, is to a creature of a higher development, with various organs, and full of veins and arteries. Up and down the Broadway passes the stream of life to and from the heart, in Wall Street. In the narrow space from water to water, on either side of this dry canal, there is comparatively little animation, and nothing at all to reward the researches of a stranger."

When Broadway has passed up half a mile from the Battery, it receives a sizable street from the east, which abuts upon a very handsome church, with a tall spire, and a graveyard and monuments around it. The church is Trinity, the richest of Protestant Episcopal corporations; the street is Wall Street, the money market of America.

Half a mile further up, Broadway passes a green triangular park of eleven acres, the acute angle of the same pointing toward the battery; this is the City Hall Park, the Charing Cross of New York, the *Place du Palais Royal.* Here the street railways converge, the newspapers are issued, the cabs wait, the eddies of people form, the City Hall, the courts, the telegraphs, the steam fire-engines, the hotels are clustered; it is a cheerful chaos. The City Hall dates back to 1803; the new court-houses behind it have been years building, have cost vast sums extravagantly, and the end is not yet, either in beauty or hooking. The new Post Office will stand before the City Hall at the point of the Park, and will be the largest building of its kind extant.

While Broadway continues straight on for a further mile and a half, lined with stately banks, hotels, shops, and theatres, another wide avenue starts from it at the Park, and sweeps to the east by a long arc, so that it rejoins Broadway nearly two miles further on; this is the Bowery, the Cheapside of New York, — the *Boulevard du Temple,* — where the German, Jewish, and cockney element resides, and it is as busy and more idiosyncratic than its great rival.

Broadway and the Bowery meet upon an oval park, three miles from the Battery, and here uniting, they make one street, possessing the characteristics of both, which crosses the island obliquely, by a course of three miles further, till it reaches the sparsely built districts, and then becomes a highway to Albany The oval park first cited is called Union Square. It is capable of being made the finest place in the world, and here stands the only equestrian statue in New York, — a Washington, twenty-nine feet high, including pedestal, which cost thirty thousand dollars.

At Union Park the city assumes much the appearance of parts of Paris, fine shops, *cafés*, and hotels, being intermixed with the opera, the circus, theatres, and assembly halls. A third of a mile further up Broadway there is another square, called Madison, of ten acres, where the resemblance to Paris is even more striking, and the theatres, hotels, and cafés are as fine as any in the world. Here Broadway, continuing on obliquely, is crossed by the noblest avenue of residences in the city, the world-noted Fifth Avenue, bordered entirely by churches and residences for a mile and three-quarters, and at that distance, caught between Fifth and Eighth Avenues, and clipped by Broadway, the Central Park stands, in the centre of the island, the pride and monument of the city; eight hundred and sixty-eight acres of rock, lake, and rolling table-land, rising in places to the height of one hundred and thirty-eight feet. It is two and a half miles long, and half a mile wide; in the midst of it is a gigantic reservoir, around which wind thirty-five miles of carriage-drive, foot-path, and bridle-road. It is a model of exquisite engineering, and its bridges, cascades, and copses, malls, gondolas, swans, museums, and flocks of deer and sheep stand in profile between the city and the sky, as in the hanging gardens of Babylon. All the suburbs of the great city are revealed from this pleasure height; all its wealth of water wherein it stands, maritime like Venice, and mountainous like Brescia. The city of the island — which, to the lament of its inhabitants was not originally named "Manhattan," after its Indian site — has had its troubles: its fire (1835), which burnt twenty millions of property; its cholera, its panics, and its riots; but when its second conflagration came, gold came also from its kindred harbor on the Pacific, and its triumphs have since been those of Antony, its charms like Cleopatra's. The whole island was originally bought for twenty-four dollars; its assessed property tax was lately about twelve millions. It has three hundred churches. Its real estate is esteemed the most secure and profitable investment in America.

There are computed to be two hundred and twelve miles of streets in the city of New York, of which eighty-one miles are in block, and five miles in wooden pavement. The remainder are either subjected to cobble-stones, or await pavement.

The amount of money to be raised by taxation, in the city of New York, in 1869, and expended under the direction of the Common Council, was four million one hundred and fifty-three thousand dollars and seventy-five cents.

The amount to be raised in the same way, during the same period, and expended under the direction of the Board of Supervisors, was one million three hundred and two thousand four hundred and ninety-eight dollars and forty-eight cents.

The assessed valuation of real and personal estate, in New York city, for the year 1869, will be about one billion dollars, an increase of ninety million dollars over the assessment of 1868.

All the great series of works now undertaken in New York come under the two heads of increased communication and improved lodgings. The little spike-shaped island of Manhattan is over-populated, at the lower end, and at the upper end completely absorbed by speculators in city lots. There is almost universal desire expressed to live cheaply in town, or to get safely and expeditiously out of town. Yet, at present, there is no city in the world which it is so difficult to quit. The depots of the two steam railroads which have their termini on the island are three or four miles from the seat of business. But one horse railroad traverses the entire longitudinal extent of the island. These are the only land outlets for nearly a million people, — two steam roads, and one tram road. On the water side there are about twenty regular ferries; but a ferry involves the breaking of bulk, the changing of seats, a scramble and accident, and it makes the city doubly dear to fifty per cent. of those who would otherwise get away. With the present facilities for doing business, and residing in or near New York, one must take his choice of these three extreme cases: —

1. Take the horse cars, and stand up for sixty minutes, holding to a strap, doubtful about one's pocket-book, oppressed with stench; dismount near a depot, walk to it in the dismal suburb, and stand the chance of having missed the train. Catching the train, stand up, perhaps, again, and dismount in some deep defile, with the road to one's home pointing upwards at an angle of forty-five degrees, and no conveyance waiting. Total time from business to bed, two hours. Total effect, disgust; perhaps to redound upon one's children and wife, in satiety and a bitter spirit. Repeat this trip next morning, and keep at it twelve times a week.

2. Walk to a ferry down dismal streets, and squeeze through a gate, carrying one's parcels, baggage, etc. Across the river stand in a gang, and rush for a seat in the cars. Stand or sit in the cars, as the lottery directs, and, dismounting about dusk somewhere ten or twenty miles from New York, walk home, imagining each bush a highwayman. If one misses the night-boat or the night-train there is no alternative but to stay in the city all night, to the distress and apprehension of his family. If he goes down to the ferry late, he may beguile himself with dreams of garroters.

3. Pay from eighteen hundred dollars to four thousand dollars a year in the city for house rent; or,

4. Board, and eat "hash."

These are the alternatives of life in New York, — a city with the best markets in the world, yet expensive without parallel; or a suburban home of difficult and irregular accessibility. A stranger looking at the various and exquisite shapes of the villas about New York, and seeing the picturesque perches of the villages, is unable to feel the penalty of a winter in the suburbs. The metropolitan problem has always been how to put steam highways down this long, pin-shaped island, already swamped with vehicles, and clamoring for streets. The problem is nearly solved; for at last a tunnel underground has been duly chartered by the Legislature of New York, and the experiment of a mid-air railroad has proved a success. I have seen the cars travelling twenty feet above ground safely and swiftly, and apparently with inconvenience to nobody; and I have ridden in them to my exceeding profit; for the whole panorama of the street is exposed, from house-cornice to curb-stone. The rails are supported by single posts of iron, of the girth of a common street lamp-post, and the effect of a cross-section is that of a series of very tall and narrow letters T. Before next winter (1869) this "air-line" railroad will be in operation from the Battery to Central Park. In three or four years the tunnel will be finished, and from breakfast to business, from the last tableau of the theatre to one's country home, will be but a step and an express train.

Our "palaces" in America are for the masses of the people,— our great hotels,— and even for the poor. What Mr. George Peabody imperfectly, but generously, provided for the London poor, Mr. Alexander T. Stewart has more wisely provided for the poor of New York: mammoth hotels arranged in series of apartments, with *tables d'hote* on the French plan. *Table d'hote* means the host's family table, where all are invited to eat in common. The two splendid hotels of Mr. A. T. Stewart will cost six millions of dollars, and they compare with the palaces of emperors in size and convenience. They are six stories high, fire-proof, built of iron, and two hundred and five feet long by one hundred and ninety-two feet deep, covering forty-one thousand square feet. They are provided with steam elevators to ascend to the lofty floors, and with spacious court-yards. Three dollars a week will pay the expenses of each person in these splendid palaces. Mr. Stewart is an Irish-American, and the richest dry-goods merchant in the world. His income in 1869 was upwards of three millions of dollars. The Metropolitan Hotel, for the general public in New York, cost one million of dollars with its furniture; and its water and gas pipes measure twelve miles; it has thirteen thousand yards of carpet, and nearly five hundred rooms. The St. Nicholas Hotel cost one million, and has six hundred rooms. Even larger hotels are in course of construction at present (1869), and perhaps the noblest hotel of them all is the Fifth Avenue, named for the street on which it stands. The Grand Hotel in Paris cost about two and a half millions of dollars, and is arranged somewhat on the American plan. Instead of one great office, it has offices on every floor.

If the experiment of Mr. Stewart fails, it will be because the people of New York are neither metropolitanized nor republicanized enough. For great cities, cheapness must come from organization, as Paris has long ago learned.

The effects of these lodging-houses and these multiplied railways upon the social life of New York may well awaken inquiry. The solution of the first must lie more largely in the cookery than in the morals. The question of the age is this: "Has hash had its day?" For, as a friend of mine in New York on whom I called, said grimly: —

"We are moving our boarding-house for the ninety-fifth time. We can't stand the hash. And," he concluded, "now I know why the wandering Jew was named Ahas(h)ueras!"

Such is New York in epitome: the Hercules of cities, with its hands full of golden fruit, and its labors only begun. How will it compare in another century, when our civilization is softened, with Paris, the metropolis of art and pleasure?

All the years of glory have burst upon Paris, and more than two millions of people, exclusive of three hundred thousand strangers, make it their home. The visitors here equal the population of St. Louis, Chicago, or Cincinnati.

A hundred miles by river from the sea its water highway is a running stream, moving at the rate of forty inches in a second; and in its widest part this is only six hundred feet across. Yet by various devices steamboats and tugs ascend to Paris, few in number, and of shallow draught; but there are a million of people here that never saw a full-rigged ship, except one old mock-frigate that stands for a bathing-house and *café*, rotting at her cables. Lyons and Rouen are far better interior sites for a city; but Paris has grown rich circumstantially.

When Julius Cæsar, before Christ's birth, invaded Gaul, he found the banks of the Seine to be a dense forest, broken by gloomy marshes, while in the middle of the river a fierce tribe of Gauls, called Parisii, worshipped under Druid priests. Five hundred years of Roman conquests found the city scarcely bigger than this little island, and its aqueducts and baths in part remain to-day. The first prominent Christians here were St. Denis, and St. Genevieve, and the latter, a beautiful young girl, converted King Clovis, the final conqueror of the Romans, and became the patron saint of Paris. The great Charlemagne did not love Paris, and after a while the Normans sailed, or poled, up the river, and burnt it. At last, when the kings would not help them, the Parisians proposed to whip the Normans on their own hook, and their most successful leaders founded the Capet dynasty, which confirmed Paris as the capital, and began the line of kings which, in our own day, the people have beheaded or driven into exile. While the British Empire dates from a conquest by foreigners, the French took its rise from a war of independence. Thereafter the priests and the kings endowed Paris with rich monasteries, abbeys, and palaces. Out of it went crusaders, long armies of invasion, and parties of faction bent on spoil and murder. Its greatest patrons were Francis I., Henry IV., Louis XIV., and the Napoleons. The histories of all these battered times have been more fully written than the romance of any modern city, by Dumas, and Sue, and Hugo. The grand revolution, the most wondrous and glorious ferment of men that the world ever knew, was entirely Parisian in origin, and, during twenty years of victory over the combined tyrants of the world, Paris was the government and pulse of France. Bonaparte beautified her; Louis Philippe, the citizen-king, turned her superfluous palaces into public picture-galleries, fortified her, and made her the railway centre of the kingdom; the existing ruler has taxed every chestnut-roaster and washerwoman to make her gorgeous. Her influence in arts, letters, thoughts, examples, sympathies, and arms is foremost amongst the cities of the world; and this can be ascribed only to the fact that she is the capital of a great, elastic, courteous, gregarious, and intellectual nation, the head of the Celtic races. Our American estimates of her are all derived from the English, who have made war upon her, whether her government was free or despotic.

Let us go up among the windmills of Montmartre, — a hill that retains the same relation to Paris that Central Park Heights has to New York, being the highest ground, and standing on the northern flank of the city. Down beneath us, on the slopes of a ridge of hills like ours, and in the level valley of the Seine, Paris stretches in an atmosphere, pure and clear as Philadelphia's, every one of its hundred domes, spires, and towers, cut sharp against the rolling and wooded horizon, and the river bending almost through the middle, flowing from east to west, and spanned by thirty bridges, like some crystal ladder. In the centre of the whole, the Seine makes two small islands, each of the size of three of our city blocks, and of these, the larger and lower one is ancient Paris, the Island of the City, where the Cathedral of Notre Dame and the Courts of Justice lie. You can see from your perch on Montmartre Hill, the two grand gothic towers, and the leaping buttresses of the former, its great flamboyant window aflame, and half a thousand carved saints in its canopies and pinnacles. The Palace of Justice is marked by the dark towers of the Conciergerie prison, where Marie Antoinette suffered for the sins of her class. A swaying, lofty, dense mass of venerable houses chokes up the quays, and this was once the great Paris, — no more to day than the two glasses of your spectacles dropped in the middle of a large newspaper. Look now at the dense environs of this island, and its companion the island of St. Louis. Both shores of the Seine are populated four miles across, and for six miles lengthwise of the river. Within these square miles of yellow stone houses (of the average height of six stories), two concentric streets, a hundred feet wide, planted with shade-trees, make the circle of the city. They are called *Boulevards* (Bulwarks), or streets built on the *site* of ancient walls (*Boule*, wall, and *vert*, green). The inner set describes a circle, with the Seine for its diameter, at least four miles in length, and you can see the eternal multitude of men and women, from where you stand, strolling down the splendid avenues of the gilded theatres, hotels, and cafés, making life the pursuit of happiness. Traversely crossing these Boulevards, two mighty streets go, straight as arrows, across Paris. One of them cuts the island of the city nearly in half, and is called the *Boulevard of Sebastopol;* the other passes on the north side of the Seine, at right angles to its rival, and leaves a broad shelf between itself and the river. This is the famous *Rue de Rivoli*, whereon those wonderful palaces of the Emperor, the Tuileries, and the Louvre stand, as well as the gardens of the Palace, and of the *Champs Elysées*, and at one end it is bounded by the Arch of Triumph; at the other by the monument of the Bastile. For pleasure-seekers, these *Boulevards*, and the *Rue Rivoli*, make the whole of Paris.

The annexed diagram will convey some idea of the relative positions of the principal streets of Paris: —

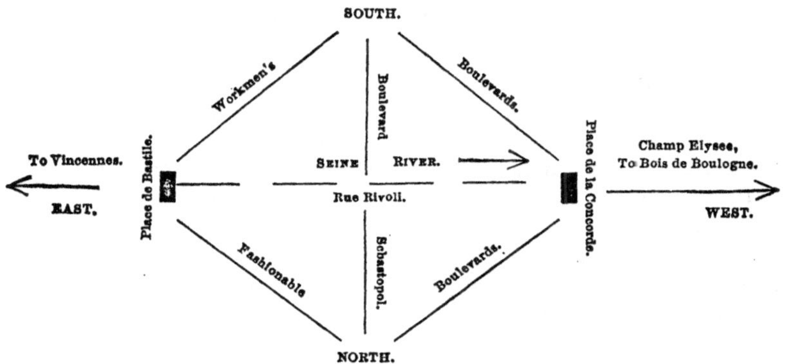

But these are new streets, with the smell of paint upon them. The labyrinthine and venerable quarters lie away yonder across the river. If you look from Montmartre again, you will see three separate domes; the middle one, rising from a green garden, is the Palace of the Luxembourg, and it divides the southern side of the river into two very different halves, of which that to the right is the old aristocratic quarter, the *Faubourg* (or suburb) St. Germain, with the dome of Bonaparte's tomb dominating it; and the other is the students' quarter, or the *Quartier Latin*, high over which the Church of St. Genevieve, or the Pantheon, lifts its fluted dome of granite. Beside Napoleon's tomb, the tall circle of the World's Exhibition stood in 1867. The half of the Seine nearer to you is the larger and more populous. That side of it to the right is the English and foreign aristocratic quarter; in the middle is the quarter of shops and hotels, with the *lorette*, or gay, or "fast" quarter, between it and the eye. Next, to the left, is the manufacturing district, the densest of all; and then the terrible suburb of St. Antoine, out of which the Red Republicans come when a throne is to dash to pieces. Around the city, on our own side of the Seine, there are steep hills extending afar off into the country, and two of these are cemeteries packed with the common and the eminent dead; the further ones are fortified, and their lean bastion towers pierce the sky.

On this hill, under the creaking windmills, was fired the last cannon for France, when Bonaparte went down, with twenty flogged despots lunging at him. This city, in the blue air below, has wild and painful contrasts in it. The highest genius, the wildest ignorance, prevail here. A martial city, where to be brave is to be human, and men are born with polish, like a varnished boot, woman has no separate existence but as man's momentary creature, to command his brief admiration and be forgotten. Five thousand girls a year come to Paris. They can earn no more than thirty cents a day, and one-third earn but twelve cents. In a city of twenty thousand students, and three hundred thousand rich, pleasure-seeking strangers, the temptation to accept a profitable friendship is not long declined. Moreover, matrimony is often a commercial contract here. Women are cheap, and those who would be wives must pay their way. When he proposes marriage, the gallant young Frenchmen calls up his lady's father, and demands that her "*dot*," or apportionment, be settled. If it is insufficient, he can refuse her hand. It is men who give the "mitten" here. Out of this commercial matrimony respect is seldom generated; love did not inspire it; therefore husband and wife will love elsewhere. The man sees a face worthy to wear, not to wed, and gallantly spends his wife's money to engage it; the wife, freshly entered into the world from the parent's rigid custody, has all her coquetries, and love of dress yet to ensue. There is a double marriage with many a couple here. No such crimes as breach of promise of marriage, or seduction, are known to Salic or Gallic law. Hence infanticide is an hourly act, and seven thousand foundlings a year go into pauperism. The Frenchman is a natural gambler, and every *café* is a gambling-house, where you dare not show the money for which you play. The treason of the State Church to the nation, in the French Revolution, has made scepticism almost national in Paris, and Sunday, in French acceptation, is a day that is consecrated to horse-racing. Among the noble classes of France the most accomplished courtiers of the world are to be found, and intellect is the prince of qualifications in society. Foreigners are always welcome at the most brilliant séances. It is neither polite nor safe to quarrel here. A blow is a high crime. The mode of settling differences is the duel. Every day in the year there is a hostile meeting; but it is not generally a barbarous one like those in pioneer states. You are not forced to fight, if you put yourself in the way of a challenge, by any personal fear, or moral cowardice, but by society, that holds it worst of all to be a coward.

Wealth buys a husband and pleasures here, but not recognition. Spirit, wit, talent, and person are welcome anywhere in Paris. It is a society to disgust an Englishman.

"Paris," says Jules Janin, its liveliest and most incisive critic, "is the history of all the provinces, of all the men, of all the passions of France. He who would be thoroughly acquainted with the great city of Charlemagne and of Napoleon, would be, at the same time, the most learned antiquarian and the greatest politician in the world."

With more fervor, Victor Hugo calls it "the model city; that pattern of well-formed capitals; metropolis of the ideal; august country of the initiative of impulse and enterprise; centre and abode of mind; a native city; a hive of the future, compounded of Babylon and Corinth."

There is no city of modern times that, by its mere mental and magnetic influence, so controls its empire as Paris. London, as a corporation, is a grand piece of feudal furniture, her oracle being the united voice of her shopkeepers. New York is essentially a vast port for the United States, but her opinion is not of binding consequence upon the national destinies. Rome is beloved and impotent in Italy, like the beautiful portrait of something dead. But Paris is generally the will of France. Her impulses obtain, from Brest to the Alps, almost awful respect. She rules by no chicanery, nor tradesman's fear, nor ecclesiastic's nod, but by her electrical beauty and mind, — a Cleopatra conquered, but then most conquering. The quickness and truthfulness of her perceptions, her sensitiveness for France's sake, without selfishness for herself; her proud and undisputed conceit of standing guard for the country, keeping its honor bright, and its rank the noblest; her courage tremendous, yet sagacious, with which, when France suffers insult, she transforms herself from her summer carnival to a fortress of barricades, and every smile of yesterday looks frosty down a bayonet. Not in these grand popular resistances only, but in defence of the nation's art, ethics, and philosophy, Paris is the same vigilant, magnetic, conscientious sentinel. Her university, and schools of science, art, and philosophy are inhabited by thousands of ardent youths, wearing the perpetual flush of high spirit and patriotism; and these, not their instructors, are the faculty of France. Before their united indignation, any professorship is put to rout. In 1863, a contest raged three days in the Faubourg St. Germain, because a professor in the Art School spoke with palpable disrespect of Eugenie Delacroix. When Victor Hugo began to write for the stage, the students carried him to success against the fiercest conservative opposition from priest, courtier, and literary rival. The schools are to-day the only element of Paris that the Emperor has despaired of controlling. In vain was Laboulaye threatened for his lectures eulogistic of the Republic of America. Vainly does the crown destroy the Professorship of Renan. Yet these mercurial boys, transformed Parisians from the day they cross the barriers, stand in military silence when acknowledged genius comes to teach them. At *L'Ecole des Beaux Arts*, when Gerome enters, there is that respect that the masters love to receive, like the breaking of the wands of the rejected suitors, in Raphael, when Joseph is wedded to the virgin. At every birthday of Beranger, the best of all the lyrists freedom has had, the students used to carry him the circuit of the *Boulevards*, and crown him with laurel. The Institute of France is the galaxy of great intellects, that Louis Napoleon would enter when he proffered the life of Cæsar for a vote. He has no seat there. The journalism of the city is not journalism in either the English or American sense, — the collection of news and correspondence, — but a medley of the most scholarly editorial, and the wittiest running commentary upon the topics of the day. The newspaper is the bellows here; the book is the coal of fire. The literature of France has produced, in this reign, two pre-eminent books, — the "Miserables," by Victor Hugo, and the "History of the Consulat and Empire," by Thiers; but it is doubtful that, except in painting, the arts and literature stand as high as in the reign of Louis Philippe, and during the Republic of 1848–50. The most courted receptions here are those of the great authors, savans, and painters. The returns for literary labor are princely. The jealousies of scholars are seldom coarsened by asperities, and the government of Paris labors to conciliate men of talent. Six public libraries, open free to all, contain one million six hundred thousand volumes; three vast picture-galleries, free to all, contain forty-eight thousand paintings, and statues of every age. A menagerie, and garden of plants, free to all, numbers one thousand three hundred living animals, and eleven thousand trees and plants. These give no idea of the inexhaustible arena of art and thought treasures gathered here, dispensed as freely as the elements of the world. And this is the glory of Paris, not her cloisters of nameless shames, the deceitfulness of the love of her men and women, nor — as some out of freedom's countenance would have us believe — the ungovernable nature of her citizens, but in the majesty and brightness of her intellect, and the love of country that inspires it. You read here no petty jealousy of Lyons, Lille, Rouen, and Marseilles. Confident in herself and her rightfulness,

Paris marches on; and when America has such a metropolis she will find no discussion as to her title.

It is consequent upon such a city as I have described that it should stand arrayed against the present government of France. Paris has never been else than republican. She shared in the ardor with which the people at large welcomed back Louis Napoleon, — the name of Bonaparte, and a republican author, — to the people's cause. In his scheme of usurpation she was incorruptible; he usurped France by baptizing her Boulevards with Parisian blood, and all the franchises of the city fell at once; her present government is a dual one, there being two administrative heads, — the Prefect of the Seine, and the Prefect of the Police, neither of them Parisians. Paris is really a department now, and not a municipality. Five thousand policemen, or *sergeants de ville*, armed with swords and pistols; five hundred mounted policemen; a garrison varying from thirty to sixty thousand troops, — these inspire obedience here, but no terror. The city, as the sentry of France, keeps picket duty, but does not fire on the enemy. Her caprices, when they come, will be as organized and desperate as ever. She has seldom returned a government member to the *Corps Legislatif*, or lower house, and one of the chief glories of the Emperor's reign has been the eloquence of the Parisian deputies, Favre, Carnot, Picard, Thiers, Ollivier, Pelletan, Gueroult, Pages, the first living orators of Europe. To avoid exciting Paris unduly, she has been undisturbed in those more refined patriotisms which are her pride. The effort of the government is to destroy her influence without, by embarrassing communication through the mail and the press, and by exciting jealousies against her. In superficial respects it has succeeded; in realities, Paris is yet the watch-tower of the country.

I can only try in some figures to give an idea of the splendor of Paris. Here there are forty-two licensed theatres, fifty-four licensed halls, eight race tracks, and sixty-four churches. The city is supplied with water by four artesian wells, that are one thousand eight hundred feet deep, and required seven years to bore them; by six steam-pumps on the Seine, and three aqueducts; and it consumes every day four hundred and eighty thousand cubic feet of the worst water in the world. The Ourcq aqueduct is eighty miles long, and cost five million dollars. Three new aqueducts have been "decreed" to bring water from the head-waters of far streams, to measure unitedly two hundred and sixty miles, and to cost twelve millions of gold dollars. One of these is under way. The sewers and subterranean streets of Paris measure, altogether, the incredible length of four hundred and five miles, and yet are so admirably constructed that one hundred and fifty workmen manage them. The catacombs under the city contain bones and skulls that represent the bodies of one million two hundred thousand dead men. There are eighty thousand manufacturers of all sorts here, and of these only eight thousand employ more than ten persons; the various departments of clothing manufacture involve a capital of fifty-five millions of dollars; the building interests of all sorts, thirty millions; gloves, millinery, etc., thirty-two millions; jewelry and personal ornamentation, thirty millions; the printing, book-binding, stationery, etc., of all sorts, twelve millions; the Custom House of Paris takes a million and a half dollars a year; the *octroi*, or municipal tax, imposed upon wines, forage, and eatables entering the gates, amounts to the sum of nine and a half millions; tobacco, pawn-brokering, and undertaking (burying the dead) are here government monopolies. The tobacco factory hires two thousand five hundred hands, half of them women, and no man can sell a cigar in France that is not bought there; nor can anybody keep a tobacco-shop except by appointment. Old soldiers and their orphans get the shops. One of them on the *Boulevard* has a net income of thirty-six thousand dollars a year. A government funeral costs from three and a half dollars to fifteen hundred dollars. There are nine classes of funerals. The hospitals of Paris, with its other public charities, cost three and a half millions of dollars a year. There are five thousand persons in prison here at any time, and thirty thousand enter the prisons during a year. The great government pawn-shop, or Mt. de Piete, lends five million dollars a year on one million five hundred thousand articles. The stall rents of the principal markets make three hundred thousand dollars annually. There are only five butcheries in Paris, and together they cost three and a half millions of dollars.

I recommend the gentlemen of the New York Common Council to move out here, if indeed the majority of them are not here already in spirit; for the freedom and munificence with which the Emperor uses other people's money requires some help from the builders of the Metropolitan Court House, and the Harlem bridge. The Rue Rivoli cost thirty millions of gold dollars; five new bridges three hundred thousand dollars apiece; the new Louvre palace, fourteen millions of dollars, though the Emperor alleged that it should cost but five millions; the imperial stable cost six hundred thousand dollars, and one carriage in it eighteen thousand dollars; one hundred and eighty carriages and three hundred grooms are among the purchases of the Emperor.

The new opera house cost five and a half millions of dollars; the great central market, twelve millions, with the demolitions it necessitates; the *Boulevard Sebastopol*, twenty-five millions; the *Boulevards* Hausmann, Malsherbes, and Beaujou, sixteen millions; the avenues concentrating at Arc de Triomphe, ten millions; the Rue Lafayette, four millions; Boulevards Magenta, Richard Lenoir, Prince Eugene, and St. Germain, twenty-two millions; five new churches, one million and a half; the belt railway around Paris, three millions; the great exhibition three millions. Here are one hundred and forty-nine millions of dollars, not including the vast sums spent in perfecting the military organization, and supplying the luxurious tastes of a parvenue court, that when it came to France could hardly pay its fare.

These disbursements the city of Paris has to pay, besides contributing her quota to the universal building schemes that agitate all the empire. Twenty-five per cent., two-thirds of it direct, is the actual government levy upon the average of incomes, besides the optional fines one must pay for being conscripted, and relieved from National Guard duty. The revenues of Paris, in 1862, were seventy-five millions of francs, or fifteen millions of dollars. The expenditures for the same year were two hundred and five millions of francs, or forty-one millions of dollars, making a debt of twenty-six millions in one year, and more, by thirty-six millions, than all Switzerland spent in the same year; thirty-one millions more than all Denmark, and thirty-four millions more than all Sweden and Norway. Since 1862 the budget has been even more staggering, and the government is charged with incurring vast expenses not referred to in it.

A twenty-fifth of all the French nation lives in Paris; twenty-four twenty-fifths of all great Frenchmen live there, twenty twenty-fifths of all sad, sinning Frenchmen live there. Genius and shame,—mysteries to each other, and therefore half affinities,—redeemed by love of abstract truth and love of country, survive in Paris the almost universal licentiousness. A stranger arriving there on Sunday, cries aloud: "The city is doomed! It has reached the pitch of Babylon and Sodom!"

But the secret of her preservation lies in this: that licentiousness in Paris slays only the body, and not the citizen. The Parisian's intellect does not expire in a debauch. His loves are all caprice, and what he loses of deep affection for his wife and home, he seems, by some anomaly of his nature, to add to his patriotism and abstract reverence. For, what the old Roman writer had to say, is patent yet: "The Gauls are a warlike and gregarious race, jealous of all but their women. These have no other law but the whim of their master, whom they love too gratefully. The men have chiefs; but these are not hereditary, and last only with their talent for war and government. The people are subordinate only to their country; mutinous against even their priests; and when they become warlike without a cause, the best cause their chiefs and priests can see is — the enemy."

CHAPTER XIX.

NAPOLEON III. AND NAPOLEONISM.

The Emperor of France, his origin, adventures, official and private life, and his predecessors on the throne. — Notes upon members of his family, and particularly upon his American relations.

On the site of some ancient brick tile yards (Tile-ries), which had moulded and baked tiles for the roofs of Paris for four hundred years, Catharine de Medicis began to build the Palace of the Tuileries (pronounced Twill-e-rie), in 1567, twenty years before Virginia was discovered and named. In this palace, his birthplace, dwells Charles Louis Napoleon Bonaparte, aged sixty-one years (1869), Emperor of the French, by the title of Napoleon III. He has the largest salary of any monarch in Europe: five millions of dollars in gold per annum, direct revenue, besides the income of certain crown domains, the confiscated lands of the Orleans family, and other matters, bringing a gross salary or civil list of eight million four hundred thousand dollars; and yet the debts charged against this revenue already amount to twenty million dollars.

The palace itself stands on the flat banks of the river Seine, a quay on one side, a street on the other, and a garden in front. The rear of the palace is flanked by side walls, which in turn connect with a series of palaces called the *Louvres*, the whole enclosing two immense courts. The width of these palaces and gardens is nearly one thousand feet, and the entire length is more than half a mile. Within them are contained every necessity of an Emperor, — the home of his court, his state apartments, chapel, theatre, vast stables, enormous and invaluable museum, relics of art and virtuoso, a great library, a garrison, triumphal arches, flowers, fountains, drives, trees, *cafés*. A part of the palace which the present Emperor built cost twelve and a quarter millions of dollars, and one hundred millions have been estimated as the value of the combined palaces and collections. To open a street, the Rue Rivoli, beside this palace, cost thirty millions of dollars, and caused the destruction of a thousand houses.

REGALIA OF STATE.

1—Queen's Diadem. 2 and 3—Queen's Coronation Bracelets. 4—Prince of Wales Crown. 5—Old Imperial Crown. 6—Queen's Crown. 7—Spiritual Sceptre. 8—Temporal Sceptre. 9—Bishop's Hat. 10—Pope's Hat. 11—Regalia of Scotland.

The Emperor's "stud" consists of three hundred and twenty horses; he has one hundred and eighty carriages, and three hundred grooms. His special State Carriage cost eighteen thousand dollars, and the body of it is almost entirely plate glass; a gilt eagle is at each corner; it is lined with white satin covered with gold bees, and the straps and cords are of gold lace. The Tuileries contains the Throne Room, carpeted with Gobelin tapestry, which for this and three adjoining rooms cost two hundred thousand dollars. The hangings are of dark-red Lyons velvet, inwrought with gold palm-leaves and wreaths. The throne itself is canopied with the same material, inwrought with small medallions of the letter "N," and the drapery suspended from it is studded with golden bees. Three steps lead to the Throne, which is a richly carved chair, backed by drapery representing an escutcheon, — the imperial eagle encompassed by a wreath, surmounted by a helmet with the imperial crown; through this escutcheon passes a cross made by a sceptre and a hand of justice.

To know how the Emperor looks holding court in this palace, I addressed a letter to Colonel John Hay, who was for a long time Secretary of Legation and *Chargé d'Affaires* at the Court of the Tuileries, during the Ministership of Messrs. Dayton, Bigelow, and Dix, and he very kindly forwarded me a circumstantial description. The occasion was the presentation of General Dix and his legation at Court, in the year 1866: —

"A few days after his presentation to the Marquis de Moustier, General Dix received a letter from the Grand Master of Ceremonies, informing him that he would be received by the Emperor on Sunday, the 23d December, at two o'clock. He afterwards received a note from the Duke de Tascher la-Pagerie, stating that the Empress would receive him immediately after his audience with the Emperor. Colonel Hay hired a carriage and two servants, in the Rue Boissy d'Anglais, for himself and the associate Secretary, Hoffman. It was a highly respectable seeming affair, not fresh enough to look hired, with a couple of owlishly solemn flunkies that seemed to have been in the family for at least a generation. They went to the General's, and in a few moments came in the Baron de la Jus, Master of Ceremonies. He said he was very much crowded to-day with *besogne*, that he had five ministers to bring to the palace, and that therefore we would please excuse his hurry. Upon which we all rose and went to the door, where we found a court carriage, the imperial arms blazing on the panels and the harness, drawn by four horses, and accom-

63

panied by two mounted outriders; everything covered with tawdry, tarnished gold lace. It seemed like the triumphal car in a flourishing circus. Into this vehicle mounted the General and the Chamberlain, Hoffman and Hay following in their sham-private remise. All were in army uniform. They had the honors of a stare from the English on the asphalt of the Champs Elysées, as the party lumbered down to the Tuileries.

"We were shown into a warm, cheery anteroom, with a superb wood fire and a view of the Tuileries Gardens, the Avenue, and the Arc de Triomphe. The Columbian Minister and several violet-colored Chamberlains were there. We talked small talk. The Chamberlains all looked alike, in their violet coats and imperial mustaches. You never know which one you are talking to.

"Fane, the British Minister ad interim, came in. He was co-author, with Owen Meredith, of 'Taunhäuser.' Hay presented him to General Dix. They talked Alabama, Fenians, and stuff. Then a stiff, gaunt Bavarian, Pergler de Perglas, and his Secretary, who seemed moved by rusty springs. Several more, — a Peruvian; a blue-blooded Brazilian. Bigelow, our retiring minister, at last, a head taller than anybody.

"There came some more violet people, and moved us into a larger salon. There we were presented to the Duc de Cambacérès, — a jaunty old gentleman, lean and shaven and wigged. He bowed lavishly, and begged us to sit down; which we wouldn't.

"Bigelow in a few moments was called for to make his parting speech. When his audience was over, General Dix, followed by Hay and Hoffman, was then ushered into the PRESENCE. The General looked anxiously around for the Emperor, advancing undecidedly, until a little man, who was standing in front of the Throne, stepped forward to meet him. Everybody bowed profoundly as the Duc de Cambacérès gave the name and title of the General. The little man bowed, and the General, beginning to recognize in him a dim likeness to the Emperor's portraits, made his speech to him, — in English, as was proper. The Emperor listened like a wooden man.

"I looked around the room, admiring, as I always did on great ceremonial occasions in France, the rich and tasteful masses of color which the various groups of great officers of the crown so artistically present. Not a man's place is left to accident. A Cardinal dashes in a great splash of scarlet. A *Cent-garde* supplies an exquisite blue and gold. The yellows and the greens are furnished by the representatives of law and legislation, and the Masters of Ceremonies fill up with an unobtrusive violet. Yet these rich lights and soft shadows are accessory to the central point of the picture, — the little man who is listening, or seeming to listen, to the General's address.

"The General finishes, — hands his sealed letter of credence to the Emperor. He receives it, and gives it to the Duke of Bassano, who stands at his right. The heavy Dutch face breaks up with ungainly movements of the mustache and the eyelids. He speaks in a wooden voice, rather rapidly, and not very distinctly. He slurs half his words, as rapid writers do half their letters. He makes his set speech (French, of course), which (with the General's) is published the next day in the 'Moniteur.' He then drops his official manner, and comes, sidelong, up to us, and talks, in English now, which he speaks with great satisfaction and bad grammar, about the coming Exposition and the American *milice*, etc., etc. After the General he turns to the Secretaries. He tells Hay he is very young to be Col-o-nel, and talks a little about the war, etc., etc., etc.

"He bowed, and we bowed, and backed out of the door, everybody bowing. We were then taken to the apartments of the Empress. She was charming, in a lilac walking-dress and invisible bonnet. She had just come from church, and received in her promenade costume. Time has dealt gently with her. She is still full of those wheedling fascinations that won her a crown. She was especially gracious to the General; talked of Johnson, and the 'swing around the circle,' etc.

"The Secretaries came in for their share of smiles and pleasant words. She spoke English with a charming Castilian accent, which is prettier than the French.

"We left the graceful blonde Spaniard, and passed down through avenues of flunkeys. Found at the door the Chief Piqueur, to whom we gave two hundred and fifty francs! (fifty dollars!) Then took the General in our carriage (the Emperor brings him to the palace, but lets him find his own way back, you know), and drove back to the Rue de Presbourg, Place de l'Etoile, the residence of the American Minister." *

* As a companion to the above sketch, I give the scene of the introduction of the American Minister, Rush, to the Prince Regent George IV.: —

"The Ambassador was received by the Prince Regent, almost alone, the Foreign Secretary, however, being present. Advancing with the letter of credence in his hand, signed by James Monroe, Mr. Rush stated in a very few words what its purport was, adding that he

From this immense palace, shooting its truncated pavilions into the sky, made brilliant by the most brilliant court in Europe, and resonant in all its courts with the beating of drums and the coming and going of couriers, it is a long descent to take up the life, family, and adventures of Louis Napoleon Bonaparte.

He is one of three presumed heirs to the French crown. The originally anointed and so-called "legitimate" royal family is represented by the Count de Chambord, whom some call Henri V., now in exile; he represents the Bourbon family, who were driven out of France by revolution in 1830. The constitutionally appointed royal

had been directed by the President to use all his endeavors to strengthen and prolong the good understanding that happily existed between the two countries. The Prince took the letter, handed it to Lord Castlereagh, and spoke briefly and courteously of his desire to maintain and extend the friendly relations existing between the two nations. That was the formal reception, but the Prince detained his new acquaintance to congratulate him on his arrival, and to inquire particularly for Mr. Adams, and other American diplomats, going as far back as Mr. Pinckney and Mr. King, and particularly eulogistic of the beauty of Mrs. Patterson, afterward Marchioness Wellesley, and her sisters, the Misses Caton, of Maryland. A word or two more about the climates of the two countries closed the audience. The new Neapolitan Ambassador was received immediately after the levee, which succeeded. Mr. Rush presented his Secretary of Legation and one of the *attachés* to the Prince, who was King in all respects except the mere title. When the levee was over, Mr. Rush had to perform a duty imperative upon every foreign minister, after having been received by the sovereign. This was to 'call' — which means to write his name in a book at the residence of each — upon every member of the royal family. As there were then seven royal dukes and their five sisters, besides Prince Leopold (afterwards King of the Belgians), and the wives of the Dukes of York and Cumberland, he must have had a long drive that day. The letter of credence from our republican President commenced by stating the names and offices of the writer and receiver, addressed the latter as 'Great and Good Friend,' and ended by 'Your Good Friend, James Monroe.' When the British Sovereign sends a letter of credence to the President of the United States, it commences and ends precisely in the above manner. When sovereign writes to sovereign, the letter begins, 'Sir: My Brother.' It may be remembered how, in 1853, the Czar Nicholas, in reply to Louis Napoleon's letter announcing his election to the French throne, did not address him as 'My brother,' but as 'My friend' (*Mon ami*); how Napoleon, with a grim smile upon his unimpressible face said, 'Ah! this is well, — our brothers are accidents *born* to us; but we *choose* our friends;' and how, not very long afterward, he contrived the Anglo-French alliance, which poured the thunders of war upon the Crimea, humbled the might of Russia, and broke the heart of Nicholas. It is dangerous to jest with a tiger." — *Dr. R. Shelton Mackenzie.*

Mr. Motley's reception by Queen Victoria, was officially announced in the London "Gazette," of Tuesday, June 22 (1869), as follows: —

"WINDSOR CASTLE, June 18.

"This day, had audience of Her Majesty, John Lothrop Motley, Esq., Envoy Extraordinary, and Minister Plenipotentiary of the United States of America, to deliver his credentials; to which audience he was introduced by the Earl of Clarendon, K. G., Her Majesty's principal Secretary of State for Foreign Affairs."

family is represented by the Count of Paris, — who was an aide-de-camp to General McClellan in 1862, — now also a French exile; he represents Louis Philippe and the Orleans family, driven out by revolution in 1848.

Louis Napoleon represents the Corsican family of Napoleon Bonaparte, and he is the nephew both of Napoleon and of Josephine, his wife; for Napoleon compelled his younger and better brother, Louis, to marry Hortense, the unwilling coquette and daughter of Josephine by her first husband. Hortense had been a milliner girl, and Louis had been an artillery cadet. They soon hated each other; but she had three children who took the name of Napoleon, and the present Emperor is the third of these. His father was King of Holland at the time of his birth, but soon gave up that throne, and separated from his wife, who had also illegitimate children, notably one born in 1811, or only three years after the Emperor, who was the son of Hortense and the Count de Flahault; this was the celebrated Duke de Morny, afterward President of the *Corps Legislatif*, who was adopted by a nobleman of Mauritius for the sum of eight hundred thousand francs, and to whom Hortense left of her fortune eight thousand dollars a year.

Many Frenchmen believe that Louis Napoleon is also illegitimate; he certainly has not French features, nor spirit; but Napoleon Bonaparte believed that he was, and great rejoicings were made at his birth; for at that time he was one of the heirs of the throne, as the sons of Lucien and Jerome Bonaparte had been declared ineligible on account of their common marriages, Jerome marrying Elizabeth Patterson of Baltimore, Maryland, and Lucien marrying Christine Boyer, and refusing the crowns of Italy and Spain rather than divorce her. Two years after his birth Louis's mother left her husband, and when, four years afterward, the great Napoleon was exiled, she took her children to Arenenberg, in Switzerland, where she had an estate. There young Louis and his brother had tutors by the Lake of Constance, and we have several glimpses of how Louis behaved himself.

At one time he paid his court to a married woman who lived on the Mainau island. As soon as the lady's husband detected the intrigue, and learned that his wife at times went to Arenenberg by night in a boat, he locked up his faithless better half. The latter jumped out of window, and broke her legs. This lady's daughter married a general officer; but her mother's blood flowed in her veins, and she eloped with an adjutant of her husband's. When the latter heard that the bird had flown, he contented himself with exclaiming: "Poor adjutant! how unhappy you will soon feel!" This lady, who possessed a fascinating beauty and a wonderful clear complexion, was just of the age to be the daughter of the man at Arenenberg whom her mother blessed with her love. Persons living at Arenenberg can perfectly well remember how the elder came across to the *chateau* in a boat on those evenings when Hortense held large receptions; and Louis Napoleon was thus enabled to slip unnoticed from the *salon*, and secretly pay the honors to the pretty woman who visited him.

The prince, in his youth, was a passionate billiard-player, and frequently went over to Constance to play there. On one occasion he had a dispute with a butcher's journeyman in Leo's coffee-house. From words they came to blows; and there are people still living in Constance who can remember Louis being thrashed by the butcher.

Growing older he was sent to Augsburg, in Bavaria, to school, and proved tolerably apt. When, on September 2, 1862, the old pupils of the Augsburg Gymnasium from 1807 to 1828, four hundred and fifty in number, assembled at Augsburg, Napoleon III. sent his ex-school-fellows five hundred bottles of champagne, and the following letter, in which five thousand francs for the poor of Augsburg were enclosed: —

"St. Cloud Palace, August 30, 1862.

"Monsieur le President: — I have heard with the greatest interest of an assemblage of the former scholars of the Augsburg Gymnasium, who wish to celebrate by a banquet the memory of former student-years passed together, — and wish at least, as an ex-pupil, to take part in thought at this pleasant festival. I have never forgotten the time which I spent in Germany, where my mother found a noble hospitality, and I enjoyed the first benefits of education. Exile offers melancholy, though useful, experiences; it teaches us to become better acquainted with foreign nations; to estimate their good qualities and worth at the right value; and if we are hereafter so fortunate as to tread once again the soil of our native land, we still retain the most friendly recollections — which keep alive in spite of time and politics — of the regions in which the years of youth were passed. Your meeting affords me the opportunity to express these, my feelings, to you. Receive them as a proof of my hearty sympathy, and the esteem with which I am your well-disposed

"Napoleon."

When Louis was still the homeless son of the Count de St. Leu, he said at a masked ball in Florence to Fenimore Cooper, the American novelist, "The world is little more than a masquerade." When still quite a boy, he went on to say to Mr. Cooper that he had also performed a masquerade, though unconsciously. During the few days between his father's abdication of the throne and the incorporation of Holland with France, he was titular King of Holland; and, in that quality, was one morning, just as he was eating some cakes, requested to receive a deputation. While the orator was praising the virtues of the abdicated King, his father, the thought of being deprived of his cakes produced such a violent effect upon him that he burst into a loud roar. "The gentlemen of the deputation, and all the courtiers present," Louis Napoleon went on to say, "outvied each other in exclamations of delight at my excellent and gentle temper, as if it had been so affected by love for my father. But I had played my first masquerade."

Louis Napoleon, according to some autnorities, was very piously trained by his mother. He was expected to pray, on his knees, every morning and evening. Hortense frequently went to the chapel of Schwaderloh, where she confessed to the chaplain, who was acquainted with the French langnage. In the evening, too, when she went on the lake with Louis, she often let her guitar fall, and prayed fervently, to which the evening bells from nearly twenty village-churches certainly invited her.

Hortense was undoubtedly an accomplished woman, and fond of her children, but absorbed in pleasure; and the two brothers took lessons in soldiering, so that when a revolution broke out in the Pope's government, both the boys engaged in it, when the eldest died of fever and fatigue, and Louis would have died but for his mother. After this, the son and mother wandered about, expelled from place after place, Bohemian in every sense but poverty, and always finding rest at last in Arenenberg. The young man kept at his studies, and pondered upon what use the world had for him, when, in 1832, the captive son of Napoleon Bonaparte died at Vienna, and this made Louis the heir of the Bonaparte party, if there should be any left of it. From this time forward he began to court publicity, to publish democratic books, and military essays; in short, to draw upon himself the attention of whatever Frenchmen were dissatisfied with the government of Louis Philippe. In 1836 he so far satisfied himself that he had partisans in France, that he put himself at the head of a set of adventurers, and attempted to seize the fortified city of Strasbourg. The failure was ridiculous, and he was marched to Paris, but the government was afraid to try him by a French jury, on account of the popularity of his family; so he was shipped off to the United States, at the age of twenty-eight.

When Louis was preparing for the Strasbourg affair, and friends warned him of the dangerous nature of the undertaking, he said, "The French will understand me, even if it fails; the rest of the world will take me for a fool — and that is good."

"How could you hope," said his aunt, "to govern this ungovernable land, even supposing that a *coup de main* succeeded?"

"My dear aunt, there is a very simple way of governing France, — she must have a war every three years."

At New York, Louis was an object of interest; but his stay was short.

He went to Baltimore, and visited his brother-in-law, Murat. The latter was thirty-five years of age at the time, and had passed through a life of adventure. Born at Milan, in 1801, as the son of General-of-Division Joachim Murat, he was afterwards Duke of Cleve, and Crown-Prince of Naples; but after the death of his father he returned to the obscurity of a poor life. On passing over to America, he existed for years as postmaster in a small town, until the European movement of 1830 urged him back to the Old World. Once again a bright star seemed to have arisen for him, when he commanded the foreign legion in Belgium, in 1831. But this part was speedily played out, and the Colonel soon exchanged the sword for the pen again. He returned to America, which country he was so thoroughly acquainted with, that he wrote a book about it, in favor of slavery. He became first a lawyer in Georgia, and then a planter in Florida; but neither profession was very flourishing. Hence he proceeded with his family to Baltimore, where the Pattersons gave him a chance. Supported by them, he started as a merchant in Baltimore, and in a short time made a very considerable fortune. One day the ex-Prince of Cleve was standing at his desk, and looking through the glass door at the office in which his clerks were at work; Summerson, the head clerk, came in, and announced a stranger: "Mr. Louis Napoleon Bonaparte, from Europe."

The brother of the above Murat married in America, as also did Jerome Napoleon, that younger brother of the first Emperor, who fired the first shot at Waterloo; the latter was requested to divorce his wife by his brother, and he cravenly did so, marrying the daughter of the King of Wurtemberg, by whom he had children, now in high favor in Paris, while Jerome Patterson Bonaparte still lives in Baltimore, and is said to bear a striking resemblance to his immortal uncle.

On the day when the death of old Prince Jerome, ex-King of Westphalia, became known in Paris (1863), his wife, Madame Patterson, then nearly eighty years of age, might be seen going through the streets in her usual dress, quite careless, as if nothing had happened. She was aware of the death; but what was Jerome to her, from whom she had been parted for fifty-five years? "Everybody," says an anonymous writer, "was acquainted with Madame Patterson's eccentricities, in Baltimore. The lady might frequently be seen making purchases at the public market; she frequently, too, collected her own rents, and dabbled in the funds. She always wore an elegant coronet, glistening with diamonds of the purest water. Her arms were white and plump as those of a girl of sixteen. She was a most zealous royalist, and considered republics low. Her greatest ambition was to hear from her grandson, Jerome, who was serving in the French army. He received the greater portion of her income. She is supposed to have left him her considerable fortune, as she was on bad terms with her son. He always kept too expensive a house for her. He is a thorough gentleman, and a member of the Baltimore aristocracy, although he is not remarkable for anything beyond a passion for fine horses. He is considered the best judge of horses in Baltimore, and keeps a magnificent stud.

"In order to save the expense of a separate household, Madame Elizabeth Patterson Bonaparte lived in a boarding-house, where everything was on the cheapest and most modest scale. For this reason she was considered miserly. She could be seen daily on the wharves, in the business regions, and on the Exchange. She had the sum of five hundred thousand dollars at her disposal at any moment.

"In her religious views she was as original as on other points. She went daily to church, accompanied by a negro, who held an open umbrella over her. The negro had a prayer-book under his arm, and was elegantly dressed, like a dandy. Madame Patterson was supposed to be an admirer of Tom Paine; and, though she attended church daily, she abused the clergy terribly.

"Her grandson, whom she educated at the military school of West Point, is serving as an officer in the French army. She has been

64

estranged for years from her brothers, who are respectable merchants in Baltimore."

All of which, being in the library of the Capitol, is here reproduced, and left for solemn reflection.

Louis Napoleon was summoned home to see his mother die, and he was by her side when she expired, at the age of fifty-four. Immediately afterward, Louis Philippe demanded his expulsion from Switzerland, and he was forced to go to England, where he meditated his destiny anew.

"What he always longed for," says Kinglake, "was to be able to seize and draw upon himself the wondering attention of mankind; and the accident of his birth having marked out for him the throne of the first Napoleon as an object upon which he might fasten a hope, his craving for conspicuousness, though it had its true root in vanity, soon came to resemble ambition; but the mental isolation in which he was kept, by the nature of his aims and his studies, the seeming poverty of his intellect, his blank, wooden looks, and above all, perhaps, the supposed remoteness of his chances of success,—these sources of discouragement, contrasting with the grandeur of the object at which he aimed, caused his pretension to be looked upon as something merely comic and odd. Linked with this, his passionate desire to attain to a height from which he might see the world gazing up at him, there was a strong and almost eccentric fondness for the artifices by which the framer of a melodrama, the stage-manager, and the stage-hero, combine to produce their effects."

In England, Louis Napoleon Bonaparte became a subject of curiosity, and there he published the "Idées Napoleonnes," which attracted attention, chiefly in France. He became acquainted with many young noblemen, and during a period of riot was sworn in as a London constable. In 1840, the remains of the first Napoleon were brought home to France with much pomp, and Louis hastened to take advantage of the revived popularity of his family name, by hiring a steamboat, filling it with a recruited party of his adherents, and making a descent upon the town of Boulogne. The patience of Louis Philippe now gave out, and after a trial, when the filibuster broke down in making a speech, he was condemned to perpetual imprisonment at Ham, a fortress. He worked at authorship here for five years, and then escaped. Immediately afterward, his father, Louis, died at Leghorn, in Italy, aged sixty-eight. Lucien Bonaparte died in 1840, and

Joseph in 1844. The latter lived long at Bordentown, in New Jersey, and he was perhaps the best of his family.

The English papers, now very deferential to Louis Napoleon, were in these days very sharp on Louis Napoleon. "Punch" represented him running through the streets of Boulogne, with an eagle under his arm, and his uncle's hat on the point of his sword. In another article, cle, headed "The Marriage Market," the later Prince President was represented as a desirable bridegroom. The firm of Coburg, which has from time immemorial been prepared to supply all the courts of Europe with brides and bridegrooms at the shortest notice, feels the liveliest pleasure at Louis Napoleon's election as President, because he is still a bachelor; and as the firm has not as yet supplied a Presidentess, it will be proud to serve his republican highness most promptly and respectably. This was resolved on at a family congress, somewhere in Saxony, as "Punch" happened to know.

In 1848, the French people found Louis Philippe intriguing for a more arbitrary government, and they drove him out of France. A republic was declared, and Louis Napoleon hastened to Paris, where the provisional government, being acquainted with his ambitious designs, and his unscrupulous character, ordered him to quit the country. His old fellow-filibusters, the gamblers in his name and star, Persigny, Maupas, and De Morny, set the wires to work, however, and he was elected a deputy to the National Assembly from four places. His character and patriotism being challenged, he gave up his seat temporarily, and left the country; but his crafty agents remained behind to manage his brightening fortunes. Three months afterward he was again elected to the Assembly by five places, and he returned, took his seat, and offered himself to the French people for the Presidency. By the popularity of his name, and the notoriety of his adventures, as well as by the dexterous and active management of his friends, he was elected to the Presidency of the Republic by five and a half million out of seven and a half million of votes. Victor Hugo describes his inauguration: —

"It was about four o'clock in the afternoon. It was beginning to grow dark, and as the great hall of the Assembly was hidden in semi-obscurity, the chandeliers were let down from the roof, and candles placed in the tribune. The President gave a signal; a door on the right opened, and a young man dressed in black, with the star of the Legion of Honor on his chest, rapidly advanced into the hall, and ascended the tribune. All eyes were fixed upon this man. His pale, sickly-looking face, with the projecting, thin cheeks, which stood out the more in the lamp-light, his large, long nose, his upper lip overshadowed by a mustache, a lock of hair hanging over a narrow forehead, his eyes small and dim, his whole appearance timid and shy, — not the slightest resemblance with the Emperor, — such was the citizen Charles Louis Napoleon Bonaparte.

"During the murmur which arose upon his entrance, he remained for some minutes, with his right hand thrust into his buttoned-up coat, stiff and motionless on the tribune, whose three sides bore the dates '22, 23, 24, February,' above which the words 'Liberty, Equality, and Fraternity' were inscribed.

"When silence was at length restored, the President of the Assembly tapped several times with his mallet on the table in front of him, and said, when perfect quiet prevailed, 'I will read the form of oath, which is to this effect: 'In the presence of God, and before the French nation, which is here represented by the National Assembly, I swear to remain faithful to the sole and indivisible Republic, and to fulfil all the duties imposed on me by the Constitution.' The President stood as he read this binding oath, after which, citizen Charles Louis Napoleon Bonaparte raised his right hand, and said, in a firm, full voice, 'I swear.'

"The President of the Assembly, still standing, continued: 'We call God and men as witnesses of the oath just sworn.'

"The National Assembly accepted the oath, and ordered it to be printed in the 'Moniteur,' and published in the same manner and form as the discussions of the Legislative Assembly.

"The matter now appeared settled, and it was assumed that citizen Charles Louis Napoleon Bonaparte, from this time up to the second Sunday in May, 1852, President of the Republic, would descend from the tribune. But he did not do so; he felt an internal impulse to bind himself, if possible, more tightly, — to add something to the oath which the Constitution had demanded from him, and to prove how arbitrarily this oath was interpreted by him.

"He requested permission to address the Assembly. 'Speak,' said the President; 'you have the word.' A deeper silence and greater attention than before prevailed. The citizen Louis Napoleon unfolded a paper and read a speech. In this speech, by which he appointed a chosen body of his own friends to offices, he said: —

"'I wish, in union with you, representatives of the citizens, to establish society upon its true basis, to introduce democratic institutions, and discover means calculated to alleviate the sufferings of a noble and intelligent people, which has just given me such a marked proof of its confidence.'

"But that which especially struck every one, which each stamped on his memory, and which found an echo in the heart of every honorable man, was the explanation with which he commenced his address. 'The voice of the nation and the oath I have just taken rule my future conduct. My duty is clearly laid down for me; and I shall carry it out as a man of honor. I shall regard all those as enemies of our country who seek by illegal measures to alter that which the whole of France has established.'

"When he had finished his speech, the Constituent Assembly rose, and raised, as if from one mouth, the loud shout of 'Long live the Republic!'"

The President, who was called "Prince" in social intercourse, was given a fair opportunity to make good his better promises, and for a little while he lived in apparent quiet at his palace of the Elysée, not far from the Tuileries. To most people he seemed dull and slow; but those who knew best his subtle and silent character feared most that, when thus phlegmatic, a storm was moving in the fog.

"There were always a few who believed in his capacity," says Kinglake, "and observant men had latterly remarked that from time to time there appeared a State Paper, understood to be the work of the President, which teemed with thought, and which showed that the writer, standing solitary and apart from the gregarious nation of which he was the chief, was able to contemplate it as something external to himself. His long, endless study of the mind of the first Napoleon had caused him to adopt and imitate the Emperor's habit of looking down upon the French people, and treating the mighty nation as a substance to be studied and controlled by a foreign brain."

The policy of the President, however, was stubbornly adverse to republicanism; he suppressed the rising of the republicans in Rome by a forced intervention, and his plotters were at work throughout France to fill the army with ambitious dreams, and break the confidence of the people in the republic. He and they resolved upon a *coup d'etat*, or armed overthrow of the government, on the 2d of December, 1851, and one by one the Generals of the Army were bribed over to assist the President in breaking the oath he had taken. The work was to be done by Maupas and St. Arnaud. Maupas assembled twenty Generals, whom he had under his command, and gave them to understand that they might soon be called upon to act against Paris, and against the Constitution. They promised a zealous and thorough-going obedience, although every one of them, from Maupas downwards, was to have the pleasing shelter of an order from his superior officer; they all seem to have imagined that their determination was of the sort which mankind call heroic; "for their panegyrist relates with pride, that when Maupas and his twenty Generals were entering into this league and covenant against the people of Paris they solemnly embraced one another."

From time to time the common soldiery were gratified with presents of food and wine, as well as with an abundance of flattering words; and their exasperation against the civilians was so well kept alive, that men used to African warfare were brought into the humor for calling the Parisians "Bedouins." There was massacre in the very sound. The army of Paris was in the temper requiredff for, during Louis Philippe's time several bitter conflicts had taken place between the people and military, and the latter had been worsted.

The night before the coup d'etat, proclamations were stealthily prepared by the conspirators, and placarded about the city.

By these proclamations the President asserted that the Assembly was a hot-bed of plots; declared it dissolved; pronounced for universal suffrage; proposed a new constitution; vowed anew that his duty was to maintain the Republic; and placed Paris and the twelve surrounding departments under martial law. In one of the proclamatio s he appealed to the Army, and strove to whet its enmity against civilians by reminding it of the defeats inflicted upon the troops in 1830 and 1848.

The same night all the leading republican deputies, and the influential men of Paris not in the plot, were seized and hurried off to prison, as well as all the Generals of the Army, and the National Guard, who could not be bought over.

The object of these night arrests was that, when morning broke, the Army should be without Generals inclined to observe the law, that the Assembly should be without the machinery for convoking it, and that all the political parties in the state should be paralyzed by the disappearance of their chiefs. The number of men thus seized in the dark was seventy-eight. Eighteen of these were members of the Assembly.

Whilst it was still dark, Morny, escorted by a body of infantry, took possession of the Home Office, and prepared "to touch the springs of that wondrous machinery, by which a click can dictate to a nation. Already he began to tell the forty thousand communes of the enthusiasm with which the sleeping city had received the announcement of measures not hitherto disclosed.

"When the light of the morning dawned, people saw the Proclamation on the walls, and slowly came to hear, that numbers of the foremost men of France had been seized in the night-time, and that every General to whom the friends of law and order could look for help was lying in one or other of the prisons.

"The newspapers, to which a man might run in order to know, and know truly, what others thought and intended, were all seized and stopped."

Paralysis, as had been supposed, seized the city; nobody could be found to head a demonstration, or to propose any measure of action.

In the course of the morning, the President, accompanied by his uncle, Jerome Bonaparte, and Count Flahault, the father of his bastard half-brother, and attended by many general officers, and a numerous staff, rode through some of the streets of Paris. "It would seem that his theatrical bent had led Prince Louis to expect from this ride a kind of triumph, upon which his fortunes would hinge; and certainly the unpopularity of the Assembly, and the suddenness and perfection of the blow which he had struck in the night, gave him fair grounds for his hope; but he was hardly aware of the light in which his personal pretensions were regarded by the keen, laughing people of Paris."

A part of the Assembly got together, however, and upon the motion of the illustrious Berryer, they resolved that the act of Louis Bonaparte was a forfeiture of the Presidency, and they directed the judges of the Supreme Court to meet and proceed to the judgment of the President and his accomplices. "These resolutions had just been voted, when a battalion of Chasseurs de Vincennes entered the court-yard of the Mayoralty, and began to ascend the stairs. One of the Vice-Presidents of the Assembly went out and summoned the soldiers to stop and leave the chamber free.

"Presently afterwards, several battalions of the line, under the command of General Forey, afterward conqueror of Mexico, came up, and surrounded the Mayoralty where the Assembly was meeting. The Chasseurs de Vincennes were ordered to load. By and by, two Commissaries of Police came to the door, and, announcing that they had orders to clear the hall, entreated the Assembly to yield. The Assembly refused. The whole Assembly declared that they resisted, and would yield to nothing short of force. In the absence of Dupin, M. Benoist d'Azy had been presiding over the Assembly, and both he and one of the Vice-Presidents were now collared by officers of police, and led out. The whole Assembly followed, and, enfolded between files of soldiery, was marched through the streets. General Forey rode by the side of the column.

"At night a large number of the windowless vans, which are used for the transport of felons, were brought into the court of the barrack, and into these the two hundred and thirty-five members of the Assembly were thrust. They were carried off, some to the Fort of Mount Valerian, some to the Fortress of Vincennes, and some to the prison of Mazas. Before the dawn of the 3d of December all the eminent members of the Assembly, and all the foremost Generals in France were lying in prison; for now (besides General Changarnier and General Bedeau, General Lamoricière, General Cavaignac, and General Leflô, and besides Thiers and Colonel Charras, and Roger du Nord, and Miot and Baze, and the others who had been seized the night before, and were still held fast in the jails) there were in prison two hundred and thirty-five of the representatives of the people, including, amongst others of wide renown, Berryer, Odillon Barrot, Barthêlemy St. Hilaire, Gustave de Beaumont, Benoist d'Azy, the Duc de Broglie, Admiral Cecile, Chambolle, De Corcelles, Dufaure, Duvergier de Hauranne, De Falloux, General Lauriston, Oscar Lafayette, Lanjuinais, Lasteyrie, the Duc de Luines, the Duc de Montibello, General Radoult-Lafosse, General Oudinot, De Remusat, and the wise and gifted De Tocqueville.

"Amongst the men imprisoned there were twelve statesmen, who had been cabinet ministers, and nine of these had been chosen by the President himself.

"These were the sort of men who were within the walls of the prisons. Those who threw them into prison was Prince Louis Bonaparte, Morny, Maupas, and St. Arnaud, formerly Le Roy, all acting with the advice and consent of Fiulin de Persigny, and under the propulsion of Fleury."

A portion of the citizens got together, and threw up some barricades between the Hotel de Ville, or City Hall, and the wide Boulevards.

Notwithstanding the panic of the *coup d'etat* there was a remnant of the old insurrectionary forces, which was willing to try the experiment of throwing up a few barricades; and there was, besides, a small number of men who were impelled in the same direction by motives of a different and almost opposite kind. These last were men too brave, too proud, too faithful in their love of right and freedom to be capable of acquiescing for even a week in the transactions of the December night. The foremost of these was the illustrious Victor Hugo. He, and some of the other members of the Assembly who had escaped seizure, formed themselves into a Committee of Resistance, with a view to assert by arms the supremacy of the law. This step they took on the second of December.

By their personal energy these men threw up a slight barricade at the corner of the Rue St. Marguerite. Against this there marched a battalion of the 19th Regiment. "And then," says Kinglake, "there occurred a scene, which may make one smile for a moment, and may then almost force one to admire the touching pedantry of brave men, who imagined that, without policy or warlike means, they could be strong with the mere strength of the law." Laying aside their firearms, and throwing across their shoulders, scarfs, which marked them as representatives of the people, the Deputies ranged themselves in front of the barricade, and one of them, Charles Baudin, held ready in his hand the book of the Constitution. When the head of the column was within a few yards of the barricade, it was halted. For some moments there was silence. Law and force had met. On one side was Code Democratic, which France had declared to be perpetual; on the other, a battalion of the line. The officer in command refused to concede what logicians call the "major premiss." He gave an important sign. Suddenly the muskets of the front rank men came down, came up, came level, and in another instant their fire pelted straight into the group of the scarfed deputies. Baudin fell dead, his head being shattered by more than one ball. One other was killed by the volley; several more were wounded. The book of the Constitution had fallen to the ground, and the defenders of the law recurred to their firearms. They shot the officer who had caused the death of their comrade.

There was a fight of the Homeric sort for the body of Charles Baudin. The battalion won it; four soldiers carried it off.

The greatest barricade was raised across the Boulevard in the eastern quarter of Paris, and against this the main army of the usurper was directed. Victor Hugo himself describes the scene, and from him the subjoined account is mainly taken: —

"Facing this little barricade, at a distance of about a hundred and fifty yards, was the head of the vast column of troops, which now occupied the whole of the western Boulevard, and a couple of field-pieces stood pointed toward the barricade. In the neutral space, between the barricade and the head of the column, the shops, and almost all the windows, were closed; but numbers of spectators, including many women, crowded the foot-pavement. But westward of the point occupied by the head of the column, the state of the Boulevards was different. From that point home to the Madeleine, the whole carriage-way was occupied by troops; the infantry was drawn up in subdivisions at quarter distance. Along this part of the gay and glittering Boulevard, the windows, the balconies, and the foot pavements were crowded with men and women, who were gazing at the military display. These gazers had no reason for supposing that they incurred any danger, for they could see no one with whom the army would have to contend. It is true that notices had been placed upon the walls, recommending the people not to encumber the streets, and warning them that they would be liable to be dispersed by the troops, without being summoned; but of course, those who had chanced to see this announcement naturally imagined that it was a menace addressed to riotous crowds which might be pressing upon the troops in a hostile way.

"Suddenly, the troops at the head of the column faced about and opened fire; some of the soldiery fired point blank into the mass of spectators who stood gazing upon them from the foot-pavement, and the rest of the troops fired up at the gay, crowded windows and balconies. The impulse which had thus come upon the soldiery, near the head of the column, was a motive akin to panic, for it was carried by swift contagion from man to man, till a column of some sixteen thousand men, facing eastward toward St. Denis, was suddenly formed as it were into an order of battle fronting southward, and busily firing into the crowd which lined the foot-pavement, and upon the men, women, and children who stood at the balconies and windows on that side of the Boulevard.

"When there was no longer a crowd to fire into, the soldiers would aim carefully at any single fugitive who was trying to effect his escape; and if a man tried to save himself by coming close up to the troops and asking for mercy, the soldiers would force or persuade the suppliant to keep off and hasten away, and then, if they could, they killed him running. This slaughter of unarmed men and women was continued for a quarter of an hour or twenty minutes.

"It was thus the Prince President was keeping his oath, and meantime the police offices in his interest were at work.

"Great numbers of prisoners were brought into the Prefecture of Police; but it appears to have been thought inconvenient to allow the sound of the discharge of musketry to be heard coming from the precincts of the building. For that reason, as it would seem, another mode of quieting men was adopted. Each of the prisoners destined to undergo this fate was driven with his hands tied behind him into one of the courts of the prefecture, and then one of the Maupas police officers came and knocked him on the head with a loaded club, and felled him, — felled him in the way that is used by a man when he has to slaughter a bullock."

At the same time the soldiery continued their butchery, and one officer declared that his regiment alone had killed two thousand four hundred men. "Supposing that his statement was anything like an approach to the truth, and that his corps was at all rivalled by others, a very high number would be wanted for covering the whole quantity of the slaughter."

In the army which did these things the whole number of killed was twenty-five.

Paris being thus crushed, France was to be wheedled by Morny, the new Secretary of the Interior.

Morny, stealing into the Home Office, had entrusted his orders, for instant and enthusiastic support, to the zeal of every prefect, and had ordered that every mayor, every juge de paix, and every other public functionary, who failed to give in his instant and written adhesion to the acts of the President, should be dismissed.

In France, the engine of state is so constructed as to give the Home Office an almost irresistible power over the provinces, and the means which the office had of coercing France were reinforced by an appeal to men's fears of anarchy, and their dread of the sect called "Socialists." Forty thousand communes were modestly told that they must make swift choice between socialism, and anarchy, and rapine on the one hand, and on the other a virtuous dictator and lawgiver, recommended and warranted by the authority of Monsieur De Morny.

Every department which seemed likely to move was put under

martial law. Then followed slaughter, banishment, imprisonment, sequestration, and all this at the mere pleasure of Generals.

"Speaking within the limits of historical truth," says the London "Times" of that date, "and upon the evidence of many eye-witnesses of these events, we affirm, that the bloody and treacherous deeds of the 4th of December will be remembered with horror, even in that city which witnessed the massacre of St. Bartholomew and the 'Reign of Terror.'

"None will ever know the number of men, who, at this period, were either killed, or imprisoned, in France, or sent to die in Africa or Cayenne; but the panegyrist of Louis Bonaparte, Granier de Cassagnac, acknowledges that the number of people who were seized and transported, within the few weeks which followed the 2d of December, amounted to the enormous number of twenty-six thousand five hundred.

"Some thousands of Frenchmen were made to undergo sufferings too horrible to be here told, enclosed in the casemates in the fortresses, and huddled down between the decks of the Canada and the Duguesclin. These hapless beings were, for the most part, men attached to the cause of the Republic. It would seem that, of the two thousand men whose sufferings are the most known, a great part were men whose lives had been engaged in literary pursuits; for amongst them there were authors of some repute, editors of newspapers, and political writers of many grades, besides lawyers, physicians, and others whose labors in the field of politics had been mainly labors of the intellectual sort. The torments inflicted upon these men lasted from two to three months."

The massacre having been effective, Louis Napoleon submitted to the nation that he be declared President for ten years. The choice given to the electors did not even purport to be anything but a choice between Louis Bonaparte and nothing. According to the wording of the Plebiscite, a vote given for any candidate other than Louis Bonaparte would have been null.

An elector was only permitted to vote "yes," or vote "no," and it seems plain that the prospect of anarchy involved in a negative vote would alone have operated as a sufficing menace.

One thing only remained to do, — to go through the appearance of legitimizing the Empire, — and this was submitted to a like farcical form of vote.

"Let us do homage to Napoleon!!!" Thus ended the lithographed circulars of the prefects after the *coup d'etat.* The three marks of admiration were generally taken for a Roman III., "and this," says one, "gave the Prince the idea of calling himself Napoleon III., which was the origin of many difficulties, as diplomacy had never recognized a Napoleon II."

To cover this murder with glory was the next thing, and a pretext was found for embroiling England with France in a war against Russia, whose Emperor had addressed the new Emperor cavalierly.

A short time after the *coup d'etat*, the Queen's speech announced to Europe "that the Emperor of the French had united with Her Majesty in earnest endeavors to reconcile differences, the continuance of which might involve Europe in war;" and she declared that "acting in concert with her Allies, and relying on the Conference, then assembled at Vienna, Her Majesty had good reason to hope that an honorable arrangement would speedily be accomplished." The war with Russia and great glory followed, and the blood-stained government was secured. Perjury had been confirmed, and the adventurer was the richest Emperor in Europe.

The French imperial succession is circumscribed very nearly as the first Napoleon arranged it, the families of Louis and Jerome Bonaparte being the only recognized channels of entail, and the descendants of all the other brothers merely belong to the "Family of the Emperor," — simple subjects with precedence above the high dignitaries. The imperial dignity is hereditary in the male and legitimate descendants of Napoleon III., in the order of primogeniture. If he shall have no male child, the Emperor may choose to adopt any of the male descendants of Napoleon I.; but this privilege of adoption does not belong to his successors. If he should die without a successor, born or adopted, the Presidents of the two legislative chambers, jointly with his Council of State, elect a Sovereign, and submit the choice to a vote of the people. In December, 1852, Napoleon nominated his Uncle Jerome, and the male and legitimate descendants of his marriage with Catherine of Wurtemberg. This would have made Prince Napoleon Joseph, born 1822, the heir, — commonly called Prince Napoleon, — but in 1853 the Emperor married Eugenie Marie de Montigo, of Spain, and her child, Napoleon Eugene Louis, — or the Prince Imperial, — born 1856, is heir to the purple.

As early as 1848, Napoleon offered his hand to Eugenie, in London; but she is said to have declined it, with the words: —

"You will go to Paris, and strive there to acquire power, become

Consul, President, or Dictator. Supposing you have attained your first object, will you remain standing? Will it satisfy your ambition? Will you not rather soar higher? You will! But, in that case, what a burden a wife will be to you! If a man wishes to become Emperor, he must leave the choice of an Empress open. But if you were to be unsuccessful in your efforts, — if things did not go as you wished; if France did not offer you what you expect from her, — then, but only then, return; then I will give you an answer to your offer; then remember that a heart beats in my bosom, which feels it has the strength to requite you for all your grief and all your foiled expectations."

This sounds like an extract from a play at the *Porte Saint Martin*, but it is solemnly put down by reverend clergymen, like Mr. J. S. C. Abbott, and ought to be valid. Had Mr. Abbott himself made that response, its authenticity could have been sworn to.

Eugenie, like every woman connected with the Bonapartes, except Marie Louise, who supplanted Josephine, was pretty and interesting, and the physical and mental superior of any Empress in Europe. She was sixteen years younger than her husband, and her child is like her, smart, and forward, and spirited. Eugenie has, it is said, a striking likeness to the celebrated Queen of Scots; the same nose, the same characteristic eyebrows, the same golden hair, the same white complexion.

As a girl she was very rich, and had an income of five hundred thousand francs. She is said to have assisted Louis Napoleon during the presidency by selling a valuable set of pearls. The latter had left London owing three years' rent, without counting his numerous tradesmen's bills.

The Parisians do not like the Empress, as she is a devoted adherent of the Pope; but considering her place and her origin, she has certainly been a brilliant woman, and given the lustre of beauty and benevolence to the dynasty. Her son has a dangerous path before him, and she must often lament that he was born upon such heights of dizziness. At present, all of them have means and pleasure in abundance. Their palaces are numerous; but St. Cloud is their suburban palace, and Fontainebleau and Compeigne their principal summer chateaux. The Emperor is an abstruse politician, sufficiently French himself to take naturally to war, oratory, and public excitement, and sufficiently Dutch, perhaps, to blend with these brilliant parts the cold, phlegmatic judgment of the house of Orange. In

America he would be called an astute, selfish politician, anxious to achieve public glory, provided it were attributed to himself. In Europe he receives the additional significance of descent, which on one side makes him hated by the aristocrats, and on the other reverenced by the ignorant peasantry. Between the two the Republicans recognize his adroitness, upbraid him as a traitor to the liberties of his country and of Europe, and employ all the abilities they can command with safety, to destroy the illusion of his name, and to counteract the power of his policy. He also is conscious of his weakness and his strength, and is no despiser of his enemies. Perhaps he feels that

> "Things bad begun make bad themselves by ill ;"

and he is at work industriously to make his reign an example of beneficence and glory, so that its remembrance shall be its bulwark when his crafty hands are folded upon his breast.

The Emperor's mode of life is, for periods, very regular and moderate. He rises at an early hour, and spends a very considerable portion of the day at his study-table. His learning is great, and his education was a conscientiously German one. He speaks French, German, and English well, understands Latin and Italian, has carefully studied geography, history, and social economy, is well versed in mathematics and physics, and is a well-trained artillery officer. He very moderately indulges in the joys of the table ; but in other indulgences is far from blameless. In his character he unites the cold tranquillity and unbending obstinacy of the Dutchman with the lively resolution of the Frenchman. In the Italian campaign of 1859 he is said to have displayed much cold resolution. As to his real talent as commander, the voices of the French officers are greatly divided. Many assert that he possesses it, and that himself drew up in great measure the plan of that campaign, while others ascribe the plan to Maréchal Niel, although they allow the Emperor to be possessed of the valuable quality of recognizing the excellence of other plans, subordinating himself to them, and carrying them out energetically. He is, at any rate, a good, if not a brilliant, soldier, and possesses the confidence of his army, if he does not arouse its enthusiasm. He has not the least wit or talent for declamation ; has no fancy, artistic talent, or the slightest taste for any art ; and though he may favor the arts, and lavish millions on prominent artists, he only does so because he believes that it heightens the lustre of his government. He is very cold toward the creations of the poetic art, and even in his youth he did not write a single verse, though he translated many German lines into French. Thus, for instance, he translated Schiller's "Ideal" in his Strasburg prison.

Napoleon, as a rule, enjoys excellent health. It is true he no longer has the elasticity of youth, and the signs of age are gradually becoming more prominent. His back is getting bent, his step more measured, his eye watery, his forehead wrinkled, his hair scanty, and his expression weak. But, then, the Emperor was never a handsome man.

Strollers in the forest of Fontainebleau notice, on returning at a late hour, a lighted room in the corner of the château, with the windows usually open to admit the evening breeze. The inhabitants know it to be the Emperor's study; and when they wish to learn whether the Emperor is at a concert or ball, they take a glance at the eastern pavilion, where the lamp frequently burns till one A. M. The Emperor rises at an early hour, and takes a sharp walk with an adjutant or the Imperial Prince. He returns at eight o'clock. He goes through the letters with his private secretary, and the newspapers, especially the London "Times" and a German journal. After this, he breakfasts with the Empress and the Prince. As a rule, only three persons are invited to breakfast, generally belonging to the department. At noon the auditor of the Council of State attends him in his Cabinet, with the despatch-bag from Paris. Very frequently a minister works with the Emperor till two o'clock; then he rides out with the Empress and his guests. At the dinner-table there is very great ceremony, in which the Imperial Prince takes but little pleasure. The ladies and gentlemen are in full dress; and the Prefect, General, Bishop, or other notabilities of the department, occupy the seats of honor. If, after dinner, there is no *soirée*, concert, or ball, the guests do what they please. The evening parties are neither musical nor learned, but all the more amusing. There is generally a good deal of noise near the Empress' *salon;* for the Imperial Prince has his guests too, who are apt to forget rank, etiquette, and discipline. The party breaks up at eleven o'clock, after the Empress has arranged the programme for the next day, which, however, binds nobody. The Emperor often rides out in the evening. On his return, at eleven o'clock, he is accustomed to arrange his work for the next day in his Cabinet.

The principal other ladies of the imperial family are the Spanish mother of Eugenie, who has become very rich by speculating on government secrets, and whom the Parisians call the "Crocodile;" the Princess Mathilde, Prince Napoleon's sister, who is divorced from her Russian husband, Prince Demidoff; Clotilde, daughter of the King of Italy, who is married to that gifted sensualist, Prince Napoleon, nineteen years her senior; the latter is the most popular member of the imperial house.

The national republican song of France, the "Marseillaise," has been set aside by the Emperor, for a song composed by his mother, Hortense, entitled "Partant pour la Syrie."

So much of politics has been said in this book that my lady readers may be diverted by some notes of a visit that I made to the tombs of the Emperor's mother and grandmother, Hortense and Josephine, in the year 1864. They lie buried in the little village church of Rueil, nine miles from Paris, and I passed through the town with some friends to look first at their home of Malmaison, near by.

Stealing away from the church square, passing a flower and vegetable market, turning into the high road again, and leaving Rueil behind, we came at last to a green lane with high stone walls on either side, and, after a few moments' thoughtful walking, stood at the gate of Malmaison.

Malmaison had received its name "Mala-Domus," from having once been the home of Norman adventurers, who had been cursed by the people. But since that time it had been exorcised and sanctified as a monastery, and finally had been turned into a country-house. Bonaparte, before embarking for Egypt, had written to Josephine to secure a country residence for his return. She hesitated some time between Ris and Malmaison, but decided in favor of the latter.

When the General became First Consul, he installed himself in the Luxembourg; but the Palace of the Medicis was only his political residence; his leisure hours were spent at Malmaison. The dignified silence and severe etiquette which became afterward the law at the Imperial Palaces of St. Cloud and the Tuileries were then unknown. It was at that time not an uncommon thing to play at "prisoner's base" here. On one side were Bonaparte, Lauriston, Rapp, Eugene, and the Demoiselles Anguie; on the other, Josephine, Hortense, Jerome, Madame Caroline Murat, Isabey Didelot, and DeLacay. They were all young people. The game would be followed by a cotillon, and in the evening by a play performed by themselves.

After many pleasant years passed here with Josephine, the house was given to the Empress after her repudiation. When Bonaparte resolved to divorce Josephine, childless to him, Hortense and Eugene, her own children, were, strangely enough, selected by the Emperor to convey the sad intelligence to the Empress; but he knew that he could rely upon their boundless devotion. The scenes that followed have been described by a Prefect of the Palace, in his "Memoirs." The same children were also summoned to be present at the nuptials of the Emperor and Maria Louise, and the Queen of Holland, Hortense, was one of the four to bear a corner of the mantle of the Empress, who usurped the place of her own mother.

Malmaison now belongs to Louis Napoleon. An old wounded grenadier kept the lodge, but was prohibited from granting us admission; so he chatted with us as we looked through the bars upon the long, white building, steep-roofed, and flanked by turrets and huge chimneys. A carriage passed round the smooth lawns; there were few large trees save beyond the house, where a beautiful wood bordered a hill-side; but close by the gate were flower-beds, whose perfumes blew upon us, as if to give us some sweet thing to carry across the seas. Here Josephine received visits from the Czar, and King of Prussia; but all her days were sad ones. She could not drive from her mind the memory of the grand court, and her sunburnt soldier, slumbering beside his young princess, and the gossip of the court ladies pitying her, who used to be their Queen. Here she died, in the arms of her children, in the spring of the year, in the month of May, neither poor nor unloved, but repudiated! Soon after her entombment the beaten Conqueror came back from Waterloo, and bade his few attendants adieu from this threshold, and turned into the deserted place to see the relics of the only being who ever loved him. Soon he lay on the rock of Saint Helena, and she was at rest in the vault of Rueil.

Critics have been divided as to the influence and merits of Josephine, but the ladies cling devotedly to the superstition of her goodness. Whatever be the cold historic truth, this remains: he was a tryant, she was unhappy. With all our reasoning, we feel that Josephine is the only soft, human episode in the biography of Bonaparte. Love, redeeming love, whether in cottage, or palace, covers a multitude of sins. We turn with relief from the glaring sun of Austerlitz, from the glory of Marengo, and the marvel of Jena, and the long, bloody trail of Moscow, to this fond, foolish, beautiful woman, the thought of whom lightened the conqueror's bivouac dreams.

Returning to the little church of Rueil, we turned at the end of the mass, to the high altar, and saw set in the wall, on either side, the tomb of Josephine to the right, and that of her daughter Hortense to the left. The first of these was the grandmother, the second, the mother of the present Emperor of the French.

The tombs were each of Carrara marble, fifteen feet high perhaps; Josephine's was by Castellier, and represented the Empress in the long, rich robes of the court, kneeling upon a cushion, and with clasped hands, before a marble *prie-dieu*. The latter was too low. The statue, while not a *chef d'œuvre*, was a correct and pleasing one, representing a beautiful woman, with a saddened, resigned face, and it was enclosed by columns and an entablature, the latter oddly carved. Below was this inscription: —

A.

Josephine.

Eugene. Et Hortense.

1825.

Her son and daughter raised the monument. The tomb of the beautiful, wilful, and gifted Hortense stood opposite.

The remains of Queen Hortense were transferred from Switzerland to Rueil, by Count de Tascher de la Pagerie, her cousin (Josephine was a De Tascher, de la Pagerie), and were deposited in a catacomb opposite to that of the Empress Josephine, in this ancient church of the Lords of Burenval. A mausoleum was raised over the vault in 1845, by Bartolini, of Florence; but one of the first melancholy duties of Louis Napoleon was to save the Church of Rueil from the ruin by which it was threatened.

Partner in brightness and sorrow with Josephine was Marie Antoinette, her predecessor upon the throne, and there is an anecdote told about the present Emperor and those beheaded Bourbons which may be worth relating: —

When Hortense went to live in the palace in the Rue d'Anjou St. Honoré, she found that Louis XIV., and Marie Antoinette were buried at no great distance from the Madeleine church-yard. An old royalist, Duseausaux, had guarded and tended the graves for upwards of twenty years. He had a cottage close by. Hortense visited him, and asked to be shown the graves. She at once shared with the old man the duty of keeping this grave in order, and it continually grew more and more charming; ere long it was entirely concealed by a mound of Parma violets. The old man died, and Hortense became the sole keeper of the graves. The children accompanied her when she visited them from time to time; they did not know who slept beneath the fragrant violets, — they only saw the tears in their mother's eyes, and clasped their hands as they saw their mother clasp hers.

"Louis Napoleon," says a rapturous Englishman, "praying at the grave of Louis XIV. and Marie Antoinette, and not knowing for whom he prayed! What a picture!"

The Court of the Tuileries alone might fail to satisfy curiosity in a volume, and it has been the subject of many; and the subordinate palaces of the Emperor would of themselves make the whole contents of a book like this. Each of the imperial country residences have immense forests attached, that of Fontainebleau being sixty-three miles in circumference, and containing forty-two thousand acres.

In the year 1863 I made the tour of the forest of the Palace of Compeigne, and resided in the town of the palace for two months. A description of this imperial residence will conclude the chapter. We reached the edge of the forest at a little village called St. Sauveur, at nightfall, and in the morning we entered one of the straight, deep defiles of the ancient and wonderful forest of Compiegne. When I would think of any vastness achieved by nature and artifice combined, I recall the long, canopied continuity of shade through which we made this day's journey. Here is a solid forest, fifty miles in circumference, patrolled, and guarded, and worked by eight hundred men, producing every year seven hundred thousand francs' worth of wood, and three hundred thousand in game. It is traversed by three hundred and sixty roads, meeting at two hundred and ninety *carrefours*, all arranged in such superb geometry, that from each *carrefour* you can see down straight lines of verdure, in from eight to twenty-four directions, and from horizon to horizon. Twenty-seven brooks wind through this wonderful forest; sixteen lakes glass it; nine villages are pent up in its perpetual shadows; fourteen hunting-lodges stand by its waysides, where all the night the baying of hounds startles the lonely traveller; two ranges of not inconsiderable mountains, curtained with foliage, shut in most of its area; the ruins of eleven castles and abbeys are buried in its fastnesses or crown its steeps; a real Roman road, with Roman villages disentombed beside it, passes through its largest diameter; and where its mighty oaks, and elms, and beeches, and maples darken and murmur now, there have their ancestors held this realm for all the Christian era. It is this that makes the Forest of Compiegne remarkable in France; but, to me, the crowning wonder was the patient labor and embellishment which had softened such wild nature to its own conceit. Over every roadway the huge trees had been taught to arch in perfect aisles; so that the whole seemed some Druidical Cathedral, where every open *carrefour* was a lantern, and whose choirs were the million birds that trilled all day, while at night the cuckoo shouted her stentorian note, and the owl laughed like a maniac unchained. Still in these miles of lofty arbor the wild boar made his home unchallenged, save once a year, when the Emperor and his game-keepers come up to Compiegne with horn and rifle, and the woods are filled with galloping courtiers. We walked among the hares and rabbits, and heard the whirr of pheasants, and now and then a fox stared down the long carpet of grass, amazed at the distinctness of the distance: but it is at bodily peril that you discharge a pistol, or stone a wren, or light a fire, or pluck a twig in this Imperial domain. The laws are written at every *carrefour*, where, also, index-boards relieve you from the dread of wandering astray and purposeless, and while this vast shadow-land is clean and thrifty as a lady's lawn, yet you will roam for hours and hours and see no human face, nor hear the reverberations of an axe. We call our western hemisphere a land of boundless forests; but I have never found in it a roof of shade like this of Compiegne. Industry has reduced our woodland to "scrub;" the "wilderness" of Virginia is chiefly brush-land, swamp and barren, and even in Michigan, the lumberman's State, it is rare to see a square mile of stalwart towering tree-boles. The Forest of Compiegne is only sixty miles from Paris, and it is not so large as that of Fontainebleau, but for quality the aboriginal Indians might have been proud of it.

In the middle of this deep forest at the little village of St. Jean au Bois, we found this sign set up against an inn: —

THE DOCTOR LARREY,
A FAMOUS AMERICAN DENTIST,
Now making a tour of the
DEPARTMENT OF THE SEINE AND OISE,
will be here
ON THURSDAY AND FRIDAY NEXT,
and at
PIERREFONDS FOR THE WEEK SUCCEEDING.
M. Gardette, the Priest, and M. Bouille, the Aubergiste,
are his references.

Our little party, solemnized by our insignificance amid this vegetable sea, came now and then to relics of a former era. At Champlieu we found a Roman theatre in perfect restoration, guarded by an old veteran, who talked of Leipsic and Waterloo; and near Fontenoy a score of laborers were working with pick and shovel in a Roman village to find material for Louis Napoleon's "Life of Cæsar." For this book there must have been, at one time or another, ten thousand men employed. I saw about a regiment of them digging up the palace of the Cæsars in Rome, and from Marseilles to Calais they unearthed every old coin, pot, and spear-head. At Pierrefonds we saw the most original and beautiful restoration in France, — the feudal castle of that name battered down by Richelieu's order, but the designs for which, being happily preserved, it had been rebuilt by the Emperor with all the massive elaborateness of its model, complete in buttress, battlement, postern, portcullis, donjon, chapel, and moat, so that if gunpowder could be abolished to-day, Pierrefonds would be less pregnable than Fort Richmond, or Drury's Bluff. Of this revived castle is to be made a mediæval arsenal, bristling with armor, and lances, and axes; and as we strangers gazed upon it in the sunset, sharply cut, machicolated, graceful, yet serene, we looked into each other's eyes.

There were but twelve thousand souls resident in the town of Compiegne, but it had a historical reminiscence for every man. By the aid of Lambert de Ballyhier, conscientious antiquarian, we made every dumb wall speak. Here were wide convents used for no better purpose than storing pork and flour, groined cloisters for horse-stalls, and ruined abbeys in the midst of the town eaten by ivy. Standing by the river's side, haunted by pigeons, is the very tower whose draw-bridge, raised by treachery, gave the Maid of Arc to Burgundy and Britain. She said her last prayer in liberty here, in the church of St. Jacques, and on the bare heights across the Oise the besieging armies pitched their tents. In this chateau lived the son of Charlemagne, whose father gave him the world, but whose feeble hands could not retain it. Beyond the village, at Choisy lay the body of the wife of Pepin, and at Villers Cotterets, not far away, Dumas, the novelist, was born. The forest, whose black edges made night perpetual on our east, had been the seat of desperate robbers, hedged in castleholds whose memory lived in every peasant's fears. Here, by Compiegne, Bonaparte received Marie Louise, pouring the perjury of love into her ear; and once in twelve months the dissolute and varnished court of the present adventurer congregates here to hear lewd plays, and to coquette in the forests. There is a museum in the old Hotel de Ville, filled with the relics of this region, and every Sunday the military band gives practice in the chateau gardens.

Ensconced in the deep forest with our pipes and books, we might lie all day, approached by none save perhaps a strolling wood-cutter, or a woman beating her panniered donkey. Still, the strong call of the cuckoo drove away all this, and the herds of deer came upon us unaware, and gazed and burst into the covert. The violets soon began to weave devices in the moss, and buttercups came, as at home, to look for tardy summer; then there were stawberries on the knolls, and so, pace by pace, the warm weather fell upon Compiegne, and brought upon us the noisy and imperious court.

CHAPTER XX.

THE FRENCH GOVERNMENT.

A comparison of bereaucracy under the empire with simple Jeffersonian administration in America. — The legislature, the ministry, and the departments.

In France, and upon the continent of Europe, which, willingly or unwillingly, looks to France for example, we shall find an innumerable number of officials, infinite jurisdiction, the pomp of government, and ubiquitous uniforms, so that it is almost as impossible to get out of government as to get out of nature there; at the birth-couch the Emperor's officer steps in to enrol the name of the child for the conscription, and a certificate of birth or paper "*de naissance*" must be carried upon the person perpetually by every French man and French woman; at the grave the government is near by to prescribe the cost of the funeral, and unwilling to release its hold even upon the carcass of the subject.

The first great distinction between France and the United States, in the mind being that one is a personal, and the other a popular government, the more visible distinction is that France is a bureaucratic government, and the United States is merely a constrained federal administration, omitting to take cognizance of any matters save those which affect its own dignity and permanence, and leaving to the people, in their local and individual way, to carry out their own fortunes and the destinies of the state.

Bureaucracy is derived from the French word *bureau*, a writing-desk or a business office, and signifies that kind of government where a host of officials, responsible only to their respective chiefs, interfere with, and control, every detail of public and private life. In France, bureaucracy is the distinguishing feature of the government, and also in the German States, where critics call it *vielregieren*, or much government. There is little bureaucracy in the United States; for Jefferson overthrew it in his simple definition of free government, notwithstanding which, the motto of the "Congressional Globe" to the present day is, "We are governed too much."

1

2

3

GREAT STATE CEREMONIES.

1—The Fête at Venice. 2—The Pope Blessing on Christmas-Day. 3—Coronation of the Queen of England.

An American visiting France is apt to fall in love with the admirable system of protection afforded there, the regulation of monopolies by government, the safety of the person, the splendor and dimensions of the national enterprises, the civility and the rich costumes of the police, the railroad guards, the firemen and the merchant captains, and he insensibly thinks of the coarse equality of subordinates at home, the brusqueness of officials, the unrestrainable avarice of corporations, the facility for contriving monopolies, the cheapness of life, and the petty penalty for violence against the person. But the observing man, looking beneath society, and above his own transient convenience, will ascribe to bureaucracy all the misfortunes of France since the downfall of the first Napoleon. That sleepless and versatile suggester covered France with administration, and gathered into his imperial hand the skeins of the largest and the least of his infinite establishments. He accustomed every Frenchman to look to the government for relief in every inconvenience, and at every time of deprivation. He took from the people the consciousness and the necessity of individual exertion, and he put a bureau at every elbow, and an official in it, to anticipate the wishes of his subjects; the consequence is, that the individual character of Frenchmen is almost extinct, and they are unstable as petted children. Having several times conquered opportunities for free government, and being in large majority sincere wishers for a Republic, they fasten upon the Republic, when they get it, the whole burden of their necessities, stifle it with bureaux, and make it ridiculous by compelling it to be the vehicle of their dreams and experiments. A Republic that shall keep bread cheap, hold corn in "Warehouses of Abundance," and support "National Workshops," is bound to become the victim of its magnanimity, to arouse expectations that cannot but be disappointed, and to disappear at last under the anarchy of its upbraiders. The founder, expositor, and administrator of that restricted Republicanism which alone is durable, Thomas Jefferson, taught the American people that the best government is that which is least seen, and, adopting his sentiments, the American people have become the most self-reliant, adventurous, and enterprising people on the globe. Always out of sight of their government, yet finding it strong when there is real necessity, they have fewer officials and smaller expenses than any great nation, and are a rebuke to bureaucratic despotism, which, except in England, characterizes the whole of Europe.

In all France there are five hundred and thirty-four thousand eight hundred office-holders, exclusive of servants, counting neither the Army nor the Navy; the salaries of the clerks at the departments in Paris alone amount to one million three hundred thousand dollars a year. The Emperor's household consists of an immense number of officials, amongst whom are twenty-five physicians and surgeons, sixteen *aides-de-camp*, and eight chaplains and ecclesiastics; the Empress has a lady reader, and the Emperor's son has three tutors. The Minister of State is also the patron of letters, theatres, and science. All the monuments, museums, palaces, and schools of fine arts, are controlled by the Minister of the Imperial household. The Emperor's body-guard consists of two hundred and twenty-two mounted men, gorgeously apparelled; the Empress has also her own escort, and the Imperial Guard consists of eight regiments of infantry, six of cavalry, two of *Gendarmes* and *Chasseurs*, and sixteen batteries of artillery. There is no such array of gorgeous official costumes in England as we find in France, where it is a stated belief that fine uniforms give dignity and effect to authority, — a statement disputed by a French traveller in America: —

"I am inclined to believe that the influence which costumes really exercise, in an age like that in which we live, has been a good deal exaggerated. I never perceived that a public officer in America was the less respected whilst he was in the discharge of his duties, because his own merit was set off by no adventitious signs."

We are getting out of our attachment to non-uniformed officials since Mr. James Fisk, the steamboat "Admiral," and the "Imperialist" newspaper have developed amongst us; but it is remarkable that with more uniforms we have less respect for our officials than we used to have when they wore plain citizen dress.

The possession of office in France, as in most of the monarchies in Europe, is considered somewhat of an aristocratic distinction, and hence De Tocqueville says: —

"I look upon the entire absence of gratuitous functionaries in America as one of the most prominent signs of the absolute dominion which democracy exercises in that country. All public services, of whatsoever nature they may be, are paid; so that every one has not merely a right, but also the means of performing it."

If De Tocqueville lived in our time he would see that many of our officials are so indifferently paid that they are, in all but name, reduced to the means of gratuitous functionaries, while they achieve no corresponding distinction.

France is at present undergoing a radical change of government; but the reforms proposed by the Emperor have not, at this writing, gone into effect, and, judging by the inconstant and despotic course of Napoleon, there is less probability of their continuing, than of his whole government being swept away by some attempt that he may make to resume his autocratic authority. We are assured, however, that they are to consist of self-government by the two legislative bodies; the selection of a ministry from the two chambers; more independence in proposing amendments to laws; the right of interpellation, and of voting the yearly budget in detail; open sessions of the Senate except by its own wish to the contrary; the right of legislators to address questions to the government as in England, and co-operation of the CORPS LEGISLATIF with the Emperor in initiating new laws. These reforms will bring the government very nearly to the condition in which it stood under Louis Philippe, and will reduce the Emperor almost to a limited sovereign. When this programme shall be carried out, as it doubtless will be before this book goes to press, France will compare with America, as De Tocqueville drew the distinctions thirty years ago in the following six paragraphs: —

"The sovereignty of the United States is shared between the Union and the States, whilst in France it is undivided and compact; hence arises the first and the most notable difference which exists between the President of the United States and the King of France. In the United States the executive power is as limited and partial as the sovereignty of the Union in whose name it acts; in France it is as universal as the authority of the state. The Americans have a federal, and the French a national government.

"Sovereignty may be defined to be the right of making laws; in France the King really exercises a portion of the sovereign power, since the laws have no weight till he has given his assent to them; he is, moreover, the executor of all they ordain. The President is also the executor of the laws, but he does not really co-operate in their formation, since the refusal of his assent does not annul them.

"But not only does the King of France exercise a portion of the sovereign power; he also contributes to the nomination of the Legislature, which exercises the other portion. He has the privilege of appointing the members of one chamber, and of dissolving the other at his pleasure; whereas the President of the United States has no share in the formation of the Legislative body, and cannot dissolve any part of it. The King has the same right of bringing forward measures as the chambers, — a right which the President does not possess. The King is represented in each Assembly by his ministers, who explain his intention, support his opinions, and maintain the principles of the government. The President and his ministers are alike excluded from Congress; so that his influence and his opinions can only penetrate indirectly into that great body. The King of France is, therefore, on an equal footing with the Legislature, which can no more act without him than he can without it. The President exercises an authority depending upon that of the Legislature.

"The President of the United States is a magistrate elected for four years. The King of France is an hereditary sovereign. In the exercise of the executive power the President of the United States is constantly subject to a jealous scrutiny. He may make, but he cannot conclude, a treaty; he may designate, but he cannot appoint, a public officer. The King of France is absolute within the limits of his authority. The President of the United States is responsible for his actions; but the person of the King is declared inviolable by the French charter.

"The King's government in France penetrates in a thousand different ways into the administration of private interests. Amongst the examples of this influence may be quoted that which results from the great number of public functionaries, who all derive their appointments from the government. This number now (1837) exceeds all previous limits; it amounts to one hundred and thirty-eight thousand nominations, each of which may be considered as an element of power. The President of the United States has not the exclusive right of making any public appointments, and their whole number scarcely exceeds twelve thousand."

In this chapter we are to consider the French administration as it has existed for nineteen years, and as much of it will continue to exist, notwithstanding any modifications which may be adopted.

The Constitution of France bears the date of 1852, and was "decreed" by Louis Napoleon, in virtue of the powers delegated to him by the French people. There are five powers in the state: the *Executive;* the *Ministers*, whom he solely nominates; his *Council of State*, preparing laws under the direction of himself and ministers; a *Legislative Body*, and a *Senate*. The government in its general working is one of the most arbitary and despotic in the world, but at the present writing the Emperor has made another of his frequent promises of reform; for, by the elections of 1867, it was evident that a tremendous reaction had commenced against his government, — the harbinger of an oft-postponed revolution.

By the Constitution of 1852, the Emperor is irresponsible; his person is inviolable; he has the right to pardon criminals; to make treaties, and to confer honors and dignities; he has the sole initiative in legislation; he commands the Army and Navy; no law is valid unless sanctioned by him; no person can hold any office without taking the oath of fidelity to him; and he nominates to all charges, appointments, and offices, whatsoever.

The Emperor's ministers receive twenty thousand dollars a year, and are eleven in number, as follows:—

Minister of State (Premier); Minister of Justice and Keeper of the Great Seal; Minister of Finance; Minister of the Imperial House; President of the Council of State; Minister of War; Minister of Marine and Colonies; Minister of Foreign Affairs; Minister of the Interior; and Minister of Agriculture, Commerce, and Public Works. The Minister of State is the medium of communication between the Emperor and the other ministers, as also with the Council of State, the Senate, and the Legislative Body; he has, besides exclusive direction of the official newspaper, which is called the "Moniteur." These ministers are responsible to the nation, but only for their individual acts, and the Senate is the only body which can accuse them, — the Senate itself being, like themselves, the creature of the Emperor. In the Council of State there are about fifty members, each with a salary of five thousand dollars. These Councillors prepare projects of law, to be laid before the Legislative Body.

The French Senate is composed of the Cardinals, Marshals, and Admirals of the realm, and, besides, of a number of other members nominated by the Emperor. Every Senator holds for life, unless he resigns, and his salary is six thousand dollars a year. The Senate is a more powerful body than the *Corps Legislatif*, which is precisely contrary to the condition of things in all constitutional governments, as in England and the United States. The object of the Emperor in the composition of his Senate seems to have been to place all apparent legislation in the hands of his favorites, and leave the people little to do except to vote for representatives, who are themselves powerless. The Senate is the only body that can receive petitions, or change the fundamental law, and no vote of the Legislative Assembly is effective without the Senate's sanction. The Emperor nominates the President and Vice-President of the Senate, each for the period of one year. They are charged especially to oppose all laws contrary to freedom of conscience, to the constitution, religion, and the equality of citizens before the law.

The members of the Legislative Body are elected by universal suffrage; there are upwards of ten millions of voters in France, about three-fourths of whom appear at elections. Every member sits six years, and receives an annual salary of five hundred dollars; if five members request it, the public may be excluded; and thus it is in the power of the Emperor to keep all obnoxious proceedings silent, for he is also the custodian of the public press; besides, he nominates the President and Vice-President of the lower house, and they keep such order as he wishes, ruling down, and ruling out, and menacing members, and having large garrisons of troops at their command, within a few yards of the legislative palace. It is thus apparent that the government of France is merely an Emperor and a series of ceremonies. There is an abundance of voting, but little fair representation, and the only privilege of the people is revolution, unless the Emperor occasionally should agree, of his own pleasure, to loosen the cords of his despotism. Nevertheless, immense interest is taken by Frenchmen in their elections, and, under the menace of the Emperor, a splendid galaxy of opposition orators has arisen in the lower house.

To ascertain the popularity of some of the leading governments of the world, we subjoin an account of the number of representatives in the lower and the upper house (1867), and the number of people to one representative, in the popular branch of the Legislature.

	Lower House.	*Upper House.*	*Population to each Representative.*
United States,	241	68	124,000
Great Britain and Ireland,	658	462	45,000
France,	376	169	100,000
Brazil,	122	60	62,000
Canada,	181	78	2,000
Switzerland,	128	44	20,000
Chili,	98	20	20,000
Prussia,	432	255	52,000
Spain,	350	396	35,000
Italy,	493	283	40,000
Austria,	203	122	98,000
Belgium,	116	58	42,000
North German Confederation,	280	43	100,000
Sweden,	185	119	22,000

	Lower House.	Upper House.	Population to each Representative.
Denmark, ...	101	59	14,000
Holland, ...	72	89	51,000
Portugal, ...	154	115	28,000

The upper house of the Legislature, or Senate, consists of life members appointed by the Emperor. He appoints his Ministers without consultation, and the principle of the responsibility of the Ministers to the *Corps Legislatif*, though strongly demanded by Thiers and others, is denied by the constitution. It is only the *bourgeoise*, or manufacturing, mechanical, and mercantile classes of the cities and towns, amongst whom a liberal party can be formed. Even upon these, the Emperor can bring to bear an enormous power of corruption and intimidation. "We can best conceive its extent," says the "New York Tribune," "by imagining a President of the United States to have so changed the constitution that he could only be resisted by revolution; who called upon the people once in six years to vote for him, or for *chaos;* who wielded a power of patronage corresponding, not merely to that of our National Government, but of our States, counties, and cities as well; who controlled the army, the police, the courts, the press, the clergy, and the schools; who made every official a spy on every other, and on the people; who suspended newspapers at pleasure, and suppressed public meetings at will; and, finally, who limited the National Legislature to simply advising what should, or should not, be done, without aspiring to criticise the constitution (which is the Emperor), on pain of treason. Such is to-day the consolidated despotism of France, — one of the most absolute the world has ever known."

This despotism is more thorough in that there is no nobility, worthy the name, associated with it; the aristocracy of the kingdom at the revolution, and their descendants, retain their titles by courtesy only.

There is no capitol building, distinctively so called, in Paris; the Senate meets in the Palace of the Luxembourg, and the public is not admitted to witness its deliberations, while the Representatives meet in a separate palace, more than half a mile distant; these two palaces are on the unpopular side of the River Seine, and when the Emperor opens the two houses, he does not visit their chamber, like the Queen of England, but they are obliged to come to his Palace of the New Louvre, where, sitting upon his throne in gorgeous ceremony, he hears the newly elected members advance and take the oath before him. As in England, each Legislative Body subsequently discusses, and votes an address in reply. The debates in both houses are reported by stenographers, but the daily newspapers can only take the official reports, and publish them in *extenso*, or if any particular subject is discussed, they must print the whole of what is said about it, so that the Emperor shall have the last word. The legislative body, or lower house, is divided by lots into nine bureaux, or committees, each of which elects its own President and Secretary. To get an amendment to any bill proposed from the Council of State, the Legislative Body must send three of its members to the palace, to plead their amendments before the Council of State.

The palace of the Legislative Body was begun A. D., 1722, and partly built by Mansard, for the Dukes of Bourbon; it was bought for one million one hundred thousand dollars forty years ago, and is an imposing structure on the banks of the Seine, facing, with its Corinthian portico, a bridge, which crosses to the front of the Emperor's Palace Gardens, — the site of the revolutionary guillotine. Without, are statues of Sully, Colbert, and other statesmen; within are several large apartments; and in the various *salons* are busts, statues, reliefs, and paintings emblematic of the growth of French law and civilization. The Legislative Hall, which corresponds to our old Hall of Representatives, is ornamented with twenty-four marble columns, and has five hundred seats, rising in tiers, from the President's chair; the walls and ceiling are decorated in crimson velvet and gold; there are galleries and tribunes for the diplomatic body, the imperial family, and the officers of state; a library of sixty-five thousand volumes is connected with the building, and near by the President of the body has a palace.

While the Legislative Chamber is ostensibly open to the public, little accommodation is really afforded the people. The deputies are allowed two tickets per day, which they sell to parties who resell them through their agents. The seats for spectators will not accommodate nearly the number which would be present, if the daily allowance of tickets were represented by their holders at one time. There are two hundred and ninety-two members in all, and two small galleries will fall far short of accommodating twice that number. Therefore it is that there is a great rush of spectators to be present at one o'clock precisely, when the doors are opened, and generally many ticket-holders have to go away without entrance for want of room for them. "If you cross the bridge in front of the palace at one o'clock P. M., each day," says a writer in the "Hartford Post," "you will be importuned by several persons who want to sell you tickets (or '*Billets pour la Sêance du Corps Legislatif*,' as they say); and I understand they have sometimes got as high as eighty *francs* (sixteen dollars) for each of them.

"The President, Mr. Schneider (1869), a little, old, but good-looking, white-haired Frenchman, with a German name, generally springs a stationary silver bell, when he calls the members to order; if that is not sufficient he raps upon the desk, and he had occasion to do so quite often, the aforesaid armed men calling out, or ejaculating something I did not distinctly hear, but which the members seemed to. In front of the President's desk is the '*Tribune*,' or platform, on which some of the orators take their stand when they address the audience. On each side, and in front of the Tribune, are the desks of the stenographic reporters, etc. The President wears a red scarf over his right shoulder, extending below the waist on the left side. Of the officers dressed in black broadcloth, with 'swallow-tailed' coats, and white cravats, and carrying a sword, I counted twelve. Besides these were quite a number of messengers or pages, dressed in a uniform of red and blue, with trimmings of gilded lace."

The French Senate meets in the old Palace of the Luxembourg, in the midst of the Students' Quarter near the university. It was built two hundred and fifty years ago. The French Senate, in 1847, consisted of three hundred and five peers. Behind the palace are large gardens, and within it is a spacious court; the building is surmounted with Mansard roofs and pavilions, and a part of it is occupied by magnificent state apartments, and a superb picture-gallery; here Napoleon was divorced from Josephine; in the Gardens, Marshal Ney was shot. The Senate Chamber is semi-circular, vaulted, ninety-two feet in diameter, and the ceiling, supported by columns, is richly painted; in a recess are the elevated seats of the President and Secretaries, flanked by statues of monarchs, priests, and politicians; there are one hundred and sixty-five seats for Senators, besides seats for the Emperor's Ministers, near the President's chair; the library here consists of forty thousand volumes.

While there is a nominal aristocracy in France, and many of the Admirals, Marshals, and other officials have titles, aristocratic distinctions are really swept away, save in so far as to make the semblance of a court. A vast order of knighthood is the Legion of Honor, where ribbons are much coveted by American piano-makers, and the venders of sewing-machines. The most formidable question in "the trade" of recent days has been whether Chickering had more ribbon than Steinway, and in the discussion of it the subject of red tape was almost completely neglected.

The Legion of Honor, of France, is presided over by the Emperor, as Grand Master, but is administered by a Grand Chancellor and Council; it pays pensions to officers and soldiers of distinction, and its members number about fifty-seven thousand, divided into five orders, each privileged to wear a ribbon, cross, or other decoration. No French subject is allowed to wear a foreign decoration without government authority.

In the payment of pensions and salaries in France, and all European States, the tendency is toward extravagant sums in high places, and parsimony toward the lower office-holders; while the reverse is the case here, as De Tocqueville exemplified many years ago, when he said: —

"It must, however, be allowed, that a democratic state is most parsimonious toward its principal agents. In America, the secondary officers are much better paid, and the dignitaries of the administration much worse, than they are elsewhere." He gave this example to bear out his statement: —

UNITED STATES.

Treasury Department.

Messenger,	$700
Clerk with lowest salary,	1,000
Clerk with highest salary,	1,735
Chief Clerk,	2,000
Secretary of State,	6,000
The President (Andrew Jackson),	25,000

FRANCE.

Ministère de Finances.

Huissier,	1,500 *fr.*
Clerk with lowest salary,	1,000 to 1,800 *fr.*
Clerk with highest salary,	3,200 to 3,600 *fr.*
Secrétaire-général,	20,000 *fr.*
The Minister,	80,000 *fr.*
The King (Louis Philippe),	12,000,000 *fr.*

We shall now proceed to examine some of the departments and bureaux of the French Government.

It is the pride of the French Government, above that of every other nation of Europe, that it is the most thorough encourager of education, of art, and of literature. It is with education alone that we are mainly concerned in America, having but recently created a bureau in the interest of the same, at Washington; but this is simply a bureau of inquiry, of suggestion, and of statistics, while in France the central government is the Director-General of all education within the empire, and has organized it upon the mathematical principles of its army and its police. Napoleon I. established one Imperial University, consisting of all the academies in France, and in 1852 the present Emperor restored this system; so that at present there are sixteen academies, of which Paris is the central and eminent one. When we speak of the University of Paris, therefore, we mean only the Academy of Paris, a component part of the grand National University; this and all the other schools of France are subordinate to the Minister of Public Instruction, whose council is impartially composed of five Catholic ecclesiastics, one minister of the Lutheran, one of the Calvinistic, and one of the Jewish creed, three Senators, three Councillors of the State, three members of the Court of Cassation, five members of the Institute of France, two heads of private schools, and eight Inspectors-General, all appointed by the Emperor for one year. Each of the sixteen universities of France has, subordinate to it, lyceums (grammar schools), colleges, and primary schools. Every university has faculties, either of medicine, law, literature, or sciences; for example, there are six faculties of Catholic theology, and two of Protestant theology, nine faculties of law, three of medicine, and six of science and letters; each of these, except Protestant theology, is maintained in the Academy of Paris. The Academy of Paris is situated in a series of buildings, scattered through what is called the Latin Quarter of the city, chief of which is the *Sorbonne*, called for a gentleman of that name, who founded a school there six hundred years ago. The present *Sorbonne* building was erected by Richelieu, the great Prime Minister; it is a vast, dingy building, enclosing wide courts, including a fine church, and owning a library of eighty thousand volumes. Richelieu is buried in the chapel. At the *Sorbonne* the faculties of science, letters, and theology lecture. The celebrated colleges of medicine and law are close by the *Sorbonne;* in the latter there are eighteen professors, and two thousand students; in the former fifty-seven professors and tutors, and three thousand students.

Many medical students go from the United States to Paris, and the total cost of their tuition for four years is two hundred and fifty-five dollars. The College of Medicine is the most celebrated school of its kind in the world, having adjunct to it magnificent dissecting-rooms and vast hospitals; there are twenty-eight thousand physicians and apothecaries in France; of the Paris hospitals *the Hotel Dieu* contains eight hundred and twenty-eight beds, and twelve thousand patients annually, attended by thirty-three Augustinian nuns. A separate chapter might be made upon the hospitals of Paris alone. They comprise hospitals for foundlings, schools for midwives, cloisters for sick children, soup-houses, and nurseries, where poor working-women deposit their babies in the morning, return to suckle them at the proper hours, and take them home in the evening, paying four cents a day.

The charities of Paris, and of France generally, are remarkably original and efficient; many of the almshouses are organized upon plans which might well be imitated in America, and the whole system of public and private schools is worthy the attention of enlightened humanity. The schools of Paris and France are the perfection of human encouragement; one of the grammar schools has forty-two professors, three hundred and seventy boarders, and five hundred day scholars; equally large are some of the private schools, one of which — the College *Stanislas* — has one hundred and thirty professors, and twelve hundred boarders and day scholars. There are also many free schools, many schools which give valuable prizes to pupils, schools of music, declamation, commerce, design, night schools, and adult schools. Prize students at the Fine Arts College are sent to Rome to study at the expense of the state. There is a special school to encourage the study of ancient manuscripts in the libraries; of military and staff schools, there are many extraordinary ones, particularly the Polytechnic School, where two hundred and sixty pupils have the advantage of twenty professors, and pay each but two hundred dollars a year; besides all these, the libraries, museums, and collections of Paris are interesting in the highest degree; the whole city, indeed, is a prodigious university, where learning and talent receive higher rewards than anywhere upon earth; so that, in our day, France stands at the head of nations in the arts, literature, and oratory. The highest prizes in the Paris lyceums, in the year 1866, were taken by the Masters Beckwith, two American lads. At the pinnacle of the entire intellectual fabric stands the Institute of France, founded in the period of the Republic, A. D., 1795, and composed of two hundred and twenty-three members, two hundred and twenty-five correspondents, thirty-one associates, thirty-five free academicians and seven secretaries; these are divided into five academies, each of which gives annual prizes, and one of them is specially charged with the composition of the French Dictionary, and with the extension and purification of the language. The Emperor labored long in vain to become a member of the Institute of France, while some of his most dignified enemies hold seats within its charmed circle.

The only secret society in France, permitted by law, is that of the Free-Masons, which has five hundred lodges.

Religion in France is neither free as in the United States, nor is there a State church, as in England, while the Emperor and his household, and most of the great officers of the State, are Catholics. All religious sects are tolerated and supported by government, and yet no congregation can meet, no church can change its pastor, except by government permission. The Protestant and the Jewish religions are both supported by law, and at least one of the Emperor's ministers (Durny) is a Protestant, but the Pope is bound by his agreement with the first Napoleon to relinquish the temporal power within France, and the Emperor nominates to all the dignities of the Papal Church. The Calvinist Protestant Church has one thousand and forty-five places of worship in France; the Lutheran Church four hundred and three places of worship, and the Church of England about forty. There are alleged to be nearly thirty-six millions of Roman Catholics in France, but in this number all are counted who are not members of some other distinctive faith. A recent inquiry resulted in the conclusion, that of these more than twelve millions professed no faith whatever. The number of French Protestants is less than eight hundred thousand, and of Jews and other creeds one hundred and five thousand. The Catholic clergy comprise one hundred and twenty-four thousand, including fifty thousand monks, or nuns. The salary of the Catholic Archbishop of Paris is ten thousand dollars a year; the whole cost of religious worship in France is under ten million of dollars annually. The most remarkable cathedrals on the American continent are probably those of Montreal, and the Roman Catholic Cathedral, of New York; the latter (incomplete) is three hundred and thirty-two feet long, one hundred and seventy-four feet wide, and it is flanked by two towers, each three hundred and twenty-nine feet high; it contains one hundred and three windows of stained glass, and it is built in the middle pointed Gothic style of the thirteenth century, of a beautiful crystalline white marble.

Notre Dame, of Paris, is three hundred and ninety feet long, one hundred and forty-four feet wide, and its two towers are each two hundred and four feet high, while its spire is two hundred and eighty feet high; it is in florid-pointed architecture, with flying buttresses, and will hold twenty-one thousand persons. The great cathedrals of Rouen, Chartres, Amiens, Rheims, and Strasbourg are far more florid and elaborate than the Gothic cathedrals of England; they are exceeded in beauty only by the cathedrals of Cologne, Milan, and Brussels.

Napoleon is a canon of the Lateran Church in Rome, as successor of the most Christian Kings. As such, he once sent twenty-five thousand francs to Rome; Henri IV., and the following kings, up to Louis XIV., sent each four thousand louis d'or; but Charles X. reduced the sum to twenty-five thousand francs. Louis Philippe declined the honor of the canonry. The garrison of Rome is mainly French, and Napoleon has been repeatedly blessed by the old bankrupt pontiff.

There are fifteen Catholic Archbishops and sixty-nine Bishops in the empire, all of whom are nominated by the Emperor, and canonically inducted by the Pope; six of these hold the rank of Cardinals in the Senate. When the French Revolution broke out, the Catholic Church in the kingdom had a revenue of seven hundred and fifty million livres, but at present the state assumes the responsibility of maintaining worship, and it has appropriated to itself the revenues of the Church.

There are few nobles in France under the empire, and they are mainly distinguished officers of the Army and Navy, and statesmen but recently promoted to honors.

The office of the Secretary of Foreign Affairs of France is very elaborately organized: the commercial department alone has twenty-eight Consul Generals, eighty-seven Consuls, seven hundred and seventy-five Consular Agents. The Minister's Department, or Hotel, cost one million dollars, and it is situated in a narrow street of the old aristocratic quarter. France supports very expensive embassies at all the great capitals, her Ambassador at St. Petersburg receiving sixty thousand dollars a year; at London, fifty-five thousand dollars; at Rome, twenty-eight thousand dollars; and at Rio de Janeiro,

Washington, and Mexico, seventeen thousand dollars each; the American Ministers at London and Paris receive about the latter figure.

There are about eight thousand five hundred miles of railway in France, which pay five million dollars in taxes annually, and which have received one hundred and fifty million dollars from the government; they carry one billion four hundred million passengers annually, by means of seventy-two thousand trucks, carriages, and engines. A railway girdles Paris, which cost nearly four million five hundred thousand dollars. Government reserves the right to exercise espionage, inquiry, and at times arbitrary control, over all the private corporations in the empire; the stage-coaches, called "diligences," the hacks, the omnibuses, whatever undertakes in a corporate capacity to minister to the uses of citizens, is brought under the strictest government control. There are thirty-one lines of omnibuses in Paris, controlled by a single company, whose charter expires in the year A. D. 1910, and which has five hundred omnibuses, carrying eighty million passengers a year, for six cents each passenger, inside seats, and three cents outside. There is also a great hack company, which pays the city of Paris four hundred thousand dollars a year; the omnibus company pays the city two hundred thousand dollars annually for its monopoly. The French hacks were introduced into the United States in 1869, and also the English Hansom cab. There are one hundred and fourteen thousand horses in Paris, and more than sixty thousand vehicles; yet eighty-seven years before the discovery of America there was not a carriage of any kind in France. There are about four thousand five hundred post-offices in France, with thirty thousand employés; in all France there are about one thousand one hundred newspapers and periodicals, nearly six hundred of which are published in Paris. The receipts of the French post-office are about seventeen million dollars annually. The money-order system of the French post-office passes the boundary of France, and commutes with the post-offices of many other countries. There are sixty-two thousand five hundred miles of telegraphic line in France. A message sent from one quarter of Paris to another costs ten cents for twenty words. A telegraphic despatch from Baltimore to Washington, D. C., cost ten cents for ten words.

The fortifications on the French frontier, mainly the work of Vauban, a Republican in a royal age, are among the strongest in the world.

Louis Philippe fortified Paris at suggestion of Napoleon. The fortifications cost twenty-eight million dollars, and are armed with nearly three thousand mortars, cannons, and howitzers, and two hundred thousand muskets. The garrison of Paris is never less than thirty thousand men, besides forty thousand National Guards, or Compulsory Militia, four thousand four hundred and forty one *Gendarmes*, or Government Police, four thousand five hundred and ninety Municipal Police, and one thousand three hundred paid firemen, besides an unknown number of spies, secret agents, etc., etc. Some of the barracks of Paris are very beautiful; one is seldom out of the sight of a soldier or out of the sound of a drum in France, in any hour of the year.

The monetary system of France, and that of weights and measures, is one of the most thorough in the world; for measures the spherical distance from the equator to the pole was taken and divided in ten million equal parts; each part is called a *metre;* the square and cube of a *metre* were made the standards of surface, capacity, and solidity. The weight of a cube of distilled water at the temperature of 39.2° Fahrenheit, was made the unit of weight. A *metre* is about thirty-nine and one quarter inches, English measure. A *hectare* is about two and a half acres. A *litre* is about a pint and three quarters. A *kilogramme* is about two and one-fifth pounds.

Paris is very indifferently lighted with gas, except on the public streets, where there are twenty-nine thousand gas-burners, owned by a company whose charter expires A.D. 1906. This gas is furnished to the city of Paris, and government of France, for three cents per cubic *metre*, but the cost to private individuals is six cents for the same quantity. This company pays forty thousand dollars a year to the city, and all its pipes and accessories revert to Paris on the expiration of its charter, the city paying for the same four hundred thousand dollars.

In 1866, government extorted from the city of Paris three million seven hundred and fifty thousand dollars; the budget of the city itself balanced at nearly forty-four million dollars. Taxes are levied throughout France upon windows and furniture. The debt of the city is upwards of forty million dollars. Nearly eighteen million dollars are collected at the gates of Paris, by what is called the *octroi.* Every town in France pays a large part of its expenses by thus enclosing the town with toll-gates, and making the farmers pay as they enter. Paris, like Philadelphia and Boston, has gradually absorbed all the suburbs which lie within its fortifications.

Three remarkable government factories in France are those for making experimental porcelain, gorgeous tapestry and carpets, and snuff and tobacco; the latter is a government monopoly, and its sales amount to twenty-eight million dollars annually.

Wine is also provided with a special market in Paris, and its sale put under government control. The wine crop of France is raised upon eight hundred thousand acres, and it is worth one hundred million dollars annually, out of which forty million dollars are taken by national and municipal taxes.

It was only in 1863 that the government relinquished its control of the bakers, whom it formerly compelled to sell bread at its own appraisement. The price of bread in Paris is about four cents a pound at present.

In 1865 there were one hundred and thirty-three thousand two hundred and twelve persons pensioned by France, at an expense of nearly fifteen millions of dollars a year; this alone represented a capital of nearly one billion five hundred million dollars.

Like the American government, and unlike other governments of Europe, generally speaking, the French raise loans from the population at large, instead of from a few rich capitalists. The system has worked successfully. None of the greater governments of Europe pays as high rate of interest as does the United States.

Some of the great stock enterprises of France are very remarkable.

The Credit Foncier of Paris is a Stock Company, with a capital of forty millions of dollars, which lends money for first mortgages upon real estate, for not more than five per cent. a year. This mortgage must be extinguished by the borrower in payments of from one to two per cent. a year upon the sum he received. The company meantime issues bonds of twenty dollars and upwards to equal the amount of its loans; if a mortgagor fails to pay up his annuities his property is liable to be sold at auction. The government owns ten millions of stock in this company, and the Emperor names its governor and two sub-governors; there are besides fifteen directors. The Minister of Finance has authority over the company; so that here, as almost everywhere, the state regulates even the corporate financial transactions of the people. The main office of the company is in a fine building in Paris; but it has branch offices in a majority of the departments.

Another great French company is the Credit Mobilier, with a capital of twelve millions of dollars in one hundred and twenty thousand shares of one hundred dollars a share. It bids for government loans, and is a mammoth stock-broking corporation, but it does not make bargains, either optional, or on time, like private brokers.

A curious banking corporation in Paris, also under the control of the Minister of Finance, is the *Comptoir National d'Escompte*, with a capital of eight millions of dollars, and several branches. It discounts bills due at a hundred days, and bearing two endorsements, for France and for foreign parts due at sixty-five days. It receives deposits and pays two per cent. upon them, and discounts for goods deposited in government warehouses. It charges four per cent. for such discounts.

An institution partly of banking and partly of beneficence is the *Caisse des Retraites pour la Vieillesse*, which keeps money for people against old age, giving them four and a half per cent. compound interest, and paying the full sum back at death to the depositor's heirs. After reaching fifty years, the depositor gets an annuity of not more than three hundred dollars a year The funds are invested in *Rentes*.

At the head of this government insurance company is the Minister of Agriculture and Commerce. It generally has on hand about one million of dollars and upwards.

The above concern is joined with two other semi-government offices, the *Caisse d'Amortisements*, which conducts the reduction of the national debt, and the *Caisse des Depots et Consignations*, which pays four and a half per cent., chiefly upon deposits by public functionaries, and people who have received legal awards or damages. This *caisse*, or office, generally has on hand from one to two millions of dollars. It also is combined with the government substitute-office, called the *Dotation de l'Armee*, which receives annual subscriptions from young men who expect to be drafted, and pays three and a half per cent. upon deposits by soldiers and officers of the army.

Four hundred and sixty dollars is the present price of a substitute.

The great pawn-broking shop of Paris is a bureau under the Minister of the Interior and the Prefect of the Seine; it is managed by a director, and a council of twelve persons, one of whom is the Prefect of Police; it was founded during the American Revolution, for the benefit of the hospitals.

It advances four-fifths upon the value of gold and silver articles, and two-thirds upon the value of all other articles. It has one great bureau and twenty-two smaller ones, besides agents in different quarters of the town. Three thousand articles are pledged every day, two thousand dollars being the largest sum loaned, and it charges about nine per cent. ; after fourteen months all unredeemed articles are sold.

There are forty-five of these excellent institutions in the different cities of France.

The total receipts in seven years, of the Dotation de l'Armee, ending in 1862, amounted to nearly ninety million dollars, so that the conscription itself is a profitable though cruel source of revenue.

Even funerals are monopolized in Paris by a private company, which is obliged to pay government eighty-two and a half per cent. on the produce of funeral ornaments, and fifteen per cent. on articles furnished ; the cheapest funeral costs less than four dollars, including the religious ceremonies.

Private slaughter-houses are prohibited in Paris, and vast government butcheries accommodate the butchers, and help the revenues of the state.

The judicial system of France is little like our own. The Minister of Justice, one of the Emperor's Cabinet, is the supreme head of all the judicial courts, and of all public worship. The High Court of Justice judges without appeal, or remedy, all persons accused of conspiracies against the Emperor, and the security of his state ; it has ten judges and four deputy judges, annually appointed by the Emperor, and divided into two chambers, one to prosecute, the other to give judgment, through a jury composed of thirty-six office-holders.

The French Court of Cassation is ostensibly the highest court of appeal, but really it is a department of government, to inspect the administration of justice in the other courts ; but when it annuls a decision of a lower court, the case is not then determined, but returns to another court of the latter class. Sixty advocates have the monopoly of practice before the Court of Cassation, which latter has a President, three Vice-Presidents, and forty-five Councillors : attached to it are an imperial prosecutor, with six general advocates, and other officers ; eleven judges present are necessary to confirm a judgment ; the members of this high tribunal wear a red gown, doubled with white fur, and a violet velvet cap.

The next court in rank is the Court of Accounts, which has jurisdiction of the accounts and expenses of the empire.

There are twenty-seven Courts of Appeal in France, each composed of a First President, several Presidents, a number of high Councillors, and various subordinate officers; the Court of Assize is the only French court in which trial by jury prevails, and in which are tried all criminal cases excepting offences against the state; the civil tribunals of France hear and determine about one hundred and fifty thousand lawsuits every year, and the criminal courts try about four thousand cases.

In each department of France, — eighty-nine in number, — there is a Court of Original Jurisdiction; that of the department of Paris is composed of one President, eight Vice-Presidents, fifty-five Judges, twenty-four Procureurs, and forty-three Registrars; this court decides, without appeal, actions relating to the person, or to personal property to the amount of three hundred dollars.

A most extraordinary court is the Tribunal of Commerce, which exists in all large towns, and is composed of the heads of mercantile houses, elected for two years, at a meeting of influential merchants, a list of whom is drawn up by the Mayor (Prefect), and approved by the Minister of the Interior; the object of these courts is to put commercial disputes and differences under the adjudication of the merchants themselves. The Tribunal of Commerce of Paris is composed of thirty Judges, and Deputy Judges, and a President; attached to it are ten police officers, who arrest persons for debt. There are about one thousand five hundred stock companies formed every year in Paris, and there are one thousand six hundred cases of bankruptcy within the same period. These latter matters come before the Tribunal of Commerce. There is one great police tribunal in Paris, corresponding to our police courts; there are twenty judges of the peace, one hundred and twenty-two notaries, eighty appraisers and auctioneers, who are exclusively government officers, one hundred and fifty sheriffs' officers (Huissiers), who protest bills, and a board of masters and foremen, called *Prud'hommes*, who amicably settle disputes about wages, strikes, apprenticeships, etc., etc.

There are nine hundred legal advocates in Paris, and upwards of two hundred solicitors and attorneys (*avoués*); the advocates have a bureau for gratuitous advice to the poor, open every Saturday. The Palace of Justice, which is to Paris what the Tombs Court is to New York, the great centre of police hearings and confinements, is a large building on an island in the Seine, where are also the police head-quarters of Paris. Very many courts, both high and low, and several prisons, cluster about this ancient pile, and here Marie

Antoinette and the Girondins were imprisoned. Across the way is the Tribunal of Commerce; not far off is the Morgue, or dead-house. Sumptuous barracks and superb new architectures give dignity and terror to this neighborhood of crime, destitution, and dispute, where have been enacted, through successive ages, the long drama of tyranny, torture, and despair, which makes so much of the literature of France. Near by is the Cathedral, and that Chapel, where are kept, according to the superstition, the very relics of the crucifixion of Christ. It is upon this spot, also, that the enthroned Master of France visits, through his satellites, the penalties of his vengeance upon the enemies of his dynasty; for, as close by the Palace of Justice and the prisons stands the Hotel de Ville, or City Hall of Paris, the objective point of all popular uprisings, the capitol of the capital city, so Napoleon has chosen the favorite haunt of his enemies to keep his household of police agents, who are to feel in secret the pulse of Paris.

Paris has two district administrations, like New York; the Prefect of the Seine is the Mayor; the Prefect of Police is the superintendent thereof, and he has charge of the eight prisons of Paris, and of all the spies, prostitutes, scavengers, firemen, policemen, bill-posters, vagrants, lotteries, gamblers, and whatever belongs to the political, sanitary, or criminal administration of the department. The Prefect of the Seine is the superintendent of all public works, establishments, churches, markets, hospitals, public festivals, etc., etc.; under him are an immense number of officials. The annual jury list of the department of Paris contains two thousand jurors; ecclesiastics, school-masters, domestics, workmen, and illiterate people are excluded from serving on juries.

There are more than four hundred prisons in France, occupied by about seventy-one thousand people, and there is one convict station at Toulon. One great prison of Paris is modelled on the American solitary-cell plan. Condemned persons are publicly executed by the guillotine. Imprisonment for debt has been recently abolished in France. To take out any patent in France requires the payment of twenty dollars a year. Authors pay nothing for copyright. To carry a gun costs five dollars a year.

Nothing would more astound an American in France than to observe the singular administration of justice, wherein the judge browbeats the witness, bullies and inveigles the prisoner, and uses every energy to make him convict himself. In all political trials, this is eminently the case, as witness the following scene: —

PARISIAN POLICE COURT. — A citizen is charged with having excited the citizens to hate each other, etc., etc. *Prisoner.* I move that my trial be postponed. My lawyer is not ready. *President.* When will he be ready? *Prisoner.* Perhaps in three or four years, Mr. President. (Great surprise on the bench, and laughter in the audience.) *Prisoner.* Let me explain; I have confidence only in my young nephew, who has just commenced studying law. He needs time, but I tell you, Mr. President, he will make a first-rate lawyer.

Another prisoner is accused of having uttered seditious cries. *President.* Do you admit the charge? *Prisoner.* I had drunk a little too much last night. *President.* What did you shout? *Prisoner.* I shouted *Vive la Republique! President.* Have you previously been condemned on the same charge? *Prisoner.* Yes. *President.* When? *Prisoner.* About eighteen years ago. *President.* What seditious cries did you utter at that time? *Prisoner.* You must remember what it was, for you yourself sentenced me. *President.* What seditious cries did you utter? *Prisoner.* Well, I shouted then *Vive l'Empereur!* (Loud laughter in the audience.)

In like manner the police of Paris is protected in all its proceedings, requiring no warrant to enter any house, or search any baggage. To strike a French policeman is a high crime, but he has little responsibility, if he unjustly maltreats a citizen, or stranger, and during times of political excitement, the police and soldiery are encouraged to be merciless and aggressive, for the highest crime in France is to manifest ill-will to the imperial dynasty. Dr. Johnson, of Paris, a celebrated physician and journalist, gave an account, in a recent letter, of the treatment of an American, Mr. J. Q. A. Warren, of Boston, by the imperial police, during the election riots of 1869: —

"Mr. Warren was proceeding along the Boulevard Montmartre, in company with another American, when he saw the police chasing the crowd, and they turned into a side street, the Rue Richelieu, to get out of the way. They had not got far when they heard the beat of a drum. This was followed by a rush of police agents, and before they had time to remonstrate, or to state who they were, they were struck several times, and Mr. Warren was knocked down. His friend owed his exemption from further ill-usage and imprisonment, to the fact of his wearing the ribbon of the Legion of Honor; but Mr. Warren, as he was trying to rise to his feet, was seized and dragged to the Mairie in the Rue Droupt. When he arrived there he found the large court-yard full of prisoners and policemen. After a delay of about half an hour, he was taken to the Inspector's room and searched. All his papers and money were taken from him. After his name, address, and *signalement* had been taken down, his papers, and, as he supposed, his money, were replaced in his pockets; but he discovered subsequently that his funds had not been restored. A further examination was made of his person for weapons, after which he was transferred to another room, which was crowded with prisoners of almost every station in life. After remaining there about half an hour, the prisoners were formed into a body, numbering about seven hundred, and marched, guarded by soldiers and policemen, to the *Conciergerie* prison at the other side of the river.

"This was about one o'clock at night. During the march the utmost brutality was exercised toward the prisoners, and they were driven and pushed along like a herd of cattle. Mr. Warren was so badly bruised and hurt that he had to be supported by two of the prisoners. His shirt and clothes were covered with blood from the effect of the blows which had been wantonly inflicted upon him in the yard of the Mairie, by one of the Sergeants de Ville. After they reached the *Conciergerie*, about three in the morning, he fainted away, and was conveyed for the night to a separate cell, where he was attended by the surgeon of the prison, who administered chloroform and stimulants to him. He remained in the *Conciergerie* with the other prisoners, until seven o'clock on Friday evening, and they had nothing all this time but a little soup of the weakest kind and some hard bread. As evening approached, they were informed that they were about to be transferred to the fort at Bicêtre, in the suburbs of Paris; on learning which, Mr. Warren managed to get a scrap of paper, and wrote a letter to Dr. Johnson, informing him of his position. The doctor immediately forwarded it to Mr. Washburne, the American Minister, and at half-past twelve the same night, Mr. Frank Moore, Assistant Secretary to the Legation, went to the Prefecture, and demanded his release. He was told that it was then too late to do anything in the matter, but that it would be attended to early in the morning.

"Shortly after he had despatched this note to Dr. Johnson, Mr. Warren and the other prisoners were transferred in the close prison carriages to the fort at Bicêtre. They were kept standing in one of the casemates there, suffering from the heat and thirst consequent upon overcrowding, until nearly midnight. The roll was then called, and the prisoners were marched, eight at a time, accompanied by a file of soldiers, to the Inspector's room, in another building, where their names, addresses, and personal descriptions were entered in a book. This done, they were conveyed to a second casemate, and in proceeding to it each prisoner stopped by order, and picked up a bundle of straw, which, with a blanket, was to constitute his bed. There they were left in quietness for the rest of the night, but without food or drink. The heat and odor of the place were insufferable, and were aggravated by the fact that all the necessities of nature had to be provided for in that crowded apartment. To men accustomed to every luxury, as many of those confined there were, the sufferings endured during this memorable night must have been a terrible ordeal. It is stated that three of the prisoners died at the *Conciergerie*, while at Bicêtre a fourth lost his senses, and committed suicide.

"On Saturday noon an order reached the fort directing the release of Mr. Warren. He was summoned to the Directors' room, and the formality of entering in a book his name, personal description, and address in Paris, having been again gone through, he was told that he would be released the same evening. He was then taken back to the casemate, where he received a little food, and at six o'clock he was released and escorted to the railway by a corporal. Fortunately a little silver, sufficient to pay his fare, which he had in one of his pockets, had escaped or had not tempted the cupidity of his captors."

These notes will convey some imperfect idea of the civil administration of France, a government which seeks to satisfy the wants of the people, by making them dependent upon it, and so robbing them of self-reliance and personal energy, so that they are but parts of its mighty machinery, whereof there is but one engineer, and he the sole hero of France, — Louis Napoleon, the wily egotist.

The government is "an immense tutelary power," after the prophecy of De Tocqueville, "which takes upon itself alone to secure their gratifications, and to watch over their fate.

"That power is absolute, minute, regular, provident, and mild. It would be like the authority of a parent, if, like that authority, its object was to prepare men for manhood; but it seeks, on the contrary, to keep them in perpetual childhood; it is well content that the people should rejoice, provided they think of nothing but rejoicing. For their happiness such a government willingly labors, but it chooses to be the sole agent and the only arbiter of that happiness; it provides for their security, foresees and supplies their necessities, facilitates their pleasures, manages their principal concerns, directs their industry, regulates the descent of property, and subdivides their inheritances. What remains, but to spare them all the care of thinking, and all the trouble of living?

"Thus it every day renders the exercise of the free agency of man less useful and less frequent; it circumscribes the will within a narrower range, and gradually robs a man of all the uses of himself. The principle of equality has prepared men for these things; it has predisposed men to endure them, and oftentimes to look on them as benefits. After having thus successively taken each member of the community in its powerful grasp, and fashioned him at will, the supreme power then extends its arm over the whole community. It covers the surface of society with a network of small complicated rules, minute and uniform, through which the most original minds and the most energetic characters cannot penetrate, to rise above the crowd. The will of man is not shattered, but softened, bent, and guided; men are seldom forced by it to act, but they are constantly restrained from acting; such a power does not destroy, but it prevents existence; it does not tyrannize, but it compresses, enervates, extinguishes, and stupefies a people, till each nation is reduced to be nothing better than a flock of timid and industrious animals, of which the government is the shepherd."

This is the remarkable prophecy of a French author, who has been accused of rebuking republicanism, while he was really its most thoughtful and observing friend, and who lived down to Louis Napoleon's *coup d'état*, and died sorrowful because of it, and with sad contempt for its author. Let him be also the exponent of the chances of this violent dynasty for long life and for historic honor: —

"Although this government has established itself by one of the greatest crimes recorded in history, nevertheless it will last for some length of time, unless it precipitates itself to destruction. It will last till its excesses, its wars, its corruptions, have effaced in the public mind the dread of socialism, — a change requiring time. God grant that in the interval it may not end in a manner almost as prejudicial to us as to itself, — in some extravagant foreign enterprise. We know it but too well in France, — governments never escape the law of their origin. This government, which comes by the army, which can only last by the army, which traces back its popularity, and even its essence, to the recollections of military glory, — this government will be fatally impelled to seek for aggrandizement of territory and for exclusive influence abroad; in other words, to war. That at last is what I fear, and what all reasonable men dread as I do. War would assuredly be its death; but its death would perhaps cost dear."

CHAPTER XXI.

POLITICS AND POLITICIANS OF FRANCE AND THE CONTINENT.

A sketch of the leading public men of France, and of the parties which they represent, with a brief statement of the present political issues of Europe at large.

EUROPE may be compared to a crab, both in appearance and in sensibility; all alive at a touch from without, yet within of feeble circulation, and at all points wearing the articulated armor of war. The most sensitive and mobile part of this irregular aggregation of unlike states is France, which is inhabited by the most democratic and courageous population of Europe, and which is accustomed to consider itself the leading state of civilization. In every political respect this assurance is well founded; for there is but one state which can, by its own internal convulsions, make Europe rush to arms, and this is France. Prussia, Austria, and Italy may make war together; tremendous mutiny may shake the British Empire in India; Germany may move in solid body upon Denmark; the Kaiser and the Czar may crush out the Maygars, and Spain may expel its Queen, and still Europe will stay at home and read the tidings without anxiety; but when Paris rises and France concurs, the European world feels sympathy, the people of every state start to arms, and the stock markets of Christendom are seized with panic.

The cause of this is, that France is truly the state by which statesmen steer; it is not her rulers which men dread, but her people and her ideas; and therefore the ruling and wealthy classes of neighboring nations are always satisfied to see France securely folded in the arms of some despotism, whether this be the Bonapartes' or the Bourbons'.

By a different process the people of the neighboring states are readily able to soothe themselves when some adventurer or some reactionist seizes France; the self-complacency and egotism of the French people is irritating to the Germans, their highly civilized neighbors, who are at heart as anxious for free institutions as the French, and by turning to account the national jealousy of their people, the monarchs of France and Germany are able in the last resort to destroy sympathy between Saxon and Celtic republicans, and make them enemies instead of allies. With all this, the people who do not love the French, feel the contact, the magnetism, and the example of France, where there are politicians more than the equals of monarchs in organizing and in oratory, and where party spirit is not the blind rancor of traditional classes, as in England, but the intelligent apprehension of men and issues. To us, in America, there is no politics in Germany; we know nothing about it, nor about Austrian, Scandinavian, and Greek politics; but a French politician has the world for his theatre, and for his fellow-actors the most formidable partisans in Europe. Associated with France in accord upon almost all questions of political principle are Italy and Spain; like political parties exist in each, at the same time arrayed upon different sides of the same general issues, for they are all of what are called the Latin races, and geographically they uphold France as a pair of supporters in heraldry bears up a shield. At the present time we see in Italy, in Spain, and in France, a Bourbon party, a Bonaparte party, a Republican party, and a Democratic party, and the head-quarters of all these parties is in Paris, or close by; there exist the political journals which encourage party spirit; there speaks the talent which turns bias into conviction and hope into enthusiasm; thence go the suggestions and the apostles of politics, Louis Blanc to England, De Tocqueville and Genet to America, Bernadotte to Sweden. When Beranger writes a Republican song the winds blow the music of it to all the peoples; when Henri Rochefort publishes a saucy journal the Atlantic cable keeps America informed as to its contents. The French elections are the only elections that are of consequence to us or to Europe; yet France in her totality is not a state as profoundly agitated in things political as America; for a Republic has no other national life than politics. Paris is earnest in behalf of the state, but the rural provinces of France are pervaded by dense ignorance, social, political, and economical; and it is this element on which Bonapartism relies to maintain itself in its bad eminence. Glory can reach further than truth, and to this day there are said to be numbers of people in France who vote for the candidates of Napoleon III., under the impression that he is the veritable banished man returned from St. Helena.

The Imperial party of France and of Europe is almost entirely a personal party, with the bulk of it composed of the army, the navy, and the office-holders, and the rural farmers and village folks closing in by a sort of stupid necessity; there also vote with this party a majority of the commercial classes, who are not admirers of the empire, but support it, rather than risk violent change and financial embarrassment. The chances are immensely in favor of any party that it is *in;* for it has all the fears of prosperous and timid people to argue upon, and all the machinery of office to use. It is computed that two millions of votes go to the Emperor from people who take his wages and eat his *potage*. The army is powerfully in his favor, and is kept continually whetted against the people, and enlivened by bounteous treatment; the clergy are not with him of choice, but prefer him to a more liberal alternative; the conservative masses who have a dread of socialism, radicalism, and irreligion cling to Bonaparte as the most endurable horn of the dilemma; but the genuine Imperial party is made up of that small body of soldiers of fortune and adventurers who, knowing the lurking love of millions of French for the name of Napoleon Bonaparte, rallied round his exiled nephew, became members of his invading corps at Strasbourg and Bologne, and who prepared the way to the *coup d'etat* of 1850; all of them are politicians, equally desperate with the heroes of revolutionary leagues in Mexico and the South American Republics, but often men of exquisite manners and good education. There are besides, incorporated with this party, many marshals and statesmen, who are ready to serve France under any administration, and others who owe the Emperor personal gratitude. In these notices we are in part indebted to Victor Hugo, in part to Mr. Kinglake.

Most intimately associated with the Emperor was his illegitimate brother, the Duke de Morny, child of Hortense Beauharnais by the Count of Flahault, and a family name was purchased for him by Hortense's imperial father-in-law; to him, to Persigny, and to St. Arnaud, Louis Napoleon owes his largest meed of gratitude. Morny was a man of great daring, and gifted with more than common powers of fascination. He had been a member of the Chamber of Deputies in the time of the monarchy; but he was rather known to the world as a speculator than as a politician. "He was a buyer and seller of those fractional and volatile interests in trading adventures which go by the name of 'shares.' He knew how to found a 'company,' and he now undertook to establish institutions which were destined to be more lucrative to him than any of his former adventures."

Morny, when twenty-seven years of age, was a master in all bodily exercises, a passionate steeple-chase rider, a clever racket player, an excellent shot, an incomparable sportsman, and renowned for his successes in the *salons* and *boudoirs;* he concealed under frivolous habits, and the rather English elegance of a man of fashion, the happiest qualities of mind and character. At an early age, he saw that the world progressed with every new government that sprang up, and that French society was being transformed. "The Old World," (these were his words) "sacrificed everything to form, and the thing itself was of little consequence; a scoundrel with good manners was preferred to a well-bred man of honor. All these ideas were filtered into me, and my ears were rendered only too sensitive. In order to be able to live with others, and correct my judgment, I have been obliged to educate myself from the beginning again." He was President very long of the Corps Legislatif, made an immense fortune, and married a Russian Princess of surpassing grace and beauty. Persigny, however, was the arch-spirit at the elbow of Louis Napoleon. His true name is Fialin, and he was born in 1808; originally he was a Radical Socialist, but for forty years he has been a Bonapartist politician. He married a grand-daughter of Marshal Ney, and received from the Emperor at his wedding a gift of one hundred thousand dollars. Louis Napoleon was, in 1848, elected to the National Assembly by three departments, through Persigny's manœuvres. In the session of June 13, the validity of these elections was discussed, after Lamartine had declared, on the previous day, that he should apply the law of 1832, excluding all the Napoleonides from France, against Louis Napoleon, until the Assembly revoked it. The debate was long and animated, and Louis Blanc, the Socialist, was decidedly in favor of admitting the Prince. He employed the memorable words: —

"Let us guard against giving pretenders greater dimensions by removing them. It is a good thing to see them close by, for then they appear to us as they really are. What did the uncle of Louis Napoleon say? He said, 'The Republic is like the sun.' We will let the Emperor's nephew approach the sun of our Republic. I am convinced that its beams will kill him."

The prophesy was reversed. The beams of Louis Napoleon's sun killed the Republic.

Guizot expressed his opinion about Persigny in the following words: "Persigny is no statesman; he is a diplomatic *gamin.*" Calm judges, however, admit that, with all his errors, Persigny is the very ablest man in the Napoleonic party. He has been Ambassador to Russia and to England.

Two distinguished partisans of the Emperor have been Maupas and Fleury, the latter being thus described: —

"The man who was the most able to make the President act, to drive him deep into his own plot, and fiercely carry him through it, was Major Fleury. Fleury was young, but his life had been checkered. He was the son of a Paris tradesman, from whom, at an early age, he had inherited a pleasant sum of money. He plunged into the enjoyments of Paris with so much ardor, that that phase of his career was soon cut short; but whilst his father's friends were no doubt lamenting ten times a day that the boy had 'eaten his fortune,' young Fleury was at the foot of the ladder which was destined to give him a control over the fate of a mighty nation."

He enlisted in the army as a common soldier; but the officers of his corps were so well pleased with the young man, and so admired the high spirit with which he met his change of fortune, that their good will soon caused him to be raised from the ranks. It was perhaps his knowledge about horses which first caused him to be attached to the staff of the President.

Maupas, one of the most despised of the Bonapartists, as the chief of his police spies, and a fit successor to Fouquier Tinville, has been sketched in aquafortis by Kinglake: —

"This person had been Prefect of the Department of the Upper Garronne. Of him, his friends say that he had property, and that he had never been used to obtain money dishonestly.

"His zeal had led him to desire that thirty-two persons, including three members of the Council-General, should be seized and thrown into prison on a charge of conspiring against the government. The legal authorities of the department refused to suffer this, because they said there was no ground for the charge.

"Then this Maupas, or De Maupas, proposed that the want of all ground for accusing the men should be supplied by a stratagem, and with that view he deliberately offered to arrange that incriminating papers and arms and grenades should be secretly placed in the houses of the men whom he wanted to have accused. Naturally, the legal authorities of the department were horror-struck by the proposal, and they denounced the Prefect to the Keeper of the Seals. Maupas was ordered to Paris. From the indignant and scornful presence of M. Faucher he came away sobbing, and people who knew the truth supposed him to be forever disgraced and ruined; but he went and told his sorrows to the President. The President of course instantly saw that the man could be suborned. He admitted him into the plot, and. on the 27th of October, appointed him Prefect of Police."

A gentler spirit, who is now a member of the Emperor's ministry, is Victor Duruy, a Protestant. Duruy, the Minister of Instruction, characterized the Emperor in the following words: "The most liberal man in the empire is the Emperor."

Duruy owed his present appointment to a clever and opportune bit of flattery. He said about the Emperor's "Julius Cæsar:" "I could not have written it better myself. I say this to the author, not to the Emperor."

Duruy is the author of a biography of Napoleon III., which, so soon as he became minister, he introduced into the French schools as a standard historical work. He has also charged the common-school histories of France with adulation of the Emperor, whom he appears sincerely to admire.

Drouyn de L'huys, the leading Napoleonic diplomatist, is sixty-four years old, and he was not an actor in the *coup d'etat;* neither is he at present in the favor of the Emperor.

Drouyn de L'huys inherited from his father a fortune of four million francs. His father was a great miser; and after his death a cask was found in his cellar, containing a million in gold.

With his wife, Drouyn afterwards married a fortune of two hundred thousand francs a year. He was, under Guizot, Director of Commerce in the foreign ministry, but voted with the opposition, so that Guizot at length let him drop. It is said that Guizot formed the following judgment about him: "The man wants to be a minister, and is not even a good clerk." When Drouyn quitted the ministry and the Senate, in 1854, he was so opposed to the existing system, that he had engraved on his cards, "Non-Senator." When, in September, 1862, Louis Napoleon offered him the portfolio of foreign affairs, which he had thrice held, he replied, "I shall not accept it to-day; but I may do so to-morrow."—"What do you mean by that?" Napoleon asked. "I must first know the conditions. I will not enter on office through a door where I shall be obliged to stoop." When he eventually accepted the portfolio, in October, he said, "I am willing to be the driver, but I must protest against the string being pulled in the middle of the drive, and being ordered to turn back."

Thouvenel has been another leading minister of the Empire, and an anecdote in his life shows that there is petticoat government even in France.

Two months before the Emperor himself dismissed Thouvenel, the latter not only sent in his resignation, in consequence of a violent scene with Eugenie, but declared that he would leave Paris and France, unless satisfaction were afforded him. Upon this, Eugenie stated she was sorry for having gone too far, and insulted a tried servant of the Emperor. After giving this explanation, however, the Empress seized her son's hand, hurried to the Emperor's Cabinet, to which he had retired after the above scene, and said to him, "You are deceived, Louis. Thouvenel wishes to induce you to overthrow the papacy, because social order and the existence of our dynasty depend on its preservation." The Emperor answered, "Who tells you that I wish to overthrow the Pope?" — "Yes, I am sure they want to destroy the papacy," the Empress interposed. "Calm yourself, madame," the Emperor continued; "everything will be arranged in accordance with your wishes."

Both Eugenie and the young Prince Imperial figure unduly in the political gossip of the empire.

The Imperial Prince attended one of the recent series of manœuvres at Châlons, on horseback, and always dined by the Emperor's side. At the grand dinner, with which the manœuvres concluded, Marshal Randon rose and said, "I drink the health of the Imperial Prince, the hope of the army." All present joined in. The little Prince, for whom his father poured out some champagne, drank a few drops, and replied, without any suggestion, "I drink the health of the army, and hope to become a good soldier."

As a soldier and a writer, the Emperor is without doubt clever, like all his family.

The Napoleonides were all authors. It is well known that the first Napoleon wrote tragedies. His brother Joseph published, in 1799, a romance, — "Moyna;" Lucien Bonaparte wrote a romance, — "Stellina" — and an epic poem, pointed against his brother, "Charlemagne; or, the Liberated Church," the *honorarium* for which was the principality of Canino, given him by the Pope. Louis Bonaparte (the father of Napoleon III.) wrote a romance — "Marie;" then another, "The Torments of Love; or, the Dutchman;" and lastly a work, — "Holland under Louis." Achille Murat, the son of the ex-King of Naples, who went to America in 1821, wrote a book about America. The works of Napoleon III. are well known.

St. Arnaud, properly named Leroy, who was Minister of War at the time of the *coup d'etat*, and Commander-in-Chief of the French in the Crimea, was also a brilliant writer, though unprincipled, and Kinglake says of him what may almost as truthfully be said of Louis Napoleon's writings: —

"It would be impossible for the most skilful novelist, for the most practised and successful elaborator of dramatic incidents, to exceed in tragic power the effect De St. Arnaud's correspondence has upon the mind of the attentive reader. With all the charm of familiar pleasantries, unguarded verdicts on men and events, playful endearments, realizing most completely the strictly private nature of these letters, now given to the world, there is a dark figure in the background, to which the eye turns constantly. This figure — struggling with an inexorable disease, impelled hither and thither by an ambition that knew no bounds; heroically rising to do battle, with the livid hues of death upon its brow — is that of the Marshal."

Passing by the Napoleonist party for the present, we come to the other two personal parties of France, the Bourbons and the Orleanists.

The House of Bourbon, which has intermarried with almost all the old Catholic dynasties of Europe, derives its name from the castle of Bourbon, in the centre of France; the *Seignors* of this castle intermarried with the royal family, Capet, six hundred years ago, and a branch of the House mounted to the throne in the person of the Huguenot King, Henry IV.; one of the grandsons of Henry IV. was Louis XIV., the Grand, and another was Philippe, Duke of Orleans; hence arose from the same stock the rival houses of Bourbon and Orleans. When Louis XVI. was condemned to death by the Republicans, the Duke of Orleans voted for his execution; when Charles X., the last reigning Bourbon, was driven from France, Louis Philippe, Duke of Orleans, accepted his crown. The Bourbons intermarried with the royal families of Naples, Parma, Placenza, and Spain, while the House of Orleans intermarried with the royal family of Belgium. The highest family connection of the Bonapartes is the House of Savoy, — the oldest in Europe and now dominant in Italy, — if we omit the marriage of Napoleon Bonaparte with the House of Hapsburg, which gave him a child, whose mother afterward married her Chamberlain during her husband's life. Harriet Martineau affectingly describes the exodus of the last Bourbon King from France in the person of Charles X.: —

"When the train arrived on the heights above Cherbourg, the spectacle that met the eyes of the travellers was very affecting. The vessels in the harbor carried the tri-color, all but two, — two ships in the distance, whose sails were hung out, and all evidently ready for immediate departure. These were American vessels engaged to carry the royal family into exile. The travelling-party drove through the town without stopping, and immediately went on board the 'Great Britain,' the soldiers on the quay presenting arms, and their officers saluting in grave silence, as the exiles passed. An officer waited on the King, to inquire whither he should have the honor of escorting him. 'To Spithead, England,' was the reply."

The French clergy has been at all times even a more formidable enemy of liberal institutions than the French nobility, and in the indignation of patriotic sentiment against them arose much of that infidelity and irreligion which characterize a large minority of Frenchmen. The first Napoleon adroitly managed to encourage the national priesthood, while he intimidated the Pope, and he extorted from the latter the privilege of regulating the churchmen within his own dominions; there are, therefore, two religious political parties of French Catholics, — the *Gallicans* and the *Ultra-Montanes*, — which, in some degree, correspond to the Ghibellines and Guelphs of feudal times; the *Gallicans* are headed, of course, by the Emperor, and while they recognize the primacy of the Roman Pontiff over the universal church, they assert the independence of national churches in self-government and local discipline; the *Ultra-Montanes* are headed by Montalembert and others, who hold that the Papal prerogative should have more weight than the self-government of national churches. Montalembert, a brilliant orator and writer, and a most consistent and uncompromising advocate of his church, and of religious and political liberty, stands at the head of a small, but intellectual body of Catholics, who claim that worship should be free, not subject to political restrictions, and who also belong to the radical opposition party in politics, holding the Emperor's *coup d'état* to have been a usurpation which neither the present age nor posterity will forgive Montalembert is an admirer of the English government, and during the American civil war he wrote a most vigorous pamphlet in favor of the Union, and the triumph of its arms.

The Legitimate party of France is still of some decaying social prominence, and at the head of it stands the Count of Chambord,—the grandson of the last Bourbon King, now (1869) forty-nine years of age; he goes by the name, among his party, of Henri V., but he dare not appear on French territory, and spends his time alternating between Venice, Vienna, the German gambling baths, and London, holding, as he goes, pompous drawing-rooms, attended by a few sentimental old nobles; like all the later French Bourbons he is an imbecile, and being childless, he consented a few years ago to combine the claims of his line with that of the Orleans family, so that at present the Count of Paris, Louis Philippe's grandson, and formerly aide-de-camp to General Geo. B. McClellan, may be considered, next to the Napoleons, the favorite of the whole limited monarchical party for the succession to the crown of France; the latter—young, not yet in the prime of life—has passed his years for the most part in England and in Spain; he has intermarried with his cousin, a member of the House of Bourbon, and bides his time, in the possession of wealth, if not of contentment. Louis Napoleon, who was treated with too tender consideration by Louis Philippe, has pursued the Orleans family with zealous severity; he confiscated their vast private estates; he forbade the King of Italy to receive the chivalrous young Orleanists into his army as volunteers in the war of 1866; and when these princes espoused the cause of the Union Army in 1862, the Emperor hastened to make overtures to England to recognize the disruption of the United States. A prince of this sort may wear the conceit of Augustus, and write the life of Cæsar; but he will fail to receive the serious admiration of the worthy part of mankind. The Orleans princes, whose grandfather was a school-teacher, and whose fathers were sent to the public schools, while the children of a reigning King, have behaved with such dignified, yet Republican simplicity as to obtain praise in mouths of wisest censure; the mass of Americans at this day are undoubtedly their well-wishers, if not their partisans.

M. Berryer, who died recently, was born in 1790, and was one of the most amiably bigoted of royalists and *legitimists*, besides being the most fervid and classical orator of France; he owed his popularity to the uprightness of his life, and the honesty of his convictions, and also to the pains he took to defend people of all parties, whom the government prosecuted. He defended Louis Napoleon after the failure of the Boulogne filibustering raid, and he defended Montalembert when prosecuted in 1848. Berryer is one of those characters who seem irreconcilable with popular government, preferring the feeling of loyalty to that of independence, and wishing to be a subject, though of an unworthy King. The young imbecile, who goes by the name of Count de Chambord, he called to the end of his days, Henri V., and addressed a dying letter to him in the terms of "Henri, O mon roi!"

Guizot, the head of Louis Philippe's cabinet, was born in 1847, in the south of France, and is a Protestant. He is an unloved, austere, scrupulous, and educated man, an author and historian of rare accomplishments, and a writer upon American history. As a politician he has been voted into obscurity, under the empire. Thiers, who was associated with him under the Orleans government, was born in 1797, of poor mechanical parents, and is considered one of the most formidable debaters, and one of the best politicians in France. He was the French Palmerston, the positive man of a negative and commercial sovereign, and he is the author of the greatest historical work which recent France has produced, while he has also made the most comprehensive and nettlesome speeches against Louis Napoleon from his place in the *Corps Legislatif*. Thiers made his entrance into public life as a journalist, like the best of French politicians, and was an ally of Armand Carrel, who perished in a duel with Emile de Girardin, the best of living newspaper editors in France, and perhaps in the world.

Girardin, like several eminent Senators of the United States, is an illegitimate son, and a smart, unstable politician. It was he, though Republican, who nominated Louis Napoleon for President, and he was the earliest to turn against the arch-traitor.

Girardin is a man past middle age, and of middle height. His hair, which is scanty behind, but fuller on the temples, falls in a carefully folded curl over his forehead, under which, clever but unsteady eyes stand forth. The slight squint in one eye produces a disagreeable impression; but even more disagreeable is Girardin's harsh voice, especially when he is speaking loudly and eagerly. Girardin appears most pleasant and natural when alone. In the Chamber he often produces the effect of an actor, through the tricks he employs, owing to his deficiency in oratory.

Girardin is immensely rich. As he was accused of venality, he said in the Chamber, "I am accused of mercenary motives in order to estrange the sympathies of the nation, although those who spread these wretched calumnies know as well as you, gentlemen, that there is no one rich enough to buy me. My ambition has nothing in common with avarice. All France cannot offer me a post which would secure me even one-half of my income." Other great journalists of France are Picard and Pelletan, both obdurate Democrats. De Tocqueville made a comparison between French and American journalists, which was truer of forty years ago than of the present day: —

"The characteristics of the French journalist consist in a violent, but frequently an eloquent and lofty manner of discussing the politics of the day; and the exceptions to this habitual practice are only occasional. The characteristics of the American journalist consist in an open and coarse appeal to the passions of the populace; and he habitually abandons the principles of political science, to assail the characters of individuals, to track them into private life, and disclose all their weaknesses and errors."

The narrow jealousy with which Napoleon and the monarchs of Europe regard the newspaper press is really a cause of its power. The enlightened mind of the greatest of French critics upon America observed that: —

"The extreme license of the press tends indirectly to the maintenance of public order. The individuals who are already in the possession of a high station in the esteem of their fellow-citizens are afraid to write in the newspapers, and they are thus deprived of the most powerful instrument which they can use to excite the passions of the multitude to their own advantage.

"The personal opinions of the editors have no kind of weight in the eyes of the public; the only use of a journal is, that it imparts the knowledge of certain facts, and it is only by altering or distorting those facts that a journalist can contribute to the support of his own views.

"But, although the press is limited to these recourses, its influence in America is immense. It is the power which impels the circulation of political life through all the districts of that vast territory. Its eye is constantly open to detect the secret springs of political designs, and to summon the leaders of all parties to the bar of public opinion. It rallies the interests of the community round certain principles, and it draws up the creed which factions adopt; for it affords a means of intercourse between parties which hear, and which address each other, without ever having been in immediate contact. When a great number of the organs of the press adopt the same line of conduct, their influence becomes irresistible, and public opinion, when it is perpetually assailed from the same side, eventually yields to the attack. In the United States, each separate journal exercises but little authority; but the power of the periodical press is only second to that of the people."

The Republican party of France is properly the Orleans party, believing in a constitutional government, and if necessary, a citizen King. The Democratic party is the old party of the Revolution, which has learned little more moderation and caution than the Bourbons. The American Republicans, except in the indicated permanence of their institutions, are little remarked in France, although the resident American population of Paris is from five to fifteen thousand. It is ordinarily no more than the former figure. It supports in the city of Paris eight special restaurants, four American physicians, four dentists, and five banking-houses. It has no newspaper, truthfully speaking, the Franco-American being printed, not in Paris, as alleged, but in London, and folded in Paris. The Paris "Times" is an English weekly, dated at Paris, likewise, and devoted to praising all the hotels which will advertise. "Galignani's Messenger" (pronounced Gally-nanny) is the only daily paper in the English language published on the continent, if we except the "Levant Herald," at Constantinople, which is sometimes a daily and sometimes a monthly. The Galignanis were Italians, resident in England, and in 1814, when Napoleon was beaten to Elba the enormous number of Englishmen that came pell-mell to Paris, to triumph in the humiliation of France and see its monuments, suggested to them a bookstore and reading-room, and afterward a news circular. This was a mere tract at first, but in the long peace that ensued twenty thousand Englishmen a year crossed the Straits of Dover, and ten thousand of these settled in Paris; the little daily paper grew apace, until now it is of ordinary size, and the subscription price of it is thirty dollars a year in gold.

It is cheaply edited, being in great part reproductions or translations of news, and editorials from French, German, and English journals; and is so closely managed that if you desire to buy five copies of any number you must order them the night before issue. The Galignanis report an income of twenty-five thousand dollars a year. The senior brother has been decorated with the cross of the Legion of Honor, and, together, they have founded a small hospital for Englishmen at Neuilly, near Paris. Their guide-book of Paris is the best in the English language, and they have published better editions of Byron than any English house.

The Galignanis, however, neither in their paper nor themselves, are of the slightest political influence in France, but are a copartnership of shrewd and prudent money-makers, who are probably Imperialists, if anything, and who take particular care to stir up no imperial enmity to their flourishing trade. The French Republicans, indeed, get little sympathy from any recognized American official instrumentality in France, and the Imperial government seems to master all our ministers in turn, so that even General Dix, when he gave up his mission on the eve of an important French election, devoted his last official appearance to a eulogy upon the Emperor. We generally send amiable gentlemen to represent us abroad, but seldom gentlemen who seem to be aware of political proprieties.

These defects of understanding in our agents are particularly annoying if not embarrassing to French republicans, who expect countenance, certainly not opposition, from us, as the model nation by whose example they appeal.

Chief amongst the radical Democrats is probably Jules Favre, the great classical advocate of Paris. This orator is the Mirabeau of the era: the man who means mischief to the empire, and never conceals it; who never took the personal oath to the Emperor, but evaded it, by standing up in his seat and saying: "*Je jure.*" He is an old-time Republican, austere and bilious, and a long hater, who will never serve when appointed on any committee to the throne, but maintains himself prince-like, by the practice of law, and is the conscience of the future and the past, in the face of this temporary despotism. Standing in court, on a trivial political cause, his presence is like that of Daniel Webster, in the height of his national fame, pleading a civil matter. Favre is scarcely more than fifty-five. His voice is clear, and powerful as Spurgeon's. His separate arguments, on whatever subject, are monuments of pure and beautiful construction, and with a wit that is of the basis of cold steel, he flashes it so dexterously that you do not see the murder in it. Out of this deadly by-play, rising into gladiatorial stature, he gives direct and thunderous assault, never faltering, nor gathering breath, his eyes burning yellow under their inexhaustible reservoirs, flinging a baneful light upon the arena, and his own goodly height, rising and expanding till, in the end, there is no audience, nor disputant, nor tribunal, but only this magnificent intellectual engine, silent at the foot of the pyramid of argument he has spontaneously erected.

This is Jules Favre, with his grayish-brown hair pushed straight back, leonine, like Calhoun's, — more imperial in the minority, than he who decrees and it is done. He is of the temperament of Thomas H. Benton, with the elastic manners and facilities of Clay, provided you tell them both to carry their point without awakening a lion in the same room, that would be apt to eat them if he got up.

The oratory of France in the present age is far in advance of that of all contemporary legislative bodies, and immeasurably fine by the side of that of the American House of Representatives, where it is still the rule, as M. De Tocqueville remarked, that "there is hardly a member of Congress who can make up his mind to go home without having despatched at least one speech to his constituents; nor who will endure any interruption until he has introduced into his harangue whatever useful suggestions may be made touching the States of which the Union is composed, and especially the district which he represents. He therefore presents to the mind of his auditors a succession of great general truths (which he himself only comprehends and expresses confusedly), and of petty minutiæ, which he is but too able to discover and to point out. The consequence is that the debates of that great assembly are frequently vague and perplexed, and that they seem rather to drag their slow length along than to advance towards a distinct object."

The Democratic party of France includes some terrible spirits, and no less terrible superstitions, of which latter are Socialism and Communism.

Communism is a more radical and extravagant form of Socialism, the latter aiming to redistribute property and labor, and organize society upon the principle of co-operation instead of by competition as at present; the Communist, however, proposes to abolish domestic government, parental authority, and the relation of husband and wife. The Socialist does not strike at the roots of domestic life, but argues that many of the vicissitudes and privations of the bulk of mankind are due to the unequal distribution of the soil; the Socialist, therefore, is merely a very radical Republican, but the Communist often urges that not alone are the distinctions of wealth unfair, but that the family relation itself is artificial. The greatest of the Socialists is Louis Blanc; the most illustrious of the Communists was Fourier, while the father of the latter sect was St. Simon.

Louis Blanc was born in Spain, in 1813, and in early life was a lawyer's clerk, and a teacher; later he became an editor, an author, and an orator, and in 1848 he was driven from France to London, where he became a remarkable journalist and historian, writing with facility in both languages; his history of the French Revolution is a book of immense research, and in part is probably the best account of that great popular uprising. Blanc, has hundreds of thousands of disciples among the French working-men; his principal socialistic work is entitled "The Organization of Labor," and it advocates the absorption of the individual in a vast "solidality," where each would receive according to his needs, and contribute according to his abilities. A huge series of national workshops were actually constructed in Paris, upon Blanc's plan; but they proved unsuccessful, and were abandoned. Louis Blanc has shown much dignity of character, and his life has probably been useful to mankind; his writings have been translated into almost all languages, and he has adherents in every country, even in England.

St. Simon was a French nobleman, descended from Charlemagne, born at Paris in 1760, well educated, and given a commission in the French army, which he accompanied to America, and he fought with distinction at the capture of Yorktown, receiving the personal encomium of Washington; he sympathized with the French Revolution, became immensely rich, and set himself to work with a wonderful method and perseverance to discover and elaborate a system of reorganizing society and government; in the prosecution of this inquiry he spent enormous sums of money in entertaining men of science and of literature, and finally he became poor, to hunger and beggary; the latter part of his life was made comfortable, and he became the head of a sect which still exists to hold his name in reverence. The story of St. Simon's life is entertaining and startling beyond that of almost any man of letters. His theory was, that religion ought to direct all the social forces toward the moral and physical amelioration of the class which is at once the most numerous and the most poor; he conceived a social hierarchy, which should direct this amelioration, — a new spiritual church, sanctifying science and industry, regulating vocations, fixing salaries, dividing heritages, and taking the best measures to make the labors of each conduce to the good of all. St. Simon's system is therefore reactionary against the Christianity which pays no attention to science; for he conceived that Christianity was by nature progressive, and meant to be modified by the changing circumstances of times and countries, whereas he alleged that it had been stiffened into dogmas, and that its clergy was ignorant of the thoughts, manners, and studies of modern times.

Fourier died in 1837; he had been a merchant's son and a traveller, and in the Revolution had lost both his fortune and his liberty; but while employed at Marseilles in superintending the destruction of an immense quantity of rice, held for higher prices in time of famine until it had rotted, his attention was called to the frauds and duplicities of commerce, and he set to work to invent some plan, whereby the people might be made independent of grasping capitalists; the consequence was, his system of Socialism, which he elaborated by patient years of thought and writing, living meantime in the most frugal manner, alone, and befriended chiefly by his own enthusiasm; at the close of his life a small group of intellectual men gathered around him, learned of his system from his own lips, and became its apostles. Amongst these were some Americans, who translated and published one of his large books in New York. Fourier believed that association would produce general riches, honesty, attractive and varied industry, peace, health, and happiness; he therefore projected associations, or phalansteries, to consist of four hundred families, or eighteen hundred persons, living in one immense edifice in the centre of a large and highly cultivated domain, furnished with workshops, studios, and instruments of industry and amusement. When the earth is covered with such palaces, they will unite in groups and series under a unitary government; there will be but one language; the only armies will be great armies of industry, to irrigate, drain, and plant. Fourier does not make war directly upon morals or religion. The property of his associations is to be held in shares, five out of every twelve shares of which are due to labor, four to capital, and three to talent. In his phalansteries the expense of living would be reduced two-thirds, and the products of labor quadrupled.

Fourier and his disciples have worked incessantly to obtain enough capital to make experiments upon this plan; an eccentric Englishman — Robert Owen — started three phalansteries, one in America, one in Scotland, and a third in England.

The most remarkably educated of all Socialists was Auguste Comte; the most extravagant, was probably Proudhon. Auguste Comte, one of the pupils of St. Simon, is the author of what is called the "Positive Philosophy," which has an immense number of disciples in France, and throughout the world; he considers theology and metaphysics to be disturbing elements in civilization, and proposes a new religion, and a new philosophy, based entirely upon discovering the laws of phenomena, and discarding as vain all inquiries into the causes and essences of things.

The extraordinary dissemination of socialistic principles from France throughout the world is attributable to the success of the French Revolution, which broke up the great landed estates of the aristocracy, redistributed property in small parcels, and immensely elevated the condition of the laboring classes. Panting for still more extended benefits, radical Republicans of France have conceived the distribution did not go far enough, that the Revolution became conservative too soon, and that the evils of mankind can in great part be avoided by annihilating the property, and even the family institution.

One of the strictest and most penurious business men this country has had — Stephen Girard — was at the same time a Jacobin Republican; his vessels were named the "Voltaire," the "Rousseau," and the "Montesquieu." He directed in his will that no clergyman should be allowed to enter the grounds of the Girard College, which he endowed, and the only religious people in whom he had any confidence were the Quakers.

Socialistic experiments have been frequently made in this country, and some of them continue to this day, while in some places Communism has been mixed with extreme superstition. The most successful phalanstery that we have, is of the latter class, and it is called the Oneida Community, wherein gross sensuality, blasphemy, and industry are about equally represented. Of communistic associations organized directly upon the plans of Robert Owen and Fourier, we have had recent examples in the environs of New York, at Red Bank, and at Modern Times. While it is common to say that France is eminently the land of Socialism, the remark is not unfrequently made in Europe that America is also filled with socialistic biases; in 1866

1

2

3 4

HALLS OF LEGISLATION.

1—The Saloon of State, Paris. 2—The Senate of France. 3—The House of Commons, London. 4—The House of Representatives, Washington.

Mr. Hepworth Dixon filled a large book with accounts of communistic sects and bands which he had visited in the United States. It is not improbable that, as our country grows more densely populated, we shall have in some form socialistic agitations amongst the working people, and these may become embittered by the strides of great corporations and by combinations of capitalists to affect the prices of the necessaries of life.

The French student, and the student-class generally on the continent of Europe, is more liberal and generous than the student-class of England, where reaction begins in the nursery.

It was to me almost incomprehensible to witness one day, before *L'école des Beaux Artes*, a prolonged riot between the art-students and the *Sergeants de Ville*, all because of an obnoxious professor.

What had he done? Insulted them, refused their sketches, made unfair discrimination in awards?

No! His crime was far greater. He had expressed a doubt of the power of Eugene Delacroix; and for this transgression of the truthful perception of art he was mobbed, and his resignation demanded. We once had a riot in our own country over the disputed merits of two actors; but it was international, not æsthetic, and its heroes were butcher boys. Shall we ever reach that enthusiasm for art when we will stand guard over a picture with cudgels, or break a statue simply because it is bad?

The irreligious party of France is represented by such men as Ernest Renan, the author of the "Secular Life of Christ." Napoleon III. expressed to the Italian ambassador in Paris his displeasure that Renan had been granted a decoration by Victor Emmanuel. "Sire," the envoy replied, "we believed we were acting in accordance with your intentions, as you, in your speech from the throne, entered decidedly on the liberal path." — "I shall turn back," Napoleon said to this; "the nation are ungrateful; by granting their wishes, it only makes their mouths water for fresh concessions." To which the envoy retorted, "The people of Paris will soon take occasion to display their ingratitude; and they will elect Picard" (the government candidate), "and not Pelletan." — "You are mistaken," the Emperor replied. "Pelletan will be elected, and I shall be glad at its happening; for the result of this election will prove that the destructive parties in France still have a broad bottom, and that I am still a necessity."

A fierce political campaign in France was well exemplified in the election of Louis Bonaparte for President, when, through the exertions of Persigny, legions of emissaries were sent into the country to work on the fancy of the people by fabulous promises, pamphlets, and songs. Peddlers of every description smuggled his portrait into everybody's hands; upon snuff and work boxes, upon everything that offered the space, appeared the inevitable physiognomy with the goat's beard and mustache. An army of organ-grinders was sent through all the towns, and sang, to the tune of the "Trois couleurs," the praise of the hero of Boulogne and Strasbourg. Absurd rumors were spread about: at one place it was said the candidate intended to give a million to the troops; at another, that he had promised a *milliard* to the workmen. Electoral committees, agents, newspapers, — all praised the man who was scarce able to keep his English milliner and his horse, and who was still in debt for the brilliant-mounted grand cross of the Legion of Honor, and the plumed hat in which he looked like a circus-rider. The organ-grinders sang in the streets of all large towns, "*Français, voulez-vous du bon, Choissez Napoleon!*"

The elections in France for the *Corps Legislatif*, in 1869, resulted as follows: government candidates elected, one hundred and ninety-three; opposition candidates elected, ninety. The number of the opposition party in the previous *Corps Legislatif* was forty-five. This result gave the greatest alarm to the Bonaparte party, and led to the proposed reforms as cited in the preceding chapter; for although Napoleon's candidates were still in the majority, even a loss of position is scarcely less a disaster where one's enemies are so uncompromising.

"On how many votes can the Opposition count?" Napoleon asked Persigny, prior to a previous election to the Legislative Assembly.

"They will get twenty-five," Persigny replied.

"That is a great deal too many," the Emperor said, earnestly. "The Opposition which eventually overthrew the Restoration was at first only seventeen strong."

The main features of the late Parisian elections, according to a newspaper correspondent are, on the one side, the annihilation of the government interest in that great city, and on the other side the cold-blooded and successful resolution of the electors to send to the House not only decided opponents, but the most dangerous, the most inimical, or, as is said in Paris, the most "irreconcilable" of opponents. MM. Garnier-Pages and Carnot are eliminated, not as suspected, but as not sufficient for the deadly war. M. Gueroult is swept away for parleying with Prince Napoleon, as Ollivier did with the Emperor. M. Jules Favre is in danger for having shown too much politeness to M. Rouher, and for having asserted in the House that habit of complimentary exordium, which is a rule and an ornament of the bar. And if you will get at the true reason for the clean sweep of the Parisian representatives, you will find in the end that they are blamed and dismissed for having sat six years in the House without having contrived any great and decisive event, and for having confronted the government during six years without having been able to overthrow it.

In 1863 about five million three hundred thousand electors voted for official candidates, and one million eight hundred thousand against them. This year (1869) we have about four million electors true to official or agreeable candidates, and three million two hundred thousand against them; and that is to say, only a majority of about eight hundred thousand voices is left in France to the existing government.

"The last of the public political meetings," says the correspondent, "was held last night, the law forbidding any assemblages of this sort during the five days next preceding the opening of the polls. The first day on which they were permitted was the 2d of May (1869). During this fortnight we have had in the Department of the Seine two hundred and fifteen of these meetings. The restrictions with which the law that permits them hedges them about have hitherto been noticed. Considering the irritating nature of these restrictions, and considering that all persons taking part in them, under the age of forty-nine years, namely, nine-tenths of all the participants, were exercising their right of assembling for the first time in their lives, it ought to be admitted that the Paris people have creditably carried out their share of the experiment. And even the authorities — considering what they are — almost deserve a good mark. They have not dissolved more than twenty or thirty meetings during the fortnight."

When we pass French politics and come to the wider arena of European politics, we shall find that Italy is the most restless state in Europe,— the land of Mazzini, Garibaldi, and their great party of compatriots; while Switzerland is the neutral ground where the discontented public spirits meet,— Poles, Bohemians, Magyars, Germans, and French; that little space of mountain land, as in the days of the Grütli, is still the scene of holy midnight conspiracy, and the most remarkable of its refugees has been Joseph Mazzini, born in 1808, the founder of the Young Europe Party,— an ardent, eloquent, and unfortunate patriot and author, and the political father of Garibaldi, whose political views he has himself expressed as follows : —

"The birth and growth of national life in Italy were Republican, and gave origin to our Communes before the days of Rome. Our national life was Republican, and creator of the idea of unity in Rome, before the Empire ; and Republican in its new birth and growth in our cities of the Middle Ages, repealing the Italian mission in Europe, and extending the link of moral unity from people to people, through religion, art, industry, and commerce. All our great records are Republican, and nearly all our great men, whether of heart or intellect, were Republicans. The tendencies and customs of our civil life, and of our dawning social institutions, are Republican. Italy has had Patriarchs, but no *patriciate condottieri;* merchant rulers who had raised themselves above their fellow-citizens, by arms or wealth, but not an aristocracy similar to those of other European lands, compact, united, guided by universally accepted leaders, and directed by a single political aim."

Garibaldi, one of the most famed names in modern history, was a poor fisherman's boy, born in Nice, sixty-one years ago. The first thing remembered of him is that he nearly lost his life, to save a poor washerwoman from drowning. He saw his country divided into twenty little states, each subject to a tyrant whose power lay in mercenary foreign soldiery ; and foreign kings, under the affectation of a protectorate, commanded these petty tyrants, so that the people were kept poor, ignorant, and servile. Great, fat convents and abbeys, free from taxation, covered the land, the occupants of which held fealty only to the Pope, and these had no sympathy with freedom. Garibaldi learned to hate the name of the King. He became a Republican while yet a boy, and, visiting Rome, saw that ancient and glorious city, the natural and traditional capital of Italy, full of ignorance and violence. He joined a secret society of patriots, was detected by spies, and compelled to fly to a foreign land.

He became a sailor, and, after many voyages, arrived in South America, where the people were throwing off the yoke of their despots. He raised the flag of the Republic of Uraguay, put to sea in a schooner, and fought several desperate engagements. At last shot down on his deck, he was dragged ashore, chained in a dungeon, and tortured ; but escaping, raised the Republican flag again, and battled till the day of independence. Then, in 1848, with his Italian troops he sailed from South America for his own country, carrying back his wife Anna, a noble and courageous woman, who had ridden often into action at his side. Soon afterwards the people rose against their tyrants, over all the peninsula. Garibaldi marched to Rome at the head of his command. There Frenchmen and Neapolitans had beleaguered the city. The Pope had run away. Garibaldi beat the French and the Bourbons in several splendid engagements. Finally enormous numbers overturned the Roman Republic.

Garibaldi took to the mountains for the cause of the union of Italy, saying in his proclamation, "I offer you hunger, thirst, cold, war, and death; he who accepts these terms, let him follow me!"

His conduct in this desperate engagement was the perfection of generalship. Sherman never moved men more skilfully, nor did Sheridan ever make more sagacious battle. The Austrians, the French, and the Neapolitan mercenaries closed round his gallant little band; and the hero's wife, refusing to desert him, died of hunger and fatigue at his side. Death was proclaimed to whoever should give him shelter now. He escaped at last and sailed for New York, an exile. For three years he worked with Signor Meucci, his countryman, on Staten Island; and seeing, at last, the people's cause rising again, he returned to Nice, his birthplace.

In 1859, Italy declared war. Garibaldi's services were gladly accepted against the Austrians, and his command was called "The Hunters of the Alps." He did the severest and noblest service of the war. In 1860, in the month of November, Garibaldi sailed by night, through the foreign fleets at Genoa, with a handful of brave men, landed at Sicily, drove out the mercenaries, marched through to the island, conquering, crossed the Straits, advanced upon Naples, and gave half of the whole country to Victor Emmanuel. His campaign, in this case, was equal to any of Napoleon Bonaparte's. Still the superstition of Europe maintained the Roman State, — a patch, a blot, upon the map of Italy. In 1862, Garibaldi, with the watchword of "Rome, or death," moved upon the imperial city. The minister of the King, Ratazzi, a pupil of the Jesuits, and then, as now, a paid creature of Louis Napoleon, ordered regular troops to capture Garibaldi.

The hero would not permit his volunteers to fire upon their countrymen, who, not so generous, shot down two hundred of the red-shirts, and kept Italy disunited still.

The present Kingdom of Italy, twenty-four millions of men, has grown out of four millions, and of these fifteen millions were the gift of Garibaldi, single-handed. He would never accept money, nor a title. They wished to make him Duke of Naples. He preferred, instead, to be a simple farmer, upon the Island of Caprera, where he has remained with his sons, in virtuous, manual labor, study, and thought.

The appearance of the man is beautiful and simple, like his life. He has a pair of soft, kind, brown eyes; his head is a little bald; a gray curling beard encircles his brown face. His dress is quiet, like his manner. His home is a rocky island, almost valueless, but by his loving consecration. All these Italian patriots are enemies of Louis Napoleon. Garibaldi said of him, at Varignano: —

"He has destroyed two republics, — the French and the Roman. The third, the Mexican, will repay him for all. There is a God and a judgment."

When Garibaldi was told that Drouyn had been appointed a minister, he said: —

"Of what consequence is it who is the valet? Tell me that another man has become the master, and I shall be glad."

It would be an unpardonable omission to make no biographical mention, in this book, of De Tocqueville, whose observations have guided us so frequently, and he may be presented as the best type of the philosophic, moderate, yet liberal statesman that France or Europe can show.

De Tocqueville was of gentle family, and great grandson of the intrepid lawyer who defended Louis XVI., and he inherited fine estates in Normandy. In early youth he engaged in politics with matchless ardor, and with an ambition the more intense that it was absolutely free from the slightest taint of personal interest. He pursued this noble enterprise for fifteen years, in the contests of Parliamentary debate, in the paroxysms of revolution, in the ranks of a Constituent Assembly, in the service of the President of the Republic, and in the direction of the Department of Foreign Affairs. He witnessed the catastrophe which extinguished the liberties of his country, and realized the darkest of his own marvellous predictions; but subjection to despotic power wasted him like an incurable disease, and amongst the causes which doubtless contributed to exhaust his delicate and sensitive frame was the ever-recurring thought that he who survives the freedom and the dignity of his country has already lived too long.

M. De Tocqueville was not thirty years old when his great work on America appeared. He awoke one morning, like Byron, and found himself famous.

The publication of his last book, in 1856, was followed, in 1857, by his last journey to England. The reception he met with here was in fact the last triumph of his life. He was received on all sides with demonstrations of respect and affection; and when the time came for his return to Normandy, the Lords of the Admiralty, hearing that there was no direct steam communication from England to Cherbourg, placed a small vessel at his disposal, which landed him within a mile or two of his own park. Three years afterwards he died.

The Free Trade party of France is small but enthusiastic, and they have the disadvantages of free traders in all lands, to make popular an intricate and statistical subject, to make common people think a step further than what is apparent, and to meet the national antipathy of France for England, in whose interest, it is argued by French protectionists, the advantage of reciprocity would be. The most illustrious names amongst French Free Traders, are those of Frederick Bastial and Michel Chevalier, the latter still living at the age of sixty-three; he visited the United States under the Orleans government, to inquire into our system of canals and railways. He is a Professor in the College of France, an anti-Socialist, and an Orleanist. Chevalier, and a few other Frenchmen, are favorably impressed toward England, and look to it for economical suggestions.

The vast questions of continental policy with which the European people have to deal have little interested the native American heretofore, yet amongst us are representatives of all these nations, and to their kinfolk is due at least some sympathy, and perhaps some inquiry.

We sell much of our crops to those people; we buy much of one sort or another back from them; we look to them for the grand caravans of emigration that are to make ports on our eastern slope, and States on our western. Also, with or without our will, we are partners in the topics which arise here. Busied with our vast material concerns, we still insensibly derive from Europe the social, refining, and intellectual *confitures* that comfort life, if they do not shape it.

I have never heard of a man that cracked his head studying American politics, until he got to the financial question. But the study of Europe, as I have said, is very much like the study of a crab. There are so many legs, all moving, and so much hard shell, and such an infinity of articulations and spikes, that one does not know where to take hold of the creature first. We have a broad zone of continent; its outlines are clear; we interlap with nobody that we fear. How to get money to build our railroads, and how to whip the Indians mercifully, are our only unevadable topics.

But here are eight or nine great races, each of them nearly of the size of all our population, interlocked, intersubjugated, cramped, trying each for itself to get out into comfortable daylight, like so many eels out of a box. Then every race wants to get out in its own way; to extend its boundaries according to what it calls the natural law of development; to collect all its natural family, with all their hereditary traps and acres, and afterward to rule them all together by one Federal will. In this aspiration it surely happens that each race will get on the toes and outrage the proprieties of every other race. Geography is too much for them. Upwards of two hundred millions of people, dwelling in a space considerably less than that occupied by our thirty-five, will make the most refreshingly incomprehensible wriggle and ferment in the world, when they all get going; and this is just their present condition. They all have their traditions. They differ in religion somewhat; in temperament vastly more; in their ideas of propriety, reverence, and comfort more than all. Let us see how preposterously unlike are some of their claims.

The farthest off of the great agitations, and one which may yet culminate in the earliest crisis, is Pan-Sclavism, or the extrication and consolidation of all the Sclave races in one empire. There are in Europe eighty millions of Sclaves, half of them in Russia, where they are the dominant race; the rest in Austria, Turkey, and Prussia. The Czar of Russia is a Sclave; so are the Poles, the Moravians, the Bohemians, and the Servians. They have their poets, and stump-speakers, and great literati, and castle-builders, and are all imbued with the idea that the time has come to unite and make the great Eastern nation of Europe. When you read of revolts in Servia, and a dozen other dimly known states in the south of Europe, you may set them down to the general insubordination of Pan-Sclavism. In the great city of Prague, which is the Philadelphia of Austria, second only to Vienna, the people refuse to hear speeches made in the German language. No country but Switzerland has ever been well governed where there is more than one legal language; still, the Bohemians of Austria, four millions strong, write novels in their own Tcheck tongue, and insist upon making the laws in it. To carry out the dream of Pan-Slavism would despoil Prussia and totally disrupt Austria and Turkey, and bring Russia almost out to the Atlantic Ocean, or within three hundred miles of France. Western Europe would submit to massacre rather than see it; yet at least ten millions of Sclaves are on the verge of revolt for this idea, and you might set all the stump-speakers and missionaries and newspapers of the world to persuading these that they were unreasonable, to no effect whatever. Again, inside the movement for Pan-Sclavism two or three agitations for individual territorial empire are afoot. The Poles, who are Sclaves, want any alliance but Russia, which is also Sclave. The Poles want a republic of aristocrats, to meet on horseback once a year in the open air in a vast cavalry legislature, and hoist the venerable flag of Poland again. The Russians want the Pan-Sclave empire to take the name of Russia, and be ruled by the Czar. One war of races, and two wars of dominion, lie in the single issue.

The next great question is that of all Germany, or united "Fatherland." In the heart of Europe are forty-five millions of Germans. They have never had a single nation, though they all speak alike, and have the same literature. For seventy years they have all sung songs, declaring that they would be one people. Now, they swear that this grand consolidation shall be deferred no longer. Encouraged by the victories of Prussia, they declare that there shall be no exception to a total blending of all the German provinces.

When this shall happen, there will be a nation close beside France fifteen millions stronger than she. Away will go France's supremacy in the affairs of Europe. She will have no influence as in the past over this divided family, and possibly will have to give up the city of Strasburg, and provinces on the Rhine that she has held more than a century. Sooner than do this every Frenchman will die on the Rhine, or across it. It was the cry of "Faderland" that robbed Denmark of Schleswig, four years ago. The same idea threatens to absorb Holland. It might even disrupt Switzerland, and put Prussia along the line of the Alps, neighbor to Italy, for half the Swiss are Germans. Yet the Germans everywhere are arming for this idea. There are three millions of needle-guns ready for the war to-day; a million of Chassepot rifles, and no end of infernally ingenious artillery. The Pan-German empire would take the city of Vienna out of Austria, and make Amsterdam a port of Berlin.

"Italy shall be free," is only another way of saying that all Italian people shall subscribe to one government. The exceptions to a united Italy at present are the city and small environing state of Rome, the Istrian coast, and the city of Trieste, which are Italian in blood and language, and the mountain region north of Venice as far as the Tyrol. It is Roman territory, however, that the Italians first demand, on grounds of tradition as well as of policy. Rome is in tradition, more than all Italy besides; it was once the world. The Italians feel that they have no natural or consecrated capital without it. The Roman people are continually crying: "Brethren, come over and deliver us from these mercenary soldiers!" and the Roman ecclesiastical government is, besides, an intestine enemy to the unity of Italy.

Italy could do without Rome if she could do without memory and heart. And it would not be an arduous task to overrun all the State of the Church, but unfortunately, the question of religion is a concern of government in Europe. Nearly all the sovereigns hold title from the Pope. One is "Most Catholic Majesty;" another, "Holy Apostolic Majesty;" a third, "Defender of the Faith;" and another, "Eldest Son of the Church." Napoleon was married by the Pope in person. Francis Joseph of Austria owes many a good turn in land and matrimony to the same pontiff. Spain is attached to this century only by the lessening link of the Church. Each of these powers would go to war with Italy in the Pope's behalf. Besides, the conservative sentiment of Europe is against Italy in this matter; Kings and Princes somehow feel that when the ancient Church goes down, reverence for more worldly titles will lessen. Kings are also as superstitious as anybody, and, having very little idea of getting to heaven on their own merits, prefer not to strike the only man on earth who keeps a passport office. Napoleon is, like all French sovereigns who have lived before him, the worst enemy of Italy, because her ally. If his son should die — and he will never have another — Prince Napoleon would be Emperor, and Prince Napoleon is son-in-law to the King of Italy. Therefore King Victor Emmanuel dare not go to war with the Pope, and offend his strong kinsman.

The Italians have great expectations of their town, Brindisi, which will be, as in the Crusades, the place of debarkation for Suez and the

East, after the completion of the Alpine tunnel. Brindisi is six hundred miles nearer Suez than is Marseilles. The Alpine tunnel is to be more than seven and a half miles long.

By Pan-Hellenism I express the aspiration of all the Christian people east of Italy and south of Austria, for independence. The war in Crete was an exhibition of Pan-Hellenism. About four hundred years ago the Turks first got into Europe, nearly at the time that Columbus got into America. They conquered all of what is now Turkey in Europe, and Greece, and the outlying islands, and established among Christian people their intolerant and almost barbarous worship and government. For four hundred years the people revolted and submitted alternately. At last Greece was made free; but the big powers, like England, were afraid to give her much territory, as she was a first-class commercial country, and might like to adopt a republican form of government. Therefore they saddled upon her a little German prince, made her pride of state wretched, and ever since have propped up the sick Turk, to the disgrace of Christianity and humanity.

A large proportion of the people of Turkey, all the Greeks, Cretans, and other islanders are Greek Christians, which is one of the three great Christian families. They want to build up the Christian Confederation of Greece, to include the whole of Turkey, and drive the Turk into Asia again. In this desire they have only two friends, Russia and the United States; because the Catholic powers have no more sympathy with the Greek Church than with the Mohammedan. The Russian royal family invariably intermarry with Protestant Princes. It is for this Pan-Hellenic idea that all south-eastern Europe is in ferment, and on this question all Europe may be involved in war. Western Europe fears, in the expulsion of the Turk, the advance of Russia to the Mediterranean. France, England, Italy, Turkey, and Spain would probably meet in this issue Russia, Prussia, Austria, and Greece.

All the great peoples of Europe are curiously interested and amazed in the rise of America, and their rulers at present compete for our friendship. "Europe," said the Prince Talleyrand, long ago, "must have an eye on America, and take care not to offer any pretext for recrimination or retaliation. America is growing every day. She will become a colossal power, and the time will arrive when (discoveries enabling her to communicate more easily with Europe) she will want to say a word on our affairs, and have a hand in them.

Political wisdom requires therefore of the government of the old continent to exercise the most scrupulous care lest any pretext be given for any such intervention. When America acquires a foothold in Europe, it would be all over with peace and security for a long time."

I close this chapter with an entertaining account of the greatest of French Republicans at home, General Lafayette, as described by William H. Seward, then (1833) a correspondent of the "Albany Evening Journal." The sketch will serve to illustrate the character of a pure Franco-American republican, and also to illustrate the household life of a French nobleman.

"We were met," says Mr. Seward, "by a servant of Gen. Lafayette who waited with a plain, neat coach, to carry us to LaGrange, his estate. We entered the domain as soon as we left the village, and a ride of something more than half a mile brought us to a grove, so rich and dense as to exclude the chateau from view. A winding of the road now discovered to us a venerable castle, built of stone, on the three sides of a square with an open court in the centre. The chateau is three stories in height, and at each angle is flanked by a circular tower. It is surrounded by a moat or canal filled with water, and traversed by bridges. An ivy clusters upon its front wall, which was planted by Charles James Fox. The coach stopped in the paved court, at the entrance of the chateau. We entered a large hall containing a grand staircase in the centre. At the foot of the stairs were two small brass cannon, mounted, and facing each entrance. The cannon bore inscriptions, stating that they were captured from the royal troops by the people of Paris in the revolution of the three days, and presented to Gen. Lafayette. Over them, and in front of the ascent of the stairs, is a triumphal ornament composed of flags taken from the royal troops in the same revolution. At the top of the staircase is an ornament, not less appropriate and characteristic; it is formed of the graceful foldings of our own standard, with its stars and stripes. We were received by Madame Maubourg, the General's oldest daughter, and by two of his grandsons. The lady spoke to us in English, but, being unaccustomed to the language in ordinary conversation, she found it so difficult that she gave me to understand we must use my bad French instead of her difficult English. She is a middle-aged woman, plainly dressed, exceedingly well-informed, vivacious, and agreeable. In half an hour the General appeared, well, cheerful, and animated, and we passed an hour in conversation upon French and English politics. The apartment which is the common parlor is still more plainly furnished than the rooms in the General's house in town. The floor is of polished oak. The room contains a bust of Washington at the age of fifty-eight, and portraits of all the Presidents of the United States except the present incumbent (Jackson). The General informed us that one of the latter had been forwarded by his friends in America, but had been lost on the way; he had written for another, but it was not yet received.

"In the course of the morning (afternoon) the several members of the family appeared, and warmly welcomed us to La Grange. The conversation was redundant in incidents of the Revolution. The General alluded to the difficulty he encountered in learning the English language, so as to pronounce it well, saying, that soon after he joined the American army he was requested to name the watchword for the day. He gave "Paris." He was himself challenged by an American sentinel, and pronounced a spy, because he pronounced the password Pa-re. He alluded to Col. Burr's visit to France; said he did not visit the colonel at Paris,—he could not—he had recently killed one of his friends (Hamilton), and conspired against another (Jefferson). I mention this as an evidence of the catholicism of the General's attachment to America, which embraced these two rival politicians, and widely opposed statesmen, without marking by a single expression his consciousness of their mutual opposition to each other. After sitting two hours, the General called a domestic, and proceeded to show us to our rooms. The one prepared for S—— was in the first story, comfortably warmed, in consideration of his ill health. He conducted me through long winding corridors of brick pavement, to the tower in the angle of the chateau in the third story, saying, 'You see, sir, that this is a very old house.' But although it was old, it was, in all that concerned the comfort of guests, perfectly *au fait*. 'We dine,' said the general, 'at half-past six. Here are paper and materials for writing. My library is on this floor; if you want anything, you will ring for a servant.' I wanted no books. I was reading the choicest history and character from the lips of Lafayette himself, and husbanded my time so as to lose nothing of the precious treasure. He spoke again in our interview this afternoon, and very freely of Louis Philippe; said that he distinctly engaged to him, that the new monarchy should be surrounded by republican institutions, to be of temporary duration, and to prepare the way for a republic; but he had a chosen to build up a dynasty, and had made a bad choice. 'Had he fulfilled his engagements,' said Lafayette, 'he might have been King twenty-five years; but to secure the support promised him by the other powers of Europe, he preferred building up his own dynasty, to make it perpetual. In the former case, the great revolution of France would have ended in four acts. Now it would be five. The people would be educated and prepared for a republic in twenty years. When that time should come France would not be content to be governed by kings. Louis Philippe and his family were sure to come down some time, and that not distant; he (Lafayette) did not think they had twenty years to reign.

"One cannot be an hour at La Grange, without discovering that Lafayette and his family are all American in their attachments and feelings. The conversation is animated beyond measure when it turns upon American affairs, reminiscences, anticipations, and hopes. The drawing-room is adorned with pictures of the American Presidents; the grand staircase with the American flag; the antechamber with busts of Washington and Franklin, and American maps. The library contains a choice collection of American books, and the sleeping-rooms have no pictures but those of American battle-fields, naval victories, landscapes, Mount Vernon, Hancock's house, Quincy, etc., etc. Would there were among American statesmen such lofty and exclusive devotion to the republic! At the dinner hour we met the entire family, consisting of twenty-two persons. The dining-room was a large and plain apartment on the ground floor. The General occupied the centre; on his right, Madame Maubourg, at the upper end of the table, and Madame Perier at the other end of the table. The dinner was served with a degree of republican simplicity which would shame our dinners in our cities. The viands were good, and the wine abundant; all, with the exception of a bottle of champagne, and a bottle of Madeira, the produce of La Grange. The General told many anecdotes of his tour in the United States, and expatiated upon the different parts of the Union. That spot, of all others, which he most admired, was Goat Island, at Niagara Falls. He described its beauties to his family, and said that he never thought of it, without feeling a desire to purchase it, and make it his residence. Madame Maubourg, by whose side I had the honor to be seated, interested me exceedingly. She described to me the Castle of Olmutz, and her stay there with her mother and sister during the imprisonment of her father, and I felt that I had not now a wish ungratified, since I had seen the hero, and the survivors of the three heroines of that dungeon. 'I will subscribe,' said Lafayette to the agent of the Prussian government, who proposed to him a renunciation of his republican principles, as a condition for his release, 'I will subscribe no declaration inconsistent with my duties as an American citizen.' Such was his language forty years ago, when the American Republic was in its infancy. 'I will not support,' said he, in 1830, 'a government which is inconsistent with my principles as an American citizen.' Was ever human character, through all vicissitudes, so consistent as that of Lafayette? Madame Maubourg said that the most sincere and unmingled pleasure she had ever enjoyed was in reading the American newspapers which recorded her father's arrival and progress through the United States. It was the triumph, the reward, the crown of a life of sacrifices, perils, and sufferings in the cause of human freedom.

"The General's tour was spoken of with no more apparent self-complacency than if it had been a ride in his little glass coach from La Grange to Paris, and the revolution of the three days was treated with no more effort at effect than if it had been an election of a Congressman in our own country. The party (rather the family) remained at the table about an hour and a half, and then retired to the drawing-room, where the evening was spent in free and unrestrained conversation. The ladies, as if they were the females of a farmer's family, had their sewing and knitting-work; the elder being employed principally in the homely operation of mending, with conversation upon books and music and the newspapers, which were by turns resorted to. At precisely ten o'clock each of the younger members of the party saluted the General, who retired upon taking leave of us for the night, and saying to us that we should take breakfast at ten o'clock.

"The General said he rose every morning at six, and I found all the gentlemen had been abroad over the plantation. From breakfast the ladies retired to the shade-trees on the lawn in front of the chateau. Mademoiselle Clementine, the daughter of George Lafayette, and an adopted daughter of the General, accompanied us in a long walk over the grounds, until we reached a small artificial lake, containing several islands planted with evergreens.

"On our return to the chateau we found the General waiting for us. He first exhibited to us the beautiful barge which had been presented to him by the Whitehall boatmen, after they had won the boat race against the Thames barge. He has built a house over it, with a substantial tiled roof, and enclosed by a network of iron which excludes it even from the touch. He next walked with us through every department of his farming affairs, which were in the most perfect order. He showed an entire familiarity with the whole, and is passionately fond of the pursuit. His horses, cattle, sheep, and swine were all housed and taken care of in the most systematic manner. I could not but mark the economy which prevailed. Even the acorns were all hoarded as food for the swine. The farm attached to the chateau contains about eight hundred acres. Besides this, he has another and larger farm in the south of France. George Washington Lafayette resides there during the summer and takes charge of it. The care of La Grange is intrusted to one superintendent. Regular daily accounts are kept, and these are carefully posted and examined every Saturday. A portion of the concern, such as the dairy, etc., and the use of what is required in the family, is subject to the supervision of his daughters. I was struck by the homage paid him by every domestic and laborer. It was merited, for his manner toward them was parental.

"At dinner he descanted to his family in glowing terms upon the homage universally exhibited in America to the soldiers of the Revolution, as witnessed by him on public occasions.

"On parting with the General, I said to him that we had a long time anticipated his return to America to spend the evening of his days there. 'My dear sir,' replied he, 'I should be very sorry to think that I shall never see America, but you know how it is. I am confined to France for two or three years to come by my office, as a member of the House of Deputies, and what may happen within that time God only knows.'"

1

2

3

4

5

REPRESENTATIVE HOMES OF CITIZENS.

1—Palace of the Prince of Prussia. 2—Duke of Wellington's Home, 3—Chateau of Duke de Lynnes, France. 4—Residence of A. T. Stewart, New York. 5—Home of Bayard Taylor.

CHAPTER XXII.

A GENERAL VIEW OF CONTINENTAL FINANCE AND GOVERNMENT.

The nations of Europe paragraphed, with particular accounts of the salaries of sovereigns, and sketches of diplomatic life, and biography.

To institute a comparison between Europe and America, geographically, would be for the sake of familiar illustration, rather than to prove any definite resemblance. Both continents face upon the Atlantic, and as we recede from the sea into each we approach, at opposite points of the compass, the frontiers. Russia is the Great West of Europe, stretching to its Rocky Mountains, vast, rolling, cold. The Mediterranean is its Mexican Gulf; Spain is an exaggerated Florida, projecting into the sea; the Baltic is the Great Lakes; the Danube is the European Ohio River, and the Valley of the Black Sea is the Mississippi Valley; the Rhine is the Susquehanna of Europe; the Alps are its Alleghanies, in which are the sources of the greater streams; Paris is New York, and Great Britain is New England. Chicago becomes Dantzic; St. Petersburg, Milwaukee; Odessa, Galveston; Constantinople, New Orleans; Venice, Mobile; Lyons, Philadelphia; Copenhagen, Buffalo; Vienna, Cincinnati. The most highly civilized regions are on the ocean; the most growing, formidable, and warlike, near the frontiers; grain and kine come from the plains of Russia, as from the prairies of America; fruit and manufactures from the valleys of the Atlantic. Three interior cities compete with jealousy for precedence: Chicago, Cincinnati, St. Louis, — St. Petersburg, Berlin, Vienna. The money is in the cities by the sea; the energy of improvements, in the far interior; but there is no vast emigration to the interior of Europe, as to the interior of America, unless it shall hereafter come from Asia.

Let us pass in review the most characteristic governments of Europe.

The Emperor of Russia, past fifty years of age, had for a mother, a Prussian Princess, and his wife is a daughter of the Grand Duke of the semi-extinct State of Darmstadt. He belongs to the House of

Romanof, and he is almost completely Teutonic in blood and origin. The Emperor's lands, forests, and salary, amount altogether to twenty-eight million five hundred thousand dollars a year. His direct income from the state is about eight million dollars annually. There are four million Protestants in Russia, but the Jews are excluded. Finland and Poland have partially independent governments. In Russia there is an extraordinary mixture of liberalism and despotism, the ballot and the *ukase*, so that the mighty empire, which comprises one-seventh of the territory of the globe, is really the most imperfect, and the most colossal of civilized states, deriving the most philosophical of its notions from the Germans, its financial theories from the French and Dutch, and its military spirit from its own Tartars.

The Government of Russia is an absolute hereditary monarchy. The whole Legislative, Executive, and Judicial power is united in the Emperor, whose will alone is law. There are, however, certain rules of government which the Sovereigns of the House of Holstein-Gottorp have acknowledged as binding. The chief of these is the law of succession to the throne. Another fundamental law of the realm, proclaimed by Peter I., is that every sovereign of Russia, with his consort and children, must be a member of the Orthodox Greek Church. The Princes and Princesses of the Imperial House, according to a decree of Alexander I., must obtain the consent of the Emperor to any marriage they may contract; otherwise the issue of such union cannot inherit the throne.

The administration of the empire is entrusted to four great boards, or councils, possessing separate functions, but centring in the "Private Cabinet of the Emperor." The first of these Boards is the *Council of the Empire*. The second is the *Directing Senate*. The third College is the *Holy Synod*. The fourth Board of Government is the *Council of Ministers*. The latter is divided into twelve departments, as follows: —

The Ministry of the Imperial House.
The Ministry of Foreign Affairs.
The Ministry of War.
The Ministry of the Navy.
The Ministry of the Interior.
The Ministry of Public Instruction.
The Ministry of Finance.
The Ministry of Justice.
The Ministry of the Imperial Domains.

The Ministry of Public Works.
The General Post Office.
The Department of General Comptrol.

The Emperor of Austria belongs to the House of Hapsburg, which intermarried with the House of Lorraine in France. Napoleon compelled this house to renounce the Imperial Crown of Germany, and in 1804 its heir assumed the name of Emperor, or *Kaiser*, of Austria; the heir of the present Emperor is eleven years old, and his mother is a Bavarian. The Empire consists of a German Monarchy, and a Hungarian Kingdom, each possessing its own laws, parliament, and ministers; in the German Monarchy there are fourteen Provincial Congresses (Diets), partly clerical and aristocratic, and partly popular, while at Vienna there is a Central Diet (Reichsrath), consisting of a House of Nobles, and Clergy, and a Lower House elected by the fourteen Provincial Diets. In Austria the Catholics outnumber the Greeks, Jews, and Protestants, nearly two to one; one of the Catholic Archbishops receives sixty-three thousand dollars a year. The Austrian Government pays eight per cent. for its later loans; the navy of the state carries less than one thousand guns. Austria is now a constitutional government, forced to become so by the deserved misfortunes of its rulers, and at the head of its statesmen is Baron Von Buest, a Saxon, and the enemy of Bismarck, who was received by the Emperor of Austria, after Bismarck had almost annihilated him, and now displays his diplomatic abilities at the head of the second state in Germany. Both Buest and Bismarck were aristocrats, with little love of the people; but both have been forced by different fortunes to help the popular cause.

The North German Confederation, of which Prussia is the bulk, is composed of about twenty states, exclusive of those which Prussia absorbed, which have formed themselves into an "eternal union," whereof the King of Prussia declares war, concludes peace, and appoints ambassadors; he commands besides all the naval forces, and the military rules of his kingdom extend to the whole federation. The King of Prussia, who represents North Germany, belongs to the House of Hohenzollern; so called for a family castle, near the Danube. The first King of Prussia was crowned seventy-five years before the American Declaration of Independence; the early rulers of Prussia saved their money, and Frederick the Great used it to enlarge his state by war. Since the war of 1866, Prussia contains a population of twenty-three millions. The King receives about two million five hundred thousand dollars a year. The heir to the Prussian Crown is now nearly forty years old, and his wife is a daughter of Queen Victoria. The Prussian Legislature is composed of a House of Lords and a Chamber of Deputies, and the government is partly Parliamentary like that of England, while in parts it resembles the arbitrary government of Louis Napoleon. There are ten members of the Prussian Cabinet; every province of the kingdom has a Governor, with a salary of forty-three hundred dollars per annum. The royal family belongs to the Calvinistic Church. The Navy carries less than six hundred guns, and is manned by less than four thousand conscripted sailors and marines; the biggest ship (1867) in the Prussian Navy carries sixteen guns of seven tons each, but many iron-clad vessels of greater power and armament have since been built for Prussia by the English.

Count Otto Von Bismarck, who, next to Frederick the Great, has been the greatest aggrandizer of Prussia, is Minister of Foreign Affairs; he is fifty-six years old, well educated and despotic; but the latter part of his life has been marked by respect for popular rights, and by enormous devotion to the interests of Prussia. In 1869, Bismarck presented his budget, and replying to the strictures of Doctor Lowe, a Republican, he made a speech from which we glean a paragraph to show the good-humor, and the style of speaking of the great Prussian Premier: —

"The last speaker appears to have been pretty sharply cut by what I said yesterday about eloquence. [Laughter.] He draws upon his imagination to find expressions that never fell from my lips. My whole life shows that I intend to adhere to a strictly parliamentary system. To prevent parliamentary power from becoming too strong does not mean to contest it. We would bring upon us the dangers of dilletanteism in politics if the strong overbalancing power lay in the parliamentary assembly, as it certainly is not at present. This speaker left the stand with his *ceterum censeo* against the army budget. I would venture to go surety for the security of the state, according to his meaning, if a victorious army could be held at bay on the borders of a state through the power of eloquence. [Laughter.] The history of Rome tells us of a case in which the enemy was kept off by the mere power of eloquence; but this enemy was composed of very uneducated people. [Great laughter.]"

The King of the Netherlands belongs to the House of Orange-Nassau, and his mother was the daughter of a Czar of Russia; he married a daughter of the King of Wurtemberg, and his son, the heir, is an Admiral in the Dutch Navy. The King receives two hundred and fifty thousand dollars a year, and the rest of the royal family receive one hundred and twenty-five thousand dollars collectively every year. The private fortune of the royal house amounts to about ten million dollars, which was amassed by the grandfather of the present King in mercantile speculations; the present King's uncle continues these speculations, and is even richer than the King. The Senate of the Netherlands consists of thirty-nine members, elected by the Provincial Legislatures from among the largest tax-payers; the House of Representatives consists of seventy-two paid members elected, by ballot, from those who pay taxes amounting to fifty dollars per year. There are seven ministers in the Cabinet, each receiving one thousand dollars per annum. The government is closely modelled after that of England. There are nearly sixty thousand men in the Army, and nearly one thousand guns in the Navy. The government clears about two million dollars a year from its colonies, but makes little or nothing upon its American colonies.

Switzerland is a United Confederacy, made so by a civil war of 1848. It has no Executive, strictly speaking, but both legislative and executive authority is vested in a State Council, and a Federal Council (*Nationale Rath*), the first of forty-four members, chosen by the twenty-two Cantons of the Republic, the second, chosen in direct election by all the citizens; the United Chambers are called the Federal Assembly, a committee of which represents the Supreme Government; the President and Vice-President of this Committee of Seven are the first magistrates of the Republic; they serve for one year for two thousand dollars, and one thousand seven hundred dollars, respectively. There is also a Federal tribunal, which is a High Court of Appeal, and arbitrates between the Cantons. Switzerland presents the anomaly of a state, where Protestants and Catholics are nearly equally divided, and only the baneful order of Jesuits is excluded, a complete toleration prevailing. The revenue of the state is upwards of five million dollars, and the expenditure little more than four million dollars (1863); the Republic had a surplus of assets in 1861 of nearly two million dollars. An honorable instance of Swiss patriotism is that of the purchase by the nation of the estate of Grütli for eleven thousand dollars. Grütli is the spot on Lucerne Lake where the Swiss patriots swore to free their country from Austrian rule; to prevent its falling into the hands of a speculative hotel company, the people, by subscription, bought it and gave it to the nation. There is no standing army in Switzerland, but every man must bear arms when called upon; and in 1862 there were three hundred and forty thousand men ready to send out, or ten times the standing army of the United States. Out of two million five hundred and thirty-four thousand five hundred and forty-two inhabitants, less than one-fifth are without land; there are eight hundred and twenty miles of railroad in Switzerland.

The King of Italy, Victor Emmanuel II., is nearly fifty years old, and is an elective King, the son of one Austrian Archduchess, and the husband of another; one of his daughters is married to Prince Napoleon, and another to the King of Portugal; his heir is twenty-seven years old, a Major-General, and the origin of the House is a German Count, who, in the eleventh century, established himself at the foot of the Alps. In 1864, the King gave up six hundred thousand dollars of his income to the almost bankrupt country, and he contents himself with about one million seven hundred thousand dollars, while several of his relatives receive smaller sums. He has nine ministers. The Roman Catholic is the established religion, with forty-five Archbishops and one hundred and ninety-eight Bishops. There are sixty-five provinces in Italy. The government is a moderated form of the French Empire, with certain English adaptations attached to it. Not only are all worships tolerated in Italy, but the bloated estates of priests have been confiscated to support public education, and to help the thirteen National Universities. The Italian Navy consisted (1866) of one hundred and six war vessels, carrying one thousand four hundred and sixty-eight guns. By the last census, Italy, as a kingdom, contains nearly twenty-two millions of people; there are nearly four hundred newspapers in the nation, and a sea-faring population of one hundred and sixty thousand, capable of making a greater navy than Austria and Prussia combined.

The Pope of Rome has an income from his own little state of 655,000 dollars a year; but contributions from abroad swell it to 5,000,000 dollars. A Pope is elected by the ballot of Cardinals, each Cardinal writing his own name and that of his candidate on a ticket, every Cardinal saying a prayer as he votes. The present is the two hundred and fifty-eighth Pope. The present Pope is seventy-seven years old; he has six ministers, at the head of which is Antonelli, the son of a wood-cutter, — a man of bad family, the most hated of all the parasites of European despots, and who is believed to have gained immense riches by filching the revenues of the mendicant Pope. The Pope is absolute, irresponsible, and infallible, never seeking advice but from his college of less than fifty Cardinals, all but thirteen of whom are Italians and Princes of the Church. The Pope expended in 1864, as in most other years, three times his income, and he is in debt in every part of the world; yet he kept, in 1860, twenty-five thousand soldiers, upon less than seven hundred thousand inhabitants. There are only eighty-four miles of railroad in his state, which generally loses money, and the Jesuits seem to have mastered the old man. The Jesuits numbered, in 1863, seven thousand five hundred and twenty-nine, the majority of whom were in France, while three hundred and fifty were in America. The Pope's winter palace, called the Vatican, contains four thousand four hundred and twenty-two rooms, and is one thousand one hundred and fifty-one feet long, and seven hundred and sixty-seven broad; his principal church (St. Peter's) cost fifty million dollars, covers eight acres, and required three hundred and fifty years to build and finish it.

The King of Portugal receives 410,000 dollars a year, of which he returns nearly 100,000 dollars to the educational bureau; but his court costs the state 760,000 dollars annually.

The Sultan of Turkey is said to receive 48,000,000 dollars a year, or three-fourths the whole revenue of his dominions; his *Grand Vizier* gets 65,000 dollars annually, and his ministers from 50,000 dollars to 41,000 dollars each, a year.

The King of the little State of Greece gets 274,000 dollars a year, in addition to 60,000 dollars from other sources.

The Grand Duke of Baden receives 313,000 dollars a year for himself and family.

The King of Wurtemburg receives 370,000 dollars a year.

Bavaria has the most aristocratic army, in officers, in Europe, and its King receives for himself and family 1,250,000 dollars a year. King Ludwig stole besides, from the public exchequer, nearly 640,000 dollars to support Lola Montez and his other mistresses, which sum he was obliged to return from his private purse, under threat of revolution. The Catholic Church in Bavaria is endowed with 42,000,000 dollars' worth of property.

The Prince of Schwarzburg Rudolstadt, with 72,000 subjects, has 60,000 dollars a year salary, exclusive of real estate revenues; the Prince of Schwarzburg Sondershausen, with 65,000 people, has 112,000 dollars a year, or one-fourth the revenue of the country besides the revenue of immense private estates derived from his predecessor, who insisted upon brewing and selling all the beer in his dominions.

The Prince of Reuss-Schleiz, with 83,000 people, receives 100,000 dollars a year, and owns almost his entire state.

The Prince of Schaumburg-Lippe, with 31,000 people, has 125,000 dollars a year, and his crown domains are mortgaged to the amount of 2,500,000 dollars.

The most starveling and pitiable Prince of Lippe-Detmold, with 108,000 people, who was obliged to sell part of his territory to Prussia, gets 50,000 dollars a year.

The Prince of Waldeck, whose ancestors sold 1,225 of his subjects to England to subdue America, three-fourths of whom never returned, has 58,000 subjects, and 186,000 dollars yearly salary, yet he is so poor that he must keep gaming-tables and sell mineral waters.

The Duke of Saxe-Altenburg, with 138,000 people, gets 108,000 dollars a year.

The Duke of Saxe-Coburg-Gotha, brother of Prince Albert of England, has 160,000 subjects, and about 80,000 dollars a year salary.

The Duke Anhalt, with 182,000 people, gets 150,000 dollars a year, and owns private estates, in various parts of the world, of more than 200 square miles of land; these miserable Princes, in anticipation of being driven out to grass, have managed to sweat, to steal, and to pick from their subjects large sums of money to lay up nest-eggs in foreign parts. A poor *Prince* was never known to escape from his country; a rich Republican exile has never been seen. While Joseph Bonaparte lived at Bordentown upon a vast estate, Moreau, the French Republican, and victor of Hohenlinden, lived opposite Trenton in a cottage, just able to find his bread. When Prince Albert married the Queen of England, with true German princely thrift, he made the first demand upon Parliament for a large annuity, and spent his married life in laying up the ingots for future use.

The Duke of Saxe-Weimer gets, out of his 278,000 people, thousands of whom are coming to America, 205,000 dollars a year.

The Duke Saxe-Meningen gets 94,000 dollars a year.

The Duke of Mecklenberg-Strelitz, with 98,000 people, gets the enormous sum of 1,110,000 dollars a year, or seventy dollars for every soul, and while on the one hand he is losing a thousand people a year bound to America, on the other he is selling parcels of his property to Prussia.

The Duke of Brunswick, who was driven out of his little realm by a riot in 1830, took with him enough extorted money to live in Paris at the rate of 1,000,000 dollars a year, while the present Duke gets 175,000 dollars annually out of 282,000 people; in 1850 one-fifth of all the births in his duchy were illegitimate.

The Duke of Oldenburg, with 295,000 people, receives 156,000 dollars a year.

The Duke of Mecklenburg-Schwerin, who claims to be the only reigning family in Europe of Sclavonic origin, and to be the oldest sovereign house in the Western World, and who calls himself Prince of the Vandals, supports a feudal state of 550,000 people, has a salary of 600,000 dollars a year, owns a railroad fifty-five miles long, and his estates comprise one-fifth of his realm, and are worth 60,000,000 dollars. In 1860 one child out of every three and eight-tenths in his domains was illegitimate; only one-half his people can read, and his government imposes restrictions upon marriage, so that he is indeed King of the Vandals! In 1864 his Diet passed a law investing all landed proprietors with power to condemn their laborers, for simple "neglect of service," to a week's imprisonment, and twenty-five blows with a stick. In one district of Hesse-Cassel young girls were, until a recent period, shipped to England, to be sold into infamy for the price of an export duty.

The King of Saxony receives 640,000 dollars a year, out of 2,225,000 population.

The King of Denmark gets 350,000 dollars a year, and his heir 14,000 dollars, levied on 1,608,000 people.

The King of Belgium receives for himself 550,000 dollars annually, and, including the expenses of his court, 840,000 dollars.

Such are some of the monstrous figures which are paid to the Sovereigns of Europe, and in view of these we are seriously advised by certain adventurers that Imperialism is the panacea for all the errors of a Republican people. The combined scandals of every Republican administration, from the days of Washington to the present time, will not match the vices of one generation of some of the pettiest ducal houses of Europe. In 1869 the banished King of Hanover was driven by the Prussians to Vienna; but though banished he was not beggared, for he and his ancestors had put by certain little morsels for rainy days, and from all these sources the bereaved monarch has a little competence, of which no one can deprive him, of about 1,500,000 dollars per annum.

Some time ago, before one of the chancery courts in London, a suit in which the King of Holland was plaintiff, and the Bank of England defendant, was heard and decided. It was a demand for a little sum of 3,000,000 dollars.

In the year 1783 a large sum was realized out of the revenues of the then Electorate of Hanover, which George III. invested in bank annuities. It now amounts to 3,000,000 dollars in gold, and was specifically designed to cover the exigencies of the King and Queen of Hanover, as well as the minor princes and princesses. In 1867 the King of Prussia protested against this sum being paid to the King of Hanover; but the English courts decided it to be his property.

The following were the amounts of the principals of the national debts of the great states of Christendom, in 1867: —

Great Britain and Ireland,	$3,907,500,000
United States,	2,775,000,000
France,	2,700,000,000
Russia,	1,325,000,000
Austria,	1,250,000,000
Italy,	1,180,000,000
Spain,	800,000,000
Holland,	425,000,000
Turkey,	350,000,000
Prussia,	295,000,000
Portugal,	235,000,000
Bavaria,	250,000,000
Belgium,	140,000,000
Brazil,	120,000,000
Peru,	108,000,000
Victoria, South Australia, New South Wales, Queensland,	86,000,000
Denmark,	75,000,000
Canada,	75,000,000
Sweden,	33,000,000
Norway,	7,500,000
Chili,	18,000,000
Argentine Republic,	25,000,000
Switzerland,	800,000

The following are the amounts of annual interest on the debts of a few of the principal states (1867).

United States,	$140,000,000
Great Britain and Ireland,	130,000,000
France,	125,000,000
Italy,	85,000,000
Austria,	65,000,000
Russia,	55,000,000
Turkey,	17,000,000
Spain,	20,000,000
Prussia,	10,000,000
Holland,	12,500,000
Brazil,	10,000,000
Peru,	10,000,000
Canada,	3,750,000
Portugal,	7,000,000
Switzerland,	15,000

To form an idea of the relative cost of some of the leading governments of the world, we cite from the statistics of 1867, the expenditure per head of population: —

New Zealand,	(per head, annually,)	$62.00
Great Britain,	" " "	16.12
United States,	" " "	15.00
Canada,	" " "	4.72
France,	" " "	10.08
Russia,	" " "	4.06
Italy,	" " "	6.18
Brazil,	" " "	2.90
Victoria (Australia),	" " "	24.00
New South Wales (Australia),	" " "	26.60
Prussia,	" " "	6.68
Sweden,	" " "	2.76
Austria,	" " "	5.26
Peru,	" " "	8.51
Switzerland,	" " "	1.66

A good idea of the business prosperity of a country may be obtained from statements of the value of its exports. A country which imports more than it sends away is, for the time being, certainly getting out of pocket. Appended are the values of the total exports and imports of some of the great countries as they were in 1867: —

	Total Imports.	*Total Exports.*
United States,	$400,000,000	$275,000,000
Great Britain and Ireland,	1,475,000,000	1,195,000,000

	Total Imports.	Total Exports.
France, ...	685,000,000	790,000,000
Germany, ...	750,000,000	700,000,000
Austria, ...	120,000,000	155,000,000
Belgium, ...	250,000,000	235,000,000
Italy, ...	195,000,000	140,000,000
Russia, ...	125,000,000	125,000,000
Holland, ...	180,000,000	150,000,000
Canada, ...	80,000,000	65,000,000
Chili, ...	25,000,000	30,000,000
Brazil, ...	60,000,000	75,000,000
Spain, ...	85,000,000	60,000,000
India, ...	250,000,000	350,000,000
China, ...	225,000,000	170,000,000
Australia, ...	145,000,000	140,000,000

Here is what soldiering alone has cost France under Napoleon III. :—

Crimean war, ...	$269,000,000
Italian "	69,000,000
Chinese "	33,200,000
Occupation of Rome, ...	10,000,000
" " Syria, ...	5,600,000
Mexican war in aid of Maximilian, . . .	120,000,000
Extra refreshments, ...	18,000,000
The total fiddling, ...	$524,800,000

Not one of these wars was of any material advantage to France, nor to anybody befriended, the Italian war included, which had to be fought over again in 1866. As to the Mexican war, modern times have seen no such melancholy failure.

In 1851, when the Emperor had just taken his throne, France owed	$1,069,127,472
In 1861, when our civil war began, France owed .	1,943,835,383
In 1867. France owed	2,700,000,000

Or the annual interest upon this debt is $125,000.000, or about $3.28 for every man, woman, and child in France.

The revenue of France, in the year 1867, was about three hundred and seventy-five millions of dollars; seven and one-half millions of dollars in excess; or it cost every human being in France ten dollars to be protected by the central government.

The greatest banking-house in Europe, and one which is intimately identified with the politics of all the leading nations, is that of Rothschilds.

The family of Rothschild was founded by Meyer Anselm, of Frankfort, who died in 1812. He was born in the Jews' alley, was brought up to be a priest of the Hebrew faith, but becoming a money-broker, he was employed to raise a loan to relieve Frankfort from an invasion of French Republicans; here Rothschild became associated with American history, for the money he obtained from the Elector of Hesse-Cassel, to aid Frankfort, was doubtless the indentical gold paid by Great Britain to hire Hessian troops to subdue her American colonies. The Elector had in his possession about five millions of dollars, and when at a later date Napoleon marched upon him, Rothschild became the repositor of this immense sum, for which he paid no interest. It is therefore remarkable that the greatest banking-house in Europe owes its beginning to the hire of British mercenaries against the United States, and the sums thus infamously paid by England were efficacious, fifty years afterward, to give the first Jew admission to the English Parliament, in the person of a grandson of Meyer Rothschild.

The five sons of the first Rothschild scattered over Europe: Nathan going to London, Solomon to Vienna, James to Paris, and Charles to Naples, while the fifth son, Anselm, remained with the old man at Frankfort. All these united in the wealthiest copartnership of the present, or probably of any other age; in 1848 they lost forty million dollars by the revolution against Louis Philippe and his allies; but their solvency after this disaster was their greatest advertisement. Anselm died childless, leaving a fortune of fifteen million dollars. Nathan, the eighth Rothschild, distributed the enormous subsidies which the British gave the Germans to war against France, and one of these payments, after the treaty of Toeplitz, amounted to sixty million dollars in gold. This same Nathan made one million of dollars by obtaining the result of the battle of Waterloo several hours before the English government.

The Emperor of Austria made Nathan a Baron of the Empire, and this title descended to his eldest son, Lionel, who was the first Jew, as we have said, to enter the British Parliament, and he represented London city for several years. The Rothschild cousins all intermarry, and as they obtain all the good loans of Europe, and refuse all the bad ones, their house seems destined to last as long as that of

Hapsburg, or Savoy, unless, like all royal lines, they suffer premature mental degeneracy.

When Fould, French minister, brought on the *tapis* the conversion of the *rentes*, he only employed Pereire, French banker, in the operation, which terribly offended Rothschild. Fould, who heard of this, and was afraid of Rothschild's influence, hastened to pay him a visit, but was very coldly received. In alarm he drove to the Emperor, and said to him : —

"Sire, I have made a mistake in passing over Rothschild in the conversion of the *rentes*. I am afraid he will pay us for it, for though he cannot upset the operation, he can injure it."

"Leave me to act," Napoleon replied, "I take the affair on myself."

The Emperor sent for Rothschild, and said to him : —

"How is it with your *chateau* of La Ferrière? I hear that it is finished, and splendid beyond all description."

"It is worth looking at, sire, although it is an exaggeration when people say that it cost five-and-twenty millions."

"Twenty-five millions! it must really be something wonderful! Within a week I will come with the Empress to La Ferrière, and breakfast there. After breakfast we will go out shooting."

Rothschild offered no obstacle to the conversion of the *rentes*.

Two money-dealers — Rapallo and Solari — advanced Louis Napoleon the funds for his Strasburg filibustering attempt. They went into speculations, which the confusion in the money-market produced by the expedition would render profitable. The money they advanced to the Prince is said to have amounted to a million of francs (two hundred thousand dollars).

Louis Napoleon wanted three hundred thousand dollars, in order to become President. Thiers procured him the sum, and merely took a simple acknowledgment from the Prince. Not a word was said about interest. The President could not sufficiently express his gratitude, and pressed Thiers' hand, with a tear of emotion in his eye What a different man was this from the old bearded Jews, to whom Louis Napoleon had often applied in vain!

Eugenie has insured her life in the Paris Company, the Nationale, for two million francs. The original proposal was for five millions, or one million dollars; but the company only accepted two, of which it reinsured one with other offices. The Germania, at Stettin, accepted one hundred thousand francs. The Empress's proposal was signed by Napoleon as her guardian. The insurance is in favor of her natural heirs, or of her son in the first instance.

The richest state at present on the Continent is Prussia, having more surplus money in its treasury, than any other, and every day increases its importance. The "Zollverein" is a mutual Customs League, dating in its incipiency from 1828, and owing its origin to Prussia, the most advanced state in Germany; it was reformed and rearranged in 1867,and now comprises most of the German States, Austria excepted. It is composed of delegates with a central government at Berlin, and has a common exchequer, into which all customs are paid, and thendistributed pro rata amongst the different states according to population. The chief sources of German revenue are import and export duties, and taxes upon spirits, wine, beet-root sugar, and tobacco. There are two hundred and fifty-two beet-root sugar factories in Prussia alone. The object of the "Zollverein" is to dispense with custom-houses between the petty states of Germany. A note in the next chapter will further speak of Germany and Eastern Europe.

CHAPTER XXIII.

THE NEW WEST AND THE NEW EAST.

Some notes upon the Western territories and coasts of the United States, and the problems of civilization in Eastern Europe. — Advances of America and Europe toward the Pacific. — The contest for preponderance in Asia. — Inquiry into the permanence of Russia's friendship for America, and into the stability of the British Empire in Polynesia and North America. — America's diplomatic relations with the world.

RUSSIA and the United States have been occupying the attention of the world for a century, and within the past twenty years have been curiously studying each other. Apparently antipodes in origin, religion, mission, and position, they have the sympathy of magnetic poles with each other, — farthest apart, yet closest in communication, — and each is assured that the axis of empire passes through itself. They have never been rivals; if they have not always pursued the same principles, their separate material ambitions have commanded mutual respect. We shall all be glad in America when Russia absorbs the Turk, and Christianity resumes the capitalship of the Greek empire on the Bosphorus, and Russia has voluntarily subscribed to the "Monroe doctrine" by parting with her only possession on the American continent. It seems to be without the range of probabilities that our two empires can collide; the superstition in the American mind that we are the gigantic twins of Christendom, starting from Europe in opposite directions to mould the destinies, the one of the West the other of the East, has well-nigh reached the American heart, and when we read of our mutual fleets in the Dardanelles manning the yards and mingling hurrahs and "hourras," we feel a thrill akin to that of a lover discovering reciprocal passion in his sweetheart.

The differences between the American and the Russian States are not so profitable subjects for investigation as their resemblances. Each has a work to do, and its temperament and system are adapted to its separate mission. The tribes which accept civilization at the point of the Russian's sword would be irreverent scholars of the

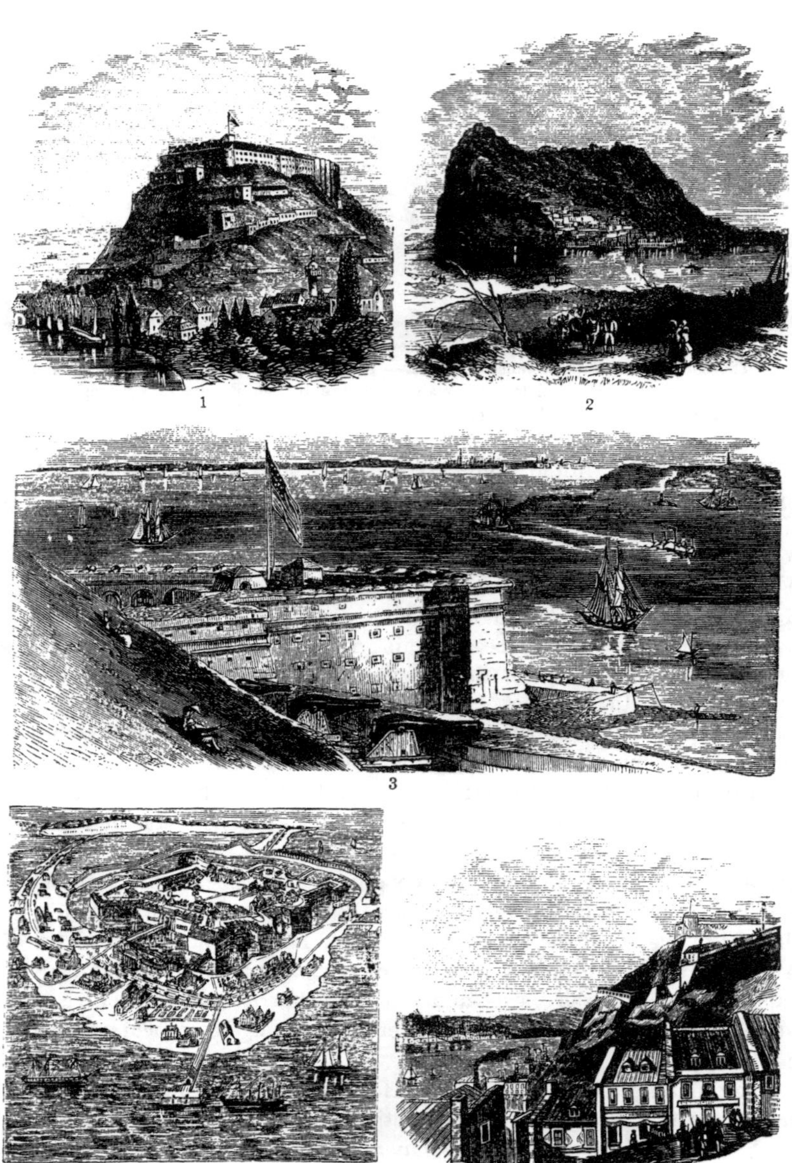

HARBORS AND FORTRESSES.

1—Ehrenbreitstein. 2—Gibraltar. 3—The Narrows. 4—Fortress Monroe. 5—Citadel, Quebec.

American ballot. Russia must civilize the nations in bulk; we initiate them into Republicanism, man by man. And who can say that the condition of the Asiatic is not improved by the prowess of Russia as much as the European by the institutions of America? These are some of the resemblances between the United States and Europe in which Russia takes a prominent place: —

The same geographical and ethnological circumstances mark both. The Atlantic coasts are jagged and broken, and they were first civilized by various races, so that there had nearly been as many distinct nations in Florida, Louisiana, Canada, Virginia, and New York, as in Spain, France, England, and Holland. The interiors of the two continents are broad, compact, of vast agricultural resources, similarly marked by plains, prairies, steppes, and irrigated by an immense river system, and the aborigines of both continents, entering from the frontier, had to be pushed back, absorbed, or civilized from the Atlantic. The Gulf of Mexico and the Mediterranean, on the south, were first discovered, developed, and became the seat of the mythology of their respective continents; Mexico and Italy, Cuba and Sicily, recall each other as do the cities of Rome and Mexico, the careers of Romulus and Cortes, Columbus and Æneas, the Buccaneers and the Saracens; the northern races triumphed over the Latins, the Saxon over the Spaniard and Gaul in both cases. The Gulf and River of St. Lawrence and their lakes suggest the English Channel, the North and the Baltic Seas; St. Petersburg, in its rapid rise, growth, and influence, may be likened only to Chicago, at the heads of these frozen courses, respectively. The dense population, the more perfect cities, the historic landmarks and memorials are by the slopes of the Atlantic; Russia, like the American Western States and Territories, busied with its immense material projects, has also a like imperfect social organization; the principle of civilization, and the germ of art and literature are in both cases at war with the rapacity of the savage, the violence of the pioneer and outlaw, the heathen tradition of the Mormon or the Turk, the anarchy of the Mexican or the Tartar; the knout and "Judge Lynch" suggest each other; and as America is retarded, in its march to the South and the Isthmus, by European influences in the West Indies and the indolent patriotism of Mexico and Spanish America, so Russia is pushed out of the short course to the Indies by Turkey and "balance of power," and compelled, like the United States, to go overland to the Pacific. The lines of Ural and Rocky

Mountains stand between America and Russia, and their broad frontier empires; out of these two ranges come their precious minerals; beyond them lie their grandest problems and resources; by the Caspian Sea, the largest inland salt lake in the world, Russia has a natural highway toward the Pacific, as have we by the Missouri, the longest of all rivers, and the Caspian is connected by canal directly with the Baltic, as is the Missouri with the St. Lawrence; and by the Amoor River, which they have navigated at low water for two thousand miles, the Russians have hopes of a better route than the Pacific Railroad's to reach the Pacific Ocean by steam. The Isthmus of Suez, purchased by an enterprising Frenchman, to the surprise and jealousy of Russia and England, and successfully pierced by a canal, reminds and warns us of the impending fate of the Central American Isthmus, which offers Europe the sole remaining and shortest route to the Pacific, and of the late design of France to seize Mexico and Central America also. The latest aspect of European emigration to America, the Scandinavian, and the settlement of large numbers of Swedes and Norwegians about the peninsulas of Michigan, Wisconsin, and Minnesota, show us how remarkably America has become a reproduction of Europe. Not more truly does the blowing seed seek like soil to that of its birthplace, than does every European race find a land like its native land in America.

A paragraph upon the races of Europe and America will indicate another analogy in our Continents: North America has (1860) nearly fifty millions of people, more than three-fifths of whom are in the United States; and Europe has two hundred and eighty millions, nearly one fourth of whom (sixty-seven millions) are in Russia. Of the five great types of man, two are practically absent from our Continent, the Mongol and the Malay, and three are absent from Europe, the American, the African, and the Malay. The great problems of the United States have been the American Indians and the African, — to subdue the one and to fix the status of the other; the great problem of Europe has been to resist and expel the Mongol and his Caucasian kin. For a thousand years the Moor and the Turk have been the insoluble element of Europe, irreconcilable, intractable, incapable of conversion. At times Christendom has united against them; oftener divided its energies against itself. In America we have never had a distinctive war of races or of religions. Until these years in which we write, we have never had upon this Continent a decided and organized heathen element, and we fondly hope that even the Chinese will be made useful and peaceable in the crucible of our tolerant institutions.

There are three great subdivisions of Christian Europeans generally received, whom we shall call, for crispness, Germanes, Sclaves, and Latins. The Germanes make the great bulk of our American population, and they comprehend the offspring of Germans, English, Scandinavians, and Dutch. The Latins are those nations which are derived from the mixture of the ancient Romans with peoples who make the modern nations of Italy, France, Spain, and Portugal; of these we have a small percentage in America blended with us. The last great division of Sclaves is almost entirely absent from America: namely, the Russians, Poles, Moravians, Bohemians, Croats, etc. These latter, situated in the east of Europe, have never felt the great impulse of Western emigration, and Russia is the New World to them, being comparatively sparsely peopled, having vast reserves of land in Asia, and ambitious prospects in Turkey and the Orient. From the Latins, South and Central America have been peopled, by amalgamation with Indians and negroes. It may be broadly said, therefore, that the three great groups of civilization are, 1. The United States, Great Britain, Germany, Scandinavia, and Australia. 2. South and Central America, France, Italy, and Spain. 3. Russia and her dependencies. It is these immense human families, artificially or geographically separated and intermixed, which are contending for dominion. The Latins are practically out of the contest; in South America they are fixed, and busied with their own concerns; in Europe they are poor colonizers, but enterprising adventurers. The Germanes are divided into three vigorous commercial families: 1. The (North) Americans; 2. The English; 3. The true Germans, including the Dutch prospectively. The Russians (4.) are a mighty unit, bearing southward and eastward at once. And the prize of all these four colonizing and commercial powers is the trade of America, Asia, and Polynesia.

In America there are but two promising contestants for trade and influence, the United States and England, Russia having withdrawn from the contest, and France having been beaten off the Continent by American diplomacy and Mexican perseverance. In Southern Asia there are four contestants: England, which possesses the Indian Empire; France, which has seized the most available route overland through the isthmus of Egypt; Holland (or the Netherlands), which possesses Java, Sumatra, Borneo, and other colonies in the Indian Ocean, containing a population of eighteen millions; and Russia, whose empire extends in fact to the Pacific Ocean and in the near future to the Indian Ocean. In the Pacific Ocean these four powers are squarely met by the United States, which, without possessions or the wish for them, has paramount influence in Japan, the favor of China, the friendly countenance of Russia, and good feeling with all the great English colonies planted there. The United States is the only power on the Pacific which has not been guilty of intrigue, of double-dealing, of envy and of bitterness, and it has taken the front rank in influence without awakening the dislike of any of its competitors, possibly excepting those English who are never magnanimous. After years of Portuguese wheedling and Dutch cringing, the Americans stepped in with the cordial manliness of their character, and carried home as guests many Princes and scholars of the Japanese Empire, since which time we have been on frank terms with Japan, and the Japanese are becoming our fellow-citizens in California. After years of English and French cannonading and blustering, marked by the disgraceful imposition of opium upon China, and the occupation of her ports, an American Minister has quietly gained the confidence of the Chinese, and he is teaching the nations how universally captivating are the principles of a republic, and how much better is citizenship than diplomacy to understand and reach the affections of jealously civilized people.

Since the consolidation of the greater part of Germany under the mailed hand of Count Bismarck,* it is not improbable that Holland

* I have perhaps passed over German politics too hastily, and therefore summarize it in a note: —

The reigning houses of Austria and Prussia had honorable origins. Rudolph, of Hapsburg, called to the Kaisership of Germany in the year 1273, for his valor and virtues, founded a line which united with the House of Lorraine, in 1740; the twenty-six sovereigns of these lines have ruled for average terms of twenty-two years. The House of Hohenzollern began with one of Charlemagne's Generals, and was afterward given control of certain Baltic provinces by the Hapsburg Emperors. The three predecessors of Frederick (II.) "the Great" established a standing army and a handsome treasury, with which Frederick, the cotemporary of Washington, increased his kingdom from two and a half millions of people to five and a half millions. By other additions, and by the war of 1866, Prussia became a stronger power than Austria, with nearly twenty-three millions of people.

The rivalry between Austria and Prussia began in Frederick's time. Prussia had Protestant and liberal institutions, and aspired to become the leading state in Germany. Her people were mainly of the German race, while Austria, governing a variety of dissimilar people, and inheriting absolute ideas upon monarchy and religion, grew away from the age and its sympathies. The German republicans, in 1848, mastered both dominions, and offered the crown of consolidated Germany to the King of Prussia, who, had he accepted it, might have anticipated the results of Sadowa by eighteen years, and dispensed and her colonies in the East will become subordinate to the polity of Prussia, and Amsterdam and Rotterdam either yield to Bremen and Hamburg, or become partners with them in the same clear-headed Saxon nationality. Bremen is coming up at present as the German Liverpool, and her great maritime company of the North German Lloyd maintain about a dozen fine steamships in the American trade. The Netherlands Trading Company, with head-quarters at Amsterdam,

with Bismarck. When Austria and Prussia, acting in concert, forced Schleswig and Holstein from Denmark, in 1864–5, their rivalry could no longer smoulder, and they prepared for war. The speedy result was the complete humiliation of Austria, and the advancement of Prussia to the head of all the German peoples. The French people, jealous of Prussia's promotion, were clamorous for war, and a dispute over the little state of Luxembourg seemed likely to produce a rupture, but Napoleon held back, and subsequently Austria conceded liberal institutions to her subjects, rebuffed her reactionary clergy, and granted the Hungarians their ancient privileges, while Prussia greatly improved the material affairs of North Germany; and, by the peace, France also seems about to realize under Napoleon a more liberal charter than she has enjoyed for thirty years. Since Sadowa, and, by reason of the peace which has prevailed on the continent, Spain also has accomplished a tranquil revolution, and expelled the disgraceful woman whose career at her court resembled that of Messalina. Even Denmark, humiliated and reduced, seems happier than before her partition, and in the autumn of 1869 the only agitations in Western Europe seemed to be among the Sclavonic races of Austria, several millions in number, which dislike the German language, laws, and character, and in Italy, which is dissatisfied with the foreign and priestly occupation of Rome. It is remarkable that this liberalization of Europe has not rewarded, but obscured, the careers of those three great pioneers of liberty and nationality; Kossuth, Mazzini, and Garibaldi. Kossuth is still in exile, although Hungary is as far redeemed as the majority of her people seem to wish, and the favorite of the hour is Deak, the moderate leader. A paragraph upon Magyar and Sclave politics may not be out of place. The leading names in Hungary, after Kossuth, are Batthyanyi, Teleki, and Deak. Casimir Batthyanyi belonged to an ancient family, and was made Minister of Foreign Affairs during Kossuth's insurrection; he died in exile; his kinsman, Louis, became the head of the revolutionary government, proved incompetent, and notwithstanding his moderation, the Austrians executed him. After the "pacification" of Hungary, the moderate party of that kingdom was led by Franz Deak, an eloquent lawyer, and the extreme party by Ladislas Teleki. The latter died in 1861, and Deak lived to see the complete triumph of his policy in 1867. The object of Deak was to preserve Hungary as a component of the Austrian Empire, but to retain all its ancient privileges of a separate ministry, all in short that Hungary rebelled to recover in 1848; this would never have been granted but for the reverses of Austria in 1866, when Von Beust, the new Austrian Prime Minister, advised it. At present Transylvania, Crotia, and Sclavonia, non-Hungarian provinces, are united with Hungary against their will, and sit in the Hungarian diet at Pesth. The Sclave population of Austria outnumbers both the German and the Magyar elements, separately; the Sclaves hate the Germans, and they made the Hussite celebration at Prague, in 1869, an occasion of political manifestation. While progress continues to be the rule for the present, it must not still be inferred that Europe is at peace. A hundred little questions perpetually in ebullition, may coalesce and make a mælstrom at any instant. In general terms, it may be said that Norway has now the freest government in Europe, and the Papal States the most illiberal.

has a capital of sixteen millions of dollars, and its shares sell at 149, with annual dividends of ten per cent. Its capital is Batavia, with a population of one hundred and twenty thousand, the emporium of island India, as Hindostan is of mainland India. Singapore is the British rival of Batavia on the Indian islands. Prussia, Holland, Hanover, Bremen, Hamburg, Oldenburg, and North Germany, unitedly possess about six thousand four hundred and sixteen vessels of all sorts, of one million one hundred and seventeen thousand tons altogether. Prussia has never had colonies, but the Dutch are old hands at establishing distant empires, and they are noted as amongst the most unfeeling, tyrannical, and phlegmatic taskmasters in the world. Holland is probably losing rank amongst commercial nations, and can only be electrified by the energy, statesmanship, and resources of Germany. But even thus absorbed she can be no match for the United States, England, and Russia, in controlling the Pacific and Indian seas.

At the southern part of Germany, with her outlet upon the Adriatic, Austria, like Prussia, stands without a colony, yet with no insignificant commerce, and with a naval spirit which availed in 1866 to redeem the disaster of Sadowa, by the victory of Lissa. Austria possessed, in 1864, nine thousand six hundred and forty-three vessels in her commercial marine, of three hundred and thirty-one thousand two hundred and eighty-seven tons, and manned by thirty-seven thousand men. Her Bremen is the city of Trieste, which stands nearly opposite Venice, at the head of the Adriatic, and her naval station is Pola, seventy-five miles further south. Trieste is the head-quarters of a celebrated maritime company, called the Austrian Lloyd, which has a fleet of seventy-four steamers, plying to all parts of the Mediterranean, and competing with the maritime companies of Genoa and Marseilles. The only outlet besides the Adriatic, for Austria, is the Danube River, which gives unreliable and roundabout access to the Black Sea and Western Asia. Two thousand vessels, of eight hundred thousand tons, of all nations, navigated the Danube, in 1860. The Turks had undisputed possession of the Black Sea (which is about twice the size of Lake Superior) until the beginning of the American Revolution, when Russia obtained the privilege of trading in it. Since that day, the Russian, like the American eagle, has crossed the continent, and drawn near the tropics. The Danube Steam Navigation Company, of Vienna, advertised, in 1869, that it possessed one hundred and forty light draught steamships.

Austria can probably never become a great naval power, unless by some good fortune she could reanimate and conciliate the Italians, who owe her so long and so remorseless misery. Italy has one hundred and sixty thousand superior sailors, and Greece has twenty-five thousand admirable watermen. The prostrate condition of Italy, and the cramped and unprofitable state of Greece, are the results of the short-sighted and greedful policy of what has been called, for a century, the "statesmanship" of the Great Powers. Afraid to give Greece a republic, and to accord her space commensurate with her spirit, they have fastened to her destinies, now a crowned beer-drinker, and now a mere lad of a decayed house, subjected Christian Crete to massacre, and kept in pinafores the countrymen of Ypsilanti and Bozzaris. Their alliances have been with Haynau and Hapsburg, instead of Garibaldi and Cavour, and at the end, behold! Italy regenerated, but in rags; the Russia they were at such pains to summon against the march of republican France, grown aware of its power, and threatening to devour them; and the Austria, with which their holy alliances were made, which had a monarch ready for every dilemma, and a groom for every princess, smitten one blow by the stripling Prussia of yesterday, has tumbled into a heap of old purple clothes, and pawnbrokers' tickets. The sympathies of the American people are with Greece and Italy, but with the fate of the provinces of Austria the same statesmanship must deal which first violently flung them together. Common sense would seem to indicate that the first step would be for the German part of Austria to join the North German confederation; the second, for the Hapsburgs to retire upon their laurels,—Mexico, Sadowa, Pesth, — and lastly to make Hungary a new state, with such neighbors as will share her fortunes, and quietly permit her and Greece to consume as much of Turkey as will agree with them; the residue, being Italian, will fall by gravity to the Kingdom of Italy.

As we approach Russia, going eastward, we feel a similar sensation to that with which we pass the River Mississippi, and enter upon the broad plains of the United States. Behind us, on either hand, are Berlin and Vienna, the last great cities of elderly Europe, like Chicago and St. Louis. Before us, wider apart, on the verge of this mighty empire, are Warsaw and Pesth, which, like our battle-fields where perished two rude but gallant Indian tribes recall their names as we pass through, — Poland, the land of Kosciusko; Hungary, the land of Kossuth. Pesth is one hundred and seventy-one miles east of Vienna, and possesses one hundred and thirty thousand people. Warsaw is three hundred miles east of Berlin, and contains two hundred and forty thousand people.

We have crossed the frontier of Russia, and spread before us to the Pacific Ocean, to the Arctic Sea, to the streams which flow into the Indian Ocean, the domain of Russia lies, — in round numbers, eight millions of square miles. Before us is Kiev, perhaps the future capital of Russia, on the latitude of Brussels, Newfoundland, and Vancouver. Due north of Kiev, six hundred and fifty miles, is St. Petersburg, the present capital, on the latitude of Greenland, and Mt. St. Elias, Russian America. Due south of Kiev, two hundred and fifty miles, is Odessa, the great grain port of Russia, on the latitude of Switzerland, Quebec, and Portland, Oregon. Due east of Odessa, eight hundred miles, is Astrachan, on the Caspian Sea, twelve hundred miles south-east of St. Petersburg, and on the air line between these two latter cities stands Moscow, four hundred miles from the capital. East of Moscow, two hundred and fifty miles, is Niznii Novgorod; west of Moscow, five hundred miles, is Riga. These seven cities are, in present or future importance, the most considerable of Russia. Moscow was the old capital, and is at present the main manufacturing city of Russia, — its Philadelphia, with four hundred thousand people. It is very nearly at the centre of Russia, near the sources of its river systems, and at the junction of its railway system, and besides its industrial and historical attractions it is the seat of Russia's greatest university. Niznii or Nijnii (lower) Novgorod is the seat of an immense intercontinental fair, held for a month every summer, during which the population of forty thousand rises to two hundred thousand; every great nation being represented in it, from America to China. The mighty River Volga, the largest in Europe, flowing past Novgorod, and close by Moscow, reaches from near St. Petersburg to Astrachan, twenty-three hundred miles. Astrachan is the Omaha of Russia, with forty thousand people; it stands on the delta of the Volga, and receives from Persia, on the opposite shore of the Caspian Sea, silks, precious drugs, and the manifold products of the East. Kiev, on the Dnieper River, is admirably situated for a political capital to control the politics of Turkey, Poland, and Hungary together, and it contains about one hundred thousand people. It is the city where Christianity was first proclaimed in Russia; has a university and a sanctuary, and is altogether better adapted for an influential capital city than St. Petersburg. Riga is on the River Dwina, five miles from the Gulf of Riga, and three hundred and seventy-six miles on the way to middle Europe, from St. Petersburg; it is a sort of Baltic Quebec, with one railroad, like the Grand Trunk, and its exports, amounting to twenty million dollars, go chiefly to England; they consist of flax, hemp, linseed, corn, timber, tallow, and tobacco. It is a dingy, gloomy town, cold and unbeloved. Odessa has one hundred and twenty thousand people, mainly Jews, Greeks, and Italians. It is a free port, and owes its prosperity largely to a French nobleman, the Duc de Richelieu, who was expelled from France in the Revolution, and made Governor here by the Czar Alexander; but the town is older than the Christian era, and it is now the third commercial city of Russia, outranked only by St. Petersburg and Riga. The English nearly destroyed its fleet in 1854, and shot Richelieu. The city, itself, like Chicago, has poor river communication with the interior, and but two railways, one still incomplete. The surrounding soil is arid and poor; building stone lies close by, out of which many handsome edifices have been constructed, and, like Chicago in former days, Odessa has exceedingly poor water; the former city stands on a prairie, while Odessa is upon a cliff, and its harbor is better than that of Chicago, being very deep, seldom frozen, and capable of holding two hundred vessels. The roads around and in Odessa are almost impassable in muddy weather, and the thermometer frequently rises there in summer to 120°. The city exports about twenty million bushels of wheat a year, and this comprises half its entire exports, which are valued at thirty million dollars annually, or two-thirds more than its imports. America sends thirty-one per cent. of all the wheat imported into the English United Kingdom, and Canada seven per cent.; Germany and Russia together send about as much as all America combined. The growth of Odessa bears no proportion to that of our great Western cities, and as an example of the latter we may cite Chicago, the Odessa of the North-west.

Chicago is now the most extensive grain and lumber market in the world. In 1838 the first shipment of wheat consisted of seventy-eight bushels; in 1862 there were exported in flour and grain of all kinds from the port fifty-six million four hundred and eighty-four thousand one hundred and ten bushels. During the year there were shipped one million eight hundred and twenty-eight thousand one hundred and sixty-four barrels of flour. In 1863, one million five hundred and thirty-seven thousand eight hundred and sixteen barrels of flour, or flour and grain of all kinds equal to about fifty-five million bushels.

The receipts of lumber in Chicago in 1865 were six hundred and six million six hundred and forty-two thousand three hundred feet; shingles, three hundred and four million two hundred and sixteen thousand; lath, sixty million three hundred and forty thousand; sent by lake and railroad transportation to all points in Illinois, to Indiana, Ohio, New York, and westward to Iowa, Missouri, Dakota, Nebraska, Kansas, and the lower Mississippi. The trade in staves, railroad ties, telegraph posts, fence posts, and other similar materials, is very extensive, and the amount of capital invested in the lumber traffic immense.

Chicago city holds an equally leading position in the pork and beef trade of the West, and next to New York is the greatest cattle market in the United States. The trade is also very extensive in salt, lead, hides, tallow, the products of the dairy, orchards, in distilled spirits, and other articles. The lake tonnage of the port, in 1864, was two million one hundred and seventy-two thousand eight hundred and sixty-six tons in arrivals, and two million one hundred and sixty-six thousand nine hundred and four in clearances, and during the season eight thousand nine hundred and thirty-nine vessels and propellers arrived, and eight thousand eight hundred and twenty-four cleared, — the tonnage engaged wholly in the Chicago trade amounting to one hundred and ninety-eight thousand and five.

The cost of buildings erected in the city, in 1865, was seven million five hundred and ten thousand dollars, and the number in 1866 was nine thousand.

The wholesale dry goods business forms a large interest, the sales having reached thirty-five million dollars a year, and the trade in boots, shoes, and clothing, twenty-five million dollars. The neighborhood of Chicago is fruitful of large and vigorous municipalities. Springfield, the capital, near the geographical centre, in the rich and beautiful valley of the Sangamon, is one of the handsomest cities in the West, and rapidly increasing in population, wealth, and refinement. Galena, Aurora, Quincy, and Alton on the Mississippi; Cairo at the mouth of the Ohio, and Peoria on the Illinois, are enterprising and growing cities.

The educational interests of the State are in a most flourishing condition, nine thousand seven hundred and fifty-three school-houses having been reported on 30th September, 1866, with six hundred and fourteen thousand six hundred and fifty-nine pupils, and over seventeen thousand two hundred teachers; the revenue for the year ending 30th September, 1866, in support of the school interest, amounting to four million four hundred and forty-five thousand one hundred and thirty dollars.

In 1860, there were in the State eighteen colleges, two thousand nine hundred students, and an income of ninety-seven thousand four hundred and twelve dollars; two hundred and eleven academies with thirteen thousand two hundred and five pupils, and an income of two hundred and thirty-three thousand two hundred and sixty-two dollars.

There were at the same time eight hundred and fifty-four libraries, two hundred and forty-six of which were public; two hundred and forty-three for schools; three hundred and thirty-nine for Sunday-schools; seven college and nineteen church libraries; with a total of two hundred and forty-four thousand three hundred and ninety-four volumes.

The finances of the State of Illinois are in a very encouraging condition, and the debt contracted in the construction of its extensive railroad lines is being speedily reduced by annual payment of the interest and gradual liquidation of the principal.

St. Petersburg, in its origin, reminds one of Washington City, and while it has grown to be one of the most magnificent cities in the world, it is bleak, expensive, unloved, and a perpetual sacrifice to the great interests of the empire. As Washington was selected for our capital in deference to General Washington, St. Petersburg was made the capital of Russia by the direct order of Peter the Great, the Russian Washington. Peter, who died seven years before the birth of Washington, inherited a cramped empire, at war with the Poles, the Tartars, the Turks, and the Swedes; but he had the advantage of a homogeneous race for his subjects, and his state, like England, Sicily, and France, owed its original vigor to an infusion of Normans. He was an intellectual savage, of fierce appetites and boundless aspirations, and he modelled his empire upon the dictates of his personal will, without regarding the natural or national bent of his people. Engaged at that period in war with the disciplined Swedes, Peter founded his capital upon Swedish soil, and proceeded to conquer his way to the coasts of the Baltic, the Black, and the Caspian Seas. He visited civilized lands and imported their arts, their artists, and their disciplinarians, and he had himself been in part the creation of German, Genevese, and Scotch adventurers. He married his Swedish mistress, executed his own son, became a ship carpenter in Holland, was made a Doctor of Laws by Oxford University, and died drunk. The Russians are, like himself, a savage people, ardent for acquisitions, mental and material, and deriving them from the more polished world, but revealing the seams of these enforced additions, — a people whose destinies have grown too fast for their education, and who behold themselves masters of a seventh part of the globe, and yet have created nothing and discovered nothing; but who borrow on the left hand the appliances of civilization to subjugate barbarism on the right hand. Their dynasty is German, and in crimes, in acquisitiveness, in cold, calculating, unfeeling, mathematical ability, it may be considered the extreme development of Teutonic statesmanship; the people are Sclaves, and their obedience bears out the derivation of their name; their civilization, as far as it goes, is Latin, at court French, in trade Greek and Jewish, in commerce Italian. But all the elements of civilization are uneasily at work in Russia, — a literature, a democracy, an opposition party on every question, — and it may prove that with so much cleared from her path by the foresight and ferocious energy of her Czars, Russia is to realize within her boundaries a lustrous civilization, when Western Europe has passed to languor and decay.

The wife of Peter the Great died intoxicated, like himself, and the successor, Catharine II., who paved the way for Russia to oppose the French Revolution, was an infamous woman of ability, successful in her favorites. Paul, who followed her, hated England and its policy in Europe, and was strangled by his family; and Alexander, the subjugator of Napoleon, became afterward a religious fanatic, and an enemy of popular progress everywhere. Nicholas was a surly tyrant, who discovered in his war with the Western powers, that Europe was not endowed with the weak heart of Asia, and when France, England, and Italy invaded Russia on the South, the mighty empire proved to be almost bankrupt in purse, and its seat of danger perilously remote from its seat of power. The present Emperor, of a more cheerful heart, has made his reign beneficent by abolishing serfdom, and by happy coincidence, at nearly the same time that slavery ceased in America, twenty-two millions of bondmen recovered their freedom in Russia; soon afterward, the Dutch emancipated throughout their dominions, and except in Spanish and Portuguese colonies, and

Brazil, slavery perished amongst the Christian nations of the earth. St. Petersburg is scarcely older than Pittsburg or Cincinnati, and occupies amongst cities of modern growth a place half-way between New York and Chicago. It has about the population of Philadelphia, is about the same distance from its seaport, Cronstadt, as New York from the ocean, covers forty-two square miles, is fifty-six feet aobve the sea, and contains sixty-four public squares, and five hundred streets. It is like Chicago in its temporary bridges of piles, is intersected with a river and water courses, built upon a marsh, and while the thermometer varies between 99° and —51°, the ice in the river Neva is frequently a yard and a half thick! There are many enormous things in St. Petersburg, — a street of palaces one hundred and thirty feet wide and four miles long, a palace seven hundred feet square, which, when full, in the court season, contains six thousand inhabitants, a library of four hundred and fifty thousand volumes, immense government factories of bronzes, mirrors, tapestry, porcelain, playing cards, — for Russia is a high-tariff country, where every domestic industry is "protected," — and a freshet every year; but the magnificent city is gray, sombre, cold, dreary, — a metropolitan Sitka, — and it is very far removed from the great destinies of Russia, so that not improbably, the capital of Peter the Great will one day be left to its own resources, and Kiev become the ruling place.

Within the Russian Empire the disaffected party at present is the nobility, which seems to perceive that the present drift of polity there is to raise the common standard of citizenship by education and reward, and quietly soften all distinctions between the autocrat and the populace; but so stupendous are the projects of Russia, and her energy in developing them, so uniform is her success, and so much wider than any internal dissensions are her exterior interests, that there can scarcely be said to be any disaffected organization in Russia. The struggle of the empire is to get a solid footing on the sea. And at present Russia is using every power to conquer her way to the Indian Ocean, where Western Europe and particularly England, have everything to fear from her advent. To be a great empire she must abut upon the temperate seas; for at present she is in the plight of Canada, frozen up on the east and the west all winter long, and the inland waters to the south of her are held by her rivals. In past times Russia was one of the great highways between India and Europe; the traffic which afterward took the routes of Venice, Constantinople, Egypt, or the Cape of Good Hope, once climbed the Volga and sought the outlet of the Baltic. To recover the trade of the East, the precious commerce in gold, gems, spices, drugs, coffee, cotton, and fabrics of fine wool and silk, — Russia is resolved to become a commercial power on the Indian and Pacific Oceans, and here she becomes a party to the great "Eastern Question."

The United States now possesses two lines of communication with the Pacific Ocean, the Panama Railroad and the Pacific Railroad, and these are the only avenues yet open on our continent; the Panama Railroad was finished in 1855, and it is forty miles long.* The Isthmus of Suez furnishes, at present, the only rival steam communication between Europe and the Pacific, and the Suez Railroad was opened in 1858. Two years previously, one M. de Lesseps, a Frenchman, planned and obtained a charter for a ship canal through the isthmus, and the same year which witnessed the opening of the Pacific Railroad recited the triumph of this canal, which had been at the beginning pronounced impracticable by George Stephenson, the English engineer, and regarded to the last by English writers and politicians with jealousy and mortification. Its total cost was about eighty millions of dollars. Its success seems to have been complete, and it will probably be considered the most extraordinary monument of the reign of Napoleon III., replacing as it does the canals of Pharaoh, Trajan, and Amrou.

Having denounced the Suez Canal as visionary and unprofitable, no sooner is it done than the English are crying aloud for a highway of their own to India, and this they propose to secure by a railroad from Constantinople to the Euphrates River, thence connecting with steamers to Kurrachee or to Bombay; they now remember bitterly how they called the Pacific Railroad in 1858 a "speculator's dream;" yet the latter road, five hundred miles longer than their long contemplated one, is as accomplished as the English character, while India and England are united only by telegraph poles, and by the permission of the French canal-makers. The proposed Euphrates route would revive long-decayed cities of antiquity, and would drain the rich regions of Persia, Arabia, and Asia Minor; it is to the interests of civilization to see it opened up, but France and Russia would make

* In 1695 the Scotch organized a Darien Company to occupy and control the Isthmus of Panama. Four millions and a half of dollars were subscribed, and twenty-five hundred men actually founded on the isthmus the "city" of New Edinburgh. They were opposed by a bigoted home government, deserted by the American colonies of England, and finally driven off by the Spanish.

of its concession by Turkey a political affront, and either threaten or bribe the Sultan to refuse it. Russia, meantime, has also projected a route to the Indian Ocean from the head of the Caspian Sea, to pass through Persia; for Persia is as dependent upon Russia for existence as is Turkey upon England, while Egypt is allied with France. And this is the great "Eastern Question," of which we hear so much: Shall England, France, or Russia, or any two of them, become paramount in the politics of Egypt, Persia and Turkey, so as to control the highways and trade of the East?

So far as Persia is concerned, the nearest great neighbor of British India, this precedence is already settled: Russia by a series of wars, lasting nearly forty years, and by subsequent intrigue at the Persian Court has completely succeeded in making Persia her creature. The Shah surrenders deserters from the Russian army, and permits the building of Russian ships-of-war in his ports of Resht and Astrabad. Persia is a despotism, corrupt like Egypt and Turkey, with a population of ten millions and an army of one hundred and twenty thousand men, thirty thousand of whom are cavalry equal to the Russian Cossacks. Between Persia and India stands only the dreary waste of Afghanistan to protect British India from the Russian, and the fortified town of Herat, near the Persian border, is the only considerable bulwark that the English have against Russia. The latter power is constantly inciting her vassal, Persia, to capture this place. The most amusing thing in Teheran, the capital of Persia, is to see amongst the mud residences of its one hundred thousand people the big advertising palaces of the Russian and the English ambassador, each striving to outwit, or outbid, or outthreaten the other. At present, the British believe that by eight years of inglorious warfare they have impressed themselves upon the resolute Afghans; but Mr. Dilke, an English traveller, showed the hollowness of this assurance in 1867; for the Afghans are mere dependents of Persia, and Persia is the vassal of Russia. In 1866 the Russians occupied much of Turkestan, the region north of Herat, and at the present writing they are probably not more than two hundred miles from Peshawur, the most northwesterly British outpost. Able to meet the English in front with Persians, Afghans, and Cossacks, and to stir up a Mohammedan mutiny in their rear, the perilous days of British India seem to have come. And if, as diplomatic rumor runs, the French in Egypt, and the Russians in Persia, are ready to act in concert at the proper time, it is hard to say what defensive course the British can adopt. They have been hitherto unable to obtain a practicable concession of the Euphrates route, owing, it is supposed to the influence of French Egypt upon Turkey.

Egypt is nominally an hereditary Viceroyalty of Turkey, its reigning family being descended from Mehemet Ali, a Turkish general; but it is really more powerful than Turkey itself, having an army arranged and drilled by European tactics, and a navy of seventy-three vessels of war and transports. Its population is about five millions, and its chief cities, Cairo and Alexandria, contain, respectively, two hundred and fifty thousand and one hundred thousand inhabitants. France has loaned Egypt about forty millions of dollars; and the Egyptian army is largely officered by French emissaries and adventurers. Turkey nominally controls thirty-five millions of people, but only two-thirds of these are, in any sense, Mohammedans, and there are so many mutinous Christians of the Russian church, and independent princes, and heterogenous tribes, that Turkey is in reality one of the weakest, most impoverished, and least effective states in the world. With a nominal army of one hundred and forty-eight thousand men, and three hundred thousand reserves, and with a navy of about forty wooden steamers and iron-clads, Turkey was obliged to seek the assistance of Egypt to suppress the Cretan revolt of 1868. Her finances stand lowest in Europe. The English have built her ships, and guaranteed her loans, but she has even greater obligations to Egypt, for the Egyptian tribute is all-essential to her, and Egypt, backed by either of the Great Powers, could speedily rise to opulence and power on the ruins of Turkey. The English have abundant reason to fear that notwithstanding the alliance of the Crimean war, France and Russia mean to work in harmony, and leave England out "in the cold." Russia and France are commercially weaker than England; their objects and routes do not conflict with each other, but both conflict with England. They are both interested in seeing her defeated in opening the Euphrates railway, and they can work upon her through Turkey's obligations to Egypt. Many Englishmen are urging that the concession of this route be forced from Turkey; but a step so bold would probably lead to general warfare amongst the three great Jesuits and expose their double dealing.

The study of this Eastern Question is complicated by a great schism between the orthodox and dissenting Mohammedans (Sonnites and Shiites), who hate each other as fiercely as Greek and Catholic Christians; the Persians and Afghans are dissenters; the Turks, Egyptians, and Hindostans, are orthodox. Amongst them all, the military prowess of Russia is irresistible.

"The vast experience of the Russians in wars, conducted alike upon the grandest and the most limited scale, — at one time carried on by great masses on the level and unobstructed plains of Europe, at another, by small detachments in the rugged mountains of Caucasus and Asia Minor, or on the frontiers of Tartary and China; the great perfection to which military science has been carried in her schools and special corps; the intelligence, skill, and courage they have so often evinced, both in attack and defence," * — all these considerations render probable what proportions a campaign between Western Europe and Russia would assume on the plains of Asia. England has grown well weary of contemplating a struggle of this magnitude, and her pacific attitude of late years has made the nations of the continent believe that she is anxious to retire from the field of European politics. An English authority, citing this superstition, thus quotes it and comments upon it: —

"'If I were an Abyssinian, or a Hindoo, or even an American,' says the Frenchman, 'I might, perhaps, care what England thinks; but being a European I do not.' A power that does not fight is no longer a power. She may still be summoned to European Congresses, — so is Turkey. Her envoys may be listened to with an affectation of respect, — so was the envoy of Greece. But the moment will come when each country of Europe has to support its counsel with the sword. France will throw hers into one scale, Prussia hers in another, and on one side or the other Russia will fling hers, and probably Austria hers, and even Italy hers. But England! England knows, and Europe knows, that in that supreme moment the power which used to subsidize one-half the continent, and fight the other, must abandon the place which she has ceased to be able to maintain by force. She must renounce her political authority, and shelter herself behind an impotent neutrality. There are men in both parties like Mr. Bright, and Lord Stanley, who look forward contentedly to such an hour; but the mass of Englishmen do not. They do not want to resume the old system of perpetual interference, but they want to be free to declare war, when interest or honor bid them."

The extent of the jealousy of the English toward the Russians can be understood from Mr. Dilke's way of stating the Eastern

* General George B. McClellan.

Question. "Drunken, dirty, ignorant, and corrupt, the Russian people are no fit rulers for Hindostan. A barbarous horde, ruled by a German Emperor and ministry, who are as little able to suppress degrading drunkenness and shameless venality, as they are themselves desirous of promoting true enlightenment and education. Russia must be beaten. A country that was fifty years conquering the Caucasus, and that could never place a disposable force of sixty thousand men in the Crimea, need give no fear to India, while her grandest offensive efforts would be ridiculed by America, or by the England of to-day."

Thus does the same gentle author refer to the Suez Canal, and his French fellow-christians: —

"It is evident enough that the Suez Canal scheme has been from the beginning a blind for the occupation of Egypt by France, and that, however interesting to the shareholders may be the question of its physical or commercial success, the probabilities of failure have had but little weight with the French government. The foundation of the Messagerie Company with national capital, to carry imaginary mails, secured the preponderance of French influence in the towns of Egypt.

"The English railway-guards have lately been dismissed from the government railway line, and a huge tricolor floats from the entrance to the new docks at Suez, while a still more gigantic one waves over the hotel; the King of Egypt, glad to find a third power which he can play off, when necessary, against both England and Russia, takes shares in the canal. It is when we ask, 'What is the end that the French have in view?' that we find it strangely small by the side of the means. The French of the present day appear to have no foreign policy, unless it is a sort of desire to extend the empire of their language, their dance-tunes, and their fashions; and the natural wish of their ruler to engage in no enterprise that will outlast his life prevents their having any such permanent policy as that of Russia or the United States. An Egyptian Pacha hardly put the truth too strongly when he said, 'There is nothing permanent about France except Mabile.'"

We may now profitably open the inquiry, What is the Pacific Ocean, and why do the nations struggle for supremacy in it? The venerable and vigorous Atlantic Ocean, on which Christian civilization first spread its sails, has been for nearly four hundred years the greatest of the world's highways. Columbus had crossed it twenty-one years before the Pacific was ploughed by Magellan; it has borne over the seventy millions of men who people North and South America, and yet to the newer ocean of the Pacific it is only a larger sort of strait, as narrow, between Brazil and Africa, as sixteen hundred miles, and at the widest only a fifth part of the earth's circumference. The Pacific, on which we are to try our fortunes, is at its greatest, — on the latitude of the Isthmus of Panama, — ten thousand and five hundred miles wide, and its area comprises two-fifths of the surface of the globe. The Pacific is in shape almost like a diamond, with the corner toward South America missing. The north-east side of the diamond is North America, the north-west side is Asia, the south-west side is the archipelago of the East Indies and Australia and New Zealand. Across the widest diameter, due west from Panama, is the riven isthmus of Malacca, through which the traders of Europe have been wont to sail on their way to China. Close to the centre of this ocean are the Sandwich Islands, where American influence has long been paramount. Due west of the United States is Japan; on the latitude of Mexico is China; on the latitude of Central America is Cochin China; the East India Islands are on the line of Peru; Australia and New Zealand are on the latitude of Chili. Yeddo is nearly west of San Francisco, Pekin of Salt Lake City, Hong Kong of Havana, Manilla of Acapulco, Batavia of Pernambuco, Sydney of Valparaiso, and Melbourne of Concepcion.

The American channel of the Pacific is nearly clear of islands, but they abound toward Southern Asia and Australia. New Zealand, the most isolated of all the great islands of the South Pacific, is almost equidistant from Hindostan and South Patagonia, and is as neighborly to the Southern polar Continent as to Australia, its British kinsman. Sailing due west from San Francisco, we reach *Japan;* the nearest mainland is *China;* descending the Chinese coast we come to *Cochin China;* beyond is *Malacca*, which turning, we enter the Indian Ocean, and reach *Hindostan;* off China in the Pacific lie the *Philippines* and numberless islands; off Malacca are the mighty series of great islands, — the Great Antilles of the East, — *Sumatra*, *Java*, *Borneo*, *New Guinea*, and *Australia*, and at last *New Zealand*, standing sheerly off in the South Pacific. The struggle in Christendom, at present, is that which agitated the world before the discovery of America,— to possess this East. Let us, therefore, pass in crisp review the above several groups of land.

Japan has an executive presumptive, educated in France. At its head is the Mikado, the divine Emperor, and the Tycoon, the hereditary Executive; the government is a sort of heathen England, with an immense aristocracy of Princes or *Daimios*, some of whom have revenues of four million dollars a year. The Japanese are the ablest nation of Asiatics; they number almost as many people as the Americans, and their country is as large as all our Middle States. The Americans are the most popular foreigners in the empire, and have every reason to anticipate that the present intimate and profitable relations with Japan will grow closer and vaster every year.

China is an absolute patriarchal government, deriving its religious traditions, like Japan, from the philosopher and school-teacher, Confucius. The population is said to be four hundred millions, the area one million three hundred square miles, and British influence is paramount in Chinese commerce. The products of Japan and China are much of the same sort: tea, tobacco, silk, and manufactured articles of steel, staples, and wood. At the most eligible part of the Chinese coast the British have an independent colony, Hong Kong.

Hong Kong, the British "factory" in China, was ceded to Great Britain in 1841, and had a population in 1865 of one hundred and twenty-five thousand, two thousand of whom were Europeans; it is an island, lying close under the China coast, of twenty-nine square miles' surface.

Cochin China, where the French have played the same avaricious and unscrupulous part as the British in China, is a peninsula, south of China, and is said to contain thirty millions of people; it is in products and civilization much like China.

The Philippine Islands, opposite Cochin China, are twelve hundred in number, comprising one hundred and fifty thousand square miles of land, and inhabited by five millions of people. They are therefore as large as the six middle States of the United States, and two-thirds more populous than all New England. Spain partly holds the Philippine Islands in subjection. Manilla, the capital, has one hundred and fifty thousand inhabitants, twenty thousand of whom are cheroot makers. The people are industrious, and many Chinese — the Anglo-Saxons of the East — are mixed with them. The revenue of these islands amounts to eleven millions of dollars annually, and the chief exports are sugar, tobacco, cigars, hemp, coffee, rice, dyewoods, gold-dust, beeswax, and all tropical fruits. Americans and English divide the business of these islands, the former growing more formidable every year. The Philippine Islands are nearer to New York by San Francisco than to London by Suez. Papua, or New Guinea, between the Philippine Islands and Australia, is the second island on the globe in greatness of dimensions, and is alternately mountain and swamp; it is twelve hundred miles long and three hundred wide, contains eight hundred thousand natives, and is claimed by the Dutch; but its deadly climate has not encouraged foreign occupation, and its exports of ebony, pearls, spices, slaves, etc., go chiefly to the neighboring islands.

Malacca, the most southerly tip of Asia, whose cape is nearly midway between British Calcutta and British Hong Kong, and is the half-way place between London and San Francisco by canal and sea, is a British colony forty by twenty-five miles in dimensions, with sixty thousand inhabitants, and productive of little, although fertile. Sumatra, separated by a navigable strait from the Malacca mainland, is a Dutch colony, with an area of one hundred and sixty-eight thousand square miles and seven millions of people, only two thousand of whom are Europeans; it illustrates the prolific vegetation and animal life of the East Indies, and its great staples are rice, coffee, oil, ivory, drugs, india-rubber, spices, and tobacco. At the southern end of Sumatra, separated by a strait, is Java, which extends to the neighborhood of Australia, and contains more people than all our middle States, one hundred and eighty thousand of whom are Europeans, Chinese, and Arabians. It is the greatest Dutch possession, and in thirty years has sent to Holland one hundred and thirty million dollars. North of Java is Borneo, the third island in size in the world, or as large as Virginia, North Carolina, Tennessee, Kentucky, Missouri and Arkansas together, yet with only two million five hundred thousand people. It has been but little explored, is unhealthy and very productive, contains all the precious metals and gems, has two hundred and fifty thousand Chinese, and is ruled jointly by Dutch, British, and natives.

Australia is the Pacific coast of England, — her California, Nevada, Utah, and New Mexico, — the only one of her colonies which has bounded, like states of the American nation, from desolation to opulence. Australia is half as large as all South America. There are seven colonies in it, numbering unitedly (1862) one million three hundred and thirty-six thousand one hundred and thirty-one people. The Pacific States of America numbered at the same time about eight hundred thousand, but even at that time Australia's ratio of increase showed decline, while the American Pacific region was growing with undiminished vigor. Victoria, the most flourishing colony of Australia, contained five hundred and seventy-four thousand people to California's three hundred and eighty thousand, and Melbourne, its capital, had one hundred and thirty-nine thousand nine hundred and sixteen inhabitants to San Francisco's one hundred and three thousand; three thousand and twenty-three vessels of nine hundred and ninety-five thousand and eighty-two tons entered and cleared from Melbourne in 1861, and three thousand eight hundred and seventy vessels of one million three hundred and forty-two thousand two hundred and ninety tons entered and cleared from San Francisco in 1863.

Sydney, the second city of Australia, contains ninety-four thousand people, and has a university building five hundred feet long; its bay is the best in Australia, and it may be called the Portland (Oregon) of the British Pacific coast.

Australia has reached its present importance by the discovery of gold, by the gratuitous shipment of British people to it, which still continues, and by the influx of Germans and Chinese. But its resources and promise are not to be compared with the American Pacific; it is a narrow reef of fertile land, enclosing an immense desert, so terrible that it has been proposed to pierce the reef and admit the ocean; it has no good harbors, and dangerous coasts; at one stretch for seven hundred coast miles not a drop of fresh water flows into the sea; deluge and drouth alternate, so that once at Sydney it did not rain for thirteen months in 1838–9; at a later period travellers found in a dry river-bed the footmarks of people who had ascended it three years before to perish, and within the past three years one exploring party to the great interior desert, died of thirst with their camels, while a second party, sent after them, was nearly drowned by a flood. The rivers of Australia are unreliable; it has contributed no plant to agriculture, and its waters contain few fish. Its staple is wool, and it contains an immense number of merino sheep, but frequently thousands of these die of thirst or by the parching of the grass. Gold, coal, iron, and the metals distinguish Australia like California, though in less abundance, and the American possessions have, in addition, the richest quicksilver mines in the world, magnificent timber forests, splendid rivers, and the fruits of all pleasant lands.

There are but four hundred miles of railway in all Australia, — far less than the amount possessed by the infant State of Wisconsin.

The sums spent upon the Victorian lines have deterred the colonists from completing their railway system; £10,000,000 sterling were spent upon two hundred miles of road, through easy country in which the land cost nothing. The United States have made nearly forty thousand miles of railroad, for less than £300,000,000 sterling; Canada made her two thousand miles for £20,000,000, or ten times as much railroad as Victoria for only twice the money. Cuba has already more miles of railroad than all Australia.

New Zealand is six thousand five hundred miles due west of South America, and twelve hundred miles south-east of Australia; it consists of three islands with a total area of ninety-five thousand square miles, one hundred and seventy-five thousand white inhabitants (three-fifths males), and forty thousand fierce savages, who keep constantly employed seventeen thousand British troops. New Zealand was settled by English and American whalers, who went ashore for shelter and provisions, and courted the native women; the British took formal possession in 1840. New Zealand is a more available colony for commercial uses than Australia, having good harbors and lands, water power, pleasant climate, and various cereals and fruits, the whole set in most noble sceneries, with mountains that reach the height of fourteen thousand feet. New Zealand is almost as large as Great Britain and Ireland, and it hopes to be the British island of the Southern Zone. Hokotika, its chief town, had, in 1866, ten thousand people, having grown more rapidly than San Francisco; gold was the magnet that drew the people to New Zealand.

Now let us see what natural advantages America has to trade with the above regions.

From London to Melbourne, Australia, via the Suez canal, is three thousand three hundred and seventy-nine miles further than from San Francisco to Melbourne, and three hundred and seventy-nine miles further than from New York by the Pacific Railroad. Yokohama, Japan, is six thousand nine hundred and eighty-four miles nearer San Francisco than London; Shanghai, China, four thousand nine hundred and fourteen miles nearer; British Hong Kong, three thousand three hundred and fourteen miles nearer; Manilla, three thousand five hundred and four miles nearer; and even British Singapore is four hundred and fifty-four miles nearer San Francisco than London. London, however, by Suez, is one thousand seven hundred and nineteen miles nearer Calcutta than is San Francisco. If war should ever close the Suez canal to England, Calcutta will be four thousand eight hundred miles further from London than above, and Melbourne's distance will be increased three thousand miles.

The part of our country that must directly compete for the trade of the East, is the States of the Pacific.

The Pacific slope of the United States is one thousand miles long, and six hundred and eighty miles wide, with a shore line of two thousand two hundred and eighty-one miles, and two harbors which are scarcely surpassed on the globe. It has produced, since 1848, eleven hundred millions of dollars in gold, and its agricultural capacity is equal to the support of one hundred millions of inhabitants.

What has the East to reward us for commercial enterprise? The soil of the Indies and of Southern Asia is characterized by a highly developed force, pervading vegetation, by which an abundance of aromatic and balsamic juices is yielded; it is marked by a gorgeous vegetable and animal life, and the precious gems and metals are no less distinctive of its soil, than are the labor, the patience, and the ingenuity of its people. By looking over the commerce of the United States at the latest reports, we shall see that the products of the East are the chief objects of expenditure with us.

Out of our total imports (one hundred and thirty-seven millions dollars) of 1869, the principal articles were, sugars seventy-three millions, coffee twenty-five millions, iron and steel goods twenty-one millions, silk goods eighteen millions, dress goods fifteen millions, tea eleven millions, linen goods ten millions, flax above ten millions, hides ten millions, *wood* seven and one-half millions. The chief articles of export, out of a total export of three hundred and forty-four millions, were cotton one hundred and sixty-two and one-half millions, petroleum thirty millions, tobacco twenty-five millions, wheat twenty-four millions, flour nineteen millions, lumber nine millions, lard nine millions. The imports exceeded the exports by ninety-three millions; the duties on the imports were one hundred and fifty millions; one half upon tea, coffee, sugar and molasses; and eighteen thousand eight hundred and seventy-five foreign vessels were engaged in the whole trade above represented, to nine thousand nine hundred and seventy-four American vessels. The East is in want of just those things which we possess, and the basis of reciprocal trade is laid in nature. To show the prolific vegetation of the East it only needs to be remembered that, by the necessities of the American war, India cotton increased in amount from twenty-five million dollars in 1859, to one hundred and ninety million dollars in 1864, and the population of the city of Bombay rose from four hundred thousand to one million.

Southern Asia and the East India Islands produce about six millions dollars of gold annually; Australian gold was discovered by a returned California miner, and the total gold and silver yield of Australia and New Zealand in sixteen years has been nearly nine hundred million dollars.

What have we done to secure the trade of the East? We have established a flourishing empire on the Pacific; we have entangled ourselves in none of the jealousies of the Europeans in the East; we have bribed nobody, and so have not a career of prosperity founded upon the perishable pinions of duplicity; and we have set on the Pacific one of the greatest maritime companies of the earth, and connected it with the Atlantic by railroad.

The Colorado, the first steamer of this China line, — which is liberally subsidized, — made her first voyage to Shanghai in twenty-seven days, and returned from Japan in twenty-one. The trade of America with China quadrupled the year this steamship line was introduced. The China steamer, America, for example, is three hundred and eighty feet long, fifty feet beam, has thirty-two feet depth of hold, and six decks. Her measurement is five thousand six hundred tons, and her engines are of two thousand horse-power. She was built by Steers, at Greenpoint, New York city, and is fitted up in magnificent style.

What remains to be done?

To deal generously and equally with Eastern people amongst us; to respect their religion, their dress, and their peculiarities of manner, and to give them a chance. Also, to lose no time in purchasing the first right of way through the Isthmus of Central America, that we may not find ourselves outwitted like England, at Suez. Already Europe is looking covetously toward this narrow bulwark, the remaining short cut to the Orient.

In the spring of 1863, an Englishman, Captain Marshall, was in Paris, who entertained the idea of piercing the Isthmus of Panama, and was the author of a book called, "The Fate of the Pacific." On the eve of his leaving Paris, he sent a copy of his book to the Emperor, and, on the next morning, received an invitation to attend the Tuileries.

When he entered Napoleon's cabinet, he found him perusing the last pages of his work. As usual, Napoleon looked sorrowful and worn. "The man has but little rest and little amusement, and will not yet learn from the other princes how a monarch can render his life easy and agreeable." — "Your work has so interested me," said Napoleon, "that I have devoted a portion of the night to it. The Panama question is one of those, however, which have always occupied me, as you can convince yourself by looking over my books." Louis Napoleon then went into all the details of the matter, and asked the captain whether he was disposed to take the bearings again on the spot. Captain Marshall replied, that he desired nothing more. The Emperor drew a draft on the banker, Pereire; and, on the same evening, the Englishman proceeded to Havre, and thence to Central America. Lastly, to become absolute on the American Pacific, we must possess by persuasive means, the harbors of Vancouver, so as to be ready for that Pacific Railroad which will unite Lake Superior with the India. Canada, thus losing the last chance of Empire in America, will close her eyes and take the inevitable separate leap.

The latest English authority, Dilke, says: —

"The future of the Pacific shores is inevitably brilliant; but it is not New Zealand, the centre of the water hemisphere, which will occupy the position that England has taken in the Atlantic, but some country such as Japan or Vancouver, jutting out into the ocean from Asia or from America. . . The political power of America in the Pacific appears predominant; the Sandwich Islands are all but annexed; Japan is all but ruled by her, while the occupation of British Columbia is but a matter of time, and a Mormon descent upon the Marquesas is already planned. The relations of America and Australia will be the key to the future of the South.

"If, as is probable, Japan, New Zealand, and New South Wales, become great manufacturing communities, San Francisco must needs in time take rank as a second, if not a greater, London.

"Russia and England are said to be nearing each other upon the Indus; but long before they can meet there they will be face to face upon the Amoor; Anglo-Saxon America representing England."

In general terms we may conclude that up to the present hour the liberality of our institutions, the vigor of our race, and the resources of our empire, have made us the most generally enlightened people on the globe, and we impress mankind as being the safest, and the strongest of contemporary nations. No other government in North America can be said to be successful; we are regarded in the Southern American continent as the common friend and protector of all there, and our American policy has been at all times positive, yet magnanimous.* In this prosperous period we shall find old friends presuming, and old enemies suave, and many offers will be made us to go into business, politics, intrigue, warfare, adventure. But all that we are, we have become single-handed, accepting for teachers the original precepts of our Republican Fathers; and happy shall we be if we make all our national emulations subordinate to happiness and liberty, and guide our future foreign policy by the laws of sincerity, reciprocity, and peace.

"Our commercial policy," said Washington, "should hold an equal and impartial hand; neither seeking, nor granting exclusive favors or preferences, for it is folly in one nation to look for disinterested favors from another, and it must pay with a portion of its independence for whatever it may accept under that character."

* "In all history nothing can be found more dignified than the action of America upon the Monroe doctrine. Since the principle was first laid down in words, in 1823, the national behavior has been courteous, consistent, firm; and the language used now that America is all powerful, is the same that her statesmen made use of during the rebellion, in the hour of her most instant peril. It will be hard for political philosophers in the future to assert that a Democratic Republic can have no foreign policy." — *Dilke.*

CHAPTER XXIV.

EUROPEAN AMERICA.

A sketch of those portions of the Western Continent which are governed by European princes, or are subordinate to European influences : Spanish America, Brazil, and the subject West Indies — The commerce of our continent and the contestants for it — The American republics, our wards — Conclusion.

If Africa and Arabia were out of the map, Asia would bear a noticeable resemblance to North America, and Australia to South America, the long-ruptured peninsula of Malacca, Sumatra, and Java answering to Panama and Central America, when we shall sever them by canals. Europe would be an exaggerated copy of Alaska, ravelling off into the western ocean; Kamschatka is the counterpart of Greenland; Japan of Newfoundland and Nova Scotia; the Indies of the West and the East make archipelagoes between the two pairs of continents; the United States would then correspond to the broad belt of China, Turkistan, Persia, and Asia Minor, Mexico to Hindostan, and Siberia to British America. There are six considerable governments in Australia as in South America. Patagonia terminates one continent as Van Diemen's Land the other. In the East India Archipelago as many nations are represented as in the West India Islands; the Dutch government in Java is as avaricious as the Spanish in Cuba.

The spirit of political independence is almost as active in Spanish South America as in English Australia, and self-dependence and dignity are correspondingly wanting in both. The capitals of Sydney, Melbourne and Adelaide, suggest the similar situations of Rio de Janeiro, Buenos Ayres, and Valparaiso. Batavia is the Havana of the East Indies, Singapore the Panama.

The dreams in which England has indulged as to her empire on the St. Lawrence, Russia is repeating upon the Amoor. Pekin and Washington are upon nearly the same line of latitude; Havana and Hong Kong are upon another line; Constantinople and San Francisco are also parallels.

But Asia is almost all heathen, and America is almost entirely

Christian. There are but three families of our race influential in America, — English, Spanish, and Portuguese. There are three races with infinite families in Asia, — Caucasian, Mongol, and Malay. Asia is ridden by Europe in the nineteenth century as tyrannically as America was ridden by Europe in the eighteenth. There is no discoverable unity of life, purpose, or coalition amongst the races of Asia; Confucius, Mohammed, Brahma, Zoroaster, Buddha, have planted it with their traditions, and a tangled outgrowth of creeds inexplorable and indestructible as its jungles covers Asia with gorgeousness which is yet darkness. With a single clue like Aladdin's lamp, the European scholar explores, as in a cavern, the pathway of some seer or sage; gems of thought, poesy, and science sparkle about him as he advances; but the darkness closes up behind and before, and humanity despairs. In South and Central America the Christian faith, however misinterpreted, binds all the people to one ultimate civilization of "peace on earth and good-will to men." The feuds of Spanish America, which seem to us so frequent, bear no proportion to the interminable savage warfares of Asia, and are scarcely more bloody than the steady strifes of Europe, and they will be found in almost every case to arise, whatever be their pretexts, from the mortal collision between Americanism and Europeanism, between Society and Priest, Man and Prince, Equality and Vanity, Republic and Tradition.

Let us arrive at some distinct notions of our continent.

For all exterior purposes the United States acts through three cities, New York, New Orleans, and San Francisco. Quitting New York, southward, by sea, the nearest foreign soil is the Bermuda Islands, belonging to England, distant, say, eight hundred miles, and from England five thousand four hundred and fifty miles; the next foreign port is Nassau, in the Bahama Islands, about nine hundred miles from New York, and six thousand two hundred and fifty-five miles from England, which also owns them. Nearly eleven hundred miles from New York is Havana, which is about seven hundred miles from New Orleans, and less than two hundred miles from an American post in Florida. Nassau and Bermuda are merely coaling and military stations for British trade and war; they hang upon the verge of the United States, like groups of camp followers, to pick up a dishonest living when we are too much engaged to attend to them. England maintains steamship connection with Bermuda from Halifax, and with Nassau from St. Thomas.

80

Havana is the third port in the North American seas in point of promise and position, ranking after New York and San Francisco, and while it could be put by rail and ferry via Florida within three days' journey of the capital of the United States, it is as far from us in freedom and influence as Spain, which is its master. It is a city of two hundred thousand people, holding the bones of Columbus, and it is the key to the American continent, distant from New Orleans no farther than from New York to Cleveland, from Vera Cruz not so far as from New York to Chicago, from Panama and from St. Thomas the distance of New Orleans from New York, while the island of Cuba, on which Havana stands, is only one hundred and twenty miles from the Mexican mainland, and one hundred and forty from the American.

Standing at Havana one might be said to be at the most central city of the world; he will be on the longitude of Columbus, Ohio, and of Macon, Georgia; England will be six thousand five hundred miles distant; the steamship routes to New Zealand, to San Francisco, to Japan, to Valparaiso, to Rio de Janeiro, to Spain, to New Orleans, to Mexico, and to New York, will converge at his feet. Wherever the isthmus between the two Americas may be cut, Havana will be the neighboring great city; for it has the only great port in the tropics. It is this island which is engaged, while we write, in one of its many hopeless struggles with Spain, and it is doomed perhaps almost in the sight of our coasts, and despite our sympathies, to relapse into bondage anew. Here at Havana is the proper place to consider the condition of our continent in relation to the United States and to Europe.

Out of the entire population of America (seventy-five millions) the United States possesses fully one-half. Other English-speaking countries and colonies make nearly five millions more. Spanish countries and colonies make about twenty-five millions. Portuguese Brazil possesses eight millions, and is somewhat stronger in numbers than Mexico. More than sixty millions are nominally republicans; about twelve millions are adherents of monarchy; the rest are merely colonists. Assuming the population of the globe at one billion, Americans of all sorts make more than one-thirteenth of mankind; they have nearly four times the territory of Europe, and nearly a fourth of Europe's population. Great Britain, France, and Spain, together, outnumber all Americans between Alaska and Patagonia.

The two great divisions of the American continent may be likened to two large clusters of grapes, united by a jagged tendril; the southern cluster is compact and symmetrical, and it is suspended much farther eastward than the larger and more ravelled northern continent. There are six nations in the tendril between the two clusters, and there is also a web of islands spun, farther eastward, between the clusters. The tendril, quitting the United States on the Pacific side, comprises Mexico, Guatemala, San Salvador, Honduras, Nicaragua, Costa Rica, and it joins the southern cluster at New Granada. The web, quitting the United States at Florida on the Atlantic side, comprises the Bahamas, the Great Antilles and the Little Antilles islands, and it is spun to the southern cluster at Venezuela. Between the web and the tendril lie two oval seas, the Gulf of Mexico and the Caribbean Sea, which are nearly sundered by the island of Cuba. The Gulf of Mexico is five times the size of the Baltic Sea, and is encompassed by three states only, the United States, Mexico, and Cuba.

The Caribbean Sea is the greatest inlet on the Western Hemisphere, sixteen hundred miles wide by one thousand miles in diameter, and it empties into the Gulf Stream with the force of three thousand Mississippi Rivers, drawing upon the South Atlantic Ocean to supply this volume, and therefore the waters of the Amazon and Orinoco Rivers really flow into the Gulf of Mexico, return round Florida, and sweep along the coast of the United States northward, warming our air and mitigating our climate. In fact, therefore, the Gulf is the pool of the Mississippi and Rio Grande, while the Caribbean Sea is the pool of the Amazon and Orinoco; the river which they both form is the ocean river of the Gulf Stream, whose shores are civilization.

In this web of islands, the West Indies, began the life of both Americas. There Columbus saw land; there Spain began her baneful and brilliant Western Empire; thence Cortez departed for Mexico, De Soto for the Mississippi, Balboa for the Pacific, and Pizarro for Peru. The history of the United States was separated by a beneficent Providence far from this wild and cruel history of the rest of the continent, and, like a silent seed, we grew into empire, while empire itself, beginning in the South, was swept by so interminable hurricane that what of its history we can ascertain is read by the very lightnings that devastated it. The growth of English America may be likened to a series of lyrics sung by separate singers, which coalescing at last make a vigorous chorus, and this, attracting many from afar, swells and is prolonged, until presently it assumes the dignity and proportions of epic song. Spanish America began like the celebration of a wondrous mass; the relics, the trophies, the perfumes, and the gorgeousness of the highest piety and power were expressed in it. To its proportions the Israelitish song on the farther shore of the Red Sea was the anthem of a handful of savages. But in the ecstasy of the celebration, frenzy came over the singers; the hyssop ran blood; blasphemy took the place of praise, and the coals from the overthrown altar set the cathedral aflame. The first tragedy was the massacre of the innocent natives, or their reduction to slavery; the second was the fruit of the monopoly of all the New World claimed by Spain, whereby the Buccaneers of other nations ravaged the Spanish coasts for one hundred and seventy years, and left the pirates for their progeny; the third was the introduction of African slavery; the fourth was the universal revolution against Spain; the fifth was the war of races, and the present is the war of all these precedents.

When the English settled America they were new experimenters on the seas; when the Dutch settled it they were a new nation, snatched from the jaws of Spain; when the Portuguese settled it they were flushed with their great achievement of doubling the Cape of Good Hope, and ardent for larger dominions; when the French settled it they were the nation of military chivalry, without other purpose than not to be all forestalled; but when the Spanish settled it they bore title-deeds from God, stamped by his vicar, to reward them for saving his earthly kingdom from Jew, heretic, and infidel. Not colonization, but treasure, was their object; not a home, but only gold. They were the best sailors and soldiers of Europe, and while they ransacked the new hemisphere for the precious gems and metals, they offered land to the apostate Jews and Moors of Spain, that these might make food to sustain the Spanish soldiery. These and other renegades made the pilgrim fathers of Spanish America, and having no women to marry they cohabited with Indians. Priests in multitude soon appeared to convert savage and half-breed; the Pilgrim fathers hung out the sign of the three golden balls, and when the Spanish troops, laden with gold and gems, reappeared, they gambled them away, or parted with them to these pawnbrokers. A race with scarcely a civilized component in it sprang up,— negro, Indian, Jewish, Moorish, Spanish, — and not a ray of light fell upon this offspring of lust and greed but what the church afforded, and the church itself shared in the lust and avarice of the time and clime. Three aristocracies appeared after a chaos of crime and war, wherein every nation of Europe had taken part, — rich tradesmen and planters of renegade descent, Spanish officeholders and their descendants, and Spanish churchmen, — all indolent, proud, and rich, in the midst of slavery. But, gorged with greed, broken by the climate and by excesses, the Spanish race was also changed, and when the great upheaval of the French Revolution came, Spain, the mother country, was the easy prey of her neighbors: her Kings were set aside, her soil overrun, and her colonies revolted. We can imagine the dignity of the Spanish American revolutions by the races which performed them. Laden with ten times the burdens of the British colonies, the Spanish Americans took up arms at first, not for freedom, but for the deposed Spanish King. Their torch of liberty was lighted at length, not from America, but from France. Yet their ally was not France, but England; for when Napoleon was overthrown, the English, studying the situation in the light of profit and loss, concluded to ally themselves with Portugal and with the Spanish republics, as against France and Spain, now allies. Therefore English adventurers and English secret money were the life of the war of independence in the South. The naval hero of Peru and Chili was the same Lord Cochrane whom we have seen, in a previous chapter, expelled from Parliament. Miranda and Bolivar, South American leaders, always had British protection in the last resort. And one of the earliest powers to recognize the independence of our neighbors was England. In this policy England has learned that a service to freedom is never without profit; for her hold upon the trade and affection of Brazil and Spanish America generally is complete, and she has felt the return wave of benefit in her own ameliorated charity and constitution. British capital yields in no place safer returns than in South American investments, and her material influence in our tropics and southern hemisphere very nearly balances our own moral influence. Still the great sympathetic fact even in these devastated republics is that we are not only a variety of Englishmen, but also the great republic.

Let us now proceed to review the countries to the south of us. And first the West Indies, as the key to the tropic mainland.

Cuba has more area than South Carolina, and more inhabitants than Virginia, these latter constituting one-fourth of all the colonial subjects of Spain, now five millions in number, or less than one-third the number in Spain herself. Half the one million three hundred and fifty-nine thousand people of Cuba are whites, and more than a fourth slaves. Cuba is as long as from Boston to Detroit, and of only forty miles' average breadth. Its long mountain range reaches heights of six thousand nine hundred feet; its railways date back to 1838, and are now quite numerous. Only nine thousand of its children go to school. It has been permanently settled for more than three centuries and a half. Its government is a despotism, in the Spanish rendering of the word, and despotism aggravated by corruption. More than a hundred years ago, the English took Havana by siege and assault. Havana contains two hundred thousand people, and ranks tenth amongst cities of population on the American continents, while in position and harbor it is second to none.

Hayti, east of Spain, is nearly the size of Scotland, or of South Carolina, and it has nearly the population of Wisconsin. In 1843 the island divided into two governments, Hayti, Negro French, French and Dominica, Negro Spanish, Spanish, both anarchies and despotisms, alternately, and the United States has been repeatedly offered the protectorate or purchase of both.

Porto Rico is half the size of Massachusetts, and has half as many people as Georgia. Half the imports and exports are from Great Britain. It is Spanish and slave.

Jamaica, the largest British island in the West Indies, is smaller than Massachusetts, and has about the population of West Virginia. It lies south of Cuba. As a colony of note, the English pronounce it a failure, and their administration of it, coupled with the name of Eyre, its satrap, is a reproach to them.

The lesser islands of the West Indies reach up to Florida, — the Bahamas, and down to Venezuela, — the windward and leeward "Lesser Antilles." In possession they are either Danish, British, French, Dutch, Swedish, or Venezuelan.

The Swedish island of St. Bartholomew — her only colony — has eighteen thousand people, and an area of thirty-five square miles, and here slavery was abolished in 1848. Sweden was the first anti-slavery state.

The Danish islands are St. Thomas, St. Croix, and St. John. St. Thomas is the great entrepot for British steamers, and the focus of their radiating lines, and it has a commodious harbor. It stands in the elbow of the Antilles, nearest Europe, and its people, with decided enthusiasm, voted to be annexed to the United States, in 1868, notwithstanding British commercial influence. The Dutch islands are Saba, St. Eustatius, Buen Ayre, Curacoa, and Oruba. They are in nothing considerable, except as exhibiting the hard, stolid government of the Dutch, which has been compared to the respect felt by the fish for Jonah, in its belly. The French islands are Deseada, Guadeloupe, Marie Galante, and Martinique. St. Martin belongs to both French and Dutch. The French are the best-regulated islands in the West Indies; their occupants are citizens of them, not mere traders in them. Martinique was the native land of Bonaparte's Josephine, and is fifty miles long by sixteen wide. The British islands are Barbuda, St. Christopher, Antigua, Dominica, St. Lucia, Barbadoes, St. Vincent, and Trinidad. Barbadoes is populous, nlightened, has newspapers, and is freer from storms than its neighbors. Magarita and Tortuga are the principal Venezuelan islands. All these islands produce sugar, tobacco, rum, and the other luxuries.

The main land of Southern North America is, in misfortunes, a proper preface to the history of Spanish America. Mexico is a federative Republic of nineteen States, each State with a Legislature, and the President and Vice-President are elected by a federal Congress. Juarez, at present the President, and as well known for his virtues as Lopez of Paraguay for his crimes, was born in 1807. The nation was established in 1821; its area is about equal to all that part of the United States east of the Mississippi River, and its population is about one-fifth of ours. In 1866 the revenue was sixteen and one-half million dollars, and the expenditure nearly double. The debt, according to Juarez' computation, was thirty-five million dollars, while the French government, and its gamblers in Mexican concerns, claimed the liabilities of the republic to be three hundred and twenty million dollars. Napoleon even claims the cost of the war he made against the Mexicans to be a Mexican obligation. It will lie more heavily upon the conscience and the solvency of his own reign. The pure whites of Mexico are only three hundred thousand in number. The President is an Indian. Mexico is shortly to open a line of railway from Mexico city to Vera Cruz, three hundred miles. The celebrated Tehuantepec ship canal route passes through southern Mexico. M. Michael Chevalier thinks it the best.

Guatemala, the next neighbor to Mexico, is larger than Louisiana, and nearly as populous as North Carolina; it is an oligarchy, with a petty tyrant at the head of it, and may be considered, scarcely excepting Paraguay, as the worst government in America. The Jesuits are all powerful; the English do three-fourths of all the commercial business. The capital city contains sixty thousand people. Through this state a ship canal is contemplated by foreign engineers. Balize, a coast strip of Guatemala, is an English colony of twenty thousand people, double the area of New Jersey.

Honduras is nearly as large as Pennsylvania, and has more inhabitants than New Hampshire; it is a republic. Nicaragua, the state which sought the aid of General William Walker in 1855, is a semi-liberal republic, with the population of Arkansas, and the area of Michigan; through it passes the American route to the Pacific, called by the name of the state.

San Salvador is a small state on the Pacific coast, larger than New Hampshire, and with three hundred thousand people. It has the highest population in Central America.

Costa Rica, the last state in North America, going southward, contains half as many people as Connecticut, and is half the size of Maine; it has a revenue of about one hundred thousand dollars, and three-fourths of its imports came from England. Hon. E. G. Squier is the best authority on Central America.

New Grenada, next beyond Costa Rica, the nearest state in South America, has as many people as Ohio, and as much land as Texas, Louisiana, and Mississippi together. It is one of the most liberal and enlightened states in South America, and its government is a federal union of state soverèignties, almost precisely like the United States. The great sites of Panama and Carthagena are in the Granadian confederation. There is every variety of climate in it; the Andes mountains rise to the heighth of eighteen thousand feet, and through their ridges run the Rivers Magdalena and Cauca, navigable for five hundred miles, northward to the Caribbean Sea. Bogota, the capital, stands higher above the sea than the highest passes of the Alps, yet in perpetual salubrity, the Magdalena and the great River Orinoco flowing from the foot of its plateau to outlets twelve hundred miles apart; it has forty thousand people, and is very picturesque; the fare from the Caribbean coast to Bogota is said to be one hundred and thirty dollars in specie.

Venezuela, the next state to the east, is more than ten times the size of Ohio, and has more than the population of Massachusetts, and it has a coast line of sixteen hundred miles. Its exports amount to six and a half million dollars annually; its interior is forest and mountain, in great part unexplored, and the tropical animals are found in the jungles and morasses of the Orinoco, which, flowing parallel to the sea, empties its great bulk of nineteen hundred and sixty miles, by many mouths, into the ocean between British

Guiana and British Trinidad. The Orinoco is navigable to Angostura. Caraccas, the city of Bolivar and earthquakes, has forty thousand people, and stands sixteen miles from its Caribbean seaport, La Guayra, which has but six thousand people. Trinidad, an English island above referred to, is nearly half the size of Connecticut, and has nearly the population of the District of Columbia; it is the second British West India island in importance, and its chief town, the Port of Spain, is one of the finest in the whole archipelago. Angostura is the Venezuelan chief city of the Orinoco, two hundred and fifty miles from the sea, and with water two hundred and fifty feet deep at the city; it is now recovering from the long night of civil war.

Simon Bolivar the "Liberator" of Northern South America died in 1830, at the age of forty-seven. He had wealth, family, and education, corresponding to Washington's. In 1816 he proclaimed the abolition of slavery, — probably the first to do so on the continent. He liberated Venezuela, New Grenada, and Peru, and Bolivia is named for him. As a soldier, he was famed for his perseverance and his long marches; as a statesman, he had well-meant egotism, and little judgment. His memory is revered, but he was in nothing like Washington, to whom he has been compared. Bolivar is said to have written late in life, to General Flores, of Ecuador: "This country will inevitably fall into the hands of the unbridled rabble, and become the prey of petty tyrants of all colors and races. The Europeans will not deem it worth while to conquer us. America for us is ungovernable."

Guiana, the territory on the Atlantic coast between Venezuela and Brazil, is in many respects a counterpart of Louisiana; a rich, unhealthy delta-land along the Atlantic, with muddy and yielding banks and streams, which come down from savage interiors laden with detritus. The British, Dutch, and French divide amongst them this region, the French making it a depot for their most infamous criminals, and their most eminent patriots. The French part is large as Ohio, and contains twenty-five thousand people, and it is the only mainland of the American continent held by France. Dutch Guiana is large as Tennessee, and has half the population of Delaware; through Parimaribo its capital, with eighteen thousand inhabitants, Dutch Guiana does a great trade with the United States. British Guiana is about the size of Maryland, though the English claim land enough from Brazil and Venezuela to make it big as Kansas; sugar, rum, and timber are its products; it contains one hundred and fifty thousand people, and its capital, Georgetown, with twenty-five thousand people, is intersected by canals, like Amsterdam. Dutch task-mastership and greed have left imprint over all Guiana, and we can imagine, from the present condition of the country, what New York might have looked like had it continued a Dutch Colony.

Let us now, from the margin of Brazil, retrace to Panama, cross the American railroad, and descend the line of nations on the Pacific coast. First Ecuador, nearly five times the size of New England, and with the population of New Jersey, Guayaquil for its port, Quito for its capital, one of the dullest states, even in South America.

Quito stands in the air half as high again as the Tip-Top House on Mt. Washington, and at two-thirds the height of Mont Blanc. It has fifty thousand people, is very difficult of access, and its port of Guyaquil, itself sixty miles from the ocean, is two hundred miles distant. Mr. Frederick Hassaurek, our late minister resident there, reports that one hundred and twenty pianos have been dragged to that difficult height, that the people conceive the only great nation besides themselves to be the French, and that, lying upon the Equator, nature is yet more attractive there than man. Guyaquil stands on the best river on the Pacific coast of South America; the river is navigated by American steamers, and the town of twenty thousand people is lighted by American gas, preserved by a Baltimore steam fire-engine, and made occasionally noisy by an American iron foundry. But the English do the commerce.

Peru, the ancient El Dorado, commemorated so well by Prescott, is now in as sorry plight as Rome to bear so rich a name. Peru has more than twice the area of Texas, and more than ten times that of New York, while its population is nearly equal to Ohio's; its coast line is one thousand six hundred miles long, but it has not a single good harbor. Guano islands, lying in Peruvian waters, contain, even at present, it is thought, fifteen millions of tons, and good guano sells for sixty-five dollars a ton in England. Peru has mountains which reach the altitude of twenty-two thousand feet, and cities, like Cuzco, higher than the Great St. Bernard. Among the valuable deposits of Peru is nitrate of soda, a powerful fertilizer, of which there are sixty-three million tons in the country. Guano absolutely supports the state of Peru, its revenue of twenty-one and one-fourth million dollars, in 1862, being three-fourths obtained from the sale of this article. The Republic, like Elijah, is fed by the ravens. The whole of Peru's debt of one hundred and fifteen million dollars is secured by these guano islands. Here is a beneficent bird of freedom, indeed, which not only perches on the standard of Peru, but lends it money. There is no religious toleration in Peru, and though the constitution is based upon that of the United States, the exceptions seem to make the government. Here, then, is a rich country a beggar, for want of peace and enterprise.

Lima, the capital, the handsomest of Pacific coast cities, is six miles from the ocean port of Callao, with which it is connected by a railroad, owned by three persons, and this is said to net them fifteen thousand dollars a day. It has a very agreeable climate, and one hundred thousand people. Peruvian steamers connect at the border of Brazil with Brazilian steamers on the Amazon, and ascend to Jaen, only two hundred miles from the Pacific coast, or twenty-four hundred from the mouth of the Amazon!

Bolivia has the population of Illinois, and the area of all our Atlantic and Gulf Southern States, except Texas. It has no seaport worth speaking of, and only a desert sea-coast on the Pacific, its natural outlet being the Amazon also. Its capital, Chuquisaca, with twenty-five thousand people, stands nine thousand feet above the sea in a territory of silver mines, and its second city, Potosi, with thirty thousand people, stands four thousand feet higher, on a mountain pierced with five thousand mines, which has yielded two billion dollars, and its deposits are inexhaustible. Bolivia is the South American Minnesota, the La Plata rising in it as well as the Amazon.

Chili is a long veneered and bevelled strip of Pacific coast and Andes, one hundred and twenty miles wide and ten times longer, lying in the relative southern latitude of California. It is undoubtedly the most prosperous republic in South America, and, with the area of New York, New England, and Pennsylvania, has the population of Massachusetts and Connecticut. It has several seaports, chief of which is Valparaiso, with nearly one hundred thousand people, situated ninety miles from Santiago, the capital. In 1866 the Spanish bombarded it, and destroyed ten million dollars' worth of property. Santiago is grandly and beautifully situated on a terrace of the Andes, and is in social complacency and education the Boston of South America, with a rich population of one hundred and ten thousand. A sketch of Chili was published by D. J. Hunter, in New York, as late as 1866.

The Chilian President is elected by Electors, as with us, and holds five years. The Senators, twenty in number, sit nine years; the

Deputies (Representatives) sit three years. The President has four Cabinet Ministers, and also an auditory Council, composed of cabinet, judges, ecclesiastics, and civilians. It will thus be perceived that the Chilian government is less representative than ours. The railways of Chili are four hundred miles in length, and will soon be one thousand miles; and the merchant marine comprises two hundred and sixty vessels and three thousand soldiers. Two thousand Germans have settled in Chili, and are active politicians; December, January, and February are the summer time there; the people are scarcely taxed at all; tobacco is a government monopoly; American patents are popular; the mint of Santiago is the finest edifice in South America; a Yankee established the first printing-office in 1812; the state has a homestead law; it is proposed to stretch an American telegraph on land from Panama to Valparaiso; the portraits of Washington and Lincoln are placed side by side in the Chilian Foreign Office by law; an American town in Chili is Caldera, with a railroad fifty miles long leading to silver and copper mines; religious toleration was stingily granted in Chili very recently.

Patagonia, which terminates the continent of South America, contains one hundred and twenty thousand people, or one being to three square miles, and is a region of desolate steppes and of volcanoes, intersected by the broad Straits of Magellan, where the Chilians are about to put tow-boats to speed vessel navigation. These straits are three hundred miles long and from five to thirty miles wide. Off these straits in the Atlantic are the Falkland Isles, two hundred in number, with the aggregate area of Massachusetts, Rhode Island, and Connecticut, belonging to England, and settled, to be of use to her commerce, as late as 1833; they now contain seven hundred people. These are the only settled islands in the Southern oceans, except Juan Fernandez, four hundred miles off Chili, settled by Americans and Sandwich Islanders, and the St. Felix isles, also in the Pacific. The Galapagos Islands are on the equator, almost due south of New Orleans. The Cape Verde islands stand in the Atlantic between the mouths of the Amazon and the Mediterranean, nearly midway, and the Azores between the mouths of the Mediterranean and the Chesapeake. Turning into the Atlantic Ocean and ascending, we come to the Argentine Republic, lying between Chili and the great River La Plata, the noblest of South American streams. Two cities hold the gulfy outlet of the La Plata, — Montevideo in Uruguay, and Buenos Ayres in the Argentine State.

The Argentine Republic, which is the Chili of the Atlantic coast, has as great a population as Missouri, and it is nearly five times the size of all our Middle States. There are eighty thousand Italians in it, and sixty thousand French and pure Spanish. Its foreign debt is owing mainly to the English and the Brazilians, and the English have subscribed nearly the whole capital for its six hundred. and fifty miles of railroad projected or accomplished. The city of Buenos Ayres once beat off the English; vessels must anchor at low water there from five to nine miles off shore, and at high water from a mile to three miles; the population of the city is one hundred and twenty-five thousand, and French and English newspapers are published.

Uruguay, probably to be soon absorbed by Brazil, or to lead to another war between Spanish and Portuguese South America, is nearly as large as the two Carolinas, and has about one-third the population of South Carolina. In 1865 Uruguay exported first in quantity to France, second to England, third to Italy, and fifth to the United States. Montevideo, its capital, has nearly fifty thousand people. The La Plata River has three great arms inland, two of which pierce to the depths of Brazil, and yet both flow to sea through Uruguay and the Argentine Republic; caught between the forks of the upper two, seven hundred miles from the sea, is the so-called republic of Paraguay, which is ten times the size of Massachusetts, and as populous as Indiana; one half the state belongs to the bloody dictator Lopez, one of those demons of wickedness who choose the name of republic to make mankind despise it. He inherited the country from his father, who had it willed to him by the executors of the fiendish Francia, the first usurper of the republic. Paraguay is the most despotic state on the American continent, and it is about passing into the hands of its own people, unless its conquerors quarrel over it and Brazil succeeds in annexing the whole as well as Uruguay. The quarrel on the La Plata is primarily between the Portuguese and Spanish Atlantic empires, intensified by the desire of the Brazilians to have the free navigation of the La Plata, and by the efforts of despots, like Rosas and Lopez, to prevent it. The behavior of Paraguay, however, was as insufferable to her Spanish allies as to Brazil, and they have made common cause against Lopez. Two American Ministers disagreeing in this war, we may take the opinion of Professor Agassiz: —

"In her conflict with Paraguay, Brazil may truly be counted among the standard-bearers of civilization. The facts which have come to my knowledge respecting this war have convinced me that it originated in honorable purposes, and, setting aside the selfish intrigues of individuals, inevitably connected with such movements, is carried on with disinterestedness. It deserves the sympathy of the civilized world; for it strikes at a tyrannical organization, half clerical, half military, which, calling itself a republic, disgraces the name it assumes."

Brazil is two thousand six hundred miles long, and two thousand five hundred miles broad, not so broad as the United States by three hundred and fifty miles, but longer from north to south by one thousand miles, exclusive of Alaska. Brazil has nearly one hundred thousand square miles more area than the United States, but, counting Alaska, we have about five hundred thousand square miles in excess. It has been settled about three hundred and forty years, and has a population of eight millions, or less than that of New York, Pennsylvania, and Ohio combined. It forms a frontier of every nation in South America but one, Chili, and is, generally speaking, exempt from the drouths and earthquakes which annoy them. In 1868 its public debt was about two hundred and forty million dollars, and its expenditure was double its revenue. It is the only large state in Christendom which maintains slavery at home, only half its population being free, and it has fewer children at school than the State of Iowa. Its river system, long unimproved, has been at length opened to the world, but the La Plata River, which is the Mississippi of the South Temperate Zone, debouches through foreign states, and in time of sullenness or war is closed to Brazil. Three or four railways penetrate a little distance into the country from the coast; the humid soil and luxurious vegetation make good common roads almost impossible. The exports of Brazil are valued (1860) at about sixty-five million dollars, or one-sixth of those of the United States. Immense portions of the interior are unexplored; the mouth of the greatest river of Brazil is directly on the line of the equator; the capital, Rio de Janeiro, is upon a latitude corresponding to that of Havana in our hemisphere, and is the largest city of South America, with the population of Baltimore. Its harbor is superior to those of New York, San Francisco, or Havana, being only a mile wide at the outlet, very deep, and girdled with mountains, while its surface of seventeen miles by twelve, is made picturesque by islands, one of which is nearly half the size of New York Island.

Rio stands four miles from the ocean around seven hills, like Rome.

A mountain within sight sends fresh water by an aqueduct; gas lights the streets, fountains play in the squares; opera, libraries, and colleges exist as in our northern cities; the city has been the capital since 1822, when Brazil became independent. Bahia City, also on the coast, has one hundred and twenty-five thousand people; Pernambuco, the sugar-mart, one hundred thousand, and Para, at the mouth of the Amazon, thirty thousand. The Amazon River drains an extent of country equal to all Europe, and affords inland navigation of fifty thousand miles, twice the circumference of the globe; from its sources the Pacific Ocean is visible; it is navigable for three thousand three hundred and sixty miles from the Atlantic! yet its seaport, Para, does a business in imports and exports amounting to only two millions of dollars yearly. It requires two weeks to ascend the Amazon to the Peruvian line; poor steamers traverse it, but the English are already preparing to make it a highway. There is not a decent hotel nor a large town on the river; mosquitoes are its bane; the river bottom is unreliable. The Brazilian people are a weak race, with poor morals, worse courage, and abominable nastiness. The virility of the children is lost by the proximity of slaves and the universal incontinence; the Spanish allies of Brazil on the La Plata despise the morals of the latter's soldiery. What of strength there is in the nation is a popular and prudent ruler, and good foreign advisers, chiefly English. The nation has never passed through the bloody centuries of its Spanish neighbors, and peace has generally favored it. It was a colony of Portugal till 1807, when Bonaparte invading the mother country, the royal family set sail, and raised the throne anew in Brazil. The King of Spain was at the same time on the point of sailing for Peru. When the time came to return to Portugal, the King was loth to make the exchange, and he finally endeavored to marry his daughter *to her uncle*, and so keep Portugal in the family, while his son Pedro kept Brazil. Pedro was unfortunate and was driven out, and the present well-behaved King is his son, Pedro II. A branch of the family still keeps Portugal, also, and the English, whose bond of attachment is port wine and bills of lading, are the patrons of both countries. King Pedro II., of Brazil, is allied by marriage with the Orleans family of France, and his wife is the sister of "Bomba," ex-tyrant of the Sicilies. His salary is four hundred thousand dollars a year, and his wife's fifty thousand dollars. The palace in Rio is an old stone and stucco building, painted yellow, two and three stories high, a hundred feet wide, and six hundred feet deep, connected by a gallery with the royal library and chapel. Here all the court ceremony of the Braganzas is kept up, — a guard of halberdiers, state liveries of green trimmed with silver, lancers, state coaches, robing rooms.

Brazilian Senators are selected by the Emperor from a number nominated in election by the people. The Representatives are not directly elected. Every inscribed voter *must* vote under penalty. Only Catholics can be Representatives. There are seven ministers, — one of "Justice." The police administration of Brazil is despotic. People are impressed into the army. The "native" race is uppermost. Titles of nobility are not hereditary.

The railroad from Rio to the River Parahyba, sixty-seven miles, was built by American engineers. The first steamer of the Pacific Mail Company which sailed to China took, on her maiden trip from New York, Louis Agassiz and a company of American naturalists, who explored the Amazon. Agassiz introduced the American lyceum lectures into Brazil, and for the first time the ladies there attended them. Mrs. Agassiz ascribes the evils of Brazil to slavery, to the character of the clergy, to the want of education, to Portuguese civilization, and to the non-popular form of the government.

There remains to be considered only the influence of the United States in the waters of America. England is now the leading power amongst our associate republics. Let us instance her steamship lines.

And first, the Royal Mail Steam Packet Company, with headquarters at Southampton, England; it has an annual aggregate subsidy from the British government of one million three hundred and fifty thousand dollars, and twenty vessels of twenty-nine thousand four hundred and fifty-four tons, nine thousand three hundred and six horse-power, and one thousand six hundred and sixty-seven men. They make two trips a month between England and Aspinwall in twenty-two days, stopping at St. Thomas and Carthagena. Six branch lines go from St. Thomas to Nassau, Jamaica, Barbadoes, Tobago, Porto Rico, Havana, and Vera Cruz; the whole converging at St. Thomas, the island which Mr. Seward wisely wished to buy, and which Congress would not. The same company sends a monthly steamer to Brazil by Lisbon, and it touches along the Atlantic coast. A third British line, the Pacific Steam Navigation Company, has the monopoly of mails and passengers along the Pacific coast of South America from Panama to Valparaiso. A fourth line leaves Liverpool every fifteen days for Northern Brazil. A fifth British line leaves London and Antwerp for the ports of Brazil. A sixth leaves Panama for New Zealand, making the longest unbroken steamship passage in the world, six thousand six hundred miles. The Cunard line, with twenty-two vessels, is heavily subsidized to New York. The Montreal ocean line, subsidized by Canada, owns eighteen steamships. The Inman line with seventeen steamers, the Williams and Guion, the Anchor, the London, and the National lines send together at least a steamer a day to New York, so that there is probably in the American trade one hundred British steamships. The Spanish run a semi-monthly line between Havana and Porto Rico and Cadiz. The Germans run eleven steamers from Hamburg to New York, and a line from Hamburg to New Orleans, and a line of nineteen steamers from Bremen to New York, Baltimore, and New Orleans. The French despatch a heavily subsidized weekly line from Havre to New York and a monthly line from Bordeaux to Brazil and Buenes Ayres. The aggregate of all these vessels is probably not below one hundred and fifty, of two hundred thousand tons' capacity, and manned by twelve thousand men.

To this large mercantile steam navy of Europe, employed in the waters of the American continent, we oppose only three steamers which sail to St. Thomas and the ports of Brazil, three which run to Havana, three steamboats to St. John, New Brunswick, and the Pacific Mail Steamship line to Yokohama and Hong Kong. Three or four slow, irregular, and aged steamers to Liverpool, Bremen, or Antwerp, keep up the infrequent apparition of our flag on the Atlantic. The rest is our coastwise commerce, from which foreign bottoms are excluded. There are causes and explanations of this maritime poverty, but no American can forget that he was formerly a citizen of the second commercial power in the world, and no republican will forget that on this continent, particularly, every American flag in sight at a masthead is an encouragement to the self-governing.

In the old Spanish days Chili communicated with Spain once a year. In 1840 a Mr. Wheelwright, of Rhode Island, began steam navigation on the Pacific with two small English-built steamers, the "Peru" and the "Chili;" out of this experiment has come the Pacific Steam Navigation Company, before mentioned, and now entirely English, which connects every port between Patagonia and Panama. The Chilian subsidy to this line is nearly sixty thousand dollars a year; during the numerous revolutions and wars along the coast, these steamers make immense sums by transporting troops and munitions of war. The fares on the line are among the highest in the world, costing from Panama to Valparaiso two hundred and thirty dollars in the cabin, sixty dollars in the steerage, and for freight eighteen dollars per ton, and so large are the dividends that they are announced secretly. The fare from Panama to Lima is one hundred and thirty-five dollars, and cabin to Guyaquil seventy-five dollars. Complaint is made of the food and the rate of fare by the people on the line, and competition by an American line has long been hoped for. A small native Chilian line began in 1851 to run to ports south of Valparaiso, and, with a capital of seventy-four thousand dollars, it cleared forty thousand dollars in two years. The Chilian government offered, in 1853, a subvention of sixty thousand dollars a year for a French line which should make eight yearly voyages between Valparaiso and Liverpool around Magellan; and in 1865 the Chilian Congress offered one hundred thousand dollars yearly. So much have our interests on the Pacific declined, that, in 1863, to thirty-six thousand nine hundred and three letters carried by the Pacific Steam Navigation Company on account of Europe, two thousand seven hundred and sixty-nine only were credited to the United States. "Thus England, France, and Germany," says Don Ramon Paez, in 1868, "have secured the monopoly of the South American trade, with total exclusion of this country, which has to pay cash for what the former obtain in exchange for the produce of their manufactories. All these nations, moreover, appoint permanent representatives, chosen from among their ablest diplomats, and keep them there as long as they choose to remain, while America has sent few, as yet, but broken-down and quarrelsome politicians."

Amongst her export friends, England rated, in 1868, Germany as the first, British India as the second, United States third, *Brazil tenth*, Canada twelfth, *New Granada fifteenth*, Cuba and Porto Rico seventeenth, British West Indies nineteenth, Argentine Republic twentieth, Chili twenty-third, Peru twenty-seventh, Mexico thirty-first, and Uruguay thirty-third. In the same year the British rated amongst the nations from whom they took imports, *the United States first*, France second, Germany third, *Brazil tenth*, British West Indies fourteenth, Chili seventeenth, Peru eighteenth, Cuba and Porto Rico twentieth, British Guiana twenty-fifth, *British North America twenty-sixth*, *New Granada thirty-first*. By that time France had become the second mercantile marine power on the seas, superseding the

United States; she had of steamers four hundred and seven, of one hundred and thirty thousand tonnage; England two thousand nine hundred and thirty-one, of nine hundred thousand tonnage; France had fifteen thousand six hundred and thirty-seven sailing vessels, and England twenty-eight thousand seven hundred and seventy-three. Beside these figures we may well be amazed at our place in the waters of America.

The American ship is America's only foreign possession. Wherever it appears, it is a colony, an apostle, an invitation, an ambassador. It was an American ship that reinforced Garibaldi at Messina, that destroyed Miramon at Sacrificios, that carried the last Bourbon from France, and that covered Kossuth with its flag. We shall cease to regret the rebellion only when that familiar hull is frequent again, and when in every port to which we go our colors shall appear among the masts.

The political anarchy of Spanish America is apparently as incurable as its social components are incapable of union. The Spanish American, as we comprehend him, is not worthy of absorption into a country whose institutions have been vindicated by its people. But Spanish America is endeared to us by cousinly geographies, by the sympathy we hold with every rod of both Americas, and by the belief we have that to this tenacious sympathy an according destiny must come. This belief is implanted in every American boy; it continues equal and undaunted amidst the scepticisms of old age; it is chastened, perhaps, but not forgotten, after wasting war. With the multitude it is mainly a material ambition; with practical statesmen, a consideration of mankind's opportunities postponed by our inaction; in minds of rarer nature, it is a waiting yet an ardent faith. While it is a national faith, it is also a republican faith, steadily ignoring the possibility that either Canada, or Cuba, or Brazil can continue subject or independent monarchies. Not that the democratic spirit can suffer from the contiguity of such examples, but that the democratic spirit will not rest while it may influence. And perhaps the American desire for universal dominion on this continent is only a ruder form of the democratic spirit, — the missionary ship which bears our principles.

Canada and Brazil are equal failures as governments, — safer but duller realms than Mexico, — disappointing the immigrant with their political atmosphere, and mocking his dreams. But the United States' spirit always discriminates between the achievements and the capacities of our neighbors, between a torpid present and a future which may be made galvanic by our contact. The American spirit leaps up at every project of colonization or commerce in the foreign dominions of this continent; in our practical homesteads the infrequent imagination becomes almost the poet's, at the mention of some impending "annexation;" but all these ardent aspirations cluster about The Ship!

The ship is the American spirit abroad. The flag which arouses it never waves so handsomely as at the masthead. With shipping we can put the republic at the piers of every city on the New Continent, and make paramount again our waning prestige at Valparaiso, Callao, Rio, and on the La Plata. Our warlike marine does not carry our institutions; its sailors are neither colonists nor traders; they do not, like our merchant sailors, sow principles in their enterprises and plant them together.

Railroads across the continent are triumphs of perseverance; canals ensure union no less than wealth; but the interior works of many aged and tottering nations are also wonderful, dragged to the light by some indomitable traveller, who tells of the extent of their fields of tea, their boundless harvests, and their vast methodized and frugal toil. Still, the reader will ask for their ships; for, with wings, Holland is greater than China without them.

This is the strong wish of the national heart, the cry of the new crusader, with "God wills it" upon his lips, as he sees the continent which he can regenerate falling to dulness, or to anarchy, or back to its illiberal origin. Restore our commerce on the sea. If our ship-yards cannot be repeopled, bring ships, meantime, from elsewhere, that the sailor's spirit may not die. At this time there are two hundred thousand American men bred by or upon the salt water, who are about to put by the tiller for the plough, there being no chance for them on their native element. They are of the mettle of Ward, of Rhode Island, who made the American climate better known in China than any Minister Plenipotentiary we ever sent there; who could barely read, yet he led the armies, and espoused the sister of an Emperor.

When our commerce shall revive by a return of wisdom and patriotism to Congress, our interest in the kindred states of our continent will also revive. We have had experience with Spanish America already; we have met it, with many of its evils, in California, Louisiana, and Florida, and its hosts of anarchy have vanished at our coming. As late as 1789 a Capuchin priest arrived at New Orleans, charged by King Charles IV., of Spain, to set up the Holy Inquisition in the province of Louisiana. We may imagine what would be the condition of the Mississippi Valley at this interval of only eighty years, when it has developed under toleration to be a greater empire than Spain, had that holy beneficence been permitted to naturalize itself amongst us. The priest was kidnapped by the Spanish governor, Mirò, and sent home, with the apology "that the mere name of the Inquisition uttered in New Orleans would not only check immigration, but would drive away the people who have already come."

In like manner we shall find the perversities sown by monarchy, military government, and a corrupt priesthood, to fly before us when we arrive, in the destiny of things, at Havana, at Comayagua, at Tehuantepec, or elsewhere. All philosophical foreign observers have remarked upon the power of the North American character to civilize and to organize new communities. Froebel, who was in California in 1850, thus published this judgment in London: "The whole process of development through which the social life of California has passed in a few years is a striking and most instructive instance of the origin, organization, and improvement of human society, from motives of advantage and necessity; while the result bears a strong testimony in favor of the political and social forms and usages of the North Americans, without which the Californian experiment could never have succeeded. No European nation would have had sufficient experience and skill in self-government to answer the wants of a situation such as that of Californian society in its nascent state."

The American feeling is no less earnest, decided, and yet affectionate, toward British, than toward Spanish America.

We have come to the period when the grandchildren of British loyalists in Nova Scotia cry aloud for our star to arise; when British Columbia pines for the delay of our coming; when Quebec lifts up her voice in open day to ask release from England, and Toronto murmurs "Amen." But we should be worth coming to without warfare; our invitation should have no less dignity than our sword. "Peace," says Senator Sumner, "is for us a universal conqueror. Through peace the whole world will be ours. Filled with the might of peace, the sympathy we extend to the struggling will be next to alliance."

INDEX.

A

D

www.ingramcontent.com/pod-product-compliance
Lightning Source LLC
LaVergne TN
LVHW021048110826
845150LV00001B/9

* 9 7 8 1 4 2 5 5 6 8 6 4 1 *